GLOBAL ENVIRONMENTAL HISTORY

Global Environmental History introduces this rapidly developing field through a broad and thought-provoking range of expert contributions.

Environmental history is a subject especially suited to global and transnational approaches and, over the course of the present generation, an increasing number of scholars have taken up the challenge that it presents. The collection begins with a series of chapters offering truly global visions; they range from reflections on the role of animals in environmental history to a summary of environmental change over the past ten millennia.

Part II switches to a sharper focus, featuring essays that characterize the distinctiveness of certain key regions such as China, Russia, West Africa, South Asia, Europe, and Latin America. The final part of the book examines different forms of modern environmentalism, ranging from the U.S. and its obsession with wilderness, to Japanese concern with human health, and on to Peru and India, where the environmental debate centres on access to resources.

Global Environmental History will be an essential resource for students of Environmental History and Global History.

J. R. McNeill is University Professor in the Department of History and the School of Foreign Service at Georgetown University. His previous works include *Mosquito Empires: Ecology and War in the Greater Caribbean,* and *Something New Under The Sun: An Environmental History of the Twentieth-century World*, winner of the World History Association Book Prize.

Alan Roe is based at the Department of History, Georgetown University.

REWRITING HISTORIES
Edited by Jack R. Censer

HAITIAN HISTORY: NEW PERSPECTIVES
Edited by Alyssa Sepinwall

THE INDUSTRIAL REVOLUTION AND WORK IN
NINETEENTH-CENTURY EUROPE
Edited by Lenard R. Berlanstein

THE ISRAEL/PALESTINE QUESTION
Edited by Ilan Pappé

MEDIEVAL RELIGION: NEW APPROACHES
Edited by Constance Hoffman Berman

NAZISM AND GERMAN SOCIETY, 1933–45
Edited by David Crew

THE NEW SOUTH: NEW HISTORIES
Edited by J. William Harris

THE OLD SOUTH: NEW STUDIES OF SOCIETY AND CULTURE
Edited by J. William Harris

THE ORIGINS OF THE BLACK ATLANTIC
Edited by Larent DuBois and Julius S. Scott

THE ORIGINS OF THE COLD WAR:
AN INTERNATIONAL HISTORY
Edited by David Painter and Melvyn Leffler

PRACTICING HISTORY: NEW DIRECTIONS
IN HISTORICAL WRITING
Edited by Gabrielle M. Spiegel

REFORMATION TO REVOLUTION
Edited by Margo Todd

THE RENAISSANCE: ITALY AND ABROAD
Edited by John Jeffries Martin

REVOLUTIONARY RUSSIA: NEW APPROACHES
TO THE RUSSIAN REVOLUTION
Edited by Rex A. Wade

THE REVOLUTIONS OF 1989
Edited by Vladimir Tismaneanu

SEGREGATION AND APARTHEID IN
TWENTIETH CENTURY SOUTH AFRICA
Edited by William Beinart and Saul Dubow

SOCIETY AND CULTURE IN THE SLAVE SOUTH
Edited by J. William Harris

STALINISM: NEW DIRECTIONS
Edited by Sheila Fitzpatrick

TWENTIETH CENTURY CHINA: NEW APPROACHES
Edited by Jeffrey N. Wasserstrom

GLOBAL ENVIRONMENTAL HISTORY

An introductory reader

Edited by
J. R. McNeill and Alan Roe

Routledge
Taylor & Francis Group

LONDON AND NEW YORK

First published 2013
by Routledge
2 Park Square, Milton Park, Abingdon, Oxon OX14 4RN

Simultaneously published in the USA and Canada
by Routledge
711 Third Avenue, New York, NY 10017

*Routledge is an imprint of the Taylor & Francis Group,
an informa business*

British Library Cataloguing in Publication Data
A catalogue record for this book is available from the British Library

Library of Congress Cataloging in Publication Data
McNeill, J. Robert.
Global environmental history : an introductory reader / J. R. McNeill and
Alan Roe.
p. cm.
Includes bibliographical references and index.
1. Human ecology–History–Cross-cultural studies.
2. Global environmental change–History–Cross-cultural studies.
3. Environmental policy–History–Cross-cultural studies. 4. Environmental
protection–History–Cross-cultural studies. I. Roe, Alan. II. Title.
GF13.M385 2012
304.209–dc23   2012022062

ISBN: 978-0-415-52052-2 (hbk)
ISBN: 978-0-415-52053-9 (pbk)

Typeset in Times New Roman
by Taylor & Francis Books

MIX
Paper from
responsible sources
FSC
www.fsc.org   FSC® C004839

Printed and bound in Great Britain by the MPG Books Group

CONTENTS

vii

CONTENTS

CONTENTS

SERIES EDITOR'S PREFACE

Although environmental history possesses more distant roots than many historical subjects, its study only really took off in the last several decades. This is not to deny interest in the environment and its change over time, but historians and other scholars pursuing this subject remained few in number. Recently, fuelled by concerns with pollution, overdevelopment, and sustainability, environmental history has burgeoned. The field now includes multiple perspectives on global trends, regional studies, and topical approaches such as the relationships between class and gender in the impact of humans on the globe. This book brings into sharp relief some of the best interpretations to date.

ACKNOWLEDGEMENTS

The permission of the authors and the publishers to reprint the following articles is gratefully acknowledged:

Chapter 1, William R. Dickinson, "Changing Times: The Holocene Legacy," *Environmental History*, Vol. 5, No. 4 (Oct., 2000), pp. 483–502.

Chapter 2, Teresa Kwiatkowska and Alan Holland, "Dark is the World to Thee: A Historical Perspective on Environmental Forewarnings," *Environment and History*, Vol. 16 (2010), pp. 455–82.

Chapter 3, W. Jeffrey Bolster, "Opportunities in Marine Environmental History," *Environmental History*, Vol. 11, No. 3 (Jul., 2006), pp. 567–97.

Chapter 4, Carolyn Merchant, "Gender and Environmental History," *Journal of American History*, Vol. 74, No. 4 (Mar., 1990), pp. 1117–21.

Chapter 5, Stephen J. Pyne, "Consumed by Either Fire or Fire: A Review of the Environmental Consequences of Anthropogenic Fire." In: Jill Ker Conway, Kenneth Keniston, and Leo Marx, eds., *Earth, Air, Fire, Water: Humanistic Studies of the Environment* (University of Massachusetts Press, 1999) pp. 78–102.

Chapter 6, Donald Kennedy and Marjorie Lucks, "Rubber, Blight, and Mosquitoes: Biogeography Meets the Global Economy," *Environmental History*, Vol. 4, No. 3 (Jul., 1999), pp. 369–83.

Chapter 7, Harriet Ritvo, "Animal Planet," *Environmental History*, Vol. 9, No. 2 (Apr., 2004), pp. 204–20.

Chapter 8, Edmund Russell, "Evolutionary History: Prospectus for a New Field," *Environmental History*, Vol. 8, No. 2 (Apr., 2003), pp. 204–28.

Chapter 9, Alfred W. Crosby, "Ecological Imperialism: The Overseas Migration of Western Europeans as a Biological Phenomenon." In: Donald Worster, ed., *The Ends of the Earth* (Cambridge: Cambridge University Press, 1989), pp. 103–17.

Chapter 10, Elizabeth Dore, "Environment and Society: Long-Term Trends in Latin American Mining," *Environment and History*, Vol. 6 (2000), pp. 1–29.

Chapter 11, Joachim Radkau, "Exceptionalism in European Environmental History," *Bulletin of the German Historical Institute*, Vol. 33 (Fall 2004), pp. 23–44.

Chapter 12, Mark Elvin, "Three Thousand Years of Unsustainable Growth: China's Environment from Archaic Times to the Present," *East Asian History*, Vol. 6 (1993), pp. 7–46.

Chapter 13, Douglas R. Wiener, "The Predatory Tribute-Taking State: A Framework for Understanding Russian Environmental History." In: Edmund Burke III and Kenneth Pomeranz, eds., *The Environmental and World History* (Berkeley: University of California Press, 2009), pp. 276–314.

Chapter 14, James L. A. Webb Jr., "Ecology and Culture in West Africa." In: Emmanuel K. Akyeampong, ed., *Themes in West African History* (Athens: Ohio University Press, 2006), pp. 33–51.

Chapter 15, William Cronon, "The Trouble with Wilderness: Or, Getting Back to the Wrong Nature," *Environmental History*, Vol. 1, No. 1 (Jan., 1996), pp. 7–28.

Chapter 16, José A. Padua, "'Annihilating Natural Productions': Nature's Economy, Colonial Crisis and the Origins of Brazilian Political Environmentalism (1786–1810)," *Environment and History*, Vol. 6, No. 3 (1 August 2000), pp. 255–87.

Chapter 17, Catherine Knight, "Conservation Movement in Post-War Japan," *Environment and History*, Vol. 16 (2010), pp. 349–70.

Chapter 18, Ramachandra Guha, "The Authoritarian Biologist and the Arrogance of Anti-humanism: Wildlife Conservation in the Third World." *The Ecologist*, Vol. 27, No. 1 (Jan.–Feb., 1997), pp. 14–20.

EDITORS' INTRODUCTION

J.R. McNeill and Alan Roe

Global environmental history is both a daunting prospect and a logical endeavor. It is daunting because trying to make sense of the entirety of the history of human interaction with planet Earth seems to require more than one lifetime spent sifting through an ever-growing quantity of relevant information. It is logical because in the environment, as in history, everything is connected to everything else and nothing stands on its own. As one of the patron saints of American environmentalism, John Muir, put it: "When we try to pick out anything by itself, we find it hitched to everything else in the Universe."[1]

What is global environmental history?

Let's begin with environmental history, and deal with the 'global' part later.[2] As a scholarly field, it dates back to the 1970s, although one can easily point to earlier works that, without using the same vocabulary, take on some of the same subjects. Many but not all of the early pioneers were historians of the American West. Environmental history has always been the province of scholars from many disciplines, not just history but others from anthropology to ecology to geography. This entails certain differences of approach. Scholars trained in ecology, for example, might employ pollen cores to reconstruct vegetation patterns of the past. Geographers might examine soil deposition at a river's mouth to draw conclusions about past land use practices upstream. Historians are trained to rely on texts and to ferret out their meanings. Collectively, using one another's work, scholars can provide better understandings of environmental change through time than any single discipline can do alone.[3]

The authors represented in this book are mainly historians. Several of them, however, have leaned upon the work of scholars in the natural or social sciences to help them build their stories. And some of our authors are themselves natural scientists, another is a sociologist, and two are philosophers. When reading these chapters – indeed when reading anything – it is advisable to look for clues about where the authors got their information and what kinds of data they prefer over others. That will help you understand why some subjects receive more emphasis than others, and why some things might be left out entirely.

The broad vistas of environmental history invite varied approaches. There are, we claim, three principal areas of inquiry in environmental history.[4] They overlap and have no firm boundaries.

First is the study of environmental change through time, or material environmental history. This is the story of human involvement with forests and frogs, with cholera and chlorofluorocarbons. This approach involves the examination of human impact on the physical, biological, and chemical environment as well as nature's influence upon human affairs. These influences – human upon nature and nature upon humans – are reciprocal and always undergoing adjustment. Changes to nature generate changes to society, and changes to society generate new changes to nature in an endless co-evolution. There is no determinism here: culture and nature help shape one another. This form of environmental history puts human history in a fuller context, that of Earth and life on Earth, and recognizes that human events are part of a larger story in which humans are not the only actors. In practice, most of the environmental history written in this vein stresses the economic and technological side of human actions, and concentrates on the last 200 years when industrialization in particular greatly enhanced the human power to alter environments.

A second approach is cultural and intellectual environmental history. It concerns what people have thought, believed, and written dealing with relationships between society and nature. It emphasizes representations and images of nature in art, literature, religious texts, and oral traditions, how these images have changed, and what they reveal about the societies and cultures that produced them.[5] The great majority of cultural environmental history is drawn from published texts, and often treats the works of influential (and sometimes not-so-influential) authors from Lucretius and Mencius to Mohandas K. Gandhi and Al Gore. This sort of environmental history tends to focus on individual thinkers but it can also embrace the study of popular environmentalism as a mass cultural movement. The largest debate within this wing of environmental history, however, has been the relative impact of various religio-cultural traditions on the natural world. This scholarship evaluates the texts and practices of Judeo-Christian, Islamic, East Asian, and indigenous spiritual traditions, attempting to determine their effects on the environment and their influence upon environmentalism.[6]

The third main approach is political and policy-related environmental history. It concerns the history of deliberate efforts to regulate the human impact on nature, and to address struggles among social groups in matters concerning nature. Early examples of soil conservation, air pollution control, and royal efforts to protect charismatic animals for a monarch's hunting pleasure go back many centuries (yes, there were air pollution regulations in medieval London!).[7] But normally policy-related environmental history extends back only to the late nineteenth century. Since 1880 more and more states and societies have gone beyond addressing single environmental issues (e.g. coal-smoke in London) and mounted systematic efforts to regulate interactions with the environment generally. Between 1880 and 1965 these efforts were normally spasmodic and often modest in their impacts. Since 1965, these interventions – both by states and environmental NGOs – have been both more pervasive and more effective. As a result of this recent flurry of environmental regulation, much of this sort of environmental history deals with the decades since 1965. Political environmental history is the approach that most easily dovetails with the conventions of mainstream history. Its practitioners use familiar sorts of source materials: government archives, printed documents, laws, and so forth. It also often uses the nation-state as its unit of analysis, although political and policy environmental history is occasionally done on international scales, and sometimes on local ones. Other types of environmental history tend to overlook political boundaries, following ideas or sulphur dioxide plumes wherever they might waft.

Now let's consider the logic of environmental history with global scope. Many ecological processes are global in scale. Consider climate change, sea-level rise, or biological invasions for example.[8] Some other environmental processes occur widely around the world, such as soil erosion, river channelization, or urban air pollution. Many cultural trends concerning the environment have been nearly global too, most obviously the post-1960s expression of ecological anxiety, although of course it took different forms in different cultures.[9] The political urge to regulate the environment is, in the twenty-first century, almost fully global.

Global-scale environmental history, like global and world history in general, stands upon the foundation of detailed local work and regional surveys. No single historian can master the complexities of soil history or the history of water pollution everywhere around the world, just as no one can fully master the global history of labor movements or stone tool technology of the Paleolithic. No one can read all the languages, nor all the relevant texts and scholarly studies. All global and world history has this problem, and for many historians this alone has sufficed to make any attempt at world history suspect.

But something is gained and something lost with any choice of scale. There is no purely intellectual reason to prefer microhistory to macrohistory. That goes for labor history, cultural history, military history, and every other subfield, environmental history included. There are of course practical reasons to prefer micro scales: bringing coherence to the subject of the global history of air pollution is much more difficult than, say, to the history of the killer fog event in London in December 1952 – itself a challenging and rewarding subject.[10] Global perspectives may be harder for authors to present clearly, but they are inherently no more or less valid than smaller ones. Just as it is useful to have both maps that show the whole world and maps that show only the streets of midtown Manhattan, it is helpful to have histories on different scales. And in environmental history, where there are truly global-scale processes sometimes at work, global-scale history is not only just as valid as smaller-scale history, but (depending on the topic) sometimes essential to anything more than a fragmented picture.

Varieties of global environmental history

Scholarly work in global environmental history is now about two decades old. There were some tentative steps and false starts before the late 1980s. For example, the prolific English world historian, Arnold J. Toynbee, in the summer of 1973 at the end of his long career, wrote a book which he entitled *Mankind and Mother Earth*.[11] In his Introduction, he referred to the book as "a retrospective survey of the history, to date, of the encounter between Mother Earth and Man, the mightiest and most enigmatic of all her children."[12] That sounds like environmental history. But unfortunately the book was nothing of the sort, merely a reworking of political, military, and religious history of the sort Toynbee had written often enough before, with a few unoriginal laments about pollution tossed in. Toynbee had seen the logic of global environmental history, but as an octogenarian could not re-program himself as an historian sufficiently to follow that logic and fulfill the promise of the book's title and Introduction.

The first global environmental history syntheses came not from professional historians such as Toynbee, but from outsiders to the discipline. They were, therefore, less inhibited by their training and the expectations of the historical profession. British geographers and a former civil servant of the United Kingdom wrote the first popular general surveys, the former in sober style and the latter with the panache of a muckraking journalist.[13] Sociologists too joined the fray.[14] Eventually natural scientists offered global historical treatments of subjects such as nitrogen and soil.[15] A multi-disciplinary magnum opus from 1990, B.L. Turner et al, *The Earth as Transformed by Human Action* helped spur global historians to action. It drew on the skills of dozens of scholars from at least a dozen disciplines to describe and explain environmental change around the world, on every scale, since 1700.[16]

Professional historians began prudently by taking on slices of the whole. As far back as 1972, Alfred W. Crosby penned an influential history of the Columbian Exchange, a term he coined to refer to the transfer of plants, animals, and disease-causing pathogens back and forth across the Atlantic in the aftermath of 1492. He followed that in 1987 with a more ecologically sophisticated study of the environmental components behind successful European imperialism in the Americas and Australasia.[17] A synopsis of that book appears here as Chapter 9. Richard Grove authored a study of environmental ideas and practices in the British and French empires.[18] Stephen Pyne, who like Crosby appears in this volume, wrote books on global fire history, while Ramachandra Guha – also among our authors – published a short history of environmentalism around the world.[19] Pyne's work, which grew out of his earlier studies of fire in American history, sought to discuss every aspect of the human relationship with fire, from cooking and the physiology of digestion to the cultural perceptions of wildfires. Guha's treatise on modern environmentalism emphasized the contrasts among the many social movements that go by that name.

Joachim Radkau was perhaps the first to bring the training and sensibilities of the historian to general global scale environmental history. His *Natur und Macht: Eine Weltgeschichte der Umwelt*, now available in English,[20] was not a survey aiming at worldwide coverage, but a sprawling series of reflections on everything from animal domestication to contemporary eco-tourism. It reads a bit like Arnold Toynbee's *A Study of History* with its bold comparisons and juxtapositions across time and space. Unlike Toynbee, whom Radkau read in his youth, the German was reluctant to offer grand pronouncements, preferring to honor historians' traditional respect for the particularities of different times and places.[21]

A platoon of professional historians brought out global-scale environmental histories of one sort or another around the same time as Radkau's. Brief surveys, apparently intended for classroom use, poured forth from Europe and the U.S.[22] A pair of longer studies took on slices of time that, their authors claimed, exhibited some coherence: John Richards surveyed the early modern centuries so strongly affected by European expansion, and J.R. McNeill portrayed the twentieth century as an era of unprecedentedly tumultuous environmental change.[23]

Other scholars presented thematic slices of global environmental history, such as deforestation or malaria, over several millennia.[24] Wide-ranging anthologies added to the sudden outpouring – and sidestepped the main limitation of global history, the inability of any single author to know enough.[25] The British Empire, on which the sun famously never set, provided a framework that added coherence to global environmental history as shown in the overview by William Beinart and Lotte Hughes.[26] To date no one has chosen to follow their example with respect to any other modern empires, such as the French, Dutch, or Japanese, all of which would make good subjects for environmental historians.

Global environmental history has come a long way in a brief time. The persistent presence of environmental issues in modern life has made environmental history a permanent fixture of historiography, unlikely to wither away any time soon. The mounting salience of climate concerns, deforestation, water shortages, and loss of biodiversity has convinced some historians, previously working far from environmental history, that it is no longer appropriate to write history without taking the environment, especially climate change, into account.[27] Furthermore, global-scale environmental history has benefited from the rise of world or global history, an intellectual response to the recent surge of globalization and, in the U.S. at least, a practical response to political pressures upon school curricula.[28] Over time, the teaching of world history has slowly legitimized, or at least begun to legitimize, world history scholarship, including global environmental history. Much has indeed been done, but, as always, further opportunities abound. Some day someone will write a global environmental history of railroads, of mining, of war, of cattle, of the oceans, of religion, of odors, of things as yet unimagined. Global environmental history still has a long way to go.

The purpose and contents of this book

The goal of this book is to provide a measure of orientation and introduction to the nascent field of global environmental history. It is intended for students, for teachers, and the curious public at large. The editors hope the selections are accessible to readers with no background whatsoever in environmental history, but also useful for those who already have some grounding in the field but seek to widen their horizons.

Organized into three parts—(I) Global Perspectives, (II) Regional Perspectives, and (III) Environmentalisms, this collection incorporates themes that have wide resonance for environmental historians Taken together, these pieces included here will give readers a sense of the multidisciplinary nature of this young field. While the chronological scope in the Global Perspectives part varies from centuries to millennia, the subjects of these essays are all trans-regional if not always fully global.

In "Changing Times: The Holocene Legacy," William R. Dickinson, an American geoscientist, provides a *longue durée* view of human-induced and naturally occurring changes to the environment during the Holocene. The Holocene is the geological epoch that began with the melting of the Pleistocene ice sheets nearly 12,000 years ago. Dickinson's long view reminds us that some environmental changes only become evident over the course of thousands of years. Taking this into account, environmental historians rarely accept the notion that there are certain "environmental baselines," or natural equilibria that should inform environmental policy. This is especially relevant to debates within restoration ecology, because when restoring anything one has to ask: restore it to its condition as of when?

Ecological ideas, such as "environmental baselines," emerged in the modern era. While no concept such as conservation existed until recently, in "Dark is the World to Thee: A Historical Perspective on Environmental Forewarnings," Teresa Kwiatkowska and Alan Holland (philosophers based in Mexico and the U.K. respectively) demonstrate that environmental problems and resource depletion long predate the development of industrial society and concern for these issues existed long before the birth of modern conservation. The authors also examine early proto-scientific views that informed classical philosophers' views of the place of humans in the larger order. This essay also illuminates the prevailing Western view until the twentieth century that uncultivated nature was gloomy, dreadful, and even terrifying – a subject that occupied many of the early environmental histories of ideas. It is instructive to read it together with Pádua's essay (Chapter 16 in this volume).

Because the life beneath its surface long remained out of view for most people, historians have frequently viewed the ocean as standing outside the realm of history. Moreover, with the exception of some species of whales, it was long held that marine life was inexhaustible. With advances in marine biology over the past few decades, the astonishing toll that the fishing industry has taken on marine life has become increasingly apparent. Environmental historians have only recently started writing about the world's marine environment, but the American historian Jeffrey Bolster's call for further research in this area has begun to spur a reponse.[29]

Carolyn Merchant, an American historian and one of the pioneers of environmental history, argues in "Gender and Environmental History," that environmental historians also failed to give gender its due. She states that issues of production and reproduction are two important ways in which gender analysis can and should enrich the field. The field has, in part but only in part, heeded her call. This piece remains important because it provides a glimpse of the development of the field and points to many directions for further research that are still far from exhausted.[30]

While most environmental historians focus on environmental changes within a specific polity, the American historian and polymath Stephen Pyne has made his mark on the field by studying fire throughout human history. In "Consumed by either Fire or Fire: A Review of the Environmental Consequences of Anthropogenic Fire," Pyne argues that by capturing fire humans began the era of large-scale anthropogenic environmental change. While Pyne's approach is historical in many parts of the article, he begins with a thorough scientific discussion of fire ecology. This is unusual (but not unique) as an approach within environmental history. Moreover, while most of the pieces in this book follow a chronological sequence, Pyne's reads more as a reflective piece about fire and its role throughout history.[31]

Global commerce has undoubtedly been the most important agent of species translocation over the past few centuries. Lately, historians such as Crosby have explained this from the perspective of the spread of pathogens. Yet as Donald Kennedy and Marjorie Lucks (environmental scientist and earth scientist respectively) argue, in "Rubber, Blight, and Mosquitoes: Biogeography Meets the Global Economy," environmental historians have paid relatively little attention to this from the perspective of ecosystem change, including species extinction. The authors also show the near impossibility of understanding resource depletion within a given place without understanding the broader market forces at work.

Arguing that animal histories have moved into the mainstream of environmental history in the two decades prior to the publication of this piece, historian Harriet Ritvo's "Animal Planet" examines the multiple ways that animals have or could fit into the field. From hunting, to domestication, to species extinction, to animals' places in some cultural narratives, environmental history, even much of human history in general, is difficult to delineate from the history of animals. And as she shows, while much of environmental history depicts humankind as an agent of harm, the history of animals can be central in thinking about the symbiotic links between humans and the rest of nature.[32]

Historian Edmund Russell's "Evolutionary History: Prospectus for a New Field," demonstrates the far-reaching applications and definitions of environmental history and hence the field's openness to innovation and new approaches. Throughout the latter half of the twentieth century, the humanities proved reluctant to embrace the insights and advances of evolutionary biology, but, as Russell demonstrates, few fields could stand to benefit from it more than environmental history. Evolutionary history stands to provide much insight into questions of both short- and long-term environmental change.[33]

Largely a synthesis of his two seminal works[34] in the filed of environmental history, historian Alfred W. Crosby's "Ecological Imperialism: The Overseas Migration of Western Europeans as a Biological Phenomenon," provides one example of an environmental historian employing the ideas of evolution and ecology in a broad explanation for the course of political, economic, and social history over the past few centuries. Crosby's vision of European expansion, and the role of plants, animals, and pathogens in bringing it about, is one of the classic and most influential arguments ever made in environmental history. It has its critics, of course, who by and large take issue with what they see as an overly determinist view that slights human agency and moral responsibility.

The Regional Perspectives part includes pieces about Europe, Russia, China, South America, West Africa, and Latin America. In "Environment and Society: Long-Term Trends in Latin America Mining," U.K.-based historian Elizabeth Dore examines environmental change in Latin America in five different periods – pre-conquest, colonial, neocolonial, capitalist modernization, and the debt crisis that began in the 1970s. She takes on the myth of the 'ecologically noble savage' by showing how recent research has demonstrated that the Aztecs and Mayas hardly lived in harmony with nature. But Dore also shows how technological advancement has exacerbated environmental despoliation. This has been especially true in Latin

America during the twentieth century when mining technologies grew more powerful, the profit motive took full precedence over long-term environmental stability, and when governments were reluctant to enact or enforce environmental laws.

Joachim Radkau's "Exceptionalism in European Environmental History" examines what has made the European relationship with the natural world distinctive. World historians and historians of Europe have argued for more than a century whether or not Europe has had a special path, and if so why. These arguments have typically been made with respect to European culture, which might – or might not – be especially helpful in achieving economic growth. Radkau – a German historian – finds that from an environmental history point of view, Europe's path has indeed been distinctive. His analysis is grounded in a comparative perspective that demonstrates how the trajectory of European environmental history differed from that of other regions in several fundamental respects.[35]

Mark Elvin's "Three Thousand Years of Unsustainable Growth: China's Environment from Archaic Times to the Present," provides a good example of long-term environmental history within a specific region. Elvin wrestles with whether environmental change can be best explained by demographic changes or by external forces – in this case, policies of the state. Through his nuanced treatment of the different periods of Chinese environmental history, he concludes overwhelmingly that demographic changes were secondary to the policies enacted by imperial China's dynasties. Moreover, Elvin, a historian who made his career in Australia, demonstrates that the state's efforts at environmental conservation sometimes imposed hardships on peasant groups, which depended on natural resources for their subsistence. While forest cover retreated consistently over the three-thousand-year period that Elvin examines, the carrying capacity of the land expanded.[36]

Doug Weiner's "The Predatory, Tribute-Taking State: A Framework for Understanding Russian Environmental History," also takes the view that state policies or governing style was central to understanding environmental change. Emphasizing state actions more than any other piece in this collection, Weiner, a historian at the University of Arizona, attributes environmental change in Imperial Russia and the Soviet Union to the very specific political culture that took root with the emergence of Muscovy in the fifteenth and sixteenth centuries. While some twentieth-century environmental historians have viewed capitalism as the primary agent of environmental destruction in the twentieth century, Weiner reminds us that the Communist system of the Soviet Union held its own in this category.[37]

James L. A. Webb Jr's "Ecology and Culture in West Africa," provides a long view of environmental change in West Africa's diverse landscapes of woodlands, desert, and savanna grasslands. A historian working in the U.S., Webb pushes the reader beyond simplistic notions of geographical determinism and argues that indigenous Africans caused changes in the landscape, often burning forests to make room for agriculture or to lessen the risk of sleeping sickness by reducing the habitat of the tsetse fly. Moreover, he shows how evolutionary adaptations especially to malaria helped African populations survive and flourish within these landscapes.[38]

The third part is the most circumscribed chronologically, as environmentalism is a twentieth-century, mainly a post-World War II, phenomenon. William Cronon's "The Trouble with Wilderness: Or, Getting Back to the Wrong Nature," was a seminal piece in the "great wilderness debate" that weighed heavily on the field during its first few decades, but especially during the 1990s. According to Cronon, a U.S. historian, the American obsession with the particular cultural construct of wilderness – the myth that America was pristine prior to interference by Euroamericans – and the juridical status it attained through the Wilderness Act (1964) has diverted environmentalists from environmental issues related to social justice. Cronon's plea for a wider view by environmentalists is an example of how environmental historians can bring perspective to contemporary environmental concerns – and ignite firestorms of controversy.[39]

Catherine Knight's "Conservation Movement in Post-war Japan," demonstrates that Japanese environmentalism was grounded in conventional calculations of national welfare. Human health, rather than the ecological concerns that strongly influenced U.S. environmentalism, served as the catalyst. Furthermore, as the New Zealander historian of Japan shows, expected economic benefits provided almost the only basis for the construction of the first Japanese national parks. While the Japanese Environmental Agency has focused much of its attention on pollution abatement, the nation's headlong push towards economic development made this project exceptionally difficult in the post-war era.

José Augusto Pádua, a Brazilian environmental historian, in his chapter "'Annihilating Natural Productions': Nature's Economy, Colonial Crisis, and the Origins of Brazilian Political Environmentalism (1786–1810)," uncovers a lost discourse from colonial Brazil that has a modern ring to it. Many Brazilian intellectuals in the decades prior to independence voiced concerns over the inefficient use, and indeed outright squander, of Brazil's forests and soils. They felt in particular that Brazil's agricultural techniques were backward and hamstrung by the reliance on slavery, so that arguments in favor of environmental stewardship and in favor of the abolition of slavery coincided. One of the authors Pádua studied even objected to over-harvesting of whales. While in some analyses the European Enlightenment of the eighteenth century is associated with reckless exploitation of resources, in Brazil, Pádua finds, intellectuals of the Enlightenment spoke out clearly for careful conservation of nature's bounty.[40]

Ramachandra Guha, a sociologist and historian from India, is our final author. In his chapter, "The Authoritarian Biologist and the Arrogance of

Anti-humanism: Wildlife Conservation in the Third World," he launches a searing attack on one form of environmentalism, conservation biology. Drawing on comments, mainly from the 1980s, made by biologists with respect to wildlife in Africa and India, Guha shows their insensitivity to the human beings living in wildlife-rich areas. These biologists, mainly American and European, failed to grasp the circumstances of farmers and pastoralists who seek their livings in landscapes shared with elephants, lions, and tigers. While conservation biology has evolved since Guha (and others) launched this critique, the conflict in values over how best to manage such landscapes remains. Should people be displaced to save tigers from extinction? Should tigers be relocated to save people from their attacks? For some people these are easy questions. For others, they are not.[41]

Of the thousands of short pieces in environmental history, we chose eighteen. They include authors who are titans in the field, and authors who (as yet) have not attained such status. Some chapters are calls for work in new arenas of research, such as the chapters of Bolster and Russell. Some are efforts to blend environmental perspectives with longstanding concerns of historians such as empire and gender in the chapters of Crosby and Merchant. Some – Dickinson, Pyne, and Elvin – deal with millennial time scales while those focused on environmentalism – Cronon, Pádua, Knight, and Guha – confine themselves to decades. Some put the state at the center of their analysis, Elvin and Weiner for example, while others emphasize culture, such as Kwiatkowska and Holland. Some are explicitly comparative, such as Radkau and Guha, while others, such as Webb and Dore are macro-regional in scope.

They could be lumped together in any number of ways, not just the one way we chose. With a little imagination, you can find them in conversation with one another, respectfully disagreeing about the role of the state, just what constitutes 'environmentalism,' or the ideal geographic or chronological scale on which to do environmental history. In any case, we hope you enjoy reading them, and are inspired to explore further the expanding universe of global environmental history.

Notes

1 Muir, *My First Summer in the Sierra* (Boston: Houghton Mifflin, 1911), ch. 6 (accessed at: http://www.sierraclub.org/john_muir_exhibit/frameindex.html? http://www.sierraclub.org/john_muir_exhibit/writings/misquotes.html)

2 Among useful primers, see J. Donald Hughes, *What Is Environmental History?* (Cambridge, UK: Polity Press, 2006).

3 E. Le Roy Ladurie, *Histoire du climat depuis l'an mil.* (Paris: Flammarion, 1967). Le Roy Ladurie revised his positions substantially in *Histoire humaine et comparée du climat* (Paris: Fayard, 2004–9), 3 vols. A sample of more recent climate history: Georgina Endfield, *Climate and Society in Colonial Mexico: A Study in Vulnerability* (Oxford and New York: Wiley-Blackwell, 2008); Franz

Mauelshagen, *Klimageschichte der Neuzeit 1500–1900* (Darmstadt, 2009); Sam White, *Climate of Rebellion* (New York: Cambridge University Press, 2011); Wolfgang Behringer, *A Cultural History of Climate* (Malden MA: Polity, 2010); Sherry Johnson, *Climate and Catastrophe in Cuba and the Atlantic World in the Age of Revolution* (Chapel Hill: UNC Press, 2011); Hubert H. Lamb, *A History of Climate Changes* (London: Routledge, 2011), 4 vols (these volumes contain reprints of Lamb's pioneering work from 1966 to 1988); a fascinating essay that attributes great significance to climate change is Richard Bulliet, *Cotton, Climate, and Camels in Early Islamic Iran* (New York: Columbia University Press, 2011).

4 The following paragraphs revisit arguments made at length in J.R. McNeill, "The Nature and Culture of Environmental History," *History and Theory* 42(2003), 5–43.

5 Remarkably the most comprehensive work in this vein as regards the Western world was written over 40 years ago, Clarence Glacken's *Traces on the Rhodian Shore: Nature and Culture in Western Thought from Ancient Times to the End of the Eighteenth Century* (Berkeley: University of California Press, 1967). Glacken's massive work explored the conceptions of nature among several dozen prominent writers from ancient times through the European Enlightenment. Other examples include Donald Worster's *Nature's Economy: A History of Ecological Ideas* (New York: Cambridge University Press, 1985) and Peter Coates, *Nature: Western Attitudes since the Ancient Times* (Cambridge: Polity Press, 1998).

6 See, for example, Lynn White, "The Historical Roots of Our Ecologic Crisis," *Science* 155 (1967): pp. 1203–7; Yif-fu Tuan, "Discrepancies between Environmental Attitude and Behaviour: Examples from Europe and China," *Canadian Geographer* 3 (1968): pp. 175–91; Hussein Amery, "Islam and the Environment," in: Naser I. Faruqui, Asit K. Biswas, Murad J. Bino, eds., *Water Management in Islam* (Tokyo: United Nations University Press, 2001), 39–60. A useful overview is Joachim Radkau, "Religion and Environmentalism," in: J.R. McNeill and Erin Stewart Mauldin, eds., *A Companion to Global Environmental History* (Oxford: Wiley-Blackwell, 2012), 493–512.

7 See Peter Brimblecombe, *The Big Smoke* (London: Methuen, 1987).

8 No single biological invasion affected the whole world except the spread of humans. But biological invasions of one sort or another have affected every square meter of the Earth's surface and possible every cubic meter of the oceans. A useful introduction to the phenomenon is Daniel Simberloff and Marcel Rejmanek, eds. *Encyclopedia of Biological Invasions* (Berkeley: University of California Press, 2011).

9 See Joachim Radkau *Die Ära der Ökologie: Eine Weltgeschichte* (Munich: Beck, 2011).

10 A recent treatment is Michelle Bell, Devra Davis, and Tony Fletcher, "A Retrospective Assessment of Mortality from the London Smog Episode of 1952," *Urban Ecology* (2008): pp. 263–68.

11 (Oxford: Oxford University Press, 1976).

12 Ibid, 18.

13 Ian G. Simmons, *Changing the Face of the Earth: Culture, Environment, History* (New York: Blackwell, 1989); Antoinette Mannion, *Global Environmental Change: A Natural and Cultural Environmental History* (Harlow, UK: Longman, 1991); Clive Ponting, *A Green History of the World* (Harmondsworth: Penguin, 1991). For Simmons' latest entry: *Global Environmental History* (Chicago: University of Chicago Press, 2008).

14 B. Vries and J. Goudsblom, *Mappae Mundi: Humans and Their Habitats in Long-term Socio-ecological Perspective* (Amsterdam: Amsterdam University Press, 2002.)

15 Donald Vasey, *An Ecological History of Agriculture: 10,000 B.C. to 10,000 A.D.* (Lafayette, IN: Purdue University Press, 1992); Vaclav Smil, *Energy in World History* (Boulder: Westview, 1994); G. Leigh, *The World's Greatest Fix: A History of Nitrogen and Agriculture* (Oxford: Oxford University Press, 2004); J.R. McNeill and Verena Winiwarter, eds., *Soils and Societies: Perspectives from Environmental History* (Isle of Harris: White Horse Press, 2006); Antoinette Mannion, *Carbon and Its Domestication* (Dordrecht: Springer, 2006); David Montgomery, *Dirt: The Erosion of Civilizations* (Berkeley: University of California Press, 2007).

16 *The Earth As Transformed by Human Action* (New York: Cambridge University Press, 1990).

17 Alfred W. Crosby, *The Columbian Exchange: Biological and Cultural Consquences of 1492* (Westport CT, Greenwood Press, 1972); Crosby, *Ecological Imperialism: The Biological Expansion of Europe, 900–1900* (New York: Cambridge University Press, 1987).

18 Richard Grove, *Green Imperialism* (New York: Cambridge University Press, 1995).

19 Stephen J. Pyne, *World Fire: The Culture of Fire on Earth*. Seattle: University of Washington Press, 1995; Ramachandra Guha, *Environmentalism* (New York: Longman, 2000).

20 Joachim Radkau, *Natur und Macht: Eine Weltgeschichte der Umwelt* (Munich: Beck, 2000); the English translation, made by Thomas Dunlap, is *Nature and Power: A Global History of the Environment* (New York: Cambridge University Press, 2008).

21 See his essay on his own work, "Nature and Power: An Ambiguous and Intimate Connection," *Social Science History* forthcoming.

22 Sverker Sörlin and Anders Öckerman, *Jorden en ö* (Stockholm: Natur och Kultur, 1998); J. Donald Hughes, *An Environmental History of the World: Humankind's Changing Role in the Community of Life* (London: Routledge, 2001); Joachim Radkau, *Mensch und Natur in der Geschichte* (Leipzig: Klett 2002); Stephen Mosley, *The Environment in World History* (London: Routledge, 2006); Verena Winiwarter and Martin Knoll, *Umweltgeschichte* (Cologne: Böhlau, 2007); Anthony Penna, *The Human Footprint: A Global Environmental History* (Malden MA: Blackwell, 2009).

23 John F. Richards, *The Unending Frontier: An Environmental History of the Early Modern World* (Berkeley: University of California Press, 2003); J.R. McNeill, *Something New Under the Sun: An Environmental History of the Twentieth-century World* (New York: Norton, 2000).

24 Michael Williams, *Deforesting the Earth: From Prehistory to Global Crisis* (Chicago: University of Chicago Press, 2003); James L.A. Webb Jr., *Humanity's Burden: A Global History of Malaria* (New York: Cambridge University Press, 2009).

25 Three examples of several: Alf Hornborg, J.R. McNeill, and Juan Martinez-Alier, eds., *Rethinking Environmental History: World-System History and Global Environmental Change* (Lanham, MD: Altamira Press, 2007); Edmund Burke III and Kenneth Pomeranz, eds., *The Environment and World History* (Berkeley: University of California Press, 2009); Timo Myllyntaus, ed., *Thinking through the Environment: Green Approaches to Global History* (Cambridge, UK: White Horse Press, 2011).

26 William Beinart and Lotte Hughes, *Environment and Empire* (New York: Oxford University Press, 2007).

27 Dipesh Chakrabarty, "The Climate of History: Four Theses," *Critical Inquiry* 35(2009): pp. 197–222.

28 In the U.S., where the ethnic origins of populations plays a role in the formation of political blocs, and where political blocs often interest themselves in school curricula, world history is the easiest compromise among the possible ways of presenting history to young people because – in theory at least – it leaves no one's ancestors out.

29 One recent example, better researched than most, is Bo Poulsen, *Dutch Herring: An Environmental History, c. 1600–1860* (Amsterdam: Aksant, 2008).

30 Merchant's most influential works in ecofeminist environmental history are *The Death of Nature: Women, Ecology, and the Scientific Revolution* (San Francisco: Harper & Row, 1980); *Ecological Revolutions: Nature, Gender, and Science in New England* (Chapel Hill: University of North Carolina Press, 1989).

31 A sample of Pyne's fire history is *Fire: A Brief History* (Seattle: University of Washington Press, 2001).

32 For Ritvo's work in animal history, see *The Animal Estate: the English and Other Creatures in the Victorian Age* (Cambridge, MA: Harvard University Press, 1987); *The Platypus and the Mermaid and Other Figments of the Classifying Imagination* (Cambridge, MA: Harvard University Press, 1997).

33 Russell has lately explored these themes at length in *Evolutionary History: Uniting History and Biology to Understand Life on Earth* (New York: Cambridge University Press, 2011).

34 Cited in note 16.

35 Radkau's major works are cited in notes 9, 20 and 22.

36 Elvin's magnum opus in this field is *The Retreat of the Elephants: An Environmental History of China* (New Haven: Yale University Press, 2004). A co-edited work of his remains important: Elvin and Liu Ts'ui-jung, eds., *Sediments of Time: Environment and Society in Chinese History* (New York: Cambridge University Press, 1998).

37 Weiner's work is best exemplified by *Models of Nature: Ecology, Conservation, and Cultural Revolution in Soviet Russia* (Bloomington: University of Indiana Press, 1988) and *A Little Corner of Freedom: Russian Nature Protection from Stalin to Gorbachev* (Berkeley: University of California Press, 1999).

38 Webb's most notable work on Africa (he has written on Sri Lanka and on the world scale as well) is *Desert Frontier: Ecological and Economic Change along the Western Sahel, 1600–1850* (Madison: University of Wisconsin Press, 1995).

39 Cronon's reputation rests chiefly on *Changes in the Land: Indians, Colonists, and the Ecology of New England* (New York: Hill & Wang, 1983) and *Nature's Metropolis: Chicago and the Great West* (New York: Norton, 1991).

40 Pádua explores these issues in *Um sopro de destruição: pensamento político e crítica ambiental no Brasil escravista, 1786–1888* (Rio de Janeiro: Zahar, 2002).

41 Guha's major works in environmental history (he also writes on Indian history and current affairs generally) include *The Unquiet Woods: Ecological Change and Peasant Resistance in the Himalaya* (Berkeley: University of California Press, 2000) and *How Much Should A Person Consume?: Environmentalism in India and the United States* (Berkeley: University of California Press, 2006).

Part I

GLOBAL PERSPECTIVES

1

CHANGING TIMES

The Holocene legacy

William R. Dickinson

Environmentalism has become a powerful force in global scientific and political affairs. Part of its influence stems from the truism that a viable environment is not just a lofty ideal but a practical necessity for the future of humanity. Another part comes from a reawakening of prehumanistic thoughts that humanity is not necessarily the sole measure of all things. These two threads of modern environmental thinking underscore the age-old question of the place of humankind in nature. Alternate concepts about the relationship of human beings to nature depend largely on philosophical attitudes independent of any external reality, but accurate perception of environmental history is a prerequisite for valid environmental concepts. Understanding how the global environment we observe today has evolved from antecedent conditions is indispensable as part of the basis for guiding future environmental management. An adequate appraisal of environmental history must include a geological perspective.

Holocene time

In geological parlance, the time since the last great Pleistocene ice sheets melted away is termed the Holocene, which has not been a long chapter in the history of the Earth. Together, the Pleistocene and Holocene make up the Quaternary period, marked by waxing and waning of polar glaciers. The round number of 10,000 years ago is commonly taken to mark the beginning of Holocene time, although improved calibration of radiocarbon dating indicates that 11,500–11,600 years is a better estimate (see Figure 1.1). The time span of the postglacial world has been surprisingly brief, and in geological terms, most modern environments have a short time depth.

The glacial world of the Pleistocene was dramatically different from our own. At times of glacial maxima, the most recent of which was only 20,000–22,000 years ago, great ice sheets covered most of North America as far south as Seattle, Chicago, and New York City. In Europe (see Figure 1.2),

3

a curved line connecting the capital cities of London, Berlin, Warsaw, and Moscow delineates the approximate ice limit, with a variety of those locales overrun by ice during periods of intense glacial advances and lying just beyond the ice limit during lesser advances. At such times, the Baltic Sea and the shallower part of the North Sea between Great Britain and Norway disappeared beneath ice cover that crowned Scandinavia, and northern Europe closely resembled modern Greenland in its climate and overall aspect.[1]

When Pleistocene ice was in place, the geographic tracts of North America and Europe that are now temperate grasslands and mixed forests were very different places. Tundra and open steppe occupied most of Europe south to the Mediterranean littoral, and a belt of tundra fringing the ice fields in North America met a broad band of coniferous forest, much like the modern Siberian taiga to the south, extending across the midsection of the United States and reaching down perhaps as far as the southern borders of Tennessee and Oklahoma (see Figure 1.3). None of the familiar landscapes of Euroamerican tradition, nor of Amerindian tradition, existed at the beginning of Holocene time.

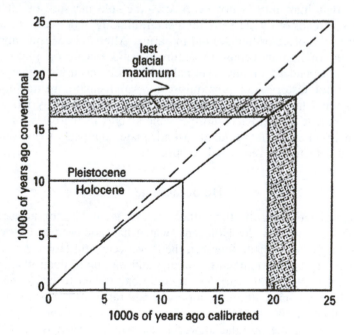

Figure 1.1 Conventional vs. calibrated radiocarbon ages. Dashed line is locus of equal ages. Solid line is actual approximate correlation of conventional and calibrated ages, with the latter derived from tree-ring chronologies for Holocene time and from independent uranium/thorium isotopic dating for Pleistocene time.[2]

Continental and island shorelines were also impacted in dramatic fashion by Pleistocene glaciation, and the direct effects extended worldwide because the continental ice sheets drew water from all the oceans. During peak glaciation, global sea level stood an estimated 410 feet lower than today (see Figure 1.4). Modern shorelines, together with their associated estuaries, tidal flats and coral reefs, cannot have occupied their present positions for more than a few thousand years. Coastal ecosystems have been forced to migrate staggering distances since the waning of Pleistocene glaciers began to drive the postglacial rise in global sea level, termed *eustasy* by geologists. Sea level was still perhaps 300 feet below its modern position as recently as 15,000 years ago. Typically, the postglacial biotic migrations were much greater than just the distances landward from synglacial positions of the strandline directly offshore. Climatic zones and water masses shifted latitude as glaciation waned, meaning that many littoral species also had to move hundreds of miles laterally along coastlines to arrive at congenial Holocene environments.

Coastlines near regions of Pleistocene glaciation paradoxically experienced an opposite change in relative sea level when the ice sheets melted. Removal of the weight of thick glacial ice caused the landscape to be uplifted at rates that outpaced the eustatic rise in sea level. Geologists term such postglacial uplift *isostatic rebound* because it stems from changes in isostasy, which refers to the processes that balance rock masses at different elevations above the fluid interior of the Earth. Because of isostatic rebound, Pleistocene paleoshorelines in formerly glaciated areas are now exposed far inland or well up the flanks of coastal mountain ranges. Along the Pacific coast of Canada, for example, paleoshorelines of Pleistocene age stand 150–500 feet above modern sea level. The isostatic rebound was time-delayed, because it could only be accomplished through slow worldwide flowage of viscous mantle lying below the stiff crust of the Earth.

Simultaneously, continental margins distant from regions of Pleistocene glaciation were tilted downward toward adjacent ocean basins when the weight of glacial meltwater was added to seawater volumes. Even at sites far removed from circumpolar ice masses, isostatic changes in local relative sea level resulting from the additional weight of ocean water left a subtle imprint on coastal landscapes. Regional isostatic adjustments to deglaciation affected sea level much less than the eustatic change in average global sea level resulting from the addition of glacial meltwater, but were quite important locally. For most Pacific islands, postglacial isostatic effects led to a relative highstand of five to eight feet in regional sea level during mid-Holocene time, peaking perhaps 4,000 years ago.[3]

Holocene humankind

The remarkable changes in the physical environments of the Earth during the Holocene have been more than matched by the cultural evolution of humankind. At the end of the Pleistocene, none of our ancestors had access to any tools more sophisticated than could be fashioned by hand from pieces of stone, bone, or wood. Virtually all the technology upon which we now rely has been developed during Holocene time in less than five hundred human generations. Human civilization as it exists was produced by opportunistic adaptations of the human species to emerging postglacial environments.[4]

Given the fact that glaciations have waxed and waned at least a dozen times, and probably a score or more times, for well over a million years, the Holocene can be viewed as just the latest of a long series of interglacial time intervals, and destined like the others to be succeeded in due course by yet another glaciation. In one crucial respect, Holocene time has been unique among interglacial intervals. It is the first interglaciation during which anatomically modern humans existed (see Figure 1.5). Whether modern human beings emerged only 50,000 years ago, as many have

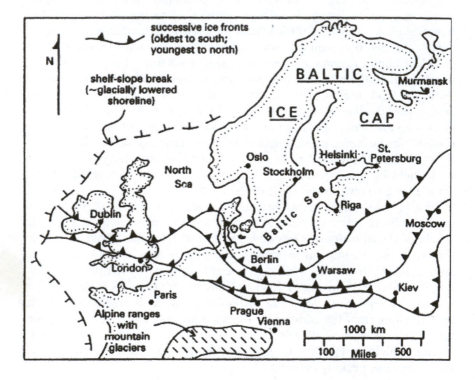

Figure 1.2 Southern limits of Pleistocene glaciations in northern Europe. Successive ice fronts mark southward extent, at various times during the Pleistocene epoch, of the vast continental glacier that blanketed the entire landscape farther north, including marine shelves exposed to the air by eustatic drawdown of sea level.[5]

thought, or have existed for nearly 100,000 years, as some now argue, none were present during the last interglaciation approximately 125,000 years ago. Interglacial climatic conditions analogous to historical experience lasted only 12,000 to 20,000 years, not markedly longer than the duration of the Holocene to date.[6]

The impact of the emerging human species on global environments during the last glaciation is moot because the conditions that prevailed then were so extensively modified by the climatic transition to Holocene time. As modern Holocene environments evolved from Pleistocene precursors, people of essentially modern aspect, driven by familiar impulses, were active on most parts of the continental landmasses from the very initiation of post-glacial conditions. The same cannot be said of oceanic islands or polar regions that people were unable to occupy before acquiring adequate maritime technology and the skills to survive under extreme climatic conditions. Exploration and settlement of the Pacific islands of Oceania, remote from the Australian and Asian landmasses, did not begin until approximately

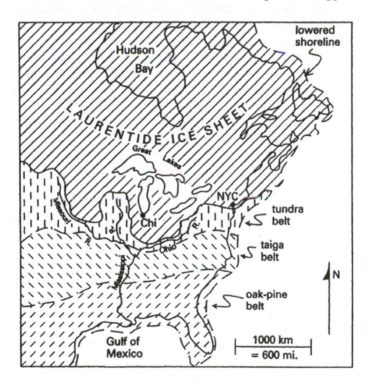

Figure 1.3 Environmental belts of eastern North America at peak glaciation – 20,000 years ago; taiga is spruce-pine evergreen forest analogous to the forests of modern Siberia; varied broadleaf tree species accompanied the oak-pine woodlands farther south.[7]

3,500 years ago. The peopling of Oceania by the Polynesians and their ancestors is one of the great sagas of prehistory but was delayed until after the middle of Holocene time.[8]

In most global environments, the Holocene landscape never established itself without human influence. Landscapes and cultures coevolved over the same intervals. Knowing the propensity of human beings to alter their surroundings indicates that the nature of Holocene environments was in part determined by human activities, even as people learned to adapt to them and exploit them for their own purposes. The environmental impact of human dispersal through Oceania over several millenia before European contact with island cultures is instructive. In island group after island group, human arrival was followed closely by environmental alteration involving forest clearance, with consequent upland erosion and downstream sedimentation, or replacement of virgin forest by agroforest developed through human silviculture.[9]

The seductive notion that the world was a pristine place before people gradually hewed their way into it, culminating their impact with the environmental insults of the industrial age, is out of focus. The landscapes of yesteryear, so beloved in our cultural memories, did not spring up wholly untouched by human hands. Nor should we view overt human manipulation, or inadvertent alteration, of the environment during prehistory as necessarily or uniformly deleterious to ambient conditions. The postglacial Holocene world was inherently in flux, and successful aboriginal cultures must have adjusted their environmental practices to modes that improved, rather than reduced, resources for subsistence.

Shoreline evolution

The glacial drawdown in global sea level has had lingering effects through much of Holocene time. In the protohistoric period of 7000–9000 BC, when many civilizations of the ancient world had their first tentative beginnings, global sea level was still more than seventy-five feet below its modern level, not rising to within fifteen feet of its present stand until about 5,000 years ago (see Figure 1.4). Massive encroachment of the sea on almost all landmasses was the rule during the first half of Holocene time. During the Pleistocene lowstand, the entire Persian (or Arabian) Gulf, down to the Strait of Hormuz, was dry land, though perhaps dotted with lakes, and the ground where ancient Mesopotamia later thrived stood roughly 600 miles from the open marine waters of the Indian Ocean. Following the postglacial eustatic rise in sea level, some 250 miles of riverine lowlands along the Tigris-Euphrates valley of the Fertile Crescent were flooded by saltwater as recently as 6,000 years ago, to be reclaimed later as dry land by fluvial aggradation. Even the seaport of Charax, founded by Alexander the Great, now lies ninety miles from open water.[10]

As the rate of rising sea level gradually slowed, rivers began to build deltas from retreating shorelines into the encroaching seas. This process became important after about 6000 BC, and led to dramatic impacts on coastal landscapes. The Holocene Mississippi River has extended its delta about 150 miles into the Gulf of Mexico, adding more than 12,000 mi^2 of land surface south of Baton Rouge to the coastal lowlands (see Figure 1.6). All the resulting diversity of levee and marshland, with its resident aquatic wildlife, occupies an area that was drowned under shelf sea at the dawn of Old World civilizations. In Egypt, the arcuate front of the Nile delta, with its classic deltoid shape, has prograded steadily into the Mediterranean at a mean rate of approximately one kilometer per century over the last 5,000 years.[11]

Recent human modifications to river regimens have now begun to reverse delta growth in key instances. Essentially all deltas subside slowly from their isostatic loads on the Earth's crust and from the time-delayed compaction of delta sediment accumulations. Without continuing deltaic sedimentation,

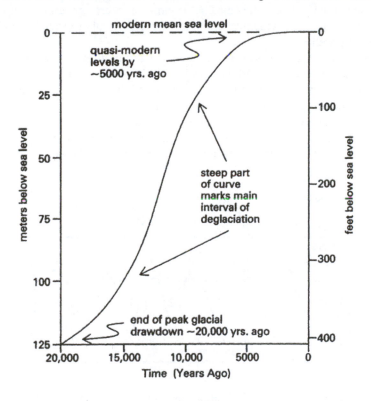

Figure 1.4 Approximate latest Pleistocene and Holocene rise in mean global sea level from eustatic change in seawater volume as deglaciation transferred mass from circumpolar ice fields to the world ocean.[12]

9

seawater encroachment is inevitable along delta margins. Upstream dams and dense networks of irrigation or drainage canals that trap sediment inhibit delta growth, as does the dredging of ship channels to funnel riverine sediment directly into deep water offshore. As a result, the Mississippi delta is currently losing subaerial delta plain at a rate nearly ten times the average rate of outbuilding over the past 8,000 years. Accelerated erosion of the front of the Nile delta has been underway for the past century, with current rates of shoreline retreat locally exceeding 250 feet per year in some years.[13]

The signal changes in worldwide strandlines during the Holocene and the comparable changes that repeatedly accompanied successive glacial-interglacial transitions throughout the duration of the Pleistocene had surprisingly little net effect on strandline biotas. We know little about shoreline faunas during Pleistocene lowstands in sea level, because drawdown in sea level placed them at sites now underwater and far offshore. From study of successive interglacial faunas, it is clear that Quaternary extinction rates of coastal marine organisms were generally unexceptional. Coastal life evidently endured the stress of repeated migration remarkably well.[14]

Analysis suggests that species survived as habitats migrated with changing times because each individual species shifts location independently, in response to its own unique tolerances and requirements, rather than as part of intact coadapted biotic communities. This picture of flux suggests that no modern coastal ecosystem is yet fully adjusted to current conditions. Each may represent a metastable state still in process of adjusting to postglacial changes in surroundings, drawing on species pools available on nearby

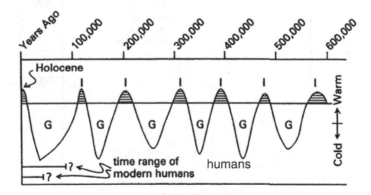

Figure 1.5 Principal climatic fluctuations over the past half million years, between glacial (G) and interglacial (I) conditions, in relation to the evolutionary emergence of anatomically modern human only 50,000 to 100,000 years ago.[15]

10

marine shelves as local conditions vary. The living biotas of modern coastal ecosystems are likely ephemeral associations caught at an arbitrary point along a spectrum of gradual change. If lasting stability of habitat and biota has been reached along any present coastline, such a state of affairs could not possibly have an antiquity of more than a few thousand years.[16]

Terrestrial surface

As Pleistocene ice masses retreated, massive biotic migrations also swept across much of the Holocene land surface as global climates changed. In Japan, far from any continental ice sheets but joined into one elongated island by drawdown in sea level during full glacial times, the extensive conifer forests of modern-day Hokkaido on the north replaced preexisting Pleistocene tundra, and the existing deciduous and evergreen broadleaf forests of the more southerly Japanese islands in turn replaced conifer forest that prevailed during glacial times.[17]

In the United States, stark latitudinal changes in vegetative cover were prominent during the transition from Pleistocene to Holocene conditions (see Figure 1.3). In the east, the southern limit of abundant spruce retreated from the Ohio Valley to the Canadian taiga north of the Great Lakes, and an irregular boundary between coniferous and deciduous forest migrated northward in its wake. In the west, during the last glaciation, mountain ranges of the Great Basin now cloaked by pygmy conifers – pinyon and juniper – harbored subalpine conifer forests analogous to those of the modern Rocky Mountains. Similarly, pygmy conifer woodlands characteristic of the modern Colorado Plateau spread southward, during the last glaciation, over much of the present Desert Southwest, which lies at distinctly lower elevations and is now occupied by a mixture of cactus and thornscrub.[18]

As the climate warmed across the American Southwest, plant assemblages in its many mountain ranges migrated upward in elevation by a minimum of at least 1,300 feet and a maximum of fully 2,600 feet to escape increasing temperature and aridity. Pleistocene floras of the intermountain region included unfamiliar plant associations unmatched exactly by any that exist today. Inland biotas experienced individualistic floral migrations, species by species in response to climatic change, that produced uneven displacements of species along both latitudinal and elevational gradients. Present plant communities are evidently ephemeral aggregations controlled by intersecting gradients of floral change. Fossil analogues are not precisely equivalent to the observed communities, and a seeming permanence of observed plant associations in the absence of modern disturbance is probably an illusion fostered by the short time frame of historic observation.[19]

The effects of deglaciation on tropical regions are not fully understood, but ambient temperatures at equatorial latitudes were cooler by approximately 5°C during the last glacial maximum. Available evidence from the Amazon basin indicates that the rain forests so prevalent in the tropics today were more restricted in extent during Pleistocene glaciation, probably broken into less continuous tracts, and composed in part of species adapted to cooler conditions than those that now prevail. Forests were nevertheless widespread in the Amazon basin even at peak glaciation.[20]

Human influences

Few of the dramatic postglacial changes in global environment escaped the attention of aboriginal humans. Even in the Americas, the last continents to be invaded by the human species, Clovis migrants from Eurasia had spread from Canada to Patagonia, and from Arizona to Boston, by thirteen thousand years ago. Several aspects of the growth of human culture suggest that the impact of human activities became an integral facet of Holocene environmental evolution. Many deltas felt the influence of human occupation almost as soon as they began to grow seaward after 6000 BC. Irrigation in lowland Mesopotamia, which lengthened steadily as the Tigris-Euphrates delta built itself into the Persian Gulf, was practiced at least locally by that time. Rice culture, with its elaborate systems of paddies and terraces, was also born about that time on the delta surfaces of southeast Asia.[21]

Across the wider terrestrial landscape, perhaps no aboriginal impact was greater than the results of broadcast fire. Aboriginal peoples burned the land deliberately, to flush small game and drive big game, to deny cover to dangerous animal predators, to clear the growth that might provide cover for enemy ambushes around their settlements and camps, to foster fresh shoots of vegetation that attract favored game, to keep woodlands clear of underbrush and easy to traverse, and to keep relatively unproductive woodlands from encroaching upon grasslands richer in usable resources. In precontact Australia, firing of native vegetation was so intensive, to nurture plant communities favored as food by either humans or their game, that native fire practices have been called "firestick farming." When people turned to growing domesticated crops, they resorted even more assiduously to wildfire to clear garden plots and fields, developing a pattern of behavior that survives today as so-called "slash-and-burn" agriculture. Although "slash and burn" has distinctly pejorative connotations for lovers of forested lands, the distributions of different tree species in many present forests owe much to the recurrence of past anthropogenic fires.[22]

Human impact

Despite decades of general knowledge about the near ubiquity of anthropogenic fire in prehistory, we are still far from comprehending its full import. On the one hand, we acknowledge that fire was the greatest invention of humankind, having in mind its critical application for cooking food, but tending to overlook the fact that it was also the most effective tool of land management available to aboriginal peoples. The grasslands and savannahs of the temperate and tropical regions might owe their very existence to anthropogenic burning, either to remove woodlands or to prevent their initial advance into tundra or steppe inherited from Pleistocene glaciation. Studies throughout the tropics have shown repeatedly that savannah grasslands are dependent for their maintenance, if not their initial creation, on the persistence of anthropogenic fires to combat forest encroachment.[23]

The alternate origin suggested for the development of grasslands is the effect of climate. In some semiarid grasslands, tree growth is precluded by lack of sufficient soil moisture. A fortuitous "experiment" shows, however, that aboriginal peoples were capable of converting forest to open land by deliberate use of wildfire. The arrival of Polynesian migrants roughly a thousand years ago was followed within just a few hundred years by removal of approximately half the previously dense New Zealand forest by repetitive firing to produce grassland, food-rich fernland, and open woodland (see Figure 1.7).[24]

The impact of wildfire on the nature and density of vegetative cover and the influence of vegetative cover on erosion rates and consequent sedimentation rates suggest that the cumulative effects of anthropogenic fire have exerted a strong control over the evolution of the Holocene landscape. Wildfire could not make mountains or govern the general courses of rivers and streams, but fine-tuning the contours of hill slopes, river bottoms, and stream terraces seems well within the scope of possible results from broad-cast burning conducted since the end of Pleistocene time.

Human behavior has also influenced evolving Holocene faunas over much of the world in two salient ways. First, Eurasian domestication of familiar pastoral animals – cattle, goats, horses, sheep, and swine – early in Holocene time affected the viability of wild counterparts over wide areas. Second, the spread of aboriginal peoples to previously unoccupied landmasses, including previously isolated islands, resulted in the extinction or local extirpation of many animals, both mammals and birds, as a result of intensive hunting. The effect was most notable on large animals, the megafauna, with long gestation periods that make population maintenance or recovery difficult in the face of steady attrition. Megafaunal extinctions were not synchronous globally, but phased sequentially from place to place as aboriginal peoples reached different continents and islands. Only in sub-Saharan Africa, where the native fauna coevolved with humankind and prehistoric domestications were a minor factor did a diverse megafauna survive into modern times. By altering fauna, aboriginal peoples might indirectly have affected the flora of many regions as well. In Australia, the extinction of large herbivores following the late Pleistocene arrival of humans to that continent apparently

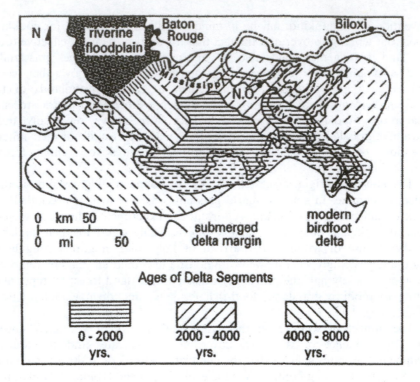

Figure 1.6 Approximate growth pattern, shown as age ranges of key delta segments, of Holocene Mississippi River delta below Baton Rouge, Louisiana (symbols dashed for submerged parts of delta lobes). In detail, time-space relations are more complex than depicted, for more than fifteen successive delta lobes or subdeltas have been distinguished from landscape feature and coring of the delta plain. "N.O." denotes New Orleans, lying just above the head of the youngest component of the delta plain.[25]

altered the floral balance, leading to conditions that encouraged the setting of wildfires to control vegetation.[26]

On many oceanic islands, destruction of habitat by intensive human occupation and anthropogenic introduction of exotic nonhuman predators probably contributed, along with hunting pressure, to the population crashes of the prehistoric past. Within the broad Pacific arena, occupying nearly half the globe, the arrival of Polynesian voyagers over the past few millennia led rapidly to the successive decimation of local bird species, and to other pervasive environmental changes in island group after island group.[27]

Environmental restoration

Although we live in a world of four dimensions, the dimension of time is unique. We may proceed east or west and north or south, retracing our steps at will, and with the aid of aircraft we can move up or down. But we can only move forward in time, with no hope of ever moving backward. We cannot recover past environments, although we might be able to regenerate them as a means of restoration.

From a geological perspective, the grand sweep of Holocene environmental changes that are largely irreversible make the likelihood of full success in regenerating or restoring lost environments seem quite slim. Returning to where we began at the outset of Holocene time is certainly impossible, and any expectation that a beneficent Nature could restore itself spontaneously to some admired state that existed in the more recent past seems quixotic. Modern industrial civilization and burgeoning population growth have injured the global environment far beyond the perspective or ability of aboriginal peoples to attempt, but the preindustrial environment was already the contingent product of multiple influences, among them the impact of our distant ancestors.

Environmental management

The burden of environmental management rests inevitably on human shoulders, and a clear sense of environmental history over the full course of Holocene time is a prerequisite for wise environmental decisions. Simply trying as human beings to make no mark on our surroundings may not achieve what we desire. Avoiding some practices, such as burning the landscape, which once were pursued with vigor by aboriginal peoples, introduces wholly new factors into the environmental equation. The popular concept of wilderness as pristine wildland free of any human influence is largely a psychocultural myth, springing more from an uplifting vision of the proverbial Eden than from any historical reality. For charting the future, we will have no substitute for understanding the dynamics of varied ecosystems and the rules of landscape evolution well enough to be able to gauge in advance the results of specific actions that we are able to control.[28]

The challenge to our powers of insight is daunting. In the environmental arena, the temptation is strong to label everything that is "natural" as "good," and anything that seems "bad" as "unnatural," but none of those terms is easy to define in a continuously changing world. Ever since the dawn of Holocene time, when global conditions remotely like those of the present day first evolved from the ice ages, humans have always impacted the natural environment. Reducing human impact toward a nil level is not only unattainable in practice, but quite literally unprecedented. The task for future human culture is to acquire the knowledge of environmental history and dynamics needed to choose the sorts of human impact that will lead to a posterity of our liking. Faith in a self-regulating and self-restorative nature, independent of humankind, cannot guide us into any environmental harbor where we would wish to moor.

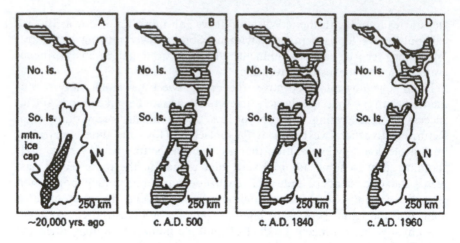

Figure 1.7 Changing forest cover (ruled areas forested) in New Zealand: A) pre-Holocene at last glacial maximum; B) Holocene prior to arrival of Polynesian migrants; C) after 750+ years of Polynesian occupation; D) after 120 years of European settlement. Anthropogenic firing of the landscape largely accounted for Polynesian forest clearance, with further reductions in forest cover made by European farmers, stockmen, and city builders. During Pleistocene glaciation, owing to drawdown in sea level, New Zealand was actually one large island half again as large as the two present islands combined (not shown as such here because the nature of synglacial vegetative cover on surrounding marine shelves is unknown from any direct evidence).[29]

Holistic history

Existing intellectual traditions have addressed Holocene history from four largely independent standpoints, none adequate alone for a holistic environmental history. From humanism sprang the discipline of history, basing its insights principally on the written record and deriving much of its basic posture from times when even the most rudimentary facts about Pleistocene glaciation and its lingering effects on the Holocene aftermath were unknown. From the social sciences, archaeology came later upon the scene with a primary focus on strictly human prehistory in the sense of cultural events prior to the advent of comprehensive written records. From the physical sciences, Quaternary geology developed as a discipline that was initially almost entirely divorced from considerations of human behavior. From the life sciences, ecologists and biogeographers have evaluated modern and historic biota with increasing sophistication but with minimal attention to prehistoric antecedents, except for documenting evolutionary taxonomic trends.

Each of these disparate approaches leads to only partial understanding of the full tapestry of the Holocene past. Casting off discipline-oriented blinders might allow us to achieve a more integrated vision of Holocene history by working from the premise that environmental and human history are parallel tracks along the same road map across an ever-changing Holocene landscape. Our very ability to forecast the environmental future with any accuracy may depend upon the blending of insights from diverse intellectual wellsprings.

Notes

1 For an overview of the Pleistocene world, see A. G. Dawson, *Ice Age Earth* (London: Routledge, 1992), 1–293. For the southern limit of North American ice sheets, see G. H. Denton and T. J. Hughes, *The Last Great Ice Sheets* (New York: Wiley, 1981), 1–484. For accurate (calibrated radiocarbon) timing of the last glacial maximum, see A. M. Tushingham and W. R. Peltier, "Implications of the Radiocarbon Timescale for Ice-Sheet Chronology and Sea-Level Change," *Quaternary Research* 39 (January 1993): 125–29.

2 For the correlation shown by the curve, see Minze Stuiver and Bernd Becker, "High-Precision Decadal Calibration of the Radiocarbon Time Scale," *Radiocarbon* 35 (Calibration 1993): 35–65; Edouard Bard, Maurice Arnold, R. G. Fairbanks, and Bruno Hamelin, "^{230}Th-^{234}U and ^{14}C Ages Obtained by Mass Spectrometry on Corals," *Radiocarbon* 35 (Calibration 1993): 191–99. Cosmic-ray bombardment of nitrogen in the upper atmosphere produces radiocarbon (a radioactive isotope with a half-life of 5730 years), which is incorporated into the carbon dioxide present in air, and dissolved in waters of oceans and lakes exposed to the atmosphere. Living organisms acquire a characteristic minor fraction of radiocarbon by equilibrating with the carbon dioxide of ambient air or surrounding waters. After death, their body parts lose radiocarbon at its known radioactive decay rate, allowing fossil materials such as wood, charcoal, bone, and shell to be dated (up to a limit of about 40,000 years, after which the amount of remaining radiocarbon is too low to measure with confidence). Conventional and calibrated radiocarbon ages differ because conventional ages are calculated with the assumption of constant atmospheric radiocarbon production, which actually varies through time as fluctuations in the magnetic field of the Earth modulate the intensity of the cosmic-ray flux reaching the atmosphere from outer space, as discussed by Carlo Laj, Alain Mazaud, and J. C. Duplessy, "Geomagnetic Intensity and ^{14}C Abundance in the Atmosphere and Ocean During the Past 50 Kyr," *Geophysical Research Letters* 23 (1 August 1996): 2045–48; H. Kitagawa and J. van der Plicht, "Atmospheric Radiocarbon Calibration to 45,000 yr B.P.: Late Glacial Fluctuations and Cosmogenic Isotope Production," *Science* 279 (20 February 1998): 1187–90. The round number of 10,000 years ago was proposed for the beginning of Holocene time by D. M. Hopkins, "Time-Stratigraphic Nomenclature for the Holocene Epoch," *Geology* 3 (January 1975): 10, and coincides well with the end of the Younger Dryas glacial readvance in conventional (uncalibrated) radiocarbon years. The best current estimate for the beginning of Holocene time is 11,530 calibrated (calendar) years BP (before AD 1950) by Steinar Gulliksen, H. H. Birks, Goran Possnert, and Jan Mangerud, "A Calendar Age Estimate of the Younger Dryas-Holocene Boundary at Krakenes, Western Norway," *The Holocene* 8 (May 1998): 249–59. The chronological implications of calibrating radiocarbon dates for the prehistory of the Americas is discussed by S. J. Fiedel, "Older Than We Thought: Implications of Corrected Dates for Paleoindians," *American Antiquity* 64 (January 1999): 95–115.

3 For Pleistocene paleoshorelines in British Columbia, see J. J. Clague, "Glacio-Isostatic Effects of the Cordilleran Ice Sheet, British Columbia," in *Shorelines and Isostasy*, edited by D. E. Smith and A. G. Dawson (London: Academic Press, 1983), 321–43. For the mid-Holocene highstand in relative sea level on Pacific islands, see J. X. Mitrovica and W. R. Peltier, "On Postglacial Geoid Subsidence over the Equatorial Oceans," *Journal of Geophysical Research* 96 (10 November 1991): 20,052–71. For the general background theory of world-wide glacio-hydro-isostasy, see R. I. Walcott, "Past Sea Levels, Eustasy, and Deformation of the Earth," *Quaternary Research* 2 (July 1972): 1–14; John Chappell, "Late Quaternary Glacio- and Hydro-Isostasy, on a Layered Earth," *Quaternary Research* 4 (December 1974): 405–28.

4 The impact of the Pleistocene-Holocene transition on the development of human culture has been discussed recently by Andrew Sherratt, "Climatic Cycles and Behaviourial Revolutions: The Emergence of Modern Humans and the Beginning of Farming," *Antiquity* 71 (June 1997): 271–87.

5 Positions of European ice fronts adapted from B. G. Anderson and H. W. Borns, Jr., *The Ice Age World* (Oslo: Scandinavian University Press, 1994), 1–208.

6 The timing of the last interglaciation has been established within narrow limits by R. L. Edwards, J. H. Chen, T. L. Ku, and G. J. Wasserburg, "Precise Timing of the Last Interglacial Period from Mass Spectrometric Determination of Thorium-230 in Corals," *Science* 236 (19 June 1987): 1547–53; J. H. Chen, H. A. Curran, B. White, and G. J. Wasserburg, "Precise Chronology of the Last Interglacial Period: ^{234}U-^{230}Th Data from Fossil Coral Reefs in the Bahamas," *Geological Society of America Bulletin* 103 (January 1991): 82–97; C. H. Stirling, T. M. Esat, M. T. McCulloch, and Kurt Lambeck, "High-Precision U-Series Dating of Corals from Western Australia and Implications for the Timing and Duration of the Last Interglacial," *Earth and Planetary Science Letters* 135 (October 1995): 115–30; Carsten Israelson and Barbara Wohlfarth, "Timing of the Last-Interglacial High Sea Level on the Seychelles Islands, Indian Ocean," *Quaternary Research* 51 (May 1999): 306–16. Recent discussions of the duration of the last interglaciation include B. J. Szabo, K. R. Ludwig, D. R. Muhs, and K. R. Simmons, "Thorium-230 Ages of Corals and Duration of the Last Interglacial Sea-Level High Stand on Oahu, Hawaii," *Science* 266 (7 October 1994): 93–96; I. J. Winograd, J. M. Landwehr, K. R. Ludwig, T. B. Coplen, and A. C. Riggs, "Duration and Structure of the Past Four Interglaciations," *Quaternary Research* 48 (September 1997): 141–54; C. H. Stirling, T. M. Estat, Kurt Lambeck, and M. T. McCulloch, "Timing and Duration of the Last Interglacial: Evidence for a Restricted Interval of Widespread Reef Growth," *Earth and Planetary Science Letters* 160 (August 1998): 745–62.

7 Synoptic maps depicting the pollen record of synglacial and postglacial vegetation in eastern North America have been presented by P. F. McDowell, Thompson Webb III, and P. J. Bartlein, "Long-Term Environmental Change," in *The Earth as Transformed by Human Action*, ed. B. L. Turner II, W. C. Clark, R. W. Kates, J. F. Richards, J. T. Matthews, and W. B. Meyer (Cambridge: Cambridge University Press, 1990), 143–52 (Fig. 9-6); Thompson Webb III, P. J. Bartlein, S. P. Harrison, and K. H. Anderson, "Vegetation, Lake Levels, and Climate in Eastern North America for the Past 18,000 Years," in *Global Climates Since the Last Glacial Maximum*, ed. H. E. Wright, Jr., J. E. Kutzbach, Thompson Webb III, W. F. Ruddiman, F. A. Street-Perrott, and P. J. Bartlein (Minneapolis: University of Minnesota Press, 1993), 449–50

(Fig. 17.10); I. C. Prentice, P. J. Bartlein, and Thompson Webb III, "Vegetation and Climate Chnage in Eastern North America Since the Last Glacial Maximum," *Ecology* 12 (June 1993): 2038–56 (Figs. 7–9).

8 The expansion of Oceanian cultures across the Pacific arena is recounted by Paul Rainbird, "Prehistory in the Northwest Tropical Pacific: The Caroline, Mariana, and Marshall Islands," *Journal of World Prehistory* 8 (September 1994): 293–349; Matthew Spriggs, *The Island Melanesians* (Oxford: Blackwell, 1997), 1–326; P. V. Kirch, *The Lapita Peoples* (Cambridge: Blackwell, 1997), 1–353. The varied settings and diverse environments of islands within the ocean basins are outlined by P. D. Nunn, *Oceanic Islands* (Oxford: Blackwell Publishers, 1994), 1–413

9 An extensive literature describing precontact environmental changes on Pacific islands is typified by P. V. Kirch and D. E. Yen, *Tikopia: The Prehistory and Ecology of a Polynesian Outlier* (Honolulu, Hawaii: Bishop Museum Press, 1982): 1–396, esp. 346; P. V Kirch, "Man's Role in Modifying Tropical and Subtropical Polynesian Ecosystems," *Archaeology in Oceania* 18 (April 1983): 26; Atholl Anderson, "Faunal Depletion and Subsistence Change in the Early Prehistory of Southern New Zealand," *Archaeology in Oceania* 18 (April 1983): 1–10; B. V. Rolett, "Faunal Extinctions and Depletions Linked with Prehistory and Environmental Change in the Marquesas Islands (French Polynesia)," *Journal of the Polynesian Society* 101 (March 1992): 86–94; J. S. Athens and J. V. Ward, "Environmental Change and Prehistoric Polynesian Settlement in Hawai'i," *Asian Perspectives* (fall 1993): 205–23; P. V. Kirch, "Late Holocene Human-Induced Modifications to a Central Polynesian Island Ecosystem," *Proceedings of the National Academy of Sciences* 93 (May 1996): 5296–5300; Dana Lepofsky, P. V. Kirch, and K. P. Lertzman, "Stratigraphic and Paleobotanical Evidence for Prehistoric Human-Induced Environmental Disturbance on Mo'orea, French Polynesia," *Pacific Science* 50 (July 1996): 253–73; J. S. Athens, J. V. Ward, and G. M. Murakami, "Development of an Agroforest on a Micronesian High Island: Prehistoric Kosraean Agriculture," *Antiquity* 70 (December 1996): 834–46; P. V. Kirch and T. L. Hunt, eds., *Historical Ecology in the Pacific Islands* (New Haven, Conn.: Yale University Press, 1997), 1–331.

10 The Holocene geohistory of Mesopotamia is outlined by Michael Sarntheim, "Sediments and History of the Postglacial Transgression in the Persian Gulf and Northwest Gulf of Oman," *Marine Geology* 12 (April 1972): 245–66; T. A. Al-Asfour, *Changing Sea-Level along the North Coast of Kuwait Bay* (London: Kegan Paul International, 1982), 1–182; G. A. Cooke, "Reconstruction of the Holocene Coastline of Mesopotamia," *Geoarchaeology* 2 (January 1987): 15–28.

11 The timing of Holocene delta initiation has been established by D. J. Stanley and A. G. Warne, "Worldwide Initiation of Holocene Marine Deltas by Deceleration of Sea-Level Rise," *Science* 265 (8 July 1994): 228–31. Subsequent growth of the Nile Delta is outlined by Vincent Coutillier and D. J. Stanley, "Late Quaternary Stratigraphy and Paleogeography of the Eastern Nile Delta, Egypt," *Marine Geology* 77 (August 1987): 257–75.

12 Curve redrawn from combined data of John Chapell and Henry Polach, "Post-Glacial Sea-Level Rise from a Coral Record at Huon Peninsula, Papua New Guinea," *Nature* 349 (10 January 1991): 147–49; Edouard Bard, Bruno Hamelin, Maurice Arnold, Lucien Montaggioni, Guy Cabioch, Gerard Faure, and Francis Rougerie, "Deglacial Sea-Level Record from Tahiti Corals and the Timing of Global Meltwater Discharge," *Nature* 382 (18 July 1996): 241–44.

13 See S. M. Gagliano, K. J. Meyer-Arendt, and K. M. Wicker, "Land Loss in the Mississippi River Deltaic Plain," *Gulf Coast Association of Geological Societies Transactions* 17 (1981): 295–300; D. J. Stanley, "Nile Delta: Extreme Case of Sediment Entrapment on a Delta Plain and Consequent Coastal Land Loss," *Marine Geology* 129 (April 1996): 189–95.

14 See J. W. Valentine and David Jablonski, "Biotic Effects of Sea Level Change: The Pleistocene Test," *Journal of Geophysical Research* 96 (10 April 1991): 6873–78.

15 Glacial-interglacial cycles adapted after R. B. Morrison, "Introduction," in *Quaternary Nonglacial Geology: Conterminous* (U.S.), edited by R. B. Morrison (Boulder, Colo.: Geological Society of America, The Geology of North America, Volume K-2, 1991), 1–12. Alternate dates for the advent of modern humans are discussed by Chris Stringer, "The Dates of Eden," *Nature* 331 (18 February 1988): 565–66.

16 The individualistic past migration of littoral organisms is discussed by J. W. Valentine and David Jablonski, "Fossil Communities: Compositional Variation at Many Time Scales," in *Species Diversity in Ecological Communities: Historical and Geographical Perspectives,* ed. R. C. Ricklefs and Dolph Schluter (Chicago: University of Chicago Press, 1993), 341–49. The dispersal of marine organisms from available species pools is discussed by M. A. Buzas and S. J. Culver, "Species Pool and Dynamics of Marine Paleocommunities," *Science* 264 (3 June 1994): 1439–41.

17 See Matsuo Tsukada, "Vegetation in Prehistoric Japan: The Last 20,000 Years," in *Windows on the Japanese Past: Studies in Archaeology and Prehistory,* ed. R. J. Pearson (Ann Arbor: University of Michigan Center for Japanese Studies, 1986), 11–56.

18 Postglacial vegetation changes in the Great Basin and the Desert Southwest are summarized by D. K. Grayson, *The Desert's Past: A Natural Prehistory of the Great Basin* (Washington, D.C.: Smithsonian Institution Press, 1993), 1–356; J. L. Betancourt, T. R. Van Devender, and P. S. Martin, eds., *Packrat Middens: The Last 40,000 Years of Biotic Change* (Tucson: University of Arizona Press, 1990), 1–467.

19 Elevation contrasts in the habitats of modern and similar but somewhat different Pleistocene floral communities in the American Southwest are discussed by J. L. Betancourt, "Late Quaternary Biogeography of the Colorado Plateau," in *Packrat Middens: The Last 40,000 Years of Biotic Change,* ed. J. L. Betancourt, T. R. Van Devender, and P. S. Martin (Tucson: University of Arizona Press, 1990), 259–92; W. G. Spaulding, "Environmental Change, Ecosystem Responses, and Late Quaternary Development of the Mojave Desert," in *Late Quaternary Environments and Deep History,* ed. D. W. Steadman and J. I. Mead (Hot Springs, S.Dak.: The Mammoth Site of Hot Springs Scientific Papers, Volume 3, 1995), 139–644.

20 Synglacial temperatures in the tropics have been discussed by T. P. Guilderson, R. G. Fairbanks, and J. L. Rubenstone, "Tropical Temperature Variations Since 20,000 Years Ago: Modulating Interhemispheric Climate Change," *Science* 263 (4 February 1994): 663–65; M. Stute et al., "Cooling of Tropical Brazil (5°C) During the 1st Glacial Maximum," *Science* 269 (21 July 1995): 379–83. The historical ecology of tropical rain forests was discussed on a global scale by J. R. Flenley, *The Equatorial Rain Forest: A Geological History* (London: Butterworths, 1979), 1–162, and the overall distribution of floral provinces in South America at peak glaciation by C. M. Clapperton, "Nature of Environmental Changes in South America at the Last Glacial Maximum,"

Palaeogeography, Palaeoclimatology, Palaeoecology 101 (April 1993): 189–208. For the pollen record of synglacial Amazon forests, see K. B. Liu and P. A. Colinvaux, "Forest Changes in the Amazon Basin During the Last Glacial Maximum," *Nature* 318 (12 December 1985): 556–57; P. A. Colinvaux, P. E. De Oliveira, J. E. Moreno, M. C. Miller, and M. B. Bush, "A Long Pollen Record from Lowland Amazonia: Forest and Cooling in Glacial Times," *Science* 274 (4 October 1996): 85–88; S. G. Haberle and M. A. Maslin, "Late Quaternary Vegetation and Climate Change in the Amazon Basin Based on a 50,000 Year Pollen Record from the Amazon Fan, ODP Site 932," *Quaternary Research* 51 (January 1999): 27–38; P. A. Colinvaux, P. E. de Oliveira, and M. B. Bush, "Amazonian and Neotropical Plant Communities on Glacial Time-Scales: The Failure of the Aridity and Refuge Hypotheses," *Quaternary Science Reviews* 19 (January 2000): 141–69.

21 Dating of Clovis sites in terms of calibrated radiocarbon ages is appraised by R. E. Taylor, C. V. Haynes, Jr., and Minze Stuiver, "Clovis and Folsom Age Estimates: Stratigraphic Context and Radiocarbon Calibration," *Antiquity* 70 (September 1996): 515–25. Early human agricultural development on delta surfaces is reviewed by D. J. Stanley and A. G. Warne, "Holocene Sea-Level Change and Early Human Utilization of Deltas," *GSA Today* 7 (December 1997): 1–6.

22 For extended discussions of aboriginal wildfires, see S. J. Pyne, *Fire in America: A Cultural History of Wildland and Rural Fire* (Princeton, N.J.: Princeton University Press, 1982), 1–654; *Burning Bush: A Fire History of Australia* (New York: Holt, 1991), 1–520. Specific studies of pre-contact fire practices by Native Americans (USA area) include Galen Clark, "Yosemite – Past and Present," *Sunset Magazine* (April 1907): 79–81; G. M. Day, "The Indian as an Ecological Factor in the Northeastern Forest," *Ecology* 34 (April 1953): 329–46; Homer Aschmann, "The Evolution of a Wild Landscape and its Persistence in Southern California," *Association of American Geographers Annals* (Supplement 1959): 34; D. R. Harris, "Recent Plant Invasions in the Arid and Semi-Arid Southwest of the United States," *Association of American Geographers Annals* 56 (September 1966): 408–22; H. T. Lewis, "Patterns of Indian Burning in California: Ecology and Ethnohistory," *Ballena Press Anthropological Papers No. 1* (1973): 1–101; Jan Timbrook, J. R. Johnson, and D. D. Earle, "Vegetation Burning by the Chumash," *Journal of California and Great Basin Anthropology* 4 (winter 1982): 163–86; William Cronon, *Changes in the Land: Indians, Colonists, and the Ecology of New England* (New York: Hill and Wang, 1983, 1–241, especially 49–51); Robert Boyd, "Strategies of Indian Burning in the Williamette Valley," *Canadian Journal of Anthropology* 5 (fall 1986): 65–86. The term "firestick farming" was introduced by Rhys Jones, "Fire-Stick Farming," *Australian Natural History* 16 (September 1969): 224–28; although his concept that anthropogenic fire has played a key role in fostering the structure of Australian plant communities has been disputed by D. R. Horton, "The Burning Question: Aborigines, Fire, and Australian Ecosystems," *Mankind* 13 (April 1982): 237–51; R. L. Clark, "Pollen and Charcoal Evidence for the Effects of Aboriginal Burning on the Vegetation of Australia," *Archaeology in Oceania* 18 (April 1983): 32–37, detailed accounts of current Aborigine fire practices tend to support Rhys Jor; Richard Kimber, "Black Lightning: Aborigines and Fire in Central Australia and the Western Desert," *Archaeology in Oceania* 18 (April 1983): 38–45; D. B. Rose, ed., *Country in Flames* [Proceedings of the 1994 Symposium on Biodiversity and Fire in North Australia] (Canberra: North Australia Research Unit, Australian National

University, Biodiversity Series Paper No. 3, 1995), 1–127. For the influence of anthropogenic fires on the distribution of forest species, see J. G. Saldarriaga and D. C. West, "Holocene Fires in the Northern Amazon Basin," *Quaternary Research* 26 (November 1986): 358–66; P. A. Delcourt, H. R. Delcourt, C. R. Ison, W. E. Sharp, and K. J. Germillion, "Prehistoric Human Use of Fire, the Eastern Agricultural Complex, and Appalachian Oak-Chestnut Forests: Paleoecology of Cliff Palace Pond, Kentucky," *American Antiquity* 63 (April 1998): 369–85; J. S. Athens and J. V. Ward, "The Late Quaternary of the Western Amazon: Climate, Vegetation, and Humans," *Antiquity* 73 (June 1999): 287–302.

23 Pioneeering studies that demonstrated the dominant role of anthropogenic fire in protecting tropical savannahs from tree invasion include Gerard Budowski, "Tropical Savannahs, a Sequence of Forest Felling and Repeated Burnings," *Turrialba* 6 (June 1956): 23–33; M. J. Eden, "Palaeoclimatic Influences and the Development of Savanna in Southern Venezuela," *Journal of Biogeography* 1 (June 1974): 95–109; R. N. Seavoy, "The Origin of Tropical Grasslands in Kalimantan, Indonesia," *Journal of Tropical Geography* 40 (June 1975): 48–52; R. A. Pullan, "Burning Impact on African Savannahs," *Geographical Magazine* 47 (April 1975): 432–38; G. A. J. Scott, "The Role of Fire in the Creation and Maintenance of Savanna in the Montana of Peru," *Journal of Biogeography* 4 (June 1977): 141–67. Recent studies showing its importance for replacing forest with savannah on newly occupied Pacific islands include Janelle Stephenson and J. R. Dodson, "Paleoenvironmental Evidence for Human Settlement of New Caledonia," *Archaeology in Oceania* 30 (April 1995): 36–41; J. R. Dodson and Michiko Intoh, "Prehistory and Palaeoecology of Yap, Federated States of Micronesia," *Quaternary International* 59 (October 1999): 17–26.

24 Fire as the prime tool of aboriginal land management was argued by O. C. Stewart, "Burning and Natural Vegetation in the United States," *Geographical Review* 41 (April 1951): 317–20; "Fire as the First Great Force Employed by Man," in *Man's Role in Changing the Face of the Earth,* ed. W. L. Thomas, Jr. (Chicago: University of Chicago Press, 1956), 115–33. An example of semiarid grassland persistent without anthropogenic influence is described by M. E. Meadows, "Late Quaternary Vegetation History of the Nyika Plateau, Malawi," *Journal of Biogeography* 11 (May 1984): 209–22.

25 Extent and age of delta lobes generalized after D. E. Frazier, "Recent Deltaic Deposits of the Mississippi River: Their Development and Chronology," *Gulf Coast Association of Geological Societies Transactions* 17 (1967): 287–311; W. J. Autin, S. F. Burns, B. J. Miller, R. T. Saucier, and J. I. Snead, "Quaternary Geology of the Lower Mississippi Valley," in *Quaternary Nonglacial Geology: Conterminous U.S.,* ed. R. B. Morrison (Boulder, Colo.: Geological Society of America, The Geology of North America, Volume K-2, 1991), 547–82; J. M. Coleman, H. H. Roberts, and G. W. Stone, "Mississippi River Delta: An Overview," *Journal of Coastal Research* 14 (summer 1998): 698–716.

26 The process and results of animal domestication are addressed by Jared Diamond, *Guns, Germs, and Steel* (New York: Norton, 1997), 1–480, especially 157–75. Megafaunal extinctions were treated for the Americas by P. S. Martin, "The Discovery of America," *Science* 179 (9 March 1973): 969–74; for Australia by Tim Flannery, *The Future Eaters* (Melbourne: Reed, 1994), 1–423, especially 180–86; and in sequential global overview by P. S. Martin, "40,000 Years of Extinctions on the Planet of Doom," *Palaeogeography, Palaeoclimatology, Palaeoecology (Global and Planetary Change Section)* 82 (May 1990): 187–201;

P. S. Martin and D. W. Steadman, "Prehistoric Extinctions on Islands and Continents," in *Extinctions in Near Time,* ed. R. D. E. McPhee (New York: Plenum, 1999), 17–55. For the inferred effect of megaherbivore extinctions on Australian flora, Tim Flannery, "Pleistocene Faunal Loss: Implications of the Aftershock for Australia's Past and Future," *Archaeology in Oceania* 25 (July 1990): 45–67.

27 For depletion of avifauna within Oceania, see S. L. Olson and H. F. James, "The Role of Polynesians in the Extinction of the Avifauna of the Hawaiian Islands," in *Quaternary Extinctions,* ed. P. S. Martin and R. G. Klein (Tucson: University of Arizona Press, 1995), 768–80; D. W. Steadman, "Prehistoric Extinctions of Pacific Island Birds: Biodiversity Meets Zooarchaeology," *Science* 267 (24 February 1995): 1123–31; D. W. Steadman, "Extinctions of Polynesian Birds: Reciprocal Impacts of Birds and People," in *Historical Ecology in the Pacific Islands,* ed. P. V. Kirch and T. L. Hunt (New Haven, Conn.: Yale University Press, 1997), 51–79.

28 For the myth of wilderness, W. M. Denevan, "The Pristine Myth: The Landscape of the Americas in 1492," *Association of American Geographers Annals* 82 (September 1992): 369–85; Arturo Gomez-Pompa and Andrea Kaus, "Taming the Wilderness Myth," *BioScience* 42 (April 1992): 271–79.

29 The areal extent of New Zealand forests at different times is indicated; M. S. McGlone, "Polynesian Deforestation of New Zealand," *Archaeology in Oceania* 18 (April 1983): 11–25; Atholl Anderson and Matt McGlone, "Living on the Edge – Prehistoric Land and People in New Zealand," in *The Naive Lands,* ed. John Dodson (Melbourne: Longman Cheshire, 1992), 199–241; M. S. McGlone, M. J. Salinger, and N. T. Moar, "Paleovegetation Studies of New Zealand's Climate Since the Last Glacial Maximum," in *Global Climates Since the Last Glacial Maximum,* ed. H. E. Wright, Jr., J. E. Kutzbach, Thompson Webb III, W. F. Ruddiman, F. A. Street-Perrott, and P. J. Bartlein (Minneapolis: University of Minnesota Press, 1993), 294–317. The timing of Polynesian arrival in New Zealand is documented by Atholl Anderson, "The Chronology of Colonization in New Zealand," *Antiquity* 65 (December 1991): 767–95; M. S. McGlone and J. M. Wilmshurst, "Dating Initial Maori Environmental Impact in New Zealand," *Quaternary International* 59 (October 1999): 5–16.

2

DARK IS THE WORLD TO THEE

A historical perspective on environmental forewarnings

Teresa Kwiatkowska and Alan Holland

> Our universe is a sorry little affair unless it has in it something for every age to investigate. (...) Nature does not reveal her mysteries once and for all. We believe that we are all her initiates but we are only hanging around the forecourt.
>
> Lucius Annaeus Seneca, *Natural Questions* VII.30

> The child, like a sailor cast forth by the cruel waves, lies naked upon the ground, speechless, in need of every kind of vital support, as soon as nature has spilt him forth with throes from his mother's womb into the regions of light.
>
> Lucretius, *De Rerum Natura,* Book V, 222–25

In our time the life sciences offer us various indicators that signal impending environmental problems. Permanent and unwelcome repercussions of ecosystem alterations may be observed at different levels of biological organisation. Biochemical and molecular effects (changes in genes, cells, and body tissues) can be detected at sub cellular levels. Our ancestors did not have the advantages of molecular biology, nor of the *International Early Warning Program* launched by the United Nations in 2000. The only bioindicators they could rely upon were destroyed landscapes, eroded soils, abandoned pastures and villages, and deforested slopes. With regard to this last, the late Michael Williams wrote: 'It is a common misconception that deforestation is a recent occurrence, gaining momentum in the tropical regions of the world since about 1950. But its history is long, and stretches far back into the corridors of time when humans first occupied the earth and began to use fire deliberately, probably some half-a-million years ago.'[1]

However, the mere existence of evidence of environmental harms is not enough; in order to have some impact this evidence must also register as such in society at large. And history records an abundance of early forewarnings that were not listened to and did not penetrate the social fabric. They were present, although not always explicit, both in what we now think of as more 'philosophical' writings and also in (what we now think of as) more 'scientific' texts. Currently, there are an increasing number of analyses looking at the historical roots of modern environmental problems. However, there is a clear need to extend these reflections to include an investigation of the early signs of warning of serious environmental degradation, to see who registered them, how they were responded to by mainstream thought and policy, and what lessons those examples and attitudes might provide for the future.

We also should bear in mind that all human actions take place within the context of ecosystems, and interact with them in ways that differ enormously over time and space. Humans compete with other species of animals and also plants for resources like water and soil, the other species themselves being active agents of environmental transformations. Environmental factors such as a harsh climate, together with the varying demands of the ecosystems to which humans must accommodate themselves, play a crucial part in the human-nature relationship. An excellent illustration is afforded by the history of the Mesopotamian region over recent millennia, as documented by Magnus Widell.[2] Here, plagues of locusts were among the main factors with which humans had to contend, closely followed by extremely cold winters and severe droughts.

Not surprisingly, the human intervention in natural processes that is unavoidable for our survival has permanently affected and in some cases irrevocably damaged many fragile natural ecosystems. A lack of ecological knowledge and the unplanned pattern of human development, exacerbated in some cases by uncompromising belief systems, have led to unexpected and unpredictable consequences. The environmental history of the earth provides clear evidence of the inadequacy of our present knowledge, past judgments and future predictions. Many writers have noted the environmental degradation that started more than four thousand years before the rise of the Sumerian civilisation, even though their voices, restricted mostly to the small community of intellectuals, have been largely ignored. The most universal and ancient features of 'humanscapes' arise from a conscious strategy to improve food supplies, provisions, safety, and comfort – or perhaps to create the landscapes that we prefer, given our savannah ancestry. The domestication of species, the creation of open fields, the raising of crops and the building of shelters and settlements are the most obvious of intentional human activities, each practised for millennia.

The Marquis de Condorcet once argued that the lessons of the past could serve for the future – that we learn from the ancients by studying their mistakes and by properly applying scientific findings.[3] There are two major problems with this. One is that it presupposes a confidence in our 'present' understanding – whenever this 'present' might be – that is wholly unfounded. The other is that many of the environmental and climatic disasters of the past survive only as a dim reflection in our legends and myths. The memory of previous natural events like droughts, exceptional storms, excessive floods, unusual colds caused by climatic changes or human activity fade quickly with passing generations. Such evidence as there is can often only be indirectly and falteringly recovered through archaeological and other associated forms of investigation.

1. Not the first and not the last

In recent years, investigation by archaeologists and geomorphologists working in southern Greece has brought to light compelling evidence for the destructive effects of human activities over the past 8,000 years. Deforestation and at times disastrous soil erosion triggered by escalating agricultural practices and growing human populations were already evident in pre-classical times, and continued through classical antiquity, challenging the belief that pre-industrial peoples were better stewards of the natural environment than were peoples in later industrial Western societies.[4]

In fact, environmental history has recorded many voices apparently warning of the effects of certain human activities on the environment. Plato and others refer repeatedly to the wooded hills and rich lands of the remote past. Whether the disappearance of this lush landscape, if it ever existed, was due to natural or human causes has been debated passionately since antiquity. Generally, it is true that landscapes have been reinvented by tragedians and comic poets to suit their dramatic purposes.[5] Yet, it is also a common misconception that deforestation is a recent occurrence, gaining momentum in the tropical regions of the world since about 1950. In fact its history is long, and stretches far back in time to the period when humans first occupied the earth and began to use fire deliberately, probably some half-a-million years ago. What has changed since the mid-twentieth century is that an ancient process has accelerated. The process of deforestation jointly with its consequences such as soil erosion and floods, well studied in the Mediterranean basin, was already evident, according to Williams,[6] in the 'deep' past around 1500 B.C. and became, as H. C. Darby suggests, 'probably the most important single factor that has changed the European landscape (and many other landscapes also) ... '.[7] This happened in several phases and was regionally diverse. Mainly it was Greeks, Carthaginians and Romans, who were involved, and later, the Arabs, Venetians, Turks and Spaniards. The consequences were enormous: for example, the 'corn chambers' of the Roman Empire, such as modern day Tunisia, became virtual deserts.

J B HEISER
CORNELL UNIVERSITY
STIMSON HALL
ITHACA, NY 14853
USA

| Order Number | 34159160 – 241622 | | Date. | 1/03/2013 |
| Customer Reference | | | Despatch Note: | 20130225914801 |

ISBN	Title	Qty	Status	Returns Reason
9780415520539	Global Environmental History	1		

Returns address:

SuperBookDeals
1101 Business Parkway, South
Westminster, MD 21157
USA

CUSTOMS/DOUANE   *** PALLET TL ***
DESCRIPTION   BOOKS
VALUE   28.99
NET WEIGHT   .89 kilos
TOTAL VALUE   28.99
SIGNATURE

Returns address:

SuperBookDeals
1101 Business Parkway, South
Westminster, MD 21157
USA

34159160 – 241622

For office use only

J B HEISER
CORNELL UNIVERSITY
STIMSON HALL
ITHACA, NY 14853
USA

00000

20130225914801

2. Causes and responses

How far was this due to human insensitivity and indifference to the environmental degradation that was occurring, and how far was it due to natural
climate change? There has been long-standing debate on the causes and
effects of Holocene erosion and alluviation in the Mediterranean lands.
Van Andel et al., referring to the land use of the Southern Argolid, write:

> The soils of the gently rolling hill country of the southern peninsula
> (...) mainstays of agriculture during the 4th through 2nd
> millennia B.C. were not especially vulnerable to erosion (...). In the
> semiarid climate of the eastern Mediterranean, landscape stability is
> naturally maintained by the vegetation, and even after a major
> disturbance *maquis* and pine woods will quickly establish a
> protective cover provided that the disruption by burning, brush
> cutting, or overgrazing does not continue too severely.[8]

Vita-Finzi[9] indicated that Mediterranean landscape transformation was
often characterised by 'punctuated-equilibrium' rather than being a process
of prolonged and gradual change. However, recent studies suggest more
complex multi-causal explanations in which local interactions between
environmental context, climate fluctuations and human impact are being
envisaged as affording appropriate clarifications of landscape alteration.
So, for example, and without contradicting that hypothesis, John Bintliff
draws attention to the over-emphasis of the human factor and the exclusion
of the equally important natural processes with regard to late Classical and
early Hellenistic landscape transformation:

> It has been natural to blame human impact as the sole reason
> for these (coastal changes), which the plentiful historic sources for
> Classical Greek, Hellenistic and Roman Imperial times allow us
> to reconstruct in this way. (...) Major changes in depositional
> behaviour are often inferred to reflect major changes in settlement
> and land use, for which archaeological evidence is lacking or very
> circumstantial.[10]

Nevertheless, as early as the ninth century B.C. Homer compared the noise of
the battle to a 'crashing sound where woodmen fell the trees' in 'mountain
dells'. Although evidence for forest clearing is erratic, its consequences such
as soil erosion have been more reliably documented. In the fourth century
B.C. Plato understood and discussed the effects of deforestation. Equally,
Theophrastus mentions the disappearance of *Tetraclinis articulata,* also
known as the sandarac tree, from Cyrene by saying: 'There was an abundance of those trees where now the city stands, and people can still recall

that some of the roofs in ancient times were made of it.'[11] Many other Greek and Roman thinkers were aware that the extensive exploitation of natural resources, depletion of biodiversity and changes of the environment could degrade the natural world and lead to unexpected consequences.

We have to acknowledge that the causes of environmental degradation have been a source of controversy, and that the examples of early warning voices that have been entirely ignored illustrate the difficulties that we have to confront when attempting to document our relationship with natural systems. The factual knowledge of our impact on natural systems, still deficient today, was little more than fragmentary at the earlier stages of human civilisation. And it is easy to imagine that the undiscriminating and irregular accumulation of facts, coupled with speculation rather than empirical research could be highly misleading. In addition, a lack of ecological knowledge, combined with a bewildering variety of myths and world visions, not to mention the simple economic necessities, are likely to have played a decisive role in ensuring that, for the most part, the warning voices fell on deaf ears.

The state of mere mortals is graphically captured in words that the ancient Greek playwright Aeschylus ascribes to Prometheus in his play *Prometheus Bound:*

> First of all, though they had eyes to see, they saw to no avail; they had ears, but they did not understand; but, just as shapes in dreams, throughout their length of days, [450] without purpose they wrought all things in confusion. They had neither knowledge of houses built of bricks and turned to face the sun nor yet of work in wood; but dwelt beneath the ground like swarming ants, in sunless caves. They had no sign either of winter [455] or of flowery spring or of fruitful summer, on which they could depend but managed everything without judgment, until I taught them to discern the risings of the stars and their settings, which are difficult to distinguish.

Yet, regardless of the many gifts and benefits that Prometheus had supposedly conferred on mortals, societies should not necessarily be taken to task for their lack of response to environmental alteration, in part because many changes did not appear obviously harmful in their early stages. Indeed, such changes might well have been regarded not as degradation but as simple transformations. It was only the accumulation of these imperceptible changes over time that led to major and visible environmental alteration. As van Andel et al. indicate, during the fourth and early third millennia B.C. we encounter no evidence that the spread of settlements and clearing of the land had a seriously destabilising effect on the landscape, even though, ultimately, damage was inevitable.[12] Human activity in the classical period had little immediate and adverse impact on the Mediterranean peoples. Therefore, there was no pressing need for them to be environmentally minded. They could view the spontaneously self-regulating order of nature as largely independent of human will.

3. It is better to light the candle than to blame the darkness

All things are easy for nature, (…) especially the things she has decided to do from the beginning, which she approaches not suddenly but after giving warning.

Seneca, NQ, III, 29, 8–30.2

Williams wrote: 'That natural processes were accelerated with tree cutting and cultivation is obvious, but all in all, it is strange that in such a literate and observant world no evidence has arisen of consciences disturbed by the exploitation of forests, no general alarm about depletion, no treatise on forest management, nor examples of efforts to plant trees other than olive trees.'[13] Although some nature conservation practices date to the early days of our civilisation, like the hunting conservation of waterfowl in the Middle Kingdom in Egypt, these efforts were mostly restricted to wild-life reserves, and had as their objective the protection of bird and game for hunting and pleasure. The origins of what we might call 'real' nature conservation, or conservation for its own sake, cannot plausibly be dated earlier than the nineteenth century, when it emerged partly under the influence of the Romantic Movement and its views of the natural world.

The question which we now take up in more detail, of why – despite the various words of warning – humanity was to wait many centuries before acknowledging and recognising the seriousness of environmental changes, does not have easy answers. But we begin with a clue which comes from distinguishing two types of what can be considered early admonitions: one, which comes out of theoretical reasoning and a broadly 'philosophical' outlook on nature; the other, although as well reflected in philosophical writings, was derived from everyday observation.

Landscape is a form of culture and history, the form in which culture and history have been absorbed. The intellectual belief in universal order, accordingly, was reflected in what people perceived, in their aesthetic taste, the pleasure of sight and senses. Given that Greek and Roman sensibility relied on symmetry, it is no wonder, therefore, that little value was attributed by them to the irregularity, variety and roughness of wild and disorderly nature, both spontaneous and capricious.

Nevertheless, the seeds of the 'precautionary principle', a strong feature of any modern analysis of environmental problems, were also sown a long time ago. Indeed, the fact that human activities bring about consequences which defy our original intentions, or that they lead to completely unexpected catastrophes, marked early Greek mythology and art. It was manifested in the mysterious games that capricious gods were thought to play with helpless human beings. Then, in the sixth century B.C. when more 'rational' approaches were beginning to emerge, it continued to modify the perceptions of Nature and the way Nature functions. 'You never step twice into the same river', wrote Heraclitus around 500 B.C. He believed that most natural processes are constantly in flux, that chance and change are the rule, and that the future is as unpredictable to other organisms as it is to us. It is a view plainly endorsed by modern ecology.[14] 'If you do not expect the unexpected you will not find it, for it is hard to be searched out and difficult to compass', he warned.[15] Thus the suggestion emerges that this view was a very early foreboding of the chaotic features of natural systems. In Plato's case too, though one might prefer to think his 'disenchantment' with the sensory world and retreat into the 'world' of forms to be due mainly to his experience of radical cultural instability, Aristotle, for one, thought it strongly influenced by Heraclitus' views on nature.[16]

However, even Heraclitus himself believed in a ceaseless recurrence; and in a deep-seated need for predictability the Greeks in general preferred to believe in intelligibility, perfection and order. It was a 'blasphemy' to assume the existence of chance events in the universe. But taking for granted the certainty of Nature's conduct helped to mask the unforeseen consequences of human impacts on the physical world. Marcus Tullius Cicero (106–43 B.C.) expressed a typical Roman, and Stoic, view when he wrote:

> When we (...) speak of nature as the sustaining and governing principle of the world, we do not mean that the world is like a clod of earth or lump of stone or something else of that sort, which possesses only the natural principle of cohesion, but like a tree or an animal, displaying no haphazard structure, but order and a certain semblance of design.[17]

In spite of the fact that already by around the year 500 B.C. Greek coastal cities had become landlocked as a result of deforestation and soil erosion, up to the time of the late middle ages people nestled in a stable social structure gave little heed to deforestation, soil erosion and invasive species. Weather, with its impact on human health, was perhaps the most apparent and, therefore, most debated variable.[18] Even though Theophrastus, who is considered by some the forerunner of ecological studies, reminded them that order should not be presumed in Nature, the Greeks rarely ventured into the fascinating world of change and chance. Nature as humans wanted to see it was governed by gods or reason according to some sort of a general plan. They maintained the view of the world as exhibiting both excellence and harmony, whose regularity was assured by a rational arrangement. As Aristotle noted: 'Absence of haphazard and the conduciveness of everything to an end are to be found in Nature's work in the highest degree ... '[19]

The perception of a benevolent and harmonious Nature which was the product of heavenly design led to the belief in its capacity to return to its former state when disturbed. The concept of a 'balance of nature' can be found in the classical vision of a Mother Earth. It was introduced by Hesiod in his *Theogony* written about 700 B.C. Equilibrium theory discounted physical and geological and climatic forces such as fire, strong winds, rainstorms, and the impact of human activities. Any disturbance was a damage, which, it was believed, set in motion forces leading to a recovery. Nature's plan or Divine Order guaranteed a return to its original state once the stress factor was reduced. The philosophical faith in a steady nature was usually connected with the conviction that nature can never be destroyed. The first century (B.C.) Roman author Lucretius declares that everything in nature is continuously being renewed but nothing is ever irreparably damaged:

> For time changes the nature of the whole world, and one state of things must pass into another, and nothing remains as it was: all things move, all are changed by nature and compelled to alter. For one thing crumbles and grows faint and weak with age, another grows up and comes forth from contempt. So therefore time changes the nature of the whole world, and one state of the earth gives place to another, so that what she bore she cannot, but can bear what she did not bear before ... [20]

This belief, repeated in the centuries ahead, was often instrumental in turning away attention from the human destruction of nature. Over and above popular belief in a world subject to the whims of a pantheon of gods, only one or two philosophers at most had seen nature as an unpredictable and mischievous troublemaker. In *De Causis Plantarum* Theophrastus avers that 'Anything which is contrary to nature is dangerous'. In the first century A.D. Lucius Annaeus Seneca, traumatised by the earthquake that shattered Pompeii (later destroyed by the volcanic eruption in A.D. 79), accentuated nature's omnipotent powers: 'Any deviation by nature from the existing state of the universe is enough for the destruction of mankind' (NQ 3.27.3 cf. NQ 6 – 'de Terrae motu'). In the modern age his conviction resounded in the neglected words of Francis Bacon that 'the subtlety of nature is greater many times over than the subtlety of argument ... '.[21]

It has to be said, however, that the significance of the Stoic directive to 'follow nature' (e.g. Seneca, Letter 5) is hard to read. At first sight it may seem to imply the view of nature as a comfort zone, where all is 'for the best'. It can equally, and perhaps better, be read, however, as showing an acute awareness that the intelligent order of the universe encompassed many unwelcome events. These included both natural events, such as the death of a child, and humanly caused catastrophes, such as the fire which totally destroyed the Gallic town of Lyons (Seneca, Letter 91). And this awareness may well in part explain some otherwise unappealing directives. When your wife or child has died, says Epictetus (*Enchiridion* 3), say to yourself that a human being has died, and you will not be disturbed. Their loss is like the falling of the leaves, adds Seneca (Letter 104); even if they do not grow again, they are replaced. Perhaps it was only by adopting such an attitude that, in a world so full of threat, the dignity, tranquillity and freedom that they sought could be achieved.

4. Everyday observation

In the event, it was not philosophical rhetoric but the practical experiences and economic interests of people that gave rise to some kind of environmental consciousness and to a string of conservation laws and regulations. Methods of remediation tended to be adopted because they answered economic and social needs rather than environmental or ecological ones. Sometimes, for example, recommendations were made about how to conserve scarce natural resources like timber but again the conservation efforts respond mostly to economic requirements and were put into effect mainly for their instrumental and practical value. Even in the sphere of practical observation, however, there were limitations. For the most part the Mediterranean peoples understood very well the changes of the seasons, with their associated weather patterns, and arranged their crops and grazing in view of that. But they did not, for example, comprehend the hazards of irrigation such as the gradual salinisation of soils. Moreover, natural processes, including those that occur in the wake of human activity, are slow and local, and mostly invisible because they are natural.

Nevertheless, there are hints in the literature of recognition of some of the more unwelcome repercussions of human intervention. Pliny, for example, was aware of the increased incidence of floods as a result of deforestation. He notes how:

> It frequently happens that in spots where forests have been felled, springs of water make their appearance, the supply of which was previously expended in the nutriment of the trees. This was the case upon Mount Haemus for example, when, during the siege by Cassander, the Gauls cut down a forest for the purpose of making a rampart. Very often too, after removing the wood which has covered an elevated spot and so served to attract and consume the rains, devastating torrents are formed by the concentration of the waters. It is very important also, for the maintenance of a constant supply of water, to till the ground and keep it constantly in

32

motion, taking care to break and loosen the callosities of the surface crust: at all events, we find it stated, that upon a city of Crete, Arcadia by name, being razed to the ground, the springs and water-courses, which before were very numerous in that locality, all at once dried up; but that, six years after, when the city was rebuilt, the water again made its appearance, just as each spot was again brought into cultivation.[22]

According to Meiggs, 'destruction by flood became a well worn *topos* in Greek and Roman literature'.[23]

A contrasting example is provided by the Greek traveller and geographer of the second century A.D., Pausanias, in his famous *Description of Greece*. Here, he writes that the reason why the Echinades islands have not been made part of the mainland by the Achelous was because the Aetolian people had been driven from their homes and all their land had been laid waste: 'Accordingly, as Aetolia remains unfilled, the Achelous does not bring as much mud upon the Echinades as it otherwise would do. My reasoning is confirmed by the fact that the Maeander, flowing through the land of the Phrygians and Carians, which is ploughed up each year, has turned to mainland in a short time the sea that once was between Priene and Miletus.'[24]

As early as the fourth century B.C. Plato observed the deforestation of Attica and contrasted it with the state of plenty that characterised ancient Athens in its Golden Age. In an often-quoted passage of *Critias* he wrote that 'what now remains compared to what then existed is like a skeleton of a sick man, all the fat and the soft soil having wasted away, and only the bare framework of the land being left'.[25] True, we should take into account Glacken's cautionary note that Plato's assessments 'can be accepted neither as factual nor as evidence of deterioration of the Mediterranean landscape owing to natural and man-made catastrophes from the remote past to Plato's time'. But he goes on to add the important rider that: 'There is, however, clear evidence here of the recognition by Plato that natural erosion and human activities – such as deforestation – may in their cumulative effects change a landscape throughout time'.[26] Theophrastus too recorded human induced climate changes caused by land drainage and deforestation. He observed that:

in the country around Larisa in Thessaly, where formerly, when there was much standing water and the plain was a lake, the air was thicker and the country warmer; but now that the water has been drained away and prevented from collecting, the country has become colder and freezing more common. In proof the fact is cited that formerly there were fine tall olive trees in the city itself and elsewhere in the country, whereas now they are found nowhere, and that the vines were never frozen before but often freeze now.[27]

We see then clear hints of awareness that human activities had been producing undesirable results, degrading ecosystems and causing soil and water pollution. These are summed up by Seneca in his *Natural Questions* where he remarks: 'If we evaluate the benefits of nature by the depravity of those who misuse them, there is nothing we have received that does not hurt us ... You will find nothing, even of obvious usefulness, such that it does not change over into its opposite through man's fault.'[28]

However, we should not fail to bear in mind that the history of human culture is very much a history of human relationships with a harsh and demanding natural environment. Accordingly, the various descriptions of a golden age when people were supposed to have lived in harmony with nature, like most generalisations, are subject to numerous objections. According to Ehrenberg, in the time of Aristophanes (fifth to fourth centuries B.C.) the Attic farmer, almost naked, worked soils which 'to a large extent [were] poor, stony and often still uncultivated'. The realities of that time were much less idyllic than Aristophanes describes.[29] Closer to the truth was Pliny the Elder who, in his *Natural History* (VII, Preface), remarked that Nature 'asks a cruel price for all her generous gifts, making it hardly possible to judge whether she has been more a kind parent to man or more a harsh stepmother'.[30]

Mediterranean ecosystems have always been fragile, and intensive agricultural activities combined with difficult natural conditions tend to have damaging and unpredictable impacts. As indicated by Williams, 'compared to the deciduous forests of northern Europe the evergreen forests were easier to clear, but their regeneration was more difficult because of the marked seasonality of the regional climate, combined with the prevalence of fire and overgrazing by stock, particularly goats.'[31] It was only in Egypt, where conditions were rather different, that humans developed a more sustainable system of agriculture that lasted for at least several thousand years.[32]

5. Practical measures

Undoubtedly, agricultural activities over the span of thousands of years have wrought permanent damage on the various regions of the world. The reckoning has been slow to come, and it is in the realm of practical politics and lawmaking that we find the most obvious 'wake-up calls' to the importance of acknowledging the constraints on human dealings with the natural world. Thus in approximately 430 B.C. the Athenian authorities enacted a decree that was to prevent the pollution of drinkable water by the dye industry. Livio Rossetti cites this law as evidence that classical Athens was aware of the causal connection between environmental degradation and certain daily activities. The enactment expressly intended to eliminate pollution of the river Ilissus: '(It is not allowed) to put skins (in the river), and thus to pollute the Ilissus by the mount of Heracles' temple, or to practise tannery and dispose of waste in the river.'[33] In the Platonic dialogue *Phaedrus* Socrates describes the riverbanks of the Ilissus of his days: 'In the name of Hera, what a lovely heaven! The plane tree is tall and bushy. The osier next to it is tall and beautiful. Its flowers are full of life and there is a sweet fragrance all over the place. Under the plane tree, the cold sparkling water flowing from the charming spring cools my bare feet ... ' (230 B.C.) Were we to take it literally, this fragment could indicate that the entire area was cleaned up and water quality improved and restored to purity and beauty in the space of about twenty years.

Further evidence in Plutarch,[34] in *Laws* by Plato and in Aristotle's *Politics* suggest an understanding of the importance of water quality for the healthy city. Plato in *Laws* book VIII describes the reasons for penalties against water pollution. We may assume that he was both aware of the problem and held these rules important and necessary. In *Laws* 761 he describes the use and protection of water resources: the administrators

> shall provide against the rains doing harm instead of good to the land, when they come down from the mountains into the hollow dells; and shall keep in the overflow by the help of works and ditches, in order that the valleys, receiving and drinking up the rain from heaven, and providing fountains and streams in the fields and regions which lie underneath, may furnish even to the dry places plenty of good water.

Among the duties of the wardens of the city was the protection of 'the waters, which the guardians of the supply preserve and convey to them, care being taken that they may reach the fountains pure and abundant, and be both an ornament and a benefit to the city' (763). Further on, Plato suggests the penalties to be imposed in the event of water pollution:

> And let this be the law: If anyone intentionally pollutes the water of another, whether the water of a spring, or collected in reservoirs, either by poisonous substances, or by digging, or by theft, let the injured party bring the cause before the wardens of the city, and claim in writing the value of the loss; if the accused be found guilty of injuring the water by deleterious substances, let him not only pay damages, but purify the stream or the cistern which contains the water, in such a manner as the laws of the interpreters order the purification to be made by offender in each case.[35]

35

Plato's writings, insofar as they represent or echo actual Greek law, clearly reveal attempts by lawmakers to control natural resource use and prevent environmental degradation. Plato, conscious of the danger of diminishing wood supply, also recommends penalties for the destruction of timber. Thus in *Laws* (VIII, 843) he writes: '... if anyone sets fire to his own wood and takes no care of his neighbour's property, he shall be fined at the discretion of the magistrates'. The conservation of the purity of air and water was also a preoccupation of Aristotle who in *Politics* (VII, 1330 B) recommended that special care be taken of the water quality: 'For the elements we use most and oftenest for the support of the body contribute most to health and among these are water and air.'

It is also worthy of mention that the intense polluting effects of metals had been more widely noticed from the early times of metal smelting than had the devastation caused by deforestation. The Greek historian and military leader Xenophon (430–355 B.C.), for example, thought that the silver mines in Laurion (Greece) were too polluted to allow a son of a friend to visit the city. (Memoirs of Socrates, Book 3, Verse 6). Later on, Lucretius (*De Rerum Natura,* Book VI, 808–17) wrote:

> Again, when they follow veins of silver and gold, rummaging with their tools the innermost secret places of the earth, what smells Scaptensula exhales from below! Or what mischief do gold mines breathe out, what do they make men look like, what colours! Do you not see or hear in how short a time they are accustomed to perish?

Workers in lead and mercury mines and smelters were known to suffer from the effects of the metals, according to Rome's famous engineer Vitruvius. In his book *De architectura* probably written between 27 and 23 B.C., he commented on the extensive water pollution around mines (Book 8, verse 3):

> For it is obvious that nothing in the world is so necessary for use as water, seeing that any living creature can, if deprived of grain or fruit or meat or fish, or any one of them, support life by using other foodstuffs; but without water no animal nor any proper food can be produced, kept in good condition, or prepared. Consequently we must take great care and pains in searching for springs and selecting them, keeping in view the health of mankind.

He further remarks that:

> Springs should be tested and proved in advance in the following ways. If they run free and open, inspect and observe the physique of

the people who dwell in the vicinity before beginning to conduct the water, and if their frames are strong, their complexion fresh, legs sound, and eyes clear, the spring deserves complete approval ...

More evidence follows:

And if green vegetables cook quickly when put into a vessel of such water and set over a fire, it will be proof that the water is good and wholesome. Likewise if the water in the spring is itself limpid and clear, if there is no growth of moss or reeds where it spreads and flows, and if its bed is not polluted by filth of any sort but has a clean appearance, these signs indicate that the water is light and wholesome in the highest degree.

And finally, in chapter 7 of book VIII, on the *Water Supplies,* Vitruvius mentions that water brought to Rome through the aqueducts can be harmful to people due to its lead content (lat. *cerussa* – carbonate of lead, $PbCO_3$).

As part of his naturalist observations, Pliny (23–79 A.D.) was also concerned that the emissions from mining activities were unhealthy to all animals. He and Strabo likewise pointed out the harmfulness of sulphur dioxide SO_2 emissions from melting ovens, though its effects were only local then.[36] The Roman poet Horace was not alone among his contemporaries in detesting 'the smoke, the wealth, the noise of Rome ...', and lost no time in retreating to his Sabine farm in the hills as often as he could. The ancient Romans, as residents of what had become the largest city in the world, were well aware of the problems of air and water pollution, caused by garbage, sewage and the runoff from industries such as smelting and tanning. Therefore, in the year A.D. 80 the Roman Senate passed a law to protect water stored during dry periods so that it could be used later on for street and sewer cleaning.[37] Sextus Julius Frontinus, who was water commissioner in the capital under Trajan and Nerva, writes proudly of his achievements as follows: 'Not even the waste water is lost; the appearance of the City is clean and altered; the air is purer; and the causes of the unwholesome atmosphere (*gravioris caeli*), which gave the air of the City so bad a name (*infamis aer*) with the ancients, are now removed.'[38] And when the Roman emperor Justinian issued a legal code in A.D. 535 the first entry read as follows: 'By the law of nature these things are common to mankind – the air, running water, the sea, and consequently the shores of the sea.'

6. Registering the impacts

As we have seen, both Plato and Aristotle were aware of the importance of what we might call 'environmental quality' to the wellbeing of the city-state.

And both were aware of how the cumulative effects of natural processes and human activities might change the landscape over time. We have already noted Plato's observations on the condition of Attica in his day. Aristotle for his part realised that there are natural processes that are constantly changing the surface of the earth. In *Meteorologica* he describes the alteration of the Argive plain in this way: 'In the time of the Trojan wars the Argive land was marshy and could only support a small population, whereas the land of Mycenae was in good condition (and for this reason Mycenae was the superior). But now the opposite is the case ... the land of Mycenae has become ... dry and barren, while the Argive land that was formerly barren owing to the water has now become fruitful. Now the same processes that have taken place in this small district must be supposed to be going on over whole countries and on a large scale'.[39] But for the most part they contented themselves with giving fairly accurate accounts of phenomena such as deforestation and soil erosion, and we look in vain for any broader interpretation of their significance. For more 'philosophical' musings, we must look elsewhere.

Writing in the year 360 B.C., Xenophon pens a rather striking passage in which he claims that the earth has her own justice, a law deeper than human enactments, written in the nature of things: 'The earth, being a goddess, also teaches justice to those who can learn; for those who treat her best she recompenses with the most numerous benefits. ... Well did he speak who said that farming is mother and nurse of the other arts, for when farming flourishes, all other arts also prosper, but when the earth is forced to lie barren, the other arts are almost extinguished, both on land and at sea ...'[40] This hints at some kind of contract between farmer and the land he farms, with environmental degradation being construed as some kind of penalty should he farm the land unjustly. It also hints at the idea that a sound ecology is the basis of a sound culture.

Equally striking are the reflections of a Roman writer who shows a troubled awareness that the decline of agriculture and the depletion of earth's bounties is due to human abandonment, and he clearly rejects the pessimistic belief in the decay of nature due to its ageing. This is the Spaniard Columella (fl. first century A.D.) who wrote:

> Again and again I hear the leading men of our state condemning now the unfruitfulness of the soil, now the inclemency of the climate for some season past, as harmful to crops, and some I hear reconciling the aforesaid complaints, as if on well-founded reasoning, on the ground that, in their opinion, the soil was worn out and exhausted by the over-production of earlier days and can no longer furnish sustenance to mortals with its old-time benevolence. Such reasons ... are far from truth; for it is sin to suppose that Nature, endowed with perennial fertility by the creator of the universe,

is affected by barrenness as though with some disease; and it is unbecoming to a man of good judgment to believe that Earth, to whose lot was assigned a divine and everlasting youth ... has grown old in mortal fashion. And, furthermore I do not believe that such misfortunes come upon us as a result of the fury of elements, but rather because of our own fault; for the matter of husbandry.

(On Agriculture, Preface)

As Columella also notes, Romans knew about the art of forestry, and were well able to plant coppices and work out the yields and labour required. He himself recommends cutting chestnut underwood at five years' growth and oak at seven years.[41] No wonder then that he has no patience with those who lay the blame on nature.

7. Factors impeding environmental awareness

Summing up our discussion so far, we have found a variety of factors militating against a full and widespread recognition of the environmental degradation being induced by human activities. In the first place, the understandable focus on securing the basic necessities of life was hardly conducive to sustained reflection on the possible consequences that might ensue. Add to this the fact that such changes were for the most part not immediate but rather, both gradual and often imperceptible. But perhaps the most significant factor was the array of prevailing worldviews that all but precluded any such recognition. From classical times through the Christian period and on into early modern times the dominant view was that of a cosmos governed by providence. The earth was seen as a physical system devised by, or even (on the Stoic view) constituted by, a supreme intelligence, part of whose function was the sustenance of humankind. Within that context, even adverse environmental conditions could only be construed as a natural part of the cultural fabric, hardly matters that humans could hope to rectify, unless they were visited as punishments for human wrongdoing. Minority views, such as a fatalism that ascribed all ills to the whims of the gods, or a golden age narrative that saw current generations as inhabiting an ageing and decaying planet, likewise cast humans as helpless onlookers rather than primary agents of change. And even those deeper thinkers whose views were outside the comfort zone of providential design, such as Heraclitus and Lucretius, preached a gospel of recurrence and renewal. Hence, we must conclude that, contrary to Williams's claims, it is really not at all 'strange' that ancient consciences were not 'disturbed' by the environmental changes that they saw happening around them.

But we have yet to mention one further factor that was inhibiting the development of an environmental consciousness: a sense of the 'dreadfulness' of nature. Far back in history cultivation of soil was a symbol of civilisation, wilderness a dwelling place of evil. Even in the seventeenth century, forest was regarded as 'dreadful', a gloomy, wild symbol of barbarism and fear. The wild nature we cherish was not always beautiful. The classical ideal associated beauty with fruitfulness, order and regularity. In the history of Western thought, Nature has been often viewed as wilderness in the worst sense, full of danger and evil, lacking forms of cultivated landscape:

> The world was certainly not made for us by divine power: so great are the faults with which it stands endowed. In the first place, of all that the sky covers with its mighty expanse, a greedy part is possessed by mountains and forests full of wild beasts, part rocks and vasty marshes hold, and the sea that keeps the shores of lands far apart. Almost two parts of these lands are robbed from mortals by scorching heat and constantly falling frost. Even the land that is left, nature would still cover with brambles by her own power, but that man's power resists, well accustomed to groan over the stout mattock for very life, and to cleave the soil with the pressure of the plough.[42]

This passage reveals not just a belief in the power of human action that is quite a characteristic feature of the classical world, but also the necessity to control nature in order to survive. The same author in a later passage emphasises the more benign aspects of human intervention:

> Day by day they made the forests climb higher up the mountains, and yield the place below to their tilth, that they might have meadows, pools and streams, crops and luxuriant vineyards on hill and plain, and that a grey-green belt of olives might run between (…); just as now you see the whole place mapped out with charming variety, laid out and intersected with sweet fruit trees and set about with fertile plantations.[43]

8. The special case of trees

At the same time, and especially with regard to the harvesting of trees, we find a more appreciative attitude to nature's bounty and an accompanying sense of the need for responsible use. The later Greek geographer Strabo, describing the region of Campania north of Naples wrote the following: 'Avernus is enclosed round about by steep hill-brows that rise above it on all sides except where you sail into it … at the present time they have been brought by the toil of man into cultivation, though in former times they were thickly covered with a wild and untrodden forest of large trees.'[44] Eratosthenes, a geographer of the Hellenistic period, relates deforestation to the need for fuel and building materials, timber for navigation and mining, and governmental land policy. The associated effects of forest clearings on landscapes and climate, already highlighted by the botanist Theophrastus, were later mentioned also by Pliny. And we can trace this awareness on into the Middle Ages with Albert the Great, and further into modern times as a theme of many travellers after the discovery of the Americas. Undoubtedly, deforestation has been a leading instrument of environmental change as far back as the Egyptian period. Some researchers view the attention of Egyptian rulers to tree plantation and cultivation as an attempt to 'combat the sometimes overly exuberant use of resources'.[45] Theophrastus noted that 'in Cyprus the kings used not to cut the trees, both because they took great care of them and husbanded them, and also because the transport of the timber was difficult'.[46] Like Strabo he discussed the cultivation of trees with reference to human use and economic value.

Pliny joins in this 'hymn to the trees':

> Long, indeed, were these last bounties of hers concealed beneath the ground, the trees and forests being regarded as the most valuable benefits conferred by Nature upon mankind. It was from the forest that man drew his first aliment, by the leaves of the trees was his cave rendered more habitable, and by their bark was his clothing supplied; even at this very day, there are nations that live under similar circumstances to these. Still more and more, then, must we be struck with wonder and admiration.[47]

However, the demand for fuel imposed by Roman industrial activity suggests that, at least in areas where woodland was sparse, it was likely to have been managed as a renewable resource. Some woodland management practices are described in Roman textual sources. Cato, writing in the mid-second century B.C., mentioned willow beds, coppice woods, orchards and 'mast-wood'. The latter could be oak or beech woods, both of which provided nuts for feeding pigs. He also mentioned the planting of poplars (*Populus*) and elms (*Ulmus minor* var. *vulgaris*) as a source of leaf fodder for cattle and sheep. References to coppice woods were also made by Columella who in the first century A.D. stated that the best woods for coppicing were oak and chestnut, chestnut being cut on a five-year cycle and the oak at seven years. He also described the planting of chestnut coppices.[48]

9. Into the Middle Ages

If we continue our story into the high and late Middle Ages we find that an awareness that human activities cause undesirable consequences in the environment is constantly re-surfacing. And it is fair to say that the clearing of forests becomes the central theme around which most of the other anthropogenic alterations of the natural world revolve. The climate of northwest Europe differs considerably from the Mediterranean environment that nurtured classical culture. After the collapse of the Roman Empire (fourth and fifth centuries), it was the forest, with its ties to town and country life that became the most significant feature of the medieval period. According to Ruddiman, the most unequivocal evidence of early and extensive deforestation lies in a unique historical document – the Domesday Book. This survey of England, ordered by William the Conqueror, reported that 90 per cent of lowland natural forest was cleared as of 1086 A.D.[49] Compared with the other information provided by the Domesday Book, the evidence of clearing might be inexact, but it does show, as Darby noted, 'that along the Welsh Marches, and in East Anglia and in Kent, woodland was being cleared for one purpose or another; and there is no reason to believe that the same tendencies were not at work all over England'.[50] Indeed the great age of forest clearing extends from the fifth through the thirteenth centuries.

Simultaneously, yet at a much slower pace, arose the awareness of destruction. As in the ancient period, evidence of this awareness is found mostly in local charters, rules, and letters, in the body of rights, usages and customary laws. The Domesday Book records tilled lands 'which have been wasted' and 'all been converted into woodland'. In many other countries sections of the forest were protected for economic reasons (*afforestatio*), and as royal hunting grounds: 'That our *silva* and *foresta* be well guarded' says the thirty sixth article of *Capitulare de Villis*, one of Charlemagne's decrees.[51] In the thirteenth century a document issued by a German king Henry the VII condemned cutting trees for agricultural purposes as calamity: 'harm had come to him and to the city of the kingdom in the destruction of the forest of the kingdom and in transformation into cultivated land'.[52]

Much of England was 'forest' in a more technical sense in the centuries following the Norman Conquest (1066) that is, country set aside as royal game preserves and subject to special forest law. Following the thirteenth century, forests attained more value as demand for timber for ship-building and for other industries was rapidly outstripping supply. As early as 1257 Henry III suspended timber exploitation in many English forests 'because of the destruction caused' (*Calendar of Close Rolls*).[53] And despite the various conservation measures, the fact remains that during the medieval period monasteries had been responsible for very considerable modifications of the landscape that involved the large-scale draining of marshes, the clearance of woodland, and the extension of sheep-farming on the chalk and limestone uplands. The monks (Benedictines and Cistercians) cut down the woods, stubbed them up and levelled them; bushes gave place to barley, willows to wheat, withies to vines.[54] Equally, massive use of charcoal on an industrial scale in Early Modern Europe prompted a new acceleration of the onslaught on western forests. British Renaissance poet Michael Drayton (1563–1631), in his *Poly-Olbion* offers a picture of the fallen state of forest by 'mans devouring hand (...)'.[55]

Accordingly, woodland conservation and management made economic sense, and forests were ruthlessly protected against 'wood stealers'.[56] The Norman kings turned huge stretches of the countryside into royal forests subject to distinctive laws. The term 'forest' was used in a legal rather than a descriptive sense, for the forests were wooded only in parts and contained land that was farmed by peasants. Within the forest boundaries, however, forest laws prevented the clearing of new land for farming and protected the deer and wild boar. The Forest of Knaresborough covered most of lower Nidderdale and was the largest of all the Yorkshire forests. The forests grew to their largest extent under Henry II (1154–89) but during the following century some were 'disafforested' and by the fifteenth century most had fallen out of use.[57] A document from the time of Henry VI (1422–71) relating to Braithwaite, near Middleham, permits the cutting of underwood but 'saving evermore, abyding [remaining] and standing still there, alle okes, almes, esshes, holyns and crabtrees without any felling or hewyng down, or cropping or twisting of theym'.[58]

10. The Renaissance: confidence and caution

At this point we encounter a further element in our account of the factors that were inhibiting a full-scale environmental awareness. The Renaissance is marked by a growing belief in the human ability to control and transform the landscape through reason and technology. Yet amidst this consciousness the belief that our activities negatively affect the natural world lives on. Starting with late fifteenth-century Venice, the centuries that follow see a playing out of the conflict between these opposing tendencies. When Georgius Agricola (George Bauer) censures the idea that mining destroys nature he quotes the arguments of those who oppose it and maintain that mining devastates fields and damages the fertile land vineyards, and olive groves: 'They also argue that the woods and groves are cut down, for there is need of an endless amount of wood for timbers, machines, and the smelting of metals. And when the woods and groves are felled, then are exterminated the beasts and birds (...) Further, once the ores are washed, the water which has been used poisons the brooks and streams, and either destroys the fish or drives them away.'[59] Later on, the poet Abraham Cowley wrote: 'Woods tall and reverend, from all time appear/ Inviolable, where no Mine is near.'

Hence, in spite of the prevailing optimistic belief in human intellectual sagacity that brings about beneficial improvements of the environment, opposite voices were getting through. In the seventeenth century, the newly formed Royal Society asked John Evelyn to report on the problem of forest policy and the shortage of timber. The resulting work surveyed the destruction and its causes such as tillage, industry and shipping.[60] Following his findings Evelyn advocated the duty and necessity of planting trees to restore what had been wasted or used. Sustaining his arguments with the authority of classical writers like Virgil, Theophrastus, Pliny and Columella, he denounced the 'disproportionate spreading of tillage' and the inconsiderate human predisposition 'to extirpate, demolish, and raze, as it were, all those many goodly woods and forests, which our more prudent ancestors left standing for the ornament and service of their country'.[61] He continued: 'Truly, the waste and destruction of our woods has been so universal, that I conceive nothing less than an universal plantation of all sorts of trees will supply and well encounter the defect … '.[62] Then again, while Evelyn put the accent on the necessity of tree planting for both aesthetic and economic reasons, he also accepted as true the belief that deeply forested areas produced moist and unhealthy air. In this context forest clearings had the beneficial effect of 'letting in the air and the sun and making the earth fit for tillage and pasture', making 'those gloomy tracks' of forest 'healthy and habitable'.[63]

Evelyn's work was not the first attempt to halt deforestation in England, since the earliest conservation efforts following the classical period date back at least to the seventh century.[64] The Magna Carta (1215) contains two sections that focus on environment-related problems. The Forest Charter establishes reforestation programmes in all royal forests and along all riverbanks.[65] Two centuries later, Henry VI passed a law intended to remedy degradation of marshlands and the 'Hurt that within short Time will happen'.[66] However, in the following centuries both domestic and industrial demands took a heavy toll of the remaining woods. For quite a while, Evelyn's work positively influenced the reforestation process, and in 1758 the Royal Society of Arts offered gold and silver medals for the 'largest plantation of each kind of tree every year'.[67] It was unfortunate that much of the planting activity showed a lack of consideration for the native species, bringing about widespread use of new species or 'rubbish' as William Cobbett described them. William Wordsworth in his Guide to the Lake District (1835) shared this opinion when he mentioned ten thousand larch trees 'stuck in at once upon the side of the hill' and 'platoons' of Scots fir serving as poor surrogates for native vegetation.[68]

Facing the urgent necessity to confront the abuse of water and forests, Louis XIV proclaimed in 1669 the French Forest Ordinance. Colbert, his minister, appointed the commission to look into the abuse of forested areas, fearing that 'France will perish for lack of woods'. It penalised forest destruction and regulated cutting. It controlled the proper use of timber. It also controlled the use and penalised the abuse of the forest floor. It prohibited grazing animals in 'lands and heaths, or void and bare places on the borders of the woods and forests'.[69] The Ordinance was intended to repair the damage brought about by the destructive use of natural resources and

the waste of royal forests. It was also meant to provide for future generations, since 'it is not enough to have reestablished order and discipline,
if we do not by good and wise regulations see to it that the fruit of this shall
be secured to posterity'.[70]

The strict forest and timber legislation in England and France during the
seventeenth century had been inspired by the historical evidence of natural
resource destruction, and the growing awareness of the risks that accrued
from human inflicted environmental changes. As James I remarked in 1610,
'If woods be suffered to be felled, as daily they are, there will be none left.'[71]
The duty to reforest was written into many early customs, manorial regulations and local laws, especially in England. At the same time these practical
attempts to save damaged natural areas for utilitarian, spiritual or orna-
mental reasons stand in contrast with the prevailing philosophical image of
an increasing, technology driven, human capacity to control the natural
world. As we have seen, evidence of the destructive effects of human action,
and – here and there – regulations to remedy our reckless dealings with
the natural world, had been emerging into view ever since ancient times.
Evelyn's work dramatised the problem of disappearing woods caused by the
widespread increase of agriculture and grazing. In 1811, the Enlightenment
thinker, German naturalist and explorer Alexander von Humboldt, in his
Political Essay on the Kingdom of New Spain,[72] glimpsed the universality
of the phenomenon, writing about the *global* human impact on the environment. He talked of nature's alteration, disappearing forests, a spreading
agriculture, monotonous landscapes, and the invasion of exotic plants.
Along with Humboldt, philosopher and poet Johann Gottfried von Herder
pictured humans as 'a band of bold though diminutive giants, gradually
descending from the mountains, to subjugate the earth and change climates
with their feeble arms'.[73]

Nevertheless, awareness of the human power to control nature, also
clearly visible in the works of Count Buffon, overshadowed all the warnings
and evidence of undesirable changes in natural systems. Some writers who
focused on climatic change indicated the possibility of some unexpected
local temperature changes due to human activities. Noah Webster wrote:
'The clearing of lands opens them to the sun, their moisture is exhaled, they
are more heated in summer, but more cold in winter near the surface;
the temperatures become unsteady, and the seasons irregular.'[74] However,
our dealings with nature were for the most part based on the optimistic
view that the human mind and human technical skills could modify the
environment at discretion. In addition, preconceived views of an orderly and
teleological nature (despite the ontological doubts of Kant and Hume),
coupled with insufficient knowledge, continued to obscure the long-term
consequences of environmental modification. What is more, many intellectuals applauded the beneficial results of draining wetlands and clearing
forests. Montesquieu assumed that ocean fisheries were inexhaustible, 'that

coal pits could happily replace forests, and that more exploitation was needed'.[75] In the eighteenth century, the English poet Alexander Pope, in *An Essay on Man* (lines 281–94) captures this cavalier spirit:

All nature is but art, unknown to thee;
All chance, direction, which thou canst not see;
All discord, harmony not understood;
A partial evil, universal good:
And, spite of pride, in erring reason's spite,
One truth is clear, WHATEVER IS, IS RIGHT.

It was Count Buffon who documented the physical effects of human action on the land in more detail than any other scientist before George Perkins Marsh. However, the French Count, like some of his counterparts in the ancient period, considered these changes beneficial for the progress of civilisation. 'Wild nature is hideous and dying; it is I, I alone, who can make it agreeable and living.'[76] Yet, in spite of his belief in the inexhaustible power of Nature, and his conception of human beings as a geographical agent, like many writers before him, he warned about the threats of deforestation, thus embodying both the conflicting tendencies already noted. He encouraged the conservation of remaining forests and the reforestation of 'a part of those we have destroyed'. Following Evelyn's proposal Buffon emphasised the need for a science of forestry; for, 'Nothing is less known; nothing more neglected. The forest is a gift of nature which it is sufficient to accept just as it comes from her hands.'[77] Fifty years later Marsh in his book *Man and Nature* (1864) argued that deforestation could lead to desertification. Referring to the clearing of once-lush lands surrounding the Mediterranean, he asserted: 'the operation of causes set in action by man has brought the face of the earth to desolation almost as complete as that of the moon'. In response, he called for the restoration of devastated forests, soils, and rivers through human co-operation with nature. After having travelled the world, he came to the conclusion: 'I know no more important practical lessons in this earthly life of ours ... than those relating to the employment of the sense of vision in the study of nature.'[78]

11. Conclusions

As Heraclitus pointed out: 'Eyes and ears are poor witnesses for men if their souls do not understand the language' (Fragment 107). Centuries later, Tennyson the English poet and enthusiast for nature and her laws, in his poem *The High Pantheism,* echoes this sentiment with: 'And the ear of man cannot hear, and the eye of man cannot see.'

One might be tempted to ask; 'What would it take for men's souls fully to "understand the language"?' We eschew this question, at least insofar as it assumes that there can be some finality and completeness in our own understanding. In one of its reports,[79] the European Environment Agency complains that in trying to reduce current and future risks the lessons of history have rarely been used. But what these lessons might be is a thoroughly moot point. We should not confuse history with science. History does not normally supply us with data, on the basis of which we can make predictions. What it does do is give us some understanding of our past that we can use to gain a better understanding of our present predicament. So far as the environment is concerned, perhaps the most we can learn from the past is an understanding that the natural and mysterious world around us is in a constant turmoil even though, sometimes, the constant processes can come to an imagined impasse. This state of momentary equilibrium presents us with the illusion of an island of stability in a turbulent universe. Unfortunately, we do not, and cannot have even incomplete fore-knowledge of future events. The sad truth is that, as Peter Bernstein writes in his challenging book, *Against the Gods: The Remarkable Story of Risk:*

> The past seldom obliges by revealing to us when wildness will break out in the future. Wars, depressions, stock-market booms and crashes, and ethnic massacres come and go, but they always seem to arrive as surprises. After the fact, however, when we study the history of what happened, the source of the wildness appears to be so obvious to us that we have a hard time understanding how people on the scene were oblivious to what lay in wait for them.[80]

There is another aspect to this statement. We should not forget that 'nature resists imitation through a model' as Schrödinger once wrote, and apparently successful predictions that make some theory plausible, will not necessarily prove accurate in future. Today's physics and life sciences offer us totally new ways of looking at Nature. But Nature continues to defy easy capture. Arguably, ecology itself is more history than science. A plurality of causal factors combined with ever-changing sets of initial conditions make it very difficult, if not impossible, to determine the cause of any given phenomenon, not to mention its consequences. The 'science' of ecology does not offer unifying solutions nor produce clear-cut predictions upon which decisions and actions could be based. The most it can teach us is that life is always capable of expressing and elaborating new and unexpected potentialities. We can never predict what these will be, though we can be pretty certain that they will occur.

A more modest and more appropriate question to ask, therefore, and one which makes no assumptions of finality or completeness so far as our own understanding is concerned, is simply how modern environmental consciousness came about. For our discussion does suggest a number of key ingredients that had to be in place before our current environmental conscience could be fully awakened.

First, in contrast with notions of renewal and recurrence, there has probably needed to be a conception of the planet or biosphere as a singular, finite entity with an open ended but finite history. The sense of urgency that characterises the modern sensitivity depends in no small measure on the belief that much environmental 'damage' is irreparable – that is, is unable to be repaired either by human ingenuity or through natural processes of renewal. And clearly, among the figures who were historically responsible for the awakening of this sense we should count the likes of the geologist Charles Lyell, exponent of James Hutton's theory of uniformitarianism and, of course, Darwin.

Second, and in contrast with the belief that nature is providentially protected, there has probably needed to be a sense of the vulnerability of nature, not excluding humans. Here, it is interesting to note that Darwin's message has mixed implications. For whilst emphasising the transience, as opposed to the permanence, of forms of life, it is emphasising at the same time that succession, or 'descent', is built into the processes of natural selection. And this, of course, is seized upon by those who find themselves at odds with the prevailing environmental conscience. Hence, in response to concerns about the 'loss' of biodiversity they are apt to remark that extinctions are all part of the natural process. Equally, whilst there is growing evidence of human induced climatic change, it has to be kept in mind that the climate system varies naturally on different time scales.[81] We should remember that climate change, often of far greater magnitudes than anything human beings have seen, has been taking place throughout not only all of human history but virtually throughout the entire history of the earth.

Third, and in contrast with the confidence in human abilities that characterises Renaissance and Enlightenment thinking, there has needed to be a real and profound grasp of human limitations, both at an intellectual and socio-political level. How this confidence has been undermined is too complicated a story to attempt here, but Freud and – again – Darwin would no doubt feature strongly. But as a footnote to that story we would venture the thought that perhaps it took a century which saw two world wars before Utopian dreams of indefinite progress could be fully laid to rest.

Finally, and in contrast with 'piecemeal' views of the human race, often resting on a range of dichotomies – Greek/barbarian, male/female and so forth – we would argue that the rise of humanism, bringing with it a sense of a common humanity and of a common human agency was another essential pre-condition. For although it brings various forms of anthropocentrism in its wake, which are not usually associated with environmental sensitivity, and although it coincided with the rise of a form of science that fuelled the optimistic belief that all problems could be overcome, it was also an essential pre-condition for the development of a sense of a common human responsibility.

Notes

1 Michael Williams, 'The History of Deforestation', *History Today* **51**, 7 (July 2001): 30–37.
2 Magnus Widell, 'Historical Evidence for Climate Instability and Environmental Catastrophes in Northern Syria and the Jazira: The Chronicle of Michael the Syrian', *Environment and History* **13** (2007): 47–70.
3 Marie-Jean-Antoine-Nicolas Caritat, M. de Condorcet, *Outlines of and Historical View of the Progress of Human Mind* (Philadelphia, printed by Lange and Utrick, 1798).
4 See Michael Williams, *Deforesting the Earth: From Prehistory to Global Crisis* (Chicago and London: University of Chicago Press, 2003).
5 John Salomon and Graham Shipley (eds.), *Human Landscapes in Classical Antiquity: Environment and Culture* (London: Routledge, 1996).
6 M. Williams, 'Dark Ages and Dark Areas: Global Deforestation in the Deep Past', *Journal of Historical Geography* **26**, 1 (2000): 28–46.
7 Ibid., 28.
8 Tjeerd. H. van Andel, Curtis N. Runnels and Kevin O. Pope, 'Five Thousand Years of Land Use and Abuse in the Southern Argolid, Greece', *Hesperia* **55**, 1 (1986): 103–28.
9 C. Vita-Finzi, *The Mediterranean Valleys: Geological Changes in Historical Times* (Cambridge: Cambridge University Press, 1969).
10 John Bintliff, 'Time, Process and Catastrophism in the Study of Mediterranean Alluvial History: A Review', *World Archaeology* **33**, 3 (2002): 417–35.
11 Theophrastus, *Historia Plantarum*. 5.3.7.
12 Van Andel et al., 'Five Thousands Years of Land Use', 113.
13 Michael Williams, *Deforesting the Earth: From Prehistory to Global Crisis* (Chicago: The University of Chicago Press, 2003), 97.
14 William Holland Drury Jr., *Chance and Change, Ecology for Conservationists* (Berkeley, Los Angeles: University of California Press, 1998), 7.
15 Fragment 18, Clément Stromates, 11, 17, 4 in G. S. Kirk, J. E. Raven and M. Schoffield, *The Presocratic Philosophers, A Critical History with a Selection of Texts,* 2nd edn (Cambridge: Cambridge University Press, 1995).
16 See, Aristotle, *Metaphysics,* Book 1, translated by W. D. Ross (The Internet Classics Archive, http://classics.mit.edu/)
17 Marcus T. Cicero, *On the Nature of the Gods,* translated by H. Rackham, Loeb Classical Library (London: Heinemann, 1933), II: 82.
18 See *Airs, Water, Places in Hippocratic Writings,* ed. and intro. G.E.R. Lloyd (Harmondsworth: Penguin, 1983).
19 Aristotle, *On the Parts of Animals,* translated by W. Ogle, (London: Kegan Paul, Trench and Co., 1882) 1, 5.
20 Lucretius, *De Rerum Natura* (On the nature of things), translated by W.H.D. Rouse, 2nd edn revised by M. F. Smith, Loeb Classical Library (London: Heinemann, 1982) V. 828–36.
21 *Novum Organum,* First Book of Aphorisms, XXIV.
22 Pliny the Elder, *The Natural History,* ed. John Bostock and H.T Riley, book XXXI, chapter 30, 'Historical Observation upon waters which have

suddenly made their appearance or suddenly ceased' (London: Taylor and Francis, 1855).

23 Russell Meiggs, *Trees and Timber in the Ancient Mediterranean World* (Oxford: Clarendon Press, 1982).

24 Pausanias, *Description of Greece,* translated by W. H. S. Jones, Loeb Classical Library (London: Heinemann, n.d.) 8, 17–35.

25 Plato, *Critias* 111-B.

26 Clarence J. Glacken, *Traces on the Rhodian Shore: Nature and Culture in Western Thought from Ancient Times to the End of the Eighteenth Century* (Berkeley: University of California Press, 1967), 121.

27 Theophrastus, *De Causis Plantarum* 5.14.2–3.

28 Seneca, *Natural Questions,* 5.18.15

29 Victor Ehrenberg, *The People of Aristophanes* (New York: Schocken Books, 1962).

30 Pliny the Elder, *Natural History* (VII, Preface).

31 Williams, *Deforesting the Earth,* 35.

32 See J. Donald Hughes, *The Environmental History of the World: Humankind's Chang ing Role in the Community of Life* (New York: Routledge, 2001).

33 Livio Rossetti, 'Il piú antico decreto ecologico a noi noto e il suo contesto' [The Oldest Known Ecological Law in Context] in Thomas M. Robinson and Laura Westra (eds.), *Thinking about the Environment: Our Debt to the Classical and Medieval Past* (London: Lexington Books, 2002), 43–57.

34 See Plutarch, *Roman Lives: A Selection of Eight Lives,* trans. Robin Waterfield (Oxford: Oxford University Press, 1999).

35 Plato, *Laws* VIII, 845 E.

36 See: R. J. Forbes, *Metallurgy in Antiquity* (Leiden: Brill, 1950).

37 See: http://www.intute.ac.uk/timeline2.html – 174k.

38 Sextus Julius Frontinus, *The Aqueducts of Rome* trans. C. E. Bennett (London: Heinemann, 1925), II. 88.

39 Aristotle, *Meteorologica,* Book I, chapter 14.

40 Xenophon, *Oeconomicus,* V. 1–12, 17.

41 Columella, *De Rustica,* IV, xxxii, 4.

42 Lucretius, Book V, 198–209.

43 Lucretius, Book V, 1370–78.

44 *The Geography of Strabo,* Vol. II, ed. H. L. Jones, Loeb Classical Library (London: Heinemann, 1923), 441–45. Also http://penelope.uchicago.edu/Thayer/E/Roman/Texts/Strabo/home.html.

45 Robert M. Alison, 'The Earliest Traces of a Conservation Conscience', *Natural History* **90**, 5 (1981): 72–78.

46 Theophrastus, *Enquiry into Plants,* V.8. 1–3, 465.

47 Pliny, 31.19 (Book XII Preface).

48 See Russell Meiggs, *Trees and Timber in the Ancient Mediterranean World,* (Oxford: Clarendon Press, 1982).

49 William F. Ruddiman, 'How Did Humans First Alter Global Climate?', *Scientific American* **292**, 3 (2005): 46–54.

50 Henry Clifford Darby, 'The Clearings of the English Woodlands', *Geography* (formerly *The Geographical Teacher*), The Quarterly Journal of the Geographical Association, no. 172, vol. XXXVI, part 2, May 1952. Also: 'The Clearing of the Woodlands in Europe', in William L. Thomas (ed.), *Man's Role in Changing the Face of the Earth* (Chicago: University of Chicago Press, 1956); and Robert M. Alison, 'The Earliest Traces of a Conservation Conscience', *Natural History* **90**, 5 (1981): 76.

51 Glacken, *Traces on the Rhodian Shore*, 334.

52 Richard H. Grove, *Green Imperialism: Colonial Expansion, Tropical Island Edens, and the Origins of Environmentalism, 1600–1860* (Cambridge: Cambridge University Press, 1995), 26.

53 See, William H. Te Brake, 'Air Pollution and Fuel Crisis in Preindustrial London 1250–1650', *Technology and Culture* 16, 3, (1975): 337–59.

54 See James Westfall Thompson, *An Economic and Social History of the Middle Ages, 300 to 1300* (London: Century, 1928).

55 Michael Drayton, *Poly-Olbion: A Chronologic Description of Great Britain*, Published by Burt Franklin, 1996.

56 Neil Roberts, *The Holocene: An Environmental History* (Oxford: Blackwell Publishing, 1989, 1998, reprinted 2004), 202.

57 David Hey, *A History of Yorkshire: County of Broad Acres* (Lancaster: Carnegie Publishing, 2005), 124.

58 Thomas Dunham Whitaker, *An History of Richmondshire in the North Riding of the County of York*, 2 (Leeds, 1823), 345–46.

59 Georgius Agricola, *De re metallica*, Translated from the first Latin edn of 1556 by Herbert C. Hoover and Lou H. Hoover (New York: Dover Publications, 1950 [1912]), 7.

60 John Evelyn. *Silva: or, A discourse of forest-Trees and the Propagation of timber in His Majesty's Dominions* (York: Printed by A. Ward, 1776; first printed in 1664).

61 Evelyn, *Silva*, 1–3.

62 Evelyn, *Silva*, 3.

63 Evelyn, *Silva*, 30–34.

64 See Darby, 'The Clearing of the Woodlands in Europe', 74.

65 Darby, 'The Clearing of the Woodlands in Europe', 82.

66 Glacken, *Traces on the Rhodian Shore*, 491–94.

67 Glacken, *Traces on the Rhodian Shore*, 492.

68 William Wordsworth, *Guide to the Lakes*, with a new Preface by Stephan Gill (London: Frances Lincoln, 2004).

69 Keith Thomas, *Man and the Natural World* (New York: Pantheon Books, 1983), 198.

70 John Croumbie Brown, *French Forest Ordinance of 1669: With Historical Sketch of Previous Treatment of Forests in France* (Edinburgh: Oliver and Boyd, 1883; reprinted BiblioLife LLC, 2009).

71 Thomas, *Man and the Natural World*, 198.

72 Alexander von Humboldt, *Political Essay on the Kingdom of New Spain* (Paris: F. Schoell, 1811).

73 J. G. von Herder, *Reflections on the Philosophy of the History of Mankind*, abridged and with introduction by Frank E. Manuel (Chicago: The University of Chicago Press, 1968), 19.

74 Noah Webster, *Dissertation on the Supposed Change of Temperature in Modern Winters* [1799], A collection of Papers on Political, Literary and Moral subjects, (New York: Webster & Clark; Boston: Tappan and Dennett, 1843), 119–62.

75 Charles Montesquieu, *Pensees et fragments inedits de Montesquieu*, ed. Gaston de Montesquieu, vol. 1 (Bordeaux, 1899–1901), 179–82.

76 Georges-Louis Leclerc, Comte de Buffon, *Natural History, General and Particular*, Translated from French by William Smellie (London: T. Cadell and W. Davies, 1812), vol 12: xiii.

77 Buffon, *Natural History*, 271–90.

78 G. P. Marsh, *The Earth as Modified by Human Action,* a new edition of *Man and Nature* (New York: Scribner, Armstrong, 1874; reprinted New York: Arno, 1970).
79 European Environment Agency (EEA), Environmental Issue Report No. 22, *Late Lessons from Early Warnings: The Precautionary Principle 1896–2000* (Copenhagen: EEA, 2001) (http://reports.eea.eu.int/environmental_issue_report_ 2001_ 22/en).
80 Peter L. Bernstein, *Against the Gods: The Remarkable Story of Risk* (New York: John Wiley & Sons, 1996), 334.
81 See Lawrence Solomon, *The Deniers: The World Renowned Scientists Who Stood Up against Global Warming Hysteria, Political Persecution and Fraud* (Minneapolis: Richard Vigilante Books, 2008).

3

OPPORTUNITIES IN MARINE ENVIRONMENTAL HISTORY

W. Jeffrey Bolster

For millennia the bountiful sea provided a larder, a living, and the possibility of riches for intrepid fishermen. Its scale in time and space, however, even for experienced mariners, appeared all out of proportion to that of familiar worlds ashore; and seafarers and landlubbers alike could not help but regard the sea as inscrutable, threatening, and eternal. Suddenly, in the blink of a twentieth-century eye, the tables were turned: The sea appeared fragile and vulnerable in the face of human arrogance. Overfishing, destruction of marine habitats, and shipborne biological invasions cast the time-honored phrase "men against the sea" in a new light. Following publication in the journal *Nature* of an essay estimating that large predatory fish had declined worldwide by 90 percent, *Newsweek's* cover story on July 14, 2003, asked, "Are the oceans dying?"[1] That question, unimaginable not long ago, seemed all the more ominous for its lack of historical precedent.

The recent crisis in the ocean has been regarded rightfully as an ecological and political problem, but rarely understood in light of history – as if nature and science were somehow realms separate from the study of the past. During the 1990s the Black Sea ecosystem collapsed, literally starved to death by a bloom of invasive jellyfish that indiscriminately devoured zooplankton, phytoplankton, and larval fish, leaving virtually nothing for the rest of the food chain. For creatures in and people around the nearly landlocked Black Sea, the horror unleashed by the ctenophore *Mnemiopsis leidyi* was immediate and vivid; but ships have been carrying invasive marine hitchhikers from one sea to another for centuries, quietly reshaping the oceans of the world. The Black Sea catastrophe was different because of its scale and the presence of cameras.[2]

When the Canadian government closed the Grand Banks cod fishery in 1992, cod stocks and spawning biomass were frighteningly low, and the average size of individual fish had plummeted. Fishermen knew they were catching juveniles and that the fishery was unsustainable, but few

Newfoundlanders could imagine alternatives. To hear politicians at the time, however, one might have thought that the problem was a recent one, and that the closures would be brief. Fourteen years later the decimated cod population has not yet rebounded, the fishery remains closed, and Newfoundland's coastal economy and society are still staggering. The collapse, of course, was hardly just a few years in the making: Newfoundland's banks had been fished rigorously for centuries.[3] Initially that ecosystem's productivity was staggering. In 1578 Anthony Parkhurst wrote from Newfoundland of capturing capelin, a bait-fish favored by cod, "with a shove-net as plentiful as you do wheat with a shovel, [enough] in three or four hours for a whole city." In 1664, when European fishermen were already catching about 200,000 tons of cod each season, the *Jesuit Relations* noted "these waters so abound in codfish ... that ships are quickly filled with them." Yet as early as 1703 an Englishman lamented from coastal Newfoundland that "the fish grows less, the old store being consumed by our continual fishing." By then the five-hundred-year fishing spree that ended in 1992 was well underway. When the Canadian government finally pulled the plug, Newfoundland's marine ecosystem had changed beyond recognition from the one described by Parkhurst or the Jesuits.[4]

If the bookends of initial abundance and contemporary scarcity in the oceans are well known by now, most waypoints between them remain obscured or uninvestigated, ripe for historical analysis. It is increasingly clear that people have been using the oceans and leaving their marks for centuries, even though the marks long appeared invisible. Isn't it time to recognize the oceans as part of history? Encouraging the development of scholarship, publications, and programs in marine environmental history, this essay argues that historians are uniquely situated to reconstruct the inextricably tangled stories of people and the oceans.[5]

The need for marine environmental history

During the last forty years dramatic biological changes have occurred in New England, West Indian, and Scandinavian waters, among other places, with profound socio-cultural consequences. The centuries-old Long Island Sound lobster fishery collapsed recently, probably from toxic insecticides, throwing lobstermen out of work and accelerating the transformation of working waterfronts into condominiums and office units.[6] Caribbean coral reefs that beguiled divers during the 1970s are moribund. Stripped of life, they no longer attract local fishers or snorkeling tourists. Meanwhile, North Atlantic fishing villages from Norway to New Bedford are grappling with their identity and economic survival; dependent on cod for centuries, they are in death throes as grim as those of the Jamaican reefs. The sea around them, moreover, has not been simply depleted by overfishing: Its web of life is being restructured in profound and increasingly unpredictable ways.[7]

Within this recently constructed and chilling metanarrative of marine environmental decline, the uncontestable truth of our era, a few alternative stories have bobbed to the surface. Maine lobstermen are not complaining. Shiny new pickup trucks at town docks from Kittery to Eastport attest to record-breaking lobster landings during the last ten years, a result, some ecologists believe, of the radical refashioning of ecological relationships among finfish, kelp, sea urchins, and lobsters initiated by the virtual eradication of cod and other demersal fish.[8] Maritime Maine has not always been the lobster coast. Maine's maritime communities, however, have always trailed historic changes in near-coastal ecosystems with significant social and cultural adaptations. That tale, in all its detail, still awaits an environmental historian.[9]

While the long-term effects of humans' manipulation of the ocean have become abundantly clear in recent decades, the process itself – little understood and, until recently, generally ignored – has been underway for centuries.[10] Spencer Apollonio, former commissioner of Maine's Department of Marine Resources, suggested that human harvesters using sails, oars, hooks, and harpoons may have removed more biomass from the Gulf of Maine during the eighteenth century than did their counterparts with diesel trawlers, polyester nets, and electronic fish-finders in the twentieth century. His back-of-the-envelope figures, worthy of careful investigation, point to the impact of the colonial whale fishery, which was an early source of profits for a region that lacked a dominant export commodity such as sugar, tobacco, or wheat. New England's peak shore whaling years were 1690 to 1725. Contemporaries claimed the near shore whaling grounds had been "fished out" by 1740, and documentary-based research indicates that a minimum of 2,459 to 3,025 right whales were killed by colonists between 1696 and 1734 in the coastal area between Delaware Bay and Maine, in addition to numerous pilot whales and occasional other great whales. Other informed estimates suggest the number of whales killed was much higher. Nor was this the earliest documented overfishing in North American waters. Sixteenth-century Basque whalers depleted right whale and bowhead populations in the Straits of Belle Isle between Labrador and Newfoundland by killing tens of thousands of whales from 1530 to 1620. Then Dutch and Basque whalers in the western Arctic killed 35,000 to 40,000 whales between 1660 and 1701, reducing stocks considerably and affecting the whales' migratory patterns.[11]

Even if seventeenth- and eighteenth-century harvesters did not remove more biomass from the system than their twentieth-century counterparts, consequences followed from overfishing. Killing large numbers of whales in a relatively short time removed their qualitative contribution to ecosystem stability. Baleen whales are not apex predators. But as long-living large animals, whales embody vast biomass in stable form. Even in a relatively small area like the Gulf of Maine, the pre-harvest whale population concentrated hundreds of thousands of tons of biomass, thus imposing certain constraints on variability within the system. Ecosystems are defined by connections between biotic and abiotic components, including constraints in both time and space. Colonial hunters' overharvesting of whales freed considerable prey from capture, and may have allowed prey populations to oscillate more dramatically than they had before. Overharvesting whales probably boosted populations of birds, cod, and other fish that had competed with whales for food. Right whales' diet, for instance, consists primarily of small crustaceans such as copepods and euphausids. Larval cod eat copepods, and little else. Fewer whales meant more food for cod and other organisms. The merchantable fish stocks that colonists desired, therefore, may have been increased, albeit inadvertently, by eradication of whales along the coast. Louwrens Hacquebord has outlined a similar ripple effect beginning with whale hunting in Norway's Svalbard archipelago.[12]

Seventeenth- and early-eighteenth-century colonists clearly were not working in a pristine coastal environment: The long reach of merchant capitalism had made appreciable inroads on North American coastal ecology before the Pilgrims hit the beach.[13] The very fact that humans' modification of near coastal ecosystems in much of the settled world has been on-going for centuries, and has been ignored for almost as long, provides tantalizing possibilities for scholars to explore how human maritime communities were embedded in non-human marine communities, and what that meant for the course of history.

Several simple ideas anchor this enterprise. First, the ocean has a history; in fact, the deep ocean and its numerous near coastal environments have long histories in which people have been inextricably involved.[14] Second, those histories are worth reconstructing. Even though much of the story will remain unknowable, sources exist that make marine environmental history possible. Third, richly contextualized and subtle historical perspectives are crucially needed in discussions about future management of ocean resources. The oceans' current crisis resulted from a century of vigorous fact-finding by scientists along with managers' reliance on numbers divorced from context, and politicians' satisfaction with exceedingly short-term solutions. If there was ever a dilemma crying out for historians' sensibilities, this is it.

Professional historians routinely critique broad generalizations and essentialist arguments by providing gritty details to the contrary. We have the ability to reconstruct the actions of historically specific people who relied on ocean resources, and thus to illuminate the nature that mattered, and how it mattered, to otherwise well-known maritime people: colonial New Englanders, seventeenth-century Dutch and Danish herring fishers, nineteenth-century West Indian turtlers, twentieth-century Filipino whalers, or contemporary Alaskan salmon trollers, to name a few. Only historians have the contextual understanding of archival documents that illuminate abundance and distribution of marine organisms in pre-scientific time.[15] The unfortunate truth is that contemporary managers charged with rebuilding depleted stocks of fish or marine mammals rarely possess any genuine knowledge of those stocks' past size. Their data often reach back only a few decades at best. Painstakingly produced marine environmental history would be a significant contribution to debates on the future use of the oceans.[16]

Finally, there is history for its own sake. Scholars in the humanities retain the conviction that compelling stories communicate their own truths and that well-documented tales about the complexities of the past can be profoundly rewarding. Such stories need not be linear, or based on quantifiable evidence. They need not be inspired by a rigid work plan, or based on testable hypotheses. In fact, as every historian knows, great histories often emerge from rather open-ended inquiries or serendipitous discoveries. Historians, thankfully, still have the personal freedom to explore what they wish. Marine environmental history need not be validated by presentist justifications of the sort that drive funded scientific research. It might begin with what Richard Henry Dana called the "witchery in the sea," an attraction felt by generations of oceanographers and maritime historians. Rewriting maritime histories by considering the living ocean as a dynamic player in human dramas could generate significant contributions to what we know about people as ecological actors. And it just might lead to carefully wrought stories breathtaking in their own right.[17]

This essay makes a case for the support and development of marine environmental history. We need to better understand many things: how different groups of people made themselves in the context of marine environments, how race, class, fashion, and geo-politics influenced the exploitation and conservation of marine resources, how individual and community identities (and economies) changed as a function of the availability of marine resources, how technological innovation frequently masked declining catches, how fishermen's knowledge of localized depletions accumulated in the past, how public policy debates revealed historically specific values associated with the ocean, how collaboration between (and then antagonism among) fishermen and scientists affected marine environments, how faith in the certainty of marine science waxed and waned, how different cultures perceived the ocean at specific times, and – when possible – how past marine environments looked in terms of abundance and distribution of important species.[18]

These are the constituent parts that get to a deeper historical question: the nature of the greatest sea change in human history. Only good marine environmental history can get to the heart of the ecological and cultural transformations that have cast the twenty-first-century ocean as vulnerable rather than eternal. Despite obstacles and problems, preliminary work in this field makes it look immediately relevant, professionally challenging, and intellectually rewarding.

Historicizing the ocean

Considering why the environmental history of the oceans has been ignored so profoundly seems like a good place to begin. While an essay of this length can make only passing reference to what Philip E. Steinberg calls "the social construction of the ocean," intriguing evidence suggests that the ocean was long considered separate from nature. More significantly for historians, western civilization assumed the oceans to be timeless. These ideas have had considerable reach and endurance.[19]

Loathsome to the ancients, the ocean was a realm that early Christians regarded as distinct from the rest of creation. As Alain Corbin explains, it was "the remnant of that undifferentiated primordial substance on which form had to be imposed so that it might become part of Creation."[20] Recent scholarship, including that of Corbin and Helen M. Rozwadowski, has begun to reconstruct the eighteenth- and nineteenth-century process through which Europeans and Americans became attracted to the sea and intrigued with it.[21] But we still don't know exactly when educated Europeans began to imagine the ocean as part of nature. In *Man and the Natural World* Keith Thomas explains that during the sixteenth, seventeenth, and eighteenth centuries English people developed an intense interest in animals, trees, flowers, and landscape. They posed new and penetrating questions about the relationship of humans to the natural world. Inquisitiveness about the sea was barely noticeable, however, even though England was rapidly becoming the foremost sea power in the Atlantic world. Thomas's book on the early modern natural world ignores the ocean entirely, a reflection of prevailing cultural attitudes at that time.[22] Apparently never having succumbed, like continental landscapes, to humans' attempts to impose order on its wildness, the ocean was long imagined as distinct from other wild places.

The myth of the timeless ocean had a proud place in nineteenth- and twentieth-century literature. "We do not associate the idea of antiquity with the ocean, nor wonder how it looked a thousand years ago," noted Henry David Thoreau, "for it was equally wild and unfathomable always." Melville embroidered this theme into *Moby Dick,* as Charles Dickens did in *Dombey and Son.* Joseph Conrad, the prolific Victorian novelist who spent years as a mariner before turning to literature, peppered his prose with references to "the incorruptible ocean" and "the immortal sea." T. S. Eliot might have spoken for them all in "The Dry Salvages," when he invoked the ocean as a cosmic metronome marking something separate from "our time."

> And under the oppression of the silent fog
> The tolling bell

Measures time, not our time, rung by the unhurried
Ground swell, a time
Older than the time of chronometers ...
When time stops and time is never ending;
And the ground swell, that is and was from the beginning,
Clangs,
The bell.[23]

This literary and spiritual sense of the ocean's immortality, the idea that it rolled on before human life existed, and that it will roll on changelessly thereafter, long contributed to the fundamentally flawed assumption that the ocean, unlike forests, plains, and deserts, has always existed outside of history.

The myth of the timeless ocean has been so seductive that even professional historians have succumbed. "To stand on a sea-washed promontory looking westwards at sunset over the Atlantic is to share a timeless human experience." So begins Barry Cunliffe's *Facing the Ocean: The Atlantic and Its Peoples, 8000 BC–AD 1500.* "We are in awe of the unchanging and unchangeable as all have been before us and all will be." This is a rather ahistorical opening to a history book. It suspends attention to the viewers' cultural frames of reference and to changes in the sea. But it is remarkably similar in its mythic content to the first two lines of medievalist Vincent H. Cassidy's *The Sea Around Them: The Atlantic Ocean, A.D. 1250.* "No gesture is equal in futility to scratching the surface of the sea. Although many a momentary wake left by some frail ocean-borne craft has been of permanent significance to mankind, the ocean has made more of an impression upon men than they have made upon the ocean."[24]

This conceptual stumbling block has impeded the development of marine environmental history. A new generation of historians can make their mark by delineating how cultural assumptions about the oceans (and the oceans themselves) have changed through time, sometimes dramatically within a short span of years. People today neither use nor imagine the oceans in the same ways as their ancestors.[25]

Until very recently it has been difficult for historians to imagine the unsustainability of industrial fisheries, much less pre-industrial ones. The idea of the eternal sea, after all, had intellectual legitimacy for centuries. In the first half of the eighteenth century Baron de Montesquieu asserted that oceanic fish were limitless. J. B. Lamarck concurred. "But animals living in the waters, especially the sea waters," he wrote in 1809 in his *Zoological Philosophy,* "are protected from the destruction of their species by man. Their multiplication is so rapid and their means of evading pursuits or traps are so great, that there is no likelihood of his being able to destroy the entire species of any these animals."[26]

By the 1860s and 1870s, however, European and American fishermen expressed genuine concerns about decreasing catches. Spencer Baird, the first United States commissioner of Fish and Fisheries, tried to allay such fears. "The principle may safely be considered as established," he wrote in 1873, "that line-fishing, no matter how extensively prosecuted, will never materially affect the supply of fish in the sea." Renowned British biologist Thomas Huxley reaffirmed Montesquieu, Lamarck, and Baird. "In relation to our present modes of fishing, a number of the most important sea fisheries, such as the cod fishery, the herring fishery, and the mackerel fishery, are inexhaustible," he announced in 1883. As Huxley told his audience at London's Fisheries Exhibition, "the multitude of these fishes is so inconceivably great that the number we catch is relatively insignificant; and secondly, that the magnitude of the destructive agencies at work upon them is so prodigious, that the destruction effected by the fisherman cannot sensibly increase the death rate." Theory, bolstered by the age-old attitude that the oceans were untouchable, trumped fishermen's complaints.[27]

In hindsight it is obvious that overfishing was the precondition to scientific investigations into fisheries productivity such as those overseen by Huxley and Baird during the 1870s and 1880s. At the time, however, whether in the North Sea, in Norway's Lofoten Islands, or along the east coast of the United States, most investigators considered overfishing to be merely a localized economic problem rather than a systemic ecological problem. (A prescient dissenter from the popular mood, James G. Bertram, argued in 1865 that "there are doubtless plenty of fish still in the sea, but the trouble of capturing them increases daily, and the instruments of capture have to be yearly augmented, indicating but too clearly to all who have studied the subject that we are beginning to overfish.")[28]

The mutually reinforcing ideas that the ocean existed outside of time and beyond the pale of society, and that it remained incorruptible, became a trope tenaciously retained by western culture for centuries, despite the unsound science and unsound history on which it was based. No less an authority than Rachel Carson reiterated it in *The Sea Around Us*. Man, she argued in 1951, "cannot control or change the ocean as, in his brief tenancy of earth, he has subdued and plundered the continents."[29]

Carson rarely called it wrong. Were she alive today, she would be among the most vocal proponents of marine environmental history. Carson would want to understand why the best and brightest in her field had gotten this story wrong for so long. It is not exactly news that people have hunted and fished for millennia in polar, temperate, and tropical seas, depleting local populations of certain marine species, pushing others to extinction, like Steller's Sea Cow, last seen in 1768, and – in ships from afar – introducing invasive organisms that altered marine communities. But it was all too easy to forget how long ago these effects were felt, or how extensive they became worldwide; easy to forget that one of humanity's defining encounters with nature through the centuries occurred in salt water. Burdened by centuries of assertions that this could not be happening, keen observers were blind to dramas unfolding in plain sight.

Now that we acknowledge the crisis, well-documented and cogently-argued marine environmental histories can begin to explain what happened. More often than not such stories will be tragic, lamenting the loss of fish *and* fishermen. They also will be laced with irony. Local concerns about overfishing are hardly new: Documents from before the American Revolution acknowledged depletion of right whales, shad, salmon, sturgeon, and alewives in New England. Nineteenth-century New Englanders lamented the extinction of the Great Auk, the commercial extinction of Atlantic halibut, the disappearance of menhaden north of Cape Cod, and the depletion of cod, haddock, and pollock on inshore grounds. Astute hand-liners from Swamscott, Massachusetts, fearing the ruthless efficiency of new long-line technology, petitioned the state legislature during the 1850s to outlaw long-lines, arguing that without such a ban, cod, haddock, and other bottom fish would soon become "scarce as salmon." Meanwhile schooner crews from Beverly, Massachusetts, fishing on the Nova Scotian banks watched their seasonal landings decrease by more than 50 percent from 1852 to 1859. It is still not clear to what extent natural fluctuations or overfishing (or some synergy between them) contributed to the lack of cod during the 1850s. Fishermen at the time, however, blamed overfishing by large French factory brigs, each of which set long-lines with thousands of hooks. All of these observations, of course, occurred before mechanized fishing. Yet until quite recently, few fishermen, scientists, or politicians imagined that global fisheries would collapse to the extent that they did by the end of the twentieth century.[30]

In light of that, perhaps historians cannot be blamed for suspending attention to the sea. Publication of Carolyn Merchant's *Columbia Guide to American Environmental History,* and Ted Steinberg's *Down to Earth: Nature's Role in American History,* both in 2002, signaled the maturation of American environmental history – and the orphan status of marine environments. Merchant, one of the most thoughtful environmental historians in the United States, produced a comprehensive overview and bibliography of the current state of the field. The opening lines of her book explained that it "introduces the many dimensions of human interaction with nature over time. As people have lived and spread out over the planet, they have modified its forests, plains, and deserts." Steinberg, author of three respected books on nature in history, wrote an environmental history textbook showcasing how "the natural world – defined here as plants and animals, climate and weather, soil and water – has profoundly shaped the American past."[31]

What about the oceans? Like other authors of environmental history overviews, Merchant's and Steinberg's silence is overwhelming, save for scattered references to Abenaki and Micmac fishing, depleted shad runs in northern and southern rivers, Rachel Carson's career as a marine biologist, and the Coastal Zone Management Act of 1972.[32] Neither book explains that it covers only terrestrial environmental history, and that complementary marine histories are waiting to be told. It is as if Nantucket's whalers, Oregon's Clatsop salmon fishers, conch harvesters in Key West, and the twentieth-century swordfish crew made famous by *The Perfect Storm* were not part of America's human encounter with the natural world. Readers of *The Columbia Guide* and *Down to Earth,* and virtually all other environmental history syntheses, could almost be excused for imagining that Americans, whether aboriginal, pre-modern, or modern, were as landlocked as the Swiss. The point is not to impugn Merchant's and Steinberg's scholarship: Although more fisheries history exists than they acknowledged, including a small percentage with an environmental perspective, it is fair to say that the field they surveyed so thoroughly has ignored one of America's longest running and most profound interactions with the environment. Fishing, after all, is the oldest continuous commercial enterprise in North America. Yet the story of human-induced changes in the ocean environment is still waiting to be told.[33]

Part of the problem is that, unlike environments ashore, where humans' manipulation with axes, plows, fire, and domesticated herds wrought visible transformations (often called "improvements") in the landscape, the ocean appeared forever unchanged. Despite increasing numbers of fishing boats and the periodic deployment of more efficient gear, fishers and lawmakers easily assumed that the unchanging appearance of the ocean mirrored an unchanged biota. Meanwhile, humans on every inhabited continent compromised the estuaries that were the nurseries of marine life. Untreated sewage, garbage, and sawdust flowed into the sea, followed by heavy metals and petroleum as economies diversified. During the twentieth century otter trawls raked popular fishing banks, smashing benthic organisms and rearranging sediment forms that had provided habitat for bottom dwellers. While the extent of habitat destruction caused by trawling is not yet known, the process has gone on virtually unnoticed – and unhindered – for more than a century.[34] Benthic organisms on Georges Bank and the Dogger Bank had no defenders as did forests in the White Mountains or on the Olympic Peninsula. Recently television has been complicit in perpetuating the myth of the eternal ocean. Producers typically select footage for brilliance and biodiversity, and viewers can hardly be blamed for assuming that the ocean remains vibrant: They rarely see the dying coral reefs or denuded fishing banks that are more genuinely representative of today's marine environment. In hindsight it is apparent that deeply embedded cultural assumptions about the nature of the sea have retarded the development of marine environmental histories.

Ecologists and historians

That the oceans do not exist outside of history has been noticed recently by an unlikely group – ecologists. The assumption behind generations of ecological field work, whether in forests, grasslands, estuaries, or elsewhere, was that study sites existed in a "natural" state. Ecologists lived easily with the fiction that energy exchange, disturbance succession, predator-prey networks, and community structure and function could be, or perhaps even *should* be studied as if human impacts were extraneous. Just as historians, wearing their own disciplinary blinders, ignored the environment except as a "setting" for the real action, ecologists suspended attention to the role of humans on the systems they studied. Times have changed.

During the last few years, senior scientists such as James T. Carlton, Jeremy Jackson, Tim Smith, Robert Steneck, and Daniel Pauly have chided colleagues for paying insufficient attention to humans' role in marine ecology. Conceptually provocative papers have called explicitly for historical investigations. "Although the scholarly records of marine life – albeit frustratingly thin and almost always qualitative – reach back in a relatively accessible manner to at least the 1500s," notes Carlton, "it is safe to say that 99% of this record remains essentially unread by modern marine ecologists and marine conservation biologists." In his estimation, "what we need now is a well-supported discipline of marine environmental history." Jackson agrees. "Paleoecological, archeological, and historical data are the only means," he writes, "for extending ecological records back long enough to document the characteristic variability of marine ecosystems and the magnitude of earlier anthropogenic change."[35]

Of course, marine scientists look to the past primarily for ecosystem trends and baselines – baselines to indicate prior abundance and distribution of marine species, baselines to reveal biological fluctuations, baselines that delineate species composition in specific systems at specific times, baselines against which climate change can be charted. Driven to understand contemporary marine ecosystems, and increasingly willing to advocate for the restoration of degraded ecosystems, those scientists are looking to the past to answer their most compelling questions. They suspect that clues to vanished species, to species not yet described in the taxonomic literature, and to other changes in the sea are probably lurking in evidence from the past. This impressive work should not be ignored by historians. But ecologists' questions are not historians' questions. Interest in the past is not the same as interest in history, understood by our profession as analysis of a specific part of the past based on verifiable sources and recognizable historical methodology. To flourish as it should, marine environmental history must take a different tack from historical marine ecology.

Marine environmental historians need to keep people and human culture squarely in their sights, and to capitalize on their storytelling capabilities.

Marine scientists, even those conscious of human effects on marine ecosystems, see humans primarily as the instruments through which stocks are overfished, invasive species are transported, habitats are degraded, and pollution introduced. They are less interested in how historically and culturally specific people made themselves as they remade the world around them. Ecologists, moreover, rarely present what they know in narrative form. The challenge for historians is to create compelling accounts of the changing nature of marine environments in which contradictory human aspirations, values, behaviors, and institutions play central roles. The heart of environmental history is the observation that people always try to manage their surroundings, even as those non-human natural surroundings are influencing the peoples' economic production and culture, and that this occurs in a contingent, and thus historical, fashion.[36] This truth is as applicable to the ocean, especially to near-coastal areas frequented by mariners, as it is to the woodlands, plains, and fens with which historians have been typically concerned. To come into its own, marine environmental history must do more than provide details for an ecological jeremiad, even though overexploitation of fish stocks is one of the most compelling environmental issues of our time.[37]

Ironically, in light of its fledgling status, marine environmental history is the only environmental history subfield in which interdisciplinary collaboration between historians and scientists has been institutionalized and generously funded. That collaboration's initial successes, tensions and criticisms illuminate not only the complicated marriage of interdisciplinary work, but fundamental conceptual disagreements about the relationship of the past to the present and future.

The visionary History of Marine Animal Populations project (HMAP), initiated in the fall of 1999, received substantial underwriting from the Alfred P. Sloan Foundation "to improve our understanding of long-term ecosystem change, especially as regards the impact of humans" and to "build an institutional framework for the training of specialists in marine environmental history and historical ecology." An arm of the Census of Marine Life, a decade-long scientific assessment of the past, present, and future of life in the oceans, HMAP billed its research approach as "unique in drawing history and ecology into collaborative study."[38]

Through summer schools, conferences, funding for research, and academic centers at the University of Southern Denmark, the University of Hull, U.K., and the University of New Hampshire, HMAP has focused attention on what is knowable about past fish and whale stocks. Surveys of historical sources have been undertaken for fisheries in medieval and early modern Scandinavia, in the White and Barents seas from the seventeenth century to the present, and in South Africa, Peru, Australia, and Canada. Studies have focused on one fishery, such as whaling, or a single species, such as northwest Atlantic cod, or an ecosystem, such as Caribbean coral reefs. Dissertations and masters' theses are being produced, and important articles published as a result of HMAP's inspiration.[39] In the future the project's open-access database of marine landings worldwide, circa 1600–2000, may prove to be a boon to marine environmental history researchers. Despite some philosophical differences and communication problems among HMAP researchers, who not only straddle the epistemological and methodological divide between history and marine ecology, but other conceptual gaps within each of those fields, HMAP has successfully drawn attention to changes in the sea over time. It has, moreover, inspired a small but dedicated group of graduate students to commit to careers in marine environmental history or historical ecology, at HMAP centers and elsewhere.

Impressive as its accomplishments have been, HMAP's contribution to mainstream historical studies has been somewhat limited. Money is one reason. Initially, funding drove the agenda. Substantial grants are available for hypothesis-driven scientific work, particularly in response to perceived crises such as the unprecedented decline in fish stocks. Little funding exists for open-ended historical research. As one HMAP scientist put it, "historians are accustomed to living on a few grains of rice." Since science grants have funded the research so far, scientists' preferences for what is worth investigating and how it should be done have prevailed, and the supposedly interdisciplinary collaboration has been lopsided from the start. Though relying on data from the past, the majority of HMAP projects have not been driven by the sort of questions that most American environmental historians ask; in fact, virtually all HMAP investigations have been quantitative, as if establishing benchmarks against which to measure loss is the *raison d'être* of marine environmental history.

That thrust also reflects the bias of HMAP's founders. While its initial statement of purpose emphasized "a balance between historical and ecological studies," the two historians on the HMAP Steering Group were clearly comfortable with historical research that would illuminate the scope of pre-modern marine populations, primarily by assembling reports of catches from the past. During his opening address to the HMAP Summer Workshop in 2001, Poul Holm, a historian from the University of Southern Denmark and one of HMAP's founders, shared his philosophy of the proposed collaboration. "For historians to influence biologists," he argued, "we need to present well-defined data and recurrent phenomena and hypotheses." Narratives based on anecdotal data would not suffice.[40]

HMAP's social-science vision of an accessible past rich with predictive possibilities is shared by some historians, but not all. Many imagine the past "as a foreign country," in David Lowenthal's words, a realm whose reach is beyond all possibility of exclusion, yet nevertheless a realm so *different* from the present and future that its correlation to them is simply not linear. What this means, of course, is that it is impossible to talk about collaboration between historians and ecologists as if all historians were in lockstep about the fundamentals within their discipline.[41]

Critics of HMAP, led by historian Lance van Sittert, a former HMAP project leader, have dismissed its "unexamined cultural assumptions" and its "search for reliable facts to be pressed into the service of positivist science."[42] Calling for historicization of the ocean, and for historicization of natural science modeling, with its presumptions about correspondence to an external and factual reality, van Sittert's approach has considerable merit. That is not equivalent, however, to a monopoly on legitimacy. It has been a long time since professional history functioned, as Peter Novick reminds us, "as a community of scholars united by common aims, common standards, and common purposes."[43]

Van Sittert's outspoken critique has driven a wedge between researchers with shared interests who could more profitably be natural allies, while overlooking the very real accomplishments of HMAP. Its founders took considerable professional risk by daring to commit to marine environmental history; then compounded that risk by working on interdisciplinary projects collaboratively – strange territory for historians, even though it goes without saying that many important questions cannot be answered by individual scholars working alone, despite the norms of the historical profession. Moreover, a research plan like that envisioned by van Sittert would not have generated comparable academic interest, especially by collaborative groups, nor would it have attracted major foundation funding. Funding matters, especially in start-up ventures. HMAP's scale and gravitas have accelerated interest in marine environmental history substantially, and spin-off projects that are not primarily quantitative have already begun. HMAP should be honored as a "first" and commended for its successes, even as historians from other epistemological traditions proceed with alternative inquiries into the history of the ocean.

Historians have a great deal to add to ecologists' understanding of the sea. Although it is clear that much about past marine ecosystems will remain unknowable, several HMAP projects and similar inquiries have illuminated the magnitude of specific fish and whale stocks in the past, making concrete contributions to the sort of modeling on which fisheries managers rely. As long as modeling and policy making based on modeling remain in the forefront of humans' attempts to manage nature, those models should reach as far back in time as possible. At the very least, historians can provide perspective on the magnitude of environmental change, reminding politicians and managers of the world we have lost.

Yet it seems just as obvious that ecological modeling – which began for fisheries in a serious way during the 1930s – has failed to provide effective stewardship of marine resources. Modeling nature conveys a potential mastery of nature that simply has never existed. More data and better models seem unlikely to fix the problem of depleted resources, even if the models include data from the past. If we are serious about restoring the abundance of renewable natural resources, society as a whole (meaning politicians, managers, and judges who make decisions about natural resources) not only needs to be more precautionary, but it needs to take a new tack.

Charting a new course for the stewardship of resources will require new ways of thinking, including new stories about the relationship of people to fish, timber, grazing lands, and water. Central to such stories will be the recognition, common to some historians, that complex variables create historically specific situations – not universal ones, or replicable ones, or natural ones, but historically specific situations. Historians who honor the past on its own terms, who strive to make that past legible to the present, but who lack the conviction that the past is predictive, have something to add to this discussion. Those historians think about time in a radically different way from most scientists. They recognize that time (including ecological time) is not linear, and that long-gone contexts and now-invisible contingencies affected the past in such a way that it was qualitatively different. This is not a concession of the irrelevance of history; far from it. It is a suggestion, however, that we need to think about non-human nature in a fundamentally different way if we want different results. Assuming that nature has a history specific to different periods and circumstances, ie. that historical contexts matter, is a good place to begin.[44]

Where do we go from here?

A reflection like this would be remiss without concrete suggestions about how aspiring marine environmental historians might get their feet wet. There are at least two basic approaches, the single-species approach at the heart of Taylor's *Making Salmon,* and the regional approach central to McEvoy's *The Fisherman's Problem.*[45] Marine environmental historians of the future will regard those texts as foundational. Transcending a simple history of overfishing, Taylor embeds the salmon's story in a tale of "mining, logging, grazing, irrigation, fishing, and urbanization," all of which combined drastically to shrink salmon habitat. Central to his analysis is the tragic hubris with which scientists and managers assessed the problem. If nature couldn't make enough fish, they reasoned, hatcheries would. Yet artificial propagation of salmon by fish culturists never lived up to its expectation. While *Making Salmon* is a model for single-species studies, one caveat is relevant to those who would follow his pioneering path. Anadromous fish – none more so than salmon – created a substantially richer documentary trail than oceanic fish.[46]

Many important species like salmon warrant a multi-faceted history of their exploitation, economic value, cultural significance, and changing place in the ecosystem.[47] Alewives, menhaden, swordfish, tunas, grouper, striped bass, eels, halibut, spiny dogfish, mackerel, and the gadoid family (cod, haddock, pollock, cusk, and hake) lead the list.[48] Some are worthy of book-length studies. For others, monographs will suffice. Invertebrates, including sponges, crabs, oysters, clams, mussels, abalone, and shrimp also need their historians.[49] So do many species of marine mammals, birds, and sea turtles. Each of these organisms was tightly tied to communities of local producers, which, in turn, were affected by changing foodways and markets, evolving fisheries technology, breakthroughs in transportation and preservation, scientific studies, regulations regarding access, and contradictory opinions regarding sustainability. Many of these species' histories speak to the rise and fall of vernacular folkways, to immigration, industrialization, race, and other topics of perennial interest to historians.

Consider an environmental history of Bahamian sponging. Hardscrabble Bahamian mariners, both black and white, began harvesting sponges during the 1840s, instigated by a French entrepreneur. By the 1890s sponging was the primary maritime industry in the Bahamian archipelago. At the turn of the century over five thousand men were "on the mud," as they called it, harvesting sponges from a fleet of sloops and schooners. As Paul Albury writes, "up to 1925 it must have seemed that sponge-fishing would endure forever and get better and better. At that time, the total income earned by sponge fishermen soared to £200,000, and a local song, 'Sponger Money Never Done,' commemorated both the durability and prosperity. The series of severe hurricanes, which began in 1926, did much damage to the sponge beds, but apart from this there developed unmistakable evidence of overfishing. ... By 1932, the fishermen were finding it difficult to make a living." Six years later a "deadly malady," possibly a virus, killed off 90 percent of the remaining sponges. Albury's synopsis contains all the elements necessary for a compelling environmental history. Economic, cultural, and ecological analysis would bolster a powerful narrative that could be substantiated through archival sources and biological literature.[50]

An alternative to the single-species approach is a regional study along lines pioneered by McEvoy, in *The Fisherman's Problem,* arguably the gold standard for marine environmental history. There is a caveat: "Region" is more complicated conceptually than it appears because politically defined regions rarely correspond precisely to bioregions. Sometimes cultural regions add yet another layer of complexity. Environmental historians in the future may wish to develop bioregional histories of marine environments, or histories of cultural areas that depended on certain marine resources. While region is a useful organizing device, it needs to be carefully defined.

Recounting the "wanton destruction" of California's fisheries from 1850 to 1980, McEvoy situated his tale in light of the profound connections between ecology, law, and economic production. Ironically, as he explained, political debates during the collapse of the sardine fishery never superseded the binary opposition about whether fluctuations in catch "were due to overfishing *or* to 'natural,' that is to say unpredictable, unavoidable, and thus legally irrelevant, causes." It was both. His place-based methodology challenges historians to unpack the relationships between ecology, economic production, and law, being attentive to how they "evolve in tandem; each partly according to its own particular logic and partly in response to changes in the other two."[51]

Long-settled and culturally distinctive places such as Chesapeake Bay, Long Island Sound, Albemarle Sound, sections of the Gulf coast from the Florida panhandle to Texas, and the Florida Keys lend themselves to a regional approach. Recently defined Marine Sanctuaries, such as the Stellwagen Bank Sanctuary off Massachusetts or the Gray's Reef Sanctuary off Georgia, administered by the National Oceanic and Atmospheric Administration, also might provide a geographic focus for monographic studies, as could Marine Protected Areas, whether in American waters or elsewhere.[52] Shorelines and biodiversity have changed in all coastal areas frequented by humans, though we could know more about this. Coral reef systems worldwide are in crisis, for instance, but this did not just happen overnight. Shallow banks such as Georges Bank have been altered, some researchers claim, as profoundly as clear-cut forests. Ralph Stanley, who fished the coast of Maine as a boy, recently recollected what happened on Jones's Grounds, "12 miles southeast of Mount Desert Rock," where his father had set trawls during World War II. The bottom there, he said, "'was covered in some kind of Vegetation.' Pieces of this stuff would come up on the trawl hooks. It looked like tree limbs, pretty colors of purple, pink, and orange. It was a great place in March to set trawls for big cod, hake and cusk. In the 1950s the draggers fishing for redfish or ocean perch gradually dragged into that bottom until all the 'tree growth' was gone." To the extent possible, stories like these can be fleshed out through observations, oral histories, and data contained in the archival record.[53]

Who will write the history of the alewife, *Alosa pseudoharengus,* a bony herring averaging ten or eleven inches long that formerly swam in large schools along the coast from South Carolina to Newfoundland?[54] Like salmon, alewives are an anadromous fish. Returning to spawn in their natal river, alewives made an easy target at waterfalls and other congested choke points. In colonial America, they were the passenger pigeons of the sea. "Experience hath taught them at New Plymouth," wrote one eyewitness, "that in April there is a fish much like a herring that comes up into the small brooks to spawn, and when the water is not knee deep they will presse up through your hands, yea, thow you beat at them with cudgels, and in such abundance as is incredible."[55]

Today alewives' numbers have plummeted. Eaten, exported, used for fertilizer and for bait, alewives were central to both market-based and subsistence economies in early New England.[56] The town of Exeter, New Hampshire, honored its debt to this lowly fish by putting it prominently on the town seal in 1930. During the seventeenth century many towns with alewife runs appointed fish wardens to oversee the harvest, but concerns about depletion were apparent before the American Revolution. "The people living upon the banks of Merrimack [River]," noted William Douglass in 1755, "observe that several species of fish such as Salmon, Shad, and Alewives, are not so plenty in their seasons as formerly." Two months before shots were fired at Lexington and Concord, a group of more than thirty men petitioned the New Hampshire General Assembly requesting that all encumbrances and weirs be removed from Cohass Brook, a tributary of the Merrimack River, so that "Said fish may have free Liberty to pass and re-pass in Said Brook for the Insuing year without Molestation that they may increce their number." From 1764 to 1815, petitions submitted to the Governor, Council and Legislature in New Hampshire reveal genuine concern about diminishing stocks of alewives. Similar concerns existed in Massachusetts. "Although in several portions of the state where the *alewives* have heretofore been most abundant," noted D. Humphreys Storer in 1839, "the various encroachments of man have sensibly diminished them."[57]

Central to the history of the alewife were struggles between harvesters using different types of gear. Constituencies with spears, scoop nets, and seines (each with significantly different capitalization costs) sought privileged access for themselves while trying to convince governments to regulate the other parties. Alewives were still being harvested in New England's rivers until the late twentieth century, when annual runs had been reduced to a few paltry fish. The changing nature of the alewife fishery needs to be reconstructed there, and in other states and provinces. If possible, we need to know more about the changing size of the stock, the annual harvests, the evolution of fisheries technology and its implications, the laws regulating access and the extent to which they were honored, the incremental growth of scientific knowledge about alewives, and the constellation of conditions that encouraged people to keep fishing even though common knowledge indicated that the stock was declining.

Few species' stories match that of the menhaden for drama, local color, and corporate intrigue. While several preliminary studies have been completed, or are in preparation, menhaden deserve a full-blown cultural and environmental history. Another member of the herring family, also known as mossbunker, porgy, and bunker, this foot-long fish, each of which weighs about a pound, schools between Maine and Florida. Today "menhaden support the largest single-species fishery on the Atlantic coast," notes Richard Ellis, "the most concentrated fishery in Chesapeake Bay, and, after Alaskan pollock, the second largest fishery in America." Omega Protein Corporation, based in Houston and founded by former president George H. W. Bush, is the largest American company currently catching and processing menhaden. Although Omega Protein insists that "the menhaden resource is healthy and self-renewing," statistics tell a different story. Total American landings during the late 1990s were just 40 percent of overall landings in the late 1950s, and "in 2000 Omega Protein laid up thirteen of its fifty-three ships and grounded twelve of its forty-five spotter planes."[58]

Too oily for most tastes, menhaden were fished commercially only on a small scale with beach seines, rowboats, and small sloops until the 1850s, when processing plants to render fish oil were built along the coast of New England. Then, in one of the more dramatic fishery collapses of the nineteenth century, menhaden virtually disappeared from waters north of Cape Cod after 1879, stranding the owners and employees of the boats poised to catch them, and the factories ready to process them. For the next six years they were exceedingly scarce along the coast of Maine; for the next forty years their appearance in the Gulf of Maine was unpredictable. In 1905, when well-financed canning syndicates petitioned the Maine legislature to expand purse seining for herring, a legislator from Surry articulated the conservationist ethic of small-scale weir fishers by invoking the memory of the menhaden. As Richard Judd tells the story – from the perspective of that legislator – the village of Surry "had once reaped a $30,000 yearly harvest in menhadens, 'and it didn't take but a little money to go into the business.' The fish disappeared when 'people from Rhode Island, New York, Connecticut, and the western states ... [came] in here.' Melding concerns over resource exploitation with populist and localistic resistance to large, nonresident corporations, the Surry representative closed his argument: consider the fate of the menhadens, he asked, 'and vote for the people.'" His passionate argument carried the day and down-easters celebrated the syndicates' defeat with victory balls and galas.[59]

In the meantime, the menhaden fishery had shifted south to Virginia and North Carolina, where, in the era of hand-hauled seine nets, it attracted large numbers of black laborers and became the last bastion of American sea-chanteying in the early and mid-twentieth century. By the turn of the twenty-first century, menhaden were the chief commercial source of long-chain omega-3 proteins that health-conscious consumers ingested to fight cardiovascular disease, cancer, and arthritis. The menhaden's role in the ecosystem of the continental shelf and in the culture of the United States makes this a fish with a story worth telling.[60]

Good history begins with good sources. Thankfully voluminous sources for the reconstruction of marine environmental histories, many untapped, exist in the National Archives of the United States, in its Washington, College Park, and regional centers, and in local, state, and private archives. Similar sources exist in many other countries. Records of commercial fish landings, logbooks' daily catch records, early scientific surveys, customs receipts for the export of fish and whale products, correspondence of the U.S. Fish Commission and various state fish commissions, census records of maritime workers and their equipment, memoirs by fishermen and naturalists, legislative petitions, court cases, diplomatic papers, newspapers, and business records (including those of canneries and packing houses) all shed light on marine organisms' former levels of abundance and the relationship of people to marine resources. Accurate statistics, or at least complete sets of data, are not easy to find, however, and certain fisheries, especially inshore fisheries in small boats were notoriously underreported. Historians uncovering the papers of fish-buyers or the daily logs of fishermen have the opportunity to collaborate with statisticians to recalculate published aggregate statistics, or even to create statistics for certain years and certain fisheries in what is otherwise a pre-statistical age.[61]

Textual records are sufficiently rich that the cultural intentions as well as the actions of people harvesting marine resources are recoverable for certain historically specific fisheries. During the 1850s a controversy over seining sea fish wracked town after town along the coast of Maine. Articulated in both a conservationist discourse and a rights discourse, it illuminated how locals imagined themselves in relationship to the resources on which they depended. In 1852 fishermen from Boothbay swore that "taking Menhaden fish ... by means of Seines in our Bays, Rivers & Harbours is very destructive to said fish and if persisted in will eventually destroy them or drive them from our coast." But fishermen in neighboring Surry disagreed. They claimed "the fears of a dearth of pogies or menhaden ... are entirely hypothetical," and they demanded "free trade in pogies." Historians have more possibilities than they realize to work with such records. In a recent study of the North Sea ling and cod fisheries, circa 1840 to 1914, René Taudal Poulsen was able to combine textual records, ethnographies, and traditional social history analysis of Bohuslän county in Sweden with catch data and fisheries population modeling. His attention to a wide range of rarely-paired sources allowed him to explore that region's adaptation to ecological change in the coastal sea.[62]

The starting point for virtually any American marine environmental history is the magisterial, multi-volume series *The Fisheries and Fishery Industries of the United States,* edited by George Brown Goode, and published by the U.S. Government Printing Office between 1884 and 1887. Goode, assistant secretary of the Smithsonian Institution, had been trained as an ichthyologist by Louis Agassiz at Harvard. An active field researcher, he participated in the U.S. Fish Commission's Atlantic coast research expeditions for several summers, and later represented the United States at international fisheries meetings in Berlin in 1880 and London in 1883. Goode was one of the nation's foremost fishery scientists in the late nineteenth century. He simultaneously maintained a passionate interest in history. A founding member of the American Historical Association, he published, among other things, a history of natural science in America.[63] Goode's career is a heartening reminder that the boundaries between marine science and maritime history need not be hermetically sealed. To the contrary: Science and history can both benefit from ecologists thinking historically and historians thinking ecologically.

No matter the sources they use, would-be marine environmental historians will need to address head-on the quandary of disciplinary boundaries. Deeply rooted assumptions concerning the typology of knowledge, specifically what is of interest to whom in scholarly or scientific circles, has circumscribed the development of marine environmental history. Environmental historians (terrestrial ones, mind you) faced an uphill challenge convincing colleagues in history departments that aquifers, earthworms, forest succession, and bio-regionalism were germane to history, even though every village and city throughout time relied on biological and geophysical resources, and affected its non-human natural surroundings. It goes without saying that humans' reliance on, affection for, and intimacy with the ocean has been but a fraction of that of the land. Moreover, the results of humans' environmental impact on the ocean have essentially remained invisible, hidden below an inscrutable surface. To be accepted, much less to flourish, marine environmental historians will need to constantly reiterate how abalone, oyster reefs, Bluefin Tuna (formerly referred to derisively as "horse mackerel"), invasive jellyfish, and marine foodwebs are the stuff of history; how, in other words, humans and the living ocean share a common destiny.

The problems posed by the overstressed ocean today are not yet insurmountable according to some optimistic marine scientists, even though depletion of the oceans' living resources is clearly worsening.[64] If policies and enforcement don't encourage conservation soon, however, the species composition of the oceans will change forever, impoverishing marine ecosystems, human economies, and cultural traditions. Questions are already begging for answers: "how long have people been making an impact on the ocean," "when did warning signs first appear," "what constellation of assumptions and policies led to a virtually unrestrained plunder of oceanic resources and the cascading effects that followed"?

Those concerns, along with a desire to better understand the sociology of past maritime communities and a passion to tell a new generation of sea stories, provide a template for marine environmental history. Done well, it can add materially to our understanding of the interactions between human culture and non-human nature in the early modern and modern world. Lord Byron was wrong when he wrote in the early nineteenth century, "Man marks the earth with ruin, his control Stops with the shore." It is up to historians in the early twenty-first century to explain what happened.[65]

Notes

I would like to thank Karen Alexander, Mark Cioc, Kurk Dorsey, Matthew G. McKenzie, Helen Rozwadowski, Jay Taylor, and the referees, all of whom read this essay and improved it substantially with their critiques and suggestions.

The errors of fact and interpretation that remain are mine. An earlier version of this paper was presented at the New England Marine Environmental History Workshop in Woods Hole, Massachusetts, in May, 2005. I thank the organizers (McKenzie and Rozwadowski) and the participants for a stimulating conference and thoughtful feedback. My work in marine environmental history has been generously supported by the Alfred P. Sloan Foundation's funding of HMAP (the History of Marine Animal Populations project), and by the James H. Hayes and Claire Short Hayes Chair in the Humanities at UNH. I appreciate their faith and generosity.

1 Ransom A. Myers and Boris Worm, "Rapid Worldwide Depletion of Predatory Fish Communities," *Nature* 423 (May 2003): 280–83. Pew Oceans Commission, *America's Living Oceans: Charting a Course for Sea Change*, Summary Report (Pew Oceans Commission, Arlington, Va.: May 2003); U.S. Commission on Ocean Policy, *Preliminary Report of the U.S. Commission on Ocean Policy, Governor's Draft* (Washington: U.S. Government Printing Office, 2004).

2 Colin Woodard, *Ocean's End: Travels Through Endangered Seas* (N.Y.: Basic Books, 2000), 1–28; James T. Carlton, "Marine Bioinvasions: The Alteration of Marine Ecosystems by Nonindigenous Species," *Oceanography* 9 (1996): 36–43; James T. Carlton, "Blue Immigrants: The Marine Biology of Maritime History," *The Log of Mystic Seaport* 44 (1992): 31–36.

3 Peter E. Pope, *Fish into Wine: The Newfoundland Plantation in the Seventeenth Century* (Chapel Hill: University of North Carolina Press for the Omohundro Institute of Early American History and Culture, 2004), 1–44; Peter Pope, "Early Estimates: Assessment of Catches in the Newfoundland Cod Fishery, 1660–90," in *Marine Resources and Human Societies in the North Atlantic Since 1500: Papers Presented at the Conference Entitled "Marine Resources and Human Societies in the North Atlantic Since 1500," October 20–22, 1995*, ed. Daniel Vickers (St. John's: Memorial University of Newfoundland, 1997), 7–40; Jeffrey A. Hutchings, "Spatial and Temporal Variation in the Exploitation of Northern Cod, *Gadus Morhua:* A Historical Perspective from 1500 to Present," in *Marine Resources and Human Societies in the North Atlantic Since 1500,* ed. Vickers, 41–68.

4 Anthony Parkhurst to Richard Hakluyt (1578) in *The Fish and Fisheries of Colonial North America: A Documentary History of Fishing Resources of the United States and Canada,* John C. Pearson, ed., Part I: The Canadian Atlantic Provinces (NOAA Report No. 72040301) (Rockville, Md.: NOAA, National Marine Fisheries Service, 1972), 7–9; *Relation of what Occurred Most Remarkable in the Mission Society of Jesus in New France, 1662–63,* in *The Fish and Fisheries of Colonial North America,* Pearson, ed., 22; William Monson, *Naval Tracts* (1703), in *The Fish and Fisheries of Colonial North America,* Pearson, 85–86.

5 Despite a few noteworthy studies by Arthur F. McEvoy, Joseph E. Taylor III, and Richard W. Judd, among others, historians have produced few investigations of previous encounters with marine environments. See Arthur F. McEvoy, *The Fisherman's Problem: Ecology and Law in the California Fisheries, 1850–1980* (Cambridge University Press, 1986); Joseph E. Taylor III, *Making Salmon: An Environmental History of the Northwest Fisheries Crisis* (Seattle: University of Washington Press, 1999); and Richard W. Judd, *Common Lands, Common People: The Origins of Conservation in Northern New England* (Cambridge: Harvard University Press, 1997).

6 Kirk Johnson, "No Recovery Soon for Lobstering in West Long Island Sound," *The New York Times,* March 8, 2003.

7 Kenneth T. Frank, et al., "Trophic Cascades in a Formerly Cod-Dominated Ecosystem," *Science* 308 (June 2005): 1621–23; R. S. Steneck, J. Vavrinec, and A. V. Leland, "Accelerating Trophic Level Dysfunction in Kelp Forest Ecosystems of the Western North Atlantic," *Ecosystems* 7 (2004): 323–31; Edwin Grosholz, "Ecological and Evolutionary Consequences of Coastal Invasions," *Trends in Ecology and Evolution* 17 (January 2002): 22–27; Michael J. Fogarty and Steven A. Murawski, "Large-Scale Disturbance and the Structure of Marine Systems: Fishery Impacts on Georges Bank," *Ecological Applications* 8 (February 1998), S6–S22.

8 Robert S. Steneck, "Are We Overfishing the American Lobster? Some Biological Perspectives," in *The Decline of Fisheries Resources in New England: Evaluating the Impact of Overfishing, Contamination, and Habitat Destruction,* ed. Robert Buschbaum, Judith Pederson, and William E. Robinson (Cambridge: MIT Sea Grant Program, 2001), 131–48; Philip W. Conkling and Anne Hayden, *Lobsters Great and Small: How Scientists and Fishermen are Changing Our Understanding of a Maine Icon* (Rockland, Maine: Island Institute, 2002).

9 The groundwork has been laid in two excellent studies. See Philip W. Conkling, *Islands in Time: A Natural and Cultural History of the Islands of the Gulf of Maine* (Rockland, Maine: Island Institute, 1999); and Colin Woodard, *The Lobster Coast: Rebels, Rusticators, and the Struggle for a Forgotten Frontier* (New York: Viking, 2004).

10 J. B. C. Jackson, et al., "Historical Overfishing and the Recent Collapse of Coastal Ecosystems," *Science* 293 (July 2001): 629–38; Poul Holm, Tim D. Smith, and David J. Starkey, eds., *The Exploited Seas: New Directions in Marine Environmental History* (St. Johns, Newfoundland: International Maritime Economic History Association/Census of Marine Life, 2001).

11 For Apollonio's estimates, see Conkling, *Islands in Time,* 260–61; and Spencer Apollonio, *Hierarchical Perspectives on Marine Complexities: Searching for Systems in the Gulf of Maine* (New York: Columbia University Press, 2002), 173–75. For contemporaries' observations of depletion, see William Douglass, *A Summary, Historical and Political, of the First Planting, Progressive Improvements, and Present State of the British Settlements in North America,* 2 vols. (Boston: 1755) 1:58–62. For conservative estimates of whale kills, see Randall R. Reeves, Jeffrey M. Breiwick, and Edward D. Mitchell, "History of Whaling and Estimated Kill of Right Whales, *Balaena Glacialis,* in the Northeastern United States, 1620–1924," *Marine Fisheries Review* 61 (1999): 1–36. For more expansive estimates see Apollonio, *Hierarchical Perspectives,* 60–61. For seventeenth-century Dutch and Basque Arctic whaling, see Laurier Turgeon, "Fluctuations in Cod and Whale Stocks in the North Atlantic During the Eighteenth Century," in *Marine Resources and Human Societies,* ed. Vickers, 87–122; John F. Richards, *The Unending Frontier: An Environmental History of the Early Modern World* (Berkeley: University of California Press, 2003), 584–89.

12 On whales as constraints in ecosystems, see Apollonio, *Hierarchical Perspectives,* 14–15, 53–71. Louwrens Hacquebord, "The Hunting of the Greenland Right Whale in Svalbard, Its Interaction with Climate and Its Impact on the Marine Ecosystem," *Polar Research* 18 (1999): 375–82; Louwrens Hacquebord, "Three Centuries of Whaling and Walrus Hunting in Svalbard and Its Impact on the Arctic Ecosystem," *Environment and History* 7 (2001): 169–85. For the ecological consequences of Antarctic whale harvests, see Richard M. Laws, "The Ecology of the Southern Ocean," *American Scientist* 73 (1985): 26–40.

13 During the last three years a spirited debate over the size of whale populations before exploitation has pitted advocates of genetic population modeling against advocates of population modeling based on historical catch records. The estimates by genetic modelers are far greater, differing by an order of magnitude. See Joe Roman and Stephen R. Palumbi, "Whales Before Whaling in the North Atlantic," *Science* 301 (2003): 508–10; S. J. Holt, "Counting Whales in the North Atlantic," *Science* 303 (2004): 39–40; C. Scott Baker and Phillip J. Clapham, "Modelling the Past and Future of Whales and Whaling," *Trends in Ecology and Evolution* 19 (2004): 365–71.

14 Lance van Sittert, "The Other Seven Tenths," in "Anniversary Forum: What's Next for Environmental History?" *Environmental History* 10 (January 2005): 106–9; Helen M. Rozwadowski and David K. van Keuren, eds., *The Machine in Neptune's Garden: Historical Perspectives on Technology and the Marine Environment* (Science History Publications/USA: 2004); Helen M. Rozwadowski, *Fathoming the Ocean: The Discovery and Exploration of the Deep Sea* (Cambridge: The Belknap Press of Harvard University Press, 2005).

15 See Pope, "Early Estimates," esp. 25–28, for a careful, methodical, and insightful study that reveals the significance of historical context for interpreting early modern fisheries landings. Pope explains underreporting in a time series of Newfoundland cod landings compiled by biologists who lacked contextual understanding of seventeenth-century data.

16 Andrew A. Rosenberg, et al., "The History of Ocean Resources: Modeling Cod Biomass Using Historical Records," *Frontiers in Ecology and the Environment* 3 (March 2005): 84–90.

17 Richard Henry Dana, *Two Years Before the Mast* (1840; reprint, New York, Penguin, 1981), 462–63.

18 Papers that have begun to address some of these issues include Richard Price, "Caribbean Fishing and Fishermen: A Historical Sketch," *American Anthropologist* 68 (1966): 1363–83; Sean Cadigan, "The Moral Economy of the Commons: Ecology and Equity in the Newfoundland Cod Fishery, 1815–55," *Labour/Le Travail* 43 (Spring 1999): 9–42; Russel Lawrence Barsh, "*Netukulimk* Past and Present: Mikmaw Ethics and the Atlantic Fishery," *Journal of Canadian Studies* 37 (Spring 2002): 15–42; Connie Y. Chiang, "Monterey-by-the-Smell: Odors and Social Conflict on the California Coastline," *Pacific Historical Review* 73 (2004): 183–214; Bill Parenteau, "A 'Very Determined Opposition to the Law': Conservation, Angling Leases, and Social Conflict in the Canadian Atlantic Salmon Fishery, 1867–1914," *Environmental History* 93 (July 2004): 436–63.

19 Philip E. Steinberg, *The Social Construction of the Ocean* (Cambridge and New York: Cambridge University Press, 2001).

20 Alain Corbin, *The Lure of the Sea: The Discovery of the Seaside in the Western World 1750–1840,* trans. Jocelyn Phelps (Berkeley and Los Angeles: University of California Press, 1994), 2.

21 Two very original works charting this process are Corbin, *Lure of the Sea;* and Rozwadowski, *Fathoming the Ocean.* Margaret Deacon, *Scientists and the Sea, 1650–1900: A Study of Marine Science* (London and New York: Academic Press, 1971) points out a brief burst of interest in the ocean by the Royal Society from 1660 to 1675, followed by decades of no interest. It is noteworthy that most seventeenth-century Englishmen simply took the ocean for granted. It was a highway, barrier, and fishing ground, but not a political space to be ruled, a subject for naturalists' inquiries, or a playground. See Captain John Smith, *A Description of New England* (London: 1616); Captain John Smith,

New England's Trials (London: 1620); and Captain John Smith, *An Accidence or Pathway to Experience Necessary for all Young Sea-men* (London: 1626). Navigation books ignored the ocean itself, addressing only navigation, seamanship, and the business of shipping. See Matthew Norwood, *The Seamans Companion* (London: 1698); James Lightbody, *The Mariners Jewel: Or, A Pocket Companion for the Ingenious* (London: 1697); and James Atkinson, Senior, *Epitome of the Art of Navigation* (London: 1718).

22 Keith Thomas, *Man and the Natural World: A History of the Modern Sensibility* (New York: Pantheon Books, 1983).

23 Henry D. Thoreau, *Cape Cod* (1865) ed. Joseph J. Moldenhauer (Princeton: Princeton University Press, 1988), 148; Herman Melville, *Moby-Dick; or, The Whale* (New York: Penguin Books, 1972), 685; Joseph Conrad, *The Nigger of the "Narcissus"* (London: 1897; reprint, New York: Penguin Modern Classics, 1985), 17, 80, 87, 135, 143; T. S. Eliot, "The Dry Salvages," in *Four Quartets* (New York: Harcourt, Brace and Co., 1943). For Dickens, see John Peck, *Maritime Fiction: Sailors and the Sea in British and American Novels, 1719–1917* (Houndsmill, Hampshire, UK, and New York: Palgrave: 2001), 80.

24 Barry Cunliffe, *Facing the Ocean: The Atlantic and Its Peoples 8000 BC–AD 1500* (Oxford: Oxford University Press, 2001), 1; Vincent H. Cassidy, *The Sea Around Them: The Atlantic Ocean, A.D. 1250* (Baton Rouge: Louisiana State University Press, 1968), xv.

25 Rozwadowski, *Fathoming the Ocean.*

26 Montesquieu cited in Clarence J. Glacken, *Traces on the Rhodian Shore: Nature and Culture in Western Thought from Ancient Times to the End of the Eighteenth Century* (Berkeley and Los Angeles: University of Californian Press, 1967), 659; J. B. Lamarck, *Zoological Philosophy: An Exposition with Regard to the Natural History of Animals* (1809; reprint, Chicago: University of Chicago Press, 1984), 45. I thank James T. Carlton for the reference to Lamarck.

27 Spencer F. Baird, *U.S. Commission on Fish and Fisheries. Part I. Report on the Condition of the Sea Fisheries of the South Coast of New England in 1871 and 1872* (Washington, D.C.: Government Printing Office, 1873), xxx–xxxi; Thomas H. Huxley, "Inaugural Address," Fisheries Exhibition, London, 1883.

28 E. F. Rivinus and E. M Youssef, *Spencer Baird of the Smithsonian* (Washington, D.C.: Smithsonian Institution Press, 1992), 141–51; Tim D. Smith, *Scaling Fisheries: The Science of Measuring the Effects of Fishing, 1855–1955* (Cambridge and New York: Cambridge University Press, 1994), 38–69; James G. Bertram, *The Harvest of the Seas: a Contribution to the Natural and Economic History of the British Food Fishes* (London: Murray, 1865), 475.

29 Rachel L. Carson, *The Sea Around Us* (New York: Oxford University Press, 1951), 15. Most environmental historians know Carson through *Silent Spring* (New York: Houghton Mifflin, 1962), but she was foremost a marine biologist whose earlier books included *Under the Sea Wind* (New York: E. P. Dutton, 1952) and *The Edge of the Sea* (New York: Houghton Mifflin, 1955). For the ocean as "insulated from social forces" during the nineteenth and early twentieth centuries, see Steinberg, *Social Construction,* 112–24, quotation on 112.

30 For the Swamscott petitioners, see U.S. Commission of Fish and Fisheries, *The Fisheries and Fishery Industries of the United States,* ed. George Brown Goode, (5 secs., 7 vols.; Washington, D.C.: Government Printing Office, 1884–87), Section 1, 226; G. Brown Goode Collection, Series 3, Collected Material

on Fish and Fisheries, Box 14, folder "Misc Notes, Mss, Lists, Statistics," RU 7050, Smithsonian Institution. For drastic reductions in landings in the Beverly fleet, see W. Jeffrey Bolster, Karen E. Alexander and William B. Leavenworth, "The Historical Abundance of Cod on the Nova Scotian Shelf," in J. B. C. Jackson, K. E. Alexander and E. Sala, eds, *Shifting Baselines: The Past and Future of Ocean Fisheries* (Dordrecht: Springer, 2011), 79–113; William Leavenworth, "Opening Pandora's Box: Tradition, Competition and Technology on the Scotian Shelf, 1852–60," *Studia Atlantica* (forthcoming). For declining catches in the inshore Newfoundland cod fishery circa 1815–55, see Cadigan, "The Moral Economy of the Commons." A longer term perspective on the dynamics of Newfoundland cod stocks is found in Hutchins, "Spatial and Temporal Variation in the Exploitation of Northern Cod," in *Marine Resources and Human Societies,* ed. Vickers, 41–68.

31 Carolyn Merchant, *The Columbia Guide to American Environmental History* (New York: Columbia University Press, 2002), xiii; Ted Steinberg, *Down to Earth: Nature's Role in American History* (New York: Oxford University Press, 2002), ix.

32 Other respected environmental histories are equally silent about the marine environment, notably John Opie, *Nature's Nation: An Environmental History of the United States* (Fort Worth: Harcourt Brace, 1998). J. Donald Hughes, *An Environmental History of the World: Humankind's Changing Role in the Community of Life* (London and New York: Routledge, 2001) mentions the marine environment only in passing. J. R. McNeill, *Something New Under the Sun: An Environmental History of the Twentieth-Century World* (New York: W. W. Norton & Co., 2000) has the most coverage, with a brief section on "Whaling and Fishing." Richards, *The Unending Frontier,* contains chapters on fishing and whaling, but they are framed like traditional maritime histories, ignoring non-human nature and ecological relationships. I. G. Simmons, *Environmental History: A Concise Introduction* (Oxford: Blackwell Publishers, 1993) has three pages on the ocean.

33 Far and away the best bibliography in fisheries history, and a necessary starting point for marine environmental history, is in Taylor, *Making Salmon,* 379–410. His thorough compilation includes important questions and a brief survey of primary sources.

34 National Research Council, Committee on Ecosystem Effects of Fishing, *Effects of Trawling and Dredging on Seafloor Habitat* (Washington, D.C.: National Academy Press, 2002); Les Watling and Elliott A. Norse, "Disturbance of the Seabed by Mobile Fishing Gear: A Comparison to Forest Clearcutting," *Conservation Biology* 12 (December 1998): 1178–97.

35 James T. Carlton, "Apostrophe to the Ocean," *Conservation Biology* 12 (December 1998): 1165–67, quotations on 1166 and 1167; Jeremy B. C. Jackson, "What Was Natural in the Coastal Oceans?" *Proceedings of the National Academy of Sciences USA* 98 (May 8, 2001), 5411–18, quotation on 5411; Daniel Pauly, "Anecdotes and the Shifting Baseline Syndrome of Fisheries," *Trends in Ecology and Evolution* 10 (October 1995): 430; Robert S. Steneck and James T. Carlton, "Human Alterations of Marine Communities: Students Beware!" in *Marine Community Ecology,* ed. Mark D. Bertness, et al., (Sunderland, Mass.: Sinauer Publishers, 2001), 445–68; Smith, *Scaling Fisheries.*

36 On the importance of narrative in environmental history, see William Cronon, "A Place for Stories: Nature, History and Narrative," *Journal of American History* 78 (March 1992): 1347–76.

37 Mark Kurlansky, *Cod: A Biography of the Fish That Changed the World* (New York: Walker and Co., 1997) was a well-received call-to-arms, but his journalist's approach did not produce history as our profession understands it. Nevertheless, many capable journalists recently have turned their attention to the ocean's plight, addressing it, at least partially, in light of history. See Woodard, *Ocean's End;* John McPhee, *The Founding Fish* (New York: Farrar, Straus and Giroux, 2002); Carl Safina, *Eye of the Albatross: Visions of Hope and Survival* (New York: Henry Holt and Company, 2002); Richard Ellis, *The Empty Ocean: Plundering the World's Marine Life* (Washington, D.C.: Island Press, 2003); Trevor Corson, *The Secret Life of Lobsters: How Fishermen and Scientists are Unraveling the Mysteries of our Favorite Crustacean* (New York: Harper Collins, 2004); David Helvarg, *Blue Frontier: Saving America's Living Seas* (New York: Henry Holt and Company, 2001); David Dobbs, *The Great Gulf: Fishermen, Scientists, and the Struggle to Revive the World's Greatest Fishery* (Washington, D.C.: Island Press, 2000); Paul Molyneaux, *The Doryman's Reflection: A Fisherman's Life* (New York: Thunder's Mouth Press, 2005).

38 For HMAP, http://www.hmapcoml.org/; for Census of Marine Life, http://www.coml.org/coml.htm.

39 Holm, Smith, and Starkey, eds., *The Exploited Seas;* Rosenberg, et al., "The History of Ocean Resources"; Bolster and Alexander, "Abundance of Cod on the Nova Scotian Shelf"; Leavenworth, "Opening Pandora's Box"; Randall R. Reeves, Matthew G. McKenzie, and Tim D. Smith, "History of Bermuda Shore Whaling, Mainly for Humpback Whales," *Journal of Cetacean Research and Management* 8 (2006): 33–44; Tim D. Smith and Randall R. Reeves, "Estimating American 19th Century Catches of Humpback Whales in the West Indies and Cape Verde Islands," *Caribbean Journal of Science* 39 (2003): 286–97; Randall R. Reeves, et al., "Humpback and Fin Whaling in the Gulf of Maine from 1800–1918," *Marine Fisheries Review* 64 (2002): 1–12; Heike Lotze and K. Reise, "Editorial: Ecological History of the Wadden Sea," *Helgoland Marine Research* 59 (2005): 1; Heike Lotze, "Radical Changes in the Wadden Sea Fauna and Flora over the Last 2000 Years," *Helgoland Marine Research* 59 (2005): 71–83; Heike Lotze, et al., "Human Transformations of the Wadden Sea Ecosystem Through Time: A Synthesis," *Helgoland Marine Research* 59 (2005): 84–95; Bo Poulsen, "Historical Exploitation of North Sea Herring Stocks – An Environmental History of the Dutch Herring Fisheries, c. 1600–1860" (PhD diss., University of Southern Denmark, Esbjerg, 2005); René Taudal Poulsen, "An Environmental History of North Sea Ling and Cod Fisheries, 1840–1914" (PhD diss., University of Southern Denmark, Esbjerg, 2005); Katherine Magness, "Development of Fishing Policy in the Gulf of Maine, Late Nineteenth Century" (MS thesis, University of New Hampshire, 2005); Martin Wilcox, "Apprenticed Labour in the English Fishing Industry, 1850–1914" (PhD diss., University of Hull, UK, 2006); Susan Capes, "Overfishing the North Sea? Human Harvesting and Marine Resource Depletion, 1850–1914" (MA thesis, University of Hull, UK, 2003).

40 Poul Holm, "Exploited Seas," lecture at HMAP Summer Workshop, Esbjerg, Denmark, August, 2001. The other historian on the HMAP Steering Group is David Starkey, University of Hull, UK.

41 David Lowenthal, *The Past is a Foreign Country* (London: Cambridge University Press, 1985).

42 Van Sittert, "The Other Seven Tenths."

43 Peter Novick, *That Noble Dream: The "Objectivity Question" and the American Historical Profession* (Cambridge and New York: Cambridge University Press,

1988), 628. See also Georg G. Iggers, *Historiography in the Twentieth Century: From Scientific Objectivity to the Post-Modern Challenge* (Hanover and London: Wesleyan University Press, published by the University Press of New England, 1997); and Joyce Appleby, Lynn Hunt and Margaret Jacob, *Telling the Truth about History* (New York: W.W. Norton, 1994).

44 My thinking along these lines has benefited from discussions with Jay Taylor.

45 In the spirit of absolute accuracy it should be noted that Taylor's book discusses six species of Pacific salmon, all in the genus *Oncorhynchus*. In common parlance, however, they are often referred to simply as salmon.

46 Taylor, *Making Salmon,* 241.

47 For the single-species approach, Charles Hardy III, "Fish or Foul: A History of the Delaware River Basin Through the Perspective of the American Shad, 1682 to the Present," *Pennsylvania History* 66 (1999): 506–34; Briton C. Busch, *The War Against the Seals: A History of the North American Seal Fishery* (McGill-Queens University Press, 1985); and Charles Dana Gibson, *The Broadbill Swordfishery of the Northwestern Atlantic: The Fishery's Economic and Natural History (Early 1800s through 1995)* (Camden, Maine: Ensign Press, 1998).

48 American taxonomists group hake with the gadoids, while Europeans separate hake into a different family. From a fisherman's perspective, hake is closely related to the gadoids, and hake seem to fulfill what Spencer Apollonio calls a "gadoid function" in the ecosystem. Apollonio, *Hierarchical Perspectives,* 79–83.

49 One of the most successful accounts ever written of a single marine species won a Pulitzer Prize. See William W. Warner, *Beautiful Swimmers: Watermen, Crabs, and the Chesapeake Bay* (Boston: Little Brown and Company, 1976).

50 Paul Albury, *The Story of the Bahamas* (London: Macmillan Caribbean, 1975), 158–60, 189–90. As this article was being revised I was pleased to learn that Loren McClenachan, a graduate student at Scripps Institution, is working on the historical ecology of the Key West sponge industry along similar lines.

51 Quotations from Arthur F. McEvoy, "Toward an Interactive Theory of Nature and Culture: Ecology, Production and Cognition in the California Fishing Industry," in *The Ends of the Earth: Perspectives on Modern Environmental History,* ed. Donald Worster (New York and Cambridge: Cambridge University Press, 1988), 211–29, quotations on 229.

52 Recent examples of the regional approach include John R. Wennersten, *The Chesapeake: An Environmental Biography* (Baltimore: Maryland Historical Society, 2001); Tom Andersen, *This Fine Piece of Water: An Environmental History of Long Island Sound* (New Haven: Yale University Press, 2002); and Margaret Beattie Bogue, *Fishing the Great Lakes: An Environmental History, 1783–1933* (Madison: University of Wisconsin Press, 2000). For marine sanctuaries, see www.sanctuaries.nos.noaa.gov/.

53 Jeremy B. C. Jackson, "Reefs Since Columbus," *Coral Reefs* 16 (Suppl, 1997): S23–S32.; Sue Robinson, "The Battle over Bottom Trawling," *National Fisherman* (July 1999), 24–25; Watling and Norse, "Disturbance of the Seabed by Mobile Fishing Gear"; *Effects of Trawling and Dredging on Seafloor Habitat;* Ralph Stanley to William B. Leavenworth, personal e-mail in possession of the author, February 15, 2006.

54 For a classic meditation on the alewives by a respected naturalist, see John Hay, *The Run* (1959; reprint, Boston: Beacon Press, 1999).

55 On alewives as passenger pigeons of the sea, see William Cronon, *Changes in the Land: Indians, Colonists, and the Ecology of New England* (New York: Hill

and Wang, 1983), 23; Captain Charles Whitborne, in *The True Travels of Captain John Smith* (1616), quoted in Henry B. Bigelow and William C. Schroeder, *Fishes of the Gulf of Maine* (Washington, D.C.: U.S. Government Printing Office, 1953), 102.

56 The best work by historians on east coast anadromous fish is Gary Kulick, "Dams, Fish and Farmers: Defense of Public Rights in Eighteenth-Century Rhode Island," in *The Countryside in the Age of Capitalist Transformation: Essays in the Social History of Rural America,* ed. Steven Hahn and Jonathan Prude (Chapel Hill, 1985), 25–50; Harry L. Watson, "'The Common Rights of Mankind': Subsistence, Shad and Commerce in the Early Republican South," *Journal of American History* 83 (June 1996): 13–43; Daniel Vickers, "Those Damned Shad: Would the River Fisheries of New England Have Survived in the Absence of Industrialization?" *William and Mary Quarterly* 3rd. ser. LXI (October 2004): 685–712. Of these, Vickers is the most ecologically sensitive.

57 Douglass, *A Summary, Historical and Political, of the First Planting, Progressive Improvements, and Present State of the British Settlements in North America,* 2: 212; Petitions to the Governor, Council and Legislature, NH Division of Archives, Concord, N.H., (indexed under "alewives"), quotation February 5, 1776; D. Humphreys Storer, M.D., "A Report on the Fisheries of Massachusetts," *Boston Journal of Natural History* 2 (1839): 289–558.

58 Quotations from Ellis, *Empty Ocean,* 25–28. See also Bonnie J. McCay, "A Footnote to the History of New Jersey Fisheries: Menhaden as Food and Fertilizer," *New Jersey History* 98 (1980): 212–20; Nathan Adams, "Closing Destiny: The Menhaden Fishery of the 19th and Early 20th Century," unpublished paper in possession of the author. I thank Mr. Adams, a student at University of Connecticut, Avery Point, for allowing me to read his paper.

59 Adams, "Closing Destiny"; Judd, *Common Lands, Common People,* 245.

60 Barbara J. Garrity-Blake, *The Fish Factory: Work and Meaning for Black and White Fishermen of the American Menhaden Industry* (Knoxville: University of Tennessee Press, 1994).

61 Relying heavily on published statistics while not examining fishermen's daily logs led Wayne M. O'Leary to overlook the significance of substantial small boat fisheries in the Penobscot, Frenchmen's Bay, and Machias Customs Districts during the 1850s and 1860s. See Wayne M. O'Leary, *Maine Sea Fisheries: The Rise and Fall of a Native Industry, 1830–1890* (Boston: Northeastern University Press, 1996); and Bolster and Alexander, "The Abundance of Cod on the Nova Scotian Shelf." For historical investigation leading to previously unknown fishery statistics, see Rosenberg, et al., "The History of Ocean Resources."

62 Petition of the inhabitants of Southport, Boothbay, and vicinity, January, 1852, Maine State Archives, Legislative Laws, 1852, box 265, folder 125; Petition of the inhabitants of Surry, March 1854, Maine State Archives, Legislative graveyard, 1855, box 241, folder 9; Poulsen, "An Environmental History of North Sea Ling and Cod Fisheries, 1840–1914."

63 Rivinus and Youssef, *Spencer Baird of the Smithsonian,* 168–69; G. Brown Goode, "The Beginnings of Natural History in America," *Proceedings of the Biological Society of Washington* 3 (Washington, D.C.: 1886): 35–105; http://www.mnh.si.edu/vert/fishes/baird/goode.html.

64 Daniel Pauly and Jay Maclean, *In a Perfect Ocean: The State of Fisheries and Ecosystems in the North Atlantic Ocean* (Washington, D.C.: Island Press, 2003).

65 George Gordon Byron, "Apostrophe to the Ocean," in *Childe Harold's Pilgrimage* (London: 1818), quoted by Carlton, "Apostrophe to the Ocean."

4

GENDER AND ENVIRONMENTAL HISTORY

Carolyn Merchant

"As it was the intuitive foresight of [Isabella of Spain] which brought the light of civilization to a great continent, so in great measure, will it fall to woman in her power to educate public sentiment to save from rapacious waste and complete exhaustion the resources upon which depend the welfare of the home, the children, and the children's children." So wrote Lydia Adams-Williams, self-styled feminist conservation writer, in 1908. Her compatriot Mrs. Lovell White of California argued that reversing the destruction of the earth brought about by "men whose souls are gang-saws" was a project that required the best efforts of women. These women of the Progressive conservation crusade of the early twentieth century exemplify an overtly feminist perspective on the environment.[1]

Donald Worster's "Transformations of the Earth," while a rich and provocative approach to the field of environmental history, lacks a gender analysis. His conceptual levels of ecology (natural history), production (technology and its socioeconomic relations), and cognition (the mental realm of ideas, ethics, myths, and so on) are a significant framework for research and writing in this emerging field. His use of the mode-of-production concept in differing ecological and cultural contexts and his account of the changing history of ecological ideas in his major books have propelled environmental history to new levels of sophistication.

A gender perspective can add to his conceptual framework in two important ways. First, each of his three categories can be further illuminated through a gender analysis; second, in my view, environmental history needs a fourth analytical level, that of reproduction, which interacts with the other three levels.[2] What could such a perspective contribute to the framework Worster has outlined?

Women and men have historically had different roles in production relative to the environment. In subsistence modes of production such as those of native peoples, women's impact on nature is immediate and direct. In gathering-hunting-fishing economies, women collect and process plants,

82

small animals, bird eggs, and shellfish and fabricate tools, baskets, mats, slings, and clothing, while men hunt larger animals, fish, construct weirs and hut frames, and burn forests and brush. Because water and fuelwood availability affect cooking and food preservation, decisions over environmental degradation that dictate when to move camp and village sites may lie in the hands of women. In horticultural communities, women are often the primary producers of crops and fabricators of hoes, planters, and digging sticks, but when such economies are transformed by markets, the cash economies and environmental impacts that ensue are often controlled by men. Women's access to resources to fulfill basic needs may come into direct conflict with male roles in the market economy, as in Seneca women's loss of control over horticulture to male agriculture and male access to cash through greater mobility in nineteenth-century America or in India's Chipko (tree-hugging) movement of the past decade, wherein women literally hugged trees to protest declining access to fuelwood for cooking as male-dominated lumbering expanded.[3]

In the agrarian economy of colonial and frontier America, women's outdoor production, like men's, had immediate impact on the environment. While men's work in cutting forests, planting and fertilizing fields, and hunting or fishing affected the larger homestead environment, women's dairying activities, free-ranging barnyard fowl, and vegetable, flower, and herbal gardens all affected the quality of the nearby soils and waters and the level of insect pests, altering the effects of the microenvironment on human health. In the nineteenth century, however, as agriculture became more specialized and oriented toward market production, men took over dairying, poultry-raising, and truck farming, resulting in a decline in women's outdoor production. Although the traditional contributions of women to the farm economy continued in many rural areas and some women assisted in farm as well as home management, the general trend toward capitalist agribusiness increasingly turned chickens, cows, and vegetables into efficient components of factories within fields managed for profits by male farmers.[4]

In the industrial era, as middle-class women turned more of their energies to deliberate child rearing and domesticity, they defined a new but still distinctly female relation to the natural world. In their socially constructed roles as moral mothers, they often taught children about nature and science at home and in the elementary schools. By the Progressive era, women's focus on maintaining a home for husbands and children led many women such as those quoted above to spearhead a nationwide conservation movement to save forest and waters and to create national and local parks. Although the gains of the movement have been attributed by historians to men such as President Theodore Roosevelt, forester Gifford Pinchot, and preservationist John Muir, the efforts of thousands of women were directly responsible for many of the country's most significant conservation achievements. Women writers on nature such as Isabella Bird, Mary Austin, and

Rachel Carson have been among the most influential commentators on the American response to nature.[5]

Worster's conceptual framework for environmental history can thus be made more complete by including a gender analysis of the differential effects of women and men on ecology and their differential roles in production. At the level of cognition as well, a sensitivity to gender enriches environmental history. Native Americans, for example, construed the natural world as animated and created by spirits and gods. Origin myths included tales of mother earth and father sky, grandmother woodchucks and coyote tricksters, corn mothers and tree spirits. Such deities mediated between nature and humans, inspiring rituals and behaviors that helped to regulate environmental use and exploitation. Similar myths focused planting, harvesting, and first fruit rituals among native Americans and in such Old World cultures as those in ancient Mesopotamia, Egypt, and Greece, which symbolized nature as a mother goddess. In Renaissance Europe the earth was conceptualized as a nurturing mother (God's vice-regent in the mundane world) and the cosmos as an organism having a body, soul, and spirit. An animate earth and an I/thou relationship between humans and the world does not prevent the exploitation of resources for human use, but it entails an ethic of restraint and propitiation by setting up religious rituals to be followed before mining ores, damming brooks, or planting and harvesting crops. The human relationship to the land is intimately connected to daily survival.[6]

When mercantile capitalism, industrialization, and urbanization began to distance increasing numbers of male elites from the land in seventeenth-century England and in nineteenth-century America, the mechanistic framework created by the "fathers" of modern science legitimated the use of nature for human profit making. The conception that nature was dead, made up of inert atoms moved by external forces, that God was an engineer and mathematician, and that human perception was the result of particles of light bouncing off objects and conveyed to the brain as discrete sensations meant that nature responded to human interventions, not as active participant, but as passive instrument. Thus the way in which world views, myths, and perceptions are constructed by gender at the cognitive level can be made an integral part of environmental history.[7]

While Worster's analytical levels of ecology, production, and cognition may be made more sophisticated by including a gender analysis, ideas drawn from feminist theory suggest the usefulness of a fourth level of analysis – reproduction – that is dialectically related to the other three. First, all species reproduce themselves generationally and their population levels have impacts on the local ecology. But for humans, the numbers that can be sustained are related to the mode of production: More people can occupy a given ecosystem under a horticultural than a gathering-hunting-fishing mode, and still more under an industrial mode. Humans reproduce themselves biologically in accordance with the social and ethical norms of the culture into which they are born. Native peoples adopted an array of benign and malign population control techniques such as long lactation, abstention, coitus interruptus, the use of native plants to induce abortion, infanticide, and senilicide. Carrying capacity, nutritional factors, and tribally accepted customs dictated the numbers of infants that survived to adulthood in order to reproduce the tribal whole. Colonial Americans, by contrast, encouraged high numbers of births owing to the scarcity of labor in the new lands. With the onset of industrialization in the nineteenth century, a demographic transition resulted in fewer births per female. Intergenerational reproduction, therefore, mediated through production, has impact on the local ecology.[8]

Second, people (as well as other living things) must reproduce their own energy on a daily basis through food and must conserve that energy through clothing (skins, furs, or other methods of bodily temperature control) and shelter. Gathering or planting food crops, fabricating clothing, and constructing houses are directed toward the reproduction of daily life.

In addition to these biological aspects of reproduction, human communities reproduce themselves socially in two additional ways. People pass on skills and behavioral norms to the next generation of producers, and that allows a culture to reproduce itself over time. They also structure systems of governance and laws that maintain the social order of the tribe, town, or nation. Many such laws and policies deal with the allocation and regulation of natural resources, land, and property rights. They are passed by legislative bodies and administered through government agencies and a system of justice. Law in this interpretation is a means of maintaining and modifying a particular social order. These four aspects of reproduction (two biological and two social) interact with ecology as mediated by a particular mode of production.[9]

Such an analysis of production and reproduction in relation to ecology helps to delineate changes in forms of patriarchy in different societies. Although in most societies governance may have been vested in the hands of men (hence patriarchy), the balance of power between the sexes differed. In gatherer-hunter and horticultural communities, extraction and production of food may have been either equally shared by or dominated by women, so that male (or female) power in tribal reproduction (chiefs and shamans) was balanced by female power in production. In subsistence-oriented communities in colonial and frontier America, men and women shared power in production, although men played dominant roles in legal-political reproduction of the social whole. Under industrial capitalism in the nineteenth century, women's loss of power in outdoor farm production was compensated by a gain of power in the reproduction of daily life (domesticity) and in the socialization of children and husbands (the moral mother) in the sphere of reproduction. Thus the shifts of power that

Worster argues occurs in different environments are not only those between indigenous and invading cultures but also those between men and women.[10]

A gender perspective on environmental history therefore both offers a more balanced and complete picture of past human interactions with nature and advances its theoretical frameworks. The ways in which female and male contributions to production, reproduction, and cognition are actually played out in relation to ecology depends on the particular stage and the actors involved. Yet within the various acts of what Timothy Weiskel has called the global ecodrama should be included scenes in which men's and women's roles come to center stage and scenes in which nature "herself" is an actress. In this way gender in environmental history can contribute to a more holistic history of various regions and eras.[11]

Notes

1 Carolyn Merchant, "Women of the Progressive Conservation Movement, 1900–1916," *Environmental Review,* 8 (Spring 1984), 57–85, esp. 65, 59.

2 For a more detailed discussion, see Carolyn Merchant, "The Theoretical Structure of Ecological Revolutions," *ibid.,* 11 (Winter 1987), 251–74. For a discussion of theoretical frameworks for environmental history, see Barbara Leibhardt, "Interpretation and Causal Analysis: Theories in Environmental History," *ibid.,* 12 (Spring 1988), 23–36.

3 Sandra Marburg, "Women and Environment: Subsistence Paradigms, 1850–1950," *ibid.,* 8 (Spring 1984), 7–22; Diane Rothenberg, "Erosion of Power: An Economic Basis for the Selective Conservativism of Seneca Women in the Nineteenth Century," *Western Canadian Journal of Anthropology,* 6 (1976), 106–22; Vandana Shiva, *Staying Alive: Women, Ecology, and Development* (London, 1988); Mona Etienne and Eleanor Leacock, eds., *Women and Colonization: Anthropological Perspectives* (New York, 1980).

4 Carolyn Merchant, *Ecological Revolutions: Nature, Gender, and Science in New England* (Chapel Hill, 1989); Corlann Gee Bush, "The Barn Is His, the House Is Mine," in *Energy and Transport,* ed. George Daniels and Mark Rose (Beverly Hills, 1982), 235–59; Carolyn E. Sachs, *The Invisible Farmers: Women in Agricultural Production* (Totowa, 1983).

5 Merchant, "Women of the Progressive Conservation Movement"; Vera Norwood, "Heroines of Nature: Four Women Respond to the American Landscape," *Environmental Review,* 8 (Spring 1984), 34–56.

6 Paula Gunn Allen, *The Sacred Hoop: Recovering the Feminine in American Indian Traditions* (Boston, 1984); Riane Eisler, *The Chalice and the Blade* (San Francisco, 1988); Pamela Berger, *The Goddess Obscured: Transformation of the Grain Protectress from Goddess to Saint* (Boston, 1985); Janet Bord and Colin Bord, *Earth Rites: Fertility Practices in Pre-Industrial Britain* (London, 1982); Carolyn Merchant, *The Death of Nature: Women, Ecology, and the Scientific Revolution* (San Francisco, 1980).

7 Merchant, *Death of Nature.* See also Evelyn Fox Keller, *Reflections on Gender and Science* (New Haven, 1985), 33–65. On gender in American perceptions of nature, see Annette Kolodny, *The Lay of the Land: Metaphor as Experience and History in American Life and Letters* (Chapel Hill, 1975); and Annette Kolodny,

The Land before Her: Fantasy and Experience of the American Frontier, 1630–1860 (Chapel Hill, 1984).

8 Ester Boserup, *The Conditions of Agricultural Growth: The Economics of Agrarian Change under Population Pressure* (Chicago, 1965); Ester Boserup, *Women's Role in Economic Development* (New York, 1970); Marvin Harris, *Cultural Materialism: The Struggle for a Science of Culture* (New York, 1979); Carolyn Merchant, "The Realm of Social Relations: Production, Reproduction, and Gender in Environmental Transformations," in *The Earth as Transformed by Human Action,* ed. B. L. Turner II (New York, 1990); Robert Wells, *Uncle Sam's Family: Issues and Perspectives in American Demographic History* (Albany, 1985), 28–56.

9 For a more detailed elaboration of reproduction as an organizing category see Merchant, *Ecological Revolutions.*

10 *Ibid.,* Nancy F. Cott, *The Bonds of Womanhood: "Woman's Sphere" in New England, 1780–1835* (New Haven, 1977); Barbara Leslie Epstein, *The Politics of Domesticity: Women, Evangelism, and Temperance in Nineteenth Century America* (Middletown, 1981); Ruth Bloch, "American Feminine Ideals in Transition: The Rise of the Moral Mother, 1785–1815," *Feminist Studies,* 4 (June 1978), 101–26; Barbara Welter, "The Cult of True Womanhood, 1820–60," *American Quarterly,* 18 (Summer 1966), 151–74.

11 On environmental history as an ecodrama, see Timothy Weiskel, "Agents of Empire: Steps toward an Ecology of Imperialism," *Environmental Review,* 11 (Winter 1987), 275–88.

5

CONSUMED BY EITHER FIRE OR FIRE

A review of the environmental consequences of anthropogenic fire

Stephen J. Pyne

We only live, only suspire
Consumed by either fire or fire.
— T. S. Eliot, *Four Quartets*

Ends and beginnings

The capture of fire by the genus *Homo* changed forever the natural and cultural histories of the Earth. Nothing else so empowered hominids, and no other human technology has influenced the planet for so long and so pervasively. A grand dialectic emerged between the fire-proneness of the biota and the fire capacity of humans such that they coevolved, welded by fire to a common destiny. If humans assimilated nature's fire into their biological heritage as a species, it is no less true that virtually all biotas have come to accept anthropogenic fire, and not a few demand it. Deny anthropogenic fire and you deny humanity and many of its ancient allies anyplace on the planet.

Keeper of the flame

In effect, a pact was struck, the first of humanity's Faustian bargains and the origin of an environmental ethos. Humans got fire and, through fire, access to the world's biota; that biota, in turn, got a new regimen of fire, one disciplined by passage through human society. Of course, humans did not control all fires and had to suffer wildfire from their own or natural sources. Nor did humans always use fire prudently or with the regularity their allied environments expected. Nevertheless, once begun, the synergism proved irresistible. A uniquely fire creature became bonded to a uniquely fire planet.

Everywhere that humans went—and they went everywhere—they carried fire. The hominid flame propagated across the continents like an expanding ring of fire, remaking everything it touched. Within that ring lived humans; outside, the wild still reigned. Humans occupied preferentially those sites susceptible to fire and shunned, or tried to restructure, those that were less amenable. They sought out what needed to be burned, and burned it. Through its human agents, the biosphere in effect wrested control over ignition from lightning and other inorganic phenomena, and the structure of fire regimes responded to new patterns, its rhythms yielding new cadences.

If humans became dependent on fire (and in some cases intoxicated, even addicted to it), it is no less true that many biotas came to depend on anthropogenic fire practices for their own survival. Organisms adapted not to fire in the abstract or to individual fires but to fire *regimes*. A sudden change in a fire regime—its load, its frequency, its seasonal timing and intensities—could propagate catastrophically throughout the system. This of course is exactly the revolution that human firebrands made possible. But if fire granted them new power, it also conveyed new responsibilities. It was vital that the flame neither fail nor run wild.

The firestick was different from other implements in the hominid toolkit. It took on the attributes not only of *Homo* but of the larger biota. An ax head has the properties of the rock from which it comes; an arrowhead, of its source flint or obsidian; an awl, of bone. Fire is more protean than these. Confined as a torch or oven, it can substitute for ax or drill or desert sun. Broadcast as free-burning fire, however, it has the properties of the weather and winds that drive it, the terrain across which it propagates, and the fuels—living, dead, and dormant—that sustain it. Through these fuels, fused by a kind of biotic weld, fire shares the properties of life. Virus-like, fire becomes as complex, dynamic, subtle, and varied as the biotas that sustain it. Like life, it can propagate, amplify, reproduce. Its reach is pervasive, penetrating into every crevice of an ecosystem. Its effects are plural, and often indeterminate. Anthropogenic fire resembles less a tool in the conventional sense than a colossal symbiosis, exclusive to humans, the source of their unique power over terrestrial biotas.

In effect, humans domesticated fire. Once tamed, it had to be fed, housed, cared for, and bred. It could no longer range for its own food, or be left to fend for itself in the elements. It had to be tended. Its reproduction, too, could be guided into select "breeds"—fire for cooking, fire for ceramics, fire for heating, lighting, hardening; fire for hunting, farming, herding, clearing the land. Wherever humans ranged, domesticated fire began to replace wild fire. Much as humans killed wolves and propagated dogs, so they drove back the domain of wildfire and substituted a regime based on anthropogenic burning. Once begun, the process could become self-reinforcing; the very act of burning helped reshape ecosystems, redesigning fuel complexes in ways that shielded humans from unwanted wildfire and further promoted domesticated fire. Domestic fire could serve humans only if humans served it. The domain of one determined the domain of the other.

Fire as power

The quest for fire is a quest for power. Virtually all fire-origin myths confirm this fact. In words that in one form or another find echoes everywhere, Aeschylus has Prometheus declare that, by giving fire, he founded "all the arts of men." To possess fire is to become human, but fire is almost always denied, only rarely granted by a fire-hoarding potentate, more typically stolen by some culture hero through force or guile. Once acquired, the balance of biotic power began to shift in favor of the otherwise meagerly endowed genus *Homo*.

For all the manifold feebleness of this species, fire compensated, and more. It made palatable many foodstuffs otherwise inedible or toxic; with smoke or heat, it made possible the preservation of foods that would soon spoil; it promoted a cultivation of indigenous forbs, grasses, tubers, and nut-bearing trees; it stimulated hunting; it hardened wooden tools, made malleable shafts to be rendered into arrows or spears, and prepared certain stones for splitting; it kept at bay the night terrors, promoted and defined the solidarity of the group, and made available the evening for storytelling and ceremony. It even allowed humans to reshape whole landscapes as, in effect, humans slowly began to cook the Earth. Everywhere humans went, fire went also as guide, laborer, camp follower, and chronicler.

Fire's danger matched its power. If untended, once-domesticated fire could go wild. The extraordinary pervasiveness that made fire universally useful also threatened humanity's ability to control it. The relationship was truly symbiotic; if humans controlled fire, so also fire controlled humans, forcing the species to live in certain ways, either to seize fire's power or to avoid its wild outbreaks. In domesticating fire, humanity also domesticated itself; fire's power could come only by assuming responsibility for fire's care. The danger of extinction was ever present. The feral fire lurked always in the shadows. Even today the control of fire is far from satisfactory.

Imagine, for example, the reception that would greet someone who announced that he had discovered a process fundamental to the chemistry and biology of the planet, a phenomenon that could grant to humans the power to intervene massively in the biosphere and atmosphere, that could, in effect, allow humans to reform the living world. Some critics would object on the grounds that humans were congenitally incapable of using such power wisely and would only harm themselves and the world. Even, those who would cheer such an announcement might be quieted by the qualifying fine print, which stipulated that control would be inevitably incomplete; that even in the built environment lives and property would be lost; and that the hazards attendant with the use of this process would be so great that emergency crews and expensive equipment would need to be stationed every few city blocks, buildings would need emergency alarms and exits illuminated by separate power sources, every residence should be outfitted with instruments to detect it, special insurance schemes would be necessary—the list goes on and on. Anyone advocating the universal adoption of such a discovery would be denounced as a lunatic or locked up as a menace to society. The process itself would never make it through federal regulatory agencies. Yet of course this is exactly our relationship with fire. Its power was too great to refuse, and its nature too protean to control completely.

As domesticated fire became indispensable, moreover, its flame had to be kept inextinguishable. The communal fire joined the communal well as the earliest of public utilities. Much as the hearth became the symbol of the family, so the ever-burning vestal fire became the symbol of tribe, city, or state. Perpetual fire-keeping, or the tending of eternal flames, expressed not only the continuity of human society but its differentness. If fire was universal to humans, it was also exclusive to them. Almost certainly we will never allow any other creature to possess it.

Fire as morality

With power came choice, and with choice anthropogenic fire entered a moral universe. Humans were genetically equipped to handle fire, but they did not come programmed knowing how to use it. Their capacity for colossal power lacked an equivalent capacity for control. Environmental conditions imposed some limitations on the land's ability to accept fire, and human societies established still other parameters by which their cultures could absorb fire. Still, the range of options remained huge; individual choices, neither obvious nor singular. Fire practices would reflect values, perceptions, beliefs, economics, institutions, politics, all the things that guide humanity through a contingent universe about which it has incomplete knowledge. The capture of fire became a paradigm for all of humanity's interaction with nature.

For fire there was no revealed wisdom, only an existential Earth that could accommodate many practices and a silent creator who issued no decalogue to guide proper use. After all, fire had not come to humans accompanied by stone-engraved commandments or an operating manual; it had been stolen. Humans were on their own. The fire they seized they had to maintain. They could nurture their special power into a vestal fire for the Earth or use their torches like the spray cans of environmental vandals. They did both.

Fire became a pyric projection of themselves. It could be used wisely or stupidly, and it illuminated and assayed other acts as sound or reckless, but, until very recently, it was not itself condemned. There were good fires and bad fires but no escape from the imperative to use fire. The belief that free-burning anthropogenic fire was *ipso facto* an expression of environmental abuse by humans, that the suppression of fire was humanity's primary duty, is a very recent invention, an outcome of new combustion sources and ideologies that consider humans inevitably "unnatural." Instead, most peoples have exploited fire to define their relationship to their environment. From medieval Icelanders to the twentieth-century Kwakiutl, people have carried fire around their lands to announce their claim to them. Like Australia's Gidjingali, aboriginal peoples explain fire use as a means of "cleaning up the country," of housekeeping, of exercising their ecological stewardship; as Robert Logan Jack expressed it, burning is "the alpha and omega of their simple notion of 'doing their duty by the land'" (Jack 1881, p. 3). Not to burn is as irresponsible as improper burning. Early fire codes in colonial America, for example, required routine burning as a social obligation. Good citizens used fire well; bad ones, poorly or not at all.

In this way, fire became not merely a projection of human will but a test of human character. Thus fire history, like fire itself, is a maddening amalgamation of human and ecological history; it belongs with the humanities as much as with the sciences. Track fire, and you track human history. However, it is the special promise of fire history that one can do more, that it is possible to use anthropogenic fire to extract information out of the historic record that might otherwise be inaccessible or overlooked, much as burning often flushes infertile biotas with nutrients and cooking renders palatable many otherwise inedible foodstuffs. Fire can remake raw materials into humanly usable history. It can drive out of archival scrub the vital character of humanity. Around it—around that informing fire— humans tell the stories that make up their history, that say who they are.

Universal fire

In a universe informed by fire, fire becomes a universal tool. To the fire the planet contained, humans have added, subtracted, redistributed, and rearranged. Human societies have inserted fire into every conceivable place for every conceivable purpose, and they have done so for so long and so pervasively that it is impossible to disentangle fire from either human life or the biosphere. The alliance between hominids and fire is ancient, apparently dating from the time of *Homo erectas,* a part of our biological inheritance.

Fire and society

Fire restructured the relationship between humans and their world. It furnished light and heat. It made possible a social life after dark; redefined social roles; warmed against the cold; demanded shelter and sustenance; served as communication media; supplemented ax, knife, and drill; and allowed cooking, which revolutionized diets and food gathering. Fire assisted almost all branches of technology. The tools for recreating fire more or less at will—drills, saws, and flints—obviously derived from or coevolved with the technologies for striking, scraping, and drilling in stone and bone. Cooking inspired new technologies such as ceramics and metallurgy. The preservation of fire was an intensely practical as well as symbolic act.

Of course, fire also entered into cultural life, reshaping the cognitive world of humans as fully as their physical landscape. Fire worship and divination constituted a primitive religion; trial by fire served as a primitive legal system, and fire-based philosophies and myths formed a primitive science and literature. As a source of heat and light, fire inevitably accompanied ceremonies, and in time became indelibly associated with them as a part of their symbolic milieu. Burned offerings carried sacrifices to the heavens. The trying fire segregated dross from essence.

No dimension of human existence was untouched by fire, directly or indirectly, and the more limited was a people's technology, the more pervasive and apparent was their fire dependence. Remove fire from a society, even today, and both its technology and its social order will lie in ruins. Strip fire away from language, and you reduce many of its vital metaphors to ash. It should come as no surprise that from the Aztecs to the Stoics, from the Christian Apocalypse to the Nordic *Ragnarok,* the myth of a world-beginning or world-consuming fire is nearly universal. Humans' dominion began with fire, and it may well end with it.

Fire and land

Fire's influence on the environment extended beyond its valued service as an aide-de-camp to wandering hominids. It was also applied directly to the landscape, and it was this capacity that defined humanity's special ecological niche, that made fire something more than a surrogate for talons, fangs, fleetness, or massive muscles. Anthropogenic fire endowed whole ecosystems, not merely a species.

Of course, anthropogenic fire built upon fire adaptations already resident in the biota, humans' fire practices mimicked nature's own fire drives and slash-and-burn cycling by windstorm and lightning, and human-kindled fire rarely produced results through its own, isolated actions. Instead, anthropogenic fire reshaped the structure and composition of landscapes, recalibrated their dynamics, and reset their timings of growth and decay; fire accelerated, catalyzed, animated, and leveraged; it combined with other processes to multiply their compounded effects beyond the sum of their individual impacts, choreographing new rhythms and steps for the partners of this biotic ballet. Fire was a remarkably intricate and pervasive enabling device, without which other technologies or practices were often incompetent; for example, there could be no slashing without the capacity for burning, and no hunting without the means by which to maintain the habitat. Similarly, humans' ability to manipulate fuels redesigned the environment within which fires (either theirs or nature's) had to operate.

Thus fire interacted with the new flora and fauna that migrating humans introduced, with livestock in search of browse, with ax and sword as weapons of conquest, with plow and seed, and with humans' understanding of how they should behave. It passed into the natural environment through the cognitive and moral world of humans. What people knew about fire affected how they used it. Knowledge (or error) acquired in one place could be transferred to another. Fire ecology had to incorporate the pathways of human institutions and knowledge as fully as biogeochemical cycles of carbon and sulfur.

Aboriginal fire

Anthropogenic fire made the world more habitable for those who held the torch. Aboriginal fires kept open corridors of travel; they assisted hunting, both by drives and by controlling the extent and timing of browse; they helped cultivate, after a fashion, many indigenous plants and simplified their harvest; not least, anthropogenic burning shielded human societies from wildfire by laying down controlled fields of fire around habitations in regions prone to natural ignitions. Fire was both cause and effect for the fact that humans preferentially lived where burning was possible and shunned unburned regions as uninhabitable. The nomadism of hunting and gathering societies was intimately interdependent with the cycle of growth and regrowth that was itself contingent on a cycle of burning.

Fire made the land inhabitable, as cooking helped make environment into food and the forge reworked rock into metals. When John Smith asked a Manahoac Indian what lay beyond the mountains, he was told "the Sunne"; his informant could say nothing more because "the woods were not burnt," and without fire, both travel and knowledge were impossible (Barbour 1986, II, p. 176). John DeBrahm noted also the purgative effect of burning, the purifying passage of humanity's ring of fire: "The fire of the burning old Grass, Leaves, and Underwoods consumes a Number of Serpents, Lizards, Scorpions, Spiders and their Eggs, as also Bucks, Ticks, Petiles, and Muskotoes, and other Vermins, and Insects in General very offensive, and some very poisonous, whose Increase would, without this Expedient, cover the Land, and make America disinhabitable" (DeBrahm 1971, p. 80). To a remarkable extent, humans were able through fire to shape wholesale the environments in which they lived, to render that land accessible.

To this end, fire was both subtle and pervasive. It promoted favored grasses, forbs, tubers, and fruits such as wild rice, sunflowers, camas, bracken, cassava, and blueberries; it helped harden the sticks that dug them up; it stimulated the reeds that, woven into baskets, carried the harvest; it cooked the gatherings, leached them of toxins, or boiled them down into oils or sap; it yielded the light by which the crop was discussed and celebrated. Fire helped humans gather chestnuts in the Appalachians, acorns in California, and mesquite beans in the Southwest. It drove off insects—in certain seasons, humans lived in smoke, as reluctant to leave its sheltering cloud as to walk away from a campfire into a moonless night.

Perhaps the most spectacular practices involved hunting. It may be said that any creature that *could* be hunted by fire *was* hunted by fire. Torches assisted evening hunts and made fishing at night notoriously productive. Smoke flushed bears from dens, sables from hollowed firs, possums from termite-cored eucalypts. Fire drives were practiced for springboks in southern Africa, elephants in Sudan, turtles in Venezuela, rheas in Patagonia, kangaroos and maalas in Australia, boars in Transbaikalia. In North America, fire hunting targeted bison, deer, and antelope; aboriginal Alaskans used it against moose and muskrat, Yuman Indians for wood rats, Californians for rabbits, Great Basin tribes for grasshoppers, and Texans for lizards.

Apart from the hunt itself, fire controlled browse, recalibrating the calendar of renewal and the rich flush of nutrients that the springtime brought. Applied correctly, fire could inaugurate that first growth or stimulate a second flush in the autumn. Regardless, the pattern of burning dictated the pattern of feeding, that is, the annual migration of grazers and browsers and of course the hunters that followed them. Fire hunting and fire herding involved enticing as well as driving. Select sites could even be baited with the smoke that meant relief from flies or with the fresh grasses recharged by burning. Apaches set such traps for mule deer; Samme, for reindeer; contemporary African poachers, for rhinos.

This fire-mediated relationship was profoundly reciprocal. If humans used flame to promote their food stocks, wildlife often depended on anthropogenic burning to fertilize and ready the landscape and stimulate the fodder that they, the indigenous fauna, also required in order to thrive. The land reflected this symbiosis, reshaped into fire-sculpted hunting grounds both large and small. Where fire could burn freely—where winds, terrain, and biota favored routine, expansive fires—great steppes, *campos, llanos,* prairies, savannas, *cerrados,* and grassy veld could result.

Agricultural fire

The Neolithic revolution adumbrated these practices with others. Of course, fire alone could not create agriculture, but it is no accident that agriculture originated in fire-susceptible environments and reworked fire-adapted grasses into cereals at its biotic forges. Outside of flood-recharged riverbanks, early agriculture was impossible without burning. At a minimum, fire was mandatory for the expansion of farming and herding beyond their special environments of origin. Agriculturists needed fire to convert and catalyze, to impose an alien flora and fauna, to forge a stubborn biome into new shapes. The metamorphosis was sometimes easy, for small adjustments could reconfigure fire practices suitable for hunting into those to serve herding or allow the shift from the harvest of a fire-cultivated native flora to the harvest of a fire-catalyzed alien one. More often, the transformation was messy and complex.

The really revolutionary changes occurred not from fire *per se* but from fire in conjunction with other practices. The violence of farming was expressed with torch and ax, the fire and sword of biological imperialism. Slash-and-burn agriculture was carried into the most remote landscapes by wandering farmers: Maoris in New Zealand; Melanesians in Fiji; American indigenes where maize or cassava was cultivated; Bantus across tropical, and subtropical Africa; [jhum]-practicing tribes throughout the Indian subcontinent and southeast Asia; and, of course, Europeans, who practiced it across their varied frontiers, from the Finns in Karelia to the Norse in Iceland and Greenland, from Russians in the *taiga* to overseas colonists in the Americas, Africa, and Australia. In mixed economies fields once cleared for crops might, through subsequent burning, be kept in grass for pasture.

Meanwhile, flocks of domesticated livestock advanced like shock troops. They reclaimed range previously fired for the hunting of wildlife; they frequently forced herders to keep open fields, first cleared for farming, as pasture, again through routine burning; they forced the creation of new grazing lands or degraded the old ones. In humid environments, from Australia's northern tropics to Siberia's *taiga,* the introduction of domesticated animals typically inspired more fire, which was used as a flaming ax to slash back the encroaching woods. In more arid grasslands, from Morocco to the American West, the introduction of livestock commonly brought a reduction in burning as animals cropped fuels that would otherwise feed flames.

Eventually fire was itself domesticated no less than land, flora, and fauna. Wildland fire became agricultural fire. Field burning obeyed a new calendar, operated at reduced intensities, and altered the frequency of broadcast fire. For the most part, humans dictated these parameters. Where fire had once reflected the subtlety and complexity of the natural world, it increasingly assumed the regimen and personality of human society, responsive to the dynamics of the human mind or what a flawed human will could impose of itself on nature.

What Survey-General T. L. Mitchell said of 1840s Australia can stand as an epigraph for all the environments humans have fashioned through flame:

Fire, grass, and kangaroos, and human inhabitants, seem all dependent on each other for existence in Australia; for any one of these being wanting, the others could no longer continue. Fire is necessary to burn the grass, and form those open forests, in which we find the large forest-kangaroo; the native applies that fire to the grass at certain seasons, in order that a young green crop may subsequently spring up, and so attract and enable him to kill or take the kangaroo with nets. In summer, the burning of long grass also discloses vermin, birds' nests, etc., on which the females and children, who chiefly burn the grass[,] feed. But for this simple process, the Australia woods had probably contained as thick a jungle as those of New Zealand or America.

(Mitchell 1969, p. 306)

When those fires were removed, the jungle reclaimed what the new inhabitants did not remake. Reclaiming the land meant redefining its fire regime.

Imperial fire

Within the last half millennium, two events have rewritten the history and geography of fire. The expansion of Europe, begun with the Renaissance voyages of discovery, set in motion a colossal, mixing of the world's flora, fauna, and peoples. Old orders disintegrated, and new ones continue to emerge that have yielded a global economy, a global ecology, and a global scholarship. Even while these events were proceeding, imperial Europe became industrial Europe, and the pressures for global change accelerated. Anthropogenic fire was, as always, catalyst, cause, and consequence of these processes.

Imperial fire

Access to a global market exposed large hinterlands to revolutionary reforms. Inevitably, economic exchange brought ecological change. By both accident and deliberation, the world's flora and fauna became hopelessly intermingled and selectively exterminated, usually with the help of or at least in the presence of fire. Livestock from the Old World went to the New; cultigens from the New World went to the Old; plants and animals from both invaded Australia; Africans were forcibly shipped to the Americas, British convicts to Australia, and Russian exiles to Siberia, and an unstable alloy of hope and despair inspired a century of emigration that reduced Europe's population in roughly the same proportion as the Black Death; weeds, vermin, diseases, and insects, no less than cereals, cattle, citrus, and medicines, crossed over long-separated biotas with results that were sometimes productive, usually unexpected, and occasionally catastrophic.

The new geography of global fire followed the evolving geography of European expansion. In some places, fires increased to epidemic proportions as immigrant fires mingled with indigenous ones, all now cut loose from traditional moorings. In others, the fires flared, like a Bunsen burner speeding a critical reaction, and then ceased, the experiment completed. In still others, they vanished into field and ceremony, little more than vestigial symbols. The permutations in how fire, flora, and fauna could interact were infinite, and no single formula can encompass all the outcomes. The general effect, however, has been to reduce the amount of open burning. The Earth has far less free-burning fire now than when Columbus sailed.

This observation is counterintuitive, or, more accurately, it runs against the grain of Western, colonial mythology, populated by noble savages and virgin forests, which requires that a discovered world of innocence be ravished by a decadent and cynical Europe. Thus an influential figure has explained the fire policy of America's National Park Service as a program to restore the state of nature that existed prior to the advent of "technological man," an ambiguous state that includes the native peoples who burned sequoia groves annually but not the German immigrants who swatted those fires out with pine boughs.

Certainly, European contact led to environmental change. In locales where land clearing became extensive, horrific fires often resulted. The transitional period—when fire practices and fire regimes mixed—was metastable and prone to violent reactions. However, this scenario fails to recognize the geographic extent and longevity of anthropogenic fire. It sees the violent flash of European gunpowder but not the already smoldering land behind it. In fact, when the smoke cleared—as it soon did—there was typically less fire after settlement or colonial rule than before. Sediment cores from off-shore Central America, for example, demonstrate that burning collapsed after the Spanish conquest and has not yet returned to pre-Columbian levels. With local exceptions, this scenario could probably be generalized throughout the Americas.

As often as not, the expulsion of fire was itself frequently a cause of environmental degradation and social disintegration. Fire's abolition subverted the habitat of fire-reliant humans as it did that of such fire-adapted organisms as longleaf pine, eucalypts, fynbos, kangaroos, and rhinos. The more universal fire was a tool—that is, the fewer the alternative technologies that were available to a people—the more devastating was its removal. With the environment changed, at least partly through a new regimen of fire, recovery was impossible. Bison could not return to tallgrass prairies that had reverted to woods. Springbok fled lands overrun with scrub. The change in fire regimen meant a change in habitat.

The reasons for Europe's pyrophobia are several. For one, temperate Europe—a climatic oddity—did not experience a routine fire season. Temperature, not precipitation, defined its seasonality. Fire existed in

Europe because people put it there. It thrived because agriculture required it. It appeared to exist as a useful tool, not as an ecological necessity. To intellectuals and officials fire stigmatized land practices as primitive; they knew wildfire as an index of social disorder; they experienced it in cities, not the countryside. They saw the burning of fallow as simple waste, as indulgent, slothful farming. If they could extinguish fire from the garden, they would. In time Europe came itself to resemble a kind of fire, burned out in the center, flaming only along its perimeter. But that smoldering core held the great powers of Enlightenment Europe, its new wave of colonizers, its scientific centers, its industrial inventors. Its ideal became the eccentric norm for the planet.

For another, Enlightenment Europe had created a species of engineering, forestry, among whose charges was the management of fire. Silviculture was a graft onto the great rootstock of European agriculture, and it correspondingly condemned burning of every sort. According to European agronomists, fire not only killed trees, it destroyed the humus upon which all life depended. Without that spongy soil, erosion was inevitable, and environmental decay irreversible. Far better to exploit biological agents such as sheep and cattle, fertilize with compost and dung rather than with ash, and sponsor labor-intensive surrogates such as weeding—anything but fire.

Besides, fire threatened fixed property, or social relationships of rigidly ordered societies. Broadcast fire encouraged nomadism, the seasonal cycling of pastoralists, the long-fallow hegiras of swidden farmers, a mobility of population that made political control and taxation difficult. The ideal of the garden that prevailed in central Europe demanded that every person, like every plant, have his or her assigned place. Finnish and Russian swiddeners fled king and tsar by burning into the boreal forest. Greek, Corsican, Sardinian, and other Mediterranean pastoralists ranged as freely as their flocks, defiant of political authority and confident in the power of fire to intimidate settled communities and harass agents of the state. Control over fire meant control over how people lived.

Forestry absorbed these doctrines, and in its shock encounter with other, oft-fired biotas, it hammered these precepts into a catechism of fire exclusion. Some wildfires would inevitably occur from the striking of native flint and European steel and from lightning, arson, and accident, as, for example, railroad-powered logging sent its iron tentacles everywhere. In addition, some broadcast burning might be unavoidable in the early years of institution building, an expedient compromise until surer control was possible. However, the ultimate ambition was a forest without fire, an orchard of saw wood and pulp. As soon as it was politically and technically feasible, foresters instigated fire control measures. As often as not, fire suppression was one of the most powerful means of controlling indigenes.

This enterprise, like other imperial exercises, proceeded most smoothly where the indigenous populations disappeared before the swarm of invading colonizers and their biological allies and camp followers. Where native peoples and biotas persisted, so did native fire. Traditional burning persisted in defiance of European desires; often, in such circumstances, colonists adopted native fire practices or hybridized with them in mutual defiance of the edicts of colonial administrators and the theories of European intellectuals. Fire policy became an expression of colonial rule, and firefighters a species of frontiersman, especially where land was reserved from folk access. In response, natives burned illicitly, at once a protest and an attempt to restore traditional lands to traditional purposes. Regardless of whether they retained political access to reserved lands like forests, unless they had fire they lacked biological access to those potential resources. The character of the land changed, often irrevocably.

All this did not pass unnoticed. Typically a debate ensued, often formal and even published, that pitted European standards against local practices, fire control against fire use. The most dramatic confrontations flared in British and French colonies, where foresters nurtured in Franco-German traditions were most aggressive at imposing policies that aspired to fire exclusion. In North America, fire control triumphed; in India, Australia, and South Africa, awkward compromises resulted that first denounced controlled burning, only to recant and ultimately absorb them into official doctrine. In time, controlled burning returned to North America as well, although in a language ("prescribed burning") that denied the legitimacy of its earlier incarnation ("light burning").

Industrial fire

Not least of all, industrial Europe began to sublimate the power of fire into machines. Controlled combustion began to replace controlled burning, and the fossil fallow of coal and oil, the living fallow of traditional agriculture. Technology invented new devices to illuminate rooms, warm houses, bake bread, harden ceramics, shape metals, and the myriad other tasks fire had once performed. New sources of energy led to new sources of mechanical power and transportation, the pathways by which nutrients would be cycled in this revolutionary model of nature's economy. Guano could be shipped from Pacific islands to fertilize European fields; clover could replace indigenous grasses unpalatable to Eurasian livestock; chemical herbicides and tractors could substitute for free-burning fallow to control weeds.

The ecology of fire was no longer confined to burned sites, but cycled and ramified throughout human institutions as well. Through foresters in the service of the British Empire, the impact of teak burning in Burma could be transmitted to the fynbos of Cape Colony. Through technology transfer—the European education of American students—the fire history of the Schwarzwald could influence fire policy in the chaparral of California. Through French colonialism and scientific publications, fires in the Riviera could be felt in Madagascar, Chad, and New South Wales. Postfire succession in Nevada and Natal could be influenced by exotic grasses from Central Asia and acacias from Australia. Fire's evolutionary future had to incorporate grazers from Europe and fertilizers from petrochemicals.

Industrialization profoundly reworked the geography of fire through its engineering of fire itself. Increasingly combustion depended on fossil fuels, long abstracted from the rhythms of free-burning fire, its emissions outside the mechanics of ecological scavenging. Always in the past, fire had depended on life, on the interaction with the oxygen and fuels that life generated, on the ecological fugue between fire and fuel forged over eons of evolutionary trials. While this symbiosis had made fire possible—even necessary—it had also restricted its dominion. In contrast, industrial combustion burned without regard to the living environment. It literally stood outside the ancient ecology of fire—and outside the traditional social mores that had guided fire use.

Industrialization's impact extended still further; its reach exceeded its grasp. It redefined what in nature was a resource and what was not, what land uses were appropriate and what were not, what regions were accessible and what weren't. It compelled a full-blown redefinition of nature, rank with new values and new perceptions, many derived from the rowdy efflorescence of a global scholarship, modern science, that accompanied and sought to explain European expansion. It set into motion a counter-reclamation that redefined the basis of European land use away from traditional agriculture. The revolution demanded not only new combustion technologies for furnace and forge but new fire practices for field and forest. Europe's intellectuals had achieved their agronomic goal. They had apparently transformed fire from an ecological process into a human tool.

Like planets orbiting binary suns, ecosystems now had to revolve around the gravitational field of industrial combustion as well as biomass burning. The interplay between the two became increasingly dense, inextricable, unpredictable, even contradictory. Industrialization could strip forests through logging and, equally, restore woodlands by abolishing the need for fuelwood. Industrial societies could subject the most remote site to exploitation, yet simultaneously propose special categories of wildland that were, by law, to remain untrammeled by human consumption. For these new landscapes new fire practices had to be invented, sanctioned by neither nature nor the precedent of human history. The upshot has been the most fundamental restructuring of anthropogenic fire and global fire regimes since the Neolithic.

Vestal fire

One outcome of this extraordinary expansion was that Europe established itself as a standard and censor of planetary fire. The fire practices of its industrial and agricultural heartland—Germany, northern France, the Low Countries, England—were accepted either as the norm or as the goal to which developing nations should aspire. Not incidentally, these nations were themselves among the important colonial powers, and they, unlike Spain and Portugal, distrusted free-burning fire and promulgated modern science. To a remarkable extent, fire practices and norms have flowed one way, from Europe outward. That trend continues, qualified by the emergence of North America as a fire power, although until recent decades North Americans also accepted the anomalous European fire scene as legitimate. It is perhaps no accident that current alarms over fire as an instrument of global change—with the implied condemnation of biomass burning—have emanated from Europe.

Global fire

The contemporary geography of Earth's fire is far from stable. Perhaps it never has been. Even where the rhythms of returning fires show some regularity, two idiographic tendencies have worked to upset any putative cycles. One is climate, and the other humanity. It is among the alarming trends of contemporary times that, through fire, climate and humanity have begun to interact in new ways.

Under the impress of industrial combustion, the ancient dialectic between hearth and holocaust has skewed. In the past decade, large wildfires have ravaged landscapes as diverse as Borneo and Canada, Australia and Manchuria. Fire has been implicated in world-ending scenarios, the fast burn of nuclear winter, and the slow burn of a greenhouse summer, the epoch-ending extinctions of the Cretaceous/Tertiary boundary fires. The public imagery of fire has become both vivid and confused, with conflagrations applauded at Yellowstone National Park and denounced in Amazonia. Nearly everywhere, free-burning fire is identified with global environmental havoc, a pilot flame to apocalypse. Again, it will be both cause and consequence; uncontrolled combustion may not only provoke global warming but result from it, in the form of wildfire, as boreal and temperate forests become colossal tinderboxes.

The transition from flame to furnace has demanded new indices by which to measure the new world order of fire. In particular, air has replaced humus as the ultimate yardstick of fire effects. The role soil served in indicating environmental health for agricultural societies the atmosphere has assumed for industrial states. Combustion will be distinguished as good or bad according to whether it aggravates or ameliorates the world's airsheds and, through them, planetary weather and climate. Fires for foraging and hunting must compare not only with fires for farming and herding but with those that power turbines and automobiles; the by-products of field and forest burning, with those from the burning of coal and oil. Even so, the

Earth remains a fire planet, and humans remain fire creatures. Neither can forsake fire and be what they are.

Contemporary pyrogeography

It is clear that the dominion of fire is changing with more than usual speed, and that it is pursuing pathways not sanctioned by evolutionary trial. This new pyrogeography takes many forms and is rewriting the registry of fire excesses and deficits. Where change is sudden, where new land use or misplaced fire practices introduce ignitions, upset fuels, or scramble the wild with the rural or urban, wildfires rage. While the particulars vary the outcome has been a global surge in uncontrolled burning—in Siberia; Indonesia; Amazonia; the Mediterranean littoral; and Oakland, California. Elsewhere, anthropogenic fire, once rare, has more or less permanently established itself like a naturalized weed. Still other landscapes—grasslands, brushlands, and forests—suffer from a deficiency of burning, a fire famine. After all, biodiversity can be lost as surely through fire exclusion as through fire excess. In the United States the best minds and most aggressive programs over the past two decades have sought to *restore* fire to wildlands.

But industrialization has gone further. Much as early hominids sought to replace the flame with the torch, and early agriculturalists sought to substitute domesticated burning for wild fire, so modernized societies have striven to replace wildland combustion with industrial combustion. The furnace supersedes the hearth; the power of fire engines, the power of torches. The critical landscapes are mechanical environments, literally within machines, and those portions of the atmosphere and biosphere that directly exchange gases with them. Combustion is no longer necessarily even associated with flame.

For fire history, modernization is associated with the liberation of fossil hydrocarbons. Other aspects of industrialization, whatever their social dimension, were secondary, because they still relied for fuel and fallow on existing biomass and were thus enmeshed in the ecological cycles of growth and decay. Their output was limited by their input. European agriculture, for example, was forever trying to close the circle between fertilizer and harvest (Mediterranean agriculture seemingly tried to square it). However much damage might be done, there was a sense in which it was self-limiting.

The exhumation of fossil hydrocarbons out of the geologic past transcended that closing cycle. Combustion (and the pyrotechnologies it supported) was no longer limited by biomass; landscape features that had previously existed to grow fuel—the woods and fallow—could now be put to other purposes. Here was biochemical bullion that could accelerate nature's economy. That it has also induced biotic inflation is also true. Its excess emissions could no longer be absorbed. Agricultural fallow was lost, and its fabled biodiversity with it, except where industrial created an alternative in nature reserves.

This substitution of fossil fuels and fossil fallow for biomass, however, has been incomplete and unsynchronized, and will likely remain so. Industrial combustion burns with savage indifference to fire ecology, without regard to time of day, season, climate, or biota. Because it depends on fossil fuels, there is no ecological feedback between fuel and fire, no biological linkage between combustion, nutrient cycles, or pathways of succession. The "fires" burn outside the parameters of natural ecosystems, often beyond the capabilities of organic scavenging and biochemical recapture. Instead of liberating nutrients, their by-products may overload or poison the environment. For industrial combustion, unlike wildland varieties, it is not sufficient that ecosystems be reshaped; they must be wholly reconstituted, complete with new pathways of energy; new cycles for biogeochemical compounds; new creatures; and, of course, new fire practices.

Those practices are far from established. Worse, they are challenging more traditional expressions—reforming the domain of anthropogenic fire, subjecting the Earth, particularly its atmosphere, to a combustion load in excess of what it can likely absorb—all this while operating outside the folkways that have traditionally guided anthropogenic fire. The new practices are rewriting the history of fire on Earth and redefining the special relationship between humans and fire. Humans are less keepers of the flame than custodians of the combustion chamber. This change, if it continues, has enormous ramifications for the natural world. The transition from torch to furnace has unsettled the fire geography of the planet, and this, in turn, has upset the moral geography of anthropogenic fire.

Over the millennia, anthropogenic fire mediated between human society and its natural environment. If it broke one regime, it fused another. Through a kind of ecological pyrolysis, it dissolved certain relationships among species, yet through an equally compelling process it had welded new ones. If fire segregated humanity from the natural world, it also bonded humans to the living world through the fuels they shared and the fire-powered dynamics it made possible. What it granted in power, anthropogenic fire demanded in responsibility. The new world order is breaking this legacy in fundamental ways. Industrial fire threatens to strangle agricultural fire, much as agricultural fire practices once weeded out aboriginal fire.

What may be lost is anthropogenic fire altogether. Contemporary primitivism typically denies anthropogenic fire a role in the management of parks, wilderness, and natural reserves. As a projection of human agency, such fires, so it is argued, represent an unwarranted and unbalancing intervention into the natural order that these sites seek to preserve. Equally, the magnitude of industrial combustion is forcing biomass burning to compete with fossil-fuel burning for limited airsheds. Taken together, these processes suggest that fire is unnecessary and undesirable. But while one pyrotechnology can substitute for another, it is more difficult to substitute one pyro-ecology for another. The ecology of fire within the built environment is not identical with that of the natural environment. Replacing a wood-burning stove with an electronic oven works within the home. Using bulldozers and herbicides instead of open flame does not work so cleanly in woods or prairies. Without an appropriate fire regime, the biodiversity of many sites may fail. Without controlled burning, many biotas will not store carbon but only stoke wildfires. In one form or another, combustion will persist, and humans will remain its keepers.

Trial by fire

The history of anthropogenic fire poses two fundamental questions for any assessment of global climate change: What is the quantitative history of fire on the planet? And what is the natural fire load? It is not obvious that there is more fire on Earth now than in the past. In fact, a good case can be made that there is not enough fire, or rather that there is a maldistribution of fire—too much of the wrong kind of combustion in the wrong kind of places, too little of the right kind of burning in the right places or at the right times. In particular, the competition between furnace and flame has thrown into confusion the combustion calculus of the Earth. Put differently, it is difficult to establish a baseline for burning.

How much combustion can the Earth absorb? What is the relationship between fire and combustion? How much industrial combustion can be added and how much wildland burning withdrawn without ecological damage? What, in brief, is an appropriate standard for anthropogenic fire, and can guidelines be found in Earth's fire history, or must humanity confront an existential Earth, silent as a sphinx? The longevity and pervasiveness of anthropogenic fire not only complicate the quest for a natural norm but may condemn it as metaphysically meaningless.

Nevertheless, norms of some kind are needed. Which fires are good and which are bad? What is the right proportion of fires? How much fire should be tolerated, or even promoted? Increasingly intellectuals are looking to the atmosphere to supply these standards, and to the threat of anthropogenic climate change as a means to furnish the moral and political arguments for reform. Air has replaced humus as the European measure of environmental health. It is not just that fire may be changing world climate, but that the climate of world opinion is compelling a change in our ancient relationship to fire.

In this emerging ecological credo, burning is bad because it releases greenhouse and other noxious gases either through outright combustion or through the destruction of vegetation, particularly forests, which are viewed as carbon vaults. Fire enthusiasts might argue that fire control, like gun control, misplaces the blame, that fires don't kill forests, people kill forests. But fire's medium is also its message. The means do make possible the ends. Extinguish anthropogenic fire, and the human impact on the Earth would be rapidly snuffed out.

Measured by critical emissions, biomass burning constitutes a significant fraction of global combustion. Some 8,680 million tons of dry matter burn yearly, which in turn release 3,500 million tons of carbon yearly, about 40 percent of the world's annual production of carbon dioxide. In the past, the domain of anthropogenic fire was almost certainly much larger. How was it that the Earth accommodated so much fire? How did it breathe when its Amazonian lungs ten thousand years ago were *cerrido,* a Gondwanic savanna congested with shrubs and grasses? How did it stockpile carbon when ice sheets blotted out the boreal forests? How can the atmosphere—itself given to extraordinary variations—become a standard of reference? Just which of the many climates experienced even during the past millennium is the norm? Surely excessive emissions are a kind of environmental debt, but it is not obvious how exactly overconsumption works in this model of nature's economy. It could be argued, plausibly, that anthropogenic fire has retarded—or may be necessary to retard—the advent of a new ice age, which is surely closer to the climatic norm in which *Homo sapiens* has had to live. The protest against global warming is a cry against changing the status quo.

Regardless, Europe's air pollution has become so serious that it can project that local deterioration across the globe, just as in centuries past it projected the reckless destruction of its soils. There are good causes for alarm over atmospheric abuse, but it would be tragic if global powers once again misapplied their ignorance and mistreated fire. European fire is an anomaly, not a norm. However humans try to manipulate the Earth's climate, fire management, not fire extinguishment, will be vital.

The attempted suppression of fire by Europe's colonial powers was an ecological disaster, though one often camouflaged because it accompanied other, equally damaging and more visible practices. The extinction of indigenous burning was often a critical prelude or catalyst to other extinctions. Today European-dominated policy stands to repeat that error if, once again, it categorically seeks to expunge fire from the landscape. Carbon cannot be sequestered like bullion; biologic preserves are not a kind of Fort Knox for carbon. Living systems store that carbon, and those terrestrial biotas demand a fire tithe. That tithe can be given voluntarily, or it will be extracted by force. There can be net changes in the Earth's fire load, but to speak of eliminating burning is not only quixotic but dangerous. Eliminate fire and you can build up, for a while, carbon stocks, but at probable damage to the ecosystem upon whose health the future regulation of carbon in the biosphere depends. Stockpile biomass carbon and you also stockpile fuel, the combustion equivalent of burying toxic waste. Cease controlled burning and, paradoxically, you may stoke ever larger conflagrations. Refuse to tend the domestic fire and the feral fire will return.

For millennia—in much of the Earth, for hundreds of millennia – humans have directed those obligatory fires. They have paid the fire tithe. Now the situation has blurred; the liberation of fossil fuels has changed the identity of *Homo sapiens* as a fire creature; new fire technologies have broken down the old order without yet installing a replacement. The issues involve more than just atmospheric pollutants and human-governed combustion; fire binds humans to the biosphere. There is a legitimate place for anthropogenic fire, and it must be defended against both those who seek to replace the flame with the furnace and those who wish to abolish the torch for the lightning bolt.

It remains a valuable intermediary with regard to humanity's relationship to both the atmosphere and the biosphere. The escalation of greenhouse gases is the outcome of industrial combustion burning fossil fuels. It burns in a different ecological context, for which biomass combustion can only partially compensate; air, not fuels, links them. The suppression of biomass burning cannot, except briefly, substitute for fossil-fuel burning. On the contrary, fire yields elemental carbon as one of its products, which is then stored in soils and constitutes almost the only long-term carbon sequestration available, the only means by which to return to mineral state something akin to the exhumation of geologic carbon. It could be argued, in fact, that more rather than less fire is necessary, at least in grasslands where the fuel cycle is annual rather than decadal.

The living world also argues for the preservation of fire. After all, fire is not exclusive to humans, and in fact it binds humans to a complicated biosphere for which hominids, as unique fire-keepers, enjoy a special niche and obligation. Much of the natural world that preservationists seek to protect coevolved with anthropogenic fire. To remove that fire regime can be catastrophic: replacing anthropogenic fire with lightning fire alone does not restore a former, prelapsarian era but more likely fashions an ecosystem that has never before existed. ·

These are special environments of course, a new order of sacred groves. Their practical dimensions may be small. But their symbolism is important, a kind of vestal fire for virgin lands. They testify that humans were intended to be the keepers of the flame, not its extinguishers; they insist on an active role for humans. To preserve and use fire is the oldest of humanity's ecological duties, its most distinctive trait as a biological organism, the first of its quests for power and knowledge, the genesis of its environmental ethics.

Fire is imprecise, and anthropogenic fire imperfect. In Plato's Allegory of the Cave he describes the human condition by imagining that humanity lives in a dark cave, divorced from the true light of the sun; we shackled humans can see and know only what we see in the fire or in the corrupt shadows cast by the fire. Yet without fire humans would be helpless and hopeless. It is through fire that we still know the world, and it is through fire that we can, and ought to, relate to that Great Other, Nature.

References

Barbour, Philip L., ed. 1986. *The Complete Works of Captain John Smith (1580–1631)*. 3 vols. Chapel Hill: University of North Carolina Press.

Bartlett, Harley H. 1955–61. *Fire in Relation to Primitive Agriculture and Grazing in the Tropics: Annotated Bibliography*. 3 vols. Ann Arbor: University of Michigan Botanical Gardens.

——. 1956. Fire, Primitive Agriculture, and Grazing in the Tropics. In *Man's Role in Changing the Face of the Earth*, edited by William L. Thomas Jr., Vol. 2. Chicago: University of Chicago Press.

Batchelder, Robert, and Howard Hirt. 1966. *Fire in Tropical Forests and Grasslands. Technical Report 67–41-ES*. Natick, Massachusetts: U.S. Army Natick Laboratories.

Clouser, Roger A. 1978. *Man's Intervention in the Post-Wisconsin Vegetational Succession of the Great Plains*. Occasional Paper No. 4, Department of Geography-Meteorology, University of Kansas, Lawrence.

Crosby, Alfred. 1987. *Ecological Imperialism. The Biological Expansion of Europe from 900 A.D.* Cambridge: Cambridge University Press.

DeBrahm, John Gerar William. 1971. *Report of the General Survey in the Southern District of North America*, ed. Louis De Vorsey Jr. Columbia: University of South Carolina Press.

diCastri, Francesco, and Harold Mooney, eds. 1973. *Mediterranean-type Ecosystems: Origin and Structure*. Heidelberg: Springer-Verlag.

diCastri, Francesco, David W. Gocciali, Raymond Specht, eds. 1981. *Mediterranean-type Shrublands*. Heidelberg: Springer-Verlag.

Hall, Martin. 1984. Man's Historical and Traditional Use of Fire in Southern Africa. In *Ecological Effects of Fire in South African Ecosystems*, edited by P. de V. Booysen and N. M. Tainton. Heidelberg: Springer-Verlag.

Hallam, Sylvia. 1979. *Fire and Hearth: A Study of Aboriginal Usage and European Usurpation in South-Western Australia*. Canberra: Australian Institute of Aboriginal-Studies.

——. 1985. The History of Aboriginal Firing. In *Fire Ecology and Management in Western Australian Ecosystems*, edited by Julian Ford. Perth: Western Australian Institute of Technology.

Harris, David R., ed. 1980. *Human Ecology in Savanna Environments*. New York: Academic Press.

Jack, R. L. 1881. *Report on Explorations on Cape York Peninsula, 1879–80*. Brisbane: Queensland Parliamentary Paper.

Jones, Rhys. 1969. Fire-Stick Farmers. *Australian Natural History* 16: 224–28.

——. 1975. The Neolithic, Palaeolithic and the Hunting Gardeners: Man and Land in the Antipodes. In *Quaternary Studies*, edited by R. P. Suggate and M. M. Cresswell. Wellington: Royal Society of New Zealand.

Komarek, E. V. 1967. Fire—and the Ecology of Man. In *Proceedings, Tall Timbers Fire Ecology Conference*. Vol. 6. Tallahassee, FL: Tall Timbers Research Station.

Lewis, Henry T. 1985. Burning the "Top End": Kangaroos and Cattle. In *Fire Ecology and Management in Western Australian Ecosystems,* edited by Julian Ford. Perth: Western Australian Institute of Technology.

Lewis, Henry T., and Theresa Ferguson. 1988. Yards, Corridors, and Mosaics: How to Burn a Boreal Forest. *Human Ecology* 16(1): 57–77.

Mitchell, T. L. 1969. *Journal of an Expedition into the Interior of Tropical Australia*. New York: Greenwood Press. Reprint of 1848 edition.

Nichols, Phillis H. 1981. Fire and the Australian Aborigine—an Enigma. In *Fire and the Australian Biota*, edited by A. M. Gill, R. H. Groves, I. R. Noble. Canberra: Australian Academy of Science.

Pyne, Stephen. 1982, 1988. *Fire in America: A Cultural History of Wildland and Rural Fire*. Princeton, NJ: Princeton University Press.

——. 1990. Fire Conservancy: The Origins of Wildland Fire Protection in British India, America, and Australia. In *Fire in the Tropical Biota*, edited by J. G. Goldammer. Berlin: Springer-Verlag.

——. 1990. Firestick History. *Journal of American History* 76: 1132–1141.

——. 1991. *Burning Bush*. New York: Henry Holt.

——. 1995. *World Fire: The Culture of Fire on Earth*. New York: Henry Holt.

Sauer, Carl. 1963. Fire and Early Man. In *Land and Life*, edited by John Leighly. Berkeley: University of California Press.

Schule, W. 1990. Landscape and Climate in Prehistory: Interactions of Wildlife, Man, and Fire. In *Fire in the Tropical Biota*, edited by J. G. Goldammer. Berlin: Springer-Verlag.

Stewart, Omer C. 1956. Fire as the First Great Force Employed by Man. In *Man's Role in Changing the Face of the Earth*, edited by William L. Thomas Jr. Vol. 1. Chicago: University of Chicago Press.

——. 1963. Barriers to Understanding the Influence of Use of Fire by Aborigines on Vegetation. In *Proceedings, Tall Timbers Fire Ecology Conference*. Vol. 2. Tallahassee, FL: Tall Timbers Research Station.

Tall Timbers Research Station. 1962–76. *Proceedings, Tall Timbers Fire Ecology Conference*. 15 vols. Tallahassee, FL: Tall Timbers Research Station.

6

RUBBER, BLIGHT, AND MOSQUITOES

Biogeography meets the global economy

Donald Kennedy and Marjorie Lucks

In 1984, a species of mosquito unknown to the entomologist who collected it was found breeding in several tire dumps around Houston, Texas. The specimens were sent to the U.S. National Museum, where Dr. Y.-M. Huang identified the newcomer as the Asian tiger mosquito (*Aedes albopictus*), a species common in Japan and Korea but not previously known to breed in the United States.[1] This discovery might well have passed without much notice, but two factors lent it significance: *A. albopictus* was a known vector for malaria, dengue fever, and several forms of encephalitis, and its range appeared to be expanding.

At about the same time, travelers who had spent time in regions of South America where the rubber tree (*Hevea brazihensis*) is endemic arrived at the airport in Kuala Lumpur, Malaysia, where they were subjected to extraordinary sanitary procedures, with some even required to undergo a period of quarantine. Malaysian authorities feared, with good reason, that these travelers might be unwitting carriers of spores from the South American leaf-blight fungus, a pathogen potentially capable of destroying the plantation rubber industry in Malaysia and in neighboring parts of Southeast Asia.

A long, complex skein of historical connection links these two events. It begins with a legendary nineteenth-century act of biological relocation for commercial purposes, popularly (and probably incorrectly) magnified into an exploit of stealth and derring-do. It includes the dramatic rise and fall of distant civic and regional economies, followed by desperate efforts to revive them. It is full of surprising and apparently accidental turns of events. What is especially remarkable about this chain of circumstance is the way in which two different dimensions of globalization – the movement of benign and harmful species, through human agency, to create a biological Pangaea, and the conversion of national economies into an interdependent worldwide nexus – link up to generate the unexpected.[2]

The role of global commerce in species translocation deserves more attention than it has received. The introduction of alien species appears to have been responsible for nearly half of all human-caused extinctions of American species, and the transport of pathogens and their vectors throughout history has resulted in unforeseen and devastating consequences for human health and for the structure of native ecosystems.[3] William McNeill beautifully summarized the early role of translocated disease-causing organisms in reshaping human history in *Plagues and Peoples.*[4] Ecosystem disruption has been less thoroughly studied, but there are dramatic examples from this century. The imported European chestnut blight rearranged the ecology of deciduous forests in the northeastern United States. In Africa, the arrival of the animal virus rinderpest in Asian cattle imported to feed Lord Kitchener's army devastated both wildebeest herds and native cattle, helping to transform the Serengheti Plain from grassland to savannah and creating new ecological opportunities for the tsetse fly, the vector for sleeping sickness and *nagana.*[5]

Even where alien organisms did not directly threaten human health, ecological mismatches created by new species in unfamiliar places could generate costly results.[6] The magnitude and extent of contemporary biogeographic reorganization is enormous. In San Francisco Bay, for example, 235 exotic species have now become firmly established.[7] Much of the invasion in this and other estuarine ecosystems is directly due to global commerce. Cargo ships from distant ports arrive and pump ballast water into the bay; with it comes whatever assemblage of marine organisms were originally taken aboard, and some of these survive and prosper in their new home. The invasive species problem received high-profile political recognition in February 1999, when President Clinton signed an executive order that created a high-level Invasive Species Council and added $29 million to the administration's fiscal year 2000 budget request to support quarantine and control efforts.

The extent of this phenomenon is due in substantial part to the internationalization of the economy and the resulting intensification of commercial traffic around the world. Nowhere are these complex connections more visible than in the history of rubber, a sequence of commercial transactions in which a plant and the organisms indirectly dependent on it are moved about with unexpected consequences. The story of rubber demonstrates how economic globalization leads to rearranged biogeography, and how these rearrangements in turn generate secondary economic consequences. It provides a historical cautionary tale worth heeding as we continue our global experiment in moving species from place to place.

Brazilian rubber

The rubber saga began in nineteenth-century Brazil and unfolded in parallel with a series of post-Industrial Revolution technological developments in Europe and the United States.

Natural rubber comes from trees belonging to two different genera. Castilla rubber, called *caucho,* came from Central America. Indians had collected latex from these trees, used it, and traded it, but it never amounted to much as an object of commerce. In the Amazon, however, rubber from tree species belonging to the genus *Hevea* became more useful once Portuguese colonialists called it to Europe's attention. By the late eighteenth century, items were being sent to the Brazilian port of Belem in Para, at the Amazon's mouth, for waterproofing. By 1840, Brazil was shipping half a million pairs of rubber boots abroad each year.[8]

A vastly greater demand for natural rubber eventually came from the rapidly expanding bicycle and automotive industries in the United States and Europe, following half a century of gradual innovation. Charles Goodyear discovered the "vulcanization" process in which rubber, sulfur, and white lead are heated together, and he patented it in 1844. Vulcanization allows rubber to remain flexible in cold temperatures and solid when it is warm, and it makes items impervious to water. Along with cold vulcanization, devised by Alexander Parkes, Goodyear's process enabled rubber to claim a place in many different manufacturing applications (e.g., gaskets, joints, electrical insulation, balloons, footwear, gloves, and medical supplies). In 1846, Robert William Thompson patented the inflatable tire tube; John Boyd Dunlop's later development of the pneumatic tire increased the comfort, speed, and safety of bicycles.[9] With the advent of the automobile, the rubber industry suddenly found a new economic niche, and the rapid expansion of that industry after the turn of the century carried the demand for rubber right along with it.[10]

But rubber still had to be collected the hard way, by workers engaged in a tedious and high-risk occupation. Typical of plant distributions in species-rich tropical rain forests, individuals of the most desirable rubber tree, *Hevea braziliensis,* are scattered thinly, often at densities as low as a few trees per hectare. Rubber tappers had to travel from tree to tree, making a series of lateral cuts in the bark to expose the channels in which the milky latex runs, then returning later to collect the exudate. Excessive heat and constant malaria exposure were regular hazards of the job.

Despite the inefficiency and difficulty of collection, the rubber industry was booming in Amazonia by 1900, and rubber exports had become a mainstay of the Brazilian economy. The trade in rubber grew gradually through the first fifteen years of the new century.[11] World production was sharply accelerated by growing demand from the automotive industry. Until 1910, wild rubber from Brazil held a monopoly, fueling a wild civic boom in the city of Manaus, eight hundred miles up the Amazon from Belem. The newly rich rubber barons, who relentlessly exploited native labor, much of it imported to Amazonia to work in the forest, lived lives of extravagant luxury. They imported European craftsmen to decorate and finish the famous (and recently restored) Manaus Opera House, which attracted international singing stars. It is claimed that they sent their laundry to Europe and were the highest per capita consumers of diamonds in the world.[12]

Asia takes over

Despite such opulence, the seeds for Manaus's demise as a jungle capital of culture had already been planted in tropical Asia. According to the popular account, those seeds found their way to Asia after being smuggled out of Brazil by a British explorer named Henry Wickham and shipped to Kew Gardens, where they arrived in 1876. They were subsequently grown to seedlings, then planted in Ceylon. The original seedlings, and other shipments made later, supplied the genetic stock that eventually enabled plantation rubber to develop on the Malay Peninsula and in other parts of Southeast Asia.

The real story is somewhat more complicated. Clements Markham, the India Office functionary who had been responsible for the earlier transfer of the cinchona plant to India from Peru, was ambitious to repeat the coup with rubber. The director of Kew Gardens, the noted botanist Sir Joseph Hooker, who was a close correspondent and mentor of Charles Darwin, had encouraged at least one earlier, failed effort to transfer the seeds.[13] Then Markham noted an account of Wickham's in which the seeds and leaves of *Hevea braziliensis* were depicted. Hooker was notified, and he told Wickham of his interest in obtaining viable seeds. After some delay the collecting began. A British ship, the *Amazonas,* had arrived at the port of Santarem, at the junction of the Amazon and Tapajos rivers, near where Wickham had collected his seed. Legend asserts that the vessel had lost its cargo by theft, and thus was providentially available for lading with Wickham, his family, and his seeds, and it credits Wickham with a clever act of smuggling. In fact, there is much doubt about why the vessel was available and whether any smuggling was involved at all. Brazil had no law against the export of rubber seeds, and custom regulations specified that products "destined for Cabinets of Natural History" would be dispatched without inspection on the sworn statement of the naturalist.[14]

Whether the departure of the seed-laden *Amazonas* was by stealth or not, the result was fatal for Brazil's monopoly on natural rubber. By 1910, while they were still feeding champagne to their horses in Manaus, stately rows of *Hevea* trees on the Malay Peninsula had reached productive maturity. The advantages of plantation agriculture were dramatic.

Trees could be tapped one after another without an arduous trek through the forest, and the product was concentrated in space, reducing labor costs. More importantly, the plantations made it possible to practice agricultural genetics on rubber for the first time; high-yielding trees could be selected and then propagated as clones. The influx of Asian rubber soon reduced the market price by over 95 percent, and it became evident that Brazilian natural rubber could not compete with the plantation product from Asia.[15] By the end of World War I, production in Asia had quintupled that of Brazil. Manaus was well on its way to being a ghost town, and the exploding tire industry in the United States and Europe was being supplied from halfway around the world.

Breaking the Asian monopoly

The decline of Brazilian rubber was not good news for U.S. industrialists, especially Henry Ford. By 1925, U.S. tire manufacturers were supplying most of the tires for the world's passenger automobiles, tires made from Asian rubber. Neither the monopoly price nor the political insecurity of Asia suited American automakers, so they sought to break the Asian grip on the market by establishing New World plantations. The most spectacular in a series of failed ventures was Fordlandia, a huge plantation established by Ford along the Tapajos River (ironically, quite near the source of Henry Wickham's seeds). By 1934, 1.5 million trees had been planted on over 7000 acres, but for reasons discussed below the entire crop failed. The project was moved elsewhere for a fresh start, then finally abandoned after yet another failure.[16]

Two efforts to establish rubber production in this hemisphere were undertaken during World War II, when all the sites of plantation rubber in Malaya and the Dutch East Indies were occupied by Japanese forces. One was a crash program to create synthetic rubber in the United States; combined with recycling efforts and use restrictions, it was successful enough to meet military needs and then to fulfill a substantial part of postwar consumer demand. The second was based on an extraordinary series of efforts that had begun well before the war to establish plantation agriculture in this hemisphere in the aftermath of the Ford disasters. A cooperative rubber research program was established by the U.S. Department of Agriculture that included stations in a number of countries, with the largest and most active at Turrialba, Costa Rica. The Department of Commerce created a special unit to send botanists into the field to locate high-yielding and resistant ecotypes of *Hevea braziliensis* and its relatives; the impression among these experts was that Wickham's Tapajos seeds were from decidedly inferior genetic stock. These hazardous expeditions yielded valuable material, much of it gathered by the distinguished Harvard botanist Richard Schultes. By the end of the war the rubber experiment stations were growing trees with complex grafts that produced resistant crowns atop high-yielding trunks.[17] The entire program was taken over by the State Department in 1952, and a year later it was terminated by order of Harold Stassen.[18]

Akron joins Manaus

The United States continued to dominate the international tire production market after the war, but in the 1960s the development of radial tires and the globalization of the personal transportation market wrought a dramatic change. Supplies of natural rubber became less expensive after World War II, temporarily stalling the growth of the synthetic rubber industry. Restrictions in natural rubber imports caused by the Korean War in the early 1950s, however, ensured a role for synthetics in tire manufacture; by then it was thought superior to natural rubber for treads, and the industry expanded greatly in the 1950s and 1960s. With three rubber alternatives available to the tire industry – natural, synthetic, and recycled – prices stabilized and uses diversified.[19]

Postwar economic prosperity and governmental road-building projects in the late 1950s and 1960s increased American affection for motorized travel. More people took driving vacations and commuted longer distances to work. Similar trends followed in Europe, Japan, and a number of newly industrializing countries, brightening the future of the automotive industry and the tire industry it supported. The tire industry, global almost since its advent, now increasingly imported supplies from Asia while shipping finished products from the United States and Europe. Although Japanese (Bridgestone, Firestone), French (Michelin), and German (Dunlop) companies were increasingly active, the U.S. industry, centered in Akron, Ohio, and led by Goodyear, still held a dominant position by the mid-1960s. Several events of the late 1960s and early 1970s, however, forced a shift in the industry away from U.S. manufacturers to Japanese and French firms.

Why did the U.S. lose its market share? Until the mid-1960s and early 1970s, the world market was dominated by the bias tire, in which cords that lie between tube and tread are oriented at an angle of 25 to 40 degrees with respect to the direction traveled. Although the radial tire (in which cords are oriented at 90 degrees to the direction traveled) was invented in 1913, construction was difficult and costs were high. Early in radial history, the advantages of improved wear and lowered fuel consumption were outweighed by the disadvantages of poorer cushioning and incompatibilities with many automobile suspension systems. As automobile design evolved, the attractiveness of radials grew, and by the 1960s several European companies were expanding their radial sales.[20]

Because American automotive companies were initially indifferent to the radial tire, U.S. tire firms chose not to make the expensive factory upgrades required in order to produce them. They compromised by offering a bias steel-belted tire, which reduced wear and met the demands of American automakers, who preferred them as original equipment on large passenger vehicles. That compromise deferred entry into the radial market, but soon American tire firms received an unpleasant surprise. In the early 1970s, several of the large automotive companies announced plans to equip some new cars with radial tires. Because the U.S. tire industry had not invested in this new technology, foreign firms reaped the benefits of this market shift.[21]

More adversity was in store for American tire manufacturers. The oil embargoes and cyclical recessions of the 1970s changed the preferences of American car purchasers from large, high fuel-consumption cars to smaller, more fuel-efficient vehicles. High gasoline prices, the 55-mile-per-hour speed limit, and a second oil crisis in 1979 tightened the hold of high performance, low wear, gasoline-saving radials on the global tire market. This advantage was expanded by the popularity of the new vehicles rolling off assembly lines in Japan, and the Japanese tire industry was benefitting both from its proximity to Asian centers of plantation rubber production and from the insistent favoritism shown by Japanese auto manufacturers toward domestically produced tires as original equipment.

These were not the only forces at work. Radial tires require much more natural rubber than do conventional tires because it is the only substance strong enough and flexible enough to serve as sidewalls. It is also the only substance safe enough to use on aircraft tires. Synthetic rubber's market share was further damaged by the high cost of petrochemical feedstocks during the oil-shock years. Acting together, all these trends increased the hold of natural rubber on the tire market and shifted manufacture away from America and toward Japan. In 1995, the U.S. was a net importer of tires, with a negative trade balance of about $1.5 billion; Japan was a net exporter, with a positive balance of about $2 billion. Akron, Ohio, the center of the U.S. tire industry, suddenly found itself headed down the same economic pathway that Manaus had followed half a century earlier.

Developing alongside the new tire market was another phenomenon: the international trade in what one clever salesman called "experienced tires." The global market for used tires is a large and vigorous one, expanding as their uses have multiplied. Acceptable wear regulations vary between countries, and so do consumer attitudes. The tire a Japanese businessman considers to be completely worn may be exported to another country and used for several more years. The U.S. generates one used tire per year for each American (242 million of them were scrapped in 1991 alone).[22] That would seem to leave little room for used-tire imports, yet the United States does import them, probably because of American driving habits. Americans are heavily car-dependent, have great enthusiasm for the open road, and often find themselves imprisoned in long stop-and-go commutes. As a result, they wear tires down so severely that no international market exists for them; indeed, 88 percent of each year's discards are destined for landfill or incineration. Americans do, however, like the more lightly worn used tires discarded by Japanese drivers. Between 1970 and 1985, the United States imported 15.2 million used tires. Increasingly, these tires have come from Japan and other northern Asian countries where the Asian tiger mosquito (*Aedes albopictus*) is indigenous.[23] The used-tire market provides yet another route of biological transport, this time involving hitchhiking rather than stealth, resulting in an invasion that could have significant public health consequences.

Tires as biological transportation

The globalization of the rubber economy was connected to biological translocation from its very beginning through the introduction of rubber seeds to Asia. Much later, the circuit between Asia and the New World was completed, again through the agency of rubber. Used Japanese tires served as the essential vessels through which a potentially dangerous insect vector was brought to the American hemisphere. American used-tire stockpiles provided ample breeding grounds for these insects, in addition to posing serious fire hazards and polluting waterways.

A simple demonstration illustrates how tires can be important in the reproductive biology of insects with aquatic larvae. One only needs to attempt to remove water from a tire casing that has been left outdoors in the rain. Turn the tire upside down and the water flows serenely inside the tire to the section that is now at the bottom. Turn it on its side and the water stays within. Roll the tire desperately, or shake it as hard as possible, and a few drops fly out. It is small wonder that in the yard or on the deck of a ship, tires retain water – the same water – for weeks and months.

It appears that *A. albopictus* was an increasingly frequent passenger in such tire casings, as changes in the international tire economy expanded the opportunity for hitchhiking. The 1983 or 1984 landing in the Houston area that resulted in the permanent establishment of the species was almost certainly not the first invasion. The Asian visitor was apparently introduced to the United States twice before, in tires returning from Asia after World War II and the Vietnam and Korean conflicts, but this civilian introduction was the first to establish permanent breeding populations. In the mid-1980s, the mosquito established its presence in the American South, spreading rapidly along major interstate highways and trucking routes while breeding in the many used-tire stockpiles in the area.[24]

Unlike its relative *Aedes aegypti,* the major carrier of malaria and dengue fever, *A. albopictus* is a temperate-zone mosquito. It can enter diapause in the egg stage, a resistant state that allows it to survive in climates where there is prolonged winter freezing. By 1997 it had established itself in over twenty states, including states as far north as New Jersey and Illinois. This spread was not due to migration, as *albopictus* is not capable of long-distance movements; instead, humans were the active agents of its distribution.[25]

These invasions into temperate North America caused serious concern for mosquito control officials; the Asian tiger mosquito was described by one American entomologist as a "promiscuous biter." But that is not their primary concern. *A. albopictus* also carries a number of epidemic viral diseases, including various equine encephalitis viruses and dengue fever, an infection that causes severe flu-like symptoms. Although it is most commonly found in infants and young children, adults are not immune from dengue, and the disease can be caused by four distinct viruses. Dengue hemorrhagic fever, a complication of dengue, has a fatality rate of between 5 and 15 percent if not treated, and no vaccine exists. Thus, the threat of dengue epidemics is managed primarily by vector control. Historically, major epidemics of dengue were rare, on the order of ten to forty years between events, and the disease was considered to be a nonfatal by-product of tropical travel. Since World War II, however, a resurgence of dengue has occurred throughout the tropics. The World Health Organization (WHO) currently estimates that fifty million new infections occur throughout the world each year.

Because a new strain of one dengue serotype was introduced in 1981, a significant epidemic reached the New World. Eradication of dengue's most common vector, *Aedes aegypti,* had been successful in Central and South America in the 1950s and 1960s, but efforts to control the insect had weakened after this initial success. By the time the new dengue strain arrived, *A. aegypti* populations had recovered.[26]

From 1977 to 1994, 2,248 suspected (481 confirmed) cases of imported dengue fever occurred in the United States, and many more in neighboring states in Central America. Between January and September 1995, more than 140,000 cases of dengue were reported to the WHO's regional office for the Americas.[27] Diagnosis of dengue, even in its acute hemorrhagic form, is difficult; most physicians have had little experience with it. Thus it is likely that the number of cases is underreported.

Is *albopictus* a good candidate vector for dengue? It has many of the right qualities: aggressive biter, known carrier of the virus (at least in laboratory trials), and capable of extending its range in the United States far beyond that of *aegypti*. This potential caused great concern among public health experts; in the late 1980s, the U.S. Centers for Disease Control and Prevention (CDC) initiated a massive inspection and fumigation program for imported used tires. In 1988, provisions were added to the Public Health Service Act requiring that all used-tire casings from Asia be certified as insect-free, but such measures were already too late to be effective.[28] The CDC now believes that the program for monitoring compliance with this provision should be abandoned.[29]

To date, no dengue cases in the U.S. have been traced to *albopictus;* the likely vector has been assumed to be *aegypti,* and so far all of the cases have occurred within the known range of *aegypti.* Moreover, no *albopictus* individuals captured in the U.S. have been found to harbor dengue virus. Indeed, some epidemiologists believe that *albopictus* may be a blessing in disguise: it is able to out-compete *aegypti* over much of the latter's range, and it is less prevalent in and around houses. If it is therefore less effective because it is less likely to bite several humans in a row, thus transferring the virus, its presence might actually provide a benefit by replacing *aegypti.*[30] Nevertheless, reason for worry continues to abound. The newcomer is an efficient vector, able to load virus from an infected host at lower levels of viremia than *aegypti.* Although aspects of the history are somewhat reassuring, a dangerous combination of factors remains: a bad virus accompanied by a potential vector that can extend its reach into new and densely populated areas.

The next phase

A. albopictus is not the only potentially dangerous species with a relationship to rubber. The South American leaf-blight fungus (*Microcyclus ulei*), the organism that devastated the Fordlandia plantations seventy-five years ago, is still a pathogen for which a control strategy other than quarantine has yet to be devised.[31] Indigenous to the Amazonian rain forest (although epidemics seem not to occur there), this fungus attacks new, young leaves on developing crowns. In the forest, widely scattered trees reach maturity at different times. Partly because the trees are spaced so widely apart, and partly because only a fraction of the trees are at a vulnerable stage, infections do not reach epidemic proportions. On plantations, by contrast, the trees are even-aged, and their arrangement in closely spaced rows greatly improves the conditions for transmission.

Why the blight fungus did not accompany Wickham's seeds to Kew is not clear. He may have been fortunate in his choice of a place to collect seeds; more likely, the spores did not survive the long sea voyage from Brazil to England. For whatever reason, the plantations that developed, first in Ceylon and India and then in Malaysia and Indonesia, were free of blight. During subsequent years, the selection process – in which clones were chosen for their rubber yield and growth rates – almost certainly increased vulnerability to infection. Whenever a rigorous selection regime is practiced for some particular character, other aspects of the phenotype are likely to be affected, even if very slightly. That supposition is strengthened by the experience of the Fordlandia fiasco: some of the trees planted there had come from Asian plantations, and these were among the first to be struck by the blight.[32]

Thus, good reason exists for rubber production ministries and plantation managers in Asia to fear the prospect of yet another alien introduction, one that could destroy the earlier one. The impact of a leaf-blight epidemic on the economy of Malaysia and other Southeast Asian countries would almost certainly be devastating; for this reason, a period of quarantine is required for scientific travelers who have been working with native rubber in South America. This safety net has also been extended to aircraft. Travelers arriving in Malaysia from any country where the leaf-blight fungus is endemic are required to walk on a special surface soaked with fungicide, to pass through a tunnel with filtered air and negative pressure, and to have all their baggage subjected to forty-five minutes of irradiation with ultraviolet light.[33]

Because there is little protection against deliberate mischief, quarantines and landing restrictions provide only limited security. The value of plantation rubber to several Southeast Asian economies is enormous, making dependent nations potentially vulnerable to extortion. A determined agroterrorist could, at least in theory, mount a credible threat against an entire regional economy, with consequences not only for that region but for an international array of dependent industries. The research program that began during World War II to develop strains resistant to leaf blight was making real progress that could have made plantation rubber in the Western Hemisphere a reality. Its cancellation removed the possibility of a worldwide hedge against this next and possibly catastrophic stage in biogeographic rearrangements linked to rubber.

Conclusion

Ecologists and conservation biologists have devoted a good deal of attention to the introduction of alien species by human agency. Such introductions have, by some estimates, accounted for nearly half of the species extinctions recorded during this century, and at earlier times in human history they have profoundly influenced agriculture, industry, and the prevalence of disease.

Sometimes these transfers are deliberate, as in the stocking of exotic game fish for recreation or the introduction of new agricultural crops. More often they are accidental, with invaders arriving as passengers on human conveyances, or in the case of microorganisms, on human bodies. The long and complicated history of rubber and its fellow travelers illustrates how pervasive and how unpredictable such introductions can be. It also demonstrates how dependent such transfers are on the globalization of human economic arrangements. The introduction of *Aedes albopictus* in the United States could not have happened without a long sequence of events, beginning with the international demand for rubber and the translocation of its production, continuing with a series of technology developments and economic decisions made in Japan and the United States, and ending with the globalization of the used-tire economy. Nor could there be a contemporary threat to a worldwide industry had not rubber been transported to an exotic land and cultivated in the absence of the selection pressures that shaped its evolution on indigenous soil.

The rubber tree, the Asian tiger mosquito, and the South American leaf-blight fungus are unlikely candidates for companionship in a single eco-system, but humans have created one for them that extends from the Amazonian rain forest to the rubber plantations of Malaysia, the tire factories of Japan, and the salt marshes of New Jersey. It is the remarkable result of early exploration, adventurous entrepreneurship, and modern technology. Most importantly, it has been made possible by the forces of economic globalization.

Like so many human achievements, the elaboration of this biological-industrial ecosystem has had an unexpected and threatening result. Human disease in North America and economically devastating plant disease in Southeast Asia are both prospects that now require regulatory vigilance and scientific investment on both sides of the Pacific. Events of this sort have raised profound policy questions for nations at risk from particular pathogens. Phytosanitary protections exist in almost all countries; in the United States, for example, the Animal and Plant Health Inspection Service of the Department of Agriculture is responsible for guarding against the importation of pathogens through infected organisms or produce. These controls, however, offer no protection against the unexpected. Ballast-pumping is virtually uncontrolled, and seeds, microorganisms, and larval stages of animals move about freely when contained in innocent-looking media. Although the United States is considering regulations governing the importation of nonindigenous species, these would likely control only the most obvious and deliberate introductions.

As commerce intensifies, inspection regimes and other control measures are likely to become even less effective – even as more of them are needed – due to political backlashes. One can only imagine, for example, the public reaction if passengers arriving at O'Hare Airport in Chicago were required to undergo the decontamination routine imposed in Kuala Lumpur. Thus, it is difficult to be optimistic about our biogeographic future. As the history of rubber suggests, global shrinkage – economic as well as biological – provides one lesson after another about the Law of Unforeseen Consequences.

Notes

The authors acknowledge the generous support of the Goldman Program and Peter Bing, and thank Max Edleson for his capable assistance.
1 Daniel Sprenger and Taweesak Wuithiranyagool, "The Discovery and Distribution of *Aedes albopictus* in Harris County, Texas," *Journal of the American Mosquito Control Association* 3 (1986): 217–19.
2 The metaphor that transcontinental introduction of alien species knits up the seams now separating the continents that once belonged to Pangaea was

introduced by Alfred Crosby in *Ecological Imperialism: The Biological Expansion of Europe, 900–1900,* Studies in Environment and History (Cambridge: Cambridge University Press, 1993).

3 See, for example David Wilcove et al., "Quantifying Threats to Imperiled Species in the United States," *BioScience* 48 (August 1998): 607–15.

4 William McNeill, *Plagues and Peoples* (New York: Anchor-Doubleday, 1976).

5 *Serengheti II: Dynamics, Management and Conservation of an Ecosystem,* ed. A. R. E. Sinclair and P. Arcese (Chicago: University of Chicago Press, 1995), chap. 5.

6 For an overview of the introduced species problem, see Daniel Simberloff, "Impact of Introduced Species in the United States," *Consequences* 2 (1996): 13–22.

7 Andrew N. Cohen and James T. Carlton, "Accelerating Invasion Rate in a Highly Invaded Estuary," *Science* 279 (1998): 555–58.

8 Warren Dean, *Brazil and the Struggle for Rubber: A Study in Environmental History* (New York: Cambridge University Press, 1987), 9.

9 Michael J. French, *The U.S. Tire Industry* (Boston: Twayne Publishers, 1990), 2.

10 Ibid., chs. 1 and 2.

11 The contribution of African rubber to the world rubber total was small; cultivated rubber came predominantly from Malaysia, Ceylon, and other southeast Asian countries. See J. H. Drabble, *Rubber in Malaya, 1876–1922* (New York: Oxford University Press, 1973).

12 For colorful accounts of this history, see Wade Davis, *One River: Explorations and Discoveries in the Amazon Rain Forest* (New York: Simon and Schuster, 1990), and Dean, *Brazil and the Struggle for Rubber.*

13 It was Joseph Hooker (along with the geologist Charles Lyell) to whom Darwin wrote in 1857 after receiving a manuscript from Alfred Russel Wallace (ironically a pioneer Amazon explorer himself) in which Wallace presented a theory of evolution by natural selection. Hooker and Lyell then negotiated a resolution of the priority issue by arranging for a joint communication that preceded the publication of Darwin's *Origin of Species.* Seeds did not often survive the long voyage from the Amazon to London, which took approximately two months. Even if they did not rot and ferment in transit, which could take as little as two weeks, they often did not germinate upon receipt. In at least one case, there was no one at the India Office (Wickham's employer and the seed-requesting agency) to accept the seeds upon delivery, so they sat for over a week in London before arriving at Kew Gardens. For a thorough account of the events surrounding both this shipment and previous attempts, see Dean, *Brazil and the Struggle for Rubber,* 11–16.

14 Dean, *Brazil and the Struggle for Rubber,* 19.

15 Bradford L. Barnham and Oliver T. Coomes, *Prosperity's Promise: The Amazon Rubber Boom and Distorted Economic Development* (New York: Oxford University Press, 1996), 2.

16 Wade Davis, "The Rubber Industry's Biological Nightmare," *Fortune,* 4 August 1997, 86–98.

17 R. D. Rands and Loren G. Polhemus, *Progress Report on the Cooperative Hevea Rubber Development Program in Latin America,* Circular No. 976 (Washington, D.C.: U.S. Department of Agriculture, 1955).

18 For an engaging and scathing review of these events, see Davis, *One River,* 330–71.

19 French, *U.S. Tire Industry,* 87–90.

20 Ibid., 100–101.

21 Ibid., 110–11.

22 U.S. Environmental Protection Agency, *Solid Waste and Emergency Response: Summary of Markets for Scrap Tires,* EP 1.17: 530-SW-90-074 A (Washington, D.C.: U.S. Environmental Protection Agency, 1991).

23 William A. Hawley et al., "*Aedes albopictus* in North America: Probable Introduction in Tires from Northern Asia," *Science* 239 (1987): 1114–15.

24 R. B. Craven et al., "Importation of *Aedes albopictus* and Other Exotic Mosquito Species into the United States in Used Tires from Asia," *Journal of the American Mosquito Control Association* 4 (1988): 138–42.

25 Paul Reiter and Daniel Sprenger, "The Used Tire Trade: A Mechanism for the Worldwide Dispersal of Container-Breeding Mosquitoes," *Journal of the American Mosquito Control Association* 3 (1987): 494–501.

26 The most current information on dengue distribution is available in *Dengue/ Dengue Hemorrhagic Fever: The Emergence of a Global Health Problem,* Centers for Disease Control EID 1, April–June 1998, and at Center for Disease Control website: http://www.healthmap.org/dengue/index.php.

27 World Health Organization Press Release, WHO 72, 1995.

28 See Charles G. Moore et al., "*Aedes albopictus* in the United States: Rapid Spread of Potential Disease Vector," *Journal of the American Mosquito Control Association* 4 (1988): 356–61.

29 C. G. Moore and C. J. Mitchell, "*Aedes albopictus* in the United States: Ten-Year Movement and Public Health Importance," *Emerging Infectious Diseases* 3 (1997): 329–34.

30 The argument goes as follows: *albopictus* prefers to live outside rather than inside, thus it is an ineffective epidemic vector because it is unlikely to bite several humans in a row. This view is reinforced by the distribution of dengue in Asia, where epidemics correlate with the presence of *aegypti* and not *albopictus*. J. Gubler, CDC, Fort Collins, Colo., personal communication with the authors, 1998.

31 A useful summary of *Microcyclus* biology and attempts at control may be found in W. Bettiol, "Biological Control of Plant Pathogens in Brazil: Applications and Current Research," *World Journal of Microbiology and Biotechnology* 12 (1996): 505–10.

32 Davis, *One River,* 339.

33 Ayob Zulkifli, Director of Crop Protection and Plant Quarantine, Department of Agriculture, Malaysia, to Donald Kennedy and Marjorie Lucks, 4 September 1998.

7

ANIMAL PLANET

Harriet Ritvo

It is hard to count the ways in which other animals figure in the stories that environmental historians tell.[1] They are part of our epic tales – those with the longest chronological reach – about the movements of early hunters and gatherers. They are part of the grand narrative of domestication and the transformation of human existence through agriculture. They often have represented nature (however nature has been understood) in religious and scientific thought. Animals also play a large role in our novellas – that is, accounts of distinctively modern concerns (or distinctively modern variations on these age-old themes), such as species loss through habitat destruction, the simplification of ecosystems through monoculture and invasion, and the modification of organisms by means of biotechnology. Their ubiquitous presence has helped establish the city and the suburb as appropriate settings for environmental history. None of these stories – long or short – has yet come to a definitive conclusion: Certainly, at least from the perspective of the animals themselves, no happy endings are in sight. That may be one reason that animals have been appearing with increasing frequency in the work of environmental historians and of scholars in related disciplines. Another may be that many of the difficult issues at the intersection of academic studies of the environment (historical or otherwise) and environmental politics have an animal dimension, or even an animal-triggered flashpoint: preservation of threatened ecosystems, overexploitation of resources such as fisheries, emergent diseases, and cloning, to name a few.

Environmental historians are not alone in their heightened interest in animals, nor is scholarly attention to animals completely new. Livestock traditionally has attracted the attention of economic historians who focus on agriculture. Important animal-related institutions, from humane societies to zoos, have had their chroniclers. The history of zoology is a well-established branch of the history of science, most conspicuously in relation to the development of evolutionary ideas. People distinguished in their association with animals, whether as breeders or hunters or scientists, have had their biographers, as, indeed, have some animals distinguished in their own right – from Jumbo to Seabiscuit. Historians have investigated the moral and legal rights and responsibilities of animals, as well as animal-related practices, such as vivisection.[2]

Nevertheless during the last several decades, the attitude of historians in general toward the study of animals has shifted significantly: To put it briefly, animals have been edging toward the mainstream. No longer is the mention of an animal-related research topic likely to provoke surprise and amusement, as was the case twenty years ago. There is now enough new work and enough interest in reading it to support a book series on the theme of "Animals, History, Culture," published by the Johns Hopkins University Press, and a series of annual edited volumes, the *Colloques d'histoire des connaissances zoologiques,* published at the University of Liège in Belgium. There are several ways to understand this shift. Animals can be seen as the latest beneficiaries of a democratizing tendency within historical studies. As the labor movement, the civil rights movement, and the women's movement inspired sympathetic scholars, so have, in their turn, the advocates of hunted whales, poached tigers, abandoned dogs, and overcrowded pigs. Even in fields like agricultural history, where animal topics have been routine, farmyard creatures have become less likely to be abstracted through quantification, and more likely to appear as individuals, or at least groups of individuals. Straws in this wind include Susan D. Jones's recent study of veterinary treatment of livestock and horses, and the conference on "The Chicken: Its Biological, Social, Cultural, and Industrial History, from the Neolithic Middens to McNuggets," sponsored in 2002 by the Yale Program in Agrarian Studies.[3] In addition, of course, the vigorous growth of environmental history has helped direct the attention of other kinds of historians toward animals.

At least in the United States, environmental history originally developed from the history of the frontier. The field has moved away from these pioneer beginnings, both geographically and theoretically, as is perhaps most clearly indicated by the gradual problematization of the concept of wilderness. But concern with the relation between the sphere of human domination and what lies (or seems to lie) outside remains strong. This concern often has been mediated through the study of the relationship between people and wild animals, a focus that links modern ways of living with those of our earliest ancestors. The longest story ever told – at least the longest one with people as characters – chronicles the development of human cultures and societies. It exists in numerous variants, depending, among other things, on whether the story is limited to *Homo sapiens,* or whether it includes extinct congeners like *H. neanderthalensis* and *H. habilis,* or stretches still further back to the australopithecines, or moves laterally to embrace our living pongid cousins. All versions agree, however, on the importance of predation. Even if, as with the chimpanzees studied by Jane Goodall, hunting was a relatively infrequent activity, and meat an occasional dietary supplement rather than a dependable source of calories, the skill and cooperation required to kill small and medium-sized game provided significant social and intellectual stimulation.[4] In most pre-agricultural human groups, hunting was more routine and more important. The archaeological record suggests that small nomadic groups also had to worry about becoming the objects of other creatures' hunts, which doubtless served in a complementary way to sharpen wits and enhance cooperation.[5]

In addition, hunting provides the earliest example of the disproportionate human power to affect the rest of the environment. Even though prehistoric human populations were relatively small, they may have had a significant impact on the large herbivores who provided the most rewarding and challenging objectives and, secondarily, on the large carnivores who also ate them. It frequently has been argued, most conspicuously by the biologist Edward O. Wilson, that the spread of modern humans outside their African homeland caused the rapid decline and, in many cases, the extinction of large animal species (and even genera) along their paths of migration.[6] Certainly the coincidence between the arrival of *H. sapiens* in Australia, North America, and South America and the subsequent impoverishment of their indigenous megafauna is very suggestive, especially as these continents, in contrast to Eurasia – where the impact of modern humans appears to have been less dramatic – had not been inhabited by earlier hominid species. This account has always been controversial, however, for several reasons. Inevitably, evidence is sparse and the argument relies heavily on inference. To acknowledge that small pre-agricultural human groups could have such an overwhelming impact on large animal species is to acknowledge that there was never any period or state of human society that existed in a completely harmonious or static relation to the rest of the environment – literally or metaphorically, no garden of Eden. Reluctance to relinquish this notion accounts for some of the emotion provoked by Shepard Krech's suggestion that PaleoIndians bore some responsibility for the Pleistocene extinctions in North America.[7] There are possible alternative explanations, of which the most prominent is that the same climatic changes that encouraged human migration, especially into the Americas, also altered the habitats to which the enormous Pleistocene animals had adapted. From this perspective, the cold-adapted fauna ultimately was displaced by competitors better-suited to a more temperate climate.[8] It is probably an indication of the enduring fascination of these animals, even to people with no opportunity or desire to hunt them, that the cause of their extinction has inspired learned and popular debate since their rediscovery in the nineteenth century.[9]

In many respects, the activities of modern hunters resemble those of their earliest forebears. In an overview of hunting from the Pleistocene to the present, Matt Cartmill has shown how, nevertheless, those activities have altered or been contested, along with shifting understandings of nature. The hunter has figured variously as heroic provider, as protector of threatened outposts, as sensitive intermediary between the human and the divine prey, as gallant sportsman, as brutal butcher, and as agent of extinction.[10] The last two epithets are the most recent, and they have become increasingly prominent in the course of the last century or so. This is not to suggest that no animal species had been eliminated between the Pleistocene and the late nineteenth century, at least on a local basis. In Britain, for example, the wolf, the bear, the wild boar, and the beaver disappeared as a result of the activities of medieval hunters, and, with the possible exception of the beaver, they were not regretted. On the contrary, their absence was greatly appreciated. The last aurochs, the wild bovines from which domesticated cattle are descended, died in Poland in the seventeenth century, not long before the last dodos were killed on Mauritius. Their passing engaged the interest of naturalists and antiquaries, but it was not until the great imperial expansion of the eighteenth and nineteenth centuries that the diminution and disappearance of animal populations began to arouse concern.

Commercial interests raised the first real alarm. Overexploitation radically reduced the productivity of the North American fur trade from the middle of the eighteenth century, when the annual harvest of Canadian beaver skins was over 150,000, to the early nineteenth century, when a territory four times as large provided one-third the yield.[11] Naturalists and hunters (often the same people wearing different hats) corroborated this worrisome sense that even substantial animal populations might not be indefinitely resilient. Visitors to the Cape Colony at the southern tip of Africa observed that neither naturalists nor hunters could find much to amuse them, and that one species of antelope, the blaubok, had been killed off completely; similar complaints were made with regard to the parts of India most accessible to colonial sportsmen. Extinction even of more numerous species was ultimately recognized as a real possibility (a recognition that was inconsistent with some versions of creationist theology, although not so troublesomely inconsistent as evolution proved to be). As formerly blank spaces on the map were filled in, the sparseness or complete absence of wild animals from areas where they had formerly been abundant no longer could be explained as their retreat to the unknown interior. Response to these dawning perceptions was mixed. Like Theodore Roosevelt several generations later, many enthusiastic sportsmen accepted the diminution of game as part of the march of progress. Throughout the nineteenth century, authorities in many parts of the world subsidized the extermination of wild animals perceived as threats to or economic competitors with farmers and their livestock.[12]

The near disappearance of the vast North American bison herds in the middle of the nineteenth century, followed by the actual disappearance of the quagga, a close relative of the zebra, from southern and eastern Africa, began to convert perception into action. Still symbolic of uncivilized nature, wild game was transformed from an obstacle into a valuable resource in need of protection. Yellowstone National Park was founded in 1872 to protect the remaining animals; for several decades the success of this endeavor remained in doubt.[13] Yellowstone and the many reserves and national parks that followed it represented a novel twist on an old idea. Restricted game parks had a long history in Europe and in parts of Asia where their purpose had been at least as much to defend the exclusiveness of hunting as to preserve the animal targets. This spirit permeated the preservation laws that were enacted by many British colonies in Africa and Asia in the late nineteenth and early twentieth centuries. They often specified differential access, quotas, and licensing fees, clearly privileging colonial officials and visiting dignitaries over both indigenous inhabitants and humble European settlers. They also discriminated among animal species, so that large carnivores were excluded from the protective umbrella; indeed their slaughter was often encouraged with bounties. This complex of motives and goals was embodied in the "Conventions for the Preservation of Wild Animals, Birds, and Fish in Africa," which was signed in London in 1900 by representatives of various European governments with colonial holdings, although most of them subsequently failed to ratify it or to honor its provisions. The Society for the Preservation of the Wild Fauna of the Empire, founded in 1903 by a distinguished group of sportsmen and colonial administrators, proved more durable, although (or perhaps because) its membership encompassed strongly conflicting viewpoints. By the time of the society's diamond anniversary, the authors of its official history characterized these early members as "penitent butchers."[14]

Efforts to protect wild animal populations have continued to provoke conflict, both internal and external. Some early campaigners for wild bird preservation wore elaborate feather hats, and so opened themselves to criticism as hypocrites (by the unconvinced) or as dilettantes (by their more rigorously logical coadjutors).[15] Poaching was an issue when game was protected only for the entertainment of elite hunters, and it continued to be an issue after the animals also became intended beneficiaries.[16] Nor was the need for wild animal protection universally acknowledged. In many places, competing human interests, alternative sources of information, and inconsistent official motivations meant that protections were not enforced or even enacted until targeted populations were severely reduced or entirely gone. Thus the last thylacine (also known as the Tasmanian tiger and the marsupial wolf) died in a zoo in 1936. Legal protection for its species in Tasmania was enacted just fifty-nine days before it expired (thylacines had been hunted to extinction on the Australian mainland long before any Europeans set foot there). Subsequently the thylacine has been the object of a great deal of apparently heartfelt but inevitably impotent regret.[17] The fate of the tiger in Indonesia and Malaysia depended on the opinions of a variety of colonized and colonizing groups, possibly in addition, Peter Boomgaard gently suggests, to those of the tigers themselves.[18] And individuals always could change their minds – or be of several minds. In *Man-Eaters of Kumaon,* Jim Corbett chronicled his triumphs over numerous lethal tigers, mostly in the classic colonialist mode: That is, claiming to protect Indian villagers who could not defend themselves. By the time of its original publication during World War II, he had become an ardent conservationist (a national park in the Himalayan foothills was named in his honor after he died – in 1973, Project Tiger, which aims to save the tiger from extinction, was founded there), yet he wrote for a public that thrilled to the chase and the kill.[19] Very recent history offers many more examples of competing human claims to the resources represented by wild animals. *Eating Apes* by Dale Peterson explores one of the most extreme and problematic cases.[20]

If hunting represents the primeval relationship between humans and the rest of the animal kingdom, then domestication represents the most transformative one, from the perspectives of both the domesticators and the domesticatees. With the possible single exception of the dog, which may have been part of human social groups long before people began to settle down, animals were domesticated in conjunction with the development of agriculture. The period when domesticated dogs first appeared and the means by which wolves became dogs are highly controversial. Raymond Coppinger and Lorna Coppinger argue strongly that dog domestication was an indirect product of early agriculture – that is, that dogs who were inclined to scavenge in village waste sites domesticated themselves, much as cats inclined to hunt in rodent-infested grain stores did several thousand years later. Other zoologists prefer explanations that emphasize the human penchant for adopting wild pets and the similar hunting practices of humans and canids.[21] But cattle, sheep, goats, pigs, horses, donkeys, camels, and llamas all were domesticated by agriculturalists or proto-agriculturalists. It is a commonplace of the most sweeping environmental histories that, although domesticated animals were not essential to the development of agriculture, they made a tremendous difference. They supplemented human labor, enhanced transportation, and provided skins and fiber, as well as meat and milk (and selective pressure in favor of the evolution of adult lactose tolerance in some human groups).[22] They have often been identified by contemporary historians as the reason for the competitive success of societies ultimately derived from ancient southwest Asia, especially in comparison with the indigenous societies of the Americas and Oceania. In the nineteenth century, racialist thinkers sometimes read this comparison in reverse, and used the absence of domesticated animals or even the failure to domesticate a particular kind of animal, as a way of denigrating human groups. Africans, for example, were criticized for not taming the elephant, which had proved so valuable in Asia.

Like most aspects of what is normally celebrated as progress, the domestication of animals had a downside, although the connection was not recognized until much later. Archaeological evidence suggests that small nomadic groups were relatively untroubled by the contagious diseases that repeatedly have decimated most settled communities. The size and the mobility of these groups had contributed to this happy situation, and both these attributes altered as people settled down to farm. Increased population meant larger reservoirs for disease and fixed residences meant permanent proximity to waste, whether disposed of in middens or in nearby watercourses. If people had domesticated only plants, these changes would only have exposed them more intensively to disease organisms that they already harbored. But the domestication of wild ungulates – animals which, though mobile, lived in groups large enough to incubate contagions – brought people into contact with a new set of diseases. Such human diseases as smallpox and measles – and diseases of other domestic animals, such as cat and dog distemper – resulted from contact with viruses that originally caused livestock diseases.[23] Over the millennia, it has been theorized by environmental historians, all but the most isolated old world populations became accustomed to these diseases. Their social impact was minimized through childhood exposure and their individual impact was possibly reduced through maternally transmitted or inherited resistance.[24] But the human inhabitants of the Americas, who had left northeast Asia before the domestication of herds or flocks, had not enjoyed this protracted opportunity to adapt to the microbial cocktail to which European adventurers began to expose them in the late fifteenth century.[25] Most environmental historians of the contact have concluded that this exposure caused the dramatic drop in indigenous populations throughout the Americas in the ensuing centuries, although David Jones has recently suggested that social factors should be weighted more heavily.[26]

Of course epidemic disease was not the only effect that old world animals had on new world people. More direct, or at least more obvious, was the impact of the animals themselves, many of which escaped and multiplied vigorously in favorable habitats throughout the Americas. Elinor Melville characterizes such enthusiastic adaptations as ungulate irruptions. Unlike that of contagions, their impact was mixed. As they had done in Europe, Asia and North Africa, these animals provided food, power, and transportation to indigenous people as well as to colonists, while also subjecting some fragile environments to unsustainable strains.[27]

Although vaccines against most of these ancient scourges had been developed by the late twentieth century, and it had even become possible to contemplate the absolute extinction of a few of them, human epidemiological vulnerability to our vast dense populations of meat animals is not a thing of the past. Influenza returns each year, slightly reengineered in southeast Asia – probably a product of the mode of farming practiced there, in which people, chickens, pigs, and wild fowl live in sufficient proximity for their flu viruses to trade genetic material. Epidemiologists watched the avian flu that decimated flocks of chickens in the winter of 2003–4 with apprehension based only partly on fear of its economic impact on the poultry industry and on the few cases in which it spread (lethally) to people. They realized that the virus that caused the influenza pandemic of 1918 was derived from a different bird virus that developed the ability to infect mammals; possibly its avian origins made it more difficult for people to resist. Nor do animals need to be domesticated to transmit zoonotic disease, although when wild animals play this role, they usually have been incorporated into human economy if not human society. Thus SARS (severe acute respiratory syndrome), which shut down travel to east Asia and to Toronto in 2003, apparently has been traced to civets, as AIDS has been traced to non-human African primates (both chimpanzees and monkeys). In each case, the attribution of responsibility has a blame-the-victim aspect.

The most compelling recent episode of zoonotic transmission is mad cow disease or BSE (bovine spongiform encephalopathy), an affliction that clearly was produced by human practices and human politics. The disease, which spread widely among British cattle in the 1980s – and in a limited number of cases to members of other species, including humans and cats – seems to have originated in cattle feed enriched with material from sheep carrying scrapie, a similar disease.[28] Although feeding cattle with material derived from fellow ungulates – a practice denounced by some excitable critics as enforced cannibalism – is not traditional, in a sense it represents an extension of a well-established technique. Since the eighteenth century, livestock farmers have attempted to streamline the inherently inefficient diets of their animals. Cattle fed on food like oilcake, a much richer source of calories than the grass they evolved to metabolize, matured earlier and gained weight faster, and thus became marketable more rapidly and more profitably. But if physical factors produced BSE, it was the Conservative British government of the 1980s that turned the disease into an epizootic. A philosophy that defined government as the protector of commercial enterprise rather than of its citizens meant that official concern with beef industry profits consistently overshadowed official concern with public health. Further, the British response to BSE (shared by some members of the public as well as government officials) was shaped by such elusive factors as national pride and national passion. Of course, any significant commodity can serve as a metonym for the nation that produces or consumes it, but animals have been particularly likely to fill such roles, and beef and beef cattle had occupied a particularly powerful emblematic position in Britain for several hundred years.[29] Not only were citizens urged to show their patriotism by continuing to eat British burgers, but non-British responses often suggested reciprocal national feeling. Thus the stalwart commitment proclaimed by other European governments to defend the health of their citizens against the British bovine menace could seem less absolute when BSE was rumored in their own herds. Although American politicians recently have taken alarm at a single detected case, rather than waiting, as was the case in Britain, for animals to succumb in their tens of thousands, they seem similarly inclined to view protection of the beef industry as their first priority, and to use the national border to distinguish among cattle suffering from the same affliction.

The vulnerability of livestock to diseases also has affected the human environment in various non-epidemic ways. That is, epizootics, such as outbreaks of cattle plague or foot and mouth disease, repeatedly have wreaked economic havoc without making people sick. Since both cattle and horses are susceptible to sleeping sickness, the prevalence of the tsetse fly made it difficult for the European biological assemblage, which had proved so effective in expediting the colonization of the temperate Americas and Australia, to move into large tracts of Africa. The waste produced by industrial concentrations of animals in stockyards and factory farms continues to strain sewage facilities. Nevertheless, as greatly as domesticated animals have influenced human existence, our impact on them has been greater still. Simply in terms of numbers, these few favored species now account for a much larger proportion of the world's biomass than did their pre-agricultural ancestors. In several cases – the camel and the cow – the wild progenitors of domesticates have disappeared. In others, such as the wolf, their populations are dwarfed by those of their domesticated relatives. If *Canis familiaris* were to be reclassified as C. *lupus* on the basis of willingness to interbreed and ability to produce fertile hybrid offspring, it would be difficult to argue for the protection of the wolf as an endangered species. So domestication has given target species an enormous evolutionary advantage, if evolutionary success is measured simply in terms of quantity.

In addition to exponentially increasing certain animal populations, the process of domestication has changed the very nature of its subjects. Archaeological evidence suggests that the early stages of domestication produced similar changes in a variety of species: reduced body size in general and brain size in particular, increased diversity in superficial characteristics like ear shape and coat color, and shortening of the face (part of a set of skeletal and behavioral changes that can be explained as the retention of juvenile characteristics into adulthood).[30] It is likely that people originally selected animals for tractability and for distinctiveness – characteristics that would make it easier to manage the creatures and to tell them apart. Once domesticated populations were firmly distinguished from their wild relatives, however, people probably began to breed for more specialized qualities. Modern breeders often claim that their favorite variety of dog or horse or cow has ancient roots, but although it is clear that distinct strains existed in earlier times, it is difficult to make direct connections from them to particular modern types. (Of course every living animal has ancient forebears, just as every living human does; in both cases the problem is to figure out who they might be.) Over the past three centuries animal breeding has become a highly technical, self-conscious, and institutionalized process – a form of bioengineering before the fact. By the middle of the nineteenth century, breeding (or artificial selection) had become so widely understood, that Charles Darwin used it to introduce his audience to the less familiar process of natural selection in the opening pages of *On the Origin of Species.*[31]

When modern breeding practices were taking form in the eighteenth century or a little before, the aim of breeders was to enhance quality in ways that could be assessed quantitatively. The first kinds of animals for which elaborate public breeding records were kept – the kind that could sustain pedigrees – were the thoroughbred horse and the greyhound, both bred for speed, which could be easily measured. The first livestock breed to receive this kind of formal attention was the shorthorn cow, the subject of a herd book published in 1822. But careful breeding had been going on long before, validated by market prices if not by paper trails. On the contrary, the best-known stockbreeder of the eighteenth century, Robert Bakewell, made a point of obscuring the descent of his prized bulls, rams, boars, and stallions. The quality of his animals was a matter of judgment, guaranteed by his name rather than those of his animals. His own success was calibrated by the size of the stud fees. Although Bakewell often has been credited with developing the breeding techniques that he applied and marketed so brilliantly, it is likely that his fame obscured the earlier labors of modest breeders, whose unsung achievements served as the basis for his celebrated ones.[32]

By the nineteenth century, as pet keeping became a popular pastime among members of the middling and less-than-middling orders of western societies, the infrastructure of breeding was applied to dogs, cats, rabbits, rodents, and various kinds of birds. It often had been difficult to decide what made a cow or pig excellent – there were heated controversies over, for example, whether morbid obesity was a prime desideratum or the reverse. With animals whose major function was to provide companionship and amusement, however, such decisions could approach the impossible. Or at least, they were likely to be very arbitrary, often reflecting an appreciation simply of the human power to manipulate. Sometimes this power was exercised to the obvious disadvantage of established useful traits, and sometimes it was exercised capriciously enough to produce creatures that were perceived as monstrosities. For example, when collies became popular pets in the Victorian period, they lost many of the characteristics that made them effective herd dogs. Particularly lamented was their intelligence, which was sacrificed when their skulls were reshaped to feature a long elegant nose. As information about genetics filtered into the pet-fancying world during the twentieth century, breeders' techniques became more focused and powerful. They even were able to achieve some goals that had long eluded them, such as a canary colored red rather than yellow.[33]

The shift from breeding livestock to breeding pets was also ordinarily, although not inevitably, a shift from the country to the city. Animals are most frequently associated with rural settings, but cities always have been full of them. Before the development of modern technologies of refrigeration and transportation, towns needed to accommodate both dairies and abattoirs.[34] Dairy animals mostly stayed out of sight, while livestock bound for slaughter often marched through the streets, but both groups added significantly to the urban waste stream. Many people, including those living in tenements, kept their own chickens and even pigs. Before the twentieth century, all urban thoroughfares were choked with horses, which disappeared only gradually with the advent of the internal combustion engine. To some extent, at least in the affluent cities of the industrial world, these utilitarian animals have been replaced by burgeoning pet populations. Several zoonotic diseases typically have occurred in urban settings. Rabies is most frequently transmitted to people by dogs, and so is most feared where dog populations are densest, although rural dogs and various wild animals are also carriers. The black death of the middle ages and the early modern period, whether or not it was the same as the modern contagion called bubonic plague, was focused on cities, although its traditional association with rats and fleas recently has been questioned.[35] But whether or not they spread the great fourteenth-century plague, rats of several species would figure prominently in an animal census of most urban environments, along with other creatures similarly adapted to scavenging or parasitism (which is to say, semi-tame, if not semi-domesticated), including mice, pigeons, and stray dogs and cats. Also making their homes in cities are many animals ordinarily categorized as wild – monkeys in Calcutta, foxes in London, raccoons and coyotes in Boston.

Of course, it is as difficult to decide what makes an animal wild as to define wildness or wilderness in any other context. The Royal Ontario Museum in Toronto once introduced its display of stuffed specimens with a diorama featuring a pair of large raccoons vigorously toppling a garbage can. The diorama (now gone, unfortunately) evoked a set of incongruities or paradoxes – not only which animals are wild and which are not, but which are suitable subjects for scrutiny in cultural and educational settings. Thus most past and present zoos have preferred to collect exotic wild animals, segregating any resident domesticates into petting zoos for children; one of the things that distinguishes the Walter Rothschild Zoological Museum at Tring (now a branch of the Natural History Museum in London) is its large collection of stuffed dogs. And animals, especially domesticated ones, breach other boundaries as well. Or, to put it another way, they help expose some of the assumptions that underlie the stories that we tell, in particular stories about the extent to which we are part of or separate from our environmental subject. With animals the question of us and them is always close to the surface. Not only have they often functioned – even the most ingratiating of them – as representatives of the natural world, but they often have been selected as obvious representatives of human groups, whether as totems or national emblems or team mascots.[36]

This liminality is most obvious – and most problematic – with regard to the animals who resemble us most closely. From its Enlightenment beginnings, formal taxonomy has recognized not only the general correspondence between people and what were then known as quadrupeds (that is, mammals), but also the particular similarities that human beings shared with apes and monkeys. It was the non-functional details that proved most compelling: the shape of the external ear, for example, or the flatness of fingernails and toenails. On this basis, the celebrated eighteenth-century systematizer Carolus Linnaeus located people firmly within the animal kingdom: He constructed the primate order to accommodate humans, apes, monkeys, prosimians, and bats.[37] Humans also were claimed to demonstrate their animal affinities in ways that were less abstract and more sensational. In an age fascinated by hybrids, humans were sometimes alleged to be the objects or the originators of potentially fruitful relationships with orangutans and chimpanzees, although scientific accounts of such episodes tended to be carefully distanced by skepticism or censure.[38] Outside the community of experts, claims could be less restrained; in the nineteenth century non-Europeans who were unusually hairy or adept with their toes were ballyhooed as products of an ape-human cross. Physical and mental similarities between people and other primates often were foregrounded in zoo displays that featured chimpanzees who not only wore clothes, but ate with silverware, drank from cups, and turned the pages of books.

Such displays were not universally appealing, however, and as evolutionary theory suggested a more concrete and ineluctable connection, it provoked increasingly articulate resistance. As Darwin sadly noted at the end of *The Descent of Man,* written a decade after the appearance of the *Origin* in 1859, "The main conclusion arrived at in this work, namely that man is descended from some lowly-organized form, will, I regret to think, be highly distasteful to many persons."[39] In the century and more since Darwin wrote, his evolutionary theory has been enshrined as biological orthodoxy. But some of the questions that troubled his Victorian critics continue to complicate modern narratives, whether told for a scientific or scholarly audience or for a less specialized one. Remote from the reflections of historians, animals clog the airwaves. A majority of the extravagantly produced commercials for Superbowl XXXVIII featured animal actors, although this was not their most frequently remarked attribute. An entire cable channel is devoted to animals, and zoological documentaries appear frequently on other networks. Many of these programs present an environmental context and an elegiac environmentalist message, at the same time that they celebrate the physical triumph of fit, canny trappers or photographers (hunters transformed to suit modern sensibilities) over dangerous beasts. It is often hard to know who is the hero of the story, let alone what the moral is meant to be.

Notes

1 I will continue to assume that we are animals too, but for the sake of euphony, I will refer to nonhuman animals just as "animals" for the rest of this essay.
2 The literature on animal rights and responsibilities is relatively sparse and eccentric: See, for example, E. P. Evans, *The Criminal Prosecution and Capital Punishment of Animals: The Lost History of Europe's Animal Trials* (1906; reprint, London: Faber, 1987); and Vicki Hearne, *Bandit: Dossier of a Dangerous Dog* (New York: HarperCollins, 1991). The literature on vivisection is denser and more conventional: See, for example, Nicolaas A. Rupke, ed., *Vivisection in Historical Perspective* (London: Routledge, 1987); and Richard D. French, *Antivivisection and Medical Science in Victorian Society* (Princeton: Princeton University Press, 1975).
3 Susan D. Jones, *Valuing Animals: Veterinarians and Their Patients in Modern America* (Baltimore: Johns Hopkins University Press, 2003). For further reflections on this topic see Harriet Ritvo, "History and Animal Studies," *Society and Animals* 10 (2002): 403–6. This issue of *Society and Animals* also includes essays on the relation of animal studies to other disciplines in the humanities and social sciences.
4 Jane Goodall, *The Chimpanzees of Gombe: Patterns of Behavior* (Cambridge: Harvard University Press, 1986), ch. 11.
5 See, for example, C. K. Brain, *The Hunters or the Hunted? An Introduction to African Cave Taphonomy* (Chicago: University of Chicago Press, 1981).
6 Edward O. Wilson, *The Diversity of Life* (Cambridge: Harvard University Press, 1992), ch. 12.
7 Shepard Krech III, *The Ecological Indian: Myth and History* (New York: W.W. Norton, 1999), ch. 1.
8 Discussions of the evidence for alternative points of view can be found in E. C. Pielou, *After the Ice Age: The Return of Life to Glaciated North America* (Chicago: University of Chicago Press, 1991), ch. 12; and Tim Flannery, *The Eternal Frontier: An Ecological History of North America and Its Peoples* (New York: Grove Press, 2001), chs. 14–17.
9 Claudine Cohen, *The Fate of the Mammoth: Fossils, Myth, and History,* trans. William Rodarmor (1994; Chicago: University of Chicago Press, 2002), especially chapter 12. See also A. Bowdoin Van Riper, *Men among the Mammoths: Victorian Science and the Discovery of Human Prehistory* (Chicago: University of Chicago Press, 1993).
10 Matt Cartmill, *A View to a Death in the Morning: Hunting and Nature through History* (Cambridge: Harvard University Press, 1993).
11 For statistical analysis of the consequences of the fur trade, see Arthur Radclyffe Dugmore, *The Romance of the Beaver; being the History of the Beaver in the Western Hemisphere* (London: William Heinemann, 1914), ch. 4; and Briton Cooper Busch, *The War against the Seals: A History of the North American Seal Fishery* (Kingston and Montreal: McGill-Queen's University Press, 1985).
12 Harriet Ritvo, *The Animal Estate: The English and Other Creatures in the Victorian Age* (Cambridge: Harvard University Press, 1987), chs. 5–6.

13 For an elaborate account of the decimation and partial recovery of the North American bison herd, see Andrew C. Isenberg, *The Destruction of the Bison* (Cambridge: Cambridge University Press, 2000).

14 John M. MacKenzie, *The Empire of Nature: Hunting, Conservation and British Imperialism* (Manchester: University of Manchester Press, 1988); and Richard Fitter and Peter Scott, *The Penitent Butchers: 75 Years of Wildlife Conservation: The Fauna Preservation Society 1903–1978* (London: Fauna Preservation Society, 1978).

15 For an extensive discussion of this campaign in the United States and Britain, see Robin W. Doughty, *Feather Fashions and Bird Preservation: A Study in Nature Protection* (Berkeley: University of California Press, 1975).

16 Karl Jacoby, *Crimes against Nature: Squatters, Poachers, Thieves, and the Hidden History of American Conservation* (Berkeley: University of California Press, 2001); and Louis S. Warren, *The Hunter's Game: Poachers and Conservationists in Twentieth-Century America* (New Haven: Yale University Press, 1997).

17 Robert Paddle, *The History and Extinction of the Thylacine* (Cambridge: Cambridge University Press, 2000).

18 Peter Boomgaard broaches the possibility of writing history, environmental or otherwise, that incorporates the perspective of animals, but regretfully decides to keep to the conventional path. Both his decision and his regret are understandable. Peter Boomgaard, *Frontiers of Fear: Tigers and People in the Malay World 1600–1950* (New Haven: Yale University Press, 2001).

19 Jim Corbett, *Man-Eaters of Kumaon* (1944; reprint, Oxford: Oxford University Press, 1993).

20 Dale Peterson, *Eating Apes* (Berkeley: University of California Press, 2003).

21 Raymond Coppinger and Lorna Coppinger, *Dogs: A New Understanding of Canine Origin, Behavior, and Evolution* (Chicago: University of Chicago Press, 2001). For an alternative view, see Juliet Clutton-Brock, *A Natural History of Domesticated Mammals* (Cambridge: Cambridge University Press, 1987), ch. 3.

22 For example, William McNeill and John R. McNeill, *The Human Web: A Birds-Eye View of World History* (New York: W.W. Norton, 2003); Alfred W. Crosby, *Ecological Imperialism: The Biological Expansion of Europe, 900–1900* (Cambridge: Cambridge University Press, 1986); and Jared Diamond, *Guns, Germs, and Steel: The Fates of Human Societies* (New York: W.W. Norton, 1997).

23 For overviews of the relation between humans and other animals as mediated by disease, see Lise Wilkinson, *Animals and Disease: An Introduction to the History of Comparative Medicine* (Cambridge: Cambridge University Press, 1992); and Joanna Swabe, *Animals, Disease and Human Society: Human–Animal Relations and the Rise of Veterinary Medicine* (London: Routledge, 1999).

24 Classically, in William McNeill, *Plagues and Peoples* (New York: Anchor, 1976).

25 The process that began in 1492 or thereabouts arguably continued until the flu pandemic of 1918. For description of that event, see Alfred W. Crosby, *America's Forgotten Pandemic: The Influenza of 1918* (Cambridge: Cambridge University Press, 1990); and Gina Kolata, *Flu: The Story of the Great Influenza Pandemic of 1918 and the Search for the Virus that Caused It* (New York: Farrar, Strauss and Giroux, 1999).

26 David S. Jones, *Rationalizing Epidemics: Meanings and Uses of American Indian Mortality since 1600* (Cambridge: Harvard University Press, 2004), chs. 1–2.

For the standard explanation, see Alfred W. Crosby, *The Columbian Exchange: Biological and Cultural Consequences of 1492* (1973; reprint, Westport, Conn.: Praeger, 2003). While the fact of population decline is uncontested, the extent of the demographic disaster is highly controversial, on historical, scientific, and political grounds, as Krech explains in *Ecological Indian,* ch 3.

27 Elinor G. K. Melville, *A Plague of Sheep: Environmental Consequences of the Conquest of Mexico* (Cambridge: Cambridge University Press, 1994).

28 For a scientific discussion of BSE, see Pierre-Marie Lledo, *Histoire de la vache folle* (Paris: Presses Universitaires de France, 2001).

29 For an account of BSE in Britain, see Harriet Ritvo, "Mad Cow Mysteries," *American Scholar* (Spring 1998): 113–22.

30 Clutton-Brock, *Natural History of Domesticated Mammals,* ch. 1.

31 Charles Darwin, *On the Origin of Species* (1859; reprint, Cambridge: Harvard University Press, 1964), ch. 1. Darwin later wrote a very long book dealing exclusively with this subject: *The Variation of Animals and Plants under Domestication, 2* vols. (1868; reprint, Baltimore: Johns Hopkins University Press, 1998).

32 For accounts of early breeding, see Nicholas Russell, *Like Engend'ring Like: Heredity and Animal Breeding in Early Modern England* (Cambridge: Cambridge University Press, 1986); Harriet Ritvo, "Possessing Mother Nature: Genetic Capital in 18th-century Britain," in *Early Modern Conceptions of Property,* ed. Susan Staves and John Brewer (London: Routledge, 1994), 413–26; and Ritvo, *Animal Estate,* ch. 2.

33 Modern breeding efforts are discussed in Margaret E. Derry, *Bred for Perfection: Shorthorn Cattle, Collies, and Arabian Horses since 1800* (Baltimore: Johns Hopkins University Press, 2003); and Tim Birkhead, *A Brand-New Bird: How Two Amateur Scientists Created the First Genetically Engineered Animal* (New York: Basic Books, 2003).

34 On the development of modern abbatoirs, see Nöelie Vialles, *Animal to Edible,* trans. J. A. Underwood (Cambridge: Cambridge University Press, 1994).

35 See David Herlihy, *The Black Death and the Transformation of the West* (Cambridge: Harvard University Press, 1997), introduction and ch. 1.

36 Keith Thomas has discussed the development of the association between animals and nature in *Man and the Natural World: A History of the Modern Sensibility* (New York: Pantheon, 1983), especially in chs. 3, 4, and 6.

37 Carolus Linnaeus, *Systema Naturae: Regnum Animale* (1758; reprint, London: British Museum [Natural History], 1956).

38 For an extended discussion of eighteenth- and nineteenth-century hybrids and cross-breeds, see Harriet Ritvo, *The Platypus and the Mermaid, and Other Figments of the Classifying Imagination* (Cambridge: Harvard University Press, 1997), ch. 3.

39 Charles Darwin, *The Descent of Man* (1871; reprint, New York: Modern Library, 1950), 919.

8

EVOLUTIONARY HISTORY

Prospectus for a new field

Edmund Russell

It was, evolutionary biologist Theodosius Dobzhansky wrote in 1937, "probably the best proof of the effectiveness of natural selection yet obtained."[1] If we were guessing what Dobzhansky had in mind, we might nominate some of the classic examples from evolutionary biology and paleontology. Charles Darwin's tortoises in the Galapagos Islands? The rise and extinction of the dinosaurs? Fossils from the Burgess shale? The answer to all these suggestions is no. Dobzhansky's proof was the evolution of insects resistant to insecticides.

In the early twentieth century, fruit growers in the western United States noticed that, over time, some insecticides "lost" their ability to kill scale insects in orchards. Most entomologists blamed people. Manufacturers produced defective insecticides, they reasoned, or farmers applied legitimate products incorrectly. A few entomologists, however, noticed that their data contradicted this explanation. Insecticides lost their potency in areas where farmers bought the most reliable insecticides and sprayed them most carefully, rather than the reverse. Perhaps, these scientists ventured, some insects carried Mendelian genes for resistance to sprays. But the reason why resistant individuals should be common in heavily sprayed areas remained a mystery for the next two decades.[2]

In the 1930s, Dobzhansky solved this puzzle by discarding an unspoken assumption. Entomologists had assumed that insect species stayed constant (or evolved so little that change was trivial) in historical time. Dobzhansky suggested the opposite. Spraying was a form of natural selection, he argued. By chance, a few individuals within a species carried genes conferring resistance to insecticides. Insecticides killed off susceptible individuals and left the resistant ones behind to reproduce. Resistant individuals passed on their genes for resistance to their offspring. Every time farmers sprayed, they increased the ratio of resistant to susceptible insects in their orchards. Eventually, so few susceptible individuals remained that insecticides appeared to have lost their potency. This deceptively simple explanation solved a pair of biological puzzles: why genes for resistance should become more common over time, and why resistance should be most common in areas sprayed most heavily. It also solved an economic puzzle: why crop losses to insects should rise despite ever-greater doses of insecticides. Further, it provided the paradigmatic example for a new approach to biology, the modern (neo-Darwinian) synthesis that united evolutionary theory with genetics.[3]

Dobzhansky's findings challenged several ideas about evolution that remain common today. Many of us think of evolution as something that happened in the distant past, took eons to occur, and was done by nature. Resistant insects, however, evolved recently rather than long ago, quickly rather than over eons, and under the influence of humans rather than nature alone. Many of us think of evolution as speciation, but populations of insects evolved resistance without budding into new species. Many of us think of a species' genes as fixed in historical time and space, or as varying so little that differences are trivial. But members of insect species carried different versions of genes before insecticides arrived, and spraying increased the proportion of genes for resistance in certain parts of species' ranges enough that resistance became an economic problem. Many of us think of evolutionary ideas as tools for biologists, not humanists. But humans have shaped the evolution of countless species for millennia, reshaping human experience as well as the genes of other species.[4]

Few historians, however, have incorporated evolution into their work. Until we do, the historicism project will remain incomplete. A signal contribution of environmental history has been to historicize ways of thinking about and interacting with other species. The most visible sciences of this effort have been ecology and public health, which have helped us understand changes in the distribution, abundance, and health of organisms. We have largely ignored, however, the impact of ecological changes and public health measures on the constitutions of other species. By changing the environments in which organisms live, we have changed the selective regimes in which they evolve. In some cases, the resulting evolution has forced humans to interact with versions of those species in very different ways. The 1950 versions of orchard insects differed from 1900 versions of the same species, which forced farmers to use a new generation of technology to control them. To reach a full understanding of the history of life on earth, then, we must join hands with evolutionary biologists and paleontologists to historicize organisms themselves.

In making the case for an evolutionary historiography, this essay focuses on genetic evolution in non-human species. For the most part, it sets aside the role of human evolution. One reason is to emphasize the value of evolution for understanding the distinctive concern of environmental history – nature. Organisms have changed in historical time; those changes have mattered to human beings; and evolution offers the only cogent explanation for such change. The second reason is to emphasize that one can practice evolutionary history with a limited agenda. Studying human evolution is not necessary (or even sufficient) for evolutionary history. The third reason is to encourage a focus on aspects of evolution sometimes obscured by controversial issues, such as sociobiology and evolutionary psychology. This essay is not a brief for those fields or for biological determinism. Humans and other species have engaged in a complex dance in which genes in non-human species, along with a variety of other human and natural forces, have played roles. Nor is evolutionary history an effort to make history a subdiscipline of evolutionary biology. It is an effort to tap some of the most powerful ideas of the past 150 years to create a fuller understanding of history.

This essay begins by making a case for the importance of anthropogenic evolution. A review of the literature documents the limited role of evolution in environmental history, hypothesizes reasons for its low profile, and surveys uses of evolution in other disciplines in the humanities and social sciences. Drawing on existing works, the next section demonstrates the potential for evolutionary history to revise accounts of events as disparate as international relations, industrialization, and the collapse of natural resources. Finally, the essay suggests that evolutionary history has the potential to inform not just our understanding of the past, but a future in which biotechnology plays an increasingly important role.

Anthropogenic evolution

Anthropogenic evolution has played a venerable role in the development of evolutionary theory. Although better known for his travels in the Galapagos Islands than for his trips to English farms, Darwin drew on domestication to understand and explain evolution in the wild. The first chapter of *On the Origin of Species* is about variation and selection under domestication. Only after putting that framework in place does Darwin turn in chapter two to natural selection, which he introduces as "applying the principles arrived at in the last chapter to organic beings in a state of Nature." Darwin described another of his books, the two-volume *Variation of Animals and Plants under Domestication,* as providing "facts on which the conclusions in *[Origin]* were founded."[5]

Today's understanding of Darwinian evolution is, at heart, simple. It requires three things: variation, inheritance, and selection. *Variation* means that individuals in a population differ in some trait. It could be any trait, visible or invisible to the eye: speed, size, tolerance of drought, metabolic efficiency, and so on. *Inheritance* means that these traits pass from parent to child. Today, evolutionary biologists focus on genes as the units of inheritance. *Selection* means that variation in traits enables some individuals to contribute more offspring to the next generation than do others.[6]

141

The term for which Darwin is most famous, natural selection, derived from domestication. Darwin believed the term was less than ideal because it implied "conscious choice" on the part of nature. But the advantages outweighed the disadvantages, for "it brings into connection the production of domestic races by man's power of selection, and the natural preservation of varieties and species in a state of nature." In Darwin's day, "selection" referred to what breeders did. Darwin needed a modifier to create the new meaning, the analogous process in nature – hence, "natural" selection.[7]

Today, the meaning has all but reversed. Evolutionary biologists often use "selection" and "natural selection" synonymously, and they use "artificial selection" (Darwin's occasional phrase) to refer to what people do. This essay uses "selection" to include natural and artificial selection and attaches an adjective when necessary to draw a distinction. Artificial selection – and thus anthropogenic evolution – has been unintentional and intentional. Evolution of resistance to insecticides was unintentional. Recent plant and animal breeding has been intentional. Breeders have worked on species whose individuals varied in some inherited traits. They selected some individuals to mate and prevented others from doing so. If all went well, the next generation included relatively more individuals with the desired trait and fewer individuals lacking it. The new generation had evolved from the generation before.[8]

Artificial selection could not change frogs into princesses, but it transformed animals so radically that it seemed magical. Working hard on the heels of a revolution in animal breeding, Darwin learned that breeders imagined a perfect animal and then set out to create it. William Youatt, whom Darwin quoted approvingly, said the breeder's "principle of selection" was "that which enables the agriculturists, not only to modify the character of his flock, but to change it altogether. It is the magician's wand, by means of which he may summon into life whatever form and mould he pleases." Even farmers without such imagination, Darwin believed, transformed their stock as radically (if more slowly) simply by picking the best animals to breed over long periods.[9]

This conception of evolution allows evolution to happen quickly, to result from human actions, and to result in changes short of speciation. Breeders have not exaggerated, then, when they have described themselves as "helping evolution." One such breeder took advantage of a mutant, featherless strain of chicken. ("We call them naked chickens," he said, "just because they are naked.") This strain, the breeder thought, might solve a problem arising from the spread of enclosed, mass-production chicken raising to tropical countries at the end of the twentieth century. Conventional feathered chickens often died of heat in such enclosures. Naked chickens might dissipate heat more efficiently than their feathered cousins did. As in most evolution, however, there was a tradeoff. Naked chickens might thrive in hot, enclosed spaces, but a stroll in the sun knocked them into a stupor.[10]

The contrast between sheds and the open air, and between chickens suited to each, illustrates the inseparability of selection from environment. Organisms have not evolved toward some universally better (much less best) state. Natural selection, as Darwin put it, "acts exclusively by the preservation and accumulation of variations, which are beneficial *under the organic and inorganic conditions to which each creature is exposed* at all periods of life." "Better" makes sense only in the context of specific environments, and then it only means that some individuals are more likely to reproduce than are others.[11]

We can measure the significance of anthropogenic evolution in several ways. To lead with the trump card: Without it, our profession would not exist. Jared Diamond's *Guns, Germs, and Steel* argues that humans directed the evolution of nearly all domesticated species. Archaeological and genetic evidence suggest that humans have been domesticating organisms since the Neolithic revolution, about 12,000 years ago. Intentionally and unintentionally, humans selected for sweeter fruit, non-shattering seed pods, less aggressive animals, and fatter cows. These modifications in turn created the agricultural surplus necessary for settled societies, social hierarchies, bureaucracies, armies, contagious diseases, complicated technology, international conquest, and writing (thus our profession). More seriously, the point is not that our profession would not exist; it is that nearly everything historians study, which by definition we consider significant, would not have occurred without domestication.[12]

Another way to measure the significance of anthropogenic evolution is to tally the taxonomic range of species that humans have domesticated. This number suggests the enormous effort humans have poured into this endeavor for thousands of years. The animals have included mammals (dog, ass, horse, cow, sheep, goat, reindeer, camel, buffalo, rabbit, elephant, ferret, mongoose, yak), birds (chicken, turkey, pheasant, quail, pigeon, falcon, goose, duck, pelican, cormorant, crane, canary, ostrich), insects (silkworm, honeybee), and fish (eel, carp, goldfish, paradise fish).[13]

The list of domesticated plants is even longer. The plants thought to have originated in the Near East alone include cereals (oats, barley, rye, wheat), pulses (chickpea, lentil, fava), tubers (beet, turnip, carrot, radish), oil crops (rapeseed, mustard, safflower, olive, flax), fruits and nuts (hazelnut, melon, fig, walnut, palm, almond, apricot, cherry, pear, apple, grape), vegetables and spices (onion, garlic, leek, cabbage, coriander, cucumber, cumin, anise, purselane), fiber plants (hemp, flax), forage crops (bentgrass, rye, clover, vetch), and drug sources (belladonna, digitalis, codeine). Making use of some of these animals and plants has depended in turn on domesticating microorganisms. Bacteria turn milk into yogurt, and yeast is essential for making leavened bread, wine, and beer.[14]

A third way to judge the importance of anthropogenic evolution is to estimate economic effects. One expensive arena is agriculture. The process

Dobzhansky analyzed, the rise of resistance to pesticides, has led American farmers to spend $1.6 billion per year to apply extra insecticide. This cost has risen each year as the number of resistant species has grown. By 1986, some 450 species of insects and mites, 100 species of plant pathogens, and 48 species of weeds had evolved resistance to pesticides. In some cases, resistance has forced the abandonment of enterprises altogether. In the 1960s, farmers had to stop growing cotton on 700,000 acres because insecticides no longer controlled a major pest, the tobacco budworm.[15]

Another expensive arena is medicine. By 2000, tuberculosis infected one-third of humanity and caused two million deaths each year. Strains of tuberculosis resistant to the major drugs infected 11 percent of the new cases. (Like insects treated with insecticides, pathogens treated with antibiotics have evolved resistance as susceptible individuals died off and resistant individuals survived to reproduce.) Fallback medicines were more expensive than the drugs of first choice. Overall, antibiotic resistance cost Americans $30 billion each year.[16]

A fourth way is to measure the cost in lives. The United States Centers for Disease Control and Prevention estimated in 1995 that sixty thousand people died each year in the United States from hospital-acquired infections. Pathogens resistant to antibiotics caused a large percentage of those deaths. The combination of insect resistance to pesticides and pathogen resistance to medications fueled distressing increases in malaria mortality in the late twentieth century. After World War II, a worldwide effort to eradicate malaria relied on insecticides (such as DDT, which killed the mosquitoes that carried the malaria plasmodium) and anti-malarial drugs (such as atabrine and quinine, which stopped the plasmodium from reproducing inside human bodies). The project saved an estimated 15–25 million lives but foundered when, among other things, mosquitoes and plasmodia evolved resistance to their respective poisons. Unable to reach its goal, the World Health Organization halted the program by 1972. By 2000, malaria killed roughly two million people each year.[17]

A fifth way is to look at the geographical scale of anthropogenic change. The increase of temperatures around the globe, apparently due partly to human production of greenhouse gases, has changed the evolutionary environment for species large and small. Pitcher plant mosquitoes in North America, to pick one example, hibernate (more precisely, enter diapause) on a schedule controlled by genes. Between 1972 and 1996, pitcher plant mosquitoes across a broad swath of the continent shifted their hibernation later in the year in response to warmer weather. On a regional level, humans seem to be changing sea levels, increasing ultraviolet radiation, transferring species across continents, contributing pollutants to air and water, and changing the pH of rain through additions of sulfur dioxide and nitrogen oxides.[18]

Most of these examples illustrate that anthropogenic evolution is a two way street. Not only do humans shape other species (which is important for those species); their evolution in turn has a significant impact on humans. The exception in these examples is the pitcher plant mosquito, whose evolution is important for scientists but has little direct influence on most humans. Indirectly, though, its evolution may be significant. If the earth continues to warm, we may look back on it as a harbinger of massive evolution yet to come.

Evolution in historiography

Of all historical fields, environmental history seems the most likely to have used evolution analytically. It studies ways in which humans have shaped nature, and it has drawn on scientific ideas to understand those processes. A search of over 33,000 entries in the Environmental History Bibliography at the Forest History Society, however, produced just eight entries in which authors used evolution as an analytical tool. Authors from fields other than environmental history wrote many of those eight. (We will look at exceptions to this pattern in the section below on evolutionary history.) The Research Register of the Documenting Environmental Change database at Cambridge University lists only one individual working on what may be termed biological evolution.[19]

Many factors may have contributed to this pattern, but three seem likely. First, historians may have lacked familiarity with evolution in general and anthropogenic evolution in particular. Few graduate or undergraduate programs in history require courses in science, much less in evolutionary biology. Even scholars who have taken courses in evolutionary biology may have learned little about anthropogenic evolution. Some of the most popular textbooks have omitted discussion of the topic. Eric Pianka, author of the textbook *Evolutionary Ecology,* wrote that he had "always tried to present evolutionary ecology as a 'pure' science."[20] Small wonder, then, if historians have seen evolution as something that has happened outside historical time and separate from human activity.

Recent publications in evolutionary biology may help correct this problem. Pianka, who devoted previous editions of his textbook to "pure" science, wrote in the introduction of the sixth (2000) edition of *Evolutionary Ecology,* "Humans now dominate ecosystems to such an extent that pure ecology has all but vanished from the face of the earth! Hence, in this edition, multitudinous anthropogenic effects are interwoven into every chapter." Pianka used loss of genetic variability, extinction, and evolution of microbes as examples of these effects. Evolutionary biologist Stephen R. Palumbi brought anthropogenic evolution to the center of his 2001 book, *The Evolution Explosion: How Humans Cause Rapid Evolutionary Change.* He describes humans as "the planet's most potent evolutionary force" and points to antibiotic resistance, HIV, and shrinking fish as examples of that force's effect.[21]

Second, historians may have seen evolution as less useful or important than other sciences in their work. The workhorse sciences of modern environmentalism, ecology and public health, have held pride of place in environmental history as well.[22] A search for "ecology" and its variants in the Environmental History Bibliography turned up 1,747 entries. "Health" appeared 503 times. Their preeminence is not surprising. Environmental concerns have drawn many scholars into environmental history, influenced their choice of research projects, and probably shaped their selection of intellectual tools.[23]

More precisely, historians may have seen some fields of ecology as more valuable than others. Two – evolutionary ecology and ecological genetics – have offered environmental historians bridges from ecology to evolution all along.[24] But environmental historians have tended to focus on community, ecosystem, and population ecology. Perhaps these fields (and public health) have appeared more useful in understanding problems of concern to environmentalists and environmental historians alike, such as wilderness, national parks and forests, wildlife, human disturbance, plant and animal invasions, and pollution.[25] This essay suggests that adding evolutionary ecology and genetics to the list enhances, rather than replaces, the fields already of greatest interest.

Third, historians may have opposed the use of evolutionary ideas for intellectual reasons. Sociobiologists and evolutionary psychologists have sought to attribute much of human behavior to genes and natural selection, a direct challenge to territory humanists and social scientists have thought their own. Any use of evolutionary ideas might seem to open the door to disciplinary takeover. More broadly, the field of science and technology studies has encouraged a skepticism about truth claims by science. A related concern is political. We know that social Darwinists and eugenicists in the past have drawn on, and perhaps been inspired by, evolutionary biology. It is all to easy to read human ideas into nature, read them back out again, and justify the original ideas on the grounds that they are natural. If historians use evolutionary ideas, might they find themselves justifying biological determinism?[26]

These concerns have merit but pose no insurmountable barriers. Evolutionary biology has not subsumed any discipline with which it overlaps, even among the sciences. There is no reason to believe history is any more vulnerable than, say, ecology. Although sociobiologists and evolutionary psychologists have grabbed their share of headlines, we should not mistake them for evolutionary biologists as a whole. On the contrary, evolutionary biologists have marched among the shock troops against biological and genetic determinism. Their persuasiveness grows not out of rejecting evolution, but the opposite – mastering evolutionary theory and evidence. Paul Ehrlich, Stephen Jay Gould, Luca Cavalli-Sforza, Lynn Margulis, and Richard Lewontin have pointed out that humans carry nowhere near enough genes to encode every human trait, that applications of evolutionary biology in the past have been based on bad science, that race is a cultural rather than a biological construct, and that the environment deeply influences the expression of genetic as well as cultural traits. Imagine how much more powerful their arguments might be when joined with those from historians able to speak knowledgeably about the dimensions of human experience in which genes have or have not played important roles.[27]

Similarly, we should not let skepticism necessarily lead to rejection. Scholars in science and technology studies have made enormous contributions by historicizing ideas and demonstrating the social dimensions of what had been seen as "objective" endeavors. The outcome of this process should be to make us skeptical about all the analytical tools we use – whether from humanities, social sciences, or natural sciences – and at the same time welcoming of useful ideas, whatever their source. Finally, we must combat political misuses of any ideas, including those from evolution. My own conviction is that deeper knowledge makes citizens more, rather than less, politically effective.

Although various disciplines outside biology have created evolutionary fields, none is identical to evolutionary history. Nearly all the existing fields focus on human evolution, whether genetic or cultural, to the exclusion of non-human species. One exception is evolutionary (or Darwinian) medicine. Proponents of evolutionary medicine have argued that most physicians see the human body as a machine designed by a careless engineer. The task of the doctor is to fix broken machinery. Evolutionary physicians, on the other hand, see the body as an organism that has evolved methods to meet challenges. Faced with an infection, ordinary physicians might seek to control fever because it appears to be a problem caused by a pathogen. Evolutionary physicians agree that fever might be a problem caused by a pathogen – but, on the other hand, fever might be the body's means of killing off the pathogen by heating it to death. (Evolutionary physicians would keep the idea of coevolution front and center. They expect that humans have evolved defenses against a certain pathogen, the pathogen may have evolved a way to circumvent the defenses, which might have led to further evolution in humans.) Keeping the fever down, then, might slow recovery. For our purposes, the important point is that human experience, in this case of disease, is the outcome of a long history of reciprocal evolution. The body has evolved defenses, and organisms have evolved ways to circumvent those defenses. (The rapid evolution of the AIDS virus is an excellent example.) An ahistorical understanding of the biology of humans and other species leads to misperceptions about causes and effects of ailments, which in turn leads to suboptimal treatments. Effective medicine demands historicizing the biology of humans and the organisms with which they coexist.[28]

Evolutionary history as described here also differs from efforts across the social sciences to develop evolutionary models of culture, behavior, and institutions. Unlike sociobiology and evolutionary psychology, these efforts do not ground their analyses in genes. Rather, they treat genetic evolution as the source of useful analogies. Evolutionary economists have studied firms as analogues of organisms, markets as analogues of natural selection, and routines (repeated ways of doing things, e.g., marketing) as analogues of genes. Anthropologists (and biologists) have treated genes and culture as parallel and interacting systems of information subject to selection. The two systems resemble each other in being heritable, shaping human behavior, and transmitting information imperfectly. They differ from each other in that genes pass information only from parents to children, while culture passes among non-relatives, skips generations, and enables individuals to inherit acquired characteristics from others.[29]

Although different from each other in several ways, and although evolutionary historians need not adopt their ideas, these fields illustrate the value of defining a research program as a field. Attaching "evolutionary" to the names of disciplines has helped scholars define their approaches, find others with similar interests (including people in other fields), and develop coherent literatures. Several of these fields have grown large enough to merit their own subject headings in the Library of Congress catalog.[30]

Evolutionary history

Until now, "evolutionary history" has meant the object of study for evolutionary biologists. (Charles Darwin studied the evolutionary history of tortoises in the Galapagos.) Here we add a new meaning: evolutionary history is the field concerned with the role of evolution in human history. Attaching "evolutionary" to the name of our discipline should bring many of the same advantages we have just seen for other fields: self-definition, ideas for research, identification of common ground with other scholars, and development of a coherent literature. Ultimately, the field's value will lie in new or revised interpretations of history and biology.

Evolutionary history embraces a dynamic view of humans, nature, and their interaction. It sees:

- Humans, and a variety of social variables, as evolutionary forces,
- Organisms as plastic and adaptive rather than static or passive,
- Anthropogenic evolution as beneficial, harmful, or neutral for humans and other species, and
- Genes as parts of the environment and as historical actors.

This approach complements existing emphases in environmental history. Environmental historians have long argued that other historical fields overlook the importance of nature in history. Evolutionary history extends this insight by emphasizing the importance of organismal plasticity. Ecological history has focused on ways humans have changed environments; evolutionary history adds interest in the ways environmental changes have changed species. Ecological history has described ways in which humans have increased and decreased the populations of certain species; evolutionary history adds an interest in the ways humans have increased and decreased populations of genes. Public-health history has emphasized the importance of efforts to control pathogens; evolutionary history adds an interest in the ways pathogens evolve to circumvent control measures.

Evolutionary history builds on foundations laid by historians, biologists, and members of other disciplines. Several examples follow. A phrase at the beginning of each example emphasizes the link between a topic of interest to evolutionary biologists, on the one hand, and a topic of interest to historians, on the other. The examples illustrate the kinds of research questions evolutionary history can prompt, show the range of fields from which evolutionary historians may come and draw, begin to create a literature in evolutionary history, and suggest potential evolutionary revisions of common interpretations of the past.

Western civilization as a byproduct of artificial selection

The best known prototype of evolutionary history, physiologist Jared Diamond's *Guns, Germs, and Steel,* makes the case that adopting agriculture was the most revolutionary act in human history. As we have seen above, artificial selection – unintentional as well as intentional – was essential to that process. Other scholars, too, have found evolution a friendly framework for explaining the development of agriculture. In *Like Engend'ring Like,* Nicholas Russell challenges the idea that pre-nineteenth century breeders practiced methodical breeding. He found that "accidental, domestic-environmental selection," more than breeding for specific traits, drove increases in productivity of meat, wool, and other animal products. Domestication and controlled breeding selected for rapid growth and sexual maturation, Russell argues, simply because growers bred domestic animals as soon as they were ready.[31] If Diamond and Russell are right, accidental selection has played a surprisingly large role in Western history.

In recent centuries, science and industry have played increasingly important roles in evolution. Deborah Fitzgerald (a historian of science, technology, and the environment) has traced the rise of methodical selection in corn breeding in the United States. In the nineteenth century, farmers improved their corn by saving the best seed to plant the next year. The arrival of government and industrial scientists shifted the locus of control from farmers to scientists. Responding to their own agendas as well as those of farmers, these scientists shifted from traditional, open-pollinated breeding methods to new, hybrid methods. Because hybrids did not "breed true," farmers now had to buy new commercial seed each year. The result was a massive change in the nature of corn. In 1933, hybrids grew on 0.4 percent of the corn acreage in the United States. By 1945, the share of land devoted to hybrids had soared to 90 percent.[32]

Genes as agents of geopolitics

"Geopolitics" usually brings to mind national leaders, armies, alliances, and strategic resources. Few would include "plant breeding" in the list. John Perkins, an environmental historian with a background in genetics, has challenged this view. Wealthy and poor nations alike, Perkins argues, saw increased food production as critical to their self-interest in the Cold War. Leaders of poor countries feared that insufficient food for growing populations could lead to loss of hard currency (to pay for imports) and create fertile ground for revolutions against the government in power. Leaders of wealthy nations feared political and economic instability, the spread of hostile ideologies, and weakening of alliances against the Soviet Union. Using wheat as his case study, Perkins shows how these fears motivated rich and poor countries to fund programs designed to boost wheat productivity rapidly through locating and transferring germplasm. Green Revolution would counter Red Revolution.[33]

If the Green Revolution enlisted genetic change as ally in geopolitical struggles, evolution also has posed a threat to national security. Through most of history, disease posed bigger threats to armies than did enemy soldiers. In the Pacific theater of World War II, malaria felled eight times more Americans than did Japan. Louse-borne typhus threatened to waylay the allied conquest of Italy. The arrival of the insecticide DDT, which was effective against malaria-carrying mosquitoes and typhus-bearing lice, seemed to be a miracle. So momentous was DDT's promise that its developer received the Nobel Prize in 1948. In the late 1940s, however, insects began showing resistance to DDT. Although this development threatened agriculture as much as public health, the United States Army led efforts to understand and counter resistance. In the 1950s, the Army organized conferences, commissioned reviews, and funded research. The result was a rapid growth in the number of publications on resistance, but researchers failed to find a way to stop this form of evolution. They could only suggest developing a stream of new chemicals, a chemical arms race that one could run but never win.[34]

Genes as economic agents

For rural sociologist Jack Kloppenburg, the most important force driving evolution in agriculture has been capitalism. In *First the Seed,* he highlights three processes that facilitated capitalistic penetration of plant biotechnology between 1492 and 2000: political economy-commodification, institutions-division of labor, and world economy-germ plasm transfer. Kloppenburg notes that humans shaped the evolution of plants through dispersing, breeding, and eventually patenting life forms. Traditional plant breeding was "applied evolutionary science." With new biotechnology, such as genetic engineering, humans started "outdoing evolution" by moving genes across species. The result was that genes became a form a property, further facilitating commodification and accumulation of wealth.[35]

In *The Animal Estate,* cultural and environmental historian Harriet Ritvo argues that Victorians used animal breeding to resolve class anxieties. As industrialization twisted and strained the English class structure, breeders created elaborate class systems, replete with blue books and pedigrees patterned after those of the nobility, for horses and dogs. Published breed standards and show rings created islands of control and predictability in a turbulent world. At the same time, though, shows offered breeders from lower rungs on the social ladder a rare and treasured chance to compete against and defeat social "betters."[36]

Industrialization as evolution

At first blush, the story of industrialization might seem to be one of the poorer candidates for revision. Industrialization is, after all, the replacement of organisms (where evolution occurs) with machinery. Farm mechanization offers a classic example of the standard argument. Productivity on American wheat farms increased in the late nineteenth and early twentieth centuries. Because yields per acre remained roughly constant while yield per worker increased, economic historians have credited this increase to new machinery. This view is consistent with the large literature showing that extending or replacing human labor with machinery increased productivity in a variety of occupations.[37]

Economists Alan Olmstead and Paul Rhode have shown, however, that the received view is only about half right. The flaw lies in the assumption that organisms in wheat fields stayed constant. They did not. Farmers knew that wheat varieties "wore out" after several years, forcing them to plant new varieties to maintain yields. Wearing out resulted not from change in the wheat, but from change in the wheat's enemies. Insects, diseases, and weeds evolved to overcome a wheat variety's defenses, so breeders had to produce a stream of new varieties to keep pace.[38]

Without breeding, yields would have plummeted and productivity gains attributed to machinery would have been far smaller. Evolutionary biologists call this phenomenon, in which an organism evolves just to stay in place, the Red Queen hypothesis. Olmstead and Rhode estimate that wheat

breeding accounted for about 40 percent of the increase in wheat productivity in 1880 to 1940.[39]

The importance of plant breeding may seem obvious in retrospect, but a
number of distinguished economic historians missed it. Contrast this over-
sight with the way we think about technology. Imagine we learned that
a wheat farmer bought one tractor, never changed the oil or repaired
broken parts, and never bought new machinery over the next fifty years.
Without a second thought, we would predict a drop in productivity. We
are not trained to predict the same pattern with organisms. "Continual
innovation" is a phrase we usually associate with technology, but organisms
are past masters at this process.

Wheat is not unique. A 2002 conference at Rutgers on "Industrializing
Organisms" focused on the role of organisms in industrialization. The
papers revealed that industrialization has often relied on organic evolution.
Along with Olmstead and Rhode's work, examples include the breeding of
hogs and chickens suited to "factories in the field," hemophiliac dogs suited
to scientific laboratories, and trees adapted to industrial silviculture. Might
future historians see mechanization as the first wave of industrialization,
with biotechnology as the second wave that supplemented and replaced
machines?[40]

Resource collapse as size selection

Common explanations for the collapse of live natural resources (fish, birds,
and trees) are anthropogenic mortality and habitat destruction. A 1996
report from the United Nations Food and Agriculture Organization on
worldwide fisheries propounded this view. It concluded that 35 percent of
the world's fisheries were declining. Another 25 percent were "mature,"
meaning that catches had leveled and probably would drop. The report
blamed overfishing and damage to breeding grounds. Its policy recommendations, mainly limits on the numbers of boats and tonnage, grew out of this
interpretation.[41]

Evolutionary history can revise this interpretation by demonstrating the
effect of humans on fish genes as well as numbers. In his study of salmon in
the American Pacific Northwest, environmental historian Joseph Taylor
argues that fish hatcheries pushed salmon into "new evolutionary paths."
Hatchery fish clumped together, carried less genetic variation, and
were smaller than wild fish. These factors combined to increase mortality.
Fishways in dams reinforced these trends. By causing more damage to large
than small salmon, fishways selected for smaller and faster-maturing fish.[42]

Taylor's study emphasizes the impact of humans on fish in streams and
rivers. We can push his analysis further by drawing on fisheries biologists to
show that anthropogenic selection at sea also reduced catches. Between 1950
and 1990, the size of spawning salmon declined 30 percent. Absent humans,

conditions favored big fish. Salmon hatched, went to sea, returned to their natal stream, and either laid or fertilized eggs. Big fish were better than small fish at fighting their way upstream and at competing for spawning sites. Ocean nets changed the odds. By snaring up to 80 percent of returning fish, the nets selected against large fish and for those small enough to slip through. Small fish produced fewer and smaller offspring than large fish, driving the number and size of salmon in the next generation even smaller. Smaller fish meant smaller tonnage (the usual measure of commercial fishery harvests) even if the number of fish caught remained the same.[43]

Size selection drove catches down in another way: by selecting for and against certain behaviors. Traditionally, going to sea for eighteen months was a good strategy because it made salmon bigger than if they stayed home. A few salmon (called jack) came back a year earlier than normal, and some (called parr) never went to sea at all. Traditionally, jack and parr competed poorly against big fish for spawning sites and mates. By catching ocean-going salmon, however, fishers altered the odds. Ocean nets selected for small fish that returned early or stayed home altogether and against fish that went to sea to get big (and be caught). Now jack and parr had as much chance at reproducing as the traditionalists who ventured out to sea, although they produced fewer and smaller offspring than did large fish. The number and size of ocean-going salmon declined.[44]

Our revision of the received view becomes more persuasive when we find similar patterns elsewhere. Whitefish in North American freshwater lakes once supported commercial fishing. The average size of whitefish declined between 1941 and 1965, when the fishery collapsed. In the 1940s, the average nine-year-old whitefish weighed 2 kilograms. By the 1970s, the average had declined to 1 kilogram. Observers blamed the size reduction on removal of older, bigger fish, but it also resulted from changing whitefish genetics. Young fish grew as rapidly in 1970 as they did in 1940, but adults grew more slowly. In the 1950s, nets caught fish aged two years and up. In the 1970s, nets caught fish aged seven years and up. The 5.5-inch holes in nets had created a size threshold, beyond which fish grew at their peril.[45]

Domestication of humans

Most of the literature on domestication implies that humans have sat in the driver's seat while other species rode in the back of the truck. The first word in the title of anthropologist Yi-Fu Tuan's analysis of pets, *Dominance and Affection,* reflects this view. For Perkins, who described the Green Revolution as one stage in a long evolutionary process, this unidirectional view is inadequate. "Wheat and people *coevolved* in ways that left neither much ability to prosper without the other," he argues.[46]

This bi-directional view opens the possibility that organisms domesticated humans as well as vice versa. Biologist Raymond P. Coppinger and English professor Charles Kay Smith have argued that since the last ice age, some 10,000 years ago, much of the most important evolution has taken place within the arena of human activity. Teaming up with humans was a good strategy for organisms faced with a rapidly changing environment.[47]

Popular writer Stephen Budiansky has made this argument in two books. In *Covenant of the Wild*, he suggests that domestic animals have "chosen" to become domesticates because this path offered more chances of survival than did living in the wild. The wolves that became dogs have thrived and now number in the millions in the United States. The wolves that remained wild find themselves all but exterminated in the lower forty-eight states. Budiansky expands on this theme in *The Truth about Dogs*.[48]

Another popular writer, Michael Pollan, argues a similar thesis about plants. In *The Botany of Desire*, he points out that bees probably "see" plants as doing work for them by supplying pollen and nectar, just as Pollan had seen his plants as doing work for him by producing vegetables. But the plants could just as well "see" the bee *and* Pollan doing work for them. Wild varieties of plants had to compete for resources with other species, protect themselves against herbivores, and hope for rain. Their domesticated relatives "got" Pollan to do that work for them, which enabled their genes to become much more common than the genes of wild versions.[49]

These examples illustrate the potential of evolutionary history to suggest unconventional hypotheses about the past. The arguments are not necessarily correct. If history is our guide, we would expect future research to support some ideas and falsify others. No matter what the outcome, though, finding out whether such hypotheses are correct would be useful and exciting.

Conclusion

Humans have been shaping the evolution of so many other species, for so long, in so many ways, and for so many reasons that this process often has hidden in plain sight. In one morning, even before making it out the door, we might wake in bed sheets made of cotton, dress in clothes made of wool, put on shoes made of leather, eat a breakfast made of wheat, butter, oranges, and eggs, read a newspaper made of wood pulp and soy ink, pat a dog, and admire flowers on the table. Every one of these materials and creatures bears the mark of anthropogenic selection, from cotton bred for large bolls to flowers selected for their showy display. Every one of them has a history. Every one of these histories has resulted from social and biological forces. And every one of these histories tells us about ourselves as well as other species.

The time has come for us to understand such histories in a coherent way. Scholars in a variety of disciplines and fields have built the foundation for such an inquiry, with biology and history leading the way along parallel, but too rarely intersecting, paths. Evolutionary history offers a way to link these endeavors. To biology, history offers understanding of the social forces that create selective pressures. To history, biology offers understanding of the ways organisms respond to such pressures. Together, as evolutionary history, they offer understanding of the ever-changing dance between humans and nature. The resulting synthesis just might lead us to new understanding of historical episodes as disparate as state building, capital accumulation, geopolitics, industrialization, and domestication.

The significance of such an understanding will grow as climate change and biotechnology expand the scale of anthropogenic evolution. Humans have long changed regional environments and thus the evolution of species in those environments. Climate change means these experiments have become global. Biotechnology, in its root sense of living technology, is nothing new. But genetic engineering has introduced a novel ability to move genes across very different taxonomic groups and accelerated the rate of evolutionary change. By 1999, genetically engineered plants accounted for about 55 percent of the soybeans, 60 percent of the cotton, and 36 percent of the corn grown in the United States.[50] If we are to understand how genetic engineering shapes human experience today and in the future, it behooves us to examine ways in which anthropogenic evolution has shaped us in the past.

Notes

For helpful comments on earlier versions of this paper, thanks go to Adam Rome; James Secord; anonymous reviewers; the Science, Technology, and Society seminar at Virginia Tech; the Technology, Culture, and Communication seminar at the University of Virginia; the Documenting Environmental Change seminar at Cambridge University; and participants in the 2001 meeting of the American Society for Environmental History. Cheryl Oakes of the Forest History Society has my gratitude for searching the Environmental History Bibliography. A sabbatical leave from the University of Virginia and a grant from the National Science Foundation (SES-0220764) supported this work.

1 Theodosius Dobzhansky, *Genetics and the Origin of Species* (New York: Columbia University Press, 1937), 161.

2 San Jose scale was resistant to lime-sulphur. Black scale, red scale, and citricola scale were resistant to hydrogen cyanide. A. W. A. Brown, "The Challenge of Insecticide Resistance," *Bulletin of the Entomological Society of America* 7 (1961): 6–19. See also A. L. Melander, "Can Insects Become Resistant to Sprays?" *Journal of Economic Entomology* 7 (1914): 167–72; H. J. Quayle, "Resistance of Certain Scale Insects in Certain Localities to Hydrocyanic Acid Fumigation," *Journal of Economic Entomology* 15 (1922): 400–404; Walter S. Hough, "Colorado and Virginia Strains of Codling Moth in Relation to their Ability to Enter Sprayed and Unsprayed Apples," *Journal of Agricultural Research* 48 (1934): 533–53; Opposition to the idea of resistance continued well into the 1930s. See G. H. Cunningham, *Plant Protection by the Aid of*

Therapeutants (Dunedin, New Zealand: John McIndoe Pub., 1935); and William Moore, "Studies of the 'Resistant' California Red Scale, *Aonidiella aurantii* Mask, in California," *Journal of Economic Entomology* 26 (1933): 1140–61; both cited in in H. J. Quayle, "The Development of Resistance to Hydrocyanic Acid in Certain Scale Insects," *Hilgardia* 11 (1938): 183–210.

3 Dobzhansky, *Genetics and the Origin of Species,* 161. See also Quayle, "The Development of Resistance to Hydrocyanic Acid in Certain Scale Insects," 183–84. For more on the rise of, and response to, resistance, see Edmund Russell, *War and Nature: Fighting Humans and Insects with Chemicals from World War I to Silent Spring* (New York: Cambridge University Press, 2001). A classic example of anthropogenic evolution in insects comes from the evolution of dark moths in response to industrial soot, which made light moths more visible to predators. See H. B. D. Kettlewell, "Selection Experiments on Industrial Melanism in the *Lepidoptera,*" *Heredity* 9 (December 1955): 323; H. B. D. Kettlewell, "Further Selection Experiments on Industrial Melanism in the *Lepidoptera,*" *Heredity* 10 (Dec. 1956): 287–300; R. R. Askew, L. M. Cook, and J. A. Bishop, "Atmospheric Pollution and Melanic Moths in Manchester and Its Environs," *Journal of Applied Ecology* 8 (1971): 247–56; Stephen Mosley, *Chimney of the World: A History of Smoke Pollution in Victorian and Edwardian Manchester* (Cambridge, England: White Horse Press, 2001), 45. The species Kettlewell focused on was the peppered moth, *Biston betularia* Linn. Recently, Kettlewell's methods have come in for criticism. See Judith Hooper, *Of Moths and Men: An Evolutionary Tale* (New York: Norton, 2002).

4 All of these views have emerged in discussions with scholars from a variety of disciplines.

5 Charles Darwin, *The Origin of Species by Means of Natural Selection or the Preservation of Favoured Races in the Struggle for Life,* 6th ed. (London: Odhams Press, 1872), 64; Charles Darwin, *Variation of Animals and Plants under Domestication,* vols. I and II (1868, rev. 1883; reprint, Baltimore, Md.: Johns Hopkins University Press, 1998), 1: 2, fn. 1. Darwin wrote in his autobiography that his idea of natural selection derived from his studies of domestication (just as his idea of the struggle for existence came from Malthus). See Nora Barlow, ed., *The Autobiography of Charles Darwin, 1809–1882* (1958; reprint, New York: Norton, 1969), 119–20. Historians have debated the accuracy of Darwin's memory. Some say that Darwin worked out natural selection and then applied it to domestication; others believe Darwin's memory was roughly correct. Michael Ruse, "Charles Darwin and Artificial Selection," *Journal of the History of Ideas* 36 (April–June 1975): 339–50; John F. Cornell, "Analogy and Technology in Darwin's Vision of Nature," *Journal of the History of Biology* 17 (Fall 1984): 303–44; L. T. Evans, "Darwin's Use of the Analogy between Artificial and Natural Selection," *Journal of the History of Biology* 17 (Spring 1984): 113–40. Our concern here is with Darwin's linking of natural and artificial selection, which he indubitably did, rather than with the chronological priority of ideas.

On the history of Darwin's ideas more broadly and their impact, see Peter J. Bowler, *Darwinism* (New York: Twayne Publishers, 1993), and *Charles Darwin: The Man and His Influence* (Cambridge, Mass.: Blackwell, 1990); Michael Ruse, *The Darwinian Revolution: Science Red in Tooth and Claw,* 2nd ed. (Chicago: University of Chicago Press, 1999); E. Janet Browne, *Charles Darwin: A Biography* (Princeton, N.J.: Princeton University Press, 1996); Adrian Desmond and James Moore, *Darwin* (New York: Warner Books, 1992);

David L. Hull, *Darwin and His Critics: The Reception of Darwin's Theory of Evolution by the Scientific Community* (1973; reprint, Chicago: University of Chicago Press, 1983); Gertrude Himmelfarb, *Darwin and the Darwinian Revolution* (Garden City, N.Y.: Doubleday, 1962); Robert M. (Bob) Young, *Darwin's Metaphor: Nature's Place in Victorian Culture* (New York: Cambridge University Press, 1985); Ernst Mayr, *One Long Argument: Charles Darwin and the Genesis of Modern Evolutionary Thought* (Cambridge, Mass.: Harvard University Press, 1991), and *The Growth of Biological Thought: Diversity, Evolution, and Inheritance* (Cambridge, Mass.: Belknap Press, 1982); Daniel C. Dennett, *Darwin's Dangerous Idea: Evolution and the Meaning of Life* (London: Penguin, 1995); Michael Ruse, *The Evolution Wars: A Guide to the Debates* (Santa Barbara, Calif.: ABC-CLIO, 2000).

6 The literature on Darwinian evolution is too enormous to review here. For an introduction, see Douglas Futuyma, *Evolutionary Biology*, 3rd ed. (Sunderland, Mass.: Sinauer, 1998); G. C. Williams, *Natural Selection: Domains, Levels and Challenges* (New York: Oxford University Press, 1992); Ernst Mayr and William B. Provine, eds., *The Evolutionary Synthesis: Perspectives on the Unification of Biology* (Cambridge, Mass: Harvard University Press, 1980); and Steve Jones, *Darwin's Ghost: The Origin of Species Updated* (New York: Random House, 2000).

7 Darwin, *Domestication*, 1:6. On breeding in Darwin's era, see John Sebright, *The Art of Improving the Breeds of Domestic Animals* (London: John Harding, 1809); William Youatt, *Cattle, their Breeds, Management and Diseases* (London: Robert Baldwin, 1834); Roger J. Wood and Vitezslav Orel, *Genetic Prehistory in Selective Breeding: A Prelude to Mendel* (Oxford: Oxford University Press, 2001).

8 Futuyma, *Evolutionary Biology.* Darwin (*Origin*, 55) divided artificial selection into "methodical" and "unconscious" selection, but "intentional" and "unintentional" work better. Darwin's unconscious selectors in fact were methodical and conscious: they selected the best animals to breed with each other, making Darwin's terms misleading. (Darwin used "unconscious," I believe, because he wanted to argue that an unconscious nature could select the best individuals to mate.) His terms also do not accurately describe selection outside agriculture. When humans created insects resistant to insecticides, they did not act methodically in Darwin's sense of breeding toward some desired goal; they were selecting for traits opposite of what they wanted. Nor were they unconscious in Darwin's sense of selecting the best individuals to mate (or even in the more common sense of being unaware). They were not selecting individuals to mate, and they were conscious of results.

9 Darwin, *Origin*, 53–56.

10 James Bennet, "Cluck! Cluck! Chickens in Their Birthday Suits!" *New York Times,* 24 May 2002.

11 Darwin, *Origin*, 134, emphasis added.

12 Jared Diamond, *Guns, Germs, and Steel: The Fates of Human Societies* (New York: W.W. Norton, 1998).

13 Edward Hyams, *Animals in the Service of Man: 10,000 Years of Domestication* (London: J.M. Dent and Sons, 1972); H. Epstein, *The Origin of the Domestic Animals of Africa*, vols. 1–2 (New York: Africana Publishing, 1971); Frederick E. Zeuner, *A History of Domesticated Animals* (London: Hutchinson, 1963); S. Bokonyi, *History of Domestic Mammals in Central and Eastern Europe* (Budapest: Akademiai Kiado, 1974); Juliet Clutton-Brock, *A Natural History of Domesticated Animals* (Austin: University of Texas Press, 1989).

14 Jack R. Harlan, *Crops and Man* (Madison, Wis.: American Society of Agronomy, 1975), 69–70; B. Brouk, *Plants Consumed by Man* (London: Academic Press, 1975); Maarten J. Chrispeels and Davad Sadava, *Plants, Food, and People* (San Francisco: W.H. Freeman, 1977).

15 Stephen R. Palumbi, *The Evolution Explosion: How Humans Cause Rapid Evolutionary Change* (New York: W.W. Norton, 2001), 139–40; National Research Council, *Pesticide Resistance: Strategies and Tactics for Management* (Washington, D.C.: National Academy Press, 1986), 16–17. See also J. Mallet, "The Evolution of Insecticide Resistance: Have the Insects Won?" *Trends in Ecology and Evolution* 4 (no. 11, 1989): 336–40.

16 David Brown, "TB Resistance Stands at 11% of Cases," *Washington Post*, 24 March 2000, A14; S. B. Levy, *The Antibiotic Paradox: How Miracle Drugs Are Destroying the Miracle* (New York: Plenum, 1992); Palumbi, *Evolution Explosion*, 85.

17 "'Wonder Drugs' Losing Healing Aura," *Washington Post*, 26 June 1995. As the century closed, the World Health Organization launched a new effort called Roll Back Malaria, whose title suggested the more modest goals that seemed realistic in light of previous disappointments. R. S. Phillips, "Current Status of Malaria and Potential for Control," *Clinical Microbiology Reviews* 14 (January 2001): 208–26; J. F. Trape, "The Public Health Impact of Chloroquine Resistance in Africa," *American Journal of Tropical Medicine and Hygiene* 64 (Jan.–Feb. Suppl. 2001): 12–17; J. A. Najera, "Malaria Control: Achievements, Problems and Strategies," *Parassitologia* 43 (June 2001): 1–89; Palumbi, *Evolution Explosion*, 137–38.

18 William E. Bradshaw and Christina M. Holzapfel, "Genetic Shift in Photoperiodic Response Correlated with Global Warming," *Proceedings of the National Academy of Sciences of the United States of America* 98 (4 December 2001): 14509–11; Sean C. Thomas and Joel G. Kingsolver, "Natural Selection: Responses to Current (Anthropogenic) Environmental Changes," in *Encyclopedia of Life Sciences* (London: Macmillan, 2002), 659–64.

19 Cheryl Oakes, librarian and archivist at the Forest History Society in Durham, North Carolina, searched the database (titles and abstracts) on 9 September 2002. Although electronic searches are imperfect, the overall pattern is so strong that adding missed citations probably would have made little difference. Even omissions are telling, for they reveal that neither author nor abstracter thought evolution important enough to mention in a title, subtitle, or abstract. The database contains other works on the history of evolutionary ideas, and works that use "evolution" to mean change in general, but this search focused instead on material (genetic) evolution in action. Authors of the eight works include a popular writer, two evolutionary biologists, a paleoanthropologist, and the iconoclast Paul Shepard (twice): Stephen Budiansky, *The Covenant of the Wild: Why Animals Chose Domestication* (New Haven, Conn.: Yale University Press, 1999); Niles Eldredge, *Life in the Balance: Humanity and the Biodiversity Crisis* (Princeton, N.J.: Princeton University Press, 1998); Dan Flores, "Nature's Children: Environmental History as Human Natural History," in John P. Herron and Andrew G. Kirk, eds., *Human/Nature: Biology, Culture, and Environmental History* (Albuquerque: University of New Mexico Press, 1999), 11–30; Stephen R. Kellert, *Kinship to Mastery: Biophilia in Human Evolution and Development* (Washington, D.C.: Island Press, 1997); Lynn Margulis, Clifford Matthews, and Aaron Haselton, eds., *Environmental Evolution: Effects of the Origin and Evolution of Life on Planet Earth*, 2nd ed. (Cambridge, Mass.: MIT Press, 2000); Rick Potts, *Humanity's Descent: The*

Consequences of Ecological Instability (New York: Avon Books, 1997); Paul Shepard, *Coming Home to the Pleistocene* (Washington, D.C.: Island Press, 1998) and *The Others: How Animals Made Us Human* (Washington, D.C.: Island Press, 1996).

    The one citation in the research register was to Laura Rival's work on the coevolution of human groups and rainforests, but she may be using "coevolution" in a general rather than specifically genetic way. Documenting Environmental Change, Centre for History and Economics, King's College, Cambridge University (*http://www.kings.cam.ac.uk/histecon/envdoc/index.html*), viewed 10 September 2002.

20 Eric R. Pianka, *Evolutionary Ecology,* 6th ed. (San Francisco: Addison Wesley Longman, 2000), xiv. Douglas Futuyma's popular, 800+ page introductory textbook on evolutionary biology says little about domestication and omits Darwin's *Variation of Animals and Plants under Domestication* from its 41-page bibliography. The single indexed reference to breeding focuses on inbreeding and outbreeding in the wild. Domestication merits two brief mentions in the index to Ernst Mayr's 974-page opus on the growth of biological thought; "breeding" does not appear in the index. See, *The Growth of Biological Thought: Diversity, Evolution, and Inheritance* (Cambridge, Mass: Belknap Press of Harvard University Press, 1982). This pattern is not new. In *Origin* (31), Darwin chided his colleagues for not paying enough attention to domestic species.

    Books by agricultural scientists often make a nod to evolution and then drop the topic. Evolution does not appear in the index of F. G. H. Lupton, ed., *Wheat Breeding: Its Scientific Basis* (London: Chapman and Hall, 1987). Evolution appears once, in the context of an "evolutionary breeding method" that relies on the idea that natural selection weeds out weaker individuals, in Oliver Mayo, *The Theory of Plant Breeding,* 2nd ed. (Oxford: Clarendon Press, 1987), 175. Evolution appears on the first page and not thereafter in R. F. E. Axford, S. C. Bishop, F. W. Nicholas, and J. B. Owen, *Breeding for Disease Resistance in Farm Animals,* 2nd ed. (New York: CABI Publishing, 2000), ix. Evolution appears in the introduction and not thereafter in Everett James Warwick and James Edwards Legates, *Breeding and Improvement of Farm Animals,* 7th ed. (New Delhi: TATA McGraw-Hill, 1979), 5–7. Evolution appears three times, in each case implying that evolution ended with domestication, in Temple Grandin, ed., *Genetics and the Behavior of Domestic Animals* (London: Academic Press, 1998), 21, 146, 204. In contrast, Lewis Stevens divided the evolution of domestic fowl into three stages: evolution of the genus *Gallus,* emergence of domestic fowl from ancestors in *Gallus,* and development of current varieties and breeds. See, *Genetics and Evolution of the Domestic Fowl* (New York: Cambridge University Press, 1991).

21 Pianka, *Evolutionary Ecology,* xiv, 10; Palumbi, *Evolution Explosion,* 10.

22 The titles of early works in environmental history illustrate the pervasive influence of ecology: William Cronon, *Changes in the Land: Indians, Colonists, and the Ecology of New England* (New York: Hill and Wang, 1983); Donald Worster, *Nature's Economy: A History of Ecological Ideas* (New York: Cambridge University Press, 1977); Carolyn Merchant, *The Death of Nature: Women, Ecology, and the Scientific Revolution* (San Francisco: Harper & Row, 1980), and *Ecological Revolutions: Nature, Gender, and Science in New England* (Chapel Hill: University of North Carolina Press, 1989); Alfred Crosby, *Ecological Imperialism: The Biological Expansion of Europe, 900–1900* (New York: Cambridge University Press, 1986); J. Donald Hughes, *Ecology in*

Ancient Civilizations (Albuquerque: University of New Mexico Press, 1975); Lester J. Bilsky, ed., *Historical Ecology: Essays on Environment and Social Change* (Port Washington, N.Y.: Kennikat Press, 1980); Arthur F. McEvoy, *The Fisherman's Problem: Ecology and Law in the California Fisheries, 1850–1980* (New York: Cambridge University Press, 1986). In her popular textbook, Carolyn Merchant notes that "ecological history" and "environmental history" often have been used interchangeably; she subsumes the latter under the former. See, *Major Problems in Environmental History* (Lexington, Mass.: D.C. Heath, 1993), 1.

Public health histories that contributed to the founding of environmental history do not cluster around a single term, but "pollution" often appears. See, for example, Martin Melosi, ed., *Pollution and Reform in American Cities, 1870–1930* (Austin: University of Texas Press, 1980). Joel Tarr's pioneering work first appeared largely in journals and is collected in *The Search for the Ultimate Sink: Urban Pollution in Historical Perspective* (Akron, Ohio: University of Akron Press, 1996).

23 Keyword search for "ecolog" (ecology and its variants) and "health" in titles and non-indexed fields (including abstract) conducted 29 November 2002. Donald Worster urged environmental history to stay close to environmentalism in his comments at the plenary session, American Society for Environmental History meeting, Durham, N.C., 28 March 2001.

24 E. B. Ford, *Ecological Genetics* (London: Methuen, 1964), and Eric R. Pianka, *Evolutionary Ecology* (New York: Harper & Row, 1974). Both appeared in multiple editions.

25 Ecological ideas useful in analyzing these issues include connectivity among species (often via the ecosystem concept), stability through species diversity, limits to growth (carrying capacity), habitat change, population dynamics, and extinction. Environmental historians often have drawn on the ecologists who emphasized these issues, such as Howard Odum, *Environment, Power, and Society* (New York: Wiley-Interscience, 1971) and *Systems Ecology: An Introduction* (New York: Wiley, 1983); Eugene P. Odum and Howard Odum, *Fundamentals of Ecology,* 2nd ed. (Philadelphia: Saunders, 1959); Robert H. MacArthur, *Geographical Ecology: Patterns in the Distribution of Species* (New York: Harper & Row, 1972); Robert H. MacArthur and Joseph H. Connell, *The Biology of Populations* (New York: Wiley, 1966); Charles S. Elton, *The Ecology of Invasions by Animals and Plants* (London: Methuen, 1958); Robert E. Ricklefs, *Ecology* (London: Nelson, 1973), and *The Economy of Nature: A Textbook in Basic Ecology,* 4th ed. (New York: W.H. Freeman, 1996); Paul R. Ehrlich, Anne H. Ehrlich, and John P. Holdren, *Ecoscience: Population, Resources, Environment* (San Francisco: W. H. Freeman, 1977) and *Human Ecology: Problems and Solutions* (San Francisco: W.H. Freeman, 1973).

26 On sociobiology, see Edward O. Wilson, *Sociobiology: The New Synthesis* (Cambridge, Mass.: Belknap Press of Harvard University, 1975), and *Consilience: The Unity of Knowledge* (London: Little, Brown, and Company, 1998); David P. Barash, *Sociobiology and Behavior,* 2nd ed. (New York: Elsevier, 1982); Richard Dawkins, *The Selfish Gene* (New York: Oxford University Press, 1976); Peter Koslowski, ed., *Sociobiology and Bioeconomics: The Theory of Evolution in Biological and Economic Theory* (New York: Springer Verlag, 1999); Michael S. Gregory, Anita Silvers, and Diane Sutch, eds., *Sociobiology and Human Nature: An Interdisciplinary Critique and Defense* (San Francisco: Jossey-Bass, 1978); Georg Breur, *Sociobiology and the Human Dimension* (New York: Cambridge University Press, 1982); Alexander Rosenberg, *Sociobiology*

and the Preemption of Social Science (Baltimore, Md.: Johns Hopkins University Press, 1980); Robert W. Bell and Nancy J. Bell, *Sociobiology and the Social Sciences* (Lubbock: Texas Tech University Press, 1989); Arthur L. Caplan, ed., *The Sociobiology Debate: Readings on Ethical and Scientific Issues* (New York: Harper & Row, 1978); Ashley Montagu, ed., *Sociobiology Examined* (New York: Oxford University Press, 1980); Michael Ruse, *Sociobiology: Sense or Nonsense?* (Boston: D. Reidel Publishing Company, 1984); Matt Ridley, *The Red Queen: Sex and the Evolution of Human Nature* (New York: Viking, 1993).

Some philosophers have treated evolution as a source of new questions or approaches within their fields. Evolutionary ethicists, for example, have treated Charles Darwin's *Origin of Species* (1859) and Edward O. Wilson's *Sociobiology* (1975) as challenging them to see whether one can develop an ethics based on genetic evolution. See Paul Thompson, ed., *Issues in Evolutionary Ethics* (Albany: State University of New York Press, 1995), back cover; Emmanuel K. Twesigye, *Religion and Ethics for a New Age: Evolutionist Approach* (Lanham, Md.: University Press of America, 2001). For supporters of evolution in philosophy, see Michael Ruse, *The Darwinian Paradigm: Essays on Its History, Philosophy and Religious Implications* (New York: Routledge, 1993); Daniel C. Dennett, *Freedom Evolves* (New York: Viking, 2003) and *Darwin's Dangerous Idea: Evolution and the Meanings of Life* (New York: Simon and Schuster, 1995).

On evolutionary psychology, see Henry Plotkin, *Evolution in Mind: An Introduction to Evolutionary Psychology* (London: Penguin, 1997); Susan Blackmore, *The Meme Machine* (New York: Oxford University Press, 1999); Charles Crawford and Dennis L. Krebs, eds., *Handbook of Evolutionary Psychology: Ideas, Issues, and Applications* (Mahwah, N.J.: Lawrence Erlbaum Associates, 1998); Louise Barrett, Robin Dunbar, and John Lycett, *Human Evolutionary Psychology* (Princeton, N.J.: Princeton University Press, 2002); Steven Pinker, *The Blank Slate: The Modern Denial of Human Nature* (New York: Viking, 2002), and *How the Mind Works* (New York: Norton, 1997); David F. Bjorklund and Anthony D. Pellegrini, *The Origins of Human Nature: Evolutionary Developmental Psychology* (Washington, D.C.: American Psychological Association, 2002); Alan Clamp, *Evolutionary Psychology* (London: Hodder & Stoughton, 2001); David M. Buss, *Evolutionary Psychology: The New Science of the Mind* (Boston: Allyn and Bacon, 1999); Robert Wright, *The Moral Animal: Evolutionary Psychology and Everyday Life* (New York: Pantheon Books, 1994); Jerome H. Barkow, Leda Cosmides, and John Tooby, eds., *The Adapted Mind: Evolutionary Psychology and the Generation of Culture* (New York: Oxford University Press, 1992). For the case against evolutionary psychology, see Hilary Rose and Steven Rose, eds., *Alas, Poor Darwin: Arguments against Evolutionary Psychology* (London: Jonathan Cape, 2000).

For social studies of science and technology, see Joseph E. Taylor III, *Making Salmon: An Environmental History of the Northwest Fisheries Crisis* (Seattle: University of Washington Press, 1999), 10; Steve W. Fuller, *Philosophy, Rhetoric, and the End of Knowledge: The Coming of Science and Technology Studies* (Madison: University of Wisconsin Press, 1993); Bruno Latour, *Science in Action: How to Follow Scientists and Engineers through Society* (Cambridge, Mass.: Harvard University Press, 1987); Bruno Latour and Steve Woolgar, *Laboratory Life: The Social Construction of Scientific Facts* (Beverly Hills, Calif.: Sage Publications, 1979); Sheila Jasanoff, Gerald E. Markle, James C. Petersen, and Trevor Pinch, eds., *Handbook of Science and Technology Studies*

(Thousand Oaks, Calif.: Sage Publications, 1995); Ruth Schwartz Cowan, *More Work for Mother: The Ironies of Household Technology from the Open Hearth to the Microwave* (New York: Basic Books, 1983); Claude S. Fischer, *America Calling: A Social History of the Telephone to 1940* (Berkeley: University of California Press, 1992); Donna Haraway, *Simians, Cyborgs, and Women: The Reinvention of Nature* (New York: Routledge, 1991); Thomas Parke Hughes, *Networks of Power: Electrification in Western Society, 1880–1930* (Baltimore, Md.: Johns Hopkins University Press, 1983); Donald A. Mackenzie, *Inventing Accuracy: An Historical Sociology of Nuclear Missile Guidance* (Cambridge, Mass.: MIT Press, 1990); Ruth Oldenziel, *Making Technology Masculine: Men, Women and Modern Machines in America, 1870–1945* (Amsterdam: Amsterdam University Press, 1999); Londa Schiebinger, *Nature's Body: Gender in the Making of Modern Science* (Boston: Beacon Press, 1993); Wiebe E. Bijker, Thomas P. Hughes, and Trevor J. Pinch, eds., *The Social Construction of Technological Systems: New Directions in the Sociology and History of Technology* (Cambridge, Mass.: MIT Press, 1987).

For sharply critical views of science and technology, see Theodor W. Adorno and Max Horkheimer, *Dialectic of Enlightenment* (1944; London: Verso, 1997), 4, 6; Jacques Ellul, *The Technological Society* (1964; reprint, New York: Knopf, 1973); David F. Noble, *America by Design: Science, Technology, and the Rise of Corporate Capitalism* (New York: Knopf, 1977); Langdon Winner, *The Whale and the Reactor: A Search for Limits in an Age of High Technology* (Chicago: University of Chicago Press, 1986).

On biological determinism, see Virginia Scharff, "Man and Nature! Sex Secrets of Environmental History," 31–48, and Vera Norwood, "Constructing Gender in Nature: Bird Society Through the Eyes of John Burroughs and Florence Merriam Bailey," 49–62, in Herron and Kirk, eds., *Human/Nature;* Daniel J. Kevles, *In the Name of Eugenics: Genetics and the Uses of Human Heredity* (New York: Knopf, 1985); Nicholas W. Gillham, *A Life of Sir Francis Galton: From African Exploration to the Birth of Eugenics* (New York: Oxford University Press, 2001); Carl N. Degler, *In Search of Human Nature: The Decline and Revival of Darwinism in American Social Thought* (New York: Oxford University Press, 1991); Alexander Rosenberg, *Darwinism in Philosophy, Social Science, and Policy* (New York: Cambridge University Press, 2000); Ronald L. Numbers and John Stenhouse, eds., *Disseminating Darwinism: The Role of Place, Race, Religion, and Gender* (New York: Cambridge University Press, 1999); Mike Hawkins, *Social Darwinism in European and American Thought, 1860–1945: Nature as Model and Nature as Threat* (New York: Cambridge University Press, 1997).

27 Stephen Jay Gould, *The Mismeasure of Man* (New York: Norton, 1996); Richard C. Lewontin, *The Triple Helix: Gene, Organism, and Environment* (Cambridge, Mass.: Harvard University Press, 2000); Richard C. Lewontin, Steven Rose, and Leon J. Kamin, *Not in Our Genes: Biology, Ideology, and Human Nature* (New York: Pantheon Books, 1984); Luigi Luca Cavalli-Sforza, *Genes, Peoples, and Languages* (Berkeley: University of California Press, 2000); Lynn Margulis, *The Symbiotic Planet: A New Look at Evolution* (London: Weidenfeld and Nicolson, 1998), 3; Paul Ehrlich, *Human Natures: Genes, Cultures and the Human Prospect* (Washington, D.C.: Island Press, 2000).

28 George C. Williams and R. M. Nesse, "The Dawn of Darwinian Medicine," *Quarterly Review of Biology* 66 (March 1991): 16–18. See also Paul W. Ewald, *Evolution of Infectious Disease* (New York: Oxford University Press, 1994);

Randolph M. Nesse and George C. Williams, *Why We Get Sick: The New Science of Darwinian Medicine* (New York: Times Books, 1994). For a wider view, see J. J. Bull and H. A. Wichman, "Applied Evolution," *Annual Review of Ecology and Systematics* 32 (2001), 183–217. On HIV evolution, see Scott Freeman and Jon C. Herron, *Evolutionary Analysis* (Englewood Cliffs, N.J.: Prentice Hall, 1998); K. A. Crandall, ed., *HIV Evolution* (Baltimore: Johns Hopkins University Press, 1999).

29 On evolutionary economics, see John Laurent and John Nightingale, *Darwinism and Evolutionary Economics* (Cheltenham, England: Edward Elgar, 2001); Richard R. Nelson and Sidney G. Winter, *An Evolutionary Theory of Economic Change* (Cambridge, Mass.: Belknap Press of Harvard University Press, 1982); Jack J. Vromen, *Economic Evolution: An Enquiry into the Foundations of New Institutional Economics* (London: Routledge, 1995). For an application of evolutionary economics to the environment, see John M. Gowdy, *Coevolutionary Economics: The Economy, Society, and the Environment* (Boston: Kluwer, 1994).

On evolutionary approaches to culture, see William H. Durham, *Coevolution: Genes, Culture, and Human Diversity* (Stanford, Calif.: Stanford University Press, 1991); Richard Dawkins, *The Selfish Gene* (New York: Oxford University Press, 1976); Luca Cavalli-Sforza and M. W. Feldman, *Cultural Transmission and Evolution: A Quantitative Approach* (Princeton, N.J.: Princeton University Press, 1981); Robert Boyd and Peter J. Richerson, *Culture and the Evolutionary Process* (Chicago: University of Chicago Press, 1985); Charles J. Lumsden and Edward O. Wilson, *Genes, Mind, and Culture* (Cambridge, Mass.: Harvard University Press, 1981). For an effort to develop a common literature of evolution in social sciences, see Johann Peter Murmann, "Evolutionary Theory in the Social Sciences," (*http://www.etss.net/*), viewed 15 December 2002.

Some historians have applied selectionist models to the history of ideas. See Walter Vincenti, *What Engineers Know and How They Know It* (Baltimore, Md.: Johns Hopkins University Press, 1990); Robert J. Richards, *Darwin and the Emergence of Evolutionary Theories of Mind and Behavior* (Chicago: University of Chicago Press, 1987).

Darwin's theory of evolution through natural selection has inspired three approaches to computer programming now grouped under "evolutionary algorithms." See David E. Clark, ed., *Evolutionary Algorithms in Molecular Design* (New York: Wiley-VCH, 2000); Thomas Back, *Evolutionary Algorithms in Theory and Practice: Evolutionary Strategies, Evolutionary Programming, Genetic Algorithms* (New York: Oxford University Press, 1996); Mukesh Patel, Vasant Honavar, Karthik Balakrishnan, *Advances in the Evolutionary Synthesis of Intelligent Agents* (Cambridge, Mass.: MIT Press, 2001).

30 Library of Congress subject headings include evolutionary computation, evolutionary economics, and evolutionary programming. The heading for evolutionary ethics is "ethics, evolutionary." Evolutionary psychology appears under "genetic psychology."

31 Diamond, *Guns, Germs, and Steel;* Nicholas Russell, *Like Engend'ring Like: Heredity and Animal Breeding in Early Modern England* (Cambridge, England: Cambridge University Press, 1986), 216–18; J. Holden, J. Peacock, and T. Williams, eds., *Genes, Crops and the Environment* (New York: Cambridge University Press, 1993).

32 Deborah Fitzgerald, *The Business of Breeding: Hybrid Corn in Illinois, 1890–1940* (Ithaca, N. Y: Cornell University Press, 1990).

33 John Perkins, *Geopolitics and the Green Revolution: Wheat, Genes, and the Cold War* (New York: Oxford University Press, 1997).

34 Russell, *War and Nature;* John Perkins, *Insects, Experts, and the Insecticide Crisis: The Quest for New Pest Management Strategies* (New York: Plenum Press, 1982), and "Reshaping Technology in Wartime: The Effect of Military Goals on Entomological Research and Insect-Control Practices," *Technology and Culture* 19 (1978): 169–86; Thomas R. Dunlap, *DDT: Scientists, Citizens, and Public Policy* (Princeton, N.J.: Princeton University Press, 1981).

35 Jack Ralph Kloppenburg, Jr., *First the Seed: The Political Economy of Plant Biotechnology, 1492–2000* (New York: Cambridge University Press, 1988), 2–3, 9.

36 Harriet Ritvo, *The Animal Estate: The English and Other Creatures in the Victorian Era* (Cambridge, Mass.: Harvard University Press, 1987).

37 Willard W. Cochrane, *The Development of American Agriculture: A Historical Analysis* (Minneapolis: University of Minnesota Press, 1979), 200; Yujiro Hayami and Vernon Ruttan, *Agricultural Development: An International Perspective,* rev. ed. (Baltimore, Md.: Johns Hopkins University Press, 1985), 209; Jeremy Atack, Fred Bateman, and William N. Parker, "The Farm, the Farmer, and the Market," in Stanley L. Engerman and Robert E. Gallman, eds., *The Cambridge Economic History of the United States,* vol. 2, *The Long Nineteenth Century* (New York: Cambridge University Press, 2000), 259, all cited in Alan L. Olmstead and Paul W. Rhode, "Biological Innovation in American Wheat Production: Science, Policy, and Environmental Adaptation," paper presented at conference on "Industrializing Organisms," Rutgers University, March 2002.

38 Olmstead and Rhode, "Biological Innovation in American Wheat Production"; see also M. D. Rausher, "Co-evolution and Plant Resistance to Natural Enemies," *Nature* 411 (no. 6839, 2001): 857–64.

39 Olmstead and Rhode, "Biological Innovation in American Wheat Production" and "Biological Innovation and Productivity Growth in American Wheat Production, 1800–1940," *Journal of Economic History* 62 (June 2002): 581.

40 On genetic evolution in the history of technology, see Edmund Russell, "An Anatomy of Organismal Technology," presented at conference on "Industrializing Organisms," Rutgers University, March 2002. A revised version, titled "The Garden in the Machine: Toward an Evolutionary History of Technology," appeared with other papers from the Rutgers conference in Philip Scranton and Susan Schrepfer, eds., *Industrializing Organisms: Introducing Evolutionary History* (New York: Routledge, 2003). For applications of evolution and selection to technological development (but not organisms), see George Basalla, *The Evolution of Technology* (Cambridge, England: Cambridge University Press, 1988).

41 United Nations Food and Agriculture Organization, *The State of World Fisheries and Aquaculture-1996,* figure 27 and related text (*http://www.fao.org/docrep/003/w3265e/w3265eoo.htm#Contents*), viewed 12 December 2002.

42 Taylor, *Making Salmon,* 203–4, 206, 233, 236.

43 W. E. Ricker, "Changes in the Average Size and Average Age of Pacific Salmon," *Canadian Journal of Fisheries and Aquatic Science* 38 (1981): 1636–56, cited in Palumbi, *Evolution Explosion,* 187–88.

44 Mart R. Gross, "Salmon Breeding Behavior and Life History Evolution in Changing Environments," *Ecology* 72 (August 1991): 1180–86.

45 P. Handford, G. Bell, and T. Reimchen, "A Gillnet Fishery Considered as an Experiment in Artificial Selection," *Journal of Fisheries Research Board of Canada* 34 (1977): 954–61, cited in Palumbi, *Evolution Explosion,* 189–90.

46 Yi-Fu Tuan, *Dominance and Affection: The Making of Pets* (New Haven, Conn.: Yale University Press, 1984); Perkins, *Geopolitics and the Green Revolution,* 19, emphasis added.

47 Raymond P. Coppinger and Charles Kay Smith, "The Domestication of Evolution," *Environmental Conservation* 10 (Winter 1983): 283–92.

48 Stephen Budiansky, *The Covenant of the Wild,* (New York: William Morrow, 1992) and *The Truth About Dogs: An Inquiry into the Ancestry, Social Conventions, Mental Habits, and Moral Fiber of Canis Familiaris* (New York: Viking, 2000).

49 Michael Pollan, *The Botany of Desire: A Plant's-Eye View of the World* (New York: Random House, 2001).

50 Council for Biotechnology Information, "FAQs," (http://www.whybiotech. com), viewed 20 July 2001; Palumbi, *Evolution Explosion;* "'Frankenfish' or Tomorrow's Dinner? Biotech Salmon Face a Current of Environmental Worry," *Washington Post,* 17 October 2000; "Biotech Research Branches Out: Gene-Altered Trees Raise Thickets of Promise, Concern," *Washington Post,* 3 August 2000; "Plant's Genetic Code Deciphered: Data Called a Biological 'Rosetta Stone,' an Engineering Toolbox," *Washington Post,* 14 December 2000; Michael Specter, "The Pharmageddon Riddle," *New Yorker,* 10 April 2000, 58–71; "Biotech Corn Traces Dilute Bumper Crop," *Washington Post,* 25 October 2000.

9

ECOLOGICAL IMPERIALISM

The overseas migration of western Europeans as a biological phenomenon

Alfred W. Crosby

Industrial man may in many respects be considered an aggressive and successful weed strangling other species and even the weaker members of its own.
Stafford Lightman, "The Responsibilities of Intervention in Isolated Societies," *Health and Disease in Tribal Societies*

Europeans in North America, especially those with an interest in gardening and botany, are often stricken with fits of homesickness at the sight of certain plants which, like themselves, have somehow strayed thousands of miles westward across the Atlantic. Vladimir Nabokov, the Russian exile, had such an experience on the mountain slopes of Oregon:

Do you recognize that clover?
Dandelions, *l'or du pauvre?*
(Europe, nonetheless, is over.)

A century earlier the success of European weeds in America inspired Charles Darwin to goad the American botanist Asa Gray: "Does it not hurt your Yankee pride that we thrash you so confoundly? I am sure Mrs. Gray will stick up for your own weeds. Ask her whether they are not more honest, downright good sort of weeds."[1]

The common dandelion, *l'or du pauvre,* despite its ubiquity and its bright yellow flower, is not at all the most visible of the Old World immigrants in North America. Vladimir Nabokov was a prime example of the most visible kind: the *Homo sapiens* of European origin. Europeans and their descendants, who comprise the majority of human beings in North America and in a number of other lands outside of Europe, are the most spectacularly successful overseas migrants of all time. How strange it is to find

166

Englishmen, Germans, Frenchmen, Italians, and Spaniards comfortably ensconced in places with names like Wollongong (Australia), Rotorua (New Zealand), and Saskatoon (Canada), where obviously other peoples should dominate, as they must have at one time.

None of the major genetic groupings of humankind is as oddly distributed about the world as European, especially western European, whites. Almost all the peoples we call Mongoloids live in the single contiguous land mass of Asia. Black Africans are divided between three continents – their homeland and North and South America – but most of them are concentrated in their original latitudes, the tropics, facing each other across one ocean. European whites were all recently concentrated in Europe, but in the last few centuries have burst out, as energetically as if from a burning building, and have created vast settlements of their kind in the South Temperate Zone and North Temperate Zone (excepting Asia, a continent already thoroughly and irreversibly tenanted). In Canada and the United States together they amount to nearly 90 percent of the population; in Argentina and Uruguay together to over 95 percent; in Australia to 98 percent; and in New Zealand to 90 percent. The only nations in the Temperate Zones outside of Asia which do not have enormous majorities of European whites are Chile, with a population of two-thirds mixed Spanish and Indian stock, and South Africa, where blacks outnumber whites six to one. How odd that these two, so many thousands of miles from Europe, should be exceptions in *not* being predominantly pure European.[2]

Europeans have conquered Canada, the United States, Argentina, Uruguay, Australia, and New Zealand not just militarily and economically and technologically – as they did India, Nigeria, Mexico, Peru, and other tropical lands, whose native people have long since expelled or interbred with and even absorbed the invaders. In the Temperate Zone lands listed above Europeans conquered and triumphed demographically. These, for the sake of convenience, we will call the Lands of the Demographic Takeover.

There is a long tradition of emphasizing the contrasts between Europeans and Americans – a tradition honored by such names as Henry James and Frederick Jackson Turner – but the vital question is really why Americans are so European. And why the Argentinians, the Uruguayans, the Australians, and the New Zealanders are so European in the obvious genetic sense.

The reasons for the relative failure of the European demographic takeover in the tropics are clear. In tropical Africa, until recently, Europeans died in droves of the fevers; in tropical America they died almost as fast of the same diseases, plus a few native American additions. Furthermore, in neither region did European agricultural techniques, crops, and animals prosper. Europeans did try to found colonies for settlement, rather than merely exploitation, but they failed or achieved only partial success in the hot lands. The Scots left their bones as monument to their short-lived colony at Darien at the turn of the eighteenth century. The English Puritans who skipped Massachusetts Bay Colony to go to Providence Island in the Caribbean Sea did not even achieve a permanent settlement, much less a Commonwealth of God. The Portuguese who went to northeastern Brazil created viable settlements, but only by perching themselves on top of first a population of native Indian laborers and then, when these faded away, a population of laborers imported from Africa. They did achieve a demographic takeover, but only by interbreeding with their servants. The Portuguese in Angola, who helped supply those servants, never had a breath of a chance to achieve a demographic takeover.[3] There was much to repel and little to attract the mass of Europeans to the tropics, and so they stayed home or went to the lands where life was healthier, labor more rewarding, and where white immigrants, by their very number, encouraged more immigration.

In the cooler lands, the colonies of the Demographic Takeover, Europeans achieved very rapid population growth by means of immigration, by increased life span, and by maintaining very high birthrates. Rarely has population expanded more rapidly than it did in the eighteenth and nineteenth centuries in these lands. It is these lands, especially the United States, that enabled Europeans and their overseas offspring to expand from something like 18 percent of the human species in 1650 to well over 30 percent in 1900. Today 670 million Europeans live in Europe, and 250 million or so other Europeans – genetically as European as any left behind in the Old World – live in the Lands of the Demographic Takeover, an ocean or so from home.[4] What the Europeans have done with unprecedented success in the past few centuries can accurately be described by a term from apiculture: They have swarmed.

They swarmed to lands which were populated at the time of European arrival by peoples as physically capable of rapid increase as the Europeans, and yet who are now small minorities in their homelands and sometimes no more than relict populations. These population explosions among colonial Europeans of the past few centuries coincided with population crashes among the aborigines. If overseas Europeans have historically been less fatalistic and grim than their relatives in Europe, it is because they have viewed the histories of their nations very selectively. When he returned from his world voyage on the *Beagle* in the 1830s, Charles Darwin, as a biologist rather than a historian, wrote, "Wherever the European has trod, death seems to pursue the aboriginal."[5]

Any respectable theory which attempts to explain the Europeans' demographic triumphs has to provide explanations for at least two phenomena. The first is the decimation and demoralization of the aboriginal populations of Canada, the United States, Argentina, and others. The obliterating defeat of these populations was not simply due to European technological superiority. The Europeans who settled in temperate South Africa seemingly had the same advantages as those who settled in Virginia and New South Wales, and yet how different was their fate. The Bantu-speaking peoples, who now overwhelmingly outnumber the whites in South Africa, were superior to their American, Australian, and New Zealand counterparts in that they possessed iron weapons, but how much more inferior to a musket or a rifle is a stone-pointed spear than an iron-pointed spear? The Bantu have prospered demographically not because of their numbers at the time of first contact with whites, which were probably not greater per square mile than those of the Indians east of the Mississippi River. Rather, the Bantu have prospered because they survived military conquest, avoided the conquerors, or became their indispensable servants – and in the long run because they reproduced faster than the whites. In contrast, why did so few of the natives of the Lands of the Demographic Takeover survive?

Second, we must explain the stunning, even awesome success of European agriculture, that is, the European way of manipulating the environment in the Lands of the Demographic Takeover. The difficult progress of the European frontier in the Siberian *taiga* or the Brazilian *sertão* or the South African *veldt* contrasts sharply with its easy, almost fluid advance in North America. Of course, the pioneers of North America would never have characterized their progress as easy: Their lives were filled with danger, deprivation, and unremitting labor; but as a group they always succeeded in taming whatever portion of North America they wanted within a few decades and usually a good deal less time. Many individuals among them failed – they were driven mad by blizzards and dust storms, lost their crops to locusts and their flocks to cougars and wolves, or lost their scalps to understandably inhospitable Indians – but as a group they always succeeded – and in terms of human generations, very quickly.

In attempting to explain these two phenomena, let us examine four categories of organisms deeply involved in European expansion: (1) human beings; (2) animals closely associated with human beings – both the desirable animals like horses and cattle and undesirable varmints like rats and mice; (3) pathogens or microorganisms that cause disease in humans; and (4) weeds. Is there a pattern in the histories of these groups which suggests an overall explanation for the phenomenon of the Demographic Takeover or which at least suggests fresh paths of inquiry?

Europe has exported something in excess of sixty million people in the past few hundred years. Great Britain alone exported over twenty million. The great mass of these white emigrants went to the United States, Argentina, Canada, Australia, Uruguay, and New Zealand. (Other areas to absorb comparable quantities of Europeans were Brazil and Russia east of the Urals. These would qualify as Lands of the Demographic Takeover except that large fractions of their populations are non-European.)[6]

In stark contrast, very few aborigines of the Americas, Australia, or New Zealand ever went to Europe. Those who did often died not long after arrival.[7] The fact that the flow of human migration was almost entirely from Europe to her colonies and not vice versa is not startling – or very enlightening. Europeans controlled overseas migration, and Europe needed to export, not import, labor. But this pattern of one-way migration is significant in that it reappears in other connections.

The vast expanses of forests, savannas, and steppes in the Lands of the Demographic Takeover were inundated by animals from the Old World, chiefly from Europe. Horses, cattle, sheep, goats, and pigs have for hundreds of years been among the most numerous of the quadrupeds of these lands, which were completely lacking in these species at the time of first contact with the Europeans. By 1600 enormous feral herds of horses and cattle surged over the pampas of the Río de la Plata (today's Argentina and Uruguay) and over the plains of northern Mexico. By the beginning of the seventeenth century packs of Old World dogs gone wild were among the predators of these herds.[8]

In the forested country of British North America population explosions among imported animals were also spectacular, but only by European standards, not by those of Spanish America. In 1700 in Virginia feral hogs, said one witness, "swarm like vermaine upon the Earth," and young gentlemen were entertaining themselves by hunting wild horses of the inland counties. In Carolina the herds of cattle were "incredible, being from one to two thousand head in one Man's Possession." In the eighteenth and early nineteenth centuries the advancing European frontier from New England to the Gulf of Mexico was preceded into Indian territory by an avant-garde of semiwild herds of hogs and cattle tended, now and again, by semiwild herdsmen, white and black.[9]

The first English settlers landed in Botany Bay, Australia, in January of 1788 with livestock, most of it from the Cape of Good Hope. The pigs and poultry thrived; the cattle did well enough; the sheep, the future source of the colony's good fortune, died fast. Within a few months two bulls and four cows strayed away. By 1804 the wild herds they founded numbered from three to five thousand head and were in possession of much of the best land between the settlements and the Blue Mountains. If they had ever found their way through the mountains to the grasslands beyond, the history of Australia in the first decades of the nineteenth century might have been one dominated by cattle rather than sheep. As it is, the colonial government wanted the land the wild bulls so ferociously defended, and considered the growing practice of convicts running away to live off the herds as a threat to the whole colony; so the adult cattle were shot and salted down and the calves captured and tamed. The English settlers imported woolly sheep from Europe and sought out the interior pastures for them. The animals multiplied rapidly, and when Darwin made his visit to New South Wales in 1836, there were about a million sheep there for him to see.[10]

The arrival of Old World livestock probably affected New Zealand more radically than any other of the Lands of the Demographic Takeover. Cattle, horses, goats, pigs and – in this land of few or no large predators – even the usually timid sheep went wild. In New Zealand herds of feral farm animals were practicing the ways of their remote ancestors as late as the 1940s and no doubt still run free. Most of the sheep, though, stayed under human control, and within a decade of Great Britain's annexation of New Zealand in 1840, her new acquisition was home to a quarter million sheep. In 1974 New Zealand had over fifty-five million sheep, about twenty times more sheep than people.[11]

In the Lands of the Demographic Takeover the European pioneers were accompanied and often preceded by their domesticated animals, walking sources of food, leather, fiber, power, and wealth, and these animals often adapted more rapidly to the new surroundings and reproduced much more rapidly than their masters. To a certain extent, the success of Europeans as colonists was automatic as soon as they put their tough, fast, fertile, and intelligent animals ashore. The latter were sources of capital that sought out their own sustenance, improvised their own protection against the weather, fought their own battles against predators and, if their masters were smart enough to allow calves, colts, and lambs to accumulate, could and often did show the world the amazing possibilities of compound interest.

The honey bee is the one insect of worldwide importance which human beings have domesticated, if we may use the word in a broad sense. Many species of bees and other insects produce honey, but the one which does so in greatest quantity and which is easiest to control is a native of the Mediterranean area and the Middle East, the honey bee (*Apis mellifera*). The European has probably taken this sweet and short-tempered servant to every colony he ever established, from Arctic to Antarctic Circle, and the honey bee has always been one of the first immigrants to set off on its own. Sometimes the advance of the bee frontier could be very rapid: The first hive in Tasmania swarmed sixteen times in the summer of 1832.[12]

Thomas Jefferson tells us that the Indians of North America called the honey bees "English flies," and St. John de Crèvecoeur, his contemporary, wrote that "The Indians look upon them with an evil eye, and consider their progress into the interior of the continent as an omen of the white man's approach: thus, as they discover the bees, the news of the event, passing from mouth to mouth, spreads sadness and consternation on all sides."[13]

Domesticated creatures that traveled from the Lands of the Demographic Takeover to Europe are few. Australian aborigines and New Zealand Maoris had a few tame dogs, unimpressive by Old World standards and unwanted by the whites. Europe happily accepted the American Indians' turkeys and guinea pigs, but had no need for their dogs, llamas, and alpacas. Again the explanation is simple: Europeans, who controlled the passage of large animals across the oceans, had no need to reverse the process.

It is interesting and perhaps significant, though, that the exchange was just as one-sided for varmints, the small mammals whose migrations Europeans often tried to stop. None of the American or Australian or New Zealand equivalents of rats have become established in Europe, but Old World varmints, especially rats, have colonized right alongside the Europeans in the Temperate Zones. Rats of assorted sizes, some of them almost surely European immigrants, were tormenting Spanish Americans by at least the end of the sixteenth century. European rats established a beachhead in Jamestown, Virginia, as early as 1609, when they almost starved out the colonists by eating their food stores. In Buenos Aires the increase in rats kept pace with that of cattle, according to an early nineteenth-century witness. European rats proved as aggressive as the Europeans in New Zealand, where they completely replaced the local rats in the North Islands as early as the 1840s. Those poor creatures are probably completely extinct today or exist only in tiny relict populations.[14]

The European rabbits are not usually thought of as varmints, but where there are neither diseases nor predators to hold down their numbers they can become the worst of pests. In 1859 a few members of the species *Orytolagus cuniculus* (the scientific name for the protagonists of all the Peter Rabbits of literature) were released in southeast Australia. Despite massive efforts to stop them, they reproduced – true to their reputation – and spread rapidly all the way across Australia's southern half to the Indian Ocean. In 1950 the rabbit population of Australia was estimated at 500 million, and they were outcompeting the nation's most important domesticated animals, sheep, for the grasses and herbs. They have been brought under control, but only by means of artificially fomenting an epidemic of myxomatosis, a lethal American rabbit disease. The story of rabbits and myxomatosis in New Zealand is similar.[15]

Europe, in return for her varmints, has received muskrats and gray squirrels and little else from America, and nothing at all of significance from Australia or New Zealand, and we might well wonder if muskrats and squirrels really qualify as varmints.[16] As with other classes of organisms, the exchange has been a one-way street.

None of Europe's emigrants were as immediately and colossally successful as its pathogens, the microorganisms that make human beings ill, cripple them, and kill them. Whenever and wherever Europeans crossed the oceans and settled, the pathogens they carried created prodigious epidemics of smallpox, measles, tuberculosis, influenza, and a number of other diseases. It was this factor, more than any other, that Darwin had in mind as he wrote of the Europeans' deadly tread.

The pathogens transmitted by the Europeans, unlike the Europeans themselves or most of their domesticated animals, did at least as well in the tropics as in the temperate Lands of the Demographic Takeover. Epidemics devastated Mexico, Peru, Brazil, Hawaii, and Tahiti soon after the Europeans made the first contact with aboriginal populations. Some of these populations were able to escape demographic defeat because their initial numbers were so large that a small fraction was still sufficient to maintain occupation of, if not title to, the land, and also because the mass of Europeans were never attracted to the tropical lands, not even if they were partially vacated. In the Lands of the Demographic Takeover the aboriginal populations were too sparse to rebound from the onslaught of disease or were inundated by European immigrants before they could recover.

The First Strike Force of the white immigrants to the Lands of the Demographic Takeover were epidemics. A few examples from scores of possible examples follow. Smallpox first arrived in the Río de la Plata region in 1558 or 1560 and killed, according to one chronicler possibly more interested in effect than accuracy, "more than a hundred thousand Indians" of the heavy riverine population there. An epidemic of plague or typhus decimated the Indians of the New England coast immediately before the founding of Plymouth. Smallpox or something similar struck the aborigines of Australia's Botany Bay in 1789, killed half, and rolled on into the interior. Some unidentified disease or diseases spread through the Maori tribes of the North Island of New Zealand in the 1790s, killing so many in a number of villages that the survivors were not able to bury the dead.[17] After a series of such lethal and rapidly moving epidemics, then came the slow, unspectacular but thorough cripplers and killers like venereal disease and tuberculosis. In conjunction with the large numbers of white settlers these diseases were enough to smother aboriginal chances of recovery. First the blitzkrieg, then the mopping up.

The greatest of the killers in these lands was probably smallpox. The exception is New Zealand, the last of these lands to attract permanent European settlers. They came to New Zealand after the spread of vaccination in Europe, and so were poor carriers. As of the 1850s smallpox still had not come ashore, and by that time two-thirds of the Maori had been vaccinated.[18] The tardy arrival of smallpox in these islands may have much to do with the fact that the Maori today comprise a larger percentage (9 percent) of their country's population than that of any other aboriginal people in any European colony or former European colony in either Temperate Zone, save only South Africa.

American Indians bore the full brunt of smallpox, and its mark is on their history and folklore. The Kiowa of the southern plains of the United States have a legend in which a Kiowa man meets Smallpox on the plain, riding a horse. The man asks, "Where do you come from and what do you do and why are you here?" Smallpox answers, "I am one with the white men – they are my people as the Kiowas are yours. Sometimes I travel ahead of them and sometimes behind. But I am always their companion and you will find me in their camps and their houses." "What can you do," the Kiowa asks. "I bring death," Smallpox replies. "My breath causes children to wither like young plants in spring snow. I bring destruction. No matter how beautiful a woman is, once she has looked at me she becomes as ugly as death. And to men I bring not death alone, but the destruction of their children and the blighting of their wives. The strongest of warriors go down before me. No people who have looked on me will ever be the same."[19]

In return for the barrage of diseases that Europeans directed overseas, they received little in return. Australia and New Zealand provided no new strains of pathogens to Europe – or none that attracted attention. And of America's native diseases none had any real influence on the Old World – with the likely exception of venereal syphilis, which almost certainly existed in the New World before 1492 and probably did not occur in its present form in the Old World.[20]

Weeds are rarely history makers, for they are not as spectacular in their effects as pathogens. But they, too, influence our lives and migrate over the world despite human wishes. As such, like varmints and germs, they are better indicators of certain realities than human beings or domesticated animals.

The term "weed" in modern botanical usage refers to any type of plant which – because of especially large numbers of seeds produced per plant, or especially effective means of distributing those seeds, or especially tough roots and rhizomes from which new plants can grow, or especially tough seeds that survive the alimentary canals of animals to be planted with their droppings – spreads rapidly and outcompetes others on disturbed, bare soil. Weeds are plants that tempt the botanist to use such anthropomorphic words as "aggressive" and "opportunistic."

Many of the most successful weeds in the well-watered regions of the Lands of the Demographic Takeover are of European or Eurasian origin. French and Dutch and English farmers brought with them to North America their worst enemies, weeds, "to exhaust the land, hinder and damnify the Crop.[21] By the last third of the seventeenth century at least twenty different types were widespread enough in New England to attract the attention of the English visitor, John Josselyn, who identified couch grass, dandelion, nettles, mallowes, knot grass, shepherd's purse, sow thistle, and clot burr and others. One of the most aggressive was plantain, which the Indians called "English-Man's Foot."[22]

European weeds rolled west with the pioneers, in some cases spreading almost explosively. As of 1823 corn chamomile and maywood had spread up to but not across the Muskingum River in Ohio. Eight years later they were over the river.[23] The most prodigiously imperialistic of the weeds in the eastern half of the United States and Canada were probably Kentucky bluegrass and white clover. They spread so fast after the entrance of Europeans into a given area that there is some suspicion that they may have been present in pre-Colombian America, although the earliest European accounts do not mention them. Probably brought to the Appalachian area by the French, these two kinds of weeds preceded the English settlers there and kept up with the movement westward until reaching the plains across the Mississippi.[24]

Old World plants set up business on their own on the Pacific coast of North America just as soon as the Spaniards and Russians did. The climate of coastal southern California is much the same as that of the Mediterranean, and the Spaniards who came to California in the eighteenth century brought their own Mediterranean weeds with them via Mexico: wild oats, fennel, wild radishes. These plants, plus those brought in later by the Forty-niners, muscled their way to dominance in the coastal grasslands. These immigrant weeds followed Old World horses, cattle, and sheep into California's interior prairies and took over there as well.[25]

The region of Argentina and Uruguay was almost as radically altered in its flora as in its fauna by the coming of the Europeans. The ancient Indian practice, taken up immediately by the whites, of burning off the old grass of the pampa every year, as well as the trampling and cropping to the ground of indigenous grasses and forbs by the thousands of imported quadrupeds who also changed the nature of the soil with their droppings, opened the whole countryside to European plants. In the 1780s Félix de Azara observed that the pampa, already radically altered, was changing as he watched. European weeds sprang up around every cabin, grew up along roads, and pressed into the open steppe. Today only a quarter of the plants growing wild in the pampa are native, and in the well-watered eastern portions, the "natural" ground cover consists almost entirely of Old World grasses and clovers.[26]

The invaders were not, of course, always desirable. When Darwin visited Uruguay in 1832, he found large expanses, perhaps as much as hundreds of square miles, monopolized by the immigrant wild artichoke and transformed into a prickly wilderness fit neither for man nor his animals.[27]

The onslaught of foreign and specifically European plants on Australia began abruptly in 1778 because the first expedition that sailed from Britain to Botany Bay carried some livestock and considerable quantities of seed. By May of 1803 over two hundred foreign plants, most of them European, had been purposely introduced and planted in New South Wales, undoubtedly along with a number of weeds.[28] Even today so-called clean seed characteristically contains some weed seeds, and this was much more so two hundred years ago. By and large, Australia's north has been too tropical and her interior too hot and dry for European weeds and grasses, but much of her southern coasts and Tasmania have been hospitable indeed to Europe's willful flora.

Thus, many – often a majority – of the most aggressive plants in the temperate humid regions of North America, South America, Australia, and New Zealand are of European origin. It may be true that in every broad expanse of the world today where there are dense populations, with whites in the majority, there are also dense populations of European weeds. Thirty-five of eighty-nine weeds listed in 1953 as common in the state of New York are European. Approximately 60 percent of Canada's worst weeds are introductions from Europe. Most of New Zealand's weeds are from the same source, as are many, perhaps most, of the weeds of southern Australia's well-watered coasts. Most of the European plants that Josselyn listed as naturalized in New England in the seventeenth century are growing wild today in Argentina and Uruguay, and are among the most widespread and troublesome of all weeds in those countries.[29]

In return for this largesse of pestiferous plants, the Lands of the Demographic Takeover have provided Europe with only a few equivalents. The Canadian water weed jammed Britain's nineteenth-century waterways, and North America's horseweed and burnweed have spread in Europe's empty lots, and South America's flowered galinsoga has thrived in her gardens. But the migratory flow of a whole group of organisms between Europe and the Lands of the Demographic Takeover has been almost entirely in one direction.[30] Englishman's foot still marches in seven league jackboots across every European colony of settlement, but very few American or Australian or New Zealand invaders stride the waste lands and unkempt backyards of Europe.

European and Old World human beings, domesticated animals, varmints, pathogens, and weeds all accomplished demographic takeovers of their own in the temperate, well-watered regions of North and South America, Australia, and New Zealand. They crossed oceans and Europeanized vast territories, often in informal cooperation with each other – the farmer and his animals destroying native plant cover, making way for imported grasses and forbs, many of which proved more nourishing to domesticated animals than the native equivalents; Old World pathogens, sometimes carried by Old World varmints, wiping out vast numbers of aborigines, opening the way for the advance of the European frontier, exposing more and more native peoples to more and more pathogens. The classic example of symbiosis between European colonists, their animals, and plants comes from New Zealand. Red clover, a good forage for sheep, could not seed itself and did not spread without being annually sown until the Europeans imported the bumblebee. Then the plant and insect spread widely, the first providing the second with food, the second carrying pollen from blossom to blossom for the first, and the sheep eating the clover and compensating the human beings for their effort with mutton and wool.[31]

There have been few such stories of the success in Europe of organisms from the Lands of the Demographic Takeover, despite the obvious fact that for every ship that went from Europe to those lands, another traveled in the opposite direction.

The demographic triumph of Europeans in the temperate colonies is one part of a biological and ecological takeover which could not have been accomplished by human beings alone, gunpowder notwithstanding. We must at least try to analyze the impact and success of all the immigrant organisms together – the European portmanteau of often mutually supportive plants, animals, and microlife which in its entirety can be accurately described as aggressive and opportunistic, an ecosystem simplified by ocean crossings and honed by thousands of years of competition in the unique environment created by the Old World Neolithic Revolution.

The human invaders and their descendants have consulted their egos, rather than ecologists, for explanations of their triumphs. But the human victims, the aborigines of the Lands of the Demographic Takeover, knew better, knew they were only one of many species being displaced and replaced; knew they were victims of something more irresistible and awesome than the spread of capitalism or Christianity. One Maori, at the nadir of the history of his race, knew these things when he said, "As the clover killed off the fern, and the European dog the Maori dog – as the Maori rat was destroyed by the Pakeha (European) rat – so our people, also, will be gradually supplanted and exterminated by the Europeans."[32] The future was not quite so grim as he prophesied, but we must admire his grasp of the complexity and magnitude of the threat looming over his people and over the ecosystem of which they were part.

Notes

1 Page Stegner, ed., *The Portable Nabokov* (New York: Viking, 1968), p. 527; Francis Darwin, ed., *Life and Letters of Charles Darwin* (London: Murray, 1887), vol. 2, p. 391.
2 *The World Almanac and Book of Facts 1978* (New York: Newspaper Enterprise Association, 1978), passim.
3 Philip D. Curtin, "Epidemiology and the Slave Trade," *Political Science Quarterly* 83 (June 1968), 190–216 passim; John Prebble, *The Darien Disaster* (New York: Holt, Rinehart & Winston, 1968), pp. 296, 300; Charles M. Andrews, *The Colonial Period of American History* (New Haven, Conn.: Yale University Press, 1934), vol. 1, n. 497; Gilberto Freyre, *The Masters and the Slaves,* trans. Samuel Putnam (New York: Knopf, 1946), passim; Donald L. Wiedner, *A History of Africa South of the Sahara* (New York: Vintage Books, 1964), 49–51; Stuart B. Schwartz, "Indian Labor and New World Plantations: European Demands and Indian Responses in Northeastern Brazil," *American Historical Review* 83 (February 1978): 43–79 passim.
4 Marcel R. Reinhard, *Histoire de la population modiale de 1700 à 1948* (n.p.: Editions Domat-Montchrestien, n.d.), pp. 339–411, 428–31; G. F. McCleary, *Peopling the British Commonwealth* (London: Farber and Farber, n.d.), pp. 83,

94, 109–10; R. R. Palmer and Joel Colton, *A History of the Modern World* (New York: Knopf, 1965), p. 560; *World Almanac 1978,* pp. 34, 439, 497, 513, 590.

5 Charles Darwin, *The Voyage of the Beagle* (Garden City, N.Y.: Doubleday Anchor Books, 1962), pp. 433–34.

6 William Woodruff, *Impact of Western Man* (New York: St. Martin's, 1967), 106–8.

7 Carolyn T. Foreman, *Indians Abroad* (Norman: University of Oklahoma Press, 1943), passim.

8 Alfred W. Crosby, *The Columbian Exchange* (Westport, Conn.: Greenwood, 1972), pp. 82–88; Alexander Gillespie, *Gleanings and Remarks Collected during Many Months of Residence at Buenos Aires* (Leeds: B. DeWhirst, 1818), p. 136; Oscar Schmieder, "Alteration of the Argentine Pampa in the Colonial Period," *University of California Publications in Geography* 2 (27 September 1927): n. 311.

9 Robert Beverley, *The History and Present State of Virginia* (Chapel Hill: University of North Carolina Press, 1947), pp. 153, 312, 318; John Lawson, *A New Voyage to Carolina* (n.p.: Readex Microprint Corp., 1966), p. 4; Frank L. Owsley, "The Pattern of Migration and Settlement of the Southern Frontier," *Journal of Southern History* 11 (May 1945): 147–75.

10 Commonwealth of Australia, *Historical Records of Australia* (Sydney: Library Committee of the Commonwealth Parliament, 1914), ser. 1, vol. 1, p. 550; vol. 7, pp. 379–80; vol. 8, pp. 150–51; vol. 9, pp. 349, 714, 831; vol. 10, pp. 92, 280, 682; vol. 20, p. 839.

11 Andrew H. Clark, *The Invasion of New Zealand by People, Plants, and Animals* (New Brunswick, N.J.: Rutgers University Press, 1949), p. 190; David Wallechinsky, Irving Wallace, and A. Wallace, *The Book of Lists* (New York: Bantam, 1978), pp. 129–30.

12 Remy Chauvin, *Traité de biologie de l'abeille* (Paris: Masson et Cie, 1968), vol. 1, pp. 38–39; James Backhouse, *A Narrative of a Visit to the Australian Colonies* (London: Hamilton, Adams and Co., 1834), p. 23.

13 Merrill D. Peterson, ed., *The Portable Thomas Jefferson* (New York: Viking, 1975), p. III; Michel-Guillaume St. Jean de Crèvecoeur, *Journey into Northern Pennsylvania and the State of New York,* trans. Clarissa S. Bostelmann (Ann Arbor: University of Michigan Press, 1964), p. 166.

14 Bernabé Cobo, *Obras* (Madrid: Adas Ediciones, 1964), vol. 1, pp. 350–51; Edward Arber, ed., *Travels and Works of Captain John Smith* (New York: Burt Franklin, n.d.), vol. 2, p. xcv; K. A. Wodzicki, *Introduced Mammals of New Zealand* (Wellington: Department of Scientific and Industrial Research, 1950), pp. 89–92.

15 Frank Fenner and F. N. Ratcliffe, *Myxomatosis* (Cambridge: Cambridge University Press, 1965) pp. 9, 11, 17, 22–23; Frank Fenner, "The Rabbit Plague," *Scientific American* 190 (February 1954): 30–35; Wodzicki, *Introduced Mammals,* pp. 107–41.

16 Charles S. Elton, *The Ecology of Invasions* (Trowbridge and London: English Language Book Society, 1972), pp. 24–25, 28, 73, 123.

17 Juan López de Velasco, *Geografía y descripción universal de las Indias* (Madrid: Establecimiento Topográfico de Fortanet, 1894), p. 552; Oscar Schmieder, "The Pampa – A Natural and Culturally Induced Grassland?" *University of California, Publications in Geography* (27 September 1927): 266; Sherburne F. Cook, "The Significance of Disease in the Extinction of the New England Indians," *Human Biology* 14 (September 1975): 486–91; J. H. L. Cumpston,

The History of Smallpox in Australia, 1788–1908 (Melbourne: Albert J. Mullet, Government Printer, 1914), pp. 147–49; Harrison M. Wright, *New Zealand, 1769–1840* (Cambridge, Mass.: Harvard University Press, 1959), p. 62. For further discussion of this topic, see Crosby, *Columbia Exchange,* chaps. 1 and 2, and Henry F. Dobyns, *Native American Historical Demography: A Critical Bibliography* (Bloomington: Indiana University Press/Newberry Library, 1976).

18 Arthur C. Thomson, *The Story of New Zealand* (London: Murray, 1859), vol. 1, p. 212.

19 Alice Marriott and Carol K. Rachlin, *American Indian Mythology* (New York: New American Library, 1968), pp. 174–75.

20 Crosby, *Columbian Exchange,* pp. 122–64, passim.

21 Jared Eliot, "The Tilling of the Land, 1760," in *Agriculture in the United States: A Documentary History,* ed. Wayne D. Rasmussen (New York: Random House, 1975), vol. 1, p. 192.

22 John Josselyn, *New Englands Rarities Discovered* (London: G. Widdowes at the Green Dragon in St. Paul's Church-yard, 1672), pp. 85, 86; Edmund Berkeley and Dorothy S. Berkeley, eds., *The Reverend John Clayton* (Charlottesville: University of Virginia Press, 1965), p. 24.

23 Lewis D. de Schweinitz, "Remarks on the Plants of Europe Which Have Become Naturalized in a More or Less Degree, in the United States," *Annals Lyceum of Natural History of New York,* vol. 3 *(1832) 1828–1836,* 155.

24 Lyman Carrier and Katherine S. Bort, "The History of Kentucky Bluegrass and White Clover in the United States," *Journal of the American Society of Agronomy* 8 (1916): 256–66; Robert W. Schery, "The Migration of a Plant: Kentucky Bluegrass Followed Settlers to the New World," *Natural History* 74 (December 1965): 43–44; G. W. Dunbar, ed., "Henry Clay on Kentucky Bluegrass," *Agricultural History* 51 (July 1977): 522.

25 Edgar Anderson, *Plants, Man, and Life* (Berkeley and Los Angeles: University of California Press, 1967), pp. 12–15; Elna S. Bakker, *An Island Called California* (Berkeley and Los Angeles: University of California Press, 1971), pp. 150–52; R. W. Allard, "Genetic Systems Associated with Colonizing Ability in Predominantly Self-Pollinated Species," in *The Genetics of Colonizing Species,* ed. H. G. Baker and G. Ledyard Stebbins (New York: Academic Press, 1965), p. 50; M. W. Talbot, H. M. Biswell, and A. L. Hormay, "Fluctuations in the Annual Vegetation of California," *Ecology* 20 (July 1939): 396–97.

26 Félix de Azara, *Descripción é historia del Paraguay y del Río de la Plata* (Madrid: Imprenta de Sanchez, 1847), vol. 1, 57–58; Schmieder, "Alteration of the Argentine Pampa," pp. 310–11.

27 Darwin, *Voyage of the Beagle,* pp. 119–20.

28 *Historical Records of Australia,* ser. 1, vol. 4, pp. 234–41.

29 Edward Salisbury, *Weeds and Aliens* (London: Collins, 1961), p. 87; Angel Julio Cabrera, *Manual de la flora de los alrededores de Buenos Aires* (Buenos Aires: Editorial Acme S. A., 1953), passim.

30 Elton, *Ecology of Invasions,* p. 115; Hugo Ilitis, "The Story of Wild Garlic," *Scientific Monthly* 68 (February 1949): 122–24.

31 Otto E. Plath, *Bumblebees and Their Ways* (New York: Macmillan, 1934), p. 115.

32 James Bonwick, *The Last of the Tasmanians* (New York: Johnson Reprint Co., 1970), p. 380.

Part II

REGIONAL PERSPECTIVES

10

ENVIRONMENT AND SOCIETY
Long-term trends in Latin American mining

Elizabeth Dore

Mining has given rise to major social and environmental transformations in Latin America since the Conquest. Drawing on historical and environmental research, this essay examines long-term trends in the ways that mining affected labour and the environment.[1] The article begins with a theoretical consideration of changing conditions of labour and environmental degradation under capitalism. This is followed by a periodisation of Latin American mining, divided into six parts: pre-conquest, conquest, colony, neo-colony, capitalist modernisation and debt crisis. In each period (excepting the first) I assess the major social and environmental transformations associated with the industry. My central conclusion is that there has been an inverse relationship between long-term trends in the brutality of labour conditions in the industry and the scope of ecological destruction linked to mining. The article concludes with a discussion of two more speculative issues: first, the impact this inverse relationship has had on contemporary political concerns; second, whether the turn of the millennium marks the end of this inverse relationship.

Before proceeding, three caveats are in order. First, as my purpose is to characterise long-term trends and major turning points in the social and ecological effects of mining, my analysis eschews detail. Second, the essay in its entirety should not be read as a history of how capitalism transformed labour and the environment in Latin American mining, since prior to the twentieth century the labour process in the Latin American industry was not, for the most part, capitalist. Third, while I argue that labour conditions in the industry tended to improve in the middle twentieth century, I am not suggesting that the exploitation of labour (in a Marxian sense) decreased, or that capitalism gave rise to prosperity, limited even to working miners. These are separate issues which are not treated in this article.

Some theoretical considerations

It is widely agreed that as capitalism matures profitability comes to depend more on raising productivity through technological change than on expanding output by increasing the hours and pace of work. In the Marxian formulation, the first – productivity increases via technical change – raises relative surplus value, and the second – expanding output by increasing the time and pace of work – raises absolute surplus value.[2] As capitalism develops there is a tendency for the basis of production to shift from the latter to the former; this is part of the modernising dynamic of capitalism. Historically, technical change was forced on industries by two processes: first, workers' struggles to reduce the length and pace of work; second, competitive rivalry among firms. The result was that capitalist expansion came to depend primarily on increasing the exploitation of workers by revolutionising technology, and secondarily on intensifying the brutality associated with the appropriation of human labour in production.

This modernisation of production suggests the theoretical possibility that capitalist development might usher in more humane social conditions. However, in practice this largely depends on the character and outcome of labour struggles. While capitalist development historically has given rise to increased levels of consumption, this has characterised relatively few countries and in finite periods of time. For example, in the post-war period from 1950 to 1970, improvements in the standard of living in the West depended on a number of contingent factors. These included: 1) rapid economic growth, 2) the relative strength of trades unions and the Left, particularly in Western Europe, and 3) the threat of an alternative way of organising society which, for all of their problems, was posed by the Soviet Union, China, Vietnam and Cuba.

Part of the dynamic of capitalism is that along with the possibility of raising the average level of consumption, the competitive drive for profits exerts a downward pressure on the condition of the working class. Historically, capitalist development has tended to be associated with a widening gap between the rich and the poor both in and between countries. This was especially evident at the end of the twentieth century, when the expansion and universalisation of capitalism, or 'globalisation', was accompanied by high levels of unemployment and insecurity of work, as well as by falling incomes and standards of living for the vast majority of people across the globe. In sum, tensions within capitalist development give rise to contradictory processes: on the one hand, a pressure to modernise production and raise productivity, and with this the possibility of improving labour conditions; on the other hand, a drive to expand profits by whatever means necessary, and with this a push to reduce labour costs which often results in deteriorating social conditions.

In apparent contrast to its modernising social potential, however restricted in time and scope, capitalist development, to date, has tended to intensify environmental degradation. The drive to accumulate, based on ever-expanding production, increased natural resource consumption. However, in a process analogous to the historic shift in exploitation from the production of absolute to relative surplus value, technological change within capitalism could, theoretically, reduce environmental degradation. This would involve the introduction and generalisation of 'nature-saving' technologies, profitmaking through resource recovery and environmental rehabilitation.[3] While there has been some movement towards such environmentally-motivated technological change, at the millennium's end this change did not represent a historic shift in the nature of capitalist production.

If environmental reform of capitalism could potentially reduce ecological destruction, the question remains how such a shift might be achieved? Echoing the earlier shift in the nature of capitalist production, which was forced on the system in large part by workers' struggles, significant change in the ways companies consume energy and resources will require concerted political action. But unlike the shift in the exploitation of labour, which responded in large part to workers' straggles, a shift to more sustainable production methods might depend more on concerted action by states than by workers' organisations.[4]

In so far as degradation of nature tends to destroy, in quality and quantity, raw materials and other means of production (including people), it poses a danger to the sustainability of capitalism as a whole. Although individual companies were reluctant to adopt measures to reduce environmental degradation, especially if these jeopardised profits, political theory suggests that states might behave differently. In their role as guardians of the social order, as opposed to protectors of specific companies or economic groups, one might posit that states would enforce the use of environmentally sustainable production techniques. Notwithstanding that theoretical possibility, and the reality of strong pressure from the scientific and environmental lobbies, the scope and degree of state-sponsored environmental reform has remained modest. In the face of reasonable predictions as to the probable extent of environmental change in the short term, in the late twentieth century most states remained largely resilient to pressure for environmental reform. This suggests that short-term profitability continued to take precedence over the longer-term viability of states and societies in the political economy of the *fin du siècle*. Drawing on these theoretical considerations, this article examines how the development of the Latin American mining industry affected changes in the conditions of labour and the environment.

Pre-Columbian America, unravelling the pristine myth

The conquest of Latin America unleashed destruction of human life on a scale possibly unrivalled in history. Ironically, it may have been the single most important event of the past millennium to safeguard the plant and animal species of the New World. Notwithstanding the prevalence of scholarship and myth about a pristine pre-conquest America, there is increasing evidence that pre-Columbian peoples were systematically incapable of sustaining the ecosystems upon which their societies depended. Intense environmental degradation may have been a significant factor in the decline of pre-Columbian civilisations.

The collapse of the classical lowland Maya has long baffled scholars.[5] However, recently archaeologists uncovered evidence of acute over-cultivation and soil depletion surrounding the sites of Tikkal, Copan and Palenque dating from approximately 1000 AD, the period of the great collapse. Indications of a sharp decline in agricultural yields over a relatively short time-frame suggest that environmental unsustainability may have contributed to the Mayan crisis. These interpretations are not rooted in a Malthusian logic.[6] Rather, they propose that changing class relations were associated with the introduction of agricultural methods which proved incompatible with reproduction of the classical Mayan social order. Although Mayan belief systems enshrined the sanctity of nature, ideology may have diverged radically from social practices. If this interpretation is correct, it points to the conclusion that even though Mayans worshipped nature, their society was undermined by massive ecological change ultimately of their own making.[7]

New evidence also points to ecological unsustainability as a factor in the crisis of the Aztec Empire. Soil samples taken from Lake Pátzcuarco in Mexico show that by the early sixteenth century the landscape of the highlands of Michoacán was seriously degraded.[8] Drawing on this evidence, archaeologists have proposed that severe soil erosion provoked a crisis of food security, which may have undermined the power of the indigenous ruling classes. If this hypothesis is correct, Aztec, Tarascan and other Mesoamerican people were especially vulnerable at the time Cortés and his army of six hundred men conquered Mexico. An explicit conclusion drawn from this research is that introduction by the Spaniards of the plough and of cattle grazing, long considered ecologically unsound, may not have been more unsustainable than indigenous agricultural practices.[9]

Clearly, the popularity of ecological explanations of pre-hispanic social instability reflected the rise of environmentalism and the emergence of ecology as an academic field. Nevertheless, those who continued to brush aside new research in order to perpetuate the pristine myth of pre-Columbian America were romanticists, as the notion of indigenous peoples living naturally in symbiosis with their environment, then as well as now, seemed increasingly untenable.[10] Rather than contributing to our understanding of the causes of ecological change, the pristine myth threatened to become a barrier to unravelling the complex dynamics of sustainable and unsustainable development.

Conquest of people, liberation of nature

Before Europeans 'discovered' the Americas, the Aztec and Inca Empires were weakened by internal warfare, as well as by environmental pressures, apparently. However, the catalyst of their demise was an exogenous force, the Spanish invasion. For the next three centuries, the search for precious metals was the driving force of European conquest and colonisation. In contrast to pre-Columbian people who worshipped nature, it would be fair to say that Spaniards worshipped silver and gold. As a consequence, the mining, processing and transport of metals was at the centre of the social and ecological transformation of colonial Latin America.

In the first stage of conquest the imperial enterprise was a campaign to extract precious metals as quickly as possible from the New World. This resulted in the extermination of the indigenous population of the Caribbean within several decades of contact. Extinction of the Tainos, Caribs and Arawaks – the people Europeans first encountered in the Caribbean – was caused by disease, hard labour, and social dislocation.[11] Isolated from contact with Europe, Asia and Africa, the native population of the Americas had little resistance to the bacteria and viruses that accompanied Europeans to the New World. When Spaniards enslaved the population of the islands, and forced them to pan rivers for alluvial gold, diseases spread rapidly and proved fatal.[12] The colonials terrorised indigenous people into submission by maiming and torturing those who resisted their authority. Indifferent to the preservation of the native population, Spanish settlers worked their Indian slaves to death. When the native population of the Caribbean was extinct, Spaniards moved on to plunder the continent.

By the mid-sixteenth century it was evident that the Spanish American mainland was rich in silver. After advisers warned the Crown that mines without miners would produce no wealth, preservation of the native population become a priority of Royal policy. Although Crown and conquerors shared an overriding objective, to extract gold and silver from the New World, the immediate interests of the settlers clashed with the long-term viability of the colonial enterprise. In contrast to colonists, whose objective was to get rich quickly and return to Spain, the Crown endeavoured to safeguard the future prosperity of the Empire. To that end, the Crown enacted a number of decrees protecting the native population. These forbade enslavement of indigenous people, and all but abolished *encomiendas,* grants to privileged settlers of native communities which were obliged to pay tribute to their overlord.[13] Notwithstanding royal intention, decrees were notoriously difficult to enforce in the New World, and many of the first Indian labourers sent to the silver mines in Spanish America were enslaved in all but name.

After rich veins of silver were discovered at Guanajuato and Zacatecas in New Spain (Mexico), Potosí in Upper Peru (Bolivia), and a number of lesser sites, the locus of New World mining changed from looting and panning gold to underground silver mining. This ushered in a fundamental spatial and social reorganisation of the continent. Silver mining created a demand for draught animals to transport ore, food to feed miners, and timber to build shafts and tunnels. This, combined with forced recruitment of Indians, rapidly altered land use and social relations. The silver deposits were enormous, as were the logistical problems associated with extracting, processing and transporting ore. Cerro Rico at Potosí was particularly rich yet frustratingly inaccessible, located in the heart of the southern Andes at an altitude of 15,000 feet.

For thirty years following discovery of the great silver deposits on the continent, individual enterprise in mining continued virtually unrestrained. Notwithstanding Royal decrees, the age of conquest, from 1492 to 1570, was a period of almost unregulated violence against the native inhabitants of the Americas. History repeated itself as *encomenderos* imposed draconian working conditions to extract silver as quickly as possible. One might argue that if conquerors had sought to safeguard the health of the native population, it would have made relatively little difference to the spread of germs – the hidden conquest. Nevertheless, most epidemiologists agree that forced labour accentuated the mortal effects of disease, and exacerbated the population implosion. Although estimates vary, a majority of scholars concur that the population of Ibero-America declined from above 60 million on the eve of conquest to less than 10 million at its nadir in the seventeenth century.[14]

Ironically, demographic collapse safeguarded the ecosystems of the New World for centuries. Although diverting rivers to pan for gold, felling trees to construct mining shafts, and clearing land for grazing and agriculture all contributed to ecological change, their combined impact on the environment was relatively minor compared with the intensive cultivation, foraging and hunting which supported the large pre-conquest societies. The Latin American–Caribbean region was relatively under-populated for almost five hundred years, in comparison with Europe, Asia and Africa, and it did not recover its pre-1492 population until the nineteenth century.[15] As a result, there was considerably less human pressure on the region's natural resource base than in other parts of the world. This may explain, in part, why Amazonia and other great forests of the Americas survived into the twentieth century.

State-sponsored colonial mining

Soon after the rediscovery of abandoned Inca mines at Potosí in 1545, a 'silver rush' convulsed the Andean region. Spanish settlers, Indian labourers and fortune-seekers of all kinds flooded to the mining centre. However, by 1560 the silver boom was waning. Scarcity of labourers, exhaustion of the rich and easily extracted ores, and inefficient processing techniques threatened to close down the mines. When it was apparent that Peruvian silver production was in serious decline, the Crown reorganised the colonial state to counter the crisis.

From the 1570s onwards, expansion of the mining industry became the overriding objective of imperial rule.[16] To accomplish this, Viceroy Francisco de Toledo forged an absolutist state in Peru which directly appropriated and distributed Indians' labour. Prior to these reforms, Spanish mineowners corralled whatever labourers they could, by whatever means necessary, to extract and process ores. This resulted in chaotic use of labour, which, it was believed, exacerbated the decline of the indigenous population. Viceroy Toledo set out to increase the supply of Indians to work in the mines and at the same time to safeguard the health of the indigenous population. The instrument to achieve these two apparently incompatible objectives was a state labour draft, the *mita*. The state assumed responsibility for guaranteeing a regular supply of Indian labourers to Spanish mineowners. In the beginning the policy was successful, as Indian communities sent an estimated 14,000 men annually to Potosí alone in the late sixteenth century. In addition, the colonial administration attempted to prevent the worst excesses associated with exploitation of the indigenous population by regulating wages and working conditions. Finally, the state restricted the 'catchment' for the *mita* to highland communities where, it was hoped, men accustomed to hard labour at high altitudes would survive the work regime at Potosí.[17] However, despite its protective veneer, soon it became apparent that state intervention did not significantly reduce the mortal effects of work in the mines.[18]

The introduction of mercury amalgamation, the newest technology in silver processing, accompanied the reorganisation of labour at Potosí.[19] Mill owners adopted the patio process, which was based on grinding silver to a fine dust and mixing it with mercury. As silver adheres to mercury, which was burned off, with the patio process it was economically viable to mine lower grade ores.[20] Soon the discovery of large mercury or 'quicksilver' deposits at Huancavelica in the central Andes sparked another upturn in the industry. The state established a monopoly to produce and sell mercury to ensure expansion of silver production because, in the words of Viceroy Toledo, 'Huancavelica and Potosí are the two poles which support this Kingdom and that of Spain'.[21]

State intervention resolved the immediate problems of the mining industry in Peru. With a regular labour supply and technological innovation, Peruvian silver production rose rapidly, peaking in the final decade of the sixteenth century. But the boom was short-lived; conditions which unleashed production undermined it as well.[22] As more Indian draft labourers, or *mitayos*, were sent to Potosí, more Indians came to know the horrors of life in the mines and mills. By the light of torches miners hammered at ore bodies in underground tunnels. In low, crowded and poorly ventilated vaults the temperatures soared. *Mitayos* spent hours climbing up fragile ladders with heavy sacks of ore, to emerge into snow and freezing temperatures at the surface. They immediately descended into the inferno below to cut and carry another load. Working alongside mules, men crushed silver and mercury with their bare feet in large vats. Some died quickly of mercury poisoning; others languished with fevers and sores.

In self-preservation, many *mita* labourers fled the mines. In addition, scores of Indians deserted their villages to escape the dragnet of the draft. Flight contributed to the devastation of Andean communities, which accelerated population decline and intensified the labour scarcity at the mines. Over the next century New World silver production declined. To expand output mineowners needed more workers, more accessible veins of higher grade ores and more quicksilver.

Silver mining dictated the social and spatial organisation of the Spanish colonial world. Mines became hubs of the largest urban centres in the Americas. With a constant flux of some 200,000 people coming and going to Potosí at the turn of the seventeenth century, it was one of the western world's largest cities. Lima, Panama, Vera Cruz and Havana, stops on the official trade route from the mines to Spain, all grew rapidly. The same was true of Buenos Aires, the nexus of the contraband silver trade. In addition, secondary towns sprang into existence along the mule trails which connected mines to the cities and ports of the New World.[23]

As well as giving rise to major urbanisation, mining changed the land-scape of Latin America. Forests and fields were converted to pasture as demand for mules to carry ore led to the creation of large ranches in areas surrounding the mines. Trees were cut to make shafts and tunnels for the mines. At Potosí, a network of dams formed twenty artificial lakes which ensured a regular supply of water to the mills. Caribbean islands were deforested to provide lumber to build the galleons which carried silver to Europe. The demand for food at the mining centres gave rise to commercial farming. All of this effected environmental change, but it did not threaten the sustainability of regional ecosystems because the population of Latin America had been declining precipitously since 1492. Throughout the continent large expanses of land were returning to wilderness.

Mercury, an adjunct of New World mining almost since its inception, was responsible for the greatest environmental damage.[24] Wrapped in leather bags, mercury was transported throughout the Americas and Spain. As a result, in addition to poisoning workers at the mines and mills, mercury contaminated large areas. Once rivers became saturated with mercury, the poison was passed to the humans, animals and birds which fed on toxic fish. In addition, plants were contaminated by irrigation waters, even in areas far from the mines. Because mercury accumulates in animal and plant tissue, it created long-lasting cycles of toxicity. Nevertheless, the damage caused by mining in the early colonial era was more social than ecological. Mining was associated with extermination of entire Caribbean civilisations and massive reorganisation and dislocation of indigenous society in Meso- and South America.

Turning to the seventeenth-century, the historiography of this era traditionally focussed on the issue of economic depression. Historians writing before 1980 generally believed that New Spain and Peru suffered from a major depression, which originated in falling silver production and rising prices on both sides of the Atlantic. In contrast, later historians argued that there was little or no seventeenth-century depression in the New World. They maintained that the downturn in silver production and in transatlantic trade did not adversely affect the majority of inhabitants of Spanish America.[25] For example, because the colonial state was unable to impose the *mita* as effectively as it had in the Toledan era, Peruvian communities benefitted from the downturn in mining. In other words, they enjoyed a certain benign neglect.[26] Whichever position historians subscribed to, they tended to agree that the seventeenth century was an era of commercial retreat in the New World. Whereas, in the sixteenth century an expanding mining sector had engendered production of mules, food and timber for exchange, in the seventeenth century a contracting industry caused a downturn in these activities.

It is noteworthy, however, that historians have not addressed the environmental consequences of the mining/population decline of the seventeenth century. While there is evidence that the forest cover in Spanish America was more extensive in the seventeenth century than it had been for some time before, or since, and that the mining/population crisis created conditions for the regeneration of vegetation and wildlife, more research is needed on the environmental consequences of seventeenth-century changes in the New World. With this in mind, it is significant that historians have come to agree that the notion of a land scarcity in the sixteenth and seventeenth centuries is largely fallacious. As a number of recent studies have demonstrated, the land question in Latin America was not about shortage of land per se.[27] In the first two centuries of Spanish rule in the Americas, population pressure on land, or the 'person-land ratio', was probably lower than it had been for the preceding centuries.

Over the course of the seventeenth century, the use and abuse of mercury declined, particularly at Zacatecas. There, because of a mercury shortage, mill owners abandoned the amalgamation technique in favour of smelting, an older and less efficient method of processing silver. Consequently, the cycle of mercury poisoning which began in the Mexican mines a century earlier started to wind down. However, this was in contrast to Potosí, where mill owners used relatively more mercury to process low grade ores in order to keep the mines operating.

In contrast to the preceding one hundred years, the eighteenth century was marked by gradual demographic growth and a revival of silver mining. It would be facile, however, to conclude that one caused the other. Notwithstanding an upturn in the Andean population after one hundred and fifty years of decline, the labour shortage intensified at Potosí.[28] In the first decades of the eighteenth century about 4,000 *mitayos* worked the mines and mills of Cerro Rico. By mid-century the number had fallen to 3,000 and it remained at that level for the next sixty years. This demonstrates that although the state undertook successive reorganisations of the *mita,* in order to expand the labour force, its efforts were largely futile. The rise in silver production at Potosí was achieved by increasing the exploitation of *mita* labourers and recruiting a growing number of nominally free workers. Mineowners appropriated more labour from *mitayos* by increasing production quotas. As a consequence, the average volume of silver ore each *mitayo* extracted doubled in the second half of the century. This was accomplished by intensifying the pace of work, lengthening working time and disregarding laws which set the maximum period *mitayos* worked at the mines. However, even with these measures, mine workers frequently fell short of their production quotas. Consequently, their wives and children often worked in the mines and mills to meet the tribute obligations.

By the nineteenth century the mining industries of Peru and Mexico were robust again.[29] It is significant, however, that throughout the era of Spanish rule, with the exception of the patio process, there was little technical innovation in extraction and processing. Although shafts and adits were deeper and longer than they had been two hundred years earlier, animal powered hoists were rare and steam power unknown.[30] Consequently, mineowners continued to rely predominantly on human labour to excavate and haul ores. In the absence of technical change, increased output in the mines was accomplished by prolonging labour time and intensifying work. In the last years of Empire fewer people worked in silver mining in Peru than in the boom years of the sixteenth century. Nevertheless, instead of working conditions improving in the mines, arguably over time the labour regime had become more brutal.

Neo-colonial mining and the rise of capitalism

In colonial Latin America the ecological effects of mining were constrained by the nature of an economic system based on merchant capital. First, mining was largely limited to silver and gold, which were valued primarily as a means of exchange and a hoard of wealth. Second, technological innovation was slow, which itself tended to limit ecological change. However, in the nineteenth century, the development of capitalism in Europe and the United States dramatically increased ecological change associated with mining in Latin America. First, the industrial revolution expanded demand for an array of metals hitherto virtually ignored in Latin America. Second, the industry grew as a consequence of technological innovation in methods of production, processing and transport.

The initial phase of neo-colonial mining began with British investment in Mexican silver mines. However, these early ventures foundered, largely as a consequence of the political and social turmoil which followed Latin America's independence wars.[31] When the industry revived in the late nineteenth century, after three quarters of a century of decline, expansion was based on non-precious metals and technological innovation. Although new mining enterprises in Latin America supplied minerals for the world capitalist market, force and indebtedness continued to prevail in the labour process. For example, in Peru, although the *mita* was abolished in 1812, for another one hundred years mining companies in the Andes relied on unfree labour.

Nitrate production was the first new mining sector to emerge in post-independence Latin America; its rise was directly linked to the development of agrarian capitalism in Europe. The transformation of land and labour systems in England, following the enclosures, created a demand for fertilisers to increase agricultural yields. The sodium nitrates mined in shallow seams in the Atacama desert were among the first 'natural' chemical fertilisers to be widely used in Europe.

In the 1840s Chilean entrepreneurs set up nitrate mines in the coastal desert strip which straddled the borders separating Chile, Peru and Bolivia. They brought tens of thousands of people to work in a region which hitherto had been considered uninhabitable. In the next decades, companies, most of them British, built railroads, set up banks, and bought mines in the area. Soon British firms dominated the Chilean nitrate industry. In 1879 Chile, Peru and Bolivia went to war over the deposits in the Atacama, the first of many wars fought over mineral rights in Latin America. With British support, in 1883 Chile won and appropriated Peruvian and Bolivian territory in the desert. But nitrates were soon replaced by new petroleum-based fertilisers. By the end of the century, mining in the Atacama was all but abandoned, along with the railroads and scattered towns it spawned.[32]

Latin American petroleum production followed close on the heels of the collapsing nitrate sector. In 1872 petroleum was discovered at Talara, where the Humbolt and El Niño currents converge off the north coast of Peru. In what was considered one of the world's richest areas of sea life, the International Petroleum Company (IPC), a subsidiary of Rockefeller's Standard Oil of New Jersey, drilled Latin America's first wells.[33] With wooden oil rigs and primitive technology, there were many accidents in IPC's first decades of production. Oil spills killed fish, animal and plant life along the Pacific, which forced a number of fishing communities to abandon the zone.[34]

By the end of the century, proliferation of electrical instruments, of railroads, and the mass production of tools, machines and armaments created markets in Europe and the United States for new industrial metals. To satisfy that demand, domestic capitalists in Peru, Mexico and Chile developed small-scale copper-lead-zinc mines. Within a decade, however, most of them sold out to foreign firms, which had more capital with which to expand and modernise the industry.[35]

Around the turn of the twentieth century many Latin American governments implemented Liberal reforms which extended rights of private property to mineral deposits. These reforms hastened denationalisation of the mining industry. In Peru, for example, prior to the twentieth century mineral deposits were state owned. On a number of occasions, foreign firms had declared they would not invest in the industry because of the precarious nature of leaseholds. In 1901, responding to pressure from US capitalists, the Peruvian government enacted a new mining code which altered the property regime: mineral deposits could be privately owned. Almost immediately, a New York company purchased 80 per cent of the mines in the Cerro de Pasco region of the central Andes.[36] Many of the deposits were virtually inaccessible, situated at altitudes between 9,000 and 12,000 feet above sea level. They were in regions without roads, bridges or other infrastructure, which were subject to seasonal flooding and mud slides. Despite these climatic obstacles, the Cerro de Pasco Corporation soon dominated the economy and society of the central highlands of Peru.

Within a decade, the large-scale mining, processing and livestock operations of the Cerro de Pasco Corporation altered the ecosystem of the Andes. The company constructed networks of roads, railroads, smelters, mining camps, dams and hydro-electric plants to serve its chain of underground copper-lead-zinc mines. First the company modernised refining by introducing the Bessemer process, the most up-to-date technology of the period. Because its smelter, inaugurated in 1905, had a capacity more than five times that of the next largest processing plant in Peru, it created a seemingly insatiable demand for ore and fuel. To supply the smelter, the Corporation modernised haulage and transport systems by installing a system of carts on rails, propelled by electric and horse power. This replaced the men who had for centuries climbed up and down ladders in the mines hauling bags of ore. Finally, the company built a network of lifts, cars and railways to transport ore from their mines to the centralised smelter.

The Cerro de Pasco Corporation purchased large quantities of timber to build its infrastructure, greatly increasing deforestation and erosion in the region. The series of dams to generate electricity for its chain of mining complexes also contributed to ecological and social change. Although the steep terrain of the Andes limited the size of dams, their sheer number flooded highland valleys far from the mines. In addition, railroads altered land. Responding to the availability of transport and the demand for foodstuffs at the mines, commercial grazing and farming began to push out subsistence agriculture, especially in areas close to the tracks.

In 1922 the company inaugurated a large smelter-refinery at La Oroya, which in short order dramatically altered the environment of an area of approximately one hundred square miles. The new smelter polluted the region's air, soil and rivers with arsenic, sulphuric acid and iron-zinc residues. Vegetation withered, animals and fish died, and people developed new diseases. Thirty peasant communities and twenty-eight hacienda owners as far as 75 miles from La Oroya filed legal claims against the Corporation for acute environmental damages. After years of litigation the people whose land and livelihood had been destroyed won a pyrrhic victory: the courts ordered the company to purchase their land. In one stroke the Cerro de Pasco Company became the largest landowner in Peru.

In an example of ecological modernisation, once the company owned the barren lands it increased profits by means of reducing environmental damage. Over the next decade the company installed flues to capture lead, zinc and bismuth particles, as well as arsenic and sulphuric acid emissions. These measures gradually increased the smelters' productivity. The company sold the recovered metals, which contributed to its expanding output of lead-zinc ores. Environmental controls had another benefit: the soil of the Andean *puna* slowly regained its fertility. On the cold, dry lands at altitudes of 12,000 feet, which the courts had ordered the company to purchase, the Company developed Peru's largest cattle ranch. Nevertheless, those environmental measures did little to regenerate the flora and fauna of the La Oroya valley, closer to the refinery. There soil and rock remained bleached by sulphuric acid, and rivers and underground water continued to be toxic and lifeless.[37] More than eighty years after the Corporation opened the refinery, the Oroya valley remained a sort of lunar landscape.

Although the Corporation modernised mineral processing and transport, for over forty years its methods of labour recruitment looked to the past more than to the future. From its inception, the Cerro de Pasco Corporation found it difficult to attract workers. The Company's North American staff regularly complained that of all the difficulties associated with mining in the Peruvian Andes, worst was the shortage of labour. The root of their problem lay in the vitality of communal and household production in the Andes. Although peasant communities were changing, households remained largely self-sufficient. Consequently, rather than accepting that work in the mines was a permanent feature of life, Andeans sought wage labour in the mines only occasionally, to solve an immediate cash crisis.

Occasional labour was incompatible with the Corporation's labour requirements. The company needed permanent workers it could train in the skills of mining and metallurgy, not men who worked for short stints, then returned to their villages. To resolve this problem, the Corporation adopted an Andean tradition called *enganche* (the hook), another name for debt peonage. It sent labour recruiters into highland villages, giving cash advances to men who promised to work off their debt in the mines. In this system, peasants became tied to the company, often for long periods because not infrequently their debts mounted, rather than declined, the longer they remained at the mines.

Within a decade, environmental damage caused by the Oroya refinery contributed to resolving the labour shortage. After inauguration of the refinery at La Oroya, peasants could no longer harvest crops in the area surrounding La Oroya. Further away, yields declined and animals died. In addition, paid labour on haciendas was harder to come by as many of the region's estates were also affected by contamination. Consequently, as the viability of peasant production declined, more families came to depend on wage labour in the mines for survival. In this period, proletarianisation of the peasantry facilitated modernisation of the mining industry.

Revolution in mining

In the 1960s, underground mining was fast becoming a relic of the past as technological innovations transformed the industry. The exploitation of high-grade subterranean veins gave way to extraction of low-grade ores from vast disseminated mineral bodies. The new open-cast techniques transformed all stages of metals mining. First, modern excavation equipment was used to remove the earth's 'overburden', or surface layer, which covered shallow mineral deposits. Second, conveyer belts and pipelines facilitated the movement of large quantities of soil, sludge and rock. Third, new mechanical and chemical techniques were employed to process low-grade ores. Fourth, super-tankers and large port facilities were used in the transport of metals. All in all, open-pit techniques revolutionised copper, iron and bauxite mining, in particular. The result was a leap in the scale of production, but at tremendous environmental cost. Mountains *were* moved and valleys obliterated. Fertile soil that had supported plant and animal life was covered by toxic tailings. Often these residues were recklessly discarded, initiating a chain of soil, water and air contamination that altered the ecosystems of large areas.

Chile, among the world's leading copper-producing countries, was in the forefront of open-pit mining. The decline of its nitrate industry in the early twentieth century paralleled the rise of copper. Copper production in Chile was based on low-grade porphyry ores, which required large investments. Following the opening of the Panama Canal, which lowered transportation costs, and technological innovations in mining and refining low-grade ores, US companies rapidly bought out Chilean mining firms. By 1920 the Chilean copper industry was dominated by three US companies. To give some sense of the scale of production, one open-cast mine, Chuquicamata, the largest copper mine in the world, produced half of Chile's copper exports throughout most of the twentieth century.

In Peru, technological revolution rendered obsolete Cerro de Pasco's empire of underground mines. After the 1960s, when the Corporation's profits declined, the bulk of Peru's mineral exports, predominantly copper and iron ore, came from Cuajone, Toquepala and Cerro Verde, open-pit mines in the south. These were an extension of the rich deposits in northern Chile. In Bolivia, from the early twentieth century, tin was extracted from abandoned silver mines at Potosí, as well as from Siglo XX and Catavi, underground mines on the *altiplano*.[38] However, the development of open-cast mining in other countries contributed to the virtual collapse of Bolivia's tin industry in the 1980s. In particular, open-cast tin mining in Brazil, and the substitution of other metals, such as aluminium, for tin in a number of industrial uses undermined profitability in the Bolivian industry. Nevertheless, if environmental sustainability had been calculated in estimating the costs of open-cast mining ventures, the Bolivian tin industry might not have been written off as uncompetitive.

The open-pit mining revolution was partially responsible for the widespread substitution of aluminium for tin. In general, it was cheaper to mine bauxite, from which aluminium is derived, from surface deposits using open-pit techniques, than to extract tin from underground mines. However, this ignored the fact that aluminium production often was associated with acute environmental degradation. First, it required massive amounts of electricity; in fact, electricity was the major input in aluminium production, not bauxite. As a consequence, bauxite-aluminium production gave rise to the construction of large hydro-electric dams. For example, in Jamaica, as part of the development of bauxite mines, companies built large dams. These flooded agricultural valleys and forced farmers off their land. A second highly damaging side effect of aluminium production was the residue of vast quantities of toxic waste. So-called 'red mud', discarded by aluminium processing plants, is a highly alkaline caustic waste that frequently contaminated ground water and soil in areas surrounding bauxite mines. In Jamaica, Venezuela and Brazil companies disposed of red mud by spreading it over large areas.

While the technological revolution in mining had direct negative ecological consequences, these were intensified by national development strategies which promoted the construction of industrial complexes as spin-offs from the mines. In Latin America, petroleum and iron ore deposits in formerly inaccessible and relatively unspoiled regions frequently formed the hub of 'development poles'. Politicians, bankers and lending agencies coordinated efforts to create these new centres of industrial production.[39]

This was the case with the massive oil deposits developed in Tabasco and Chiapas in Mexico in the 1970s, where the government expropriated agricultural land for mining operations. In ten years Villahermosa, once a small river town, had refineries, ports, pipelines and almost a million people.[40] Air pollution combined with filtration of contaminated water reduced fertility of the remaining farmland. In addition, after a few years vegetation had been damaged by nitric acid rain which originated in the sulphur and nitrate emissions from the refinery.[41] By 1980 one of the few remnants of Villahermosa's past was its ironic name, 'beautiful town'. Its pollution problem was so extreme that residents of Mexico City derived consolation from comparing the toxicity of the two regions.

One of the first development poles to be established in conjunction with metal mining in Latin America was in the remote Orinoquia rainforest in Venezuela. In the 1960s the Venezuelan government nationalised U.S.-owned iron mines in the state of Bolívar to build a large iron-steel complex at Ciudad Guayana.[42] The massive infrastructure at Ciudad Guayana, where the Orinoco and Caroní Rivers converge, included open-pit mines, steel plants, a hydro-electric power plant, and as an after-thought an aluminium refinery. The aluminium refinery was put there to take advantage of electricity generated by the Guri hydro-electric dam, one of the largest in the world. In its early years of operation all the bauxite the plant processed was imported. Only later were bauxite deposits discovered at Los Pijigüaos, about 800 kilometres from Ciudad Guyana. This discovery spread environmental dislocation into a new region, inhabited by indigenous peoples and unique varieties of birds, animals, reptiles and plants. Bauxite excavated at the giant open-cast mine at Los Pijigüaos was floated up the Orinoco to the refinery at Ciudad Guayana. This initiated a chain of pollution carried by the rivers and extending from the mining-industrial complex into the surrounding rainforest.

The development of Ciudad Guayana involved careful economic planning, but little consideration for the project's impact on the tropical ecosystem. The entire river network was altered to meet the needs of the complex. The Guri Dam changed the flow of an extensive river system and flooded large areas of tropical soil. The construction of super-ports on the Orinoco, and widening the river to accommodate ocean-going tankers, aggravated the environmental transformation of the river system. In addition, the mining-metallurgical complex generated a sociopathic process of urbanisation that would be repeated at other development poles. As population growth outpaced the provision of basic urban services, the combination of human waste, debris from the mines, and airborne pollutants from the metallurgical plants turned Ciudad Guayana and the surrounding zone into an environmental disaster area.

Notwithstanding their size, Ciudad Guayana, Villahermosa, and other mega-mining projects were dwarfed by Brazil's *Programa Grande Carajás*. Begun in the 1980s, Carajás was the largest mining project in the world. Everything about Carajás was mammoth, including its threat to the global ecosystem. The project converted one quarter of the planet's largest tropical rainforest into its largest agro-industrial centre.[43] At the hub of the enterprise was an iron ore deposit which reputedly enjoyed the lowest production costs in the world. It was calculated that Carajás alone would produce ten per cent of the world's iron.

The Carajás iron mine became the heart of a vast 'integrated development project' that included a string of open-cast mines producing bauxite, copper, chrome, nickel, tungsten, cassiterite and gold. Processing plants, steel and aluminium factories, agro-livestock enterprises, hydro-electric dams, railroads and deep-water river ports all radiated out from the mines. These formed an archipelago that covered an area of 900,000 square kilometres, the size of France and Britain combined. In addition, the project was like a giant magnet, drawing farmers, gold prospectors, and enterprises of all kinds into the Amazon.[44] Like earlier mining booms in Brazil, mining in Amazonia altered the locus of the country's economy.[45] Along with ranching, it transformed Amazonia from a vast natural preserve to one of Brazil's most dynamic centres of economic growth.

Before Carajás was completed its effect on the environment was apparent, particularly repercussions from deforestation. Besides clearing the forest to make way for mines, farms, and cattle ranches, 1.6 million acres of timber was cut annually to stoke pig iron smelters and provide lumber for construction. The project included plans for reforestation; nevertheless, large areas of the forest were reduced to scrub. This contributed to climate change in and beyond Amazonia. Less rainfall, combined with soil erosion, siltation and flooding were early warning signs of desertification. Research showed that certain plant and animal species were becoming extinct. In total, the construction and operation of Carajás set in motion overwhelming negative changes in the ecosystem.[46]

Large as they were, Carajás and other industrial ventures did not monopolise mining in Amazonia. After the rise in the price of gold in 1979, an estimated one million *garimpeiros,* or prospectors, invaded the region in a gold rush of unprecedented proportions. In the 1980s, the gold which *garimpeiros* extracted from the rivers of Amazonia accounted for approximately 90 per cent of Brazil's annual output. The roads, railroads and services installed for Carajás facilitated the gold rush.[47] In contrast to the scale and technology of integrated development projects, *garimpeiros* were mining's 'informal sector'. Relying on simple machinery and artisanal methods, prospectors worked alone or for small-scale contractors.

Garimpeiros have been blamed for much of the erosion in Amazonia because their techniques involved excavating the banks of the region's waterways.[48] This activity disturbed the ecology of the river system, in particular causing siltation that choked out shallow-rooted trees and plants which had stabilised the terrain.[49] Most destructive of the environment and of *garimpeiros* themselves was their abuse of mercury. To separate gold from ore prospectors used an amalgamation technique not unlike the one developed in the sixteenth century to process silver.

Some specialists argued that small-scale prospecting caused extreme environmental degradation because it was unregulated and unplanned. In their view, prospectors' profligate use and careless disposal of mercury contaminated rivers, soil and the atmosphere more than large mining companies would have done. They argued that the scale of silt, sewage and other kinds of river contamination was an inevitable by-product of the sheer numbers of gold prospectors; this could have been avoided if the sector were dominated by large firms. Finally, critics of small-scale mining held that random logging caused more serious erosion than did projects, such as Carajás, with programmed deforestation/reforestation.[50]

Other specialists disagreed. Faced with massive industrial mining, they viewed *garimpeiros* as the lesser of two evils. Despite the damage they caused, together with indigenous tribes and small farmers, *garimpeiros* helped to resist the advance of ranchers, speculators, and mega-mining companies which were relentlessly transforming Amazonia.[51] However, the ecological damage that resulted from informal gold mining caused conflicts between *garimpeiros,* farmers and indigenous peoples of the region.[52] Indian tribes, in particular, attempted to keep prospectors out of the forest because their survival depended on hunting, gathering and fishing, all of which were jeopardised by small, unregulated mining.[53]

Environmental destruction caused by mining in Latin America increased significantly in the twentieth century, particularly following the introduction of open-cast techniques. This was in contrast to a general reduction in the brutality of working conditions in the industry. The technology of open-cast, non-selective mining transformed the labour process in metals extraction. Modern mining no longer required men to work underground in dangerous, unhealthy conditions. Men (and some women) who extracted ore from open-cast mines operated construction equipment. They drove cranes, shovels and dredgers which scraped away the earth's mantle. The mechanisation and division of labour which came to characterise industrial mining has been associated with rapid increases in productivity. For example, in 1970 on average more than ten times more metal was produced per day in Peru's open-cast copper mines than would have been possible in underground mining.[54]

In Latin America, the open-cast revolution in mining marked a turning point for the human condition of miners and the environmental sustainability of the industry. While the first tended to improve, the second tended to deteriorate. In so far as profitability came to depend on the pace of technical innovation in extraction, processing and transport, more than on prolonging and intensifying labour, it was associated with two tendencies: first, the *relative* reduction in the number of workers employed by large mining companies; second, some scope for improvement in working conditions for those in work.

In the middle twentieth century, the militancy of miners' trades unions in several Latin American countries, in the context of mechanisation associated with new techniques, brought improvements in miners' working and living conditions.[55] In general, the horrors of heavy physical labour in appalling conditions underground gave way in advanced sectors of the industry to a more 'modern' labour process. As the character of the exploitation of labour in the mines changed, work at the mines became more like that in other industries. As a consequence, by the 1960s miners' collective struggles derived less from their conditions of work than from the increasing numbers of miners who had no work at all. With underground mines closing down, unemployment became the scourge of the industry.

Transformations in the labour process, which provided the possibility for improving conditions of work, also generated massive environmental destruction. The same mechanisation and open-cast techniques which lightened the labour of working miners brought ecological disaster to large regions of Latin America. Leaps in productivity ushered in alterations of the environment on what seemed like an ever-expanding scale. The direct and indirect effects of the mining revolution degraded large expanses of the earth's surface, the impact of which was felt far beyond the continent.

Debt disaster

Environmental destruction and debt were among the major global concerns of the late twentieth century. Although apparently separate issues, their causes and effects were linked because finance capital imposed a solution to the debt crisis which almost inevitably resulted in large-scale ecological degradation.

The Third World debt crisis originated in an escalation in the price of oil in the 1970s. Flush with petro-dollars and anxious to extend credit wherever they could, banks in Europe and the US pressed loans on Latin American governments. These funds financed the construction of roads, dams, ports, pipelines and mines. The result was growth in production, in particular of petroleum and metal mining; however, income growth was not as rapid as economists had expected. Construction of some of these projects dragged on for decades, others were never completed. In many cases mega-mining projects proved to be less profitable than they appeared on paper. Instead of generating income, a number of these projects generated debt. For example, in Peru debt servicing for the mining sector alone was US$ 663 million in 1984.[56]

The North's solution to the debt crisis accentuated environmental and social dislocation throughout the Third World. The bankers' response to indebtedness was coordinated by the International Monetary Fund, which imposed structural adjustment policies on governments. The aim of these policies was to ensure that countries did not default on their debts to private banks and multilateral lending agencies. Structural adjustment, or conditionality, involved economic deregulation, denationalisation and, above all, export promotion. In Latin America, to satisfy conditionality, governments encouraged exports, almost regardless of their environmental or social impact.[57]

In the context of debt, export promotion and environmental degradation became intertwined. Petroleum was Latin America's leading export in the 1980s. Although prior to the 1970s, Mexico and Venezuela had been the only significant producers in the region, in the 1980s petroleum companies initiated ambitious exploration programmes in Amazonia as well as in offshore fields. The expansion of petroleum exploration was directly related to the debt crisis. Faced with large service payments and contracting economies, governments were anxious to exploit their petroleum reserves. Consequently, they offered companies favourable terms to develop their deposits. While these governments sometimes paid lip service to issues about the environmental impact of these programmes, in practice they were unwilling to take actions which might discourage companies from operating in the region.

In the 1980s Brazil had the largest debt of any country in the world. Although the capitalist development of the rainforest preceded the debt crisis, Brazilian politicians resolved to hasten exploitation of the resources of Amazonia to service its loans. For instance, notwithstanding low metals prices in the 1980s, Carajás and other large open-pit mines were inaugurated and enlarged. These contributed to the fastest and most ruthless enclosure movement in history. It is estimated that in twenty years, between 1970 and 1990, 50 million hectares of common lands in Amazonia were appropriated as private property. The rush to the Amazon unleashed environmental destruction and violent conflicts over natural resources on a scale few had anticipated.[58]

As I have described, Amazonian gold prospectors represented an extreme and well publicised case of environmental depredation. While less well known, the spread of an informal sector in mining occurred in other countries of Latin America, and with similar effects. Neo-liberal economics engendered widespread poverty, unemployment and deregulation, which encouraged artisanal mining to flourish in the shadows of industrial enterprises. As small-scale, 'informal' mining ventures easily circumvented regulations controlling the disposal of toxic tailings and chemical pollutants, the environmental consequences of these activities rapidly became apparent. This suggests that in mining, small is not necessarily more sustainable than large-scale ventures.[59] I propose that with regard to mining, the salient factors which condition environmental impact are the form of property relations and the political will to regulate production, not enterprise size. When capital accumulation drives production and choice of technology, ecological considerations tend to be disregarded, whatever the size of firm. This would support the conclusion that where production is consciously and collectively designed to enhance social needs, there is more possibility that choice of technique, including scale, might reflect environmental considerations. However, writing in a time when socialism seems remote, realism leads me to suggest that the nationalisation of mining activities might be a more pragmatic political agenda. And, unlike in the past, environmentalists would endeavour to ensure that the politics of nationalisation was based on environmental as well as class objectives.

Environmental destruction and human immiseration: inverse or merging tendencies?

Analysis of historical trends in Latin American mining suggests a tendency towards decline in human immiseration coupled with a rise in environmental destruction. These processes intensified with the expansion of capitalism in Latin America. Capitalism has the potential to free human beings and productive resources from limitations which characterised previous economic systems. At the same time it subordinates workers and resource use to the competitive drive to accumulate capital. The combination of 'liberation' and subjugation creates a power that is productive as well as destructive. Production expands rapidly, but in the process of accumulation capital consumes resources on an ever-expanding scale.[60] This creates a tendency within capitalism to erode ecological sustainability: however, it also contains counter-tendencies. The development of technologies which economise in the use of resources is one; another is that when profitability is constrained by environmental degradation, firms may take measures to overcome impediments to the expansion of capital, such as at La Oroya in the 1920s.[61] However, the most important force for ecological preservation stands outside capital and potentially opposes its expansion. That force is the power of people who in an organised way resist the destruction of natural resources which are crucial to their lives.

With the expansion of capitalism, exploitation of the working class tends to increase, as capitalists appropriate more unpaid labour time in the process of production. Yet inherent in capitalism is the possibility that the standard of living and working conditions of the labouring class may improve. Rising productivity provides the possibility that capitalists can increase profits and also accede to some demands by workers for improvements in their conditions of existence. That two-fold process occurred in industrial countries in the twentieth century: trade unions fought for improvements in the lives of workers, and the standard of living of the working classes rose. To a lesser extent that process characterised the mining industry in Latin America.

One might conclude that these long-term inverse tendencies – improvement in the conditions of existence of the masses of people in contrast to increased ecological deterioration – gave impetus to environmental movements which flourished in the industrialised countries in the late twentieth century. In Europe and the US, where human suffering seemed to be on the wane, people became increasingly alarmed by the devastation of the natural world. However, the experience of the 1990s underlined the fact that with the expansion of capital, improvements in the standard of living of the working class is only a possibility, not an inherent characteristic of capitalist development.

Events of the *fin du siècle* in the developing world, specifically the social consequences of the debt crisis, of neo-liberal economics and of globalisation, suggested that in so far as an inverse relationship between human and natural degradation existed, it might be drawing to an end. One could project that in the future the two tendencies will fuse into a common trend.[62] This possibility stems from trends apparent in the final decades of the twentieth century. These include: first, falling incomes and standards of living of the vast bottoms of the social pyramid in Latin America, Africa and parts of Asia; second, chronic environmental decay and acute environmental crises which eroded the quality of life of broad sections of the population throughout the developing world.

Notes

I thank John Weeks, Juan Martinez-Alier, Daniel Faber and the two reviewers for this journal for comments on an earlier draft, and Anne Worden for research assistance.

1 For historical analysis see: Elizabeth Dore, *The Peruvian Mining Industry: Growth, Stagnation and Crisis* (Boulder, CO: Westview Press, 1988); John Fisher, *Silver Mines and Silver Miners in Colonial Peru, 1776–1824* (Liverpool: Centre for Latin American Studies, University of Liverpool, 1977) and 'Silver Production in the Viceroyalty of Peru, 1776–1824', *Hispanic American Historical Review* 55:1 (February 1985); Peter Bakewell, 'Mining in Colonial Spanish America', and A. J. R. Russell-Wood, 'Colonial Brazil: the gold cycle', in Leslie Bethell, ed., *The Cambridge History of Latin America: Colonial Latin America*, Vol. II, (Cambridge: Cambridge University Press, 1984); Brooke Larson, *Colonialism and Agrarian Transformation in Bolivia: Cochabamba, 1550–1900* (Princeton: Princeton University Press, 1988); Florencia Mallon, *In Defense of Community in Peru's Central Highlands* (Princeton: Princeton University Press, 1983); Richard L. Garner, 'Long-Term Silver Mining Trends in Spanish America: A Comparative Analysis of Peru and Mexico', *American Historical Review* 93:4 (October 1988): 898–935.

For environmental analysis see: Anthony Hall, *Developing Amazonia: Deforestation and Social Conflict in Brazil's Carajás Programme* (Manchester: Manchester University Press, 1989); David Cleary, *Anatomy of the Amazon Gold Rush* (Oxford: Macmillan, 1990); Elizabeth Dore, 'Open Wounds', *NACLA's Report on the Americas* 25: 2 (September 1991): 14–21; Juan Martinez-Alier, *Ecological Economics: Energy, Environment and Society* (Oxford: Blackwell, 1991) and 'Ecology of the Poor: A Neglected Dimension of Latin American History', *Journal of Latin American Studies*, 23:3 (October 1991); Alejandro Toledo, 'Destruir el paraíso: energéticos y media ambiente en el sureste mexicano', *Ecología: Política/Cultura* (Mexico), 2 (Summer 1987): 15 ff.

and 'The Ecological Crisis of Latin America', a special issue of *Latin American Perspectives* 19:1 (Winter 1992).

2 John Weeks, *Capital and Exploitation* (Princeton: Princeton University Press, 1981) 10–49.

3 Contributions to 'Green Marxism' include Peter Dickens, *Society and Nature: Towards a Green Social Theory* (Hemel Hempstead: Harvester, 1992) and *Reconstructing Nature: Alienation, Emancipation and the Division of Nature* (London and New York: Routledge, 1996); John Foster, 'The Absolute General Law of Environmental Degradation Under Capitalism', *Capitalism, Nature, Socialism* 3:3 (1992): 77–82; James O'Connor, 'Capitalism, Nature, Socialism: A Theoretical Introduction', *Capitalism, Nature, Socialism* 1:1 (Fall 1988): 11–37; Daniel Faber, 'The Ecological Crisis of Latin America: A Theoretical Introduction', *Latin American Perspectives* 19:1 (Winter 1992): 3–16; Jean Paul Deleage, *Historia de la Ecología: Una ciencia del hombre y la naturaleza* (Barcelona: ICARIA, 1992); Tim Allmark, 'Environment and Society in Latin America', in M. R. Redclift and G. R. Woodgate, eds, *The International Handbook of Environmental Sociology* (Cheltenham and Northampton, MA: Edward Elgar, 1997) and Enrique Leff, *Ecología y capital: hacia una perspectiva ambiental del desarrollo* (Mexico, DF: Universidad Nacional Autónoma de México, 1986).

4 This was demonstrated by the limited nature of international accords, for instance the Kyoto Agreement of 1997 and the Buenos Aires Agreement of 1998.

5 Theories range from military defeat, internal insurrection, spiritual convulsion, natural disaster such as earthquakes etc. T. Patrick Culbert, ed., *The Classic Maya Collapse* (Albuquerque, NM: University of New Mexico Press, 1973).

6 Malthus argued that population tends to increase at a faster rate than its means of subsistence and that unless it is checked by a moral restraint or by disease, famine, war or other disaster, widespread poverty and degradation inevitably result.

7 For analysis of the sustainability of Mayan resource use see Mary Pohl, ed., *Prehistoric Lowland Maya Environment and Subsistence Economy* (Cambridge, MA: Peabody Museum, 1985); Elizabeth A. Graham, *The Highlands of the Lowlands: Environment and Archeology in the Stann Creek District, Belize, Central America* (Madison, WI: Prehistory Press, 1994); Ursula M. Cowgill, *Soil Fertility and the Ancient Maya* (New Haven, Conn: Transactions of the Connecticut Academy of Arts and Sciences, 42 (Oct 1961), 1–56); Helmuth O. Wagner, 'Subsistence Potential and Population Density of the Maya on the Yucatan Peninsula and Causes for the Decline in Population in the Fifteenth Century', International Congress of Americanistas, XXXVIII, Stuttgart-Munchen, Germany, 1968, v. 1, 179–96.

8 Michael Hamer, 'The Ecological Basis for Aztec Sacrifice', *American Ethnologist* 4:1 (1977): 117–33; Sarah L. O'Hara, F. Alayne Street-Perrott and Timothy P. Burt, 'Accelerated Soil Erosion around a Mexican Highland Lake Caused by Prehispanic Agriculture', *Nature* 362:6415 (4 March 1993): 48–51; and Karl W. Butzer, 'No Eden in the New World', *Nature* 362:6415 (4 March 1993): 15–17.

9 O'Hara, et al., 'Accelerated Soil Erosion'.

10 William Denevan, 'The Pristine Myth: the Landscape of the Americas in 1492', *Annals of the Association of American Geographers,* 82:3 (1986), 369–85. For arguments about the unsustainability of the pre-hispanic Amazon see B. Meggers, 'Amazonia: Real or Counterfeit Paradise?' *Review of Archeology*

13 (1992): 25–40, and 'The Prehistory of Amazonia', in J. Denslow and C. Padoch, eds., *Peoples of the Tropical Rain Forest* (Berkeley: University of California Press, 1988). For an interpretation of pristine America see Raphael Girard, *Historia de las Civilizaciones Antiguas de America* (Madrid: Ediciones Istmo, 1976), 3 vols.

11 Irving Rouse, *The Tainos: Rise and Decline of the People Who Greeted Columbus,* (New Haven: Yale University Press, 1992).

12 Alfred W. Crosby, *The Columbian Exchange: Biological and Cultural Consequences of 1492* (Westport, CT: Greenwood Press, 1987) and *Ecological Imperialism: biological expansion of Europe, 900–1900* (Cambridge: Cambridge University Press, 1986).

13 The first royal measures to protect the Indians were decreed in 1542 and called The New Laws. Africans brought to the colonies as slaves were less fortunate than the Indians: the New Laws ratified their enslavement. Their financial cost to their owners would serve, in theory, as protection. Henry Stevens, trans. and ed., *The New Laws of the Indies* (London: The Chiswick Press, 1893), iii–xvii.

14 This mid-range estimate is from William M. Denevan, ed., *The Native Population of the Americas in 1492,* 2nd ed. (Madison: University of Wisconsin Press, 1992). For contributions to the debate on the demographic collapse see, Nicolás Sanchez Albornoz, *The Population of Latin America,* translated by W. A. R. Richardson, (Berkeley: University of California Press, 1974), 37–66; Sherburne F. Cook and Woodrow Borah, *Essays in Population History: Mexico and the Caribbean* (Berkeley: University of California Press, 1971), Vol. 1, and 'The Rate of Population Change in Central Mexico, 1550–70', *Hispanic American Historical Review 37:4* (Nov 1957): 463–70; Linda A. Feinman et al., 'Long-term Demographic Change: A Perspective from the Valley of Oaxaca' *Journal of Field Archaeology* 12:3 (1985): 333–62; Thomas M. Whitmore, *Disease and Death in Early Colonial Mexico: Simulating Amerindian Depopulation* (Boulder, CO: Westview Press, 1992).

15 Juan Martinez-Alier, Conference 'Worlds in Collision', University of Portsmouth, November 1992.

16 On reorganisation of the colonial state in Peru see Steve J. Stern, *Peru's Indian Peoples and the Challenge of Spanish Conquest* (Madison: University of Wisconsin Press, 1982); Larson, *Colonialism and Agrarian Transformation,* 51–91; and Karen Spalding, *Huarochirí: An Andean Society under Inca and Spanish Rule* (Stanford: Stanford University Press, 1984).

17 The labour system in the Mexican mines was substantially different from that in Peru. The standard interpretation of the labour force at Zacatecas and other Mexican mines emphasises the preponderance of wage workers who were attracted to the mines by high pay. P. J. Bakewell, *Silver Mining and Society in Colonial Mexico: Zacatecas 1546–1700* (Cambridge: Cambridge University Press, 1971).

18 Stern, *Peru's Indian Peoples,* 51–113; Larson, *Colonialism and Agrarian Transformation,* 51–91.

19 Mercury amalgamation developed in New Spain (Mexico) in the 1550s.

20 D. A. Brading and Harry E. Cross, 'Colonial Silver Mining: Mexico and Peru', *Hispanic American Historical Review* 52:4 (November 1972): 567.

21 G. Lohmann Villena, *Los Minas de Huancavelica en los siglos XVI y XVII* (Sevila, 1949), 169–77.

22 This is a case of O'Connor's second contradiction of capitalism. 'On the Two Contradictions of Capitalism', *Capitalism, Nature and Socialism,* 107–9.

23 For the ways mining altered the spatial organisation of colonial society see Carlos Sempat Assadourian, *El sistema de la economia colonial: mercado interno, regiones y spacio económico* (Lima: Instituto de Estudios Peruanos, 1982).

24 For estimates of quantities of mercury used in New Spain and in Peru see Brading and Cross, 'Colonial Silver Mining', 572; and Garner, 'Long-Term Silver Mining'.

25 For the orthodox view see: Earl J. Hamilton, *American Treasure and the Price Revolution in Spain 1506–1650* (Cambridge: Cambridge University Press, 1934); Woodrow Borah, *New Spain's Century of Depression* (Berkeley: University of California Press, 1951); J. I. Israel, 'Mexico and the "General Crisis" of the Seventeenth Century', *Past and Present* 63 (1974): 33–57. For revisionist interpretations see: John Lynch, *Spain Under the Hapsburgs* (Oxford: Oxford University Press, 1964–69) 2 vols., 11,195; Herbert S. Klein and John J. Tepaske, 'The Seventeenth-Century Crisis in the Spanish Empire: Myth or Reality?' *Past and Present* 90 (1981): 116–35; and J. I. Israel and Henry Kamen, 'Debate – The Decline of Spain: A Historical Myth?' *Past and Present* 81 (1981): 170–85.

26 While the fall in the number of *mitayos* sent to the Peruvian mines may reflect the continued population decline, of more importance was the declining power of the colonial state. Larson, *Colonialism and Agrarian Transformation*, 92–115.

27 William Taylor, *Landlord and Peasant in Colonial Oaxaca* (Stanford: Stanford University Press, 1972); Eric Van Young, 'Mexican Rural History since Chevalier: The Historiography of the Colonial Hacienda', *Latin American Research Review* 18 (1983): 5–61.

28 This discussion is based on Enrique Tandeter, *Coercion and Market: Silver Mining in Colonial Potosí, 1692–1826* (Albuquerque, NM: University of New Mexico Press, 1993), and 'Forced and Free Labour in Late Colonial Potosí', *Past and Present* 93 (November 1981): 98–136. See Dore, *Peruvian Mining*, 71–76, for discussion of the nature of forced and free labour.

29 D. A. Brading, *Miners and Merchants in Bourbon Mexico, 1763–1810* (Cambridge: Cambridge University Press, 1971); Fisher, 'Silver Production in the Viceroyalty of Peru, 1776–1824'.

30 Brading and Cross, 'Colonial Silver Mining', 548–56.

31 Arthur C. Todd, *The Search for Silver: Cornish Miners in Mexico 1824–1947* (Padstow: Lodenek Press, 1977).

32 In 1991 it was proposed that Chile should import toxic waste and store it in these abandoned mines.

33 William Bollinger, 'The Rise of United States Influence in the Peruvian Economy, 1869–1921', M.A. thesis, University of California at Los Angeles, 1972; I. G. Bertram, 'Development Problems in an Export Economy: A Study of Domestic Capitalists, Foreign Firms and Government in Peru, 1919–30', Ph.D diss. Linacre College, University of Oxford, 1974.

34 On oil exploration and indigenous peoples see J. Kimerling, 'Oil, Lawlessness and Indigenous Struggles in Ecuador's Oriente', in H. Collinson, ed., *Green Guerrillas* (London: Latin American Bureau, 1986).

35 For analysis of this process in Peru see Dore, *Peruvian Mining*, 78–111; and Adrian DeWind, *Peasants Become Miners: The Evolution of Industrial Mining Systems in Peru, 1902–1974* (New York: Garland, 1987). For Chile, Maurice Zeitlin, *The Civil Wars in Chile: or, The Bourgeois Revolutions that Never Were* (Princeton: Princeton University Press, 1984). For Mexico,

Marvin D. Bernstein, *The Mexican Mining Industry 1890–1950: A Study of the Interaction of Politics, Economics and Technology* (Albany, NY: University Press of the State University of New York, 1965); Robert Randall, *Real del Monte: A British Mining Venture in Mexico* (Austin, TX: University of Texas Press, 1972); and Todd, *The Search for Silver.*

36 For the denationalisation of mines and the Peruvian Mining Code of 1901 see Dore, *Peruvian Mining,* 89–91.
37 Juan Martinez-Alier, 'La Interpretación ecologista de la historia socio-económica: algunos ejemplos andinos', *Revista Andina* 15 (1990). For the 'smoke controversy' see Mallon, *In Defense of Community,* 226–31.
38 On Bolivian tin mining see James Dunkerley, *Rebellion in the Veins* (London: Verso, 1984); June Nash, *We Eat the Mines and the Mines Eat Us: Dependency and Exploitation in Bolivian Tin Mines* (New York: Columbia University Press, 1979); *The Great Tin Crash: Bolivia and the World Tin Market* (London: Latin American Bureau, 1987); and Manuel Contreras, *The Bolivian Tin Mining Industry in the First Half of the Twentieth Century* (London: Institute of Latin American Studies, 1993) Research Paper No. 32.
39 F. Neto, 'Development Planning and Mineral Mega-Projects: Some Global Considerations', in D. Goodman and A. Hall, eds., *The Future of Amazonia* (Basingstoke: Macmillan, 1990). For the petroleum industry see Frank Tugwell, *The Politics of Oil in Venezuela* (Stanford: Stanford University Press, 1975); George Phillip, *Oil and Politics in Latin America* (Cambridge: Cambridge University Press, 1982); and George W. Grayson, *The Politics of Mexican Oil* (Pittsburgh: University of Pittsburgh Press, 1980).
40 Toledo, 'Destruir el paraíso', 15.
41 Joel Simon, *Endangered Mexico: An Environment on the Edge* (London: Latin American Bureau, 1998).
42 For Ciudad Guayana see María Pilar García, 'Actores y movimientos sociales en los grandes proyectos de inversión minero-industriales en América Latina', *Revista Interamericana de Planificación,* XXIII: 89 (enero-marzo 1990): 223–52. García compares the ecological impact of Ciudad Guayana to the Lázaro Cárdenas-Las Truchas iron-steel complex in Michoacán, Mexico.
43 Hall, *Developing Amazonia,* and 'Agrarian Crisis in Brazilian Amazonia: the Grande Carajás Programme', *Journal of Development Studies* 23:4 (July 1987): 522–52; Philip M. Fearnside and Anthony Hall, 'Agricultural Plans for Brazil's Grande Carajás Program: Lost Opportunity or Sustainable Local Development?' *World Development* 14 (March 1986): 385–409; J. Timmons Roberts, 'Trickling Down and Scrambling Up: the Informal Sector, Food Provisioning and Local Benefits of the Carajás Mining 'Growth Pole' in the Brazilian Amazon', *World Development* 23:3 (March 1995): 385–400.
44 Charles F. Bennett, 'The Carajás Project, Brazil: Ecological Impacts of Mineral Development in the Amazon Basin', (San Diego: *Proceedings, Pacific Coast Council on Latin American Studies,* 1987), 91–100.
45 In early colonial Brazil economic life centred around sugar exports, produced on slave plantations in the North East. The discovery of gold at the end of the 18th century in Minas Gerais began a major shift from the North East to the South. Fortunes made in gold mining built the coffee estates around Rio de Janiero, which became the fulcrum of the economy.
46 Hall, *Developing Amazonia.*
47 Marianne Schmink and Charles H. Wood, *Contested Frontiers in Amazonia* (New York: Columbia University Press, 1992).

48 D. Biller, 'Informal Gold Mining and Mercury Pollution in Brazil', Policy Research Working Paper no. 1304 (Washington, DC: World Bank, 1994).

49 For analysis of similar processes in Guyana see Marcus Colchester, *Guyana: Fragile Frontier* (London: Latin American Bureau, 1997).

50 Cleary, *Anatomy of the Amazon Gold Rush.*

51 *Ibid.*

52 Schmink and Wood, *Contested Frontiers;* G. Macmillan, *At the End of the Rainbow? Gold, Land and People in the Brazilian Amazon* (London: Earthscan, 1995).

53 On peasant agriculture and sustainability see Evaldice Eve and Christopher Eve, 'Resource Base of Peasants in the Brazilian Amazon: Planning Solutions for Current Problems of Sustainability', *Bulletin of Latin American Research* 17:3 (1988): 387–407. For effects of mining on the Yanomami see *Bound in Misery and Iron: The Impact of the Grande Carajás Programme on the Indians of Brazil* (London: Survival International, 1987).

54 This is a conservative estimate calculated from a historical series on productivity in Peruvian mining. Dore, *Peruvian Mining,* 87–159.

55 Notwithstanding these tendencies, in some countries of Latin America, particularly Chile and Peru, technologies that facilitated rising productivity were introduced in the 1980s, when trades unions suffered extreme repression. As a consequence, in this period technical change was accompanied by deteriorating working conditions and by an absolute and relative reduction in the level of employment in open-pit mining.

56 For indebtedness in Peruvian mining see Oscar Ugarteche, *El Estado Deudor: Economía Política de la Deuda: Perú y Bolivia 1968–1984* (Lima: Instituto de Estudios Peruanos, 1986).

57 For debt and ecological destruction see Elizabeth Dore, 'Debt and Ecological Disaster in Latin America', *Race and Class* 34: 1 (1992): 73–87. For causes of the debt crisis, John Weeks, 'Losers Pay Reparations, or how the Third World Lost the Lending War', in John Weeks, ed., *Debt Disaster: Banks, Governments and Multinationals Confront the Crisis* (New York: New York University Press, 1989), 41–63.

58 Susana Hecht and Alexander Cockbum, *The Fate of the Forest* (London: Penguin Books, 1990) 2nd edition.

59 On sustainibility of small-scale mining ventures see G. Burke, 'Policies for Small-scale Mining: the need for integration', *Journal of Minerals Policy, Business and Environment – Raw Materials Report* 12:3 (1997); Mamadou Barry, ed., *Regularising Informal Mining: a summary of the proceedings of the International Round Table on Artisanal Mining* (1995); and World Bank, Industry and Energy Development. Occasional Paper no. 6 (Washington, DC, 1996).

60 O'Connor, 'On the Two Contradictions of Capitalism.'

61 This is an example of 'ecological modernisation'. G. Spaargaren, *The Ecological Modernisation of Production and Consumption: Essays in Environmental Sociology* (Wageningen, The Netherlands: Wageningen University, 1997).

62 This view is developed in the 'Green Marxism' school. See, for instance, Dickens, *Reconstructing Nature;* and Tim Allmark, 'Environment and Society in Latin America'.

11

EXCEPTIONALISM IN EUROPEAN ENVIRONMENTAL HISTORY

Joachim Radkau

"Don't be afraid to say you don't know," is one of the rules which Oliver Rackham, the British forest historian, proposes in his provocative manner for historians of the environment.[1] I will try to heed this advice. Therefore, as I set out ten theses, they should be understood as cautious hypotheses about some open questions. My subject, the problem of Europe's special path (*Sonderweg*) in environmental history, appears rather ambitious; it is difficult to grasp. Moreover, the comparison between Europe, the New World, and the Third World is burdened with prejudices. By analyzing questions of this kind, one is moving on shaky ground. It is not even certain whether Europe as a whole is an appropriate unit for environmental history because in several respects the Mediterranean is a region of its own which has had characteristic environmental problems throughout its history.

In this paper, "Europe" means first and foremost Western and Central Europe, the earliest centers of industrial development. In what sense Mediterranean Europe, too, belongs to my concept of Europe or whether the whole Mediterranean should be understood as a particular environmental region remains an open question. My paper seeks to examine the connection between environmental conditions and the industrial revolution. In general, I have the impression that Western and Central Europe since medieval times can indeed be considered an environmental unit in some important respects.

But, to be sure, in many other respects the units of environmental history are much smaller, and the progress of knowledge depends on field research in these small areas. Large-scale overviews always run the risk of constructing history out of preconceived assumptions, not solid research. On the other hand, mere field studies are frequently not able to identify the truly distinctive traits of a specific region, as the comparison with other regions is missing. Important particularities of European environmental history have not been adequately recognized because of the lack of comparison with non-European regions. Reading recent works on American, Indian, or

Chinese environmental history, one gets surprising insights into character-istically European features of the relationship between man and nature. Therefore, a worldwide comparison can be justified because of the services it offers to regional research.[2]

1. A plea for caution in regard to the spiritual approach

In his Christmas lecture in 1966, which became the starting point and a sort of holy text for environmental history, Lynn White Jr. assigned the Judeo-Christian religion a prominent place among the "historical roots of our environmental crisis." "Especially in its Western form," he declared, "Christianity is the most anthropocentric religion the world has seen. ... Christianity, in absolute contrast to ancient paganism and Asia's religions ... not only established a dualism of man and nature but also insisted that it is God's will that man exploit nature for its proper ends." Modern science and technology, the immediate causes of modern alienation from nature, have—in the words of Lynn White—"grown out of Christian attitudes toward man's relations to nature."[3] This statement has deeply influenced the environmentalists' view of Western civilization in comparison with the old civilizations of the East. The history of religion and of spiritual move-ments seemed to be the royal road to writing environmental history in a worldwide perspective and overcoming the immense complexity of the material world.

Eugen Drewermann, a popular German ex-priest, presented a similar view in his German bestseller, *Der tödliche Fortschritt—Von der Zerstörung der Erde und des Menschen im Erbe des Christentums* (Deadly Progress—On the Destruction of Earth and Mankind within the Christian Heritage). "The religion of Israel," he states, "has remained, after all, a desert religion which ... has never been able to perceive the earth as good-natured and warm like a Great Mother."[4] The recent cultural turn within the social sciences seems to have endowed the spiritual approach with a new attrac-tiveness in environmental matters as well.[5] But this might in the end turn out to be a blind alley. I fear it is an illusion to believe that the history of religion offers a clear and simple structure for a world history of the relationship between humankind and nature. Religion is not an autonomous force in history. In this regard, historians have much to learn from the writings of Clifford Geertz. In a comparison of the cultural appearance of the Islamic religion in Morocco and Indonesia, Geertz discovered funda-mental differences that stood in connection with ecological contrasts. "Intensive, extremely productive wet rice cultivation has provided the main economic foundation" of the culture of Java, he writes; "and rather than the restless, aggressive, extroverted (Moroccan) sheikh husbanding his resources ..., the national archetype is the settled, industrious, rather inward plowman of twenty centuries, nursing his terrace. ... In Morocco civilization was built on nerve; in Indonesia, on diligence."[6] Elsewhere he warns of drawing direct conclusions about everyday behavior from religious ideas: "But no one, not even a saint, lives in the world religious symbols formulate all of the time, and the majority of men live in it only at moments."[7]

To be sure, religion is no trifling matter in environmental history. But it makes little sense to tear some seemingly environmentalist elements of religion, such as "Mother Earth," out of the greater context. The meaning of religion for the practical relationship between man and nature can only be discovered by analyzing everyday religious culture, not merely by contemplating its basic religious ideas. In this way, the imagined contrast of "East" and "West" becomes blurred; a much more complicated picture emerges instead.

The "dominium terrae" ("Subdue the Earth!") commandment of the Judeo-Christian god has had no clear practical meaning throughout history, contrary to the opinion of some environmental historians. In early modern times a human responsibility for nature and the duty of animal protection was deduced from this commandment, which was understood within its biblical context. Did Christianity remain a desert religion in the agrarian West? Certainly not, if one looks not only at the Bible, but also at popular religion, at the stories of the saints, the festivals of the church. Everywhere, one finds traces of the traditional agrarian world. And it is hardly a coincidence that on the whole, modern environmentalism is most widespread in Protestant countries.

On the other hand, were the great Eastern religions really non-anthropocentric? Did they really promote a brotherly relationship toward nature?[8] Herbert Franke, one of the leading German historians of China, made statements of this kind about Chinese religious and spiritual traditions; but this view has been vigorously attacked by Gudula Linck. "Yin and Yang— forget it." According to Linck, the old Chinese veneration of unspoilt nature was not a mirror of reality, but a resigned sigh from isolated individuals who retired from public life.[9] Above all, the publications of Mark Elvin have debunked the myth of Chinese harmony with nature through the millennia.[10]

The widespread belief among environmentalists that rescue will come from non-Western cultures is not well-founded. It is quite easy to find overwhelming evidence for an anthropocentric attitude toward nature not only in the history of the West, but in the history of the East as well. It is not here that we find the key to the unique European path in environmental history. To be sure, this is not to say: "Forget religion as a driving force in environmental history!" Perhaps we need a new Max Weber to discover intimate links between Protestantism and modern environmentalism. But even between Protestant Europe and Protestant America there exist remarkable differences in environmental history.

2. Outlines of an institutional approach to environmental history

If we look at institutional aspects of environmental history, we arrive on more solid ground.[11] In this context, I conceive the term "institution" in the broad sense of the institutional school of economics; as comprising not only administrative bodies and established organizations, but also rules and customs fixed for a long time. My basic philosophy is very simple: It is not ideas and individual actions that are of decisive importance in the evolution of the human treatment of nature, but rather the lasting patterns of everyday collective behavior and the institutions that generate and perpetuate those patterns.

I would argue that on this level, a distinctive European path can be recognized most clearly and concretely, though some open questions will remain. The management of environmental problems in Europe has been deeply influenced over the centuries by old European traditions of *Verrechtlichung*—regulation by law—dating back to Roman times. In the pluralistic European political tradition, where different sources of law always existed, law has frequently been a subject of discussion and controversy. Law was not only imposed by an omnipotent ruler, but was also conceived as something an individual could use to fight against the ruler. For over five hundred years, the forest communities (*Markgenossenschaften*) of the Tyrolean peasants instituted legal proceedings against the Habsburg government in order to preserve their *jus regulandi silvas;* and in the end, in 1847, they won.[12] I have the impression that it would be difficult to discover similar stories in other regions of the world—it seems that there was not even the hint of such stories. The basic conditions of environmental history have been deeply imprinted by this longtime process of legal regulation.

One could propose a hypothesis that contradicts this finding: Are institutions of this kind really so important for the treatment of nature in the course of history? Did the really decisive things not happen on a level below these institutions, on the level of the domestic economy? There is some truth in this view. Until the nineteenth, even twentieth century, the basic units of environmental behavior in most regions of the world were very small: the family, the house, the farm, the neighborhood. Until modern times, the environmental advantage gained by European traditions of legal regulation was probably not very considerable. But at least since the eighteenth century, it has been growing along with the increasing complexity of environmental problems that could no longer be regulated sufficiently within the framework of a domestic economy. The sound management of woodlands, of water resources, of pasture, and of urban problems demanded more and more institutional regulation.

In this context, we should take notice of another important point: The growth of effective institutions which are founded upon everyday behavior needs a lot of time; it cannot happen as a quick reaction to a sudden state of emergency. In the leading European countries, industrialization was—at least in comparison with the rest of the world—a relatively slow process that lasted several generations. Therefore, Europe had a better chance than many other regions of the world to build institutions that acted as a certain counterbalance against the negative side effects of industrialization.

Perhaps the greatest achievement of research on environmental history so far has been the rediscovery of the immense number of environmental conflicts in the urban regions during the period of early industrialization in the nineteenth and early twentieth centuries. At least in Germany, the most impressive research has mainly been done in this area.[13] But on the whole, the results are highly ambiguous. On the one hand, the reader is impressed by the broad scope of early environmentalist concern; on the other hand, one may be irritated by the lack of immediate and effective action against the obvious pollution of the environment. An institutionalist approach would probably be fruitful here and help advance discussion. Instead of asking the question "Was environmental protest successful or not?" one might ask: "In what way were institutions of environmental management influenced or shaped by this protest?" In this way, environmental history need not remain an endless lament. Repeated environmental protest has frequently had an institutional effect in the long run. Sometimes, the most difficult problems are not the lack of any practical measures, but the new environmental issues created by certain kinds of temporarily successful environmental management, for instance by waterworks, organized reforestation, major projects for cleaning up the cities, or nuclear energy as a remedy for the depletion of limited fossil energy resources.

The most important European success story told by the institutionalist school of economic history is the development of reliable property rights, but it is not certain whether the rise of private property was a success story in environmental history. In the era of subsistence economy, well-established property and inheritance rights may have been the best way to conserve the fertility of the soil. But under the conditions of unlimited and worldwide capitalist dynamism, unrestricted private property rights tend to become an environmental risk. Thus, the European path has definite drawbacks: even institutions that have been rather successful for a long time may become detrimental under changed conditions. Today, African agrarian scientists are complaining about the hypertrophy of private property rights in the European legal tradition: "Traditional legal doctrine sanctifies the property rights of the individual against the state, but perceives hardly any objection to the individuals appropriating more and more property rights at the expense of the public's larger interest in environmental resources as the common property of all."[14]

Yet it seems that the emphasis on private property rights is not the whole European tradition. The development of certain kinds of collective loyalties belongs to the European heritage as well, though it is difficult to say whether they are particularly European. Above all, the nation-state has been an invention with far-reaching environmental consequences. Environmental history as a whole is always much more than environmental history in the narrow sense of the word.

3. Balance and imbalance between field and pasture

For the biologist, there is a clear and simple natural foundation of Eurasian superiority: the domestication of big mammals, especially cattle and horses.[15] This success alone does not explain European superiority over the Asian civilizations, from where most European domesticated animals originated. But Eric L. Jones is probably right that in early modern times there was already a quantitative European advantage in regard to large animals. "Europeans commanded more working capital per head than Asians, mainly in the form of livestock. ... They brought more draught animals to bear on their fields than the Chinese and stronger, better-fed ones than the Indians."[16] Long before the industrial revolution, the peoples of Western and Central Europe—of "carnivorous Europe"—probably had more sources of energy and calories available to them than most Asians, if we disregard nomadic peoples. This holds true for water power, too, if we think of the multitude of rivers that were water-bearing year-round, which were the driving force of the tens of thousands of water mills that were a distinctive trait of Central and Western European development and land-scape since medieval times. Therefore, the origins of Europe's special path in environmental history as well as in the history of technology can be traced far back into premodern times.

The use of large mammals for cavalry and the deep plough certainly gave Europeans a military and economic advantage, but did it stabilize the agrarian ecosystem? A pastoral economy frequently leads to over-grazing and the destruction of woodlands. In many regions of the world there is an ancient tension between peasants and herdsmen, especially in the Asian regions that suffered from nomadic invasions. But even in European history there are many instances of hostility between agricultural and pastoral cultures. Most famous is the case of the Spanish Mesta, the powerful shepherds' organization that invaded the fields by means of royal privileges and neglected the interests of the peasantry. In the view of Douglass C. North and Robert P. Thomas, both pioneers of the institutionalist school of economics, the Mesta is the striking negative proof of the power of institutions in the course of economic history.[17] Whether the Mesta had a similarly detrimental effect on the environ-ment is not certain. Modern Spanish environmentalists are becoming enthusiastic about the biodiversity upon the *caminadas,* the old paths of transhumance.

Be that as it may, compared with the Mediterranean and with many other regions of the world, Western and Central Europe are, on the whole, characterized by relatively successful combinations of farming and herding, and that means by a relatively well-organized material flux in agriculture combined with high ecological reserves. To be sure, the balance was frequently far from perfect, but up to the nineteenth century, this balance tended to improve. This equilibrium was of decisive importance for the improvement of agricultural sustainability because prior to the introduction of chemical fertilizers, the conservation of the fertility of the soil depended on the use of animal manure. In this regard, there were significant differences between many regions of the world. This is a subject that deserves the special attention of environmental historians. With respect to manuring practices, there was even a striking contrast between the old agricultural regions of Europe and most Yankee farms in North America, which exploited the abundance of land without much care for maintaining fertility. European peasants had known since medieval times that they inhabited an area of limited resources.

The balance between field and pasture depended on institutions: the three year crop rotation system, the wood and pasture commons (*Allmende*), and contracts between peasants and pastoralists. For this reason, an institutional approach might be fruitful in analyzing the ecology of traditional agriculture as well. Nowadays, institutions of this kind are lacking. The old principle of balance between agriculture and pastoralism has been forgotten. Today, in the era of chemical fertilizers and highly specialized agriculture, the awareness of one of the most important elements of ecological stability in human existence has nearly disappeared.

4. The Western European marriage pattern

There is a widespread and well-founded opinion that overpopulation and population pressure on resources—sometimes abbreviated as PPR—is the most important environmental stress coefficient in history. This view has not remained unchallenged. The main counterargument notes that "overpopulation" is an inexact term susceptible to ideology, that the most densely populated countries are in many cases the wealthiest ones, and that population growth frequently enforces several forms of intense agriculture that are more sustainable than the old slash-and-burn economies. There is some truth in this counterargument. Environmental history cannot be reduced to mere demographic history. Chinese wet rice agriculture offers the best known example of population growth creating an economy with relatively high ecological stability. But Chinese history also offers impressive evidence that an agricultural system that encourages unlimited population growth carries a great ecological risk in the long run.

216

What are the characteristics of European reproductive behavior in comparison with other cultures? To be sure, there is no simple answer that does justice to all regions and historical periods. In his famous work, *Les paysans de Languedoc,* Emmanuel Le Roy Ladurie describes how the peasants of southern France repeatedly stumbled into the Malthusian trap of overpopulation and famine during medieval and early modern times. But in Western Europe, bad experiences of this kind ultimately contributed to a learning process. From the Middle Ages on, there was a peasant maxim, "No land, no marriage."[18] This maxim did not limit the number of children within marriage, but in the course of centuries, clear signs of fertility control emerged.

The question whether the story of birth control is a happy story of sexual know-how or a sad story of infanticide and sexual repression is one of the great unsolved mysteries of history. Be this as it may, this story exists. David Grigg remarks that "the seventeenth century is of greatest importance for the widening of the demographic options." "In the first place ... , it saw the appearance of the West European pattern of late marriage and a comparatively high proportion [of] unmarried [people]."[19] And this is not the end of the story. Fernand Braudel observes about eighteenth-century France: "Contraception by coitus interruptus is spreading like an infectious disease and is gaining more and more adherents."[20] It is curious to see how this famous historian disapproved of the environmental wisdom of his own people in this regard. At the end of the nineteenth century, doctors warned that coitus interruptus might lead to physical or mental illnesses. But a German farmer coolly replied: "I don't believe that. Otherwise everybody would be sick."[21]

It is an interesting problem whether reproductive patterns of this kind can be explained by the institutional approach. From the eighteenth century until today, the state and its institutions have frequently favored population growth and opposed contraception and other birth control practices. It was society that tacitly but stubbornly resisted the political encouragement of population growth. Sometimes, historians should look for a tacit environmental reason by reading between the lines of the sources and for informal institutions of society independent from government policy. The hidden passive reserves left over by birth control probably have been (and are) one of the most important elements of ecological stability in the past and the present. The precarious environmental situation of a country like China at least since the eighteenth century seems to demonstrate the dilemma of a land which has lost a great deal of its soil reserves.

5. Continuity, sustainability, and self-sufficiency

Donald Worster has declared that he is deeply skeptical of the term "sustainable development," which the 1992 Rio Conference named as the supreme environmentalist goal for the world economy. Worster dislikes this term in politics as well as in environmental history because he suspects that "sustainability" is simply a catchword designed to justify the unrestrained exploitation of nature. From his point of view, the preservation of untouched nature is a better goal than "sustainable development."[22] It is easy to understand his skepticism when one bears in mind the American experience in which sustainable development has never been a historical reality over a longer period. However, for an analysis of the environmental history of Europe, the criterion "sustainability" makes more sense. If there is a continuity of villages, towns, and institutions over a long period combined with a sedentary mentality as it existed in many parts of Europe—but also, to be sure, in Asian regions—then a history of sustainability can make sense. And the chances of a genuine sustainable management of resources are greater when there is a high degree of local self-sufficiency and limited dependence on external forces. It seems that many parts of Europe were characterized since medieval times—if not since antiquity—by a relatively high degree of continuity and local and regional autonomy.[23] When reading the famous stories of the rise of European commerce, one should not forget that most European regions lived mainly on their domestic resources until the nineteenth or even twentieth centuries. This self-sufficiency applied at least to the most important resources, grain and firewood.

The traditional German term for "sustainability," *Nachhaltigkeit,* stems from forestry; in this area, it comprises a history of several hundred years—to be sure, a history which reveals much of the ambiguity and the manipulative possibilities of that concept.[24] But there is no better alternative even today.

It is significant that the goal of *Nachhaltigkeit* has a peculiarly long tradition in some Central European saline forests. As early as 1661, the chancellor of Reichenhall, an old Bavarian salt-works city, stated: "God created the woodlands for the salt-water spring, in order that the woodlands might continue eternally like the spring. Accordingly shall the men behave: They shall not cut down the old trees before the young trees have grown up."[25] In these words, sustainability appears as a secular form of eternity that endows human things with an affinity to God. The condition for this kind of sustainability was the autonomous saline town, which needed huge masses of wood, which lived on its own forest resources, and which was accustomed to having salt-works running constantly over many centuries. In many mining towns there was no such spirit of sustainability because of the violent ups and downs of the mines.

The interior regions of Asia raise the interesting question of whether there is perhaps a different type of sustainability, a sustainability connected with discontinuity and mobility—a nomadic type of sustainability. Under the conditions of many steppe regions, settlement leads eventually to overgrazing and to desertification. The question of whether the nomadic economy is sustainable or not is still controversial, all the more so since it has political consequences for the treatment of nomadic tribes.[26] A definitive and general answer is not possible. One should probably distinguish between planned and inherent sustainability. The latter was as a rule more typical of traditional societies than the former. But there seems to be growing evidence that nomadic peoples not only adapted themselves to the conditions of the steppe, but, to a certain degree, *created* the steppe by the destruction of woodlands and sometimes even of agriculture. Surely, many nomads had a kind of soil awareness, but they had no methods for improving the soil, and they defined their status by the possession of livestock, not of land. At least under modern conditions, it seems that the future belongs to the sustainability of the sedentary peasant, not to that of the nomad.

6. Forest and power

Especially for the last decade, we have become remarkably well informed about many chapters of East and South Asian environmental history. Just take the two well-done, recently published anthologies on China and India/Southeast Asia, both products of cooperation between Western and Asian scholars: *Sediments of Time* and *Nature and the Orient*.[27] These are based on extensive regional research, most of which has been little known in Europe up until now. Because of this new abundance of information, a comprehensive comparison between "East" and "West" in environmental matters has become much more complicated than at the time of Lynn White's Christmas speech in 1966, and whoever studies this new mass of literature may doubt whether a well-founded comparison will be at all feasible in the future. But in the end, one point seems to be even clearer than before: With regard to the institutional treatment of forests, there has been—for at least five hundred years—a fundamental difference between China and India on the one hand and Western and Central Europe on the other. Since the late Middle Ages the protection of forests has been a manifestation of political power in Europe; in Asia, however, it has not. One would hardly expect that the environmental history of the world contains major features which are so distinctive, but as far as I can see, the evidence is overwhelming.

One may also find a love of trees in ancient Chinese literature, and certain traditions of forest protection existed in China, too. Nicholas K. Menzies has investigated these traditions: the imperial hunting reserves, the Buddhist temple and monastic forests, the Cunninghamia groves of some peasant communities, among others. But on the whole it remains clear that these examples were exceptional. "The trend of government policy during the late Imperial period was to open land for settlement and to permanent agriculture, not to exclude the population." Therefore, "administrative authority was rarely exercised to reserve forested land as government property," as was the case with many European governments.[28] Not the conservation of forests, but the clearing of forests was a manifestation of power in Asian cultures. "Traditional Chinese thought exhibited a definite bias against forests and the cultivation of trees," observes Eduard B. Vermeer. "Forest areas were seen as hideouts for bandits and rebels, beyond the reach of government authority, where uncivilized people lived their wretched lives without observing the rules of property. In this view, the clearance of forests and agricultural reclamation brought safety and political and cultural progress."[29] Although this attitude was widespread in Europe too, since late medieval times it stood in competition with a better appreciation of the forests.

In India, traditions of forest protection may have been somewhat better developed than in China; but on the whole, the situation seems to have been similar. It is true that an anthology on Indian forest history starts with the forest protection edict of the Mahrat King Shivaji of about 1670 A.D.: "... The mango and jack trees in our own kingdom are of value to the Navy. But these must never be touched. This is because these trees cannot be grown in a year or two. Our people have nurtured them like their own children over long periods. If they are cut, their sorrow would know no bounds."[30] But in all the literature so far available, this edict appears rather unique. Apart from the Indian tradition of cultivating mango and other fruit trees, the edict does not refer to any institutional traditions of forest protection. Madhav Gadgil and Ramachandra Guha, the authors of an "ecological history of India," praise the alleged traditional Indian harmony with nature, but they, too, do not present any sources on forest protection in pre-colonial India.[31] (Or do these sources exist in the archives of the Mughal period, but written in old Persian which most Indian historians do not read?) The contrast to the immense mass of forest protection documents in Central and Western Europe from the sixteenth century on could hardly be sharper.

The causes are manifold. Often the royal passion for hunting is said to have been the main motivation for European forest protection. But I believe that the high value of the woodlands for pasture—which lasted from prehistoric times until the nineteenth century—might be even more important. Here again, livestock seems to be at the core of the problem. For governments, shipbuilding was, as a rule, the primary interest that made forest protection a matter of utmost priority, whether in sixteenth-century Venice, in medieval Portugal, in Colbert's France or in John Evelyn's England. (Even in early Ming China, the building of a fleet gave a uniquely strong though transitory impetus to a gigantic reforestation project.[32]) Another strong force for institutional control of woodcutting came from the mining interests, as long as wood and charcoal were the energy base of mining and smelting. The peasants have frequently been charged with being the enemies of the forest; but this accusation was a one-sided evaluation from the perspective of governmental forestry. The peasants had their own woodlands for pasture, firewood, and building, woodlands which from the forester's viewpoint might have been of inferior quality, but were superior in regard to biodiversity.[33]

My argument can be challenged with the question whether the sharp institutional contrast between East and West in the treatment of forests truly corresponds to a contrast in actual practice. Was it really the forest laws and forest administrations that protected the woodlands rather than unwritten customs and the interests of the people? I admit this is a difficult problem still full of open questions. Many historians of forests frequently give the impression that the true history of forest laws is the history of the violation of these laws. Forest history often has been written as the history of forest destruction, at least before the great reforestation movement of the nineteenth century.

In my earlier work, I have repeatedly discussed this pessimistic kind of premodern forest history. It is a complicated matter, and a general evaluation is hardly possible. But in any case, there are good reasons to be cautious with many forest destruction stories in Europe.[34] Oliver Rackham has repeatedly ridiculed these stories, remarking that the deforestation storytellers forgot the simple fact "that trees grow again."[35] At least in most Western and Central European regions the forest easily regenerates itself even without artificial reforestation; limiting the human use of the forest is enough. Under conditions of this kind, governmental forest protection could succeed with relative ease. The European tradition of institutionalized forest protection was surely favored by European ecology. But the decisive point was probably the fact that in spite of innumerable forest conflicts between government and peasants or other forest users, there was to a certain degree a common interest in the conservation of the forests and— notwithstanding countless violations—a certain acceptance of the regulation of forest use in principle, if not in every case.

7. The advantage of European polycentrism

In the course of the present process of European unification, much hope is frequently placed in common European environmental policies. But even today, we often have to recognize that really effective environmental policies are usually best achieved within small nations like Denmark or the Netherlands. An effective consensus is best reached where society is relatively homogeneous and communication is not too complicated. The opinion that problems will be solved by European integration might therefore turn out to be a fundamental error. In the past, European polycentrism appears to have had considerable advantages in regard to the handling of environmental issues. The peculiar European process of legal regulation (*Verrechtlichung*) is conditioned by this polycentrism where every authority needs legitimation by law. Where, on the contrary, there is only one single authority far and wide, there is no strong pressure for legitimation, and no legal advantage can be obtained by individual engagement.

Even more important is another point. Effective environmental management can only be achieved by institutions that are not too far away from the site where action is demanded. Forest and water management—the two classic areas of governmental intervention in environmental matters—both present numerous historical examples of the advantage of tackling problems from nearby, not from a far-away capital. Even if the Chinese Emperor had been determined to protect the forests, he would not have been able to do so effectively because an appropriate forest policy can be organized only on a regional level, not on the level of a huge empire. In this regard, a comparison between China and Japan is instructive. Even though in Japanese cultural tradition a high estimation of woodlands does not seem to be more deeply rooted than in Chinese tradition, for strictly practical reasons Japanese institutions started a forest protection policy with remarkable effectiveness in the course of the eighteenth century.[36]

In Europe, a comparison between France and Germany is informative. Under the strong administration of Colbert and his *grande ordonnance forestière* of 1669—Colbert even warned: "France will perish from lack of wood!"—France gained European leadership in forest policy, which it held throughout the eighteenth century. But in the long run, the French centralist system was not well adapted to forest problems. At the end of the eighteenth century, German states took the leadership in forestry.[37] This success was conditioned by German political polycentrism. In various German states a plurality of regional approaches to forestry arose. It was the only way to obtain real practical progress. German nationalists complained about German particularism (*Zersplitterung*), but Wilhelm Pfeil (1783–1859), a leading Prussian teacher of forestry, emphasized that German scientific forestry was—in contrast to French forestry—"exclusively the product of the German partition into different countries."[38] In this way, the rigid Prussian dogmatism of Hartig's forestry rules was counterbalanced by other forestry schools that came out of the mixed forests of middle and southwest Germany.

The lessons of forest history could probably be transmitted to other areas of environmental policy. Consequently, one can doubt whether it is wise at the present time for many environmentalists to adopt the current "globalization" rhetoric, though it partly descended from the rhetoric of global ecological problems. There are indeed connections between environmentalism and "globalization." The *causes* of many environmental problems have analogous structures all over the world, but the *solutions* frequently demand much local knowledge and appropriate regional methods.

8. A green revival of Wittfogel's "Asiatic mode of production"

The theory of the "Asiatic mode of production," also known as "Oriental despotism," is thought-provoking, but does not have the best reputation. It was worked out by Karl August Wittfogel (1896–1988), who started as a German communist and finished as an American anti-communist, and the development of his theory was influenced by the great change in his life and outlook. Initially, it was an endeavor to apply Marxism to the history of non-European civilizations that produced neither feudalism nor capitalism; later on, it was used by Wittfogel as a weapon in the Cold War. The core of the theory is the following argument: Everywhere in the world where agriculture needs artificial irrigation on a large scale, there is little room for individual producers and a strong tendency toward bureaucratic centralism.[39] Wittfogel's theory presented a political economy of totalitarian bureaucracy. At the same time, it offered an explanation for the fundamental difference between Western and non-European cultures. It is interesting to note that Douglass C. North adopted the Wittfogel theory as an impressive example of an institutional approach to economics, arguing that in this case economic institutions are generated by nature: "Wittfogel's hydraulic society was in effect a natural monopoly, with economies of scale derived from the indivisibility of an integrated water system."[40]

In reality, however, the relationship between nature and institutions seems to be more complicated. For a long time, there has been a well-founded counterargument to Wittfogel. In most cases, even in India and China, irrigation can be managed on a local level. Natural conditions and the mode of production alone do not really enforce a central bureaucracy. The "Asiatic mode of production" is not based on simple natural causality.

Despite this argument, the problem is not yet settled. As Mark Elvin wrote to me: "[Wittfogel's] ghost cannot be exorcized." Undoubtedly, there is a historical connection between irrigation and power, though it does not consist of a simple causality. Arid regions did not, to be sure, create the *necessity* for establishing a central bureaucracy, but they did create the *possibility* for one. Even if local irrigation was sufficient, improved irrigation on a major scale could multiply the agricultural product. Central power was not enforced by natural conditions, but it could make itself indispensable through ambitious irrigation projects: through the building of waterworks as well as the subsequent demand for regulation; and, last but not least, through the demands of crisis management, because larger irrigation projects generated great risks. Big dams increased the risk of catastrophic floods if the dams failed at only one single point or if the masses of water became too powerful. Waterworks have to be supervised and repaired continuously in order to operate well. Drainage is as important as irrigation itself in order to avoid salinization and the spread of swamps and malaria. The central bureaucracies often legitimated themselves though the problems of big waterworks, but in the long run they were not able to solve these problems in an effective way. In Chinese imperial myth, the Emperor was the savior in the face of the big floods, but catastrophic floods recurred again and again. The inherent contradiction of the Asiatic mode of production originates from ecology, not so much from economy.

As a rule, it is difficult to isolate ecological causes in history, as they usually interact and work together with other forces. Peter Christensen summarizes the medieval downfall of Mesopotamia as follows: Plague and epidemic diseases made "visible the inherent environmental instability which I believe was the key factor in the decline of Mesopotamia. The large-scale colonization and expansion in Parthian and Sassanian times had created an ecological system extremely sensitive to the smallest disturbances."[41] But one should not forget that over a long period, irrigation systems offered a kind of stability by making peasants independent from the vagaries of the weather to a certain degree. The claim advanced by Clive Ponting and others that already the Sumerians had committed ecological suicide by irrigation with subsequent salinization does not correspond with the millenia of flourishing agriculture in Mesopotamia.[42] The extensive irrigation networks contained problems similar to modern industrial systems. For a long time one is mainly aware of the advantages, while the full extent of the ecological trap becomes obvious only much later.

It seems that one characteristic feature of European environmental history is the absence of large-scale systems of field irrigation (not of small-scale systems of meadow irrigation). Eric L. Jones believes that this absence proved to be an advantage in the end. "The very impracticability of hydraulic agriculture freed a fraction of European energies for other purposes. The rainfall farmers of Europe might be fewer in number than the farmers of China and India, but the former spent less time on all aspects of farmwork than the latter spent on water control work alone."[43] In the long run, the lack of major irrigation was an element of ecological stability and likewise of individual autonomy. It is an irony of history—as Marc Reisner has pointed out[44]—that in large parts of the arid American West, "Asiatic" conditions have emerged in the course of the twentieth century: a kind of agriculture totally dependent upon large irrigation networks which means dependence on governmental subsidies and threat of desertification. Reisner predicts that the agriculture of Arizona and California will have a fate similar to that of the agriculture of Mesopotamia. Under these conditions, the term "sustainable development" makes no sense.

9. Environmental repercussions of European colonialism

As to the ecological aspects of colonialism, we have two great works which have gained worldwide attention: Alfred W. Crosby's *Ecological Imperialism* and Richard H. Grove's *Green Imperialism*. Today, colonialism is one of the most discussed subjects in international environmental history. Nevertheless, the significance of colonial expansion for environmental developments in Europe has remained a neglected problem. Reading Crosby, one gets the impression that imperialism has been an ecological success story, at least from the European point of view. But Crosby does not tell the whole story. Europe not only colonized the New World with grain, cattle, and sheep, but was itself colonized with the potato, maize, and not least by the phylloxera which destroyed traditional European viticulture. The potato encouraged strong population growth and undermined European traditions of birth control which were weakened, too, by the chance to emigrate to America. Maize increased soil erosion and did not fit into the traditional crop rotation systems. Therefore, it seems that European ecology was not stabilized, but in some ways disturbed by colonialism.

Richard H. Grove discovered a lot of surprising indications that point to colonial origins of modern environmentalism. Is colonial history after all, at least seen from the environmentalist standpoint, a story with a happy ending? Considerable doubts remain. The history of ideas presented by Grove is not identical with a history of actions and real effects. But even the history of ideas seems to be ambiguous. If one carefully scrutinizes several important points in Grove's argument, one repeatedly discovers that the true origin of colonial environmental awareness lay in Europe, not in the colonies. Poivre looked at Asian agriculture with the eyes of a French physiocrat. Alexander von Humboldt's deforestation concerns presumably originated in his German homeland, where fears of that kind had become a real mass psychosis at the end of the eighteenth century.[45] In the spring of 1790, young Humboldt undertook a journey on the Rhine together with Georg Forster, then a famous world traveler. Forster's report contains long reflections on the imminent danger of wood shortage, which might cause northern peoples in the end to emigrate to the south.[46] In a recent publication, Grove himself has pointed out that Hugh Cleghorn, one of the founding fathers of Indian forestry, and several other pioneers of colonial environmentalism were influenced by their Scottish background, by the experience of a country "already made barren by the evils of the English."[47] The criticism of the ruthless soil exhaustion caused by North American farmers was inspired by the pattern of traditional European agriculture and the European agrarian reforms of the late eighteenth century.[48]

On the whole, the effects of colonialism on the European environment do not appear to be fortunate. The following effect can be identified most clearly: The lack of a durable tradition of forest protection in leading colonial powers like Spain, the Netherlands, Great Britain, and even Denmark is apparently conditioned by the ease with which these countries were able to import masses of timber from their colonies or other regions of the world. In contrast, the German states developed scientific forestry at a time when

Germany had no colonies and was forced to live on its own wood resources. Furthermore, the omnipotence of the Mesta in Spain during the sixteenth and seventeenth centuries is connected with the rise of Spanish colonialism. As for England, the mass import of Peruvian guano in the nineteenth century thwarted the efforts of agrarian reformers to improve the inherent sustainability of agriculture. The colonial world trade threatened the traditional European balance between field and pasture and nurtured the illusion of unlimited resources. The full consequences of this development, however, belong to the postcolonial period, which probably experienced the deepest ecological change in history.

10. A "European miracle" in environmental history?

In contrast to the pessimistic view of European culture that prevails in the spiritual approach to environmental history mentioned at the beginning, the institutional approach seems to present a European success story similar to the one told by Eric L. Jones in his *European Miracle*. But I fear this is not the end of history. In spite of all the achievements of environmental policies, there are no true grounds for optimism. Human institutions, even if they are effective, are never fully adapted to the complexity of environmental problems. One of the most impressive lessons of history has always been the insight that this very success may become the cause of decline in the long run.

To be sure, it was the relatively stable ecological conditions of Western and Central European soil and the relatively effective institutions of the countries in these regions that made the rise of industrial civilization possible. Only a region with rich wood and water resources and—at least to a certain extent—sustainable methods of forest utilization was able to enter a path of unlimited growth in energy-intensive industries with high water consumption. Coal did not start the industrial revolution. The pit-coal only carried on a development which had begun on the basis of charcoal and wood. Moreover, only countries with effective urban and national institutions capable of overcoming at least the worst damages caused by industry were able to make industrial development a self-sustaining and popular process. But sustainability remains an illusion in an economy that annually consumes the fossil resources that have grown over a period of a million years. Since the European path is marked by exceptional characteristics, it cannot become the model for the whole world. In some respects, it may not even be an appropriate model for the European future. Moreover, a part of the traditional foundations of European ecological stability, for instance the old combination of agriculture and animal husbandry, has been overtaken by modern developments. The stability of deep European soils is threatened by growing acidification, especially during the last decades.

Perhaps we should learn the lesson of Chinese environmental history, which is far better documented than any other non-European history. Mark Elvin described the history of the Chinese Empire as "three thousand years of unsustainable growth."[49] Perhaps he goes too far in this harsh evaluation. The great anthology co-edited by Elvin, *Sediments of Time,* suggests that the environmental decline of China is fully documented only for the last three *hundred* years. Based on the present state of research, I prefer an interpretation of Chinese history which differs a little from Elvin's. It seems to me that for many centuries, Chinese agriculture did indeed embody a high degree of ecological stability. This stability was founded mainly on three elements: (1) the wet rice cultivation that in its traditional form needed little or no manure; (2) the highly elaborated system of terraces that stopped soil erosion; (3) the systematic use of "night soil," of human excrement, for fertilization.

It was mainly the last point for which Justus von Liebig, the great chemist, praised the Chinese for being the wisest people on earth, because they gave back to the soil all they had taken away from it.[50] I presume that for a long time, a high degree of inherent sustainability did indeed exist in Chinese agriculture and may partly explain Chinese cultural continuity over the millennia. But it was precisely this stability that encouraged continuous population growth and concealed the elements of unsustainability: population pressure, deforestation, erosion, in marginal regions even desertification and, above all, the growing loss of ecological reserves. The environmental crisis of China might foreshadow the environmental crisis of Western civilization: a crisis aggravated precisely by its long-term success.

Notes

1 Oliver Rackham, "The Countryside: History & Pseudo-History," in *The Historian* 14 (1987): 16.

2 This paper is based upon my *Natur und Macht—Eine Weltgeschichte der Umwelt* (Munich, 2000); enlarged paperback edition 2002.

3 Lynn White, Jr., "The Historical Roots of Our Ecological Crisis," in *Science* 155, no. 3767 (March 1967): 1205ff. With a similar tendency, Rolf Peter Sieferle, "Europäische Traditionen im Umgang mit der Natur," in *Europas Kulturen und ihr Umgang mit der Natur,* Mainauer Gespäche, vol. 14 (Insel Mainau, 1999), 17.

4 Eugen Drewermann, *Der tödliche Fortschritt,* 5th ed. (Freiburg, 1991), 73.

5 See, for instance, several contributions to *Europas Kulturen und ihr Umgang mit der Natur,* Mainauer Gespräche, vol. 14 (Insel Mainau, 1999).

6 Clifford Geertz, *Islam Observed: Religious Development in Morocco and Indonesia* (Chicago, 1971), 9ff.

7 Clifford Geertz, *Dichte Beschreibung: Beiträge zum Verstehen kultureller Systeme* (Frankfurt, 1995), 86.

8 Tenzin Choegyal, the junior brother of His Holiness the Dalai Lama, when asked by the author about environmentalist elements in Buddhism, emphasized that the aim of Buddhism is *not* human unification with nature, but on the

contrary human deliverance from the material world! Peter Gerlitz, *Mensch und Natur in den Weltreligionen* (Darmstadt, 1998), arrives at a similar result for world religions in general.

9 Herbert Franke, "Geschichte und Natur—Betrachtungen eines Asien-Historikers," in *Natur und Geschichte,* ed. Hubert Markl, (Munich, 1983), 51–69; Gudula Linck, "Die Welt ist ein heiliges Gefäß, wer sich daran zu schaffen macht, wird Niederlagen erleiden—Konfliktaustragung an der Natur während der Umbrüchein der chinesischen Geschichte," in *Mensch und Umwelt in der Geschichte,* ed. Jörg Calließ et al., (Pfaffenweiler, 1989), 327–51.

10 See note 49; Mark Elvin, "The Environmental History of China: An Agenda of Ideas," in *Asian Studies Review* 14 (1990): 39–77; Marl Elvin, "The Environmental Legacy of Imperial China," in *The China Quarterly* 156 (Dec. 1998): 733–56.

11 My institutional approach has some affinity to the organizational approach of Frank Uekötter with whom I had many discussions; see Frank Uekötter, "Confronting the Pitfalls of Current Environmental History: An Argument for an Organizational Approach," in *Environment and History* 4 (1998): 31–52.

12 Heinrich Oberrauch, *Tirols Wald und Waidwerk: Ein Beitrag zur Forst-und Jagdgeschichte* (Innsbruck, 1952), 21. The particular Western character of this public sense of law has been stressed by the Russian liberal Bogdan Kistiakovsky, who stood in close connection with Max Weber in his criticism of Russian Intelligentsia, in *Vechi—Wegzeichen, Zur Krise der russischen Intelligenz,* ed. Karl Schlögel, (Frankfurt, 1990), 212–50.

13 See my review of the works of Arne Andersen, Franz-Josef Brüggemeier, Michael Stol berg, Ralf Henneking, Ulrike Gilhaus, Jürgen Büschenfeld, Peter Munch, et al. in *Geschichte in Wissenschaft und Unterricht* 50 (1999): 365–84.

14 J. B. Ojwang with Calestous Juma, "Towards Ecological Jurisprudence," in *In Land We Trust: Environment, Private Property and Constitutional Change,* ed. Calestous Juma and J. B. Ojwang, (Nairobi, 1996), 321.

15 Jared Diamond, *Guns, Germs and Steel* (London, 1997), 174ff; Marvin Harris, *Kannibalen und Könige* (Stuttgart, 1990), 145ff.

16 Eric L. Jones, *The European Miracle: Environment, Economies, and Geopolitics in the History of Europe and Asia* (Cambridge, 1981), 4.

17 Douglass C. North and Robert P. Thomas, *The Rise of the Western World: A New Economic History* (Cambridge, 1973), 4, 86, 129, 131.

18 Angus McLaren, *A History of Contraception* (Oxford, 1990), 141.

19 David Grigg, *Population Growth and Agrarian Change: An Historical Perspective* (Cambridge, 1980), 289.

20 Fernand Braudel, *Frankreich,* vol. 2 (Stuttgart, 1990), 183.

21 McLaren, 189.

22 Donald Worster, "Auf schwankendem Boden: Zum Begriffswirrwarr um nachhaltige Entwicklung," in *Der Planet als Patient,* ed. Wolfgang Sachs, (Berlin, 1994), 95ff.

23 At a time when Third World examples of autocentric development had been discredited, Dieter Senghaas presented several European countries as historic patterns of appropriate and autonomous development: Dieter Senghaas, *Von Europa lernen: Entwicklungsgeschichtliche Betrachtungen* (Frankfurt, 1982). For a thorough explication of that approach, see Ulrich Menzel, *Auswege aus der Abhängigkeit: Die entwicklungspolitische Aktualität Europas* (Frankfurt, 1988).

24 About the many different meanings of "Nachhaltigkeit" in forestry, see Wiebke Peters, "Die Nachhaltigkeit als Grundsatz der Forstwirtschaft, ihre

Verankerung in der Gesetzgebung und ihre Bedeutung in der Praxis," (diss., University of Hamburg, 1984).

25 Gotz v. Bülow, *Die Sudwälder von Reichenhall* (Munich, 1962), 159 f. The question whether sustainability was really obtained in the saline forests of Reichenhall remains controversial today; see Alfred Kotter, "'Holznot' um 1600: Die Energieversorgung der Saline Reichen hall," in *Salz Macht Geschichte*, ed. Manfred Treml et al., (Augsburg, 1995), 186–92.

26 H. F. Lamprey, "Pastoralism Yesterday and Today: The Over-Grazing Problem," in *Tropical Savannas*, ed. Francois Bourlière, (Amsterdam, 1983), 658, believes to recognize an "overwhelming evidence of continuing extensive ecological degradation" by nomadic pastoralism. Melvyn C. Goldstein and Cynthia M. Beall, *Nomads of Western Tibet: The Survival of a Way of Life* (Hong Kong, 1990), present a description of skillful adaptation to an extremely hard environment. But it is doubtful whether one can generalize this Tibetan example.

27 Mark Elvin and Liu Tsáui-jung, eds., *Sediments of Time: Environment and Society in Chinese History* (Cambridge, 1998); Richard H. Grove, Vinita Damodaran, and Satpal Sangwan, eds., *Nature and the Orient: The Environmental History of South and Southeast Asia* (Delhi, 1998).

28 Nicholas K. Menzies, *Forest and Land Management in Imperial China* (New York, 1994), 44. Yi-Fu Tuan, *China* (London, 1969), 32, 141, 142 mentions some cases in Chinese history where an alliance between imperial power and forest protection can be observed, but at the same time makes clear that this policy was not effective in the long run.

29 Eduard B. Vermeer, "Population and Ecology along the Frontier in Qing China," in Elvin and Liu, *Sediments of Time,* 247ff.

30 Madhav Gadgil, "Deforestation: Problems and Prospects," in *History of Forestry in India,* ed. Ajay S. Rawat, (Delhi, 1991), 13.

31 Madhav Gadgil and Ramachandra Guha, *This Fissured Land: An Ecological History of India* (Delhi, 1992).

32 Jaques Gernet, *Die chinesische Welt* (Frankfurt, 1979), 331.

33 Joachim Radkau and Ingrid Schäfer, *Holz: Ein Naturstoff in der Technikgeschichte* (Reinbek, 1987), 59–65, 157–59.

34 For France, see Andrée Corvol, *L'Homme et l'arbre sous l'Ancien Régime* (Paris, 1984), 632. "Il est donc fort délicat d'employer l'expression de 'crise forestière' puisque chaque réorganisation administrative se justifie au travers de ceux qui la conduisent." Similarly, Ingrid Schäfer, *"Ein Gespenst geht um": Politik mit der Holznot in Lippe 1750–1850* (Detmold, 1992).

35 Oliver Rackham, *Ancient Woodland, Its History, Vegetation and Uses in England,* (London, 1980), 153. I am not likewise convinced when Rackham transfers his mockery upon deforestation stories into Mediterranean history, for instance in Oliver Rackham and Jennifer Moody, *The Making of the Cretan Landscape* (Manchester, 1996). See, for the Mediterranean, J. R. McNeill, *The Mountains of the Mediterranean World: An Environmental History* (Cambridge, 1992). McNeill repeatedly characterizes Rackham's position as a "maverick opinion," 72, 311.

36 Conrad Totman, *The Green Achipelago: Forestry in Preindustrial Japan* (Berkeley, 1989).

37 Michel Devèze, *La grand reformation des forets sous Colbert* (Nancy, 1962); Heinrich Rubner, *Forstgeschichte im Zeitalter der industriellen Revolution* (Berlin, 1967).

38 Karl Hasel, *Studien über Wilhelm Pfeil* (Hannover, 1982), 137.

39 Karl August Wittfogel, *Wirtschaft und Gesellschaft Chinas* (Leipzig, 1931); *Oriental Despotism: A Comparative Study of Total Power* (New Haven, 1957). Joachim Radkau, "Der Emigrant als Warner und Renegat: Karl August Wittfogels Dämonisierung der 'asiatischen Produktionsweise,'" in *Exilforschung: ein internationales Jahrbuch* 1 (1983): 73–94.

40 Douglass C. North, *Structure and Change in Economic History* (New York, 1981), 26.

41 Peter Christensen, *The Decline of Iranshahr: Irrigation and Environments in the History of the Middle East 500 B.C. to A.D. 1500* (Copenhagen, 1993), 104.

42 Clive Ponting, *A Green History of the World* (London, 1991), 70ff.

43 Jones, The European Miracle, 8.

44 Marc Reisner, *Cadillac Desert: The American Desert and Its Disappearing Water,* rev. ed. (New York, 1993).

45 Joachim Radkau, "Holzverknappung und Krisenbewußtsein im 18. Jahrhundert," in *Geschichte und Gesellschaft* 9 (1983): 513–43.

46 Georg Forster, *Ansichten vom Niederrhein* (1791: Stuttgart, 1965), 56ff.

47 Richard Grove, "Scotland in South Africa: John Crumbie Brown and the Roots of Settler Environmentalism" in *Ecology & Empire: Environmental History of Settler Societies,* eds. Tom Griffiths and Libby Robbin, (Seattle, 1997), 144.

48 The most famous early example is Harry J. Carman, ed., *American Husbandry* (1775: Port Washington, 1939).

49 Mark Elvin, "Three Thousand Years of Unsustainable Growth: China's Environment from Archaic Times to the Present" in *East Asian History* 6 (1993): 7–46.

50 Justus v. Liebig, *Chemische Briefe* (Leipzig, 1865), 498ff. In *Sediments of Time,* one finds contradictory comments on the use of human excrements. On page 6, Elvin criticizes this method as an offspring of worm diseases; on page 503, Kerrie L. MacPherson in an article on cholera quotes D. B. Simmons (1879) that the returning of "nightsoil" to the soil reduced "the danger of contamination" to "a minimum." Both opinions may contain some truth; I presume that the favorable effect prevailed. I got the impression that the modern hygienic movement tended to overstate the danger of worm infections.

12

THREE THOUSAND YEARS OF UNSUSTAINABLE GROWTH

China's environment from archaic times to the present

Mark Elvin

Introduction

This essay looks at the history of China from about 1000 BC to the present day from the point of view of the interaction of politics, economics, and the environment.[1] It shows that there have been three main phases: an archaic 'ecological' economic system until about 500 BC; a system of developmental economics primarily driven by the needs of state power that lasted until about AD 1000; and a relatively mature economic system primarily driven by the market since that time, that is following the 'mediaeval economic revolution'[2] and on down to the establishment of Communist rule in 1949. The population expanded during this period, partly in the form of increased spatial density, and partly in the form of geographical expansion from a core in north China. To some degree, however, it was also effected by the incorporation of other peoples,[3] so that the true rate of growth may not have been quite as spectacular as it appears. In (very) round numbers, the Chinese population grew from over 50 million before the end of the first millennium BC to over 100 million shortly after AD 1000, then to over 200 million early in the eighteenth century, to over 400 million by about 1850, and finally to over 1000 million at the present day. The apparent long-term pre-modern annual rate of growth thus rose from about 0.07% during the first millennium AD to 0.1% during most of the second millennium, to about 0.5% in the eighteenth and nineteenth centuries, and then to 0.65% during the early modern epoch. It has been over 1% for most of the Communist period.

The broad characteristics of production and exchange during the three periods were as follows: In the first there was a significant component of hunting, fishing, fowling, gathering, and herding in the economy, varying regionally, with millet being the staple cereal, hemp the main clothing fibre, and small-scale drainage and flood-prevention the focus of hydraulic works. In the second there were larger states (soon of 'European' size) and then—for just under half the period—a unified Empire, some massive cities (10^5 inhabitants), a shift to a more purely agricultural economy, still mainly based on dry-field farming,[4] with large-scale artificial inland water-transport (often initially for military uses) and some large irrigation schemes, the limited and state-controlled market system being primarily driven by tax-extracted funds and the profits of large estates. In the third, as the demographic centre of gravity shifted southwards the Yangzi valley, wet-field rice agriculture dominated the most economically advanced regions, irrigation systems proliferated, cotton became the main clothing fibre, the economy was extensively monetized, and the market system was decontrolled and expanded enormously, with ordinary consumer demand now being the main driving force. In this third period there was quite significant literacy[5] and numeracy, based on woodblock printing and the abacus, and a gradually developing process of 'urban devolution'[6] that meant that additional urban population tended to be found mostly in settlements of small to medium size ($> 10^3$ and $< 10^5$ inhabitants). At the end of this third period, in the late seventeenth and eighteenth centuries, certain imported New World crops such as maize and sweet potatoes became extensively cultivated in upland areas, while extra land available for further effort-efficient late-traditional rice-farming or lowland dry-farming had virtually come to an end outside Manchuria,[7] and a 'high' level of yields per hectare by 'premodern' standards—the average rice yield per hectare being of the order of 6 kiloliters with late-traditional technology[8]—had been achieved in most regions. 'Hot-spot' modern economic growth, including an extensive acquisition by Chinese of what was then modern technology, began in the later decades of the nineteenth century in places like Shahnghaai that had been opened by the modern West to international trade and linked into the world economy,[9] but it hardly spread at all into the hinterland for a long time, and has only to a limited extent done so now.

Certain long-term patterns can be detected. For example, the climate in north China has been shown by Zhur Keezhen 竺可楨 and others to have fluctuated considerably during the historical period.[10] From 3000 to 1000 BC the mean annual temperature was about 2° C higher than it is today. A clear shift to colder weather began around the start of the first millennium BC. By the third century AD the mean annual temperature was from 1° C to 2° C below the present level, and early in the fifth century the entire gulf of Borhaai 渤海 froze solid in winter. By the seventh century this trend had been reversed, and a marked warming had occurred, reaching a brief maximum in the eighth century at about 1°C above present-day mean annual temperature.

The cold returned suddenly at the start of the twelfth century. Lake Taih 太湖, at latitude 31° N, froze solid in the winter of 1111, as it did again in 1329 and 1351, and four times in the second half of the seventeenth century. From 1100 to just before 1900 the mean annual temperature, though varying considerably, stayed at approximately 1° C below its present level. The economic effects of climate change are multiple: yields of cereal crops are sensitive both to the level of insolation and to the quantity and timing of precipitation; the altitude of possible cereal cultivation varies with mean annual temperature; many fruit trees die at temperatures below a relatively sharply defined limit; cold winters can help to control insects pests and fungal diseases; winter freezing affects the use of water-transport systems (such as the Grand Canal), and so on. It may be noted that major downturns of the mean annual temperature very roughly coincided with three major premodern political and cultural transitions: (1) the replacement of the Shang state in North China by the Zhou at the end of the second millennium BC, and, perhaps more importantly, the breaking up of the Western Zhou dominion by the end of the first quarter of the first millennium BC; (2) the gradual disintegration of the early unified Qin/Hahn/Western-Jin empire, which was under way by the end of the second century AD, and definitive by the start of the fourth century; and (3) the decline of the middle empire of the Tang/Sohng, with the loss of north China to non-Chinese rule in 1126, and the loss of the south in 1279, together with the ending of the mediaeval economic revolution. Since climate is only one factor among many, and the size of the sample of cases is three, not too much should necessarily be made of this. It is worth noting, however, that E. S. Kulpin, stressing that "the ancestors of the Chinese" in the second millennium BC lived in a narrow, fertile strip of wetlands along the middle and lower course of the Yellow River, close to extensive virgin forests full of rhinoceros, elephants, tapirs, bamboo-rats and other subtropical and tropical animals, in a climate very humid compared to that of the present day, as the summer monsoon came further north at this time, assigns a major role in the formation of classical Chinese civilization to the traumatic shift to a colder climate in the period, that is, between, approximately, the eleventh/ninth centuries and the fifth/third centuries BC.[11]

Another long-term trend was drainage and reclamation. Thus the huge inland marshes near the mouth of the Yellow River and along the central course of the Yangzi were mostly drained in the first period and early in the second. Massive reclamation of sea-coast salt-marsh in and near the mouth of the Yangzi occurred at the end of the second and at the beginning of the third, leading to the creation of a dyked polder-land area in Jiangnan that was in many ways comparable to Holland. Likewise there was deforestation and stripping of vegetation cover in north China during the second period on a scale large enough to cause, in conjunction with strategically unviable systems of river levees, extensive man-made 'natural' disasters in the lower Yellow River. This process reached a first but lesser maximum early in the third period, when the river's lower course shifted south of the Shandong peninsula, and then a grand climax towards the end of the traditional empire (eighteenth and nineteenth centuries), the process to some extent restarting *de novo* after the shift in the river's course back north in 1853–55.[12] In this last part of the third period, as the cultivation of upland crops—chiefly maize and sweet potatoes—spread, often on a shifting basis, there was a 'holocaust' of the forests in many parts of China that left most of the country short of accessible wood (Manchuria once more excepted) at the beginning of the modern age (that is, c.1900).[13]

If numerous details are ignored, it is possible to say that the long-term trend of basic exploitation of the environment was towards maximal 'arablization', that is use for cereal cultivation as opposed to rearing stock in herds, or reliance on non-farm sources of food from forests and wetlands.[14] Arable farming can support a denser population than other traditional modes of environmental exploitation. There was also a long-term trend, though with many complexities, towards the privatization of landed property, that is, away from state-run land-distribution systems, and *de facto* collective use of non-arable resources such as 'mountains and marshes' (*shanzer* 山澤), to use the traditional phrase.[15] Only hydraulic systems, which tended to be run by the state where they were large and defensive in nature (such as seawalls and levees along major rivers), and by collectivities under state supervision when they were for irrigation, escaped this trend.[16] Private landed property, both in terms of units of ownership and units of actual operation, also tended to become more and more fragmented towards the end of the empire. As regards ownership, this was the result of the Chinese system of partible inheritance combined with a relatively new disinclination of the rich to put their money into farmland and so build up new large holdings, perhaps because other forms of investment now promised better returns. As regards operation, it was the consequence of the higher productivity per hectare of garden-style ultra-labour-intensive cultivation.

The title of the present essay is therefore only a paradox in appearance. The styles of economic exploitation of the environment adopted, at least after the ecologically self-conscious restraint of the first period were not, over the very long run, sustainable in a steady form, especially given the apparently uncontrollable tendency of the population not only to grow, but to grow at an ever-increasing rate. The Chinese economy survived these millennia, and in fact did remarkably well for a time, quite possibly leading the world in the middle centuries of the middle ages, because it mastered new technological skills such as hydraulically sophisticated irrigated rice-farming, and because it was continually expanding into fresh resource areas such as Tairwan in the later seventeenth century, the far south-west in the early nineteenth century, and Manchuria beyond the Liaor river valley in the early twentieth century. The 'filling-up' of usable land, the erosion and degradation of soils opened up in unsuitable places, the difficulties of intensifying farming any further (prior to the availability of 'modern' scientific-industrial inputs), the exhaustion of profitable opportunities (in other words, of suitable places) for new irrigation projects, the disappearance of a large proportion of the accessible forests—not balanced, even for wood supplies, which are only a part of the total problem caused by loss of trees, by the commercial response of growing new timber for sale—all testified to the seriousness of the environmental pressures under which the Chinese economy was labouring by the end of the empire, and before the 'modern' period.[17]

'Modern' technology has enormously extended technological capability. For the moment China has escaped again, possibly at the cost of creating even more difficult problems for the not so distant future, including a greatly increased population.[18] The most serious single immediate question (though there are others close behind it) seems to be the absolute shortage of water in north China, for which there appears to be no economically viable solution once the possibilities of improving a still inefficient management of this resource have been used up.[19]

Such, in oversimplified form, is the general picture of the interaction between economy and environment in China over the last three thousand years. If there is a lesson to be drawn from it, when we look, as we shall later, at some of the details, it is probably that the most important single factor controlling what happens to the environment is *the social structure of the power* that makes the key decisions affecting the economic and other activities that impact on the environment. To give one simple example: unlike almost all private proprietors, tenants, and even governments (when the latter were under pressure, as for example to build ships), Buddhist and Daoist monasteries looked after their trees. Their goals and their structure of decision-making, and, above all, their time-horizons, were different from those on the basis of which the others worked. Even the few collective groups who practised conservation chiefly did this to safeguard their own and their descendants' long-term profits.[20] Again and again, power—whether in the sense of a state's requirements for the extra resources needed to achieve military superiority or simply the pattern of land-tenure—emerges as the most crucial variable, though population pressure comes not far behind it in importance.

Given this picture, however preliminary and approximate, the next question is: how do we think about it?

Conceptual perspectives

The subject-matter of environmental history is the interface where human beings have entered into a reciprocal relationship with the biogeochemical

systems of the Earth. Behind the banal word 'systems' lies an almost unbe-
lievably complex web of cycles—atmospheric, hydrologic, and sedimentary,
as well as the more particular cycles of carbon, nitrogen, phosphorus, and
sulphur. All of these, in varying degrees, are shaped to a significant degree
by biota, in particular by bacteria and fungi, the growth and decomposition
of plants and animals, and the recycling of their constituent elements.
Human beings have long played a part in this, albeit a modest one,
and there have been only a few landscapes even in the last few millennia of
premodern times that can be characterized as having been wholly 'natural',
that is completely unshaped by human intervention.

It is appropriate to say that we live in the midst of life. The elements just
mentioned are essential for life—carbon for carbohydrates and almost
everything, nitrogen for nucleic acid bases and hence DNA, as well as for
amino acids and hence proteins, phosphorus for ATP, the basic 'currency'
of biological energy, and for DNA phosphate groups, and so on.[21] Biotic
processes affect them all.[22] The general interdependence of species populations upon each other (humans included), through a variety of causal
networks, is also well known. The basic mechanisms—including symbiosis,
predation, competition, and inhibition—tend to produce loosely defined
local communities of plant and animal species that shade off into each other
along multiple gradients, and are mostly undergoing one or more forms of
change, such as community succession and cyclical variation, but of which
the most important is response to shifts of climate.[23] The concern of the
political and ideological environmental movement with 'stability' is well-
founded in many particular practical contexts, but cannot be justifed as an
absolute principle either of analysis or action.[24]

What happens, then, when economic development of a premodern variety
takes place? A Chinese-style rice-field is a useful initial example. It has to be
levelled and dyked, which requires a substantial investment of human energy
(in other words, 'land' in this context is quasi-capital). It has to be supplied
with water, which means the creation of a hydraulic system of dams, storage
basins and distributary channels. This system will almost always be to some
degree unstable, mainly because of the progressive deposition of sediments
in distribution channels (due to the slowing down of the flow of current),
siltation upstream of barrages, and degradation of the bed downstream.
Hence it will require indefinitely prolonged further inputs of energy for
maintenance if the original investment is not to be lost. This latter is a
form of premodern technological 'lock-in', the mortgaging of a proportion
of future energy resources (and often some material resources, such as pinetree trunks for the salt-water-resistant base-piles of seawalls). In return,
food production per hectare is increased, and stabilized with respect to
fluctuations in rainfall. But there is more. Rice-fields produce methane, a gas
whose 'greenhouse' effect is about twenty times more powerful per mole
than carbon dioxide, and created by bacteria in the mud splitting acetate in

organic material into methane and carbon dioxide.[25] In China (in the past but also to some limited extent still today), the widespread use of untreated or minimally treated human faecal matter as a manure in rice-fields where peasants work in bare feet led to the spread of schistosomiasis. Motile *Schistosoma* larvae (called *miracidia*) emerge from ova excreted in human waste and enter snails from which they emerge in an infective swimming form (called *cercaria*) that penetrates human skin and infects the liver or bladder.[26] All of the effects of this sort need to be taken into consideration in any long-term economic history. What is the 'true cost', and in what sense, of developing riziculture? The conceptual tools to do this have yet to be fashioned.

If we look at economic development in a more general sense, we can note that agriculture and other human economic activities have reduced the net primary productivity of the biosphere by about 40%, defining NPP as the mean annual creation of new organic matter (assimilation minus respiration) without offsetting it against the annual loss of existing organic matter by decomposition and other means. (This reduction can be estimated by means of heavy-isotope analysis of datable organic material, since plants use heavy isotopes in less than their naturally occurring proportions. Accelerated destruction of vegetable matter by burning or decomposition can thus be detected as a time-specific dilution of the atmospheric concentration of certain such heavy isotopes.)[27] Soils are of course created partly by meteorological disaggregation of parent rock that is then washed downstream by fluvial processes, and partly by the action of microbial decomposers. When soils are opened for farming, however, the organic matter content tends to diminish. Agriculture is, among other things, the reduction of biomass in order to be able to control the use of what remains. Where soils with a high clay content ('clay' being defined by a diameter of constituent grains $<2\mu$[28]) are concerned, deforestation on slopes upstream, a process that normally increases run-off, can, it seems, accelerate chemical denudation (by removing the useful cations held by the negative electric charge of clays), and hence limit the provision of the nutrients needed by biota.[29]

It also seems probable that from a medical point of view the agricultural revolution was in some respects a disaster. Not only did it reduce the variety of the human diet, especially in New World cultures dependent on maize,[30] but the denser populations that could now be supported, and their sedentarization, made it possible for 'crowd diseases' to flourish, since the micro-organisms responsible require quite a sizeable minimum accessible reservoir of potential hosts to be able to continue in existence; otherwise the death and acquired immunity of these hosts will prevent their continued propagation. Sedentarization also prevents the easy evacuation of heavily infected or polluted sites. Likewise a slow rate of pathogen transfer to new hosts tends to favour the evolution of less lethal forms, since this maintains a host in existence long enough for transfer to be effected;

and the converse is probably true, namely that the concentration of a population of potential hosts favours the evolution of more lethal forms. Clearly this formulation has to be modified to allow for the mode of transmission of a particular infection—a droplet-borne microbe will be more sensitive to host concentration or dispersion than will a waterborne one, for example.[31] Nor, presumably, will it apply to incidental zoonoses not established in a human population on a permanent basis. Many of these crowd diseases seem, however, to have been originally associated with the domestication of animals: examples, among many, are tuberculosis (almost certainly derived from cattle, since *Mycobacterium bovis* infects humans whereas *M. tuberculosis*, the specifically human form, will not infect cattle),[32] measles (which has been linked with canine distemper), and maybe even smallpox (which though it has no known animal vector may also have been linked with cattle).[33] The historical balance-sheet of agriculture is thus complicated, there being many 'pluses' and 'minuses', often apparently incommensurable. What is clear, though, is that the simple triumphalism of the older economic history is misplaced. The many health costs of industrial production (such as the celebrated Minamata disease, due to the consumption of marine animals that had concentrated derivatives of the diethyl mercury discharged in factory wastes) are well enough known to need no special comment here. But how is health to be 'costed'? The measures taken, often ineffectually, to restore it are hardly an adequate proxy; and—without going into the details, which are complex—diminished health surely diminishes the enjoyment of most other goods as well.[34]

A few orthodox economists, such as Repetto, have recently recalculated the national accounts for selected countries taking into consideration the loss of environmental assets valued by market or by shadow prices, and shown that the picture of 'success' or 'failure' can sometimes be significantly altered by so doing.[35] This is useful, but does not touch the core of the conceptual problem. What is needed is a mental model of 'nature' that goes beyond the implicit idea that resources are somewhat like the distinct and separate goods on the shelves of a supermarket ('environmental assets') and takes into account the type of *interdependencies* described in the preceding paragraphs. Outside small-scale contexts of short duration in ecological terms, the environment is not an amenity that can be reasonably handled in terms of trade-offs. It is the foundation of all the systems of production and waste disposal through which an economy functions.

A new method of evaluating both past processes and decisions affecting the future is also needed. Such a method will probably have the following features: (1) There will no longer be 'externalities' (which is what half-glimpsed interdependencies have been in effect called in the past). (2) The powerful (and often useful) 'Midas principle' that assumes that everything is quantitatively intercomparable in terms of money[36] will be critically re-examined and probably jettisoned as an overriding rule, though retained for use in limited contexts. (3) Some way will be found of handling long-term transtemporal comparisons that takes into account the horizon of predictability that chaos theory indicates, especially for systems described by non-linear equations; and some method will be found for the non-arbitrary assignation of a time-discount rate for long-term comparisons of values across periods of a length too great for there to be any meaningful trans-temporal 'futures' market. (4) There will probably be other features, such as (perhaps) a redefinition of the maximand(s) in terms other than an aggregate (based on some formally arbitrary aggregating assumption) of the 'utility' of individuals used by standard economics. An interesting guide to what such a new theory might in part look like is provided by what might be called the 'quasi-economics' (since many of its techniques are derived from conventional economics) that is used by behavioural eco-logists to analyze, and in experimental situations to predict, the behaviour of animals, birds, and insects. Ecological quasi-economics takes as its ultimate criterion the survival of specific genes (via inter-allele competition), or assemblages of genes (the genotype, or continuously mutationally intertransformable sets of genotypes, so-called 'quasi-species'), and as its proximate criterion the life-time reproductive success of individuals. It uses a variety of quasi-currencies, such as energy and time, as appropriate, and incorporates such features as the costs and benefits of varying patterns of competition and cooperation, the pay-off of resource-defence (the costs and benefits of maintaining a given size of territory, for example), and the evo-lution of predator-prey 'arms races'. Group selection appears as at most a weak force—thus systems of voluntary birth-control for the good of the group, if they ever temporarily emerged, would be unstable, as it would usually 'pay' individuals to cheat—and an interesting question is how far this remains true of human populations.[37]

The economic historian who is serious about how the world actually works has no option but to try to absorb and incorporate what his or her scientific colleagues have to tell him or her about the probable effects of the technologies that are utilized in the economic systems that he or she studies. As a result, he or she learns to see processes differently. In the case of deforestation, for example, it will become obvious that his or her economist friends tend not to see the trees for the wood (in other words, the living system for the inanimate resource). Geologists' perspectives add a modicum of reassurance: biogeochemical systems seem to have undergone greater changes in the course of geological time than even those that humanity is currently imposing on them—and survived, albeit often in changed form. What may be new is the speed of anthropogenic changes. Ecologists drive home the point, however, that unlimited population expan-sion in a system closed with respect to energy and resources inevitably leads to collapse, and the earth—apart from the influx of solar radiation—is such a closed system.[38]

For example, the annual use per person of fresh water supplied by run-off in the world grew between 1687 and 1987 by 4 times. In absolute terms, because population grew, it went up by 35 times, to a 1987 total of about 3.5×10^3 cubic kilometers a year.[39] The absolute growth-rate for the three-hundred-year period is thus about 1.2% per year. The 1987 total is a little under one-eleventh of the world's estimated total supply of fresh run-off water. It is therefore evident that if the same rate of absolute growth were to continue, the world does not have much more than 200 years—one major Chinese dynasty—before it is using every last drop.

The tool-kit inherited by the economic historian from economics, though it contains much that is still useful, is simply not adequate—and not even remotely adequate—to incorporate scientific knowledge most of which is new over the last two generations. This leaves the economic historian who faces up to the challenge in a state of serious conceptual anomia. Without a relatively well-systematized set of adequate controlling concepts it is all but impossible to formulate internally coherent and logically integrated evaluations of past economic processes, or of future proposals. I have some sympathy with those who prefer to retain a measure of internal rigour even at the cost of empirical irrelevance even if, as must be apparent, I personally regard this conventional approach as a strategic dead-end.

Powerless wisdom: the ecological economy of archaic China

Archaic China (before about 500 BC) possessed a political philosophy that put at the centre of its conceptions the conservation of a well-ordered nature. It spoke of the "constant paths of Heaven and the public-spiritedness [or, in other words, the generosity] of the Earth [*tianjing dihyih* 天經地義]." To the regular movements of the stars, the dependable recurrence of the seasons, and the growth and death of plants and animals, there corresponded the ritually correct patterns of behaviour of human beings, which were of equal importance.[40] The slightest deviation could provoke natural disorder, and until at least the end of the empire, natural disorder was seen as a symptom of moral turpitude at either a national or a local level.[41] An example from the second quarter of the first millennium BC of this ideology may be found in the *Guoryuu* 國語 [Tales of the Various States] which was put together in the succeeding epoch. It is known under the title of "Lii Ger 李革 tears up the nets":

One summer's day, Duke Xuan [of the state of Luu] spread his nets in the deeps of the River Sih. [The grand officer] Lii Ger tore up the Duke's fishing-nets and threw them to the ground. "In ancient times," he said [to the Duke], "once the period called 'The Great Cold'[42] had passed, the insects who had hidden themselves in the earth came forth, and the official who was the guardian of the waters [*shuuiyur* 水虞] would concern himself with the practices used for netting fish and for catching them in traps. Large fish that were captured or turtles that were landed had to be sacrificed at the ancestral temple. The people of the state were enjoined to act according to these rules, so as to help the [bright-male-active] matter-energy-vitality [*qih* 氣] to rise.

"When the birds and the beasts were pregnant with young, but the aquatic tribes were maturing, the official guardian of animals [*shouhyur* 獸虞] would under these circumstances forbid the use of nets to catch four-legged beasts or birds. He would [command the people only to] harpoon fish and turtles for their summer provisions, so as to help [the smaller ones] to grow in abundance. When the birds and the beasts were maturing, and the aquatic tribes were 'pregnant' with young, the official who was the guardian of the waters would, under these circumstances, prohibit the people from using either large or small fishing-nets, but let them entrap beasts in pits to provide for the slaughterhouses of the ancestral temples, so as to rear up [beasts] both for presentation and practical use.

"Furthermore, in the mountains the sprouts growing from [coppiced] trunks were not to be chopped off. In the wetlands, it was forbidden to cut the tender sprouts. It was not allowed to take fish-spawn or hatchlings. Where deer were concerned, fawns were to be permitted to grow up. It was obligatory to protect the fledglings and the eggs of birds. As to insects, the eggs and pupae [yuarn 原] of ants were to be left untouched. The teaching of ancient times is that all beings should propagate themselves in abundance.

"At this time of the year, the fish have only just ceased giving birth, and so not allowing the fish to grow up, but even spreading out nets to catch them, is insatiable greed."

When the Duke had heard these words, he said: "I was wrong. Is it not, however, well that Lii Ger has corrected me? This torn-up net is well, too, as a [warning] exemplar for me. Have the officials keep it for me, so that I never forget it."[43]

Moralizing tales of this sort were a Chinese cultural speciality, but should not be wholly discounted, since they presupposed an audience on whom they could produce the appropriate effect. Typically, everything is recounted as it ought to have happened, yet it cannot have been simply fantasy. It seems likely that this story, and others like it, reflects a time when there were already small city-states[44] where gathering, hunting, and fishing still played a major part in the economy but the pressure of population on resources was beginning to make itself felt. Thus in 524 BC Duke Mu of Shan 單穆公, a minister at the court of the Zhou high king, observed:

If it should happen that the forests of the mountains are exhausted, and that of the forests of the piedmont only scattered remnants remain, or that they have disappeared, and that the thickets and marshes have come to the last days of their existence, the forces of the people will be weakened, the farmland where cereals and hemp grow will be uncultivated, and they will lack resources. The superior man should be concerned about this problem in a spirit of altruistic urgency, and without relaxation. How could it ever delight him?[45]

The reality of this age, and its practical wisdom, were otherwise. In order to mobilize resources and build up populations to man the armies that were engaged in a warfare that was rapidly shifting from a relatively ritualized combat to a pitiless destruction—a transition that has left its literary traces in speeches attributed to realists mocking the folly of the old-fashioned military pieties[46]—statesmen turned to economic development. In the middle of the sixth century BC, Zii Muh 子木, prime minister of the state of Chuu, entrusted the following tasks to his minister of war Yaan of Weei 蒍掩.

to put the payment of taxes in good order, and to make a tally of the numbers of suits of defensive armour and of offensive weapons. [So] on the jiaawuu day [of the sexagenary cycle] Yaan of Weei listed the cultivable land in a register, surveyed the mountains and the forests, grouped together the marshlands and the water-meadows [commentators suggest as hunting-grounds], distinguished between the heights and the hillocks, marked out the poor and salty lands, enumerated the watercourses along the frontiers, circumscribed the lowlying pools, and divided with raised paths the areas between the dykes into small fields, made pastures of the alluvial lands beside the waters, and fields for the eight-family groups [jiing 井][47] in the fertile places at the feet of hills, calculated the quotas of the contributions to be paid in, the numbers of chariots to be supplied, and made a register of the horses, and determined the quotas of soldiers mounted in chariots and of those on foot, the numbers of [suits of] body-armour and of shields. This done, he presented [the list] to Zii Muh.[48]

In late-archaic China at least, economic development was both the consequence and the cause of an intensified warfare.

The scriptural or quasi-scriptural works of the classical age that followed—in broad terms the third quarter of the first millennium BC—abound in prescriptions for the restrained exploitation of nature, but there is an evident undercurrent of anxiety. In the *Yuehlihng* 月令 (Ordinances for the Months) we read, for example, that in the middle of spring "one should not exhaust the rivers and the marshes. One should not empty the pools created by dams. One should not burn the forests on the mountains."[49] And likewise, in the last month of spring, "the nets for snaring animals and birds, and those mounted on long handles [for birds], the concealment shelters [for those shooting game], and the poisons used to poison animals should not be taken through the nine gates [of the palaces, cities, suburbs, and barriers],"[50] in other words they were to be kept in storage. In the sixth month the guardians of the forest [*yurrern* 虞人] should go on patrol to stop people from cutting wood.[51] Beneath these prescriptions lies the sense that the natural world is permeated by the flow of matter-energy-vitality, and that behaving in a fashion inappropriate to the season will cause natural disasters. At the end of the summer, for example, "it is impermissible to mobilize soldiers or set 'the masses' [*zhohng* 眾, in early times perhaps a particular military corps[52]] in motion; nor may one undertake large-scale operations, lest one perturb the matter-energy-vitality that is providing nourishment [*yaangqih* 養氣]."[53] With this perception that what we think of as the inanimate world was, in effect, alive, it is understandable that sacrifices of animals were regularly made to mountains, forests, streams, and marshes.[54]

What is of central importance, though, is that towards the end of this period there was a tendency on the part of state governments to transform the traditional policy of conservation and prudent management into one of limiting access for commoners to non-agricultural land, partly to create some degree of state monopoly that could be exploited to fiscal advantage, and partly to force the population to settle down to the pursuit of farming, the primary source of taxes and conscripts. A early example of this trend was the monopoly of the Duke of Qir over forests, reeds, and salt in the late sixth century BC, which was regarded as greedy.[55] The texts are confused and contradictory, reflecting this transition and the multiplicity of objectives, and assuredly there was a vast range of circumstances differing from one locality to the next. We can, bearing in mind these cautions, take the *Book of Master Guaan* 管子, a composite work compiled towards the end of the pre-imperial age and later edited by Liur Xiahng 劉向, as an illustration of the multiple perspectives in accordance with which the question was perceived.

The symbolic and religious aspect remains. Activities have to have the appropriate seasonal character. In the summer, for example, "you should not gather together great crowds of people, nor light great fires, nor cut down great trees, nor put to death the great officers of state, nor chop down [the vegetation on] the great mountains, nor cut the grass in the great plains. If you destroy the three great natural entities [probably trees, mountains, and plains], the state will thereby be damaged. Such are the interdicts of the Son of Heaven for the summer season."[56] Prudent estate management continued.

Thus, "if the mountains and the marshes are opened at the appropriate season, the common people will not make irregular entry into them."[57] Likewise, in a chapter that implicitly uses the idea of the carrying capacity of a certain environment for a population of a certain size, it says that "even though the mountains and marshes [*shanzer* 山澤] are extensive, if there are no prohibitions on the use of plants and trees, and even though the soils are rich, if there are no quotas on the use of mulberry trees and of hemp, and even though the pasturages are numerous, if taxes are imposed on the six species of [domestic] animal, then—this situation will be [nonetheless] as if we had closed shut the door of goods and of resources."[58]

But there is another note struck as well. The people must be sedentarized:

> Though the rivers and the seas are vast, and though the pools and marshes are extensive, and the fish and turtles numerous, it is necessary to have rules governing the proper use of nets, and people should not rely entirely on fishing to make their living [*chuarn-waang buhkee yi cair err cherng* 船網不可一財而成]. It is not that We [the ruler] wish to treat the plants and trees as our personal property, or that We are grudging with respect to the fish or the turtles, but that We cannot endure that the common people neglect the cultivation of cereals. It is for this reason that it is said: "The kings of ancient times imposed prohibitions on the mountains and the marshes because they wished to oblige the common people to concentrate on cereal farming."[59]

This last point was probably a misreading of the archaic age in terms of the new motivations of the classical age. In a similar spirit, the *Shangjun shu* 商君書 (Book of the Lord of Shang), a text of brutal physiocratic *Realpolitik* that preached a militarized peasant-soldier state based on the uncompromising and predictable use of rewards and punishments, argued that if the government "had the unique power over the mountains and the marshes, then the common people who detest farming, are lazy, and want doubled profits, will have nowhere to find something to eat. If they have nowhere to find something to eat, they will be obliged to engage in the cultivation of the fields. If they are obliged to engage in the cultivation of the fields, the unfarmed grasslands will have be opened up." A traditional commentary explains that "unique power" meant interdicts on mountains and marshes, and that the people were "not permitted to gather wood, to hunt, or to fish in an uncontrolled manner."[60]

With the creation of the Chinese empire towards the end of the third century BC, control over at least a substantial proportion of non-farmland was put in the hands of the emperor's personal treasury, so that taxes could be levied with the purpose of meeting the needs of the imperial household.[61] At least in some areas, the common people continued to have access to forests and wetlands but under certain restrictions. A bamboo document of the third century BC, recently excavated in Hurbeei, and containing a section of the "field laws [*tiarnlŭh* 田律]" of the Qin state, says:

> In the spring, during the second month, they will not dare to cut wood for building or in the mountain forests, or retain water behind the dykes. Before the summer they will not dare to take armfuls[62] of hay to make ashes [to put on the soil], nor gather the *lih-grass* 荔 that is sprouting, nor take the young of animals, eggs, or fledglings ... , nor poison fish or turtles, nor emplace pitfalls, traps or nets. During the seventh month, however, these restrictions are relaxed. If, though, afflicted by the misfortune of a death they need to cut wood for a coffin, they are not obliged to take note of the season.
>
> As for the meadows near the walled cities and other parklands subject to interdicts, they will not dare to take their dogs there for hunting in the time when there are fawns about. Those of the people's dogs that have entered a parkland subject to interdicts, but have not chased or caught a wild animal, they will not dare to kill; but those that have chased or caught a wild animal, they will kill. Dogs killed by way of reprimand and repression[63] will be surrendered in their entirety to the authorities. Of other kills made in the parklands subject to interdicts, they may eat the meat but surrender the skins to the authorities.[64]

Zhu Maaichern 朱買臣, an imperial official who lived in the second century BC, cut wood and hawked it about in order to support himself, and this would only have been possible if the forests of Wur 吳, where he lived, had been open all year.[65] Nonetheless, the *History of the Hahn* notes the relaxing of the restrictions on the mountains and marshes (*shii shanzer* 弛山澤) by Emperor Wern of the Hahn as an act of exceptional generosity during a time of drought and locust plague,[66] and a Sohng-dynasty compendium on the Later Hahn dynasty states that "All the taxes on mountains, marshes, dams, and reservoirs were called 'interdict cash' (*jihnqiarn* 禁錢), and were under the control of the emperor's personal treasury (*shaaofuu* 少府)"[67] The story is more complicated than I have indicated, but it is broadly true to say that the first transformation of the regulations once designed to conserve nature as a sustainable production system was into a sort of partial state monopoly. As an indication of its subsequent continuation, we may note a decree issued by Emperor Wuu of the southern dynasty of the Liang in AD 508:

> It is from the thickets, marshes, mountains, and forests that come forth the resources that sustain us. Buildings erected side by

side depend upon axes [to cut the required wood], yet for one generation after another now [the forests] have been under ever firmer prohibitions. How could one describe such a situation as sharing the profits [of Nature] with the people, or being benevolent towards the black-haired folk [that is, Our subjects]? Wherever the frontier colonies subject to Our Court [*gongjia turnshuh* 公家屯戍] are debarred from clearing [these lands] by burning it is right that all the regular prohibitions be removed.[68]

Fine sentiments, dosed action. When the Suir dynasty reunited the empire at the end of the sixth century, however, they put a formal end to prohibitions on access to mountains and marshes.[69] Under the Tang dynasty that followed, we find that the Department of Guardians (*yurbuh* 虞部) in the Ministry of Works (*gongbuh* 工部) in the Office of the Affairs of State (*shahngshusheeng* 尚書省), the bureaucratic heirs of those long previously charged with the conservation of nature, were mostly concerned with looking after the needs of the Court and the capital. Apart from the expression of ritual sentiments that were largely empty of operational content, the rules governing what was and what was not allowed to the ordinary people applied only to special zones: the immediate environs of the capital cities, for example, and around sacred mountains and shrines.[70]

The second transformation was that the guardians, in fulfilling their duties to supply the Court with materials, from time to time at least themselves became among the most effective destroyers of the natural environment. In a poem that is loaded with political allusion—including the idea that talented men have been cut down at the Court like axed trees— the essayist and historian Liur Zongyuarn 柳宗元 (773–819) summoned up images that, although they can hardly be taken straightforwardly, must have had some reality if they were to have carried conviction:

> The official guardians'[71] axes have spread through a thousand hills,
> At the Works Department's orders hacking rafter-beams and billets.
> Of ten trunks cut in the woodlands' depths, only one gets hauled
>   away.
> Ox-teams strain at their traces—till the paired yoke-shafts break.
> Great-girthed trees of towering height lie blocking the forest tracks,
> A tumbled confusion of lumber, as flames on the hillside crackle.
> Not even the last remaining shrubs are safeguarded from destruction;
> Where once the mountain torrents leapt—nothing but rutted gullies.
> Timbers, not yet seasoned or used, left immature to rot;
> Proud summits and deep-sunk gorges, now—brief hummocks of
>   naked rock.[72]

The wisdom of the ancients was powerless.

Power and property: from classical
China to the middle empire

There is no rule that environmental wisdom can coexist with power, whether military, political, or economic. In most cases it seems that the contrary is likely to be true. The essential nature of power in the social sense is not all that far removed from its scientific definition as units of energy divided by units of time. Social power requires the creation of means to capture and direct the flow of energy in nature just as much as its flow in other human beings (sometimes known as 'exploitation'). In other words, technological mastery combined with political domination. The capture of the flux of natural energy at any given time is usually easier if it is to some extent 'stolen' in the sense that it is removed more rapidly than natural processes can restore it. Socio-political power and the over-exploitation of the environment have a tendency to co-vary, though there may be exceptions in specific cases. The *Master Guaan* states explicitly that development is indispensable for the survival of the state: "Where the territory is extensive but the state [guor 國] impoverished, this is because the untilled land has not been opened up. Where the populace is numerous but the armed forces feeble, this is because the common people have no [great] income. If secondary occupations [such as trading] be not forbidden, the untilled land will not be opened up, ... and it will be impossible to hold out against enemies from outside, or to maintain security within the borders."[73]

The state of Qin, which was in due course to unify the empire, greatly increased the effectiveness of its war-machine in the third century BC by the improvement[74] and creation respectively of two gigantic irrigation systems, using technology imported from the more advanced regions of eastern China, systems that permitted a greater, cheaper, and more reliable production of food. The first of these was that in the present province of Sihchuan where the Mim River 岷江 leaves the mountains and flows out across a sloping (0.29% to 0.42%) fan-shaped plain. The principle was simple: water, moved by gravity, was first diverted from the main stream (in such a way as to stabilize, as far as possible, the quantity entering the system, whether at the Mim River's low water [about 500 m³/sec] or peak discharge [5000 to 6000 m³/sec]); then it was directed through a network of distribution channels, used for irrigation, and the residue returned to the main course far (some 100+ km) downstream. The details required solving the problem presented by the deposition of sediments, as the slowing of the current reduced the competence of the flow to carry suspended particles, and thus the system was threatened with the infilling of its channels over time. In oversimple terms, the solution adopted was twofold. Regular dredging was carried out during low water in the winter (57% of rainfall occurs today in the June–September period) in accordance with the advice of the first director of the works, Lii Bing 李冰, to "clear out the mud-deposit deeply, and build the dykes low."[75] Second, a bend was engineered upstream of the main diversion outlet in such a way that a substantial proportion of the suspended sediments was deposited on its convex inner side, as a result of the slower flow there and the subsidiary helicoidal current in the plane at right angles to the main current.[76] These deposits were then flushed out periodically by opening another channel that led back directly into the old main course of the river, but was normally closed off, while at the same time shutting the diversion outlet, which was normally open. The flushing channel was closed by a barrage of huge bamboo baskets filled with heavy stones resting on a fixed stone sill, which also served as a spillway regulating the height of the water in the system, hence as an emergency overflow during heavy floods (or even a safety-valve, since the gabions could be swept away). Removing, and later replacing, these baskets, which were 3 feet in diameter and 10 feet long (at least in Tang times, from which these figures come),[77] required the repeated use of a large quantity of labour, as did the annual dredging. This is an early example of premodern lock-in: the initial investment, on which the productivity of the entire system rested, could only be preserved at the cost of perpetual expensive maintenance. In fact, the Mim system has proved unusually enduring, in spite of the repeated destruction of the main diversion head and the crescent-shaped dykes creating the articificial bend, and an expanded and altered version of it is still functioning today.[78]

The Zhehng Guor Canal 鄭國渠 to the north of the Weih River 渭河, in what is today Shaanxi province, and started in 246 BC, took heavily silt-laden water from the Jing River 涇水 to the Luoh River 洛水, running along higher ground for the first part of its course so that the water would be released onto the fields below where, in the words of a Hahn-dynasty ditty "it serve[d] as both irrigation and fertilizer." This was also an effective way of combating the salinity of much of the land. Its 200-kilometer course had an average slope of 0.64 per mil, which indicates a high degree of surveying skill. The canal needed continuous re-engineering because of siltation, including new added channels, and its effectiveness seems to have declined markedly over the centuries. Its critical contribution, when it was created, was to feed the population of the area 'within the passes' where the Qin and the Hahn empires had their capitals. Simaa Qian, the great historian, not only attributed the triumph of the state of Qin over the other states of the third century BC, and hence the creation of the empire, to this irrigation system, but put words into the mouth of its creator, Zhehng Guor, that suggest that in the course of building it this latter had become conscious that, although he had started with the hope of distracting the ruler of Qin from war, this ascendancy was likely to be the consequence of his work. Without adopting any simple monocausal explanations, we can observe that economic development was inextricably linked with political and military hegemony.[79]

Property is a fundamental form of social power, and in this context we may note that the early empire and the long era of political division that followed it (a period together running from the end of the third century BC to the end of the sixth century AD) was marked by a competition between the state and the owners of large estates to dominate the extraction of revenue both from the land and from the labour-power dependent on the land (which was mainly but not exclusively farmland) in the form of taxes, conscripted labour, and rents. This competition was too complex for summary here, but it is important to note that after the fall of the Hahn empire in the third century one of the main means used by the state was systems of government-directed land distribution to peasant farmers, or farmer-soldiers. Two passages will convey something of the nature of these forces that were opposed, but also linked, in that most bureaucrats and estate-owners were drawn from largely similar social groups, and could even function in both capacities in different contexts. In the third century, Zhohngchang Toong 仲長統 wrote:

> The households of the powerful are [compounds] where one finds hundreds of ridgebeams linked together. Their fertile fields fill the countryside. Their slaves [*nurbih* 奴婢] throng in thousands, and their [military] retainers [*turfuh* 徒附] can be counted in tens of thousands. Their boats, carts, and their merchants spread out in every direction. ... The valleys between the hills cannot contain their horses, cattle, sheep, and swine.[80]

It is worth observing, in passing, the importance of the part still played by herds of large animals in the Chinese economy at this date.

The second passage describes how in 243 the state of Weih 魏, in northern China, it was "desired to extend the cultivated acreage, and to accumulate a stockpile of cereals, in order to destroy the bandits [that is, its rival states]." According to Dehng Aih 鄧艾, a statesman of this time, speaking of the valley of the Huair River:

> "Though the soil is good, there is not enough water to use to the full its productive power. It will also be necessary to dig canals to provide water for irrigation, so as to stockpile large quantities of military provisions, and to serve as transportation routes for the government. ... Our concern is with the area south of the Huair River. For each large-scale military expedition more than half of the troops have to be used for transport, which is highly expensive. ... Twenty thousand colonists should be stationed to the north of the Huair, and thirty thousand to the south. At any time, twenty per cent of the men will be off duty, and so there will be a regular force of forty thousand men who

function simultaneously as farmers and as soldiers. ... Wur will be conquered."[81]

Beneath the conflict opposing large estate-owners and the state was another battle, related but not identical, in which the common people, to some extent backed by the state, fought with the estate-owners for access to land, both arable and non-arable. In 306, under the Jihn dynasty, Shuh Xi 束皙 said, in a memorial stressing the responsibility of local officals to assign land to the landless, that:

> In the thousand counties of the empire there are many who wander hither and thither in search of food. They have abandoned their own properties and have not in actual fact been assigned any by the state. ... What is more, in the ten commanderies of the metropolitan area the land is constricted yet the population dense. ... Nonetheless pastures for pigs, sheep, and horses are widespread in this region. They should all be suppressed so that we can provide for the needs of those who have no land. ... What is more, the marsh of Wur 吳澤 in the commandery of Jir 汲 [in what is today Her'nam province] contains several thousand *qing*[82] of good-quality land, but the water there is stagnant and the people have not opened it up for agriculture. I have heard the people of this principality all declare: 'It would not be difficult to drain them, so as to convert the saline wetlands into plains [*yuarn* 原], from which large profits could be derived, but the great and powerful families do not wish to give up the abundance of fish which they catch here, and they have known how to intrigue with the officials in such a fashion that in the end [this mutual complicity] has never been broken.'[83]

Here, as sometimes happens, social justice for the poorer members of society and environmental conservation by the well-to-do were directly opposed.

Another example comes from 336 in the region around Yeh [鄴] in the north-east, which was then suffering from drought. The authorities, we are told, "ordered the local magistrates to lead strong grown men into the mountains and the wetlands to gather acorns and to catch fish so as to provide help for the old and sick, but powerful families had taken possession of these places and resources of this nature could nowhere be found."[84] A crucial text from the middle of the fifth century, when the Liur Sohng dynasty ruled south of the Yangzi, shows both the fever of non-governmental economic development that already gripped parts of east-central China by this time, and the confused state of property rights:

> The Prefect of Yamgzhou ... reported to the Emperor: "Though the prohibitions regarding the mountains and the lakes have been

established since times past, the common people have become accustomed to ignoring them, each one of them following in this the example of the others. They completely burn off the vegetation on the mountains, build dams across the rivers, and act so as to keep all the advantages for their families. ... Rich and powerful people have taken possession of ranges of hills. The poor and the feeble have nowhere to gather firewood, or hay. These incursions are serious abuses that damage good government, and to which the administration should put an end. It should be reaffirmed that the old laws which defined what was beneficial and what harmful are still in force."

The authorities examined the edict of 336, which said: "To take possession of the mountains, or to put the marshes under one's [personal] protection is tantamount to robbery with violence. Those who steal more than 10 feet of land are to be beheaded in public."

Yarng Xi 羊希 stated: "This system of 336 contains prohibitions that are rigorous and severe. Since it has been difficult for the people to obey them, their principles have [in practice] been eased so as to be in keeping with the spirit of the times. Nonetheless, taking possession of mountains, and blocking rivers with dykes, have become more and more common. Because people copy each others' bad example, these places have, so to speak, become their hereditary property. Were we to take back these properties all of a sudden, this action would provoke anger and resentment. We ought now to repeal [the old rules] and create a system based on the five following provisions: (1) As regards the mountains and the wetlands, we shall not charge with an offense, nor confiscate the lands of those who have become accustomed to clearing them by burning the vegetation, and planting bamboos and all sorts of fruit in such a fashion that these can renew themselves, and to building dams and lakes, and also barrages to keep captive river and sea fish ... which they maintain in good repair. ... "[85]

He then goes on to specify maximum limits of acreage for officials of various ranks, and for commoners, and prescribes that their holdings be entered in the land-registers.

What this passage makes clear—and I have nowhere found any evidence to the contrary—is that while there was a clear concept of a *public* economic domain, of forests and wetlands in particular, to which commoners had varying rights of usually limited access, and which had to be maintained by the state, and was in some sense state land, there was no *de jure* common land in the Western sense of land belonging to a specified community, but only *de facto* common land perpetually vulnerable to encroachments as population growth put natural resources under ever greater pressure.[86] In north China, in 485, the Northern Weih emperor Xiaohwem lamented the apparent decline in the condition of the people since ancient times, commenting that in his day "the rich and powerful have appropriated the mountains and marshes, while the poor and the weak have lost hope of having the smallest plot of land."[87] In these last two passages we see the early stages of the remorseless process by which over the next millennium almost all the non-agricultural land in China eventually came into private ownership.

The details of this important story have still to be systematically researched, and there may have been several stages. One important aspect was the making available by the state of more and more of its reserved domain to the ordinary people to use as what has just been described as 'de facto common land'. For example, it is said of the Ming emperor Rem, who ruled from 1425 to 1426, that "wherever the government had placed prohibitions on the mountain work-sites, gardens [for tea, etc], the forests, the lakes, the wetlands, [sites for] kilns and founderies, fruit trees and bees, all was given to the common people."[88] In fact this can only have been true to a limited extent. He is also said to have said to his top officials, when discussing the problem of firewood for Beijing:

> In ancient times, the mountains, the rivers, and the wetlands were all shared with the people. Although there were the interdicts imposed by the guardians, and the people had to observe the proper times and seasons for gathering resources, the essential concern was to keep the people in good condition, and it was not the case that the state had a monopoly of these resources. There are several million inhabitants in the capital [in fact, closer to a million] and from where can they get their wood for heating except from the mountains? ... What is more, the mountains and marshes have been produced by Heaven and Earth in order to benefit the people. The region to the east of Yongguan 庸關 and next to Wahnshouh 萬壽 should remain closed to the gathering of firewood, but apart from this ban the people should be allowed to collect it everywhere without prohibition.[89]

From this, and from the removal of further restrictions by Rem's successor, the emperor Xuan, it can be seen that there was still not general access. It is also relevant to note that the use of the northern frontier forests as a barrier to barbarian cavalry began at this time—a form of environmental military defence.[90] The processes by which these de facto commons were then converted into the private mountain land owned by the so-called "mountain lords" (shanzhuu 山主) that characterized most of the mountainous areas in Qing times is still to be studied.

In some places what almost amounted to *de jure* common land was created by communities towards the end of the empire. For example, in Tongdaoh 通道, in the south of the province of Hur'nan (26°10' N, 109°45' E) and today an 'autonomous' county for the Dong 侗 minority, this happened in 1851 at a place called Camp Baaoshan 保山寨. The elders here created a system to protect their trees from over-exploitation and left a record of their decisions engraved on a stele:

> Was the vegetation of the forests of these mountains always the way it is today? No. It was not. A phenomenon whose age is of many centuries has met with a disaster.
>
> On the mountain of Houhlorng 後龍山 in Shahngxiang 上湘 we have always had several thousands of trees of vast girth. The people of the present time are not of a quality comparable to those of more remote ages. They have acted in their personal interest in cutting down trees in an unreasonable fashion. The result has been that the beauty of the mountain trees has undergone a change, and the mountains shine as if they had been stripped naked.
>
> This means that we have reached a moment in time when the mountains have been ruined, the arteries of vitality drained dry, and the spirits of human beings become inconstant. Our locality is in a state of decomposition and decline for which there is no remedy. Seeing that this decline is already an accomplished fact, who possesses the power to remedy this situation of rottenness, or to find the means by which the springtime may return?
>
> All the trees, on all sides of this Camp, must be cared for so that they can return to a good condition, and then surpass the past, flourishing, rich, and of a great age, and such that our children and our grandchildren may pass on their abundance from one to the other without end.
>
> We have now resolved that all the land on Mount Houhlorng, up to the summit of its slopes and as far down as the reservoirs, gardens, fields, and houses, and towards the interior as far as the crest of Liinglour, and towards the exterior as far as the fields and reservoirs of Yamchong, shall become communal land. [The term *gongdi* 公地 used here is more commonly rendered "public land," but this does not fit the context.] It will not be permitted either to buy it or to sell it. All the trees of these forests are to be conserved and placed under an interdict. It is forbidden to fell them in an unreasonable fashion. Those who do not obey this resolution approved by public discussion are wicked thieves. They will be held responsible and punished by collective action. ...
>
> We have decided that the trees around the source of the river at Camp Baaoshan provide it with a comprehensive protection and

that all of them must be cared for and placed under an interdict. It will not be allowed for them to be felled in an abusive fashion. Those who disobey will be punished.

We have decided that the second circumscription of *Cunninghamia* [*shan/sha muh*] at Camp Baaoshan, and the first of *Cunninghamia* on Mount Marqueh are to be communal mountains [*gongshan*], and they are not to be sold or bought.[91]

This unusual inscription is not easy to interpret. In the first place, cases are known of mountain cemeteries that were owned by kin-groups where the kin-group leaders put an end to the felling of trees, the collection of dead wood for burning, the gathering of chestnuts, and the growing of crops by the ordinary members of these kin-groups chiefly in order to be able to monopolize the profits for the kin-group organization, as distinct from its individual members, or in all probability for themselves. Whether this was what was going on in Camp Baaoshan, under the rhetoric of collectivity and environmental salvage, is impossible to tell from the evidence. The use of the terms "unreasonable" and "abusive" suggest that some felling continued, under some sort of control, presumably that of the community leaders. In the second place, it is evident that the formal constitution of collective land in the mountain forest areas came late here, and this has possible parallels in other contexts, such as the equally late formation in north China of collective village groups to handle the task of crop-watching.[92] Prior to the middle of the nineteenth century, at least in this remote area, there seem to have been enough resources for everyone to take what they wanted or needed, and there may have been some past buying and selling of forest lands, at least outside the area that was reserved and placed outside such transactions. Lastly, the evident need to define the reserved area in a precise geographic sense, as well as the description of rapid timber depletion, give a hint of the pressure on these resources, presumably from those encroaching as private property owners, that was building up on the forests by this period. The foregoing commentary is speculative, but indicates the most probable pattern of events on the basis of our present limited knowledge.

Unsustainable progress: the destruction of the trees

By the end of the imperial period (in round numbers, 1900), most of China Proper had been stripped of the forest cover that three millennia earlier had covered it in almost unbroken succession from the tropical rainforests of the far south to the conifer forests on the northern mountains.[93] The only large forests that remained in areas that were relatively easy of access were in Manchuria, an area mostly debarred to Hahn Chinese inmigration before the middle of the nineteenth century, and which had thus escaped

Chinese-style exploitation. If we had to create a swift characterization of this Chinese style in the last centuries of the empire, it would be in terms of a dynamic but relatively poor society that was constantly driven by population expansion to attempt to master nature in new environments, and which often achieved this in a skilful manner, marked by a patient tenacity, but which in the long run more often than not damaged or even destroyed these environments. And yet, overall, a larger and larger population was supported. This can be seen, according to one's perspective, as either a disaster or a triumph. In central China two thousand years ago it was common to cut down a whole tree in order to fashion a single coffin. In 1983 a ban was placed on using wood for floors, staircases, electricity poles, mine-props, railway sleepers, bridges, and coffins.[94]

Deforestation in China presents a complex historical and geographical pattern which is only partly known and cannot be even summarized here.[95] The process can however be illustrated by two of the most important episodes of the story: (1) the effects of the stripping of trees and the vegetation cover, as the result of economic development, in the middle reaches of the Yellow River[96]—the region, broadly speaking of the loess, a fine yellow aeolian dust—in increasing the sediment load carried by this river, and (2) the consequences of the invasion of the wooded uplands in the eighteenth and early nineteenth centuries by poverty-stricken people who destroyed an enormous, if for the moment unquantifiable, proportion of the remaining forests in order to practise a transient slash-and-burn agriculture that sent fragile topsoils pouring downstream.

Pollen analyses have shown that 5000 years ago the north China plain had a warmer and more humid climate than it has today. It was covered with wetlands and in many places the woods came down to the banks of the river. It should therefore be remembered that natural, climatic effects played an important part in the changes that are about to be described; not every new development was anthropogenic. Regions that are today semi-arid, or even arid, were then substantially wooded. Forests covered about three-quarters of Gansu province, slightly less than half of Shaanxi province, and almost two-thirds of Shanxi. In the plain lower down, Her'nam province was about two-thirds wooded, Shandong province somewhat under half wooded, and Herbeei province more than two-thirds wooded. Erosion is thought to have been slight in this period. The Yellow River was not called "yellow" at the start of the historical era slightly more than three millennia ago, but simply "The River" (*Her* 河); the adjective was added toward the end of the first millennium BC, a time when the *History of the Hahn Dynasty* says that sixty per cent of its water was "mud".[97] (The present-day mean solid content, measured slightly upriver from the mouth of the delta, is just over 25 kg/m^3).

It is no more than a plausible guess at the moment, but the likelihood is that the reason for this change was the policy of promoting the agricultural development of the north-west by the Qin and Hahn dynasties, including forced transfers of population. The grasslands that were the principal vegetation cover of the middle reaches were opened up for farming, and temperate-zone forests in the south-eastern part of this area were cut to satisfy the need for timber created by the great capital cities in the north-west, accelerating erosion.[98] During the last century or so of the first millennium BC the bed of the Yellow River, now enclosed by man-made levees, rose for the first time above the level of the surrounding plain. In the absence of man-made levees, of course, periodic overflowing of the banks would have led to the deposition of sediment outside the main bed as the overflow slowed down and its carrying power was reduced. One of the motives that had led to the techniques required for the creation of these huge embankments during the Warring States period preceding the unification of the empire had been military: several of the states of the plain used them to direct floodwaters across their rivals' territories.[99] The levees of the Warring States period were set back about ten kilometers from the riverbank, in order to provide adequate space for floodwaters, but the *History of the Hahn* tells us that within these levees "the sediments were so rich that the common people cultivated them. It would happen that [for a time] they would suffer no evil consequences, and so they would build houses there, and later these would form villages. When there were large floods, these villages would be drowned, but they would again make new dykes to defend them."[100]

During the great part of the Former and Later Hahn, 186 BC–AD 153, there was approximately one disastrous break in the Yellow River levees every 16 years, with a concentration during the period 66 BC–AD 34 when the frequency was one major break every 9 years.[101] The burden of annual repairs on the ten commanderies along the banks around the year 6 BC was described by Jiaa Yih 賈誼 as "ten thousand ten thousands" (if taken literally, 10^8) copper cash; and he added that "when there are major breaches, countless people die."[102] During the more than 400 years that followed the cessation of population transfers to the north-west and of agricultural colonization c.140, as the weather grew colder, and the frontier between pastoralists and farmers shifted south with the regrowth of a grass and forest cover, the frequency dropped to about one breach in every 50 years.[103] Barbarians were good for the environment.

During the later part of the Northern Weih dynasty 北魏 (c.500), the arablization of parts of the middle reaches recommenced (for example, in Hertaoh 河套 on the north-west corner of the great bend of the river), and then, after the middle of the eighth century, the midpoint of the Tang, the conversion of grazing-lands to cereal cultivation accelerated.[104] During the early part of the Tang dynasty, even with the Chinese becoming re-established in the north-west, the Yellow River continued to be peaceful, but the capital at Charng'an made heavy demands on the area for wood and food, and economic activity intensified.[105] Pressures for development in the north-west gradually intensified, however. Thus, in 788, when Lii Yuarn-liahng 李元諒, the military governor of Loongyouh 隴右 circuit (approximately modern Gansu), was restoring the ruined city of Liarngyuarn 良原,

> the vital territory in the eastern part of the circuit [Loongdong 隴
> 東] was being raided by the [Tibetan] barbarians who regularly
> pastured their horses there and rested their soldiers. Yuarnliahng
> set up warning beacons on mounds some distance away, filled in
> the gaps in the city walls and repaired the parapets. He led his
> soldiers in person, sharing both hard toil and leisure moments
> with them. They felled the forests, mowed the grasses, and cut down
> the thickets, waited until they had dried out and then burned
> them all. Over an area several tens of *lii* square all was farmland,
> beautiful to behold. He urged his soldiers to plant trees and crops;
> and their yearly harvest of millet and vegetables came to several
> hundred thousand *hu*.[106]

During the last 160 years of the Tang, 746–905, however, breaches in the levees along the lower course of the Yellow River happened once every 10 years.[107] During the Five Dynasties and Ten Kingdoms in the first half of the tenth century, it was one every 3.6 years.[108]

During the first phase of the mediaeval economic revolution under the Northern Sohng dynasty, 960–1126, the Yellow River broke its levees with an average frequency of once every 3.3 years.[109] This is an underestimate, as only cases where the breaking of hydraulic defence-works is explicitly stated to have occurred (sometimes in two separate places in a single year) have been included, which has meant leaving out disasters only recorded as severe floods. Official statistics, which should be taken cautiously, state that the worst of these floods, that of 1117, drowned more than a million people.[110] Even if these data are regarded as giving no more than a rough indication of an order of magnitude, it is evident that a mismanaged ecosystem can kill on a colossal scale.

It was also during this period that the river began intermittently to take a course to the sea south of the Shandong peninsula. It divided into two, one branch going north and the other south, towards the end of the twelfth century, and towards the end of the thirteenth century it shifted exclusively to the southern route. From 1324, when the definitive southern course was established, to 1853–55, when it moved north again, the lower Yellow River was, for the purposes of counting the frequency of breaks in the levees, a new river.[111]

In 1420, the Ming moved their capital to Beeijing, and the attack on the forests in the north and north-west intensified as Hahn Chinese populations re-expanded here after a period of abrupt demographic decline under the Mongols. After the middle of the sixteenth century, for example, we read of a county in Shanxi, in the basin of the Fern River 汾水, which empties into the mid-course of the Yellow River, that because of the cutting of the forests, the hills "shone in their nudity". Under the Qing dynasty that followed, the opening up of the loess lands in Gansuh province in the far west of China Proper, and through which the upper part of the middle course flows, is said to have doubled the area under cultivation there between the middle of the seventeenth century and the early nineteenth. According to one analysis, over the more than half a millennium of the river's southern course, the average frequency of breaks in the levees was once every 1.6 years, or close to two in every three years. Another puts the frequency for the period of the Qing dynasty before the course changed (1645–1855) as one disaster ever 1.89 years.[112] By either reckoning, abnormality had become the norm.

The foregoing is a crude sketch that will require extensive refining, including a systematic examination of the different locations on the river at which disasters occurred at different times.[113] Among possible causes other than the stripping of the mid-course vegetation cover and forests it is also necessary to consider changes in hydraulic practice and changes in climatic conditions. For example, the methods of Pan Jihxuhn 潘季馴, the celebrated but probably overrated hydraulic engineer of the late sixteenth century, namely unifying the multiple riverbeds and then constricting the channel in order to accelerate the current and hence increase the scour, were widely admired,[114] and the Yongzhehng emperor in 1729 ordered the implementation of Pan's idea of increasing the height of the dykes by 5 inches each year (not a sensible long-term strategy),[115] and so we should perhaps be careful not to assume that the technology necessarily always improved over time. The transitions from a relatively warmer to a relatively colder climate in (very approximately) the second century of both the first and second millennia AD correlate with *opposite* patterns in the occurrence of disasters in the lower Yellow River (improvement and aggravation respectively), and any simple climatic explanation therefore looks difficult. A study of the period 1471 to 1970, most of it falling within the later 'Little Ice Age', which also affected China, but which may not represent patterns found in earlier historical times, has however shown that in relatively colder winters the climate was drier than average in the west of China and wetter in the east, and that in relatively warm winters this pattern was reversed.[116] This suggests that any effects at work are likely to have been rather subtle and beyond our present power to detect with certainty.

Clearly, though, the historical balance-sheet of the pluses and minuses of north-western agricultural expansion in imperial China has to take into account these hydrological consequences. Simply as an illustration of the kind of costs directly involved—an example chosen simply because there are some figures for it, and not because it was of any special importance—consider the dredging of deposited sediments and the new dyking that had to be done in 1606 at Xurzhou 徐州, where the Grand Canal—supply artery for the capital—crossed the Yellow River, to keep the crossing workable. Half a million men had to be conscripted to work for six months, and the state had to pay 0.8 million ounces of silver. This was not routine, but it was not exceptional for large-scale intermittent maintenance.[117]

The second of our examples, the late-imperial forest holocaust, is a major part of the explanation of why, today, China's reserves of wood per person are about one-eighth of the world average.[118] This process was a long-term one, but it reached its premodern peak under the Qing dynasty in the last two centuries of the empire. An acute conflict had gradually developed between the needs of short-term economic survival and long-term environmental protection. Fahn Cherngdah 范成大 of the Sohng dynasty says in the preface to his poem on the cultivation of dry fields recently opened for farming:

These newly-assarted fields are lands in the defiles between the hills and they have to be ploughed by the blade [of the axe] and then burned before the seeds are sown. At the start of spring people fell a multitude of trees in these mountains until they have all been brought low. When the time comes for sowing, they wait until it is rainy weather; then, on the day before sowing, they burn [the fields] so as to use the cinders as fertilizer. The following day, when it is raining, they use the prepared soil to plant their seeds, and thus the shoots flourish and the yields are doubled. If no rain falls, the opposite occurs. The mountains are by and large of a low fertility, and the soils have little strength. ...[119]

In the same fashion a monograph on the local products of the province of Hur'narn published in 1840 says:

Between the River Yuarn 沅 and the River Xiang 湘 there are many mountains. People only grow millet there, and many of them live on the ridges or buttes. Every time they want to sow grain broadcast they first cut down the trees and make a general conflagration. They wait till the wood has become ashes and then sow in these latter. In this way the yields of their harvests are doubled. This is what the history-books call 'ploughing with the blade [of the axe] and sowing in fire.[120]

Clearing the hill-slopes for farming, followed by setting fire to any small trees that remained, had a harmful effect on the hydraulic systems downstream, as may be seen by reading a letter written by Meir Boryarn 梅伯言

(1786–1856) about the 'shed people' (*perngmirn* 棚民) or migrant squatters and settlers in the uplands south of the Yarngzii valley:

When the late Doong Wenkeh [董文格] was governor of Anhui province he wrote a memorial ... on the opening up of the mountains by the shed people. The thrust of his argument was that all those who had attacked the shed people were steeped in geomantic theories [*lorngmaih fengshuui zhi shuo* 龍脈風水之說] to the point that they let the riches in several hundred *moou* [畝] or so of mountains run to waste, and neglected to behave in the normal and proper manner, in order to safeguard land harbouring a single coffin [fearing to damage the occult forces thought to run through the earth]. The shed people were nevertheless capable of confronting difficulties and being content with insipid food in the high mountains and places that but rarely saw any traces of human beings. They knew how to assart and sow dry-field cereals in such a way as to supplement rice and sorghum. Not one of them was lazy, and the land gave forth all its benefits to them. [Encouraging them] was an appropriate policy and it was wrong to put obstacles in their way with prohibitions, which gave rise to quarrels.

When I read what he had to say, I thought he was right, but when I went to Xuancheng 宣城 [near Wurhur 蕪湖 in Anhui] and asked the country people [about this question], they all of them said that when the mountains had not been developed the soil had held firmly in place and the stones had not budged. The covering of plants and trees had been thick and abundant, and that after the rotting leaves had been heaped up for a few years they might reach a depth of two or three inches. Every day the rain passed from the trees to these leaves, and from these leaves into the soil and the rocks. It passed through the cracks in the rocks and drop by drop turned into springs. Downstream, the rivers flowed slowly. What was more, the water came down without bringing the soil along with it. When the rivers flowed slowly, the low-lying fields received their water without suffering from disaster. Furthermore, even after half a month without rain, the fields lying high up still obtained an influx of water.

These days, people used their axes to deforest the mountains. They employed hoes and ploughs to destroy the coherence of the soils. Even before a shower of rain had come to an end, the sands and gravels were coming downstream in its wake. The swift currents filled up the depressions. The narrow gorges were full to the brim, and could not retain the mud-filled water, which did not stop until it reached the lowest-lying fields where it was then stagnant. These low-lying fields became completely filled, but the water did not continue to flow in the fields up in the mountains. This was opening the sterile soils [*buh maor zhi tuu* 不毛之土] for farming, and damaging the fields where the cereals grew; and profiting 'servants' who did not pay taxes [*wur shuih zhi yong* 無稅之傭, or, more exactly, squatters on others' lands], and impoverishing [registered] households who did pay taxes.

I also listened to their words and found them to be correct. It has—alas!—always been impossible for benefit and harm to be either one of them unmixed.[121]

The practical understanding of the environment on the part of the peasants with the permanent fields downstream was well-developed, and there is at least one detailed description in an agricultural treatise of the early nineteenth century, Bao Shihchern's 包世臣 *Qirmirn sih-shu* 齊民四書 [Four arts needed for the governance of the people], of how to limit the loss of soil fertility in mountain lands by means of contoured ditches, the retention of a cap of unfarmed land at the top of each slope, and careful crop rotation.[122] The environmental destruction was not, basically, due to ignorance but to short-term economic pressures. A mobile and fragmented population of cultivators with little or no security of tenure could not afford to take long-term consequences into consideration. Growing trees for timber, fuel, fruit, lacquer, and oil, and bamboos for the markets, was in principle quite profitable, but only a practical option for those with secure property rights, and the financial reserves to cover the long period of maturation, to absorb partial losses due to fire, and to defend themselves against robbery and threats to ownership in the law-courts. Thus, once again, the structure of power in the society, here in the form of the pattern of land-tenure, shaped the pattern of decision-making that had immediate effects on the environment. It should be noted, though, that owners of large tracts of hill-lands were often attracted by the quick gains to be made from leasing allotments to farmers as opposed to the long-term gains of prudent silvicultural management. Silvicultural contracts were only given to tenants for the quickest-growing trees, such as *Cunninghamia* and *Pinus massonia*, which on good soils can be profitably cut after twenty to thirty years, though up to fifty may be needed on the poorest land.

The mountain soils of the provinces of Zherjiang, Anhui, and Jiangxi are mostly very acid (pH ~ 4 in modern times), with an annual rainfall that ranges from 1000mm to 2000mm, with a marked seasonal concentration in spring and summer. This acidity could only be tolerated by sweet potatoes, ordinary potatoes, and peanuts, which were first imported into coastal China from the New World around the end of the sixteenth century and then spread inland. The subsequent opening up of these mountains led to the destruction of the layer of humus, a complicated substance composed of the products of the mineralization and humification of organic residues, with a consequent reduction in the capacity of the soil to retain water. Podsolization occurred—that is, the formation of a hard layer in the sub-soil composed of leached-down minerals. There are also references to soils becoming "hard and red," which was presumably what is (loosely) called 'laterization', a process which leaves soil high in oxides of iron and aluminium, and with a shortage of accessible phosphates. Alternatively, what may have occurred was the stripping away of the thin humus layer to reveal the lateritic sub-soil that already existed beneath.[123] When soils were ruined, the hill-farmers just moved on. The consequences downstream were irrigation systems and fields covered with the largely infertile deposits that had followed the initial fertile topsoil layer, and often a reported rise in the price of firewood.[124]

A lament for loss of an ecosystem can be found in the local history of Yuhshan 玉山, which lies on the frontiers between the provinces of Zherjiang and Jiangxi in the south-east:

> The rural districts to the north-west [once] produced *Cunninghamia* [*shan/sha* 杉] in abundance. During the Yongzhehng reign [in the second quarter of the eighteenth century] the places opened up near to the mountains, moreover, furnished the city of Harngzhou [with wood]. Recently the population has grown, and the fertility of the soil has become exhausted. Nowhere do they wait [now] till the trees that remain have reached a hand's span in girth before the axes resound *zheng! zheng!* Only old *Liquidambar* trees [*feng* 楓], if they are useless, are to be found in association with places shaded over by pines and camphor-trees [*zhang* 樟], growing with them to old age in the recesses of the mountains. ...
>
> Old farmers say that at the beginning of the Qianlorng reign [1736], when people were opening up the mountains of Huair and Yuhshan, trees grew there in abundance, the thickets of bamboos were dense, and herds of deer wandered by or rested at the side of the paths. Pheasants and hares were everywhere in the mountains, and could be caught without difficulty. Mandarin ducks and egrets [*luh* 鷺] frequently flew back and forth along the margins of Stone Drum Creek. Human beings and animals were used to one another, and paid each other no attention, though, on the other hand, wild boars, 'field pigs' [*tiamzhu* 田豬], bears, black bears [*goouxiong* 狗熊 = *Ursus tibetanus*] and other, unknown, wild beasts, often did harm. Recently bamboos and trees have been ever more widely cleared, and human settlement grown denser. The wild beasts have not waited to be driven away, but have departed of their own accord.[125]

Dreams of a better age, gilded by nostalgia, no doubt; but too many tales from around the world tell a somewhat similar story for it to be simply dismissed out of hand.[126]

By the last few centuries of the empire there were many regions where the only oases of forest were those of sacred sites or around monasteries. The traveller Xur Xiarkeh 徐霞客 (1586–1641) left the following account of the countryside around Mount Taihher 太和山, a Daoist peak in south-eastern Shaanxi:

> Rocky walls surround Mount Huar 華山 on all sides, and it is for this reason that there are no [trees with] lofty branches or more than commonplace trunks on the lower slopes of the peaks. When one reaches the summit however, there are pines and cypresses [*song bor* 松柏] many of which would require three persons to encompass [with their arms]. ... As to Taihher the mountains surround it on all sides. Dense forests stretch for a hundred *lit* [~ 60 kilometers]. They make the sun disappear, they reach the sky. Ten kilometers or so away from the mountain there are strange pines and ancient cypresses so vast that several persons would be needed to put their arms around them. They extend across all the valleys, The reason for this is the prohibitions imposed by the state [*guorjihn* 國禁]. [In contrast] among the peaks of Song 嵩 and Shaoh 少 [in the province of Her'narn] one sees no trace [of forests] from the plains and foothills right up to the ultimate summits, because of the felling and cutting of firewood.[127]

It is noteworthy that Xur, familiar with so much of China, should have thought Taihher's forests worthy of comment.

The foregoing has merely sketched a picture, not proven a case, but it seems a reasonable working hypothesis that this endless quarrying of resources, driven by population growth, could not have been safely or successfully prolonged—at the late-imperial level of technology—indefinitely. Hence one of the justifications for my title.

Unsustainable progress: hydraulic lock-in and limited water-supply

It was not possible to double-track the Grand Canal. Nor to increase the size of the boats that travelled on it. The reason for this was an insufficiency of water with an acceptably low sediment load in certain places along the route that it took in Mirng and Qing times from Hamgzhou in the south-east to just outside of Beeijing in the north-east. Where the Canal crossed the western flanks of the Shandong hills, it went north up a staircase of 27 (later 38[128]) locks to the summit at Narnwahng 南旺, where there was also a storage reservoir, and then down a staircase of 21 locks to Lirnqing 臨清. As the system had evolved by 1503 it was mainly controlled by the Daih Village Barrage 戴村埧 on the Wehn River 汶河 in the hills above Narnwahng. The low discharge of winter and spring water had all to be directed into the Canal, because it was relatively sediment-free, but the higher summer discharge, with its heavy load of sediment that would quickly have clogged the waterway, had to be deflected into an alternative channel, the Kaan River 坎河, that descended directly to the sea. This was done by building a spillway across the mouth of the Kaan at an appropriate height. At the same time, it was necessary, when the flotilla of ships carrying the tax rice was on its way north (usually in late summer and early autumn) temporarily to direct all available water into the Canal, in order to ensure that they did not ground. This was achieved by building a temporary dyke each year across the entrance to the Kaan, and then demolishing it as soon as its work was done. This required a heavy and continuous input of labour and money. The situation was complicated by the tendency of the Wehn to shift its course entirely to the Kaan, and an embankment had to be built downstream of the spillway to prevent this.[129] Thus the Canal was not fully operational all the year every year, and as there was not enough water here to use pound-locks with opening gates (a technique first invented in Sohng China[130]), because a substantial amount of water is flushed down every time a vessel passes through one, simple closed cross-dykes had to be used here, and the boats hauled over ramps alongside them to get past. The Canal, one of the key technological foundations of the unity of the empire, since it linked southern resources with northern defences, and hence—one might say—held the empire together with engineering, had reached the limits of its possible expansion long before the end of the imperial period. For basically environmental reasons.

This example can be taken to symbolize the distinctive combination of impressive premodern economic potential, since inland water transport is remarkably cheap in terms of cost per kilometer-ton, and of environmentally conditioned long-term limitations, that was inherent in the water-based economy that underpinned the most economically advanced parts of later traditional China. The historical creation of many Chinese functional regions was due primarily to the mastery of hydraulic techniques, especially drainage of wetlands, river-levee and seawall defences against floods and tidal incursions, a variety of types of hydraulic system supporting high-yielding wet-field rice agriculture to sustain dense concentrations of population, cheap water transport to enable trading centres to access large marketing areas (in approximate terms, radii > 100 km), and systems of urban water-supply and sewerage to service large urban concentrations (populations $\sim 10^5$). A 'functional region' may be defined, following G. W. Skinner,[131] as a space within which the frequency of human interactions and transactions—commercial, political, social, and intellectual—is markedly higher than with the immediately neighbouring spaces. The functional regions of China were not in general (*pace* Professor Skinner) physiographically given, but *created*, the most striking example being that of Jiangnarn, the Chinese Holland, which 1500 years ago was little more than a vast saltmarsh ringed by settlements on the alluvial fans at the feet of the surrounding mountains. It is impossible to understand the economic history of China without an understanding of hydrology and hydraulics.

At the heart of historical Chinese hydraulic systems there was a paradoxical combination of increased stability and increased instability. The paradox can be explained in the following way. The central fact of the environment of northern and central China is the variability of the weather, and the natural disasters that arise from this variability. As a result it is difficult to stabilize agricultural yields. In so far, therefore, as farming serves as the fiscal basis of the state, instability of agricultural yields makes state revenues, whether taxes or corvées, unstable in turn. Hydraulic installations functioned, in the phrase used in the early first millennium AD, as reliable "artificial clouds and rains."[132] For about four hundred years following the end of the Hahn dynasty early in the third century, for example, a period studied in detail by Sakuma Kichiya, the majority of the hydraulic systems that appeared were created and run by the state, its generals, or its bureaucrats, often with the explicit intention of improving logistic capacity and stabilizing revenues. An example is the renovation in 444 of the dried-up Official Canal 官渠 in Nimgxiah, where the Yellow River turns from a northerly to an easterly direction. Diao Yong 刁雍, the Northern Weih official who proposed this project, explained his motives as follows:

> If we think of the farmers, although they still live on the lands around the Official Canal, they are not able to grow any great quantity of crops because it lacks the water for them to do so. Long before my arrival they were failing to pay their taxes in full. There are many soldiers here, all of them either famished or inadequately nourished. ... If we wish to look after the interests of the commoners, and assure that the state is well supplied with resources, we need a large quantity of arable land. Since there is a shortage of rain in this region, we must meet this problem by diverting [a part of] the Yellow River.[133]

He is said to have succeeded in irrigating about four million *moou*, or rather less than a quarter of a million hectares. Thus, agricultural, demographic, fiscal, and military stabilization; but probably only for a limited time. The reason that the Official Canal had earlier dried up seems to have been a gradual change in the relative heights of the Yellow River and the distribution channels.

> When I examined the old canal and its embankments, it was clearly a work of high antiquity, and not of recent date. ... [Hills] had been cut through to make a passage for the [water from the] Yellow River. On both banks they had constructed large channels more than 10 paces wide for irrigating the fields. South of the hills, the water was drawn into these channels. I calculated that when they had been built in ancient times [their beds] were only 10 feet above [that of] the water [coming from the Yellow River]. The waters of the Yellow River [at that time] had moved swiftly through them and carried away the sediment. Today [the beds of] these channels are 23 feet above [the bed of] the water from the Yellow River. What is more, when the water from the Yellow River does gradually make its way in, it often loses its momentum [lit. "subsides suddenly"—*bengtuir* 崩隤]. The channels and the irrigated land are now elevated high [above the Yellow River, because of the sediment thus deposited, and the down-cutting of its main course by the river over the centuries], and the water cannot make its way up into them.[134]

Diao cut a new inflow channel from a point higher up than the original one, but it is unlikely that this remedied the inherent long-term hydrological instability, and the need for a heavy burden of maintenance—in perpetuity—if the system was to continue to survive.

An illustration from the Mirng dynasty, about a thousand years later, is a more specific demonstration of this second aspect. According to the local history for the prefecture of Huair'an, where the Grand Canal had to cross the Yellow River (then on a southern course and debouching south of the Shandong peninsula):

> When the transport route was opened for the first time [in other words, in the early fifteenth century for this particular section], the Canal was at a higher level than the Yellow River and the River Huair. For this reason it suffered little damage. ... As the levees along the Yellow River, and the lakes alongside [the Canal, fed by the Huair], grew higher and higher, the Canal was progressively at a lower and lower [relative] level. Since the middle of the Mirng dynasty we have witnessed disasters caused by flows in the reverse direction [i.e., from the rivers into the Canal], to such a degree that there has not been one year when we have not been burdened with the need to clean it out, dredge it, construct [dykes], and block [off these inflows].[135]

In other words, simply preserving the existing situation consumed ever more resources.

During the sixteenth century the Chinese authorities tried to go round the rapids in the Yellow River near Xurzhou and a nearby section of the river that was frequently blocked with silt, by excavating the Jia River 泇河. This succeeded but at the cost of new difficulties. Here is a description of the President of the Minister of Public Works surveying the route:

> He led the public servants with the responsibility for managing the Yellow River up onto the plateaux and down into the swamps in order to calibrate the relative heights. Their route went around the Ge hills, and west of the Xihngyih mountains where the topography of the land is flat over a wide area. To the south of the Zhongxin Canal [a name for the older River Jia before this project] there was a lot of blue stone.[136] He went further south to avoid it and reached a place called Harnzhuang. The terrain here became more and more marshy, and it was possible to cut a path [for the canal]. He thereupon had them dig six boreholes to 'test the pulse'. When they had gone to a depth of several feet they found small stones and gravels, as well as soil with a texture like curdled milk, and which broke into crumbs when raked over with a hoe. ... "These are the soils we need," he said, "for cutting a canal."[137]

The unfortunate hydrological effects only appeared later. The local history for Peirzhou 邳州 made the following comments:

> There is no river greater than the Yellow River, and no river more prone to flooding than the River Yir 沂 [in south Shandong province]. These days the Yellow River flows along the ancient bed of the River Sih 泗 and ever since the River Sih was captured by the change of course by the Yellow River, the River Yir has not flowed out to the south. [In other words, it had become blocked off.]
>
> Since the Jia Canal has been opened, all the rivers in Shandong province have been forced south-eastwards. The River Yirng 營, the River Wuu 武, the [old] Jia, and the River Yir have been cut off at one and the same time. There is a multiplicity of embankments and of locks, and it has been troublesome finding how best to open and close them. [The water] has been obstructed both to the east and the west, and the pulses of the rivers thrown into confusion. ...
>
> Lake Guan ... and Lake Liarnwang near the mouth of the River Yir, and Lake Wahn ... and Lake Zhou and Lake Liur ... have all become silted up as a result of these rivers overflowing into them.

In the downstream section of the River Zhir 直河 no banks or irrigation channels have survived because of the influx of sediment laden currents.

Thus it is that the transport canal [i.e. the Grand Canal] is a sickness of our stomach and heart, while the Yellow River is a robbber who has come into the courtyard of our house. Our stomach and heart are afflicted by choking up, while the courtyard of our house has been thrown into confusion.[138]

Thus stabilization—of the Canal, and hence of the regular delivery of the imperial tribute in grain—and destabilization—of the hydrological régime of much of southern Shandong—went hand in hand.

Local conflicts over who gained and who suffered from the way in which a hydraulic system was operated or restructured were not uncommon. The Lii Canal 李渠, built in 809, and which provided the city of Yuarnzhou 袁州 (perhaps 20,000 to 25,000 inhabitants during the early Sohng) in Jiangxi province with drinking water, water for washing, water for fighting fires, and transportation, was also used for a time upstream of the city to drive watermills, and, at the other end, as a sort of all-purpose sewer. The water-mills were in due course forbidden, as they slowed down the current, and the encroachment by houses eventually made the urban part of the waterway too narrow for boats, while there was a continual battle, necessitating a permanent organization under Canal Chiefs (*qurzhaang* 渠長), to stop people from throwing rubbish and filth in the stream. It was, for example, forbidden to build kitchens or privies that abutted onto the water.[139] In other words, the use of water, as almost always, depended on the distribution of power. Another example, which is interesting as being a sort of zero-sum hydraulic game, is the long-running battle in the middle of the nineteenth century—at times an actual battle, with weapons—in Miaanyarng 沔陽, where the Hahn River debouches into the central Yangzi. The clash was between those who favoured allowing the south side to be flooded during periods of peak discharge by the Hahn, this being the preferred option of the government party, and those, the more populist hydraulic rebels, who favoured flooding the north. The rebels won for a while, and built illegal dykes to protect the south, which thereby enjoyed better harvests.[140]

Dwight Perkins has shown that by the end of the imperial period, suitable possibilities for new irrigation schemes—of course given the existing level of technology—were probably running short in China.[141] To this extent, the old style of growth can be said to have become unsustainable. A less immediately obvious problem, but perhaps of equal importance, was that of premodern technological lock-in. What this amounted to was essentially the committing for an indefinite future of the use of a proportion of income and resources simply for the maintenance of existing hydraulic systems, if the previous investment in construction and maintenance was not to be lost. It would seem that the proportion of income, resources, and organizational capacity required was large, but no systematic quantitative study has been done, and this is, for the time being, an impression only. It is also true that the evolution of an environment could, according to circumstances, either remove the burden, as when the seawards extension of a coast made it unnecessary to maintain old seawalls, or increase it, as when storm surges increased in severity. One can find examples of both in the history of Harngzhou Bay. Technological lock-in is a feature of most large-scale premodern Chinese hydraulic systems, and it seems likely that it pre-empted the use of a significant proportion of the economic surplus that might otherwise have been directed to other ends.

As an illustration of the sort of magnitudes involved, consider the rebuilding of 20,000 feet[142] of seawall in Shahngyur 上虞 county on the south side of Harngzhou Bay in 1347. The foundations required more than 60,000 pinetree trunks of a foot in diameter, presumably because pine-resin offered some protection against rotting, and more than a million cubic feet of stone. This was only on one occasion, though interlocked stone lasted longer than earth, and it was only for on the order of 6 kilometers.[143] The total length of the seawall protecting southern Jiangsu and northern Zherjiang was of the order of 400 kilometers. Repair work on seawalls, often done at the height of summer, is also said to have been responsible for numerous deaths in the labour-force.[144] Bearing in mind that the seawalls were only a part of the total hydraulic system in this area, the overall social cost is unlikely to have been negligible.

Conclusion

The effects of human activities on the environment in China can be seen almost as far back as recorded history in this part of the world (which may be regarded as starting some time not long before or after 1000 BC, depending on how one defines 'history'). They are not intrinsically a modern phenomenon. Already in 276 AD, for example, we find Duh Yuh 杜預 arguing that a substantial part of the irrigation system was environmentally inappropriate overdevelopment:

> Those who maintain waterfields [*shuuitiarn* 水田] find it convenient to "plough by burning and weed by flooding" [*huoogeng shuuinouh* 火耕水耨]. It has always been thus. This operation is, however, only applied to new farmland full of grasses and wild herbs, and located at some distance from where people live. In times past the south-east was only at the beginning of its development, and the human population was sparse. It was for this reason that they found it advantageous to farm by burning. With the continuing

expansion of the population in recent times, and the breaches that occur every year in reservoir barrages and dams, good fields have been turned into reed-swamps, people dwell on the brinks of marshes, dry land and water have lost the characteristics proper to them, [livestock] put out to pasture have died off, and trees have rotted where they stood. Such are the disastrous consequences of reservoir barrages.

If reservoir barrages are numerous, the soil becomes 'thin' [*baor* 薄] and the water 'shallow' [*qiaan* 淺 – lacking in nutrients?], so that floods do not deposit a fertilizing richness. ... A clear edict ought to be issued to the effect that while old reservoir barrages and dams dating from Hahn times, and small private reservoir barrages up in the mountain valleys, should be kept in good order so that they retain their water, all of those constructed since Weih times, and all of those that have broken and flooded because of rain and are full of reeds and *maacharng* grasses,[145] are to be breached and drained.[146]

We should need to know more than we do at present about the effects of the fall in mean annual temperature that was under way at this time before judging how far his position was well-founded, but the call for deinvestment on environmental grounds is noteworthy.

Second, some of the consequences of premodern human activity, though developing at a slow tempo compared to their modern counterparts, were on a huge scale. Long-term deforestation (especially in the eighteenth and nineteenth centuries), and the worsening hydraulic problems of the Yellow River on each new lower course to which it shifted, during periods when the stripping of its mid-course vegetation cover had intensified, and arising from the enclosure of its varying lower courses between levees, are two examples. From the point of view of the local human society these anthropogenic effects contained a complex mixture of benefits and costs that are all but impossible to evaluate overall in any reasonably objective way. In practice, after the end of the archaic period (which varied from region to region but which we may think of as occurring in general about 500 BC) two forces tended to dominate patterns of decision-making that had a major impact on the natural environment: (1) the search for state military and political power through the creation and appropriation of a growing and dependable supply of tax-resources, soldiers, and conscripted labour—especially in the early period; and (2) the pressure of a population growing at an ever-increasing rate—especially in the late period. Both forces can be said, with only slight and obvious qualifications and nuances, to be still at work today.

Third, in several respects the premodern Chinese economy also became 'locked in' to the patterns in which its technology interacted with the environment. This term can be defined by three criteria: (1) the exit costs to different and perhaps ultimately better patterns tend to be high (the inhabitants of an unmaintained polder starve even if they do not drown), (2) further expansion runs, after an initial boom period, into environmentally imposed constraints (limited supplies of water prevent the double-tracking of Grand Canals), and (3) large and often increasing amounts of resources and income have to be devoted to maintaining existing systems if the original investment incurred in creating them is not to be lost (thus seawalls can come under intensified pressure from tides and storm surges). This complex of phenomena has been illustrated from various aspects of the premodern Chinese hydraulic economy, with its massive but perpetually unstable installations, and while these are probably the most striking examples, they are not the only ones that could be given.

While the final premodern incarnation of the late-traditional Chinese farm economy had skills in soil-maintenance, and a per-hectare productivity by premodern means, that rightly impressed pre-World War Two Western agronomists like F. H. King, who were aware of the self-destructive aspects of high-technology Western farming,[147] it should not be romanticized. The overall system was not indefinitely sustainable, chiefly because of its population growth, but also because of what it was doing to its forests and upland soils.

Notes

1 The materials in this essay are drawn from the course of lectures that I delivered in January–March 1993 at the École Normale Supérieure in Paris on "L'histoire de l'environnement en Chine." I should like to thank the then Directeur Adjoint of the ENS, Dr Marianne Bastid-Bnjguière, for her kindness in making available to me this opportunity to crystallize some of my ideas on this subject in interaction with a friendly but critical audience. Steve Dodds prompted the English version with his invitation to deliver a paper at his conference on 'Sustainable Well-Being' at the A.N.U. in July 1993, and I should like also to express my gratitude to him for this challenge. An especial acknowledgement, too, to Samson Rivers (Chiang Yang-ming 江陽明), without whose help in tracking references this work would have been hard to finish. My colleague Dr Su Ninghu 苏宁浒, as always, provided indispensable bibliographic guidance in the domain of Chinese scientific literature and professional help with the hydrology, and my debt to him is evident and substantial.

The present version of this paper was the basis of the Annual Lecture of the Centre for Modern Chinese Studies at St Antony's College, Oxford, delivered 11 May 1994.

[...]

2 A term introduced and justified in M. Elvin, *The pattern of the Chinese past* (Stanford: Stanford University Press, 1973), pt 2.

3 For example, that portion of the Yueh (or 'Viet') people who lived in what is now southern Zherjiang and Furjiahn on the south-east coast.

4 The wet-field cultivation of rice may go back to the Neolithic (c.4000 BC) in places like the southern shore of Hamgzhou Bay (Zherjiang) in what is now 'China'. See Wur Weirtarng 吳維棠, "Comg Xinshirqih-shirdaih wernhuah yirzhii kahn Hamgzhou-wan liaang-ahn-de Quarnxin-shih guu dihlii" [The Holocene palaeo-geography of both shores of Hamgzhou Bay reconstructed on the basis of Neolithic cultural remains], *Dihlii xuerbaoh* 38.2 (June 1983), pp. 124–25.

5 E. Rawski, *Education and popular literacy in Ch'ing China* (Ann Arbor, Mich.: University of Michigan Press, 1979), pp. 140ff., has estimated that by late-imperial times perhaps 30% to 45% of adult males had some degree of useful literacy, and 2% to 10% of the women. 'Literacy' in a Chinese cultural context cannot be sensibly defined in an 'either/or' fashion, but only in terms of a place on an extended range that ran from keeping accounts and reading almanacs at one end to the mastery of a tersely elliptical high literary style packed with historical and literary allusions at the other.

6 A term introduced and justified in M. Elvin, "Chinese cities since the Sung dynasty," in *Towns in societies*, ed. P. Abrams and E. A. Wrigley (Cambridge: Cambridge University Press, 1978), pp. 81–82.

7 The correct historical name for the region that has become, in the present century, the so-called 'Three North-eastem Provinces' of China, but which was, aside from the valley of the river Liaor, barred to Hahn Chinese migration by the Manchu rulers until the later half of the nineteenth century.

8 See, for example, J. L. Buck, *Land utilization in China* (1937; reprint ed., New York: Paragon, 1964), p. 226, which shows China, as of 1929–33 and agriculturally still unmodernized, significantly surpassed in average per-hectare rice yields only by Italy (where its cultivation was restricted to highly favourable areas), though Chinese wheat yields per hectare were only half of those in Great Britain at this time.

9 For the core of the first industrial revolution, the engineering and machine-building industry, the two volumes of historical materials, Shahnghaai-shih Gong-shang Xirngzhehng Guaanlii-jur, and Shahnghaai-shih Dih-yi Ji-diahn Gongyeh-jur, eds, *Shahngbaai mirnzur jiqib gongyeh* [The Chinese non-governmental machine-building industry in Shahnghaai] (Beeijing: Zhonghuar Shujur, 1979), provide documentary proof that Chinese-owned and Chinese-managed enterprises in Shahnghaai had mastered all but a handful of the technologies then necessary for a modern economy (the exceptions being sectors like aviation) by the time of the outbreak of the Pacific War in mid-1937.

10 See the summary, Chu Ko-chen [Zhur Keezhen], "How China's climate has changed over 5,000 Years," *China Reconstructs* 22.9 (Sept. 1973). The Chinese-language original is idem, "Zhongguor jihn wuuqian-niam-lair qihhouh biahnqian-de chubuh yamjiuh" [Preliminary investigations into the changes in China's climate during the last 5000 years], *Kaaoguu xuerbaoh* 1 (1972). Zhur's methods, which are basically phenological (i.e. the analyis of the recorded chronological variations in the ranges and seasons of key marker plants and birds and animals), are described in Zhur Keezhen and Yuan Miinweih 宛敏渭, *Wuhhouh-xuer* [Phenology] (Beeijing: Kehxuer Chubaansheh, 1973). Some more recent studies of Chinese historical weather patterns are summarized in R. S. Bradley, *Quaternary paleoclimatology. Methods of paleoclimatic reconstruction* (Boston: Unwin Hyman, 1985), ch.11, *passim*.

11 Eduard Salmanovich Kulpin, *Chelovek i priroda v Kitae* [Man and nature in China] (Moscow: Nauka, 1990), pp. 37–41, 196. I am grateful to Dr John Fincher for most kindly bringing a copy of this book back from Russia for me.

This warm, moist phase should be seen in the context of the longer-term changes described in Wur Chem 吳忱 *Huarbeei pirngyuam sihwahn-niam-lair zihran huarnjihng yaanbiahn* [Changes in the natural environment of the North-China plain over the last 40,000 years] (Beeijing: Zhongguor Kexuer Jihshur Chubaanshe, 1992), esp. pp. 105–14. I should like to thank Dr lai Chi-kong for the gift of this book.

12 Calculations from the figures given by Xur Haailiahng 徐海亮, "Huamgher xiah-your-de duiji lihshii fazhaan qushih" [The history and trend of develop-ment of the sedimentary deposits in the lower reaches of the Yellow River], *Zhongguor shuuilib xuerbaoh* 7 (1990) indicate that for the period 1194–1855 the total vertical accretion of deposited sediment at the mouth of the southern course was 9.88 meters. On the horizontal seaward extension of some 90 km during this period see Yeh Qingchao 叶青超, "Shihluhn Subeei feih-Huamgher sanjiaao-zhou-de fayuh" [On the development of the abandoned Yellow River delta in northern Jiangsu province], *Dihlih xuerbaoh* 41.2 (June 1986).

13 For a preliminary orientation see the map on p. 66 of Naval Intelligence Division [U.K.], *China proper* (Edinburgh: HMSO, 1945), vol. 3.

14 See the comments by the Jesuits resident in Beeijing in north China in the eighteenth century, translated by M. Elvin, "The technology of farming in late-traditional China," in *The Chinese agricultural economy*, ed. R. Barker and R. Sinha (Boulder, Col.: Westview Press, 1982), pp. 14–15.

15 The concept of property in late-imperial China was not that distant from the modern West European concept, in that it was individual (with a certain familistic bias) and commercialized, though with a slightly stronger emphasis on the right to a particular technologically defined usage of a natural resource. Hence fishing with nets and with cormorants in the same given body of water might be quite distinct rights of property, and sold and bought separately. See Terada Hiroaki 寺田浩明, "Chūgoku kinsei niokeru shizen no ryōyū" [The ownership of nature in China in post-mediaeval times], in *Rekishi ni okeru shizen* [Nature in history], ed. Gotō Akira 後藤明 et al. (Tokyo: Iwanami, 1989). Mongol nomadic stock-rearing, in contrast, was founded on the interlocking non-alienable usage rights of kin-groups. See Yoshida Jun'ichi 吉田順一, "Yūbokumin ni totte no shizen no ryōyū" [The ownership of nature among nomads], in the same volume. I would like to thank Professor Shiba Yoshinobu 斯波義信 for his kind gift of a copy of this book.

16 A short overview may be found in M. Elvin, "On water control and manage-ment during the Ming and Ch'ing periods, " in *Ch'ing-shih wen-l'i* 3.3 (Nov. 1975).

17 See, for example, A. O. Osborne, "Barren mountains, raging rivers: The ecolo-gical and social effects of changing land-use on the Lower Yangzi periphery in late-imperial China" (PhD diss., Columbia University, 1989) (Ann Arbor, Mich.: UMI #9020586, 1991).

18 See V. Smil, *The bad earth. Environmental degradation in China* (Armonk, N.Y.: Sharpe, 1984), and He Baochuan, *China on the edge. The crisis of ecology and development* (San Francisco: China Books & Periodicals, 1991).

19 S. J. McGurk, "The economics of water management on the North China plain: water resource policy and planning on the Hai River plain, 1985" (PhD diss., Stanford University, 1989) (Ann Arbor, Mich.: UMI #9017888, 1991).

20 Yuam Qinglim 袁清林, compiler, *Zhong-guorhuarnjiing baaohuh shiibuah* [His-torical discussion of the conservation of nature in China] (Beeijing: Zhongguor Huanjiing Kehxuer Chubaansheh, 1990), pp. 244–51. I am grateful to Professor

Juju C. S. Wang 王俊秀教授 of the National Tsing Hua University for kindly making a copy of this scarce book available to me.

21 L. Stryer, *Molecular design of life* (New York: Freeman, 1988). The best one-page summary is on p. 10 of A. G. Cairns-Smith, *Genetic takeover and the mineral origins of life* (Cambridge: Cambridge University Press, 1982).

22 See, for example, W. H. Schlesinger, *Biogeochemistry. An analysis of global change* (San Diego: Academic Press, 1991), pp. 147–52, 169–80, 324–31; and P. Westbroek, *Life as a geological force* (1991; paperback ed., New York: Norton, 1992), pp. 137–46, 224–27.

23 C. J. Krebs, *Ecology. The experimental analysis of distribution and abundance*, 3rd ed. (New York: Harper Collins, 1985), pt 4, pp. 435–702.

24 As E. Goldsmith, a great pioneer, nonetheless tends to do in his *The way. An ecological world-view* (London: Rider, 1992).

25 Schlesinger, *Biogeochemistry*, pp. 317–18.

26 G. Tortora, B. Funke, and C. Case, *Microbiology. An introduction* (Redwood City, Calif: Benjamin/Cummings, 1989), pp. 568–69, 677. There is a detailed account of the nature of schistosomiasis and methods for its prevention in China (notably by the treatment of human sewage) in Zherjiang-sheeng jihsheng-bihng fangzhii bianxieezuu, ed. *Jihshengchoeng-bihng-defarngzhii* 寄生虫病的防止 [The prevention of parasite diseases] (Shahnghai: Rernmin Chubaan-sheh, 1972), ch. 1. The provinces principally affected are Jiangsu, Zherjiang, Anhui, Jiangxi, Hurbeei, and Guaangdong.

27 Schlesinger, *Biogeochemistry*, pp. 114–40, esp. 125–26.

28 H. Chamayou et J-P. Legros, *Les bases physiques, chimiques et minéralogiques de la science du sol* (Paris: Presses Universitaires de France, 1989), p. 8. This dividing-line at 2µ is taken to demarcate the finer particles as a fraction with relatively greater chemical activity related to their higher surface/volume ratio. Other authorities place the limit at slightly different points.

29 Schlesinger, *Biogeochemistry*, pp. 102–4.

30 Jared Diamond, *The rise and fall of the third chimpanzee* (London: Vintage, 1991), pp. 163–72, esp. 168–69 and 218–21.

31 P. W. Ewald, "The evolution of virulence," *Scientific American* 268.4 (April 1993).

32 C. Metcalf, "A history of tuberculosis," in *A century of tuberculosis. South African perspectives*, ed. H. M. Coovadia and S. R. Benatar (Cape Town: Oxford University Press, 1991), p. 2. Dr Zhang Yixia 張宜霞, however, kindly pointed out to me that New World tuberculosis may predate the introduction of cattle, citing M. J. Allison et al., "Documentation of a case of tuberculosis in pre-Columbian America," *American Journal of Respiratory Diseases* 107 (1973).

33 See the comments of R. Sallares in his *The ecology of the ancient Greek world* (London: Duckworth, 1991), pp. 287–90.

34 M. Feshbach and A. Friendly, *Ecocide in the USSR. Health and nature under siege* (London: Aurum, 1992), document the important negative health impact of many aspects of Soviet economic growth. I would like to thank Dr Paul Monk for drawing this book to my attention.

35 R. Repetto, "Accounting for environmental assets," *Scientific American* (June, 1992).

36 Midas was a king of Phrygia to whom legend attributed the power of turning everything he touched to gold, including his daughter.

37 On most of these points see J. R. Krebs and N. B. Davies, *An introduction to behavioural ecology*, 2nd ed. (Oxford: Blackwell Scientific Publications, 1987).

38 Schlesinger, *Biogeochemistry*, pp. 349–50.

39 M. I. L'vovich, G. White, et al., "Use and transformation of terrestrial water systems," in *The earth as transformed by human action*, ed. B. L Turner et al. (Cambridge; Cambridge University Press, 1990), pp. 237, 248.

40 See M. Elvin, "Was there a transcendental breakthrough in China?", in *The origins and diversity of the Axial Age*, ed. S. N. Eisenstadt (Albany, N.Y.: State University Press of New York, 1986), pp. 325–31.

41 A characteristic example of Chinese moral meteorology is that in the *Shir-chaor shehngxubn* 十朝聖訓 [Sacred instructions of ten reigns] issued by the Qing emperors, where we find in *Dah-Qing Shih-zong Xiahn-huarngdih shehngxuhn*, *j.*8, 'Jihng Tian 敬天' [Respecting Heaven], page 8a, the Yongzhehng Emperor noting that in the spring of 1729 all the districts in Zhirlih [present-day Herbeei province] had enjoyed a fall of "auspicious snow," with three exceptions. This lack of snow was 'explained' by a quarrel that had been going on for more than thirty years between locals in this area over the use of the water from the old Huihmirn Channel, which irrigated on the order of 2000 hectares. A high official had now inspected the channel and adjured the people to respect the imperial exhortation to reform themselves. Overwhelmed by imperial compassion, said this official, they had "forthwith come to their senses, shared out [the water from] the channel and irrigated [the land] together, forever putting their quarrels to rest." On the 12th day of the 3rd lunar month there had been "repeated falls of auspicious snow, covering the ground more than a foot deep, so that the spring plowing will have [moisture] to depend upon." The emperor observed that "there really does exist an ultimate pattern-principle whereby Heaven-Nature [*tian* 天] and humans mutually affect each other, for that which constitutes the heart-mind [*xin* 心] in humans is precisely that which constitutes the heart-mind in Heaven-Nature. If in a particular locality mutual suspicions and dislikes give rise to quarrels and lawsuits, and people's heart-minds are full of an unpeaceful matter-energy, then the matter-energy of Heaven-Nature will also decline or be blocked up in this place."

42 Approximately 21 January to 4 February.

43 *Guoryuu* 國語 [Tales of the various states] (Shahnghaai: Shahnghaai Guujir Chubaansheh, 1978), 2 vols., "Luuyuu," pp. 178–80, paraphrased in Yuam Qinglim, *Conservation of nature,* pp. 107–8. Translation by the present author.

44 For the justification of the use of the term 'state' at this period, see C. Blunden and M. Elvin, *Cultural atlas of China* (Oxford: Phaidon, 1983), p. 61.

45 *Tales of the states*, "Zhouyuu," p. 121, cited in Yuam Qinglim, *Conservation of nature*, p.110. Translation by the present author.

46 When Duke Xiang of the state of Sohng lost the battle of the Hong River in 638 BC because he had chivalrously refused to attack the army of Chuu before they had finished crossing the river and drawn themselves up in position, he replied to criticism by saying that "those who made war in ancient times did not ambush their foes in defiles," and implied that he would not disgrace his imperial ancestors by so doing. To this his realistic minister Zii Yur responded that if an enemy was trapped in a defile, that was a gift from Heaven and to be accepted. Armies were to be used for the state's advantage. In this exchange we can sense the passing of an archaic age when the loss of honour was felt to be more serious than the loss of victory. Zii Yur spoke for the future. *Chun-qiu Zuoo-zhuahn jinzhuh jinyih* 春秋左傳今註今譯 [The Springs and Autumns Annals with the commentary of Zuoo, modern notes and a modern translation] (Tairbeei: Shangwuh Yinshuguaan, 1971), 3 vols, Xigong 22nd year, *shahng*, p. 325.

47 That is, the so-called 'well-field' [*jiingtiarn* 井田] system attributed to archaic China, in which eight families cultivated a central field in common to provide taxes for a feudal lord.

48 *The commentary of Zuoo, zhong*, p. 945. See also F. S. Couvreur, *Tch'ouen Ts'iou et Tso Chuan* [The Springs and Autumns Annals of Luu and the commentary of Zuoo], 3 vols (Herjian-fuu: Mission Press, 1914), 2: 439. Translation adapted by the present author.

49 *Yuehlihng* 月令 [Ordinances for the months], pp. 83–100 in *the Liijib jirsbuo* [The record of the rites, with collected explanations], ed. Chem Haoh (Tairbeei: Shihjieh Shujur, 1969), p. 80.

50 *Ordinances for the months*, p. 87.

51 Ibid., p. 91, and cited in Yuam Qinglim, *Conservation of nature*, p. 113.

52 A suggestion based on an analysis of the contexts in which the oracle-bone form of this character was used by Shirakawa Shizuka 白川靜, *Kakotsubun no sekai* [The world of the oracle-bone script] (Tokyo: Heibonsha, 1971), pp. 204–13.

53 *Ordinances for the months*, p. 91. For the 2nd millennium BC it would be more appropriate to say that the Chinese saw the natural world as permeated by and controlled by spirits. See Shirakawa, *Oracle-bone world*, pp. 41–2, 46–49. *Qih* was a late-archaic and early-classical concept that partly fused with earlier ideas, and partly superseded them. Much of Shang spirit-lore—such as that relating to the phoenix (*fehng* 鳳) as the spirit of the wind (*feng* 風)—was forgotten, garbled, or rationalized by early classical times. See Shirakawa, *Oracle-bone world*, pp. 52–53.

54 E.g., *Ordinances for the months*, p. 84.

55 *Commentary of Zuoo, xiab*, Zhao-gong 20th year, p. 1219, and Couvreur, *Springs and autumns*, 3.323. Yahnzii told the duke: "The trees of the mountains are guarded by the [official known as the] Herngluh 衡鹿; the reeds and rushes of the wetlands are guarded by the [official known as the] *zhoujiao* 舟鮫 the firewood and kindling of the thickets are guarded by the [official known as the] *yurhour* 虞侯, and the salt and the oysters are guarded by the [official known as the] *qirwahng* 祈望." In other words, the ordinary people were barred by State monopolies from access to all of these resources.

56 *Guaanzii* 管子 [The book of Master Guaan], ed. Zhaoh Yohngxiarn (c.1582) (Chamgsha: Shangwuh Yinshuguaan, 1940), "Qingzhohng jii," 3.120, and partially cited in Yuam Qinglim, *Conservation of nature*, p. 118. Translation by the present author.

57 *Master Guaan*, "Xiaaokang," 1.102.

58 *Master Guaan*, "Ba guan," 1.59 and cited in Yuam Qinglim, *Conservation of nature*, pp. 117–18. Translation by the present author.

59 *Master Guaan*, "Ba guan," 1.60, and cited in Yuam Qinglim, *Conservation of nature*, pp. 119–20. Translation by the present author.

60 *Shangjun shu jieeguu dihngbeen* 商君書解詁定本. [Book of the Lord of Shang, definitive edition with explanations], ed. Zhu Shicheh (Beeijing: Guujir Chubaan-sheh, 1956), "Keenlihng," p. 7; also cited in Yoshinami Takashi 好並隆司, "Chūgoku kodai santaku ron no saikentō" [A re-examination of the theories about 'mountains and marshes' in ancient China], in Chūgoku Suiri Shi Kenkyūkai, ed., *Chūgpku suiri shi ronsbū* [A collection of essays on the history of water-control in China] (Tokyo: Kokusho Kankōkai, 1981), p. 11. Translation by the present author.

61 Yoshinami, "Mountains and marshes," p. 12.

62 Taking *yeh* 夜 as *yib/yeh* 掖/腋.

63 *Herjihn* 河禁 = *hejihn* 呵禁 approximately "reprimand and repress".
64 Yummehng Qin-jiaan zheenglii xiaaozuu 云梦秦簡整理小組, "Yurnmehng Qin-jiaan shihwem 2" [Texts of the Qin-dynasty [bamboo] strips from Yummehng, with explanations], in *Wernwuh* 文物 7 (1976). Partially cited in Yuam Qinglim, *Conservation of nature*, p. 169, and Yoshinami, "Mountains and marshes," p. 19. Translation by the present author.
65 Yoshinami, "Mountains and marshes," p. 21, on the basis of Ban Guh 班固, *Hahn shu* 漢書 [History of the Hahn] (Beeijing: Zhonghuar Shujur, 1962), *j.*64 *shahng*, p. 2791: "He did not have under his care any inherited patrimony, but regularly cut firewood to furnish himself with food. He would travel about with the bundled firewood on his back, reciting books from memory." Translation by the present author.
66 *History of the Hahn*, "Wern-dih jih," p. 131, cited in Chem Romg 陳嶸, *Zhongguor sen-lirn shii-liaoh* 中國森林史料 [Historical materials on China's forests] (Beeijing: Xinhua, 1983), p. 19. I am grateful to my colleague Dr Su Ninghu 蘇宁滸 for the gift of a copy of this book. Note the comparable relaxations mentioned for 317 and (?) 323 on p. 23.
67 Yuam Qinglim, *Conservation of nature*, p. 161.
68 Yaor Siliarn 姚思廉 *Liarng shu* [History of the Liang] (Beeijing: Zhonghuar Shujur, 1973), "Wuudih" *shahng*, p. 48; cited in Chem Romg, *Forests*, p.25. Translation by the present author.
69 It is unclear if this was fully implemented. Later, in 713 [721, see below], under the Tarng, Liur Torng 劉彤 proposed to make revenue from "mountains and marshes," more specifically salt, iron, and timber, a major source of state income that would relieve the pressure of taxation on farmers, which tends to imply that it had been, though there may have been local levies. See Liur Xuu 劉昫 et al., ed., *Jiuh Tarngshu* [Old history of the Tarng] (Beeijing: Zhonghuar Shujur), *j.*48, "Shirhuoh," pp. 2106–7. In 728 a "relaxation of the interdicts on dams and wetlands" was proclaimed, which may indicate that prior to this time it had not. See Chem Romg, *Forests*, p. 29. D. Twitchett, *Financial administration under the Tang* (Cambridge: Cambridge University Press, 1963), pp. 50–51, gives the date of Liur's plan as 721 (as does Chem), and notes that it "came to nothing."
70 See *Old Tarng history*, "Zhirguan" *ehr*, p. 1841, and Zeng Gongliahng 曾公亮 et al., ed, *Xin Tarngshu* [New history of the Tarng] (Beeijing: Zhonghuar Shujur), "Baai guan 1," p. 1202, on which see the translation by R. des Rotours, *Traité des fonctionnaires et traité de l'armée* (reprint of 2nd ed.; San Francisco: Chinese Materials Center, 1974), pp. 128–29; also cited in Yuam Qinglim, *Conservation of nature*, pp. 163–64. Only the *Old Tarng History* features the ritual formula: "All gathering, trapping, fishing, and hunting had to be done according to the appropriate season," though the *New Tarng History* says the guardians were "in charge of ... such matters as mountains, marshes, plants, and trees ... and hunting," and forbids cutting trees in spring and autumn.
71 *Yurberng* 虞衡.
72 *Liur Zongyuam* 柳宗元集 [Collected works of Liur Zongyuam] (Tairbeei: Zhong huar Shujur, 1978), *j.*43, "Xirng narn luh 行路難." 2, pp. 1240–41; cited in Yuam Qinglim, *Conservation of nature*, p. 263. I follow the commentary in reading 山孝 as 庨 'grand', 'imposing', hence, in this context, 'deep'.
73 *Master Guaan*, 1, "Jing-yarn," *san*, pp. 7–8.
74 Probably. The question of improvement versus construction is controversial, as is that of how many of the features of the Mim River scheme visible today were added much later. See Tsuruma Kazuyuki 鶴間和幸, "Shōsuikyo Tokōen

Teikokukyo wo tazunete: Shin teikoku no keisei to Senkokuki no san daisuiri jigyō" [A visit to the Zhang River canal, Du River dyke, and Zhehng Guor canal: on the formation of the Qin empire and the three great hydraulic schemes of the Warring States period], *Chūgoku suiri shikenkyū* 17 (1987), pp. 40–41. The numerical data in what follows are all taken from this source.

75 Lii Yuan 李元, *Shuu shuui-jing* [Classic of the rivers of Sihchuan] (1794; reprint ed., Cherngdu: Shuushu-sheh, 1985) 2: 11b. I would like to thank Dr Warren Wan-kuo Sun 孫萬國 for the gift of this book. See also J. Needham (with Wang Ling and Lu Gweidjen). *Science and civilisation in China* (Cambridge: Cambridge University Press, 1971), vol. 4, pt 3, p. 293.

76 H. Chamley, *Sédimentologie* (Paris: Dunod, 1987), p. 142.

77 The illustration in K. Flessel, *Der Huangho und die historische Hydrotechnik in China unter besonderer Berücksichtigung der Nörd-lichen-Sung-Zeit und mit einem Ausblick auf den vergleichbaren Wasserbau in Europa* [The Yellow River and historical hydraulic technology in China with special attention to the Northern Sohng period, together with an overview of comparable hydraulic constructions in Europe] (Tübingen: by the author, 1974), p. 74, shows much longer and narrower "Würste aus Bambusgeflecht."

78 Shuuilih Shuuidiahn Kehxuer Yarnjiuh-yuahn and Wuu-Hahn Shuuilih Diahnlih Xueryuahn, eds, *Zhongguor shuuilih-shii gao* 中國水利史稿 [Draft history of water control in China], 2 of 3 planned vols (Beeijing: Shuuilih Diahnlih Chubaansheh, 1979), 1: 66–70.

79 Needham, *Science and civilisation*, vol. 4, pt. 3, pp. 285–87; Tsuruma, "Three great hydraulic schemes," p. 44; and *Draft history of water-control*, vol. 1, pp. 118–32.

80 Fahn Yeh 范曄, ed., *Houh Hahn shu jirjiee* [History of the Later Hahn Dynasty, with collected explanations] (Tairbeei: Shangwuh Yinshuguaan, 1958), *j.* 49, *liehzhuahn* 39, "Warng Chong, Warng Fuh, Zhohngcharng Toong", p. 1775. Cited in Heh Changqum 賀昌群, *Hahn-Tarng-jian fengjiahn tuudih suooyoou-zhih xirngshih yarnjiuh* [Studies on the formation of land-tenure systems from the Hahn to the Tarng] (Shahnghaai: Shahnghaai Remmim Chubaansheh, 1964), p. 195 (but with reference given to *the History of the Later Hahn, j.* 79); also cited in Elvin, *Pattern*, p. 33. There is a discussion of this passage in E. Balazs, *Chinese civilization and bureaucracy* (New Haven, Conn.: Yale University Press, 1964), p. 219 (where the reference is also to *j.* 79).

81 Chem Shouh 陳壽, ed., *San Guar zhih* [Record of the Three Kingdoms] (Beeijing: Zhonghuar Shujur, 1969), "Weih shu" *j.* 28, "Dehng Aih," pp. 775–76; also cited in Elvin, *Pattern*, pp. 37–38.

82 One *qing* was roughly 4.5 hectares or 11 acres.

83 Farng Xuamlirng 房玄齡 et al., eds, *jihnshu* 晉書 [History of the Jihn dynasty] (Beeijing: Zhonghuar Shujur, 1974), *j.* 51, *liebzhuahn* 21, pp. 1431–32; also cited in Elvin, *Pattern*, pp. 39–40.

84 *History of the jihn, ceh* 5, *j.* 106, p. 2764 ("Shir Jih-lorng shahng"). Also cited in Sakuma Kichiya 佐久間吉也, *Gi-Shin-Nambokuchō suiri shi kenkyū* [Studies on the history of water control in the Weih, Jihn, and Northern and Southern Dynasties] (Tokyo: Kaimei Shoin, 1980), pp. 164, 196.

85 Sheen Yue 沈約, comp., *Sohng shu* [History of the Liur Sohng], reprint ed. (Beeijing, Zhonghuar Shujur, 1974) *j.* 54, "Koong Jihgong … ", pp. 1536–37.

86 Thus Eduard Vermeer comments, for a much later period, in his "The mountain frontier in late imperial China: economic and social developments in the Dabashan," *Toung Pao*, forthcoming 1992, that "all land had been staked out in the Ming or early Qing, and we do not find any communal land rights.

(In actual practice, however, it is probable that the local people had free use of the mountains for cutting grass, and gathering fuel.) All mountain land had become private property." From a proof copy kindly sent to me by Dr Vermeer.

87 Weih Shou 魏收, ed., *Weih shu* [History of the (Northern) Weih dynasty] (Beeijing: Zhonghuar Shujur, 1974), *j. 7 shahng*, p. 157.

88 *Mirngshi* [History of the Mirng], "Shirhuoh zhih", reprinted in *Zhongguor lihdaih shirhuob-zhih zhehngbiahn* [The economic monographs of the successive Chinese dynasties: principal collection] (Tairbeei: Xuerhaai, 1970), 2.937.

89 Yuam Qinglim, *Conservation of nature*, p. 135.

90 *Economic monographs*, vol. 2, p. 939.

91 Yuam Qinglim, *Conservation of nature*, p. 267.

92 Hatada Takashi 旗田巍 *Chūgoku sonraku to kyōdōtai riron* [The Chinese village and the theory of the collectivity] (Tokyo: Iwanami, 1973), esp. ch. 5.

93 S. D. Richardson, *Forests and forestry in China* (Washington, D.C.: Island Press, 1990), pp. 39–85.

94 Richardson, *Forests*, p. 115.

95 Lirn Homgrong 林鸿荣, "Sihchuan guudaih senlim-de biahnqian" [The transformation of Sihchuan's ancient forests], *Norngyeh kaaoguu* 1985.9 and 10, is a preliminary sketch of a single province. He shows how climatic change, replacement growth following logging, partial forest recovery during periods of human economic and demographic decline, the development of commercial silviculture (tea, mulberries, lacquer, fruit-trees, and so on), styles in grave-construction and palace-building that made extravagant use of wood, the demands for fuel for such activities as brine-boiling and metallurgy, and of course the extension of farming as techniques changed (as from mobile slash-and-burn to permanent hill-slope terracing), all interlocked to create a particular pattern. It is noteworthy that as early as Qin/Hahn times the catalpas (*zii* 梓) and cypresses (*bor* 柏) of the upper Mirn River valley were being assembled into rafts and floated down to the Yangzi as "timber easily obtained at slight effort and of an abundant usefulness." Lirn, "Sihchuan's forests," p. 166. Chern Qiaoryih 陈桥驿, "Guudaih Shaohxing dihqu tianram senlim-de pohhuaih (jir qir duih nomgyeh-de yiing-xiaang)" [The destruction of the natural forests of the ancient Shaohxing region and its impact upon agriculture], *Dihlii xuerbaoh* 31.2 (1965) shows how poems can be used to recreate a picture of the trees and fauna of past times in this area, which was the birthplace of Chinese nature-poetry. His later "Lihshii-shahng Zherjiangsheeng-de shandih keenzhir yuu shanlirn pohhuaih" [The place in history of the opening of the hill lands of Zherjiang province and the destruction of the forests], *Zhongguor shehuih kehxuer* 1983.4, is mostly about the introduction of New World crops and (on p. 215) quotes the *Mirngshu* 明書 to the effect that "for the first time people cleared land by burning in the mountains of Zherjiang, and the vegetation and trees on all sides were swept away."

96 The 'middle reaches' may be defined as north-western Shanxi, northern Shaanxi, eastern Gansu, the desert Ordos region, Dongsheng, and the mountainous parts of southern Nimgxiah.

97 Cited in Fujita Katsuhisa 藤田勝久, "Kandai no Kōka shisui kikō" [Flood control measures on the Yellow River under the Han dynasty], *Chūgoku suiri shi kenkyū* 16 (1986), p. 14.

98 Zhongguor Kehxuer-yuahn 'Zhongguor Zihrarn Dihlii' Bianji Weeiyuamhuih, ed., *Zhongguor zihrarn dihlii. Lihshii zihrarn dihlii* 中國自然地理-历史自然地理

[Natural geography of China. Historical natural geography] (Beeijing: Kehxuer Chubaan-sheh, 1982), p. 33.

99 Fujita, "Yellow River under the Hahn," pp. 12–13.

100 Ban Guh, *Hahnshu* [History of the (former) Hahn dynasty], quoting Jiaa Yih, cited in Fujita, "Yellow River under the Hahn," pp. 13–14.

101 Calculated from the table in Fujita, "Yellow River under the Hahn," facing p. 10. I have omitted the floods of AD 107, because they were due to rain.

102 Fujita, "Yellow River under the Hahn," pp. 7, 11.

103 Yuam Qinglim, *Conservation of nature*, p. 72, gives an even lower figure for "the Later Hahn [after Warng Jiing 王景 had controlled the course of the Yellow River in AD 69] to the Suir", namely one breach of a dyke or flood every 125 years.

104 Chinese Academy of Sciences, *Historical natural geography*, p. 33.

105 Yuam Qinglim, *Conservation of nature*, pp. 30, 90–91.

106 *Old Tarng history, j.* 144, p. 3918. Analogous examples may be found in ibid., *j.* 161, p. 4229 (Yamg Yuamqing 楊元卿), and *j.* 177, p. 4609 (Bih Xiam 畢誠).

107 The overall frequency for the entire Tarng dynasty (618–905) is given by Yuam Qinglim, *Conservation of nature*, p. 72, as one disaster every 15.6 years.

108 Yuam Qinglim, *Conservation of nature*, p. 72.

109 Calculated from Itō Hashiko 伊藤敏雄, "Sōdai no Kōka shisui kikō" [The structure of flood control on the Yellow River under the Sohng dynasty], *Chūgoku suiri shi kenkyū* 16 (1986), tables following p. 22.

110 Tuotuo 脫脫 et al., ed., *Sohng shii* [History of the Sohng dynasty], reprint ed. (Beeijing: Zhonghuar Shujur), *j.* 61, "Shuui shahng," p. 1329.

111 The frequency of "breaches and floods" in the "Mongol dynasty" in the thirteenth century and the first half of the fourteenth has been given by Yuam Qinglim, *Conservation of nature*, p. 72, as one every 3.4 years, but this figure is suspect for a number of reasons (such as implicitly starting the dynasty around 1218, when it did not rule China, including floods, and not even applying throughout to the same lower course of the river).

112 Matdsuda Yoshirō 松田吉郎, "Shindai no Kōka shisui kikō" [The structure of flood control on the Yellow River under the Qing dynasty], *Chūgoku suiri shi kenkyū* 16 (1986), pp. 34–40.

113 Sediment yield in the Yellow River above the Sanmern narrows (the terminus of the middle reaches) has risen by 32% since 1949, according to Richardson, *Forests*, p. 235.

114 Critics have however noted that increasing lower-course scour betwen 1578 and 1592 by increasing current velocity caused increased deposition of suspended sediment at the mouth of the river where the current was slowed by its encounter with the sea, hence a reduction of the overall channel gradient and renewed flooding. See Tani Mitsutaka 谷光隆, *Mindai Kakō shi kenkyū* [Studies on the history of the hydraulic works done on the Yellow River during the Mirng dynasty] (Kyoto: Dōhōsha, 1991), p. 392. I am most grateful to Professor Tani for the gift of a copy of his book.

115 Matsuda, "Yellow River under the Qing," p. 38.

116 Zhehng Sizhong 郑斯中, "Woo-guor lihshii shirqi leeng-nuaan niarndaih ganhahn-xirng" [Patterns of dryness in cold and warm decades during the historical period in our country], *Dihlii yarnjiuh* 2.4 (Dec. 1983).

117 Tani Mitsutaka, *Yellow River under the Mirng*, p. 20.

118 Approximately 10 m³ per person in 1991. See He Baochuan, *China on the edge. The crisis of ecology and development* (San Francisco: China Books, 1991), p. 29.

119 Cited in Chem Romg, *Forests*, p. 51.

120 Ibid.

121 Meir Zengliahng 梅曾亮 [Boryarn], *Borjiahn shanfarng wernjir* [Collected works from the Borjiahn Studio] in *Zbonghuar wernshii congshu*, no. 12 (Tairbeei: Jinghuar Shujur, 1968), "Jih perngmirn shih" [A record of matters relating to the shed people]; also cited in Chem Romg, *Forests*, p. 52. There is a slightly different translation in Osborne, "Barren mountains," pp. 18–19.

122 Bao Shihchern 包世臣, *Qirmirn sih-shu* [Four arts needed for the governance of the people], in *idem*, *Anwarsih-zhoong* 安吳四種, *Jihndaih Zhongguor shii-liaoh congkan*, no. 30 (1846; reprint of 1851 revised ed., Tairbeei: Wernhaai Chubaansheh, 1966), pp. 1675–77.

123 Professor W. Holzner (Universität für Bodenkultur), personal communication, 31.12.93.

124 The foregoing paragraphs are largely based on Osborne, "Barren mountains," *passim*.

125 *Yuhshan xiahnzhih* 玉山縣志 [Yuhshan county gazetteer] (1873; reprint ed., Tairbeei: Chemgwern Chubaansheh), "Dihlii zhih," p. 335, also cited, with a slightly different translation, in Osborne, "Barren mountains," pp. 92–93.

126 See, for example, J. R. McNeill, *The mountains of the Mediterranean world* (New York: Cambridge University Press, 1992), pp. 81–82 (Luciana in antiquity).

127 Xur Xiarkeh, *Xur Xiarkeh yourjih* [A record of the travels of Xur Xiarkeh], reprint ed. (Shahnghaai: Guujir Chubaansheh, 1980), *shahng*, pp. 54–55.

128 After the building of the Jia Canal described later in this section early in the seventeenth century.

129 *Draft history of water control in China*, *xiah*, pp. 2–12.

130 Needham, *Science and civilisation*, vol. 4, pt. 3, "Civil engineering and nautics," pp. 350–51.

131 G. W. Skinner, ed, *The city in late imperial China* (Stanford: Stanford University Press, 1978), pp. 211–86.

132 For example, *"yurn-yuu your rern"* 雲雨由人 in Warng Guorweir 王國維, ed., *Shuuijing zhuh-jiaoh* [The corrected annotated *Classic of the rivers*] (Shahnghaai: Shahnghaai Rernmirn Chubaansheh, 1984), *j.* 9, p. 310.

133 *Weih history*, *j.* 38, "Diao Yong, Warng Huihlorng ... ," p.867; also cited in Sakuma Kichiya, *History of water-control*, p. 364.

134 *Weih history*, *j.* 38, p. 867.

135 Tani Mitsutaka, *Yellow River under the Mirng*, p. 17.

136 Not identified. In Australia, engineers' 'bluestone' is a variety of basalt.

137 Tani Mitsutaka, *Yellow River under the Mirng*, p. 165.

138 Ibid., p. 247.

139 Shiba Yoshinobu 斯波義信, *Sōdai Kōnon keizai shi no kenkyū* [Researches on the economic history of Jiangnam] (Tokyo: Tōyō Bunka Kenkyūjo, 1988) pp. 403–22. I am most grateful to Professor Shiba for his gift of this book.

140 Morita Akira 森田明, *Shindai suiri shi kenkyū* [Researches on the history of water-control under the Qing dynasty] (Tokyo: Aki Shobō, 1974), pp. 118–34. There is a summary of this conflict in M. Elvin, "On water control and management during the Ming and Ch'ing periods," *Ch'ing-shih wen-t'i* 3.3 (Nov. 1975), pp. 92–93.

141 D. Perkins, *Agricultural development in China 1368–1968* (Edinburgh: Edinburgh University Press, 1969), pp. 60–65, 333–44.

142 The average Chinese foot (there were many variations by locality and by the purpose for which it was being used) was, very approximately, the same as the English foot.
143 Honda Osamu 本田治, "Sō-Gen jidai Settō no kaitō ni tsuite" [On the seawalls of Zherdong in the Sohng and Yuam periods], *Chūgoku suirishi kenkyū* 9 (1979), p. 12, n. 40.
144 Morita Akira, *Water-control under the Qing*, p. 289.
145 馬腸
146 *History of the Jihn, j. 26*, "Shirhuoh," pp. 788–89.
147 See F. H. King, *Farmers of forty centuries* (London: Cape, 1927).

13

THE PREDATORY TRIBUTE-TAKING STATE

A framework for understanding Russian environmental history

Douglas R. Wiener

Without embracing yet another rigid determinism, it may be proposed that certain forms of political economy leave their own footprints on the physical landscape and bequeath identifiable environmental legacies. At least one scholar has even attempted an ecological "archaeology of colonialism."[1] One problem that the environmental historian seeks to explain is how particular socioeconomic and political orders, through the values, outlook, sense of meaning, and behaviors that flow from their structuring of common sense and everyday life—their internal logics—create particular ranges of choices for decision makers and public actors which then encumber environmental consequences. (Of course, different systems with different logics may also generate similar legacies.) Such logics provide both a comfort zone and a formidable barrier to imaginable alternatives. Not infrequently, existing systems become very durable, reproducing fundamental patterns over long periods because they have succeeded in making the case—often aided by repression or the threat of violence—that their view of "the way things are" is the most realistic one around.

This essay seeks to begin to explain how the natural (and social) landscape of post-Soviet Eurasia arrived at its current, parlous condition. The core of the argument is simple. At least since the Mongol-Tatar invasion of the thirteenth century, and particularly with the rise and expansion of the Muscovite state, and later, the Russian Empire and the USSR, a succession of militarized, predatory tribute-taking regimes have dominated the Eurasian land mass. Whatever they called themselves, the attitudes of these regimes toward the human and nonhuman (natural) resources of Russia have been similar. Unbounded by the rule of law (although constrained somewhat by custom), these regimes saw the population and the land over which they ruled as a trove of resources to be mined for the rulers' purposes.

At times, those purposes have sounded noble: defense of the one true faith; the ingathering of the dispersed Russian ethnos; the creation of a just, classless society; or the engineering of a transition to a "liberal, democratic, free-market society." Nevertheless, high-minded purposes have not over-shadowed the rulers' cold understandings of the prerequisites of maintaining power (although subjectively, many of Russia's rulers probably believed that they were serving noble ends); and in pursuit of these purposes, Russia's rulers have spared neither people nor land.

The cumulative environmental legacy of Russia's regimes is edifying, but hardly heartening. One does not have to subscribe to a special environmental e-mail list such as REDfiles (Russian Environmental Digest) to appreciate the scale of environmental problems in the former Soviet Union. Images of long-standing problems (e.g., European deforestation, the Aral Sea crisis, nuclear and industrial contamination from Murmansk to Sakhalin, and deteriorating levels of public health, with unprecedented modern peacetime demographic decline in Russia) produce a composite impression of a region poisoned by a civilization gone badly awry.[2] Tracing the genealogy of this landscape of risk is important not only for the people of that region but for everyone on the planet. Just as we have all been engulfed by the environmental effects of capitalist "globalization," equally, we all find ourselves downwind or downstream of Chernobyl, Kyshtym, the Novaya Zemlya and Semipalatinsk nuclear test sites, the nuclear dumping in the Arctic and Pacific oceans, and the eroded south Siberian and Kazak steppes.

The situation appears not always to have been so gloomy. On the eve of the first millennium, the Slavs seem to have been a "free" people of the forests. They practiced slash-and-burn agriculture (*liada, podseka*) but also returned to once-cultivated, and subsequently abandoned, fields after suitable intervals to allow the recovery of soil fertility (a practice known as long-fallow agriculture, or *perelog*).[3] Fields could usually be cultivated for four to five years in succession before losing their fertility.[4] They also domesticated livestock, which they pastured in forest clearings. Described by the sixth-century Byzantine commentator Procopius as "living communally, without leaders" and by the Byzantine emperor Maurice as "freedom-loving, bold, and disinclined either to slavery or to submission," the Slavs made their redoubts in the almost impassable forests and swamps along the Dnepr and Dvina basins.[5]

However much importance one ascribes to the Viking invaders from Gotland in the consolidation of the first Eastern Slav state—Kievan Rus'—and the loose federation to which it gave rise, the evidence from the Russian Primary Chronicle (Tale of bygone years) testifies to the significant role of private property, the law and (limited) civic participation in the governance of those societies, among them the commercial republics of Novgorod and Pskov. (The more recently settled northeastern principalities of Vladimir-Suzdal and later Moscow constituted important exceptions.) Those societies were nevertheless certainly capable of exhausting their resources. As the wealth of Novgorod, in particular, was based on the export of forest products, especially pelts, that republic's energetic commercial spirit was unkind to fur bearers; the beaver was hunted out of European Russia and survived precariously on the eastern slopes of the Urals.[6] Nevertheless, the forest cover remained generally intact over Rus', yielding to a park-like mixed forest-steppe landscape only at the southern margins of Slavic settlement. Revealingly, at the time of Iaroslav the Wise (1019–54), forests blanketed 40 percent of the current territory of Ukraine (or twenty-eight million hectares), compared with 14.2 percent today.[7]

The pagan Slavs exempted areas of the forest from use, designating them either as sacred groves or as unclean places. This tradition continued even after the introduction of Christianity in 988, although these areas were now consecrated, following processions into the forest with church banners and icons. Such areas allowed the regeneration of renewable biotic resources of the forest, especially game.[8] Large oaks served as landmarks for travelers and to divide territory: felling such trees occasioned a stiff monetary fine, according to Iaroslav the Wise's law code *Russkaia pravda,* whose writ embraced Kievan Rus'.[9]

After Eurasia was absorbed into the Mongol Empire (the domain of the Golden Horde), the Russian lands evolved in a different direction. During their struggles to liberate themselves from Mongol-Tatar suzerainty (and to subjugate their rival princes), the grand princes of Moscow aggrandized their highly centralized, militarized, authoritarian polity. The commercial republics of Novgorod and Pskov were crushed and ravaged by the early sixteenth century; the grand prince, from the time of Ivan IV ("the Terrible"), was now tsar or caesar (and the successor to the *khan*). All property was subsumed into the tsar's household; the Muscovite state constituted his giant patrimonial demesne. That state had also evolved into a permanent state of belligerence. In his quest to regather the "Russian (Orthodox) lands" lost to the (Roman Catholic) Polish-Lithuanian Commonwealth and to crush neighboring (Lutheran) Livonia and the (Islamic) successor states to the Horde, Ivan IV pursued holy wars on all fronts. To support his vastly expanded military, the tsar granted estates, complete with enserfed peasants, to newly ennobled gentry on condition of service. The obliteration of Russian cities as independent commercial and political centers, a joint legacy of the Mongols and the Muscovite princes, made self-sufficient, serf-powered estates all the more necessary.[10] Society was a hierarchy of power. Gentry were "slaves" (*kholopy*) to the tsar, and enserfed peasants were bondsmen to the gentry. The autarkic, tribute-based Russian economy was coming into being.

The first environmental consequences of the Muscovite militarized service state were not long in coming. Incessant war brought in its train famine and horrific epidemics from the 1550s through the 1570s, with the consequent abandonment of plowland, exacerbated by the mass flight of peasants to the "wild fields" of the forest-steppe and steppe to escape Ivan IV's draconian policies. This flight, in turn, led to a sharp increase in the exploitation of those peasants who remained in, or were returned to, the ambit of the state's control. Increased land-based natural and money rents led peasants to intensify production by eliminating fallow, leading to a rapid loss of soil fertility and to equally devastating famine, political anarchy, and even foreign occupation during the Time of Troubles (1599–1613).[11] However, as Richard Hellie notes, the Muscovite regime did not see any alternative to the hyper-exploitation of its peasantry: "At times of economic dislocation the only means of satisfying the needs of the army, the backbone of which was the middle service class cavalry, seemed to be to limit the movement of the primary producers capable of rendering this support. This understanding was based on an unwillingness to reduce the army to a size the country could afford. Any reduction was impossible, for it would have forced the admission that Russia was indefensible or that its military aspirations were too grandiose."[12]

Russia's rulers understood that their system could function only if they closed all escape routes to their captive labor force; and that tactic in turn propelled further territorial expansion of the state. Yet expansion threatened dilution of the tsarist administration over the increasingly vast imperial territory; in consequence, the peasants and other taxable groups had to be squeezed even more, ad infinitum.

With the defeat of the Kazan and Astrakhan khanates in the 1550s, the Muscovite state expanded southward and eastward while simultaneously prosecuting an on-again, off-again war with the Polish-Lithuanian Commonwealth and Livonia (and later Sweden) in the north and west. In an attempt to secure the southern boundaries against the Crimean Khanate and its patron, the Ottoman Empire, intricate systems of defensive lines (the *zasechnaia cherta*) were constructed from the mid-1500s at the southern edge of the forest and across the forest-steppe: its culminating phase was known as the Belgorod defense line, begun in 1637. Among the most grandiose military projects in history, it included the construction of administrative garrison towns and many hundreds of miles of trenches, palisades, towers, and abatis. These were breached by the Crimean Tatars only once, in 1571, when Moscow was sacked.[13]

As late as the early seventeenth century, an unbroken ocean of grass still stretched from the Danube to Mongolia. Although the various nomadic pastoralist groups that occupied these grasslands were also skilled hunters, neither the steppe vegetation nor the fauna appear to have been noticeably affected by their presence; but we should approach with caution the conclusion that, until the appearance of the Russians, the steppe was "pristine" and untransformed. Indeed, that is the subject of an unresolved debate among ecologists and biogeographers, some of whom assert that without intensive grazing, the fescue-feathergrass assemblage, at least in the northern part of the steppe, would have yielded to a more hydrophilic meadow-type vegetation.[14] Perhaps the major effect that the nomads had on the steppe was burning, especially during wars. Most of the burning of the steppe, though, was done by Russians as a defensive measure, to deprive the nomads' horses of pasture.

By the mid-seventeenth century, the various Cossack federations (Don, Zaporozh'e, Kuban, Iaik) had been deputized by the tsarist state to protect its borders against the nomads. As they penetrated farther south and east into the steppe, they were followed by agriculturalists. Behind this advance the defensive lines, no longer needed by the end of the eighteenth century, remained undeveloped, becoming anomalous dense islands of forest amid agricultural and park-like landscapes. (The Tula abatis was preserved as the Tul'skie Zaseki Zapovednik, or "inviolable" nature reserve, from 1935 to 1951, when it was eliminated by the Stalin regime; the Kaluzhskie Zaseki reserve was established in 1992.) As such they represent one of the few "green" contributions of the Muscovite, tsarist, and Communist periods.

As the rich Black Earth region of the former western steppes in Ukraine and southern Russia became available for cropping, Slavic migrants (future Russians and Ukrainians), organized as serf labor on gentry estates, converted the steppe into a grain basket. Forest islands, especially along steppe rivers and streams, were felled for firewood, construction materials, and shipbuilding, which boomed under the patronage of Peter I ("the Great"). Whatever forest-conservation measures were promulgated by Peter, notably the ban on logging along rivers and in designated forest preserves (1722), were taken solely to ensure sufficient materials for his warships.

By the middle of the eighteenth century, these trends had already had profound effects not only on the vegetation but also on the fauna. Gone were the herds of European bison (*Bison bonasus L.*) and tarpan, or wild horse (the last one died in 1877). The last *tur,* an ancestral form of the domesticated cow, was killed in 1644, and the saiga antelope (*Saiga tatarica*), once found as far west as Moldavia, was driven back east beyond the Don River. The steppe was cleared of beaver (*Castor fiber*) and moose (*Alces alces*) as well. The once-extensive ranges of the greater and lesser bustard (*Otis tarda L.* and *Otis tetrax L.*), common and Demoiselle cranes (*Grus grus L.* and *Anthropoides virgo L.*), and other species of steppe avifauna now contracted to isolated spots. By 880 the Wild Field, as Slavs called the European part of the steppe, was no more.[15] The proportion of cultivated land had increased in the region from 26 percent in 1719 to 66 percent in 1881.[16] This proportion represented just about 100 percent of the *cultivable* land.

The revolution from above of Peter I and his successors also had serious effects on forests throughout European Russia. His wars, first with the Ottomans and then with the Swedes, led to a great expansion of serf-powered iron works, which in turn required vast amounts of charcoal. The world's biggest smelter of iron in the eighteenth century, the Russian iron industry as late as the 1880s was consuming almost twenty million cubic meters of timber annually, when the rest of Europe had converted to coke.[17] Potash, paper, salt production, tar, pitch, turpentine, distilling, domestic heating and home construction, railroads, telegraph poles, coal mine pit-props, and, by the late nineteenth century, a growing timber export trade took an enormous cumulative toll on the forest cover.

The tribute-taking mode of the central government was imitated by all those who held power at the lower levels of authority. Michael Confino's old but classic study of the landed gentry argues that they had the aspirations and attributes of "grand proprietors" but the "mentality of petty exploiters."[18] Permeated by a spirit of mistrust of their peasants (which was reciprocated), the gentry—infused with the logic of tribute—subscribed to a peculiar calculus of value. They confused sales price with profit owing to their failure to account for the cost of peasant labor, which they treated as a free good. Serfdom consigned Russian agriculture to low yields combined with soil exhaustion, as nobles had neither the money to buy the best technologies nor the willingness to entrust complicated machinery to the serfs.[19]

Exploring the logic of gentry estate management, Confino identifies three core impulses: the desire for more income, the unwillingness to make timely investments and the lack of patience to wait for investments to bear yields, and, finally, their desire to preserve serfdom intact.[20] Because improvements could not be permitted to affect the social relations and labor customs of the estate, the gentry retained the persistent hope that the acclimatization of new cultivars would produce quick wealth through an agronomic miracle. Ivan Bolotov even recommended growing cotton in Russia "regardless of region."[21] Although not wantonly cruel for the most part, nobles structured their production and consumption in a way that left little in reserve for bad times. The famine of 1833–34, for example, led to mass deaths of both livestock and peasants. The nobles had to purchase replacement animals, making the estate's margin of viability even more threadbare.[22]

Unable to make their estates financially viable after the loss of their bonded labor following emancipation, many members of the gentry sold off their forests to timber merchants. According to the calculations of M.A. Tsvetkov, forest cover declined in European Russia from 52.7 percent, or 213,416,000 hectares, in 1696 to 35.16 percent, or 172,378,000 hectares, in 1914; some provinces, such as Tver', were almost totally deforested, declining from 75.8 percent forest cover to 22.6 percent over that period.[23] At every level, tribute takers, be they the bureaucratic monarchy in

St. Petersburg, gentry on their estates, or chartered merchants, became dependent on expansion to new areas, on rent-seeking, or on confiscation— even of their own resources—as opposed to becoming more productive, developing new products, and penetrating new markets.

In an important and perceptive study, Jane Costlow notes that some sensitive Russian artists and writers—Nikolai Nekrasov, Il'ya Repin, Leo Tolstoy, Anton Chekhov, Ivan Shishkin, and others—understood the inter- connection between deforestation and what she calls "larger structures of violence and individual tales of shirked responsibility" that characterized the larger society.[24] Repin's *Procession of the Cross in an Oak Wood,* Costlow observes, shows in clear emotional terms that "the *narod* [people, masses] and the trees are both victims of violence, and inhabit a desiccated, near- apocalyptic landscape."[25]

Although some historians of the Russian Empire have suggested that a new pattern finally began to emerge after the revolution of 1905, when Tsar Nicholas II was forced to accept limitations on his powers and the creation of an enfeebled legislature (the Duma), the state continued to use its enor- mous repressive power to maintain the near-servile conditions of labor in the empire's military-industrial complex. An enormous quantity of the accumulated wealth generated by the biological potential of the Russian land and embodied in the tsarist military-industrial complex was squan- dered in World War I; even more was consumed in the resultant social explosion and civil war that engulfed the country.[26]

By perpetuating the tribute-taking state with its short-term objectives, the tsarist empire made itself less secure, not more. Promising, by contrast, a "planned," "rational," and scientific governance, the new Soviet leaders ironically ended up perpetuating the same imperial tribute-taking system, with some interesting, but ultimately unavailing, modifications.

Perhaps the most important of the novelties introduced by the Bolsheviks was the pretense of planning. Actually, the promise of a "planned economy" first beckoned during World War I, when Russian politicians and academics eagerly began to imitate the efficient and even more dirigiste German war economy.[27] To a certain extent, the new Soviet rulers initially did promote a longer view of development, as manifested in the support for Vladimir Ivanovich Vernadskii's Radium Institute and for a comprehensive geological assay of the country through the Academy of Sciences' Commission on Natural Productive Forces (KEPS, later SOPS).[28] More surprisingly, the new Bolshevik regime extended its support to the young nature-protection movement. Where prerevolutionary advocates of this cause had also spoken of a "moral duty" to nature or enthused over the aesthetic qualities of sites that they sought to protect, after 1917, in order to appeal to the mate- rialist and economic sensibilities of the new rulers, advocates highlighted the benefits to science and to rational economic planning that nature pro- tection could proffer.[29]

Also, because nature protection was not usually regarded by the Soviets (or by later Communist regimes) as particularly politically charged (even though we might think that it should have been so viewed), a certain amount of unpoliced social space also opened up for mobilization in this area. Led by eminent field biologists, the Soviet nature-protection movement for many decades was the arena for a fascinating sociological drama. During the 1920s these scientists managed to win the confidence of cultural officials such as Anatolii Vasil'evich Lunacharskii, people's commissar for education of the Russian Soviet Federated Socialist Republic, and were able to gain the creation of the world's first national environmental-impact body, the Interagency State Committee for Nature Protection (1925–31), which had a right to assess and hold up economic projects that were found to cause unacceptable ecological harm. Lunacharskii also assisted in the emergence of the world's first network of protected territories exclusively dedicated to ecological and scientific study (*zapovedniki*), which were projected to serve as baselines (*etalony*) of "healthy, integral ecological communities" against which changes in surrounding, human-affected areas could be compared. On the basis of these comparisons, it was hoped, scientists could recommend the most appropriate forms of land use for each major bioregion.[30]

By 1933 there were seventy republic- and local-level reserves across the Soviet Union with a total area of six million hectares (about fifteen million acres). Additionally, in 1924 an All-Russian Society for the Protection of Nature (VOOP) was founded, which from 1928 published the bimonthly journal *Okhrana prirody* (Protection of nature). Extensive foreign contacts were forged; Daniil Nikolaevich Kashkarov, a leading ecologist, even made a coast-to-coast tour of the U.S. national parks in 1929.[31]

In 1931, however, after Stalin's ascendancy, the Interagency Committee was abolished. Articles published in *Okhrana prirody* that implied that collectivization was unnecessary—claiming that biological control of pests through habitat protection and restoration could be just as effective in augmenting the harvest—were savaged as "land mines placed under socialist construction."[32] Recent scholarship has found strong evidence that scientist-activists began to link their own freedom with that of nature. After all, Gulag projects such as the Baltic–White Sea Canal (Belomorstroi) graphically demonstrated that violence and bondage for nature and for humans went hand in hand.[33] Courageously, nature-protection activists advanced arguments against giant hydropower projects, collectivization, and the "transformation of nature" even at the height of the first five-year plan (1928–32).

Tellingly, many of these great projects had their antecedents in the tsarist period. Collectivization, after all, was nothing more than the total reenserfment of the peasantry under a tribute regime so brutal that it generated a man-made famine in Ukraine and the North Caucasus in which between five and eight million people died (the worst modern tsarist-era famine in 1891–92 "only" killed half a million).[34] It is no surprise that most of the blueprints for Stalin's canals were developed under Peter I.[35] Because of uncooperative topography and late industrialization, railways became more cost-effective ways of shipping goods in the nineteenth century, and few canals were built before the 1930s. For Stalin, however, purely economic criteria or even engineering rationality often were not the basis for undertaking large-scale projects.

This mentality is reflected in Paul Josephson's textbook *Totalitarian Science and Technology,* which highlights a pervasive feature of Soviet technology: gigantomania. Projects seemed "to take on a life of their own, so important [were] they for cultural and political ends as opposed to the ends of engineering rationality"[36] And Loren Graham shows the path not taken in his poignant study of the suppression of a humanistic approach to engineering in the USSR in the late 1920s. That is when the first showcase of the five-year plan, the Dnepr hydroelectric station, was begun. Had the Soviets based their decision on economic rationality alone, they would have abandoned the megalithic single dam in favor of several smaller plants, including coal-fired ones, as many of their engineers were suggesting. However, "the final decision to go ahead with the giant dam was based not on technical and social analysis but on ideological and political pressure. Stalin and the top leaders of the Communist Party wanted the largest power plant ever built in order to impress the world and the Soviet population with their success and that of the coming Communist social order."[37]

Even more graphic illustrations of Stalin's display technologies were the railroad from Salekhard to Vorkuta, built at great human cost by laborers of the Gulag, which sank into the permafrost, and the notorious Baltic–White Sea Canal or Belomorstroi, which proved unnavigable by the warships and large freighters it was supposed to accommodate.

In a way, the economic rationality of the projects, conventionally understood, was almost beside the point. Their real raison d'être lay elsewhere. If the Soviet leaders ever had a clear vision of a Communist utopia, at its core presumably was the figuration of late nineteenth- and early twentieth-century British, German, and American industry, with rivers of steel flowing and smokestacks belching.[38]

Many in the Bolshevik Party were left unimpressed by "attractive pictures of stateless Communism" because it was a vision that seemed to belong to the far-distant future. Iakov Gol'tsman, representing what Thomas Remington has called the party's "technocratic left" wing, wholeheartedly supported Lenin's policies of extreme centralization against the challenge of "workers' control": "Impatient with theories of statelessness, committed to modernization, [Gol'tsman's] attitude typified a current of working-class sentiment which created a base of support for Soviet dictatorship among those proletarian activists whom the revolution had thrust into prominence."

Because of this group's conviction that socialism was unthinkable without industrialization, they argued that some kind of primitive capital accumulation for investment and reinvestment was required. As we know, this view became dominant under Stalin, and Remington argues that "the extraction of surplus labor became the *goal* of socialism, because, according to one author, 'the development of the communist revolution is the development of the productive forces.'"[39]

Lenin's electrification plan exemplified the use of technology for the transformation of nature and people. According to Jonathan Coopersmith, electricity, it was thought, "would eradicate the cultural and economic chasm between town and country, a major target of Russia's Marxist modernizers." In Lenin's own words, "electrification ... will make it possible to ... overcome, even in the most remote corners of the land, backwardness, ignorance, poverty, disease, and barbarism." H.G. Wells quipped in 1920 that Lenin "has succumbed at last to a Utopia, the Utopia of the electricians."[40]

But this utopia of the electricians could not be built without investment capital, which the mixed economy of the 1920s (New Economic Policy) was not generating quickly enough for the impatient rulers. Taking a page from Ivan IV's playbook (Stalin later "edited" Sergei Eisenstein's cinematic portraiture of Ivan to make it more sympathetic), Stalin used brute force not simply to collectivize the peasants but also to extract from them the needed "surplus" investment capital in the form of grain, and millions perished in the resulting famine. To add to the irony, the Bolshevik regime had entirely appropriated the tsarist-era style of cost accounting that treated human labor as well as natural resources as free goods, despite paying lip service to Marx's theory of labor value.

At what juncture Soviet leaders ceased to believe in the Communist future is still an open question and a very complex one. Lenin's last essays reveal a distinct agnosticism about the quick success of the Soviet project. By the late 1930s, it was clear that the Soviet economy had failed to meet elementary demands for food and shelter. Nevertheless, the existing strategies of centralized planning, monumental projects, and hyper-industrialization were retained; the regime, it appears, perceived that these features were indispensable for building legitimacy, constructing new Soviet citizens, and justifying the self-perpetuation of the enormous administrative and managerial bureaucracy on which the regime's real power rested.[41]

Peter Rutland reaches a similar conclusion, namely, that "planning" served to mask "unwelcome contradictions" at the heart of the Soviet order. "Planning offers itself as a way of asserting man's control of the economic environment, and manages to disguise the fact that it is essentially uncontrollable. It provides a rudimentary work ethic—or, in Marxist terms, it justifies the extraction of surplus labor—by telling the workers that they are laboring not merely for the wages they receive, but also for the greater good of society, in particular for the future. It functions as a device of political legitimation, i.e., it provides a further answer to the perennial question of 'why should I obey my rulers?'"[42] In this context we could comfortably substitute "the conquest of nature" for "planning."

It is possible that "planning" and "the conquest of nature" were not originally devices for the self-perpetuation of the Bolshevik elite and their new system. "Bolshevik theories of social organization," notes Thomas Remington, "although inchoate at the time of October, always presupposed that commodity exchange would be replaced by an administrative authority guided by intelligent reason. The new state would dedicate itself to developing the great natural resources of Russia that the *ancien régime,* in its folly and incompetence, had failed to exploit."[43] No one bothered to consider how "rational" economic decisions were conjured or precipitated; no one thought about the possibility of a plurality of "rationalities." That "rationality" was a social construct—always relative to some specific referent—remained unexamined before the seizure of power.

The revolution's promise of a new world even led many to devise projects "to overcome the limits of physical nature." Inventors and crackpots hatched plans to create perpetual-motion machines, to melt the glaciers of the Pamir Mountains, to warm up the Arctic, to divert the course of entire rivers, and change the climate of Eurasia. Gravity, entropy, and even death would be overcome: at least one prominent Bolshevik, the engineer Leonid Krasin, an otherwise rather reasonable political figure, "publicly stated his belief that science would one day achieve the resurrection of the dead."[44]

Conquering nature, for early Soviet ideologues, itself meant conquering death—certainly through the collective participation in the building of a utopia, whose embodiment would be monuments of metal and concrete that would survive the ages, but sometimes also in a literal sense.[45] Although "personal immortality" did not currently exist, wrote the Soviet literary spokesman Maxim Gorky, we will yield to "people who will create a new, marvelous, bright life and, perhaps, through the miraculous force of fused wills, shall defeat death."[46] For the regime, free floating without a clear blueprint for the future, without the disciplines of global and domestic markets, and unable to supply the needs of the population, a basis for legitimacy had to be found in the cultivation of "new Soviet people" and the deployment of compelling myths that would inspire loyalty, or at least the patience to accept the long wait for Communism.

Irrespective of whether the Soviet leadership actually believed that immortality could be achieved, the production of new forms of selfhood was intimately bound up with the desire to expurgate all "spontaneous," unpredictable and ungovernable traits of the old humans. Personal self-aggrandizement and individualism, although lushly practiced by the leaders as well as the people, were publicly declared impermissible "bourgeois" qualities to be rooted out. Aleksei Gastev, perhaps the most extreme theorist of the new person, promoted an Institute of Labor whose curriculum included studies of social engineering, Frederick Taylor's methods, and psycho-technology. His model for the new humans was the machine.[47] Gastev celebrated the "Americanization" of the individual, by which he meant the transformation of the ordinary individual into a completely efficient machine. Anticipating an "amazing anonymity" among future proletarians, he hailed the "steadily expanding tendencies toward standardization" in society.[48]

We remember Gorky, however, and not Gastev, as the one who linked all these transformations—nature, society, and the individual—into a single, idealistic-sounding program of action while simultaneously crafting an immense mystification to benefit the Stalinist regime. In a series of newspaper essays during the late 1920s and early 1930s, Gorky returned to an old theme: the final triumph of rationality and consciousness over spontaneity. With the advent of socialism, he averred, chaos would be banished forever from the world. Swamps, predators, drought, snakes, deserts and other "unproductive" lands, "sleepy forests," Arctic ice, hurricanes, and earthquakes would all be eliminated.[49] The propagandist of a view that humanity was a collective "god," Gorky propounded that "Man is the bearer of energy that organizes the world, creating 'second nature'—culture; man is an organ of nature, created by her as if for the attainment of self-knowledge and transformation."[50] "Imagine," he wrote,

> that in the interests of the development of our industry it is necessary for us Russians to dig a ... canal in order to link the Baltic Sea with the Black Sea. ... And so instead of sending millions to be slaughtered, we send a portion of them to this work which is vital to the country. ... I am confident that those killed during three years of war would have been able in this time to drain the ... swamps in our country, to irrigate the Hungry Steppe and other deserts, to connect the rivers of the Trans-Urals with the Kama, to lay a road through the Caucasus Mountain ridge and to accomplish still other great feats of labor.[51]

Espousing what he called "geo-optimism," Gorky decried nature worship. "There is something 'primitive and atavistic' in the sight of humans bowing before nature's beauty."[52]

As Stalin's violent collectivization and the first five-year plan were set in motion, Gorky's calls for the transformation of nature became more strident. "We live in a world of wonders created ... by that consummate revolutionary and wonderworker: reason," he exulted in "Drought Shall Be Annihilated," an article that appeared in a major daily. Humans were "omnipotent," and "there hardly exists anything impossible for the rational will of millions of people directed toward a single goal."[53] Declaring "a war to the death" against nature, Gorky in another article fumed that "the blind drive of nature to produce on earth every kind of useless or even harmful trash—must be stopped and eradicated."[54] "First nature" and "everything elemental (spontaneous)" would be effaced and transformed into rationally planned "second nature." Reflecting a profoundly monocultural vision in all respects, Gorky celebrated the disappearance of the "mottled impoverishment" of rural Russia: "The light-bluish strips of oats and, alongside them, a black parcel of upturned earth, then a golden strip of rye, and a greenish one of wheat, and, in general, a multicolored sadness of general fragmentation. ... In our day huge expanses of land are colored more powerfully, in only one color."[55] This transformation of nature could reinscribe plastic and impressionable human nature, lectured Gorky. "Upbringing, my friends," he proclaimed, "is omnipotent!"[56]

Gorky inaugurated the new literary agenda with the "collectively written" apologia for the Baltic–White Sea Canal, whose motto—"In transforming nature, man transforms himself"—he personally coined.[57] An early major project of the Gulag, the canal functioned more as an icon of modernity than as a practical military or economic facility. Praising the secret police operatives of the GPU (Glavnoe Politicheskoe Upravlenie, or Main Political Administration) as "engineers of human souls," Gorky saw them as agents who were purging the hundreds of thousands of prisoner-laborers of their "elemental" backward qualities and peasant individualism and transforming them into productive "new Soviet people."[58] "These grandiose projects," he wrote, "directing the physical energy of the mass to a struggle with nature, ... permit people to come into contact with their essential mission in life—the mastery of the forces of nature so as to put an end to their rabidity."[59]

In this drama of transformation, nature was cast as the enemy. However, nature had met its match. Pictured as an omnipotent and omniscient planner of whole continents, Stalin makes a cameo appearance in Gorky's *Belomor*. "Stalin holds a pencil. Before him lies a map of the region. Deserted shores. Remote villages. Virgin soil, covered with boulders. Primeval forests. Too much forest, as a matter of fact; it covers the best soil. And swamps. The swamps are always crawling about, making life dull and slovenly. Tillage must be increased. The swamps must be drained. ... The Karelian Republic wants to enter the stage of classless society as a republic of factories and mills. And the Karelian Republic *will* enter classless society by changing its own nature."[60]

Whether Gorky, or Stalin, authentically believed by 1933 that such pharaonic projects could really produce the people of the future we cannot know. However, the projects did promote other strategic goals of the regime. Together with the real or imagined military enemies of the USSR, nature could always be cast in the role of enemy. This view provided the justification for mobilizing the population periodically for enormous campaigns such as the Great Stalin Plan for the Transformation of Nature, Nikita Khrushchev's Virgin Lands campaign, his construction of the Bratsk Dam in Siberia, Leonid Brezhnev's plan to reroute Siberian rivers southward, and his construction of the ill-fated Baikal-Amur railroad. Writing about the civil war period (1918–21), Remington noted that "each round of mobilization sought to unlock some hidden store of energy but produced an even greater countereffect in the form of bribery, black markets, hoarding, speculation, deception, and small-scale enterprise. Thus mobilization reduced the aggregate quantity of usable resources."[61] The same could be said of all the subsequent campaigns.

By contrast with their more nakedly pragmatic analogues in the United States, Soviet acclimatization and predator control were part of a vast "plan" to reinvent nature, turning it into the obedient servant of human society. In 1929 the academician Nikolai Kashchenko wrote: "The final goal of acclimatization, understood in the broad sense, is a profound rearrangement of the entire living world—not only that portion which is now under the domination of humanity but also that portion that has still remained wild. Generally speaking, all wild species will disappear with time; some will be exterminated, others will be domesticated. All living nature will live, thrive, and die at none other than the will of humans and according to their designs. These are the grandiose perspectives that open up before us."[62]

The writer and engineer Mikail Ilin wrote a best-selling book about the "struggle against nature." Ilin celebrated Soviets as "Conqueror[s] of their Own Country" and predicted that "within a few years all the maps of the USSR will have to be revised. In one place there will be a new river ... in another a new lake. ... Man will transform deserts, change water flows, and even create new species of plants and animals. ... Man must fight the river," he admonished, "as the animal-tamer fights wild beasts."[63] That these words were not simply the utterances of academic cranks and writers is demonstrated by the vast state-sponsored campaigns for the acclimatization of exotics (including the mink, muskrat, nutria, and raccoon dog) and for predator elimination, both of which extended even into the supposedly inviolable nature reserves.[64] An order to exterminate all foxes in Ukraine was issued as late as 1958.[65] It is not difficult to hear in this, and in Trofim Denisovich Lysenko's myriad schemes, an echo of the old gentry dream that an agronomic miracle would save the decrepit estate without requiring structural changes in power relations or labor practices.[66]

Wildfire control policy represented another such campaign. The absolutist Soviet state mounted an absolute war against natural fire. By 1972, Stephen Pyne informs us, controlled burning by peasants was outlawed by the Brezhnev regime, and the state's fire brigades patrolled the skies, constituting the "largest wildland firefighting system in the world." Fires continued to burn, however, and were compounded by the furtive nature of controlled burning after 1972 as well as by the choking lack of information, including essential meteorological information. The sole reliance on fire suppression set the stage for the monumental 1987 fire in the Transbaikal region, which has been estimated to have burned over about 12 million hectares (although official reports put the area at 92,000 hectares at first and 290,000 hectares later). As Pyne insightfully concludes: "Aerial fire suppression was, in the final analysis, a political institution, an expression of the state's geopolitical will. It responded to the political ecology of a totalitarian regime."[67]

In the nineteenth century, Russian elites, unable to imagine a structurally different order, also placed their hopes for prosperity and modernity on the development of southern Siberia, along the Amur River.[68] Ultimately, they hoped that a new orientation, toward the Pacific, would transform Russia into a second United States. However, as Mark Bassin has shown, these hopes were not founded on credible geographical knowledge of Russia's Far East. This kind of wishful thinking in Russia was not limited to the nineteenth century. In fact, it reached its apogee under the Soviets— witness Stalin's infamous Arctic railroad and the more recent Baikal-Amur railroad. Although our geographies are socially constructed, not all imagined geographies are equal: there *is* still a material world out there against which we more than occasionally bump our heads. To the great cost of the Soviet human population as well as to flora and fauna, Stalin often acted and spoke as if the constraints of material reality did not matter; his was the ultimate "geography of the mind."

So strong was the regime's insistence that it was all-knowing and all-powerful that it was even prepared to defy the consensus of international science in a range of disciplines. Acting in the name of the regime, Lysenko and Isai Izrailovich Prezent's first major denunciatory campaign was launched against ecology as a science. As it happened, the leading ecologist of the day, Vladimir Vladimirovich Stanchinskii, scientific director of the Askania-Nova *zapovednik,* had advanced scientific arguments from both ecology and genetics against the acclimatization of exotic fauna. After a visit to Askania-Nova by Lysenko and Prezent in the late summer of 1933, Stanchinskii and his team were arrested as "counterrevolutionaries."[69] Not surprisingly, Lysenko and Prezent then turned to the suppression of genetics, a campaign that was crowned with success in 1948 after Stalin personally intervened. This disregard for expert counsel, particularly when such counsel implied higher costs for the regime's pet projects in order to protect humans or other "nonproduction values," was a red thread that ran through Soviet economic practices from the 1930s to perestroika.

The hostility to any limitation on the Party and state's freedom to transform and "reinvent" nature is reflected in a remark made by the chairman of a 1930s Party purge commission to Mikhail Petrovich Potemkin, a Communist and former president of the All-Russian Society for the Protection of Nature, during Potemkin's interrogation: "How can you," demanded the purge commission chair, "a member of the Party, have become involved in a cause like conservation?"[70]

Interesting parallels exist between the histories of Soviet nature protection and those of pollution control and public health during the 1920s and 1930s, although the two communities of discourse remained almost completely separate. A scientist-led field, with 1,600 public health physicians (in 1928) and environmental chemists at its core, actively pursued novel technical means of treating industrial wastes while insisting that the regime proceed with caution in its drive to industrialize. About forty research institutes were concerned with problems of air, water, and soil quality by the mid-1930s, and there was even an All-Union Conference for the Preservation of Clean Air in Kharkov in 1935. Wastewater recycling was proposed in 1934.[71]

Again, however, the repressive thirties had their dampening effect on this field. When one expert wrote in 1930 that "a new substance may be broadly introduced only after it has been determined by appropriate scientific and technical research institutes that it is harmless," the director of the All-Union Institute for Labor Hygiene and Organization rebutted: "If we took Professor Koiranskii's proposal seriously, then this would be tantamount to placing a 'veto'—in the name of science—over the industrial introduction of a whole array of new substances and new chemical production processes."[72]

The later 1930s saw mass repressions of scientists, physicians, and public figures in this area, beginning with the former chief public health inspector of the USSR and minister of public health, Grigorii Naumovich Kaminskii, whose battle to protect workers and other citizens from hazardous industrial pollution ended with his arrest in 1937 and subsequent execution. By July 1939, Vice-Premier Andrei Ianuar'evich Vyshinskii responded to entreaties for a law setting pollution standards with the rejoinder that "we have the Stalin Constitution. That is sufficient to ensure that our public hygiene and public health are the best in the world."[73]

Just as protection from pollution was textual or iconic and not real, so were some campaigns to transform nature. With the announcement of the Great Stalin Plan for the Transformation of Nature in October 1948, provinces in the steppe region were given targets of acreage for shelterbelt plantings. Vladimir Boreiko describes how the Ukrainian SSR, seeking to fulfill its plan for the Belgorod-Don shelterbelt, spent a good deal of money on an artistically designed billboard featuring the slogans of Stalin and other party leaders on the campaign. Bitterly he concludes: "It all fits. If you are producing for people, you strive for quality. If you are producing for fools, you produce something for show."[74] Because the Soviet system was not able to produce for consumers, it had to produce for show and produce a public which could consume the virtual reality.

The industrial and hydraulic models for these icons of "successful" modernity were appropriated from abroad. Because of the absence of an organic, self-propelling economic dynamism within the Soviet economy, innovations had to be borrowed continually from outside.[75] Peter Rutland writes: "Much of this 'learning from America' was largely rhetorical, but one can nevertheless see that in certain respects Soviet planners have adjusted their priorities through observation of the changing world market—the introduction of chemicals, plastics, and fertilizers, for example. But the dominant tendency in priority setting has been inertia ... the priorities laid down in the early 1930s."[76] Although such practices assured the reproduction of the *apparat* (bureaucracy) and therefore reflected the *political* rationality of the Soviet system, they ultimately cannibalized the economy and exhausted resources, with industry essentially only able to produce enough to keep itself going.

Sham communalism resulted in a repressed and intensified egoism and survivalist mentality based on kinship, small groups of friends, and clientelism, which set the stage for today's Mafia.[77] In actuality a perpetuation of tsarist serfdom, the Soviet tribute-taking system deepened a general lack of empathy, an inability to assume responsibility, and a dangerous environment for workers and the general public. Inspired by the work of Ulrich Beck, the sociologist Oleg Yanitsky characterizes Russia as the ultimate "risk society" which had sustained "genetic damage" during the long period of totalitarianism.[78] "Over the course of eighty years," Yanitsky writes, "[the USSR] was used as a testing ground for the most divergent model schemes of modernization." By the fall of the Communist regime, an area occupying 2.5 million square kilometers of the territory of the Russian Federation, or 15 percent, was considered to represent "an acute ecological situation."[79] In this area lived 20 percent of the nation's population, sixty million, and sixty-eight cities were deemed "dangerous" by Goskompriroda (the USSR State Committee for Environmental Education). In sixteen of these cities, the concentration of air pollutants was more than fifty times the norm.[80] Safe drinking water was a particularly low priority, with only 30 percent of wastes satisfactorily treated and with such major cities as Baku, Riga, and Dnepropetrovsk lacking sewage systems.[81] In Russia alone, one million tons of lethal chemicals are stored in dubious conditions of security at more than 3,500 sites. Contaminated nuclear sites, aside from the region affected by Chernobyl, include Kyshtym in the Urals, the site of a 1957 disaster;[82] Krasnoyarsk; Tomsk Oblast; and the eastern coast of Novaya Zemlya, to name only the most seriously polluted areas.

Agriculture is another prime case of the workings of the tribute economy. Again in Russia in 1989, 60 million hectares of agricultural land were eroded, 42 million hectares had elevated acidity, and another 36 million hectares were saline. The lack of economic criteria of utility or efficiency promoted an "extensive" mode of development (for example, to increase agricultural production, you cultivate more land rather than intensify production on currently cultivated land) and a disregard for such inputs as resources, labor, and appropriate techniques. Attempting to explain the discounting of resource costs and environmental externalities in Soviet-type economies, Marshall Goldman and others argued that Marxian economic dogmas such as the labor theory of value acted as constraints on economic actors.[83] Indirectly responding to this view, Joan DeBardeleben's influential study *The Environment and Marxism-Leninism* demonstrated that Marxist-Leninist dogma could (and was beginning to) accommodate the costing of resources and externalities as well as other environmental values.[84] Regrettably, the dogma's relative flexibility made little difference in the world of practices or outcomes. That is because, in the end, outcomes are governed by political economy and actual power relations—an old Marxian saw that still cuts some wood. In the last analysis, Marxism was just a fig leaf covering an insidiously plunderous iteration of Russia's traditional tribute-taking mode of economic organization.

Closely researched multifactoral case studies of actual environmental policy making and practices (as opposed to often-meaningless decrees and regulations) have provided illuminating analyses of the political economy of the Soviet Union. Amid the growing literature in this area, two studies by Thane Gustafson capture the complexities of Soviet decision making. His first book, on water policies, amplified the point made a decade earlier by H. Gordon Skilling: that Soviet officials' visions of how to pursue economic development, among other things, diverged significantly according to the specific economic sectors for which they bore responsibility—and, we might add, from which they skimmed their tribute.[85] Because natural resources, even renewable ones such as water, are ultimately finite, and certain uses of rivers, such as water storage for hydropower, work at cross-purposes with other uses—such as shipping, fishing, and irrigation—policy conflicts emerged. These conflicts reflected the physical impossibility of simultaneously maximizing all uses and cast a long shadow on the regime's dream of transcending the "kingdom of necessity" through the directed transformation of nature. They also revealed the cost-benefit logic of the regime as it was inexorably forced to trade off some goals against others.

More often than not, those trade-offs were for short-term advantage, with heavy disregard for serious long-term costs. A classic example of this was the autarkic decision to turn Central Asia into a supplier of the Soviet Union's cotton. The goal of cotton self-sufficiency for the USSR was first proposed by Lenin in 1918. However, it was under Stalin that the regime undertook to "bridle" the Amu Darya and Syr Darya rivers for this purpose, in the words of the Uzbek Party secretary Usman Yusupov. Later, under Khrushchev, the regime extended the irrigation to Turkmenistan, building the unlined Karakum Canal (whose seepage rate was 50 percent). It was a classic case of imperialist land use: by the 1970s Central Asia could no longer feed itself, owing to the substitution of cotton for food crops accompanied by rapid population increase. Now, owing to the salinization of soils as a result of over-watering and poor drainage, much of the best agricultural land has been poisoned.[86]

If that were not bad enough, the unconstrained withdrawal of water from the two rivers has resulted in a regional environmental catastrophe on a par with Chernobyl: the disappearance of the Aral Sea. Barely fifty years ago, the Aral was the fourth largest lake in the world, covering an area of 66,000 square kilometers with a volume of 1,061.6 cubic kilometers and a salinity level of 10 parts per 1,000. Now, the Aral Sea is almost gone. For almost a decade, it has consisted of two shrinking ponds: in 1998 its total area was 28,687 square kilometers and its volume 181 cubic kilometers. Owing to the unprecedented evaporation, salinity in the lake has increased more than fourfold, to 45 parts per 1,000. Fishing, once the major industry of the region, has disappeared from the southern Uzbek basin. Large, rusting trawlers lie stranded, listing on the dry seabed, looking like a scene out of a science-fiction movie. It is difficult to imagine that forty-odd years ago the annual catch exceeded forty thousand metric tons.

The entire regional landscape underwent disastrous transformation. A toxic, man-made lake, Sarykamysh, with an area of three thousand square kilometers, was formed by the discharge of drainage water from the cotton fields. The *tugai* flood-plain, a species-rich habitat of tall reeds, tamarisks, poplars, willows, and oleasters, was desiccated. Of 170 indigenous species of mammals, a mere 38 still inhabit the region, perhaps themselves doomed to go the way of the extinct Amu Darya tiger.

Epidemiologically, too, the desiccation of the Aral Sea has been a catastrophe. From the exposed seabed, tens of millions of tons of sands laden with salts, pesticides, fertilizers, and other chemicals—precipitates from irrigation wastewater discharged over decades—are carried annually to fields and towns. Dust storms, perhaps the result of regional climate change caused by the lake's disappearance, afflict the region as well. Worst hit has been the Autonomous Republic of Karakalpakstan (in Uzbekistan), bordering the former sea. A recent statistic noted that 111 children per 1,000 die before their first birthday.[87] As clean water has disappeared, viral hepatitis and typhoid fever have become widespread, as have anemia, cancers, and tuberculosis.

Finally, the desiccation of the sea poses another, global danger. During the Cold War the Soviet army tested and stored biological weapons on Vozrozhdenie Island, once located in the middle of the lake and now only three kilometers from the shore. Among the organisms were Ebola virus, plague, anthrax, smallpox, Marburg fever, and a host of other lethal diseases. No one gave a thought to the possibility that one day there might be no lake to isolate the facility. One accidental release could trigger a worldwide pandemic.

When the Party bosses of Central Asia, who had profited for decades from the cotton monoculture, realized that the Aral Sea was disappearing, they sought to counteract the damage by proposing a transfer of water from northward-flowing Siberian rivers such as the Irtysh and Ob' to their region. It was a typical reaction: solve your immediate problem by creating another one whose solution can be deferred. First considered by the Aral-Caspian Expedition of the USSR Academy of Sciences in April 1950, the proposed Sibaral Canal, dubbed "the project of the century," would have stretched for 2,200 kilometers across the Turgai trough, delivering water to the Aral. Because it considered the entire country its patrimony and therefore its testing ground, the Communist Party leadership endorsed the project, along with a similar project to divert north-flowing European rivers and waters south, to irrigate Ukraine, Kalmykia, and the North Caucasus, and to stem a further drop in the level of the Caspian Sea. Each unforeseen and undesirable consequence of the tribute-takers' "planning" was addressed by displacing the problem onto some other region, sector, or generational cohort.

When the unprecedented water diversions were proposed and then endorsed by the Brezhnev regime as another "project of the century," scientists warned of possible global-scale consequences. Such an abrupt cutoff of warmer river water to the Arctic Ocean could alter the entire heat balance of the planet, some cautioned; others drew attention to the vast amount of agricultural land in southern Siberia that would be flooded in connection with the damming of the Ob' and Irtysh rivers. Only an increasingly desperate public outcry convinced the new Soviet leaders— Mikhail Sergeevich Gorbachev and Nikolai Ivanovich Ryzhkov—to cancel the project. That decision, taken on August 20, 1986, was Gorbachev's first major signal to the educated public that there was really some kind of change in the offing. Because the Central Asian republics have been unable to shift their agricultural economies away from cotton and rice to more traditional orchard crops, the Aral Sea is now certain to disappear completely within the next two decades. At no point did the Soviet leaders or their comprador vice gerents in Central Asia look back—or forward. The crucial question is, When did a picture of the costs, or trade-offs, of development come into view? For it was then that a transparent debate should have been held. But then, transparency has never been a strong point of the militarized tribute-taking state.

In *Crisis amid Plenty,* Thane Gustafson showed how this complicated weighing of risks and trade-offs played out in energy policy. The Soviet leadership's pursuit of growth to maintain the system and shore up its legitimacy turned out to require dangerous short-term reorientations in investment. Because of existing inefficiencies, embodied in shoddy, obsolete technologies and wasteful practices, extracting or producing the energy needed to run the Soviet and CMEA (Council for Mutual Economic Assistance, or Comecon) economies required ever more exorbitant investments in the energy sector, squeezing production of consumer goods and severely limiting other investment options.

At the end of World War II the regime was presented with a windfall: the discovery of the world's second largest oil field at Samotlor in western Siberia. However, its short-term perspective led the regime to pump the field with water to extract the oil faster. By the mid-1980s, when production was at its peak, a barrel of West Siberian crude cost more to get out of the ground than it could be sold for on the world market. Nevertheless, the regime's desperation for hard-currency earnings—to purchase the food for its people that its devastated collective-farm sector could not produce— caused it to expand drilling maximally. Rather than pump out old wells more efficiently, it wastefully opened new wells. Billions of barrels of oil in the ground are now admixed with water, making future recovery extremely expensive. Because labor was used profligately in the oil fields, hundreds of thousands of people by the 1990s found themselves stuck in the world's largest Arctic swamp. Vast areas are polluted.[88] As Gorbachev found out, the investments required to make the economy more energy efficient, and thereby more durable over the long run, required intolerable short-term sacrifices on the part of the population; by the late 1980s there was almost no room to maneuver.

Precisely this desperate set of choices around energy led to the overly hasty and careless process by which the reactors at Chernobyl, for example, were designed, promoted, and allowed to go on line, as Zhores Medvedev shows.[89] In his masterful analysis of the largest industrial accident in history, Medvedev demonstrates how the crude quality of Soviet industrial welding dictated a vulnerable design, how nuclear power represented a fix for a system that squandered energy against a backdrop of steeply increasing costs for extraction of hydrocarbons and coal, and how a culture of fear and distorted information flow impeded the safe testing of a retrofitted emergency cooling system. Like the dilemma over irrigation and river diversions, the Soviet and Eastern European energy question was not simply about a natural resource; it was about the nature of the entire political and economic system.[90] Once the patrimonial regime had set its goals, the only question was how to attain them, even if all the available choices were fraught with high risk for present and future generations.

Certainly the symbolic use of technology and the arrogant, autocratic style of decision making are crucial parts of the Soviet environmental legacy. Another, however, is the pervasive militarization of the Soviet state from its very inception. Although official Soviet historians and others have long argued that "capitalist encirclement" and foreign intervention "forced" a civil war on a reluctant infant Bolshevik experiment, it is equally possible to find quotes from Lenin proving that he understood that a civil war would almost inexorably follow a Bolshevik seizure of power—and welcoming that prospect.[91] In any event, by 1921 the Bolshevik regime had already acquired a distinctly militarized profile. Equally important, the civil war provided the justification (in all senses of the term) for the imposition of an unrelenting regime of requisitioning on the peasantry, along with the forcible suppression of strikes and of independent unions, all other political parties, elected soviets, and factory councils.

Although the tsarist regime had begun the production of mustard gas in 1915, Soviet-German military cooperation during the 1920s renewed work on chemical weapons under the supervision of the OGPU, or secret police.[92] That work later expanded to the testing and production of biological weapons, one consequence of which was the accidental release of anthrax near the city of Sverdlovsk (Ekaterinburg, population one million) in April 1979, causing 64 officially reported (and, according to one scholarly estimate, 36,000) deaths.[93]

The military-industrial complex represented 30 to 35 percent of the total Soviet budget. However, its shadow over the economy was even greater. The military-industrial complex commandeered up to 70 percent of the metalworking sector for its needs and used 45 percent of the electricity in the country, 50 percent of all metal, and 30 percent of all motor transport. Little of the country's high technology saw its way to the civilian sector; the military-industrial complex monopolized more than 90 percent. Between 50 and 70 percent of all industrial production went to serve military needs. As of January 1, 1990, the number of men under arms in the various military services was 8.5 million, with 4.5 million more in reserves. As noted, the energy needs of this sector were enormous. Products of the 440 active and 85 demobilized atomic power stations (55 more are under construction), spent fuel and wastes now amount to 8,700 tons in about 100 storage sites.[94]

Incalculable areas of land have been poisoned by the Soviet military-industrial complex. More than 90,000 square kilometers in Russia alone, not counting Kazakstan, have been badly polluted by the space program. An estimated 660,000 square kilometers has been used for military maneuvers, including 200,000 in Kazakstan. Perhaps physical compacting of the land is the least of the problems; there is also heavy pollution in these test areas from fuel discharges, uranium, and lead. An additional 60,000 square kilometers was set aside for special military hunting areas.[95]

Owing to the considerable fuel needs of the military (11.8 million tons of reactive fuel in 1987—still far less than the U.S. military's 18.6 million tons),[96] oil and gas fields have been exploited with little concern for the environmental consequences. As a result, enormous areas of the sensitive West Siberian tundra have been badly polluted. At least sixteen regions of the former Soviet Union are badly polluted: the Aral Sea region; areas affected by Chernobyl fallout, extending into Belarus (Gomel') and even Russia (Briansk); the Sea of Azov; the Donbas coal and iron region of Ukraine; the entire republic of Moldova; the Black Sea and its littoral;

the Caspian Sea; the Kalmyk Autonomous Republic; the Volga River; the Kola Peninsula; the Urals region; the Kuzbas coal region; Lake Baikal; the Moscow region; the Fergana Valley in Central Asia; and the Semipalatinsk nuclear testing region (now Semei) in eastern Kazakstan. Novaya Zemlya and the Arctic Ocean could be added to this list.[97] It is estimated that only 15 percent of Russia's urbanites live in places that meet official clean-air standards. In the worst-affected areas, such as the city of Sterlitamak, birth defects are so rampant that only 16 percent of births are considered totally normal.[98]

Atmospheric as well as subterranean testing of nuclear weapons has left scars on the human population and landscape. One of the saddest legacies is that of Kazakstan, which endured 450 nuclear tests (119 above ground) between August 29, 1949 and October 19, 1989, until they were stopped under pressure from a powerful grassroots antinuclear movement in the late 1980s. Dangerous radiation exposure left hundreds of thousands of people to cope with birth defects and cancer rates of epidemic proportions. In addition, nearly twenty million hectares of land have become unusable. Eighty nuclear tests have taken place on the fragile Arctic archipelago of Novaya Zemlya, whose mainland and shallow coastal shelf also constituted a "dumping ground for enormous amounts of radioactive and mixed waste": up to 17,000 containers (150,000 cubic meters) of liquid radioactive waste, plus possibly fifteen old or damaged nuclear reactors, some still containing fuel. When a mass die-off of starfish and seals in the White Sea occurred in 1990, many saw it as the result of nuclear dumping.[99] The litany of environmental ills occasioned by the Soviet military-industrial complex would fill a very large book. But perhaps the most arresting point of all is that the military-industrial complex represented the *most efficient* sector of the Soviet economy.

Late perestroika: a new beginning stifled

Whatever Gorbachev's intentions, perestroika opened the door to new political possibilities. In the aftermath of the elections to the Congress of People's Deputies in March 1989 and right through the summer of 1990, it was still possible to believe that the Soviet Union would lead the way to an enlightened alternative to both Reagan/Thatcher-style capitalism and neo-Stalinism. After all, hadn't the Soviet electorate sent the biggest delegation of world-class intellectuals to a national legislature since the French and American revolutions? Andrei Sakharov, Nikolai Vorontsov, Galina Starovoitova, Roy A. Medvedev, Sergei Zalygin, Roald Sagdeev, and Aleksei Yablokov were only the tip of the iceberg. In the summer following the 1989 elections, Gorbachev's prime minister, Nikolai Ryzhkov, named Nikolai Nikolaevich Vorontsov, an eminent zoologist, to head the USSR State Committee for Environmental Protection. When the state committee was upgraded to a ministry in 1991, Vorontsov became the first non-Communist member of a Soviet government since the spring of 1918. Although saddled with an obstructive and parasitical bureaucracy within his agency which he was politically unable to remove, Vorontsov named able non-Party scientists, such as Aleksandr Bazykin and V.A. Krasilov, to key posts and pushed to reform thoroughly the norms and values of the environmentally hazardous Soviet economy.[100]

The fall of 1990, however, was the start of a cruel and disappointing period for the former Soviet intelligentsia. Hard-liners gained the ascendancy within Gorbachev's regime, and Vorontsov was almost completely isolated. Foreign Minister Eduard Shevardnadze quit, warning of a crackdown, and soon thereafter Soviet forces imposed repressive measures in the Baltic republics. To his credit, Vorontsov did not give up when things started to unravel. Instead, he tried to inject the perspective of a natural scientist, a biologist, and an expert on organic evolution. This perspective was one that was shaped in great measure by his teachers and mentors from the nature-protection movement of the 1920s through the 1950s, who in their time had also tried to guide policy in a more humane direction on the basis of their own understanding of science. Two examples of the way that Vorontsov's science influenced his positions on political and diplomatic issues were his efforts to keep some kind of federal connection among the successor states to the USSR and his promotion of binational *zapovedniki* on Soviet and later on Russian borders. These undertakings may both be understood as flowing from his conviction that natural history constitutes the original and most enduring common human language, and that the protection of the environment is humanity's most fundamental common concern.

Russia and the successor states

Despite his heroism during the August 1991 coup, Vorontsov was not kept on as newly independent Russia's environmental minister. Perhaps this was because he had broken a political rule in publicly revealing and criticizing the Soviet army's secret nuclear test on Novaya Zemlya. Vorontsov's colleague at the Institute for Developmental Biology, Aleksei Yablokov, who had become Boris Yeltsin's environmental adviser, was also pushed out by 1993. Viktor Danilov-Danelian, a colorless engineer, was named minister of environmental protection. The tribute-takers had placed one of their own back in the job.

Under a barrage of propaganda emanating as much from the Western leaders and media (particularly the *Wall Street Journal* and the *New York Times*) as from the Russian and post-Soviet press, readers and viewers were led to believe that a fundamental restructuring of the political economies of Russia and the other post-Soviet states had taken place with the fall of

Communism.[101] Now, more than a decade later, with large sectors of the Soviet Union's former industrial sector cannibalized to pay for a short-term consumption orgy by the "new Russians" and their post-Soviet counterparts in other republics, there is a growing recognition that despite new labels, the old tribute system has remained in place. If anything, the system's predatory features became more exaggerated as the older unitary hierarchy, enforced by the Communist Party, broke down, and a fierce jockeying for advantage ensued. In many regions, "tribute wars" broke out. Part of the issue in the two bloody wars over Chechnya was the question of who was to control lucrative franchises, such as oil refineries and pipelines.[102] Recent conflicts in Eurasia, especially within the newly independent states (Ukraine, Georgia, Russia, Moldova, and Tajikistan), whether as wars for ethnic independence, gang wars, or peaceful "political" struggles, have pitted warlords, with their own Mafia federations, against each other for the right to loot the contested territories.[103] Although state gangsterism has unquestionably made a relative few very wealthy and very powerful, it has pauperized and debilitated the state in its legitimate, civilian functions: assuring the health, safety, and well-being of the population at large and investing in their future. The immense scale of the post-1991 tribute taking has undermined the state's ability to collect legitimate taxes.

This situation has led to deindustrialization as well as the slashing of funding for science, education, public health, and the environment. One consequence of the decline of investment in industry is that the average age of the industrial plant has increased, and technologically generated accidents rose almost sixfold between 1991 and 1996.[104] Nonpayment of electricity bills has led utilities to shut off power to clients such as the Plisetsk rocket-testing facility in Arkhangelskaya Oblast in 1994, the Murmansk submarine base a year later (the admiral had his troops storm the power station), a strategic-weapons unit in Ivanovskaya Oblast in 2000 (again with a military seizure of the power station), and to the Central Urals copper-smelting refinery in Pervoural'sk in August 1998. This last incident caused a series of accidents, including a dangerous discharge of sulfur dioxide gas, which poisoned crops on five collective farms and provoked asthma attacks in the population. The chief engineer of the smelter led a small private army of Pinkertons in a seizure of that power station. An even more dramatic accident occurred in November 1999 in the same Ekaterinburg (Sverdlovsk) Oblast, when a power shut-off disabled pumps that emptied wastewater from a mineral processing plant's holding reservoir. After the coffer dam burst, the swirling waters washed away a gas line, power lines, and a bridge, and flooded apartments.[105]

Meanwhile, toxic wastes increased from 67.5 million metric tons in 1993 to 108.9 million tons in 1999, despite an unprecedented peacetime *decline* in gross industrial production of 50.9 percent. Yet, because investment in 1999 was only 23.2 percent of that of 1990, reuse and treatment of these wastes declined from 46.5 percent to 31.7 percent of waste generated. Levels of polluted wastewater generation are 74.4 percent of 1990 levels, and only 20 percent of the water treatment capacity of 1990 is in operation.[106] Perhaps the only reason that Vladimir Putin, in a moment of high drama, cast Russia's deciding vote to launch the Kyoto Protocol was the fact that his nation's carbon emissions were relatively low as a result of the unprecedented deindustrialization.

Budget allocations for science continue their downward trends, representing a shrinking percentage of a shrinking budget. Almost 40 percent of the State Hydrometeorological Service's environmental-quality measuring facilities were closed between 1991 and 1997.[107] Perhaps the logical final step was Vladimir Putin's complete elimination of the Ministry for Environmental Protection in 2000. Its functions were taken over by the Ministry for Natural Resources, a move in many ways similar to Stalin's termination of the Interagency State Committee for Nature Protection in 1931. Uzbekistan similarly eliminated its environmental ministry. American, Swedish, Korean, Japanese and other firms have not wasted time gaining access to lucrative resources in the extractive industries (including forests, oil and gas, fishing, and mining) of the former Soviet Union. Was the West's environmental critique of Communism just a ploy?[108]

Continuing to overreach domestically and on the world stage, the leaders of the Soviet Union did not feel that they had the "luxury" to protect their own people or their environment. They left a train of catastrophes in their wake. The current leaders of post-Soviet Eurasia are to an astonishing degree holdovers and products of the previous Communist system. Now they have shed the red flag and have draped themselves in national colors. Most claim to be democrats and supporters of the free market. In reality, they have simply found it to their advantage to establish successor khanates to the former Soviet "Golden Horde."[109]

In geopolitical terms, the disappearance of the Soviet Union seemed to promise a safer planet. Environmentally speaking, however, that conclusion is extremely questionable. The balkanization of Eurasian territory has had the effect of dividing water basins into national segments, often precluding any kind of coordinated management policy. Where the Caspian Sea had effectively been divided between two countries, Iran and the USSR, it is now partitioned five ways, among Kazakstan, Russia, Azerbaijan, Iran, and Turkmenistan, with growing prospects of conflicts over oil and gas. Unpoliceable Mafia clans smuggle plutonium, nuclear-weapons components, and conventional weapons, aided by distribution networks that circle the globe. Finally, the misery that has accompanied the abject dispossession of tens of millions has already contributed to the resurgence of drug-resistant tuberculosis, to outbreaks of cholera, and to a growing AIDS epidemic. Eurasia, like Africa, could well become the site of the world's next pandemic.

Could the environmental movement change Russia?

The members of the nature-protection movement of the Soviet Union displayed great courage. The All-Russian Society for the Protection of Nature even survived multiple attempts under Stalin to eliminate it. Where issues of nationality intruded, nature-protection advocates were under double threat. Vladimir Evgen'evich Boreiko's meticulously researched studies on the fate of nature protection in Ukraine paint a bleak picture. All of the voluntary scientific and professional societies of that republic, including those for nature protection, were shut down, in some cases accused of serving as cover for "counterrevolutionary nationalist groups." By Boreiko's count, about 40 percent of the leading nature-protection activists of Ukraine were executed.[110]

Miraculously, as we now know, the scientist-activists, the All-Russian Society for the Protection of Nature, and the *zapovedniki,* although strafed, managed to survive as relative islands of autonomy within the Soviet state, probably owing to their extreme marginality in the eyes of the regime (although the *kraeved* or local-lore societies, which were also deeply involved in nature protection, were closed down by 1937). Against the backdrop of Stalinism, nature reserves acquired an aura of sacred space. In the words of Sergei Zalygin: "The *zapovedniki* remained some kinds of islands of freedom in that concentration-camp world which was later given the name 'the GULAG archipelago.'"[111]

Nature-protection activism became a vehicle, from the 1930s through the 1960s (and beyond), for the defense of a prerevolutionary ideal of science as well as for the cultivation of alternative visions of economic development and resource use, even though activists were ultimately unable to prevent the destruction, authorized by Stalin in August 1951, of the 12.6 million-hectare *zapovednik* system.[112]

Other groups seeking to develop spheres of autonomy from the Soviet state, such as Estonian, Latvian, and Russian nationalists as well as university students, saw that they too could make use of the unpoliced discursive and organizational domain of nature protection.[113] A similar use of "free space" may be seen in the history of Eastern European countries and non-Russian Soviet republics, as Jane Dawson, Barbara Hicks, Katy Láng Pickvance, and Andrew Tickle have shown.[114] However, as Pickvance in particular is keen to emphasize, the larger social implications of such activism were different in Eastern Europe. As my own research has shown, the guild-like and frequently elitist nature of Soviet-era nature-protection movements, by contrast with those of Hungary and Poland, for example, precluded them from serving as enduring and effective nuclei for the defense of broader public interests. As such, they reflected the general inability of groups in the former Soviet Union—especially in Russia—to organize and cooperate across group lines. This failure was perhaps the most poignant and most damaging consequence of the thousand-year, militarized tribute-taking state.

In a cruel irony, the fall of Communism and the transition to "democracy," supported by the vast majority of environmental activists, have created even worse conditions for the growth or even the survival of environmental movements in the post-Soviet political space. "Democrats" and nationalists, who were keen to support environmental activism as part of a broad, multipronged assault on Soviet power, had little need for green politics after they gained control of the successor states. Although environmental problems are just as serious as they were during the late 1980s, the new political realities, plus the exhaustion and cynicism of the general population, have meant that the only available sources of support for post-Soviet environmental groups are foreign foundations and international environmental organizations. Because those who pay the piper call the tune, foreign sponsors imposed their own agendas on Eurasian environmental groups. As a consequence, it is difficult to speak of indigenous environmental activism in the post-Soviet world. Ironically, as foreigners assumed trusteeship over local organizations in an effort to build what they call civil society, they in fact widened the gap between local activists, who now confine themselves largely to grant writing, and a potential mass base.[115] Even so, the Putin regime effectively eliminated the presence of foreign nongovernmental organizations in Russia in 2006.[116] On the basis of the historical record, the equation of environmental groups in the former USSR with an incipient "civil society" is unsupportable. The same is true today. One continues to look in vain for social forces with the potential to take on the tribute state and rebuild the Eurasian political economy from its foundations.

Conclusions

In the last analysis, the political rationality of Soviet economic practices—owing precisely to their economic *ir*rationality in terms of providing for the long term—fatally undermined the political stability of the system.[117] Its lack of a social vision, its inability to innovate or change, and the determination of its elites to hold on to power at all costs condemned the Soviet Union to implode under the crushing weight of its environmental, health, financial, productivity, and political problems. The political problems were actually the result of the confluence of the system's structural problems. As Arran Gare observes, the Soviet tribute-taking state's complete failure to provide a vision or incentives for its people led to a "loss of meaning ... which expressed itself, among other things, in the highest incidence of alcoholism in the world."[118] As with tsarism, the long-term, systemic production of such passive and disoriented people made the vast country far easier for the Party to control, but that same process condemned the country to

Chernobyl and other environmental disasters, as well as to long-term decay of its infrastructure, resource base, and human capital. Overgrazing, disregard for crop rotation, and an overproduction of tractors has led to the annual loss of 1.5 billion tons of topsoil.[119] Instead of ending up as useful inputs somewhere else, harmful waste products are customarily dumped into the nearest convenient waterway. Between 1981 and 1988, a full 80 percent of the budget for air-pollution control went unspent, and in 1988 Kazakstan fulfilled a mere 1 percent of its environmental-protection investment plan.[120] Even when the quantity of water subject to treatment increased (by 18 percent), as between 1980 and 1990, the amount properly treated *decreased by* 40 percent.[121] Those problems have only worsened since the breakup of the USSR.

Citing the sociologist Mancur Olson, Stefan Hedlund in his provocative study underscores the persistent feelings of insecurity—geopolitical and domestic—at the heart of Russian and Eurasian leaders' rapacious pattern of rule. "If an autocratic ruler has a short-term view, he has an incentive, no matter how gigantic his empire or how exalted his lineage, to seize any asset whose total value exceeds the discounted present value of its tax yield over his short-term horizon. In other words, just as the roving bandit leader who can securely hold a domain has an incentive to make himself king, so any autocrat with a short time horizon has an incentive to become, in effect, a roving bandit."[122]

The "main question," Hedlund asserts, "both in theoretical terms and with respect to the concrete Russian case, is whether a society that has been locked into a situation of destructive roving banditry may actually find a way out. Is it perhaps even the case that there exist 'pathological' institutions, in the form of private mental models, that are immune to public policy?"[123] In other words, how can anyone ever convince the populations of Eurasia, who have been reliving and reproducing historical trauma for a thousand years, that they should begin to believe in the possibility of a more secure existence—the core psychosocial precondition for escaping the lethal clutches of the predatory, militarized tribute state?

Theodore von Laue called attention to this vicious circle forty years ago.[124] Indeed, these persistent feelings of geopolitical and internal insecurity, seared into the consciousness of rulers and ruled alike, have fired the engine of Russia's repetitions. Shattered by the trauma of the Mongol-Tatar conquest—and reinforced by such episodes as the prolonged wars with Poland-Lithuania, the Crimean Tatars, the Ottomans, and the Swedes; the Time of Troubles; a series of anarchic peasant risings; Napoleon's sweep to Moscow; Russia's defeat at the hands of the Japanese in 1905, the humiliating loss to Germany in World War I; Allied intervention during the civil war; Bolshevik perceptions and propaganda about "capitalist encirclement"; the 1927 "War Scare"; Bolshevik leaders' fears during the 1920s of domestic "encirclement" by a "petty bourgeois" peasantry, private entrepreneurs, and non-Party professionals; the Nazi devastation of the European portion of the USSR; the Cold War; and, finally, the split with the Chinese Communists—Russia's rulers were able to gain popular support, or at least acceptance, of an economically punishing, military-oriented, predatory regime that suppressed any dissent and refused to share power. Those times when the regime, inefficiently and at great human cost, succeeded in repelling foreign invasion were tirelessly celebrated so as to bolster the regime's legitimacy during peacetime, when "normal" tribute-taking resumed. A good deal of the problem resides in the fact that Russia's history experientially supports the very kind of traumatized worldview that stands in the way of dismantling the militarized tribute state.

The premature predictions for liberal-democratic transitions by the states of Eurasia (the former Soviet Union) foundered on the reefs of historical legacies and globalization. Today there is a greater need than ever for careful studies of resource politics and economics of the area. Few would disagree that its environmental problems are affecting whole regions and even the entire planet. Because the short-term, nihilistic costing calculus of the predatory tribute-taking state is still in place, and perhaps stronger than ever, a second Chernobyl is simply waiting to happen. Scholars and policy makers alike must deepen their knowledge about these issues and come up with more imaginative ways of reconciling Eurasians' desire to become prosperous, integrated participants in the global economy with the imperative to protect their environmental quality and that of the entire planet. In the process, the global West might even begin to take a look in the mirror, where the outlines of a sinister convergence have become more pronounced of late.

Notes

I am grateful to Arja Rosenholm, Sari Autio-Sarasmo, and the Aleksanteri Institute for kindly allowing me to republish a reworked version of my article "The Genealogy of the Soviet and Post-Soviet Landscape of Risk," in *Understanding Russian Nature: Representations, Values and Concepts,* ed. Arja Rosenholm and Sari Autio-Sarasmo, Aleksanteri Papers 4/2005 (Helsinki: Aleksanteri Institute, 2005), 209–36.

1 Timothy C. Weiskel, "Toward an Archaeology of Colonialism: Elements in the Ecological Transformation of the Ivory Coast," in *The Ends of the Earth: Perspectives on Modern Environmental History,* ed. Donald Worster (Cambridge: Cambridge University Press, 1988), 141–71.

2 To subscribe to REDfiles, send an e-mail to majordomo@teia.org (Transboundary Environmental Information Agency, Elena Vassilieva, editor). For a comprehensive assessment of Russia's current environmental situation, see *Environmental Performance Reviews: Russian Federation* (Paris: Organisation for Economic Co-operation and Development, 1999); and N.N. Kliuev, ed., *Rossiia i ee regiony: Vneshnye i vnutrennie ekologicheskie ugrozy* (Moscow: Nauka, 2001). On the successor states to the Soviet Union, see Philip R. Pryde, ed., *Environmental Resources and Constraints in the Former Soviet Republics* (Boulder, CO: Westview Press, 1995).

3 Slash-and-burn cultivation was usually practiced on land covered by birch forest, not evergreens, owing to the difference in productivity. Useful surveys are R.A. French, "Introduction" and "Russians and the Forest," in *Studies in Russian Historical Geography*, vol. 1, ed. J.H. Bater and R.A. French (London: Academic Press, 1983): 13–21, 23–44.

4 V.K. Tepliakov, *Les v zhizni drevnei rusi i moskovii* (Moscow: MLTI, 1992), 11.

5 Tepliakov, *Les v zhizni*, 14.

6 Viktor Nikolaevich Bernadskii, *Novgorod i Novgorodskaia zemlia v XV veke* (Leningrad: Izdatel'stvo Akademii nauk SSSR, 1961). See also Janet Martin, *Treasure of the Land of Darkness: The Fur Trade and its Significance for Medieval Russia* (Cambridge: Cambridge University Press, 1986).

7 Vladimir Evgen'evich Boreiko, *Istorioiia okhrany prirody Ukrainy, X vek— 1980*, 2nd ed. (Kiev: Kievskii ekologo-kul'turnyi tsentr, 2001), 221.

8 Tepliakov, *Les v zhizni*, 18.

9 Boreiko, *Istoriia okhrany*, 221; Tepliakov, *Les v zhizni*, 27.

10 A.M. Sakharov makes this argument in "Rus' and Its Culture, Thirteenth to Fifteenth Centuries," *Soviet Studies in History* 18, no. 3 (Winter 1979–80): 26–32.

11 See, for example, E.I. Kolycheva, *Agrarnyi stroi Rossii XVI veka* (Moscow: Nauka, 1987), esp. 172–201.

12 Richard Hellie, *Enserfment and Military Change in Muscovy* (Chicago: University of Chicago Press, 1971), 147.

13 Ihor Stebelsky, "Agriculture and Soil Erosion in the European Forest-Steppe," in Bater and French, eds., *Studies*, 1: 48–49.

14 See my discussion of this debate in *A Little Corner of Freedom: Russian Nature Protection from Stalin to Gorbachev* (Berkeley: University of California Press, 1999), 389–94, and in "A Little Reserve Raises Big Questions," *Open Country* 4 (Summer 2002): 8–14.

15 S.V. Kirikov, *Promyslovye zhivotnye, prirodnaia sreda i chelovek* (Moscow: Nauka, 1966); *Chelovek i priroda vostochno-evropeiskoi lesostepi v X–nachale XIX v* (Moscow: Nauka, 1979).

16 Stebelsky, "Agriculture," 54.

17 French, "Russians and the Forest," 32–33.

18 Michael Confino, *Domaines et seigneurs en Russie vers la fin du XVIIIe siècle* (Paris: Institut d'Études Slaves de l'Université de Paris, 1963), 10.

19 Confino, *Domaines*, 123–25.

20 Confino, *Domaines*, 134, 147.

21 Confino, *Domaines*, 164–65. See also Douglas R. Weiner, "The Roots of 'Michurinism': Transformist Biology and Acclimatization as Currents in the Russian Life Sciences," *Annals of Science* 42 (1985): 243–60.

22 Steven L. Hoch, *Serfdom and Social Control: Petrovskoe, a Village in Tambov* (Chicago: University of Chicago Press, 1986), 52, 56, 125.

23 M.A. Tsvetkov, *Izmenenie lesistosti Evropeiskoi Rossii s kontsa XVII stoletiia po 1914 god* (Moscow: Izdatel'stvo Akademii nauk SSSR, 1957), cited in French, "Russians and the Forest," 39–40.

24 Jane Costlow, "Imaginations of Destruction: The 'Forest Question' in Nineteenth-Century Russian Culture," *Russian Review* 62 (January 2003): 91–118, esp. 100.

25 Costlow, "Imaginations of Destruction," 105.

26 Industrial production was only 21 percent of 1913 levels by 1921.

27 Peter I. Holquist, *Making War, Forging Revolution: Russia's Continuum of Crisis, 1914–1921* (Cambridge, MA: Harvard University Press, 2002); Loren R.

Graham made this observation in his article "The Formation of Soviet Research Institutes: A Combination of Revolutionary Innovation and International Borrowing," in *Russian and Slavic History,* ed. Don Karl Rowney and G. Edward Orchard (Columbus, OH: Slavica, 1977), 49–75.

28 Alexander Vucinich, *The Empire of Knowledge: The Academy of Sciences of the USSR (1917–1970)* (Berkeley: University of California Press, 1984); Kendall E. Bailes, *Science and Russian Culture in an Age of Revolutions: V.I. Vernadsky and His Scientific School* (Bloomington: Indiana University Press, 1990).

29 Douglas R. Weiner, *Models of Nature: Ecology, Conservation and Cultural Revolution in Soviet Russia,* 2nd ed. (Pittsburgh, PA: Pittsburgh University Press, 2000).

30 Weiner, *Models of Nature.*

31 Weiner, *Models of Nature.*

32 These are the words of Arnosht Kol'man, an arbiter of science for the Moscow Committee of the Communist Party, in his "Sabotazh v nauke," *Bol'shevik* 2 (1931): 75. See Weiner, *Little Corner of Freedom,* 43.

33 Vyacheslav Gerovitch and Anton Struchkov, "Epilogue: Russian Reflections," *Journal of the History of Biology* 25, no. 3 (Fall 1992): 487–95, esp. 488–90.

34 On the 1891 famine, see Richard G. Robbins Jr., *Famine in Russia: 1891–1892* (New York: Columbia University Press, 1975). Robert Conquest has written the definitive work on the 1932–33 famine, *The Harvest of Sorrow: Soviet Collectivization and the Terror-Famine* (New York: Oxford University Press, 1986).

35 R.A. French, "Canals in Prerevolutionary Russia," in Bater and French, eds., *Studies,* 2:451–81.

36 Paul Josephson, *Totalitarian Science and Technology* (Atlantic Highlands, NJ: Humanities Press, 1996), 78–79.

37 Loren R. Graham, *The Ghost of the Executed Engineer: Technology and the Fall of the Soviet Union* (Cambridge, MA: Harvard University Press, 1993), 52. He relies on the earlier history of the Dnepr Dam by Anne D. Rassweiler, *The Generation of Power: The History of Dneprostroi* (New York: Oxford University Press, 1988).

38 Thomas F. Remington writes: "[The Bolsheviks] cultivated an ideology of technological modernism which linked the accumulation of national power to the liberation of society's resources from underdevelopment. Lenin, in particular, translated the older socialist ideals of justice and equality into formulas of collective power through industrial progress. Industrialism provided the mechanistic images of Lenin's vision of society: a society grown into the state, a state in which, to be sure, power was itself shared with the masses and social choice was disaggregated into millions of discrete but automatic responses. ... [N]o chaos would be tolerated" (*Building Socialism in Bolshevik Russia: Ideology and Industrial Organization, 1917–1921* [Pittsburgh, PA: University of Pittsburgh Press, 1984], 19).

39 Remington, *Building Socialism,* 143.

40 Jonathan Coopersmith, *The Electrification of Russia, 1880–1926* (Ithaca, NY: Cornell University Press, 1992), 153, 154.

41 On this question, see Ferenc Fehér, Agnes Heller, and György Márkus, *Dictatorship over Needs: An Analysis of Soviet Societies* (Oxford: Basil Blackwell, 1983).

42 Peter Rutland, *The Myth of the Plan* (La Salle, Ill.: Open Court, 1985), 252–53.

43 Remington, *Building Socialism,* 114.

44 Remington, *Building Socialism,* 125; see also V.I. Ponomareva, ed., *Ekologiia i vlast', 1917–1990: Dokumenty* (Moscow: Mezhdunarodnyi fond "Demokratiia," 1999), documents 12 (pp. 34–35), 32 (pp. 84–86), 43 (pp. 103–5), 57 (pp. 127–28), and 91 (pp. 194–96).

45 On the metaphorical Soviet discourse on immortality, see Irene Masing-Delic, *Abolishing Death: A Salvation Myth of Russian Twentieth-Century Literature* (Stanford, CA: Stanford University Press, 1992); Katerina Clark, *The Soviet Novel: History as Ritual* (Chicago: University of Chicago Press, 1985); and Rolf Hellebust, "Aleksei Gastev and the Metallization of the Revolutionary Body," *Slavic Review* 56, no. 3 (Fall 1997): 500–518.

46 M. Gor'kii, "O temakh," *Pravda,* October 17, 1933, reprinted in *Sobranie sochinenii,* vol. 27 (Moscow: Gosudarstvennoe izdatel'stvo khudozhestvennoi literaturv, 1953), 106.

47 Remington, *Building Socialism,* 138.

48 V.Z. Rogovin, "Diskusii po problemam byta i kul'tury v Sovetskoi Rossii dvadt satykh godov," *Sotsial'nye issledovaniia,* no. 7 (1971): 46–74, esp. 63–65.

49 M. Gor'kii, "Otvet," *Investita,* December 12 and 13, 1929, in *Sobranie sochinenii 25:* 77

50 Gor'kii, "Otvet," 77.

51 Gor'kii, "O temakh," 100.

52 M. Gor'kii, "O M.M. Prishvine," *Krasnaia nov',* no. 12 (December 1926) in *Sobranie sochinenii,* 24: 265.

53 M. Gor'kii, "Zasukha budet unichtozhena," *Komsomol'skaia pravda,* September 8, 1931.

54 M. Gor'kii, "O bor'be s prirodoi," *Pravda* and *Izvestita,* December 12, 1931, in *Sobranie sochinenii,* 26: 198.

55 M. Gor'kii, "Sovetskaia literatura," *Pravda* and *Izvestita,* August 19, 1934, in *Sobranie sochinenii,* 27: 322.

56 Quoted in Il'ia Shkapa, *Sem' let s Gor'kim* (Moscow: Sovetskii pisatel', 1990), 324.

57 M. Gor'kii et al., eds., *Belomorsko-Baltiiskii Kanal imeni Stalina: Istoriia stroitel'stva* (Moscow: Gosudarstvennoe izdatel'stvo "Istorila fabrik i zavodov," 1934).

58 "Rech' na slete udarnikov Belomorstroia" originally published as "Prekrasnoe delo sdelano," *Pravda,* September 3, 1933, in *Sobranie sochinenii,* 27: 73.

59 M. Gor'kii, "O kochke i o tochke," *Pravda* and *Izvestiia,* July 10, 1933, in *Sobranie sochinenii,* 27: 43.

60 M. Gorky et al., *Belomor* (New York: Smith and Haas, 1935), 306.

61 Remington, *Building Socialism,* 175.

62 N.F. Kashchenko, "Rol' akklimatizatsii v protsesse pod' ema proizvoditel'nykh sil SSSR," *Iugoklimat: Sbornik po voprosam akklimatvzatsii rastenii i zhivotnykh* (Odessa: n.p., 1929), 5. See also Weiner, *Models,* 171–228.

63 M. Ilin, *New Russia's Primer: The Story of the Five-Year Plan,* trans. George S. Counts and Nucia P. Lodge (Boston: Houghton Mifflin Co., 1931), 141 ff., 35.

64 Weiner, *Models,* 171–228; Weiner, *Little Corner of Freedom,* 44–45, 202–5, 228–29, 248, 378–81, 386–87.

65 Vladimir Boreiko, *Belye piotna istorii prirodookhrany: SSSR, Rossiia, Ukraina,* vol. 2 (Kiev: Kievskii ekologo-kul'turnyi tsentr, 1996).

66 I argue this in "Roots of 'Michurinism'" and *Models of Nature.*

67 Stephen J. Pyne, *Vestal Fire: An Environmental History, Told through Fire, of Europe and Europe's Encounter with the World* (Seattle: University of Washington Press, 1997), 521, 525.

68 Mark Bassin, *Imperial Visions: Nationalist Imagination and the Geographical Expansion in the Russian Far East, 1840–1865* (Cambridge: Cambridge University Press, 1999).

69 See Weiner, *Models,* 213–23; Weiner, *Little Corner of Freedom,* 44–61; Boreiko, *Askania-Nova; Tiazhkie versty istorii (1826–1993)* (Kiev: Kievskii ekologo-kul'turnyi tsentr, 1994), 91. On Lysenko and Prezent, see also David Joravsky, *The Lysenko Affair* (Cambridge, MA: Harvard University Press, 1970); Zhores A. Medvedev, *The Rise and Fall of T.D. Lysenko* (Garden City, NY: Doubleday, 1971); and Valery Soyfer, *Lysenko and the Tragedy of Soviet Science,* trans. Leo and Rebecca Gruliow (New Brunswick, NJ: Rutgers University Press, 1994).

70 GA RF (State Archive of the Russian Federation), fond 404, op. 1, d. 53, listy 16–17.

71 Mikhail Vladimirovich Poddubnyi, *Sanitarnaia okhrana okruzhaiushchei sredy v Rossii i SSSR v pervoi polovine XX veka* (Kiev: Kievskii ekologo-kul'turnyi tsentr and Tsentr okhrany dikoi prirody SOES, 1997), 34. Series: Istoriia okhrany prirody, fascicle 16.

72 Poddubnyi, *Sanitarnaia okhrana okruzhiaiushchei sredy.*

73 Poddubnyi, *Sanitarnaia okhrana okruzhaiushchei sredy,* 27.

74 Boreiko, *Belye piatna,* 2: 97.

75 Loren R. Graham, "The Fits and Starts of Russian and Soviet Technology," in *Technology, Culture and Development: The Experience of the Soviet Model,* ed. James P. Scanlan (Armonk, NY: M.E. Sharpe, 1992), 3–24.

76 Rutland, *Myth of the Plan,* 107.

77 See especially Arkady Vaksberg, *The Soviet Mafia: A Shocking Exposé of Organized Crime in the USSR* (New York: St. Martin's Press, 1991).

78 Ulrich Beck, *Risk Society: Toward a New Modernity* (London: Sage, 1992); Oleg Nikolevich Ianitskii, *Rossiia: Ekologicheskii vyzov (obshchestvennoe dvizhenie, nauka, politika)* (Novosibirsk: Sibirskii khronograf, 2002), 41.

79 Kliuev, *Rossiia i ee regiony,* 42 ("ostraia ekologicheskaia situatsiia").

80 Ann-Mari Sätre Åhlander, *Environmental Problems in the Shortage Economy: The Legacy of Soviet Environmental Policy* (Aldershot, U.K.: Edward Elgar, 1994), 6–8.

81 Åhlander, *Environmental Problems,* 15.

82 Zhores A. Medvedev, *Nuclear Disaster in the Urals* (New York: Vintage, 1979).

83 Marshall I. Goldman, *The Spoils of Progress: Environmental Pollution in the Soviet Union* (Cambridge, MA: MIT Press, 1972).

84 Joan DeBardeleben, *The Environment and Marxism-Leninism: The Soviet and East German Experience* (Boulder, CO: Westview Press, 1985).

85 Thane Gustafson, *Reform in Soviet Politics: Lessons of Recent Policies on Land and Water* (New York: Cambridge University Press, 1981), and *Crisis amid Plenty: The Politics of Soviet Energy under Brezhnev and Gorbachev* (Princeton: Princeton University Press, 1989).

86 On the Aral Sea crisis and the problem of cotton-based agriculture in Central Asia, see Tom Bissell, "Eternal Winter: Lessons of the Aral Sea Disaster," *Harpers Magazine,* April 2002, 41–56; Nikolai Ivanovich Chesnokov, *Dikie zhivotnye meniaiut adresa* (Moscow: Mysl', 1989); John C.K. Daly, "Global Implications of Aral Sea Dessication," *Central Asia—Caucasus Analyst* (November 8, 2000); Murray Feshbach and Alfred Friendly Jr., *Ecocide in the USSR: Health and Nature under Siege* (New York: Basic Books, 1992); Michael H. Glantz, ed. *Creeping Environmental Problems and Sustainable Development in the Aral Sea Basin* (Cambridge: Cambridge University Press,

1999); Ulrike Grote, ed., *Central Asian Environments in Transition* (Manila: Asian Development Bank, 1997); "Receding Waters May Expose Soviet Anthrax Dump," *Austin American-Statesman* (June 2, 1999); Philip P. Micklin, ed., "The Aral Crisis," special issue of *Post-Soviet Geography*, no. 5 (1992); Philip R. Pryde, *Environmental Management in the Soviet Union* (Cambridge: Cambridge University Press, 1991); and Erika Weinthal, *State Making and Environmental Cooperation: Linking Domestic and International Politics in Central Asia* (Cambridge, MA: MIT Press, 2002).

87 John C. K. Daly, "Global Implications of Aral Sea Desiccation," *Central Asia–Caucasus Analyst* (biweekly briefing), November 8, 2000, www.cacianalyst.org/?q=node/255.

88 John D. Grace, *Russian Oil Supply: Performance and Prospects* (Oxford: Oxford University Press, 2005), chapters 3 and 4.

89 Zhores A. Medvedev, *The Legacy of Chernobyl* (New York: W.W. Norton, 1990).

90 A recent study that focuses on the timber industry similarly refines our picture of the Soviet political economy, pointing out that lower-priority sectors of the economy, such as environmental protection, suffer from lower efficiency and quality of service delivery in addition to (and partly as a consequence of) constricted access to resources. See Åhlander, *Environmental Problems*. For intelligent views of Soviet-style economies from the inside, see Gennady Andreev-Khomiakov, *Bitter Waters: Life and Work in Stalin's Russia, a Memoir* (Boulder, CO: Westview Press, 1997); and Miklós Haraszti, *A Worker in a Worker's State: Piece-Rates in Hungary* (Harmondsworth: Penguin Books, 1977).

91 On Lenin's views, see Sheila Fitzpatrick, "The Civil War as a Formative Experience," in *Bohhevik Culture*, ed. Abbott Gleason, Peter Kenez, and Richard Stites (Bloomington: Indiana University Press, 1985).

92 Vladimir Birstein, *The Perversion of Knowledge: The True Story of Soviet Science* (Boulder, CO: Westview Press, 2001), 121–22.

93 Valerli Ivanovich Bulatov, *Rossiia: ekologiia i armiia* (Novosibirsk: TsERIS, 1999), 62. S.N. Volkov estimates the number of fatalities at thirty-six thousand: see his studies "Spetssluzhby i biologicheskoe oruzhie v dvukh izmereniiakh," in *Mir, demokratiia, bezopasnost'* 12 (1998): 38–55, and *Ekaterinburg: Chelovek i gorod; Opyt sotsial'noi ekologii i prakticheskoi geourbanistiki* (Ekaterinburg, 1997).

94 Bulatov, *Ekaterinburg*, 20, 23, 51.

95 Bulatov, *Ekaterinburg*, 26, 28–29.

96 Bulatov, *Ekaterinburg*, 29.

97 Philip R. Pryde, "Environmental Implications of Republic Sovereignty," in *Environmental Resources and Constraints in the Former Soviet Republics*, ed. Philip R. Pryde (Boulder, CO: Westview Press, 1995), 12, 14.

98 Boris I. Kochurov, "European Russia," in Pryde, *Environmental Resources*, 50.

99 Anna Scherbakova and Scott Monroe, "The Urals and Siberia," in Pryde, *Environmental Resources*, 74.

100 On Vorontsov, see V.A. Krasilov, ed., E.A. Liàpunova, comp., *Evoliutsiia, ekologiia, bioraznoobrazie: Materialy konferentsii pamiati Nikolaia Nikolaevicha Vorontsova (1934–2000)* (Moscow: UNTs DO, 2001), and Evgenii Panov, "Pamiati N.N. Vorontsova," *Okhrana dikoi prirody* 23, no. 4 (2001): 45–46.

101 See Stephen F. Cohen, *Failed Crusade: America and the Tragedy of Post-Communist Russia* (New York: W.W. Norton, 2000); Peter Reddaway and Dmitri Glinski, *The Tragedy of Russia's Reforms: Market Bolshevism against*

Democracy (Herndon, VA: United States Institute of Peace Press, 2001); and Stefan Hedlund, *Russia's "Market" Economy: A Bad Case of Predatory Capitalism* (London: University College London Press, 1999).

102 Anatol Lieven, *Chechnya: Tombstone of Russian Power* (New Haven: Yale University Press, 1998), 84–86. That the oil issue is subsidiary does not make the conflict in Chechnya any less of a tribute war in other ways.

103 See Hedlund, *Russia's "Market" Economy;* Martin McCauley, *Bandits, Gangsters and the Mafia: Russia, the Baltic States, and the CIS since 1992* (Harlow, U.K.: Longman Publishers, 2001).

104 Kliuev, *Rossiia i ee regiony,* 47.

105 Kliuev, *Rossiia i ee regiony,* 47.

106 Kliuev, *Rossiia i ee regiony,* 43–44.

107 Kliuev, *Rossiia i ee regiony,* 50. In 1997 science was allotted 2.88 percent of the budget of the Russian Federation. In 2001 the science budget was a mere 1.72 percent.

108 The same question can be asked of ethno-nationalist environmental opposition to Soviet projects, which strangely fell silent once nationalities gained independence from the Soviet Union. The case of the Ignalina nuclear reactor in Lithuania is a good case in point: see Jane Dawson, *Eco-nationalism: Antinuclear Activism and National Identity in Russia, Lithuania and Ukraine* (Durham, NC: Duke University Press, 1996).

109 For an acerbic but powerful exposition of this point, see Stephen Kotkin, "Trashcanistan: A Tour through the Wreckage of the Soviet Empire," *New Republic,* April 15, 2002.

110 Boreiko, *Istoriia okhrany,* 1: 50.

111 Sergei Zalygin, "Otkroveniia ot nashego imeni," *Novyi mir* 10 (1992): 215.

112 Weiner, *Little Corner of Freedom,* 63–181.

113 See Robert G. Darst, *Smokestack Diplomacy: Cooperation and Conflict in East-West Environmental Politics* (Cambridge, MA: MIT Press, 2001); Dawson, *Eco-nationalism;* Weiner, *A Little Corner of Freedom;* Oleg Nikolaevich Ianitskii, *Sotsial'nye dvizheniia: too interv'iu s liderami* (Moscow: Moskovskii rabochii, 1991).

114 Dawson, *Eco-nationalism;* Andrew Tickle and Ian Welsh, eds., *Environment and Society in Eastern Europe* (Harlow, U.K.: Longman, 1998); Katy Láng Pickvance, *Democracy and Environmental Movements in Eastern Europe: A Comparative Study of Hungary and Russia* (Boulder, CO: Westview Press, 1998); Barbara Hicks, *Environmental Politics in Poland: A Social Movement between Regime and Opposition* (New York: Columbia University Press, 1996).

115 Ianitskii, *Rossiia,* esp. parts 3 and 4. The term *civil society* is an unfortunate one because of its extreme vagueness. Its users seem to assume that the existence of a middle class with independent professional organizations is a guarantor of civility in society and of a functioning democracy. However, the example of Germany during the 1920s and early 1930s, a society with both these features, is instructive. See also the thoughtful discussion by Joseph Bradley, "Subjects into Citizens: Societies, Civil Society, and Autocracy in Tsarist Russia," *American Historical Review* (October 2002): 1094–1123.

116 "Putin Signs Restrictive NGO Bill," *Global Policy Forum,* January 17, 2006, www.globalpolicy.org/ngos/state/2006/0117putin.htm.

117 Rutland, *Myth of the Plan,* 63. Rutland prematurely concluded (contra Hillel Ticktin, "Towards a Political Economy of the USSR," *Critique,* no. 1 [1973]: 20–41), that the "continued existence of the Soviet Union is living proof

that [political and economic rationality in the Soviet context] are not mutually contradictory." Perhaps he should have waited six years before pronouncing on the issue!

118 Arran Gare, *Beyond European Civilization: Marxism, Process Philosophy, and the Environment* (Bungendore, New South Wales: Ecological Press, 1993), 84.
119 Åhlander, *Environmental Problems*, 18.
120 Åhlander, *Environmental Problems*, 61, 71.
121 Åhlander, *Environmental Problems*, 73.
122 Hedlund, *Russia's "Market" Economy*, 25, citing Mancur Olson, "Why the Transition from Communism Is So Difficult," *Eastern Economic Journal* 21, no. 4 (1995): 445.
123 Hedlund, *Russia's "Market" Economy*, 28.
124 Theodore H. von Laue, *Why Lenin? Why Stalin? A Reappraisal of the Russian Revolution, 1900–1930* (Philadelphia: Lippincott, 1964).

14

ECOLOGY AND CULTURE IN WEST AFRICA

James L. A. Webb Jr.

For tens of thousands of years, human communities in West Africa grappled with some of the most varied and challenging environments in the world. The members of these communities evolved strategies for living on the arid grasslands of the Saharan edge, in the savanna woodlands to the south, and even down in the wet green rainforests north of the Gulf of Guinea. Like the successful Stone Age pioneers elsewhere in the African and Eurasian tropics, early West Africans drew upon a shared cultural tradition of tool-making to fashion clothing, shelter, storage containers and weapons. They used fire to shape their immediate domestic and natural environments. They cooked meat, fish and plants, transforming the yields from their hunting, fishing and gathering. In order to improve their hunting prospects, they burned patches in the grasslands and woodlands to draw wild game to the resulting fresh plant growth. In the rainforests, where lightning and natural tree fall had already torn holes in the green canopies, they charred out biologically productive edge environments, or ecotones,[1] that likewise enhanced their opportunities to harvest wild game.

The ecological zones in which early West African pioneers struggled can be depicted on a map as long and narrow bands that extend from east to west across the region. These ecological bands are characterized by distinctively different annual rainfall profiles as well as different plant and animal populations. Over a mere 2000 kilometers, a succession of highly diverse ecological zones begins at the southern edge of the Sahara, known as the sahel, where only plants and animals that have adapted to very arid conditions are able to survive. Below the sahel begins the vast and open grasslands known as the savanna, and then, at the southern edge of these grasslands, begins an ecological zone with an even denser distribution of trees, known as the woodlands. These open forests in turn merge into the nearly full humidity of the tropical rainforests and lagoons along the Gulf of Guinea.

For the countless generations of early pioneers, travel within and across one or more of these ecological zones was a common experience, building up an ecological knowledge of plants, animals, insects, water supplies and mineral resources. Newly arriving groups from neighboring regions had extensive contacts with hunting and gathering communities already familiar with the local flora and fauna in the different ecological zones, and this knowledge was critical to the success of the immigrants.

The mobility and interactions of small communities of hunters, gatherers, and fishers in the early epochs of West African history also established a common linguistic framework throughout the entire region, and this helped to forge a common West African cultural identity. Indeed even today, West Africans south of the Sahara speak West African languages that are closely related and are thus considered by scholars to belong to a single West African language family.[2]

To understand historical change in more recent eras, the diversity among these ecological zones presents special challenges for interpreting the evolving relationships between ecology and culture in West Africa. Social and natural scientists now understand that these ecological zones have been shaped in part by human activities and, in turn, that the lifestyles, which have developed in the different zones, have been fundamentally constrained by a fluid set of ecological realities. Human beings in West Africa, as in other parts of the world, were not so much living in balance with nature as they were actively shaping environments that permitted more intensive human use. From these findings, social scientists have jettisoned outdated views that the 'environment' *determined* ways of life. Put another way, the realities of ecological adaptation and human inventiveness were far more complex and more interesting than simple environmental determinism would allow.

From the natural sciences has come new knowledge about the patterns of historical climate that has led social scientists to abandon the idea that the peoples of West Africa were rooted in stable environments. Over the early ages of human colonization, the rhythms of natural climate change forced humans living in certain ecological bands to shift their survival strategies and relocate to areas that offered relief from ecological stress. These ongoing movements, in combination with the fact that early West Africans lived and built with natural materials that broke down without much trace, have meant that archaeological evidence of very early communities (with the exception of those using stone tools) has been impossible to recover. But even if the early human footprints in West Africa's tropical ecological zones were ephemeral, the early accomplishments and ecological knowledge gained in these difficult tropical environments were of great significance. They laid the foundations upon which later West African communities would develop.

Ecological zones and constraints

The aforementioned pattern of elongated ecological bands is created by the interaction of a global system of wind currents. Every year, a system of humid air circulation picks up moisture over the Gulf of Guinea, and with the rotation of the earth on its axis over the course of the year, this moist wind system moves slowly north and then retreats. A countering circulation of arid continental wind blows from the Mediterranean across the Sahara.[3] This annual pattern of wind circulation results in a marked gradient of humidity that is highest near the Gulf of Guinea, where rain falls all year long, and that then tapers to a short season (at best) of intermittent summer rainfalls in the southern Sahara. Over the course of the annual cycle, variations in total rainfall are most dramatic in the northern, arid regions. The sahelian and savanna zones are thus the most susceptible to drought.

Climatological research has also uncovered the existence of long phases of arid and humid conditions in the deep past, as well as more fine-grained understandings of fluctuations in climate in more recent millennia. These natural variations forced the migrations of human communities and changed the natural conditions under which they struggled. During drier phases, such as the period 6,000–5000 BCE, the ecological bands were compressed towards the south; during wetter phases, such as the period 4,000–2,500 BCE, this compression was reversed, and the vegetation bands migrated northward.[4] Because all of West Africa is situated within the tropics and receives considerable warmth from solar radiation during the year, rainfall, rather than warmth, was the principal limiting determinant of the different ecological zones' floral and faunal productivity. Biological productivity was lowest in the arid areas and increased progressively into the rainforest zones.

These zones of diverse vegetal and animal biodiversity stretched across broad plains at three different general elevations. Along the Atlantic coast, much of the terrain is below 200 meters elevation; one set of the interior plains extends at elevations between 200 and 350 meters, and another set at between 350 and 900 meters. From the highland areas of the southwest are found the sources of the Gambia and Senegal Rivers that drift north and west to the Atlantic Ocean, and the Niger and Volta Rivers that flow in arcs north and east, and then south to the Gulf of Guinea. These rivers pass through vast flatlands, endowed with shallow top-soils and with the generally poor sub-soils that are characteristic of the entire region.

Beyond the visible and complex worlds of flora and fauna, West Africa – like the rest of tropical Africa – also harbored a lethal universe of micro-parasites. Two particular diseases – trypanosomiasis (also known as African sleeping sickness) and malaria – became the most significant of the micro-parasitic infections that influenced human settlement patterns and culture. The indigenous mammals of West Africa had developed, over evolutionary

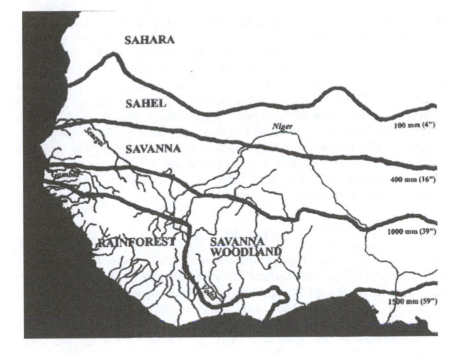

Figure 14.1 Ecological zones of West Africa.
(Source: adapted from Map 1.2 'Rainfall Patterns and Ecological Zones', in George E. Brooks, Eurafricans in Western Africa, Athens, OH: Ohio University Press, p. 3, with the permission of Ohio University Press).

time, a relationship with the trypanosomes; this allowed the mammals to serve as carriers of the parasite without suffering from the symptoms of the disease. Human beings, however, had evolved in a much more recent era and had not achieved this symbiosis. Sleeping sickness for human beings was the classic disease of the West African frontier, endemic throughout the rainforest, woodland, and grasslands. Pioneering settlers succeeded in reducing the disease threat through the extensive burning of the bush habitat required by the tsetse fly, the carrier of the disease.[5]

Malaria was a fundamental challenge to West African pioneers across all of the ecological zones, from the sahel south to the rainforest. It imposed high burdens of morbidity and mortality. To counter malaria, however, human communities evolved genetic defenses. An early mutation known as Duffy antigen negativity became common at some point after 50,000 BCE and provided immunity to *vivax* malaria, a type of malaria that caused general debilitation. So successful was this genetic defense that *vivax* almost disappeared from West Africa. A second mutation known as sickle-cell afforded some members of these early communities limited immunity to the *falciparum* malaria, the deadliest and most recently evolved type of malaria that is endemic to West Africa. West Africans still died in appallingly large numbers, particularly from *falciparum* infections in childhood, but they did not die in the numbers they would have done without sickle-cell. The downside to this imperfect form of ecological adaptation was that a minority of West Africans with the sickle-cell mutation suffered from the complications of sickle-cell anaemia.[6] Furthermore, malaria and sleeping sickness were only two – although the most important – of an array of formidable, deadly challenges to human settlement in the region. The struggles and successes of West African societies in the distant past stand out boldly when one considers that they were forged in the most difficult human- and animal-disease environment in the world.[7]

The first era

Throughout the micro-regions that were settled across all ecological zones, the most important cultural advances in early West African history were those that allowed human communities to increase dramatically the number of calories they consumed. These advances allowed for a more rapid increase in human populations, which in turn brought about rapid transformations within the West African biomes.[8] One of the most significant of these early developments was agricultural innovation, which is thought to have progressed earliest in the transition zones between the rainforest and woodland biomes.

Tens of thousands of years ago, early pioneers dug up tubers that flourished naturally in moist ecotones with partial sunlight – in woodland and rainforest clearings. Some tubers were richer in calories than others, and over thousands of years the pioneers' selection of the better tubers eventually began to develop two varieties of genetically modified yams.[9] At some much later era – perhaps at approximately 6000 BCE – human communities began to plant these yams, rather than simply gather them. And at a later period still – perhaps during the first millennium BCE – the white and yellow Guinea yams became staple food crops.[10] This was momentous; the settlement of the rainforest zone – and the extensive rainforest clearance that made it possible – was predicated upon the domestication of these two yam varieties that flourished in the wet forest environment and stored well after harvest. This horticultural revolution that began in the rainforest openings may have preceded the agricultural revolution in the more arid zones. It should be noted, however, that the horticultural revolution is not possible to date with exactness. Moist conditions do not permit the survival of plant evidence.

In the sahel and savanna, another process of agricultural innovation unfolded. Over tens of thousands of years, communities had gathered wild grasses in the floodplains and along the banks of the Senegal and Niger

Rivers and their tributaries. They had also fished and hunted in the aquatic environments. In the fourth or third millennium BCE, a long era of ongoing experimentation with wild grasses culminated in the development of millets, sorghums and wild rice. As communities began to plant these newly domesticated grains, this incipient agriculture allowed for denser human settlements along the riverbanks in the savanna and sahelian regions. Population growth was, however, very slow. The agronomic systems were adapted to the unpredictable rainfall and flood patterns, and even in good years produced very low yields by contemporary standards.

Compelling evidence of these now all but unrecoverable early ecological accommodations can be found, however, in the linguistic record. The vast array of West African languages, all related yet distinct, is testimony to the demographic impact of the horticultural and agricultural revolutions, which offered positive inducements to settlement and ultimately allowed for denser human populations and the emergence of new languages.

Even before the horticultural and agricultural revolutions had unfolded in West Africa, human communities in what are today the Sudan and Turkey began to develop their own cultural breakthroughs in the domestication of cereal grains and livestock.[11] By the sixth millennium BCE, the vast grasslands of the western and central Sahara – to the north of West Africa – had become a far frontier of these Anatolian and Nilotic centres of human innovation. A virtual continent unto itself, these grasslands were home to groups of cattle and horse pastoralists, who lived from their animals, gathered, and hunted. Some of these pastoral peoples may well have drifted west from environments along the Nile River. They spoke languages that were branches of the large Afro-Asiatic language family of northern Africa and southwest Asia.

Over time, the northern developments of animal domestication and grain production percolated into the sahelian and savanna regions of West Africa. Owing to the limitations of the evidence, it is not possible to date exactly when agriculture and livestock herding began to be incorporated into the West African lifestyles. It probably happened long before the dramatic climate shift that began in the middle of the third millennium BCE, when the Saharan grassland pastoralists were driven south during a period of marked aridity.

As the Sahara became drier, the central grasslands withered and pastoralists were forced to the margins of the desert. This resulted in a larger pastoral presence across the sahel and the northern reaches of the savanna. Over time, the practice of herding cattle, goats and sheep became widely adopted throughout the region. Although some villagers incorporated livestock directly into their agricultural systems, the major pattern to emerge was the formation of new social groups that specialized in livestock herding to the exclusion of agriculture. This development came about as people needed to move the herd animals in order to take advantage of seasonal grazing lands. The specialization of the pastoralists meant, however, that they were dependent upon settled communities for grain and other goods and services. The symbiotic relationship between livestock-herding peoples and agricultural peoples remains a prominent cultural pattern in the sahelian and savanna regions into the twenty-first century.[12] The domesticated animals were slow to find a niche below the savanna, due to the hostile disease environment. The trypanosome-carrying tsetse fly in particular injected sickness and death into domesticated livestock. The best defense against the trypanosomiasis threat to livestock – burning out the tsetse fly habitats in order to keep the fly some distance from the villages – was less practicable south of the savanna grasslands. In the first millennium BCE, a new revolutionary technology that allowed for the smelting of iron came to West Africa.[13] The new furnace designs that were capable of generating the higher temperatures that allowed for iron smelting had a profound influence on the evolution of West African history. The ability to make iron agricultural implements, land-clearing tools, and weapons of war gave dramatic advantages to those who mastered the new technologies.[14]

Continuing along the time line, which must remain highly uncertain owing to the limitations of the surviving evidence, larger human communities began to form in the southern rainforests in the first millennium BCE. This growth was possible because the ancient knowledge of fire could be harnessed to the iron-working technology, and because settled communities of good size had been able to form when the productive capacity of the cleared forest-land had been greatly increased through yam cultivation. These changes, in turn, made it possible to clear large spaces in the rainforest, although only with truly enormous investments of labor. One scholar has estimated that the clearing of a *single hectare* of mature rainforest – approximately 2.5 acres and 1400 tons of plant material – required 500 man-days.[15]

The process of Iron Age rainforest conversion, once launched, proceeded to run its course. Communities learned to draw upon the iron deposits of highly variable quality that occur throughout much of West Africa. Yet relatively dense populations took root only in a few rainforest areas. The growth of social and political complexity was principally constrained by the disease environment, the nutritional limitations of the yam-based diet, and the scarcity of people to carry out the necessary labour of forest clearance.

By the beginning of the first millennium CE, West African settled communities, which were more complex than hunting and gathering societies, were well ensconced in all of the various ecological zones. These successes were built upon a deeply rooted knowledge of the local ecologies. Yet, despite this knowledge, West African societies were engaged in an ongoing struggle to achieve social and political stability in the face of a difficult environment. They developed new ways of organizing their societies. For example, in the northern regions, the communities developed the institution of endogamous caste, which allowed for individual and small-group mobility and supported the transmission of advanced technical knowledge within specialist subgroups. In the woodlands and rainforests, the communities organized themselves around the institution of the clan, which allowed for those in authority to control access to and to assign responsibility for the agricultural fields, which had been cleared through prodigious effort. Furthermore, across all regions, people developed new cosmological systems that linked their own struggles to those which had come before them. Their artisans worked with local materials and achieved impressive artistic successes.

Over time, this more intensive human settlement generated a wealth of new ecological knowledge about regional flora, fauna, climate, and mineral resources that the growing communities could put to use. Through fire, hunting, gathering, land clearance for agriculture and horticulture, and the introduction of domesticated animals, West African communities, like other Iron Age communities elsewhere in the world, began to have a great impact on their local environments and to generate more significant environmental change. Livestock herds grazed selectively and began to modify their environments. Agriculturalists and horticulturalists burned and simplified their local biotic environments, thereby producing more biologically productive edge environments for smaller animals and birds. West Africans, like other Iron Age communities, worked to reduce their own exposure to dangerous wild animals, pushing them away from villages and their environs. Some of these initiatives were strikingly successful. To cite only one example, the elephant, once a capstone species prominent across West Africa's ecological zones, was pushed close to regional extinction.[16]

New northern influences

In the millennia before the common era, the introduction of domesticated animals and iron-making technology had profound impacts on the course of West African history. In the last centuries of the first millennium CE, new northern influences had helped to redirect the course of West African historical change. Camels came to replace horses and oxen as the principal beasts of burden in North Africa c. 300–600 CE, and by c. 800 CE camel caravans were regularly traveling across the Sahara.[17]

The more regular contact between West and North Africa had important repercussions. The complex changes taking place in the societies of the Mediterranean region, including more intensive market exchange, began to stimulate new forms of economic activity in West Africa. The demand for West African export goods was highly specialized, and because the distances from West Africa to the Mediterranean markets were great, only export goods that, in economic terms, had a high value-to-bulk ratio could bear the cost of transport. The two principal goods that met this requirement were gold and captives.[18]

Local political authorities near the sahelian gold fields built more elaborate political structures both to organize gold mining and to raise and maintain military forces capable of protecting the high-value exports. Ultimately, these military forces were bolstered by the availability of new steel weapons and cavalry horses imported from North Africa. In brief, this meant that the cultural and political implications of the export of West African gold and captives were highly significant, because the long-distance trade across the Sahara underwrote the successive growth and elaboration of the celebrated empires of Ghana (c. 800–1240 CE), Mali (1240–1464 CE), and Songhai (1464–1591 CE). This would not be the last time that international trade would prove to be a 'double-edged' sword; although the export of gold itself does not seem to have had a deleterious effect on West Africa's path of development, the political violence that generated slaves for export produced immense suffering among the societies of the sahel and savanna that found themselves under assault. The growth of empire meant that even those communities which were not raided, but which lay within the imperial sphere, were forced to give up some of their agricultural product to augment state coffers.

Even beyond the arid zones of the sahel and savanna, the influence of international economic demand was considerable. In the case of Asante, for example, which was the largest precolonial polity carved out of the West African rainforest, the export of gold to international bullion markets produced an inflow of slaves, rather than an outflow.[19] Asante's gold sales allowed for the massive importation of workers both from the savanna and from coastal lands along the Gulf of Guinea into Asante, whose labor could be committed to a truly massive clearance of rainforest. The result was the elaboration of the kingdom of Asante, a polity that replaced earlier hunting and gathering communities with the great matriclan system. These political and cultural institutions evolved along with the massive ecological transformation of the rainforest in the course of the fifteenth, sixteenth, and seventeenth centuries.[20]

The introduction of Islam was also fundamental in redrawing the cultural map of West Africa. Islam percolated south into and across the Sahara in the course of the seventh and eighth centuries and very gradually began to produce a new line of cultural demarcation between the sahel and savanna to the north, and the forest regions to the south. The Islamic worldview was conducive to trade; it also brought with it literacy, and insisted upon a code of conduct and belief that was consistent with practices of the great intercultural Muslim zone of the Mediterranean and southwest Asia. Over time, Islamic and non-Islamic societies in West Africa grew increasingly distinct; indeed, one eminent historian held that these divisions

between Islamic and non-Islamic West African societies were so fundamental that one might dispense altogether with the idea of a West African
cultural zone.[21] Yet from other perspectives, such as that of state building
in the arid zones that were later Islamized, the case for grand cultural
continuities – both before and after Islam – is very strong. The empires of
Ghana, Mali, and Songhai flourished with the same general basis of political economy before, during, and after the conversion to Islam. The cultural
impact of Islamization, however, was without doubt broad and far-reaching.
Islamic conversion brought with it some familiarity with the ethos and
worldview of Muslims in northern Africa. Cultural influences from
West Africa also flowed north across the Sahara, although at terrible
cost. Muslim merchants and raiders funneled Africans who were captured in
West African warfare into the Saharan and trans-Saharan slave trade, and
in this manner brought about a further mixing of cultural influences.

Atlantic influences

One of the staples of international trade in the period before c. 1500 CE was
the export of captives across the Sahara. This might at first appear surprising because in West African communities, owing to the difficult disease
environment and to the low caloric yields from the principal grain crops,
labor was in chronically short supply. Indeed, because an agricultural surplus was so hard won from the generally poor soils of West Africa, virtually
all West African societies across all ecological zones developed cultural
mechanisms for the control of labor, including distinctive social identities for
dependants and slaves.[22] Yet beyond the need for an agricultural surplus,
an elite ruling class required the services of a powerful military to support
its political dominance. For this reason, West African political authorities
were generally willing to sell captives in exchange for military goods.

The slave trades imposed high costs in human suffering. The economic
logic of the slave trade into and across the Sahara was cold: captives were
sold to import war horses and steel weaponry that in turn were used
to collect taxes and gather more slaves.[23] This was also the fundamental
economic logic upon which the Atlantic slave trade was built. West African
political authorities purchased iron bars (that could be transformed into
weapons and agricultural implements) and guns, in addition to consumable
goods, in exchange for captives.[24] As in the case of international trade with
North Africa, the result was the growth of larger and more complex political structures among the more powerful state participants in the trade,
and a general increase in the level of insecurity and suffering for those outside the umbrella of state protection. Beyond the political and military
realms, the consequences of the Atlantic slave trade for West African societies were complex and varied. From an ecological point of view, one large
benefit during the course of the Atlantic slave trade was the transfer of

several New World crops with very high caloric yields – particularly corn (maize), cassava (manioc), and to a lesser extent the peanut (groundnut) and potato – which set off rapid demographic growth, perhaps as significant as that caused in earlier millennia by the agricultural and horticultural revolutions and the introduction of iron technology.

From the 1830s, following the abolition of the Atlantic slave trade, communities in or near the coastal zones began to specialize in the production of vegetable oil crops such as the peanut, palm kernel, and palm oil.[25] The reallocation of labor and productive terrain along the coast had significant consequences for West African societies, because the new opportunities for production of agricultural goods for export created pressures to create a new gendered division of labour. Often, men took charge of the vegetable oil 'cash crops'; women came to specialize increasingly in the grain 'food crops'. Later these new opportunities (and in some cases, colonial requirements) for the production of other cash crops were extended into zones far from the coast in the interior by the construction of railways, and in the second quarter of the twentieth century by the construction of roads for long-distance truck transport.

This new orientation towards export agriculture thus began well before the establishment of European colonial rule and continued throughout the twentieth century and into the twenty-first. In conjunction with rapid population growth, this export orientation brought about the conversion of rainforest and savanna to agricultural fields. The ecological consequences of this conversion were a complex set of costs and benefits, depending in part upon the characteristics of the export crop, the soil endowment, and the style of cultivation. On the cost side was damage to the soil; in the sahel and savanna, the cultivation of cotton and peanuts was notorious for impoverishing the soil. In the rainforest and woodlands zones, export crops could wreak similar damage; in the cocoa regions of Ghana, for example, the soils became depleted and degraded.[26] Another cost was the fact that planting large fields of a single crop ('mono-cropping') could dramatically increase the opportunities for insect infestation and fungal blight. These difficulties, of course, had also plagued the simple fields of millets, sorghum, and rice; the difference was one of scale and the extent of vulnerability. When the root-borer struck the cocoa plantations in the Gold Coast (Ghana) in the 1930s, the entire colonial economy – and that of the local producers – was threatened.

On the benefit side, at least potentially, lay opportunities for West African farmers to increase the flow of income to their families and communities, and to improve health and future prospects. According to liberal economic theory, this new export orientation would produce an economic stimulus towards general development, as well as providing a financial foundation for the colonial state; however, the real effects were less salubrious than those imagined by the theorists, and the colonial authorities made sure that their state revenue bases were secure before passing on revenue from export sales to producers. But the increase in export trade brought larger numbers of West Africans into the margins of a rapidly evolving international commercial culture. Among the more significant cultural transformations that took place over the colonial period was an increasing familiarity with the European-style paper and metal coin currencies, which replaced the cowry shell and brass manila currencies. With the general acceptance of 'modern' European-style currencies, West Africans came to embrace a new, and increasingly global, ethos of consumerism.

Other forms of ecological change within West Africa were initiated directly by European colonialists who were guided by cultural values that were profoundly different from those of their African subjects. Late nineteenth-century and early twentieth-century Europeans in colonial service were, in general, unfavorably impressed by the low productivity of West African agricultural systems, which they understood to be a function of less advanced technology, a lack of initiative, and primitive ecological practices. They identified the agronomic practice of 'shifting cultivation' (that allowed for long fallow periods) as responsible for environmental degradation. Thus the colonialists, presuming that they had ecological knowledge superior to that of West Africans with centuries of accumulated experience, prescribed an intensification of agricultural production, to be led either by market forces or by coercion. These beliefs may seem irrational today, but they were a 'logical' extension of the hodgepodge of ideas known as 'pseudo-scientific racism' that insisted on the general inferiority of Africans. These beliefs were to prove remarkably resilient.

Colonial and post-colonial interventions

One of the principal colonial ecological beliefs was that the Sahara was expanding as a result of destructive human land-use practices. Europeans believed that the ongoing process of desertification was caused principally by the misuse of grasslands at the desert edge by pastoralists, and by the destruction of trees by villagers. Taken together, these deleterious practices were thought by European colonizers to have allowed the arid landscape to expand and thereby to threaten the viability of local economies. In this view, sahelian ecological practices were directly responsible for poverty and food scarcity. The idea that there could be dramatic shifts in regional climate that were generated by broader natural forces was not considered, and nor was there an appreciation that the historical record was closer to one of short and medium shifts in climate than to long-term equilibrium. In fact, as noted above, climate shifts were one of the fundamental forces for ecological and cultural change in earlier epochs.

The belief that West Africans were responsible for environmental degradation, combined with the general frustration the colonial masters felt with the low level of wealth creation from small-farmer export-oriented agriculture, led colonial regimes before and after the Second World War to begin planning for large-scale ecological interventions, particularly in arid regions. One French colonial project – to bring in African workers to the floodplains of the Niger River in order to develop new 'rational' models of irrigated agriculture – was a dismal failure.[27] In the post-war period, the emphasis shifted from the control of labor to more overtly technological solutions. In the second half of the twentieth century, both the French and the British, and later their international partners, joined forces to construct large storage dams on the major West African rivers (the Senegal, Niger, and Volta) to make impounded water available for irrigation and to produce hydroelectricity.

The rationale for these interventions appeared logical and purposeful to its designers, who worked 'from the top down' and did not attempt to elicit responses, reactions, and suggestions from the villagers who would be most directly affected by the interference. The building of dams dramatically reversed ancient patterns of the floodplains and rain-fed agriculture, and involved the uprooting of communities. With massive capital investments, West African watershed ecologies were reworked to an international model with mixed success. A parallel development took place in the dryland farming systems where the agricultural practices of West African farmers began to be reshaped by the ideas of international scientific agronomy. The denigration of the indigenous ecological knowledge of West African communities by outside 'development experts' has proved remarkably persistent, although in the small-farmer sector today there is an increasing appreciation of local wisdom.[28]

Another major set of ecological interventions emerged from professional ecologists' concerns about the loss of global wildlife habitat. By the 1980s, the ongoing conversion of the rainforest biome to agriculture (under the aegis of European-owned plantation agriculture as well as that of West Africans) began to cause alarm in Western conservationist circles. West Africans were once again blamed for environmental degradation, and chief among the charges was that of profligate deforestation. The empirical reality of deforestation in West Africa is extremely complex, and it is indeed certain that rainforest habitat was shrinking. The forces responsible were numerous: multinational corporations cut rainforest timber, as did West African entrepreneurs; population growth generated political pressure to open up new lands; and the net result was a loss of wildlife habitat.[29] With the rise of non-governmental organizations (NGOs) in the last decades of the twentieth century, and with the global environmental ideal of biodiversity protection honored at least in word in the agenda of the World Bank, some NGOs such as the World Wildlife Fund for Nature moved in aggressively to protect wildlife habitat. In the Central African Republic, they did this by creating a small military force to keep forest peoples away from protected areas, justifying their policies in the belief that forest peoples were ecologically destructive.[30]

In the late twentieth and early twenty-first centuries one of the most significant transformations in West African ecology and culture has come about as a result of the growth of urban centres. The roots of this recent urbanization stretch back into the early colonial period, when railroads and roads were built to facilitate the evacuation of cash crops to the ports. Over time, large numbers of West Africans left their rural communities in search of better life prospects in the dense and sprawling urban environments. These migrants, who often initially traveled to urban areas with the intention of returning ultimately to the countryside, have generally not returned. This rural-urban movement has been particularly pronounced since the 1960s, when West African governments began to subsidize the importation of staple foods for urban populations. These policies had the effect of reducing the incentives for farmers to grow food for the urban market, thereby encouraging more rural-urban migration.

In the cities, the children of first-generation urban settlers have grown up without an unbroken, intimate knowledge of rural ways of life and ecology. This cultural transformation is part of a broader pattern of increasing globalization. In urban West Africa, rice flows in from Southeast Asia; city-dwellers wear clothes woven on looms in Europe, East Asia, and North America; and families watch television shows that flood their compounds with new socio-cultural messages. These influences also spill, to a lesser extent, into the rural towns and villages of West Africa. Globalization has created new desires for participation in the culture of consumerism. Yet incomes in West Africa remain very low by global standards, and most individuals are still unable to embrace a Westernized lifestyle devoted to consumerism.

At least since the mid-twentieth century, population growth has been rapid in both the burgeoning urban centres and in the countryside. The expansion of West African population – even under the constraints of the HIV/AIDS epidemic and the continuing burden of malaria – constitutes the single most important force for ecological change today.[31] It exerts ongoing pressure to open up new lands for agriculture, livestock herding, mining, and logging, as well as urban settlement. The net result is an accelerated process of biome conversion that is part of a global pattern throughout the tropics.

Notes

1 An ecotone is a transitional zone between two biotic communities – such as forest and field.
2 With the principal exception of the Hausa speakers of northern Nigeria, whose linguistic ancestors were relatively recent arrivals.
3 The interface between these wind systems is known at the Inter-Tropical Convergence Zone. For further information on West African climate, see

Derek F. Hayward and Julius S. Oguntoyinbo, *Climatology of West Africa* (London, 1987).

4 See A.S. Brooks and P.T. Robertshaw, 'The Glacial Maxima in Tropical Africa: 22,000–12,000 BP', in O. Soffer and C. Gamble (eds), *The World at 18,000 BP, Vol. 2: Low Latitudes* (London, 1990), pp. 121–69; Susan K. McIntosh and Roderick J. McIntosh, 'West African Prehistory (from c. 10,000 to A.D. 1000)', *American Scientist*, 69 (1981): 602–13; George E. Brooks, *Landlords & Strangers: Ecology, Society, and Trade in Western Africa, 1000–1630* (Boulder, CO, 1993), pp. 7–9.

5 The classic work on this is John Ford, *The Role of the Trypanosomiases in African History* (Oxford, 1972).

6 Georges C. Benjamin, 'Sickle-Cell Anemia', in Kenneth Kiple (ed.), *The Cambridge World History of Human Disease* (Cambridge, 1993), pp. 1006–8.

7 See Emmanuel Akyeampong, 'Disease in West African History', in E. K. Akyeampong (ed.), *Themes in West African History* (Athens: Ohio University Press, 2006), 186–207, for more information on this subject.

8 A biome is a term that refers to a major ecological zone and the organisms that live in it.

9 *Dioscorea cayensis, Dioscorea rotundata:* the white and yellow Guinea yams, respectively.

10 Patricia J. O'Brien, 'Sweet Potatoes and Yams' in Kenneth F. Kiple and Kriemhild Coneè Ornelas (eds), *The Cambridge World History of Food* (Cambridge, 2000), vol. I, pp. 207–18, especially pp. 212–15.

11 The relative timing of these breakthroughs is not agreed upon by experts. Christopher Ehret has recently weighed the evidence and suggested that the complex of early human achievements in food-gathering, planting, and iron-making took place in the Sudanic region of Eastern Africa as well as in the southwestern region of Eurasia. For new historical perspectives on early Africa, see Christopher Ehret, *The Civilizations of Africa. A History to 1800* (Charlottesville, VA; Oxford, 2002).

12 Some of the most detailed and influential work has been done on the ancient communities in the Niger Bend region, where the Niger River flows north into the desert edge, before turning east to empty into the Bight of Benin. In the Niger Bend, the fluctuations in historical climate were significant enough to force populations out of settled areas and into the pastoral livestock-herding sector. This 'pulse model' of historical change might be extended to unveil new understandings of cultural identity in West Africa. Boundaries of all types – ecological and cultural – were porous and changed over time. Roderick J. McIntosh, 'Pulse Model: Genesis and Accommodation of Specialization in the Middle Niger', *Journal of African History,* 34(2) (1993): 181–200.

13 Iron smelting is believed to have originated in Turkey or perhaps in Sudan.

14 Nok culture on the great Jos plateau in what is today central Nigeria may mark the southernmost extension of large-scale settled community life in the first millennium BCE, and it is in Nok culture that one finds the earliest evidence of smelting iron in West Africa. On the importance of metallurgy in African history, see John Iliffe, *Africans: The History of a Continent* (Cambridge, 1995), pp. 18–36.

15 Ivor Wilks, 'Land, Labor, Gold, and the Forest Kingdom of Asante: A Model of Early Change', in Ivor Wilks (ed.), *Forests of Gold: Essays on the Akan and the Kingdom of Asante* (Athens, OH, 1993), pp. 58–59.

16 One of the most striking results of these initiatives is the virtual disappearance of the elephant from West Africa. See Jonathan Kingdon, *Island Africa. The Evolution of Africa's Rare Animals and Plants* (Princeton, 1989), p. 94.

17 The one-humped camel, the dromedary, was first domesticated in Arabia c. 1200 BCE.

18 Arabic texts are the principal sources for our understanding of the early trans-Saharan trade. See Nehemiah Levtzion and J.F.P. Hopkins (eds), *Corpus of Early Arabic Sources for West African History,* trans. J.F.P. Hopkins (Cambridge, 1981).

19 On slaves in early Asante history, see A. Norman Klein, 'Slavery and Akan Origins', *Ethnohistory,* 41(4) (1994): 627–56 and Ivor Wilks, 'Slavery and Akan Origins? A Reply', *Ethnohistory,* vol. 41(4) (1994): pp. 657–65.

20 Wilks, 'Land, Labor, Gold, and the Forest Kingdom of Asante', pp. 41–90.

21 Philip Curtin, 'Africa North of the Forest' in Philip Curtin et al., (eds) *African History* (Boston, MA, 1978), especially pp. 79–81.

22 See Ismail Rashid, 'Class, Caste, and Social Inequality in West African History', in E. K. Akyeampong (ed.), *Themes in West African History* (Athens: Ohio University Press, 2006), 118–140, for more information on this subject.

23 James L.A. Webb, Jr, *Desert Frontier: Ecological and Economic Change along the Western Sahel, 1600–1850* (Madison, WI, 1995); Robin Law, *The Horse in West African History* (Oxford, 1980).

24 John K. Thornton, *Africa and Africans in the Making of the Atlantic World, 1400–1680* (Cambridge, 1992).

25 Oceanic transport costs dropped sharply beginning in the 1830s, owing to the use of the steam engine on ever larger ships.

26 Kojo Sebastian Amanor, *The New Frontier: Farmers' Response to Land Degradation. A West African Study* (London, 1994).

27 Monica van Beusekom, *Negotiating Development: African Farmers and Colonial Experts at the Office du Niger, 1920–1960* (Portsmouth, NH, 2002).

28 Michael Mortimore, *Roots in the African Dust* (Cambridge, 1998).

29 James Fairhead and Melissa Leach, *Reframing Deforestation. Global Analysis and Local Realities: Studies in West Africa* (London, 1998).

30 Tamara Giles-Vernick, *Cutting the Vines of the Past: Environmental Histories of the Central African Rain Forest* (Charlottesville, VA, 2002).

31 See Emmanuel Akyeampong, 'Disease in West African History' for more information on this subject.

Recommended reading

Akyeampong, Emmanuel (2000) *Between the Sea and the Lagoon: An Eco-social History of the Anlo of Southeastern Ghana c. 1850 to Recent Times* (Athens, OH: Ohio University Press; Oxford: James Currey).

Amanor, Kojo Sebastian (1994) *The New Frontier: Farmers' Response to Land Degradation. A West African Study* (London: Zed Books).

Brooks, George E. (1993) *Landlords & Strangers: Ecology, Society, and Trade in Western Africa, 1000–1630* (Boulder, CO: Westview Press).

Fairhead, James and Melissa Leach (1995) *Misreading the African, Landscape: Society and Ecology in a Forest-Savanna Mosaic* (Cambridge: Cambridge University Press).

McIntosh, Roderick J. (1998) *The Peoples of the Middle Niger* (Oxford and Malden, MA: Blackwell Publishers).

Richards, Paul (1985) *Indigenous Agricultural Revolution: Ecology and Food Production in West Africa* (London: Hutchison).

Webb, Jr, James L.A. (1995) *Desert Frontier: Ecological and Economic Change along the Western Sahel, 1600–1850* (Madison, WI: University of Wisconsin).

Part III

ENVIRONMENTALISMS

15

THE TROUBLE WITH WILDERNESS

Or, getting back to the wrong nature

William Cronon

The time has come to rethink wilderness

This will seem a heretical claim to many environmentalists, since the idea of wilderness has for decades been a fundamental tenet – indeed, a passion – of the environmental movement, especially in the United States. For many Americans wilderness stands as the last remaining place where civilization, that all too human disease, has not fully infected the earth. It is an island in the polluted sea of urban-industrial modernity, the one place we can turn for escape from our own too-muchness. Seen in this way, wilderness presents itself as the best antidote to our human selves, a refuge we must somehow recover if we hope to save the planet. As Henry David Thoreau once famously declared, "In Wildness is the preservation of the World."[1]

But is it? The more one knows of its peculiar history, the more one realizes that wilderness is not quite what it seems. Far from being the one place on earth that stands apart from humanity, it is quite profoundly a human creation – indeed, the creation of very particular human cultures at very particular moments in human history. It is not a pristine sanctuary where the last remnant of an untouched, endangered, but still transcendent nature can for at least a little while longer be encountered without the contaminating taint of civilization. Instead, it is a product of that civilization, and could hardly be contaminated by the very stuff of which it is made. Wilderness hides its unnaturalness behind a mask that is all the more beguiling because it seems so natural. As we gaze into the mirror it holds up for us, we too easily imagine that what we behold is Nature when in fact we see the reflection of our own unexamined longings and desires. For this reason, we mistake ourselves when we suppose that wilderness can be the solution to our culture's problematic relationships with the nonhuman world, for wilderness is itself no small part of the problem.

To assert the unnaturalness of so natural a place will no doubt seem absurd or even perverse to many readers, so let me hasten to add that the nonhuman world we encounter in wilderness is far from being merely our own invention. I celebrate with others who love wilderness the beauty and power of the things it contains. Each of us who has spent time there can conjure images and sensations that seem all the more hauntingly real for having engraved themselves so indelibly on our memories. Such memories may be uniquely our own, but they are also familiar enough be to be instantly recognizable to others. Remember this? The torrents of mist shoot out from the base of a great waterfall in the depths of a Sierra canyon, the tiny droplets cooling your face as you listen to the roar of the water and gaze up toward the sky through a rainbow that hovers just out of reach. Remember this too: looking out across a desert canyon in the evening air, the only sound a lone raven calling in the distance, the rock walls dropping away into a chasm so deep that its bottom all but vanishes as you squint into the amber light of the setting sun. And this: the moment beside the trail as you sit on a sandstone ledge, your boots damp with the morning dew while you take in the rich smell of the pines, and the small red fox – or maybe for you it was a raccoon or a coyote or a deer – that suddenly ambles across your path, stopping for a long moment to gaze in your direction with cautious indifference before continuing on its way. Remember the feelings of such moments, and you will know as well as I do that you were in the presence of something irreducibly nonhuman, something profoundly Other than yourself. Wilderness is made of that too.

And yet: what brought each of us to the places where such memories became possible is entirely a cultural invention. Go back 250 years in American and European history, and you do not find nearly so many people wandering around remote corners of the planet looking for what today we would call "the wilderness experience." As late as the eighteenth century, the most common usage of the word "wilderness" in the English language referred to landscapes that generally carried adjectives far different from the ones they attract today. To be a wilderness then was to be "deserted," "savage," "desolate," "barren" – in short, a "waste," the word's nearest synonym. Its connotations were anything but positive, and the emotion one was most likely to feel in its presence was "bewilderment" or terror.[2]

Many of the word's strongest associations then were biblical, for it is used over and over again in the King James Version to refer to places on the margins of civilization where it is all too easy to lose oneself in moral confusion and despair. The wilderness was where Moses had wandered with his people for forty years, and where they had nearly abandoned their God to worship a golden idol.[3] "For Pharaoh will say of the Children of Israel," we read in Exodus, "They are entangled in the land, the wilderness hath shut them in."[4] The wilderness was where Christ had struggled with the devil and endured his temptations: "And immediately the Spirit driveth him into the wilderness. And he was there in the wilderness for forty days tempted of Satan; and was with the wild beasts; and the angels ministered unto him."[5] The "delicious Paradise" of John Milton's Eden was surrounded by "a steep wilderness, whose hairy sides/Access denied" to all who sought entry.[6] When Adam and Eve were driven from that garden, the world they entered was a wilderness that only their labor and pain could redeem. Wilderness, in short, was a place to which one came only against one's will, and always in fear and trembling. Whatever value it might have arose solely from the possibility that it might be "reclaimed" and turned toward human ends – planted as a garden, say, or a city upon a hill.[7] In its raw state, it had little or nothing to offer civilized men and women.

But by the end of the nineteenth century, all this had changed. The wastelands that had once seemed worthless had for some people come to seem almost beyond price. That Thoreau in 1862 could declare wildness to be the preservation of the world suggests the sea change that was going on. Wilderness had once been the antithesis of all that was orderly and good – it had been the darkness, one might say, on the far side of the garden wall – and yet now it was frequently likened to Eden itself. When John Muir arrived in the Sierra Nevada in 1869, he would declare, "No description of Heaven that I have ever heard or read of seems half so fine."[8] He was hardly alone in expressing such emotions. One by one, various corners of the American map came to be designated as sites whose wild beauty was so spectacular that a growing number of citizens had to visit and see them for themselves. Niagara Falls was the first to undergo this transformation, but it was soon followed by the Catskills, the Adirondacks, Yosemite, Yellowstone, and others. Yosemite was deeded by the U.S. government to the state of California in 1864 as the nation's first wildland park, and Yellowstone became the first true national park in 1872.[9]

By the first decade of the twentieth century, in the single most famous episode in American conservation history, a national debate had exploded over whether the city of San Francisco should be permitted to augment its water supply by damming the Tuolumne River in Hetch Hetchy valley, well within the boundaries of Yosemite National Park. The dam was eventually built, but what today seems no less significant is that so many people fought to prevent its completion. Even as the fight was being lost, Hetch Hetchy became the battle cry of an emerging movement to preserve wilderness. Fifty years earlier, such opposition would have been unthinkable. Few would have questioned the merits of "reclaiming" a wasteland like this in order to put it to human use. Now the defenders of Hetch Hetchy attracted widespread national attention by portraying such an act not as improvement or progress but as desecration and vandalism. Lest one doubt that the old biblical metaphors had been turned completely on their heads, listen to John Muir attack the dam's defenders. "Their arguments," he wrote, "are curiously like those of the devil, devised for the destruction of the first garden – so much of the very best Eden fruit going to waste; so much of the best Tuolumne water and Tuolumne scenery going to waste."[10] For Muir and the growing number of Americans who shared his views, Satan's home had become God's own temple.

The sources of this rather astonishing transformation were many, but for the purposes of this essay they can be gathered under two broad headings: the sublime and the frontier. Of the two, the sublime is the older and more pervasive cultural construct, being one of the most important expressions of that broad transatlantic movement we today label as romanticism; the frontier is more peculiarly American, though it too had its European antecedents and parallels. The two converged to remake wilderness in their own image, freighting it with moral values and cultural symbols that it carries to this day. Indeed, it is not too much to say that the modern environmental movement is itself a grandchild of romanticism and post-frontier ideology, which is why it is no accident that so much environmentalist discourse takes its bearings from the wilderness these intellectual movements helped create. Although wilderness may today seem to be just one environmental concern among many, it in fact serves as the foundation for a long list of other such concerns that on their face seem quite remote from it. That is why its influence is so pervasive and, potentially, so insidious.

To gain such remarkable influence, the concept of wilderness had to become loaded with some of the deepest core values of the culture that created and idealized it: it had to become sacred. This possibility had been present in wilderness even in the days when it had been a place of spiritual danger and moral temptation. If Satan was there, then so was Christ, who had found angels as well as wild beasts during His sojourn in the desert. In the wilderness the boundaries between human and nonhuman, between natural and supernatural, had always seemed less certain than elsewhere. This was why the early Christian saints and mystics had often emulated Christ's desert retreat as they sought to experience for themselves the visions and spiritual testing He had endured. One might meet devils and run the risk of losing one's soul in such a place, but one might also meet God. For some that possibility was worth almost any price.

By the eighteenth century this sense of the wilderness as a landscape where the supernatural lay just beneath the surface was expressed in the doctrine of the *sublime*, a word whose modern usage has been so watered down by commercial hype and tourist advertising that it retains only a dim echo of its former power.[11] In the theories of Edmund Burke, Immanuel Kant, William Gilpin, and others, sublime landscapes were those rare places on earth where one had more chance than elsewhere to glimpse the face of God.[12] Romantics had a clear notion of where one could be most sure of having this experience. Although God might, of course, choose to show Himself anywhere, He would most often be found in those vast, powerful landscapes where one could not help feeling insignificant and being reminded of one's own mortality. Where were these sublime places? The eighteenth century catalog of their locations feels very familiar, for we still see and value landscapes as it taught us to do. God was on the mountaintop, in the chasm, in the waterfall, in the thundercloud, in the rainbow, in the sunset. One has only to think of the sites that Americans chose for their first national parks – Yellowstone, Yosemite, Grand Canyon, Rainier, Zion – to realize that virtually all of them fit one or more of these categories. Less sublime landscapes simply did not appear worthy of such protection; not until the 1940s, for instance, would the first swamp be honored, in Everglades National Park, and to this day there is no national park in the grasslands.[13]

Among the best proofs that one had entered a sublime landscape was the emotion it evoked. For the early romantic writers and artists who first began to celebrate it, the sublime was far from being a pleasurable experience. The classic description is that of William Wordsworth as he recounted climbing the Alps and crossing the Simplon Pass in his autobiographical poem *The Prelude*. There, surrounded by crags and waterfalls, the poet felt himself literally to be in the presence of the divine – and experienced an emotion remarkably close to terror:

> The immeasurable height
> Of woods decaying, never to be decayed,
> The stationary blasts of waterfalls,
> And in the narrow rent at every turn
> Winds thwarting winds, bewildered and forlorn,
> The torrents shooting from the clear blue sky,
> The rocks that muttered close upon our ears,
> Black drizzling crags that spake by the way-side
> As if a voice were in them, the sick sight
> And giddy prospect of the raving stream,
> The unfettered clouds and region of the Heavens,
> Tumult and peace, the darkness and the light –
> Were all like workings of one mind, the features
> Of the same face, blossoms upon one tree;
> Characters of the great Apocalypse,
> The types and symbols of Eternity,
> Of first, and last, and midst, and without end.[14]

This was no casual stroll in the mountains, no simple sojourn in the gentle lap of nonhuman nature. What Wordsworth described was nothing less than a religious experience, akin to that of the Old Testament prophets as they conversed with their wrathful God. The symbols he detected in this wilderness landscape were more supernatural than natural, and they inspired more awe and dismay than joy or pleasure. No mere mortal was meant to linger long in such a place, so it was with considerable relief that Wordsworth and his companion made their way back down from the peaks to the sheltering valleys.

Lest you suspect that this view of the sublime was limited to timid Europeans who lacked the American know-how for feeling at home in the wilderness, remember Henry David Thoreau's 1846 climb of Mount Katahdin, in Maine. Although Thoreau is regarded by many today as one of the great American celebrators of wilderness, his emotions about Katahdin were no less ambivalent than Wordsworth's about the Alps.

> It was vast, Titanic, and such as man never inhabits. Some part of the beholder, even some vital part, seems to escape through the loose grating of his ribs as he ascends. He is more lone than you can imagine. ... Vast, Titanic, inhuman Nature has got him at disadvantage, caught him alone, and pilfers him of some of his divine faculty. She does not smile on him as in the plains. She seems to say sternly, why came ye here before your time? This ground is not prepared for you. Is it not enough that I smile in the valleys? I have never made this soil for thy feet, this air for thy breathing, these rocks for thy neighbors. I cannot pity nor fondle thee here, but forever relentlessly drive thee hence to where I *am* kind. Why seek me where I have not called thee, and then complain because you find me but a stepmother?[15]

This is surely not the way a modern backpacker or nature lover would describe Maine's most famous mountain, but that is because Thoreau's description owes as much to Wordsworth and other romantic contemporaries as to the rocks and clouds of Katahdin itself. His words took the physical mountain on which he stood and transmuted it into an icon of the sublime: a symbol of God's presence on earth. The power and the glory of that icon were such that only a prophet might gaze on it for long. In effect, romantics like Thoreau joined Moses and the children of Israel in Exodus when "they looked toward the wilderness, and behold, the glory of the Lord appeared in the cloud."[16]

But even as it came to embody the awesome power of the sublime, wilderness was also being tamed – not just by those who were building settlements in its midst but also by those who most celebrated its inhuman beauty. By the second half of the nineteenth century, the terrible awe that Wordsworth and Thoreau regarded as the appropriately pious stance to adopt in the presence of their mountaintop God was giving way to a much more comfortable, almost sentimental demeanor. As more and more tourists sought out the wilderness as a spectacle to be looked at and enjoyed for its great beauty, the sublime in effect became domesticated. The wilderness was still sacred, but the religious sentiments it evoked were more those of a pleasant parish church than those of a grand cathedral or a harsh desert retreat. The writer who best captures this late romantic sense of a domesticated sublime is undoubtedly John Muir, whose descriptions of Yosemite and the Sierra Nevada reflect none of the anxiety or terror one finds in earlier writers. Here he is, for instance, sketching on North Dome in Yosemite Valley:

> No pain here, no dull empty hours, no fear of the past, no fear of the future. These blessed mountains are so compactly filled with God's beauty, no petty personal hope or experience has room to be. Drinking this champagne water is pure pleasure, so is breathing the living air, and every movement of limbs is pleasure, while the body seems to feel beauty when exposed to it as it feels the campfire or sunshine, entering not by the eyes alone, but equally through all one's flesh like radiant heat, making a passionate ecstatic pleasure glow not explainable.

The emotions Muir describes in Yosemite could hardly be more different from Thoreau's on Katahdin or Wordsworth's on the Simplon Pass. Yet all three men are participating in the same cultural tradition and contributing to the same myth: the mountain as cathedral. The three may differ in the way they choose to express their piety – Wordsworth favoring an awe-filled bewilderment, Thoreau a stern loneliness, Muir a welcome ecstasy – but they agree completely about the church in which they prefer to worship. Muir's closing words on North Dome diverge from his older contemporaries only in mood, not in their ultimate content:

> Perched like a fly on this Yosemite dome, I gaze and sketch and bask, oftentimes settling down into dumb admiration without definite hope of ever learning much, yet with the longing, unresting effort that lies at the door of hope, humbly prostrate before the vast display of God's power, and eager to offer self-denial and renunciation with eternal toil to learn any lesson in the divine manuscript.[17]

Muir's "divine manuscript" and Wordsworth's "Characters of the great Apocalypse" were in fact pages from the same holy book. The sublime wilderness had ceased to be a place of satanic temptation and become instead a sacred temple, much as it continues to be for those who love it today.

But the romantic sublime was not the only cultural movement that helped transform wilderness into a sacred American icon during the nineteenth century. No less important was the powerful romantic attraction of primitivism, dating back at least to Rousseau – the belief that the best antidote to the ills of an overly refined and civilized modern world was a return to simpler, more primitive living. In the United States, this was embodied most strikingly in the national myth of the frontier. The historian Frederick Jackson Turner wrote in 1893 the classic academic statement of this myth, but it had been part of American cultural traditions for well over a century. As Turner described the process, easterners and European immigrants, in moving to the wild unsettled lands of the frontier, shed the trappings of civilization, rediscovered their primitive racial energies, reinvented direct democratic institutions, and thereby reinfused themselves with a vigor, an independence, and a creativity that were the source of American democracy and national character. Seen in this way, wild country became a place not just of religious redemption but of national renewal, the quintessential location for experiencing what it meant to be an American.

One of Turner's most provocative claims was that by the 1890s the frontier was passing away. Never again would "such gifts of free land offer themselves" to the American people. "The frontier has gone," he declared, "and with its going has closed the first period of American history."[18] Built into the frontier myth from its very beginning was the notion that this crucible of American identity was temporary and would pass away. Those who have celebrated the frontier have almost always looked backward as they did so, mourning an older, simpler, truer world that is about to disappear forever. That world and all of its attractions, Turner said, depended on free land – on wilderness. Thus, in the myth of the vanishing frontier lay the seeds of wilderness preservation in the United States, for if wild land had been so crucial in the making of the nation, then surely one must save its last remnants as monuments to the American past – and as an insurance policy to protect its future. It is no accident that the movement to set aside national parks and wilderness areas began to gain real momentum at precisely the time that laments about the passing frontier reached their peak. To protect wilderness was in a very real sense to protect the nation's most sacred myth of origin.

Among the core elements of the frontier myth was the powerful sense among certain groups of Americans that wilderness was the last bastion of rugged individualism. Turner tended to stress communitarian themes when writing frontier history, asserting that Americans in primitive conditions had been forced to band together with their neighbors to form communities and democratic institutions. For other writers, however, frontier democracy for communities was less compelling than frontier freedom for individuals.[19] By fleeing to the outer margins of settled land and society – so the story ran – an individual could escape the confining strictures of civilized life. The mood among writers who celebrated frontier individualism was almost always nostalgic; they lamented not just a lost way of life but the passing of the heroic men who had embodied that life. Thus Owen Wister in the introduction to his classic 1902 novel *The Virginian* could write of "a vanished world" in which "the horseman, the cow-puncher, the last romantic figure upon our soil" rode only "in his historic yesterday" and would "never come again." For Wister, the cowboy was a man who gave his word and kept it ("Wall Street would have found him behind the times"), who did not talk lewdly to women ("Newport would have thought him old-fashioned"), who worked and played hard, and whose "ungoverned hours did not unman him."[20] Theodore Roosevelt wrote with much the same nostalgic fervor about the "fine, manly qualities" of the "wild rough-rider of the plains." No one could be more heroically masculine, thought Roosevelt, or more at home in the western wilderness:

> There he passes his days, there he does his life-work, there, when he meets death, he faces it as he has faced many other evils, with quiet, uncomplaining fortitude. Brave, hospitable, hardy, and adventurous, he is the grim pioneer of our race; he prepares the way for the civilization from before whose face he must himself disappear. Hard and dangerous though his existence is, it has yet a wild attraction that strongly draws to it his bold, free spirit.[21]

This nostalgia for a passing frontier way of life inevitably implied ambivalence, if not downright hostility, toward modernity and all that it represented. If one saw the wild lands of the frontier as freer, truer, and more natural than other, more modern places, then one was also inclined to see the cities and factories of urban-industrial civilization as confining, false, and artificial. Owen Wister looked at the post-frontier "transition" that had followed "the horseman of the plains," and did not like what he saw: "a shapeless state, a condition of men and manners as unlovely as is that moment in the year when winter is gone and spring not come, and the face of Nature is ugly."[22] In the eyes of writers who shared Wister's distaste for modernity, civilization contaminated its inhabitants and absorbed them into the faceless, collective, contemptible life of the crowd. For all of its troubles and dangers, and despite the fact that it must pass away, the frontier had been a better place. If civilization was to be redeemed, it would be by men like the Virginian who could retain their frontier virtues even as they made the transition to post-frontier life.

The mythic frontier individualist was almost always masculine in gender: here, in the wilderness, a man could be a real man, the rugged individual he was meant to be before civilization sapped his energy and threatened his masculinity. Wister's contemptuous remarks about Wall Street and Newport suggest what he and many others of his generation believed – that the comforts and seductions of civilized life were especially insidious for men, who all too easily became emasculated by the femininizing tendencies of civilization. More often than not, men who felt this way came, like Wister and Roosevelt, from elite class backgrounds. The curious result was that frontier nostalgia became an important vehicle for expressing a peculiarly bourgeois form of antimodernism. The very men who most benefited from urban-industrial capitalism were among those who believed they must escape its debilitating effects. If the frontier was passing, then men who had the means to do so should preserve for themselves some remnant of its wild landscape so that they might enjoy the regeneration and renewal that came from sleeping under the stars, participating in blood sports, and living off the land. The frontier might be gone, but the frontier experience could still be had if only wilderness were preserved.

Thus the decades following the Civil War saw more and more of the nation's wealthiest citizens seeking out wilderness for themselves. The elite passion for wild land took many forms: enormous estates in the Adirondacks and elsewhere (disingenuously called "camps" despite their many servants and amenities), cattle ranches for would-be rough riders on the Great Plains, guided big-game hunting trips in the Rockies, and luxurious resort hotels wherever railroads pushed their way into sublime landscapes. Wilderness suddenly emerged as the landscape of choice for elite tourists, who brought with them strikingly urban ideas of the countryside through which they traveled. For them, wild land was not a site for productive labor and not a permanent home; rather, it was a place of recreation. One went to the wilderness not as a producer but as a consumer, hiring guides and other backcountry residents who could serve as romantic surrogates for the rough riders and hunters of the frontier if one was willing to overlook their new status as employees and servants of the rich.

In just this way, wilderness came to embody the national frontier myth, standing for the wild freedom of America's past and seeming to represent a highly attractive natural alternative to the ugly artificiality of modern civilization. The irony, of course, was that in the process wilderness came to reflect the very civilization its devotees sought to escape. Ever since the nineteenth century, celebrating wilderness has been an activity mainly for well-to-do city folks. Country people generally know far too much about working the land to regard unworked land as their ideal. In contrast, elite urban tourists and wealthy sportsmen projected their leisure-time frontier fantasies onto the American landscape and so created wilderness in their own image.

There were other ironies as well. The movement to set aside national parks and wilderness areas followed hard on the heels of the final Indian wars, in which the prior human inhabitants of these areas were rounded up and moved onto reservations. The myth of the wilderness as "virgin," uninhabited land had always been especially cruel when seen from the perspective of the Indians who had once called that land home. Now they were forced to move elsewhere, with the result that tourists could safely enjoy the illusion that they were seeing their nation in its pristine, original state, in the new morning of God's own creation.[23] Among the things that most marked the new national parks as reflecting a post-frontier conscious-ness was the relative absence of human violence within their boundaries. The actual frontier had often been a place of conflict, in which invaders and invaded fought for control of land and resources. Once set aside within the fixed and carefully policed boundaries of the modern bureaucratic state, the wilderness lost its savage image and became safe: a place more of reverie than of revulsion or fear. Meanwhile, its original inhabitants were kept out by dint of force, their earlier uses of the land redefined as inappropriate or even illegal. To this day, for instance, the Blackfeet continue to be accused of "poaching" on the lands of Glacier National Park that originally belonged to them and that were ceded by treaty only with the proviso that they be permitted to hunt there.[24]

The removal of Indians to create an "uninhabited wilderness" – unin-habited as never before in the human history of the place – reminds us just how invented, just how constructed, the American wilderness really is. To return to my opening argument: there is nothing natural about the concept of wilderness. It is entirely a creation of the culture that holds it dear, a product of the very history it seeks to deny. Indeed, one of the most striking proofs of the cultural invention of wilderness is its thoroughgoing erasure of the history from which it sprang. In virtually all of its manifestations, wild-erness represents a flight from history. Seen as the original garden, it is a place outside of time, from which human beings had to be ejected before the fallen world of history could properly begin. Seen as the frontier, it is a savage world at the dawn of civilization, whose transformation represents the very beginning of the national historical epic. Seen as the bold landscape of frontier heroism, it is the place of youth and childhood, into which men escape by abandoning their pasts and entering a world of freedom where the constraints of civilization fade into memory. Seen as the sacred sublime, it is the home of a God who transcends history by standing as the One who remains untouched and unchanged by time's arrow. No matter what the angle from which we regard it, wilderness offers us the illusion that we can escape the cares and troubles of the world in which our past has ensnared us.[25]

This escape from history is one reason why the language we use to talk about wilderness is often permeated with spiritual and religious values that reflect human ideals far more than the material world of physical nature. Wilderness fulfills the old romantic project of secularizing Judeo-Christian values so as to make a new cathedral not in some petty human building but in God's own creation, Nature itself. Many environmentalists who reject traditional notions of the Godhead and who regard themselves as agnostics or even atheists nonetheless express feelings tantamount to religious awe when in the presence of wilderness – a fact that testifies to the success of the romantic project. Those who have no difficulty seeing God as the expression of our human dreams and desires nonetheless have trouble recognizing that in a secular age Nature can offer precisely the same sort of mirror.

Thus it is that wilderness serves as the unexamined foundation on which so many of the quasi-religious values of modern environmentalism rest. The critique of modernity that is one of environmentalism's most important contributions to the moral and political discourse of our time more often than not appeals, explicitly or implicitly, to wilderness as the standard against which to measure the failings of our human world. Wilderness is the natural, unfallen antithesis of an unnatural civilization that has lost its soul. It is a place of freedom in which we can recover the true selves we have lost to the corrupting influences of our artificial lives. Most of all, it is the ultimate landscape of authenticity. Combining the sacred grandeur of the sublime with the primitive simplicity of the frontier, it is the place where we can see the world as it really is, and so know ourselves as we really are – or ought to be.

But the trouble with wilderness is that it quietly expresses and reproduces the very values its devotees seek to reject. The flight from history that is very nearly the core of wilderness represents the false hope of an escape from responsibility, the illusion that we can somehow wipe clean the slate of our past and return to the tabula rasa that supposedly existed before we began to leave our marks on the world. The dream of an unworked natural landscape is very much the fantasy of people who have never them-selves had to work the land to make a living – urban folk for whom food comes from a supermarket or a restaurant instead of a field, and for whom the wooden houses in which they live and work apparently have no mean-ingful connection to the forests in which trees grow and die. Only people whose relation to the land was already alienated could hold up wilderness as a model for human life in nature, for the romantic ideology of wilderness leaves precisely nowhere for human beings actually to make their living from the land.

This, then, is the central paradox: wilderness embodies a dualistic vision in which the human is entirely outside the natural. If we allow ourselves to believe that nature, to be true, must also be wild, then our very presence in nature represents its fall. The place where we are is the place where nature is not. If this is so – if by definition wilderness leaves no place for human beings, save perhaps as contemplative sojourners enjoying their leisurely reverie in God's natural cathedral – then also by definition it can offer no solution to the environmental and other problems that confront us. To the extent that we celebrate wilderness as the measure with which we judge civilization, we reproduce the dualism that sets humanity and nature at opposite poles. We thereby leave ourselves little hope of discover-ing what an ethical, sustainable, *honorable* human place in nature might actually look like.

Worse: to the extent that we live in an urban-industrial civilization but at the same time pretend to ourselves that our *real* home is in the wilderness, to just that extent we give ourselves permission to evade responsibility for the lives we actually lead. We inhabit civilization while holding some part of ourselves – what we imagine to be the most precious part – aloof from its entanglements. We work our nine-to-five jobs in its institutions, we eat its food, we drive its cars (not least to reach the wilderness), we benefit from the intricate and all too invisible networks with which it shelters us, all the while pretending that these things are not an essential part of who we are. By imagining that our true home is in the wilderness, we forgive ourselves the homes we actually inhabit. In its flight from history, in its siren song of escape, in its reproduction of the dangerous dualism that sets human beings outside of nature – in all of these ways, wilderness poses a serious threat to responsible environmentalism at the end of the twentieth century.

By now I hope it is clear that my criticism in this essay is not directed at wild nature per se, or even at efforts to set aside large tracts of wild land, but rather at the specific habits of thinking that flow from this complex cultural construction called wilderness. It is not the things we label as wilderness that are the problem – for nonhuman nature and large tracts of the natural world *do* deserve protection – but rather what we ourselves mean when we use the label. Lest one doubt how pervasive these habits of thought actually are in contemporary environmentalism, let me list some of the places where wilderness serves as the ideological underpinning for environmental concerns that might otherwise seem quite remote from it. Defenders of biological diversity, for instance, although sometimes appealing to more utilitarian concerns, often point to "untouched" ecosystems as the best and richest repositories of the undiscovered species we must certainly try to protect. Although at first blush an apparently more "scientific" concept than wilderness, biological diversity in fact invokes many of the same sacred values, which is why organizations like the Nature Conservancy have been so quick to employ it as an alternative to the seemingly fuzzier and more problematic concept of wilderness. There is a paradox here, of course. To the extent that biological diversity (indeed, even wilderness itself) is likely to survive in the future only by the most vigilant and self-conscious management of the ecosystems that sustain it, the ideology of wilderness is potentially in direct conflict with the very thing it encourages us to protect.[26]

The most striking instances of this have revolved around "endangered species," which serve as vulnerable symbols of biological diversity while at the same time standing as surrogates for wilderness itself. The terms of the Endangered Species Act in the United States have often meant that those hoping to defend pristine wilderness have had to rely on a single endangered species like the spotted owl to gain legal standing for their case – thereby making the full power of the sacred land inhere in a single numinous

351

organism whose habitat then becomes the object of intense debate about appropriate management and use.[27] The ease with which anti-environmental forces like the wise-use movement have attacked such single-species preservation efforts suggests the vulnerability of strategies like these.

Perhaps partly because our own conflicts over such places and organisms have become so messy, the convergence of wilderness values with concerns about biological diversity and endangered species has helped produce a deep fascination for remote ecosystems, where it is easier to imagine that nature might somehow be "left alone" to flourish by its own pristine devices. The classic example is the tropical rain forest, which since the 1970s has become the most powerful modern icon of unfallen, sacred land – a veritable Garden of Eden – for many Americans and Europeans. And yet protecting the rain forest in the eyes of First World environmentalists all too often means protecting it from the people who live there. Those who seek to preserve such "wilderness" from the activities of native peoples run the risk of reproducing the same tragedy – being forceably removed from an ancient home – that befell American Indians. Third World countries face massive environmental problems and deep social conflicts, but these are not likely to be solved by a cultural myth that encourages us to "preserve" peopleless landscapes that have not existed in such places for millennia. At its worst, as environmentalists are beginning to realize, exporting American notions of wilderness in this way can become an unthinking and self-defeating form of cultural imperialism.[28]

Perhaps the most suggestive example of the way that wilderness thinking can underpin other environmental concerns has emerged in the recent debate about "global change." In 1989 the journalist Bill McKibben published a book entitled *The End of Nature,* in which he argued that the prospect of global climate change as a result of unintentional human manipulation of the atmosphere means that nature as we once knew it no longer exists.[29] Whereas earlier generations inhabited a natural world that remained more or less unaffected by their actions, our own generation is uniquely different. We and our children will henceforth live in a biosphere completely altered by our own activity, a planet in which the human and the natural can no longer be distinguished, because the one has overwhelmed the other. In McKibben's view, nature has died, and we are responsible for killing it. "The planet," he declares, "is utterly different now."[30]

But such a perspective is possible only if we accept the wilderness premise that nature, to be natural, must also be pristine – remote from humanity and untouched by our common past. In fact, everything we know about environmental history suggests that people have been manipulating the natural world on various scales for as long as we have a record of their passing. Moreover, we have unassailable evidence that many of the environmental changes we now face also occurred quite apart from human intervention at one time or another in the earth's past.[31] The point is not that our current problems are trivial, or that our devastating effects on the earth's ecosystems should be accepted as inevitable or "natural." It is rather that we seem unlikely to make much progress in solving these problems if we hold up to ourselves as the mirror of nature a wilderness we ourselves cannot inhabit.

To do so is merely to take to a logical extreme the paradox that was built into wilderness from the beginning: if nature dies because we enter it, then the only way to save nature is to kill ourselves. The absurdity of this proposition flows from the underlying dualism it expresses. Not only does it ascribe greater power to humanity than we in fact possess – physical and biological nature will surely survive in some form or another long after we ourselves have gone the way of all flesh – but in the end it offers us little more than a self-defeating counsel of despair. The tautology gives us no way out: if wild nature is the only thing worth saving, and if our mere presence destroys it, then the sole solution to our own unnaturalness, the only way to protect sacred wilderness from profane humanity, would seem to be suicide. It is not a proposition that seems likely to produce very positive or practical results.

And yet radical environmentalists and deep ecologists all too frequently come close to accepting this premise as a first principle. When they express, for instance, the popular notion that our environmental problems began with the invention of agriculture, they push the human fall from natural grace so far back into the past that all of civilized history becomes a tale of ecological declension. Earth First! founder Dave Foreman captures the familiar parable succinctly when he writes,

> Before agriculture was midwifed in the Middle East, humans were in the wilderness. We had no concept of "wilderness" because everything was wilderness and *we were a part of it.* But with irrigation ditches, crop surpluses, and permanent villages, we became *apart from* the natural world. ... Between the wilderness that created us and the civilization created by us grew an ever-widening rift.[32]

In this view the farm becomes the first and most important battlefield in the long war against wild nature, and all else follows in its wake. From such a starting place, it is hard not to reach the conclusion that the only way human beings can hope to live naturally on earth is to follow the hunter-gatherers back into a wilderness Eden and abandon virtually everything that civilization has given us. It may indeed turn out that civilization will end in ecological collapse or nuclear disaster, whereupon one might expect to find any human survivors returning to a way of life closer to that celebrated by Foreman and his followers. For most of us, though, such a debacle would be cause for regret, a sign that humanity had failed to fulfill its own promise and failed to honor its own highest values – including those of the deep ecologists.

In offering wilderness as the ultimate hunter-gatherer alternative to civilization, Foreman reproduces an extreme but still easily recognizable version of the myth of frontier primitivism. When he writes of his fellow Earth Firsters that "we believe we must return to being animal, to glorying in our sweat, hormones, tears, and blood" and that "we struggle against the modern compulsion to become dull, passionless androids," he is following in the footsteps of Owen Wister.[33] Although his arguments give primacy to defending biodiversity and the autonomy of wild nature, his prose becomes most passionate when he speaks of preserving "the wilderness experience." His own ideal "Big Outside" bears an uncanny resemblance to that of the frontier myth: wide open spaces and virgin land with no trails, no signs, no facilities, no maps, no guides, no rescues, no modern equipment. Tellingly, it is a land where hardy travelers can support themselves by hunting with "primitive weapons (bow and arrow, atlatl, knife, sharp rock)."[34] Foreman claims that "the primary value of wilderness is not as a proving ground for young Huck Finns and Annie Oakleys," but his heart is with Huck and Annie all the same. He admits that "preserving a quality wilderness experience for the human visitor, letting her or him flex Paleolithic muscles or seek visions, remains a tremendously important secondary purpose."[35] Just so does Teddy Roosevelt's rough rider live on in the greener garb of a new age.

However much one may be attracted to such a vision, it entails problematic consequences. For one, it makes wilderness the locus for an epic struggle between malign civilization and benign nature, compared with which all other social, political, and moral concerns seem trivial. Foreman writes, "The preservation of wildness and native diversity is *the* most important issue. Issues directly affecting only humans pale in comparison."[36] Presumably so do any environmental problems whose victims are mainly people, for such problems usually surface in landscapes that have already "fallen" and are no longer wild. This would seem to exclude from the radical environmentalist agenda problems of occupational health and safety in industrial settings, problems of toxic waste exposure on "unnatural" urban and agricultural sites, problems of poor children poisoned by lead exposure in the inner city, problems of famine and poverty and human suffering in the "overpopulated" places of the earth – problems, in short, of environmental justice. If we set too high a stock on wilderness, too many other corners of the earth become less than natural and too many other people become less than human, thereby giving us permission not to care much about their suffering or their fate.

It is no accident that these supposedly inconsequential environmental problems affect mainly poor people, for the long affiliation between wilderness and wealth means that the only poor people who count when wilderness is *the* issue are hunter-gatherers, who presumably do not consider themselves to be poor in the first place. The dualism at the heart of wilderness encourages its advocates to conceive of its protection as a crude conflict between the "human" and the "nonhuman" – or, more often, between those who value the nonhuman and those who do not. This in turn tempts one to ignore crucial differences *among* humans and the complex cultural and historical reasons why different peoples may feel very differently about the meaning of wilderness.

Why, for instance, is the "wilderness experience" so often conceived as a form of recreation best enjoyed by those whose class privileges give them the time and resources to leave their jobs behind and "get away from it all"? Why does the protection of wilderness so often seem to pit urban recreationists against rural people who actually earn their living from the land (excepting those who sell goods and services to the tourists themselves)? Why in the debates about pristine natural areas are "primitive" peoples idealized, even sentimentalized, until the moment they do something unprimitive, modern, and unnatural, and thereby fall from environmental grace? What are the consequences of a wilderness ideology that devalues productive labor and the very concrete knowledge that comes from working the land with one's own hands?[37] All of these questions imply conflicts among different groups of people, conflicts that are obscured behind the deceptive clarity of "human" vs. "nonhuman." If in answering these knotty questions we resort to so simplistic an opposition, we are almost certain to ignore the very subtleties and complexities we need to understand.

But the most troubling cultural baggage that accompanies the celebration of wilderness has less to do with remote rain forests and peoples than with the ways we think about ourselves – we American environmentalists who quite rightly worry about the future of the earth and the threats we pose to the natural world. Idealizing a distant wilderness too often means not idealizing the environment in which we actually live, the landscape that for better or worse we call home. Most of our most serious environmental problems start right here, at home, and if we are to solve those problems, we need an environmental ethic that will tell us as much about *using* nature as about *not* using it. The wilderness dualism tends to cast any use as *ab*-use, and thereby denies us a middle ground in which responsible use and non-use might attain some kind of balanced, sustainable relationship. My own belief is that only by exploring this middle ground will we learn ways of imagining a better world for all of us: humans and nonhumans, rich people and poor, women and men, First Worlders *and* Third Worlders, white folks and people of color, consumers and producers – a world better for humanity in all of its diversity and for all the rest of nature too. The middle ground is where we actually live. It is where we – all of us, in our different places and ways – make our homes.

That is why, when I think of the times I myself have come closest to experiencing what I might call the sacred in nature, I often find myself remembering wild places much closer to home. I think, for instance, of a small pond near my house where water bubbles up from limestone springs to feed a series of pools that rarely freeze in winter and so play home to waterfowl that stay here for the protective warmth even on the coldest of winter days, gliding silently through streaming mists as the snow falls from gray February skies. I think of a November evening long ago when I found myself on a Wisconsin hilltop in rain and dense fog, only to have the setting sun break through the clouds to cast an otherworldly golden light on the misty farms and woodlands below, a scene so unexpected and joyous that I lingered past dusk so as not to miss any part of the gift that had come my way. And I think perhaps most especially of the blown-out, bankrupt farm in the sand country of central Wisconsin where Aldo Leopold and his family tried one of the first American experiments in ecological restoration, turning ravaged and infertile soil into carefully tended ground where the human and the nonhuman could exist side by side in relative harmony. What I celebrate about such places is not *just* their wildness, though that certainly is among their most important qualities; what I celebrate even more is that they remind us of the wildness in our own backyards, of the nature that is all around us if only we have eyes to see it.

Indeed, my principal objection to wilderness is that it may teach us to be dismissive or even contemptuous of such humble places and experiences. Without our quite realizing it, wilderness tends to privilege some parts of nature at the expense of others. Most of us, I suspect, still follow the conventions of the romantic sublime in finding the mountaintop more glorious than the plains, the ancient forest nobler than the grasslands, the mighty canyon more inspiring than the humble marsh. Even John Muir, in arguing against those who sought to dam his beloved Hetch Hetchy valley in the Sierra Nevada, argued for alternative dam sites in the gentler valleys of the foothills – a preference that had nothing to do with nature and everything with the cultural traditions of the sublime.[38] Just as problematically, our frontier traditions have encouraged Americans to define "true" wilderness as requiring very large tracts of roadless land – what Dave Foreman calls "The Big Outside." Leaving aside the legitimate empirical question in conservation biology of how large a tract of land must be before a given species can reproduce on it, the emphasis on big wilderness reflects a romantic frontier belief that one hasn't really gotten away from civilization unless one can go for days at a time without encountering another human being. By teaching us to fetishize sublime places and wide open country, these peculiarly American ways of thinking about wilderness encourage us to adopt too high a standard for what counts as "natural." If it isn't hundreds of square miles big, if it doesn't give us God's-eye views or grand vistas, if it doesn't permit us the illusion that we are alone on the planet, then it really isn't natural. It's too small, too plain, or too crowded to be *authentically* wild.

In critiquing wilderness as I have done in this essay, I'm forced to confront my own deep ambivalence about its meaning for modern environmentalism. On the one hand, one of my own most important environmental ethics is that people should always be conscious that they are part of the natural world, inextricably tied to the ecological systems that sustain their lives. Any way of looking at nature that encourages us to believe we are separate from nature – as wilderness tends to do – is likely to reinforce environmentally irresponsible behavior. On the other hand, I also think it no less crucial for us to recognize and honor nonhuman nature as a world we did not create, a world with its own independent, nonhuman reasons for being as it is. The autonomy of nonhuman nature seems to me an indispensable corrective to human arrogance. Any way of looking at nature that helps us remember – as wilderness also tends to do – that the interests of people are not necessarily identical to those of every other creature or of the earth itself is likely to foster *responsible* behavior. To the extent that wilderness has served as an important vehicle for articulating deep moral values regarding our obligations and responsibilities to the nonhuman world, I would not want to jettison the contributions it has made to our culture's ways of thinking about nature.

If the core problem of wilderness is that it distances us too much from the very things it teaches us to value, then the question we must ask is what it can tell us about *home,* the place where we actually live. How can we take the positive values we associate with wilderness and bring them closer to home? I think the answer to this question will come by broadening our sense of the otherness that wilderness seeks to define and protect. In reminding us of the world we did not make, wilderness can teach profound feelings of humility and respect as we confront our fellow beings and the earth itself. Feelings like these argue for the importance of self-awareness and self-criticism as we exercise our own ability to transform the world around us, helping us set responsible limits to human mastery – which without such limits too easily becomes human hubris. Wilderness is the place where, symbolically at least, we try to withhold our power to dominate.

Wallace Stegner once wrote of

> the special human mark, the special record of human passage, that distinguishes man from all other species. It is rare enough among men, impossible to any other form of life. *It is simply the deliberate and chosen refusal to make any marks at all.* ... We are the most dangerous species of life on the planet, and every other species, even the earth itself, has cause to fear our power to exterminate. But we

are also the only species which, when it chooses to do so, will go to great effort to save what it might destroy.[39]

The myth of wilderness, which Stegner knowingly reproduces in these remarks, is that we can somehow leave nature untouched by our passage. By now it should be clear that this for the most part is an illusion. But Stegner's deeper message then becomes all the more compelling. If living in history means that we cannot help leaving marks on a fallen world, then the dilemma we face is to decide what kinds of marks we wish to leave. It is just here that our cultural traditions of wilderness remain so important. In the broadest sense, wilderness teaches us to ask whether the Other must always bend to our will, and, if not, under what circumstances it should be allowed to flourish without our intervention. This is surely a question worth asking about everything we do, and not just about the natural world.

When we visit a wilderness area, we find ourselves surrounded by plants and animals and physical landscapes whose otherness compels our attention. In forcing us to acknowledge that they are not of our making, that they have little or no need of our continued existence, they recall for us a creation far greater than our own. In the wilderness, we need no reminder that a tree has its own reasons for being, quite apart from us. The same is less true in the gardens we plant and tend ourselves: there it is far easier to forget the otherness of the tree.[40] Indeed, one could almost measure wilderness by the extent to which our recognition of its otherness requires a conscious, willed act on our part. The romantic legacy means that wilderness is more a state of mind than a fact of nature, and the state of mind that today most defines wilderness is *wonder*. The striking power of the wild is that wonder in the face of it requires no act of will, but forces itself upon us – as an expression of the nonhuman world experienced through the lens of our cultural history – as proof that ours is not the only presence in the universe.

Wilderness gets us into trouble only if we imagine that this experience of wonder and otherness is limited to the remote corners of the planet, or that it somehow depends on pristine landscapes we ourselves do not inhabit. Nothing could be more misleading. The tree in the garden is in reality no less other, no less worthy of our wonder and respect, than the tree in an ancient forest that has never known an ax or a saw – even though the tree in the forest reflects a more intricate web of ecological relationships. The tree in the garden could easily have sprung from the same seed as the tree in the forest, and we can claim only its location and perhaps its form as our own. Both trees stand apart from us; both share our common world. The special power of the tree in the wilderness is to remind us of this fact. It can teach us to recognize the wildness we did not see in the tree we planted in our own backyard. By seeing the otherness in that which is most unfamiliar, we can learn to see it too in that which at first seemed merely ordinary.

If wilderness can do this – if it can help us perceive and respect a nature we had forgotten to recognize as natural – then it will become part of the solution to our environmental dilemmas rather than part of the problem.

This will only happen, however, if we abandon the dualism that sees the tree in the garden as artificial – completely fallen and unnatural – and the tree in the wilderness as natural – completely pristine and wild. Both trees in some ultimate sense are wild; both in a practical sense now depend on our management and care. We are responsible for both, even though we can claim credit for neither. Our challenge is to stop thinking of such things according to sets of bipolar moral scales in which the human and the nonhuman, the unnatural and the natural, the fallen and the unfallen, serve as our conceptual map for understanding and valuing the world. Instead, we need to embrace the full continuum of a natural landscape that is also cultural, in which the city, the suburb, the pastoral, and the wild each has its proper place, which we permit ourselves to celebrate without needlessly denigrating the others. We need to honor the Other within and the Other next door as much as we do the exotic Other that lives far away – a lesson that applies as much to people as it does to (other) natural things. In particular, we need to discover a common middle ground in which all of these things, from the city to the wilderness, can somehow be encompassed in the word "home." Home, after all, is the place where finally we make our living. It is the place for which we take responsibility, the place we try to sustain so we can pass on what is best in it (and in ourselves) to our children.[41]

The task of making a home in nature is what Wendell Berry has called "the forever unfinished lifework of our species." "The only thing we have to preserve nature with," he writes, "is culture; the only thing we have to preserve wildness with is domesticity."[42] Calling a place home inevitably means that we will *use* the nature we find in it, for there can be no escape from manipulating and working and even killing some parts of nature to make our home. But if we acknowledge the autonomy and otherness of the things and creatures around us – an autonomy our culture has taught us to label with the word "wild" – then we will at least think carefully about the uses to which we put them, and even ask if we should use them at all. Just so can we still join Thoreau in declaring that "in Wildness is the preservation of the World," for *wildness* (as opposed to wilderness) can be found anywhere: in the seemingly tame fields and woodlots of Massachusetts, in the cracks of a Manhattan sidewalk, even in the cells of our own bodies. As Gary Snyder has wisely said, "A person with a clear heart and open mind can experience the wilderness anywhere on earth. It is a quality of one's own consciousness. The planet is a wild place and always will be."[43] To think ourselves capable of causing "the end of nature" is an act of great hubris, for it means forgetting the wildness that dwells everywhere within and around us.

Learning to honor the wild – learning to remember and acknowledge the autonomy of the other – means striving for critical self-consciousness in all of our actions. It means the deep reflection and respect must accompany each act of use, and means too that we must always consider the possibility of non-use. It means looking at the part of nature we intend to turn toward our own ends and asking whether we can use it again and again and again – sustainably – without its being diminished in the process. It means never imagining that we can flee into a mythical wilderness to escape history and the obligation to take responsibility for our own actions that history inescapably entails. Most of all, it means practicing remembrance and gratitude, for thanksgiving is the simplest and most basic of ways for us to recollect the nature, the culture, and the history that have come together to make the world as we know it. If wildness can stop being (just) out there and start being (also) in here, if it can start being as humane as it is natural, then perhaps we can get on with the unending task of struggling to live rightly in the world – not just in the garden, not just in the wilderness, but in the home that encompasses them both.

Notes

1 Henry David Thoreau, "Walking," *The Works of Thoreau,* ed. Henry S. Canby (Boston, Massachusetts: Houghton Mifflin, 1937), p. 672.

2 *Oxford English Dictionary,* s.v. "wilderness"; see also Roderick Nash, *Wilderness and the American Mind,* 3rd ed. (New Haven, Connecticut: Yale Univ. Press, 1982), pp. 1–22; and Max Oelschlaeger, *The Idea of Wilderness: From Prehistory to the Age of Ecology* (New Haven, Connecticut: Yale Univ. Press, 1991).

3 Exodus 32:1–35, KJV.

4 Exodus 14:3, KJV.

5 Mark 1:12–13, KJV; see also Matthew 4:1–11; Luke 4:1–13.

6 John Milton, "Paradise Lost," *John Milton: Complete Poems and Major Prose,* ed. Merritt Y. Hughes (New York: Odyssey Press, 1957), pp. 280–81, lines 131–42.

7 I have discussed this theme at length in "Landscapes of Abundance and Scarcity," in Clyde Milner et al., eds., *Oxford History of the American West* (New York: Oxford Univ. Press, 1994), pp. 603–37. The classic work on the Puritan "city on a hill" in colonial New England is Perry Miller, *Errand into the Wilderness* (Cambridge, Massachusetts: Harvard Univ. Press, 1956).

8 John Muir, *My First Summer in the Sierra* (1911), reprinted in *John Muir: The Eight Wilderness Discovery Books* (London, England: Diadem; Seattle, Washington: Mountaineers, 1992), p. 211.

9 Alfred Runte, *National Parks: The American Experience,* 2nd ed. (Lincoln: Univ. of Nebraska Press, 1987).

10 John Muir, *The Yosemite* (1912), reprinted in *John Muir: Eight Wilderness Discovery Books,* p. 715.

11 Scholarly work on the sublime is extensive. Among the most important studies are Samuel Monk, *The Sublime: A Study of Critical Theories in XVJII-Century England* (New York: Modern Language Association, 1935); Basil Willey, *The Eighteenth-Century Background: Studies on the Idea of Nature in the*

Thought of the Period (London, England: Chattus and Windus, 1949); Marjorie Hope Nicolson, *Mountain Gloom and Mountain Glory: The Development of the Aesthetics of the Infinite* (Ithaca, New York: Cornell Univ. Press, 1959); Thomas Weiskel, *The Romantic Sublime: Studies in the Structure and Psychology of Transcendence* (Baltimore, Maryland: Johns Hopkins Univ. Press, 1976); Barbara Novak, *Nature and Culture: American Landscape Painting, 1825–1875* (New York: Oxford Univ. Press, 1980).

12 The classic works are Immanuel Kant, *Observations on the Feeling of the Beautiful and Sublime* (1764), trans. John T. Goldthwait (Berkeley: Univ. of California Press, 1960); Edmund Burke, A *Philosophical Enquiry into the Origin of Our Ideas of the Sublime and Beautiful,* ed. James T. Boulton (1958; Notre Dame, Indiana: Univ. of Notre Dame Press, 1968); William Gilpin, *Three Essays: On Picturesque Beauty; on Picturesque Travel; and on Sketching Landscape* (London, England, 1803).

13 See Ann Vileisis, "From Wastelands to Wetlands" (unpublished senior essay, Yale Univ., 1989); Runte, *National Parks.*

14 William Wordsworth, "The Prelude," bk. 6, in Thomas Hutchinson, ed., *The Poetical Works of Wordsworth* (London, England: Oxford Univ. Press, 1936), p. 536.

15 Henry David Thoreau, *The Maine Woods* (1864), in *Henry David Thoreau* (New York: Library of America, 1985), pp. 640–41.

16 Exodus 16:10, KJV.

17 John Muir, *My First Summer in the Sierra,* p. 238. Part of the difference between these descriptions may reflect the landscapes the three authors were describing. In his essay, "Reinventing Common Nature: Yosemite and Mount Rushmore – A Meandering Tale of a Double Nature," Kenneth Olwig notes that early American travelers experienced Yosemite as much through the aesthetic tropes of the pastoral as through those of the sublime. The ease with which Muir celebrated the gentle divinity of the Sierra Nevada had much to do with the pastoral qualities of the landscape he described. See Olwig, "Reinventing Common Nature: Yosemite and Mount Rushmore – A Meandering Tale of a Double Nature," *Uncommon Ground: Toward Reinventing Nature,* ed. William Cronon (New York: W. W. Norton & Co., 1995), pp. 379–408.

18 Frederick Jackson Turner, *The Frontier in American History* (New York: Henry Holt, 1920), pp. 37–38.

19 Richard Slotkin has made this observation the linchpin of his comparison between Turner and Theodore Roosevelt. See Slotkin, *Gunfighter Nation: The Myth of the Frontier in Twentieth-Century America* (New York: Atheneum, 1992), pp. 29–62.

20 Owen Wister, *The Virginian: A Horseman of the Plains* (New York: Macmillan, 1902), pp. viii–ix.

21 Theodore Roosevelt, *Ranch Life and the Hunting Trail* (1888; New York: Century, 1899), p. 100.

22 Wister, *Virginian,* p. x.

23 On the many problems with this view, William M. Denevan, "The Pristine Myth: The Landscape of the Americas in 1492," *Annals of the Association of American Geographers* 82 (1992): 369–85.

24 Louis Warren, "The Hunter's Game: Poachers, Conservationists, and Twentieth-Century America" (Ph.D. diss., Yale University, 1994).

25 Wilderness also lies at the foundation of the Clementsian ecological concept of the climax. See Michael Barbour, "Ecological Fragmentation in the Fifties"

in Cronon, *Uncommon Ground,* pp. 233–55, and William Cronon, "Introduction: In Search of Nature," in Cronon, *Uncommon Ground,* pp. 23–56.

26 On the many paradoxes of having to manage wilderness in order to maintain the appearance of an unmanaged landscape, see John C. Hendee et al., *Wilderness Management,* USDA Forest Service Miscellaneous Publication No. 1365 (Washington, D.C.: Government Printing Office, 1978).

27 See James Proctor, "Whose Nature?: The Contested Moral Terrain of Ancient Forests," in Cronon, *Uncommon Ground,* pp. 269–97.

28 See Candace Slater, "Amazonia as Edenic Narrative," in Cronon, *Uncommon Ground,* pp. 114–31. This argument has been powerfully made by Ramachandra Guha, "Radical American Environmentalism: A Third World Critique," *Environmental Ethics* 11 (1989): 71–83.

29 Bill McKibben, *The End of Nature* (New York: Random House, 1989).

30 McKibben, *The End of Nature,* p. 49.

31 Even comparable extinction rates have occurred before, though we surely would not want to emulate the Cretaceous-Tertiary boundary extinctions as a model for responsible manipulation of the biosphere!

32 Dave Foreman, *Confessions of an Eco-Warrior* (New York: Harmony Books, 1991), p. 69 (italics in original). For a sampling of other writings by followers of deep ecology and/or Earth First!, see Michael Tobias, ed., *Deep Ecology* (San Diego, California: Avant Books, 1984); Bill Devall and George Sessions, *Deep Ecology: Living as if Nature Mattered* (Salt Lake City, Utah: Gibbs Smith, 1985); Michael Tobias, *After Eden: History, Ecology, and Conscience* (San Diego, California: Avant Books, 1985); Dave Foreman and Bill Haywood, eds., *Ecodefense: A Field Guide to Monkey Wrenching,* 2nd ed. (Tucson, Arizona: Ned Ludd Books, 1987); Bill Devall, *Simple in Means, Rich in Ends: Practicing Deep Ecology* (Salt Lake City, Utah: Gibbs Smith, 1988); Steve Chase, ed., *Defending the Earth: A Dialogue between Murray Bookchin & Dave Foreman* (Boston, Massachusetts: South End Press, 1991); John Davis, ed., *The Earth First! Reader: Ten Years of Radical Environmentalism* (Salt Lake City, Utah: Gibbs Smith, 1991); Bill Devall, *Living Richly in an Age of Limits: Using Deep Ecology for an Abundant Life* (Salt Lake City, Utah: Gibbs Smith, 1993); Michael E. Zimmerman et al., eds., *Environmental Philosophy: From Animal Rights to Radical Ecology* (Englewood Cliffs, New Jersey: Prentice-Hall, 1993). A useful survey of the different factions of radical environmentalism can be found in Carolyn Merchant, *Radical Ecology: The Search for a Livable World* (New York: Routledge, 1992). For a very interesting critique of this literature (first published in the anarchist newspaper *Fifth Estate*), see George Bradford, *How Deep is Deep Ecology?* (Ojai, California: Times Change Press, 1989).

33 Foreman, *Confessions of an Eco-Warrior,* p. 34.

34 Foreman, *Confessions of an Eco-Warrior,* p. 65. See also Dave Foreman and Howie Wolke, *The Big Outside: A Descriptive Inventory of the Big Wilderness Areas of the U.S.* (Tucson, Arizona: Ned Ludd Books, 1989).

35 Foreman, *Confessions of an Eco-Warrior,* p. 63.

36 Foreman, *Confessions of an Eco-Warrior,* p. 27.

37 See Richard White, "'Are You an Environmentalist or Do You Work for a Living?': Work and Nature," in Cronon, *Uncommon Ground,* pp. 171–85. Compare its analysis of environmental knowledge through work with Jennifer Price's analysis of environmental knowledge through consumption. It is not much of an exaggeration to say that the wilderness experience is essentially consumerist in its impulses.

38 Compare with Muir, *Yosemite,* in *John Muir: Eight Wilderness Discovery Books,* p. 714.
39 Wallace Stegner, ed., *This Is Dinosaur: Echo Park Country and Its Magic Rivers* (New York: Knopf, 1955), p. 17 (italics in original).
40 Katherine Hayles helped me see the importance of this argument.
41 Analogous arguments can be found in John Brinckerhoff Jackson, "Beyond Wilderness," A *Sense of Place, a Sense of Time* (New Haven, Connecticut: Yale Univ. Press, 1994), pp. 71–91, and in the wonderful collection of essays by Michael Pollan, *Second Nature: A Gardener's Education* (New York: Atlantic Monthly Press, 1991).
42 Wendell Berry, *Home Economics* (San Francisco, California: North Point, 1987), pp. 138, 143.
43 Gary Snyder, quoted in *New York Times,* "Week in Review," 18 September 1994, p. 6.

16

'ANNIHILATING NATURAL PRODUCTIONS'

Nature's economy, colonial crisis and the origins of Brazilian political environmentalism (1786–1810)

José A. Pádua

I.

Of all the elements that God created for His glory, and for the use of man, certainly none is more worthy of contemplation than the Earth, the common Mother of all living creatures. She still gives us the same protection that she offered to those born in the beginning of the world. Not even the immense multitude of families who have inhabited her, nor the terrible flood and shipwreck that it suffered with all its sinful children, nor the numerous and fearsome revolutions that so many times have almost thrown her off of her axis, nor the long succession of centuries that change and consume everything, were able to sterilise the fruitful germen of her fertility. She will always be, until the end of the world, as liberal and generous as she was in the beginning ... *despite the ungratefulness of men, who seem to work continuously to destroy and annihilate her natural productions, and to consume and weaken her primitive substance.*

José Gregório de Moraes Navarro (1799: 7)

The author of these words was a magistrate in the interior of Minas Gerais, in Brazil, at the end of the 18th century, when the region was experiencing the decline of a relatively short but historically remarkable cycle of extraction of gold and precious stones.[1] Little is known about this man, except that he studied Law at the Universidade de Coimbra, in Portugal, between 1778 and 1782 (Moraes, 1969: 257).[2] We also know that he served as a judge in Paracatu do Príncipe, deep in the western section of Minas Gerais, having been responsible for the official installation of that village, in 1798 (Barbosa, 1971: 340).

In 1799 Navarro published in Lisbon a small and fascinating volume entitled *Discurso sobre o Melhoramento da Economia Rústica no Brasil* [*Discourse on the Improvement of Brazil's Rustic Economy*].[3] As far as we know, it was in this booklet that Navarro – after indulging in formalities common to the learned texts of the times, including a tribute to the Portuguese royal prince and an Arcadian poem in which he imagines a golden age when Aster could again return to the live on the Earth[4] – for the first and only time formally presented his reflections about the contrast between the generosity of the earth and the ungratefulness of men, creatures who continuously strive to 'destroy and annihilate her natural productions'. He did not remain at this generic level, though, as he also made important critical observations about the behaviour of Portuguese colonisers in Brazil. In Navarro's words, they

> successively founded large cities, remarkable villages and many other smaller places. But how are all these old population centres today? They resemble lifeless bodies. This is so because the neighbouring farmers, who supplied them with their basic goods, with their agriculture, *after reducing all trees to ashes, after depriving the land of its most vigorous substance*, left it covered with grasses and ferns ... and abandoned their houses, mills, workshops and corrals, establishing themselves in new plots.
>
> (Navarro, 1799: 11. The emphases in all the
> citations from Navarro are mine.)

Although he recorded the state of abandonment of many population centres and productive areas of the colony, as a consequence of destructive action affecting the natural environment, Navarro's text stops short of stating that any and all attempts of human settlement were necessarily doomed. On the contrary, he foresees the possibility of lasting social progress, overcoming the destructive trend, if a beneficial and intelligent environmental behaviour is adopted:

> Let us suppose now that, better advised, men have conserved the trees that bear fruit and are useful and that, *using each plot according to its natural characteristics, they have aided the fertility of the earth through means that experience and industry revealed to be the most convenient.* Would they not be much happier? Would the land not be as bountiful and beneficial to them as it was in the beginning to its first settlers?
>
> (Navarro, 1799: 9)

It is easy to see that Navarro's ideas, discussed further in this text, are quite unique, if we consider their time and place. Under the guise of a narrative typical of the style of the time – mixing biblical citations, elements of natural history and Graeco-Roman Arcadian references – what emerges from Navarro's text resembles a set of topics and perceptions usually associated only with the contemporary world. Navarro develops topics and perceptions familiar to the ecological debate of the last decades, which many consider to have emerged only after the great transformations – objective and subjective – caused by the planetary expansion of urban-industrial civilisation. Some aspects of Navarro's text seem to establish a startling connection between this 18th century magistrate from Minas Gerais and certain key questions of culture and politics at the close of the 20th century.

Navarro presents the earth, for example, as an availing and creative force, in a global and abstract sense. This is not the eulogy of the fertility of a specific place, something quite common in human cultures since antiquity, but the assertion of the permanent fecundity of the earth as a whole, the 'common Mother of all living creatures'. In Navarro's mind the planet acquires a sense of personality, a feminine gender and a will to survive that overcome all the many obstacles and difficulties posed since remote eras – such as Divine punishment (the deluge), the working of cosmic mechanics (the revolutions) or the exponential and potentially destructive growth of human presence.

When Navarro discusses the relationship between humanity and the earth, on the other hand, he sees that there is a potential ecological antagonism between them. What is most significant in this vision, as in the previous one, is its generic, abstract and continuous sense, going beyond local or specific contexts. The capacity of humans for environmental destruction does not stem from random or occasional actions, but translates a basic trend to consume the 'primitive substance' of the planet. It is true that Navarro argues, as we shall see, that this trend is stronger among young and immature cultures, having the potential to decrease through time by learning from its tragic consequences. In the case of colonial Brazil, a society that was living 'as if in its infancy' (Navarro, 1799: 8), devastation was growing and its results could already be felt in dramatic fashion. Several communities and productive activities were collapsing forever because of environmental degradation.[5] The nature of this collapse, in Navarro's mind, was not based on warfare among humans, nor on the exogenous irruption of some natural factor, but on the negative consequences of aggregate social action upon the natural environment. This natural environment starts to deny its 'vigorous substance' to mankind, which is thus deprived of its material base of existence. But the earth does not do so on its own, because it is by its own nature fertile and generous. It does so in response to human behaviour that 'consumes' and 'weakens' this substance. The earth is at once passive and active. Passive, because it takes human aggression silently. Active, because this silence is temporary, actually the incubation of revenge. The earth changes from beneficial to mean, from fecund humus to the proliferation of

366

noxious weeds. Here we see an extremely modern theme – well expressed by Michel Serres (1991: 24) – of the passing 'from the war of all against all to the war of all against everything'. The issue of the opposition between humanity and the natural environment is no longer a moral one, a stark display of ungratefulness. It becomes an eminently political problem – a threat to the collective survival of the human community.

Despite composing a picture of environmental crisis and decay in 18th century Brazil, the author was not pessimistic about the future. Not only was it possible to learn to live harmoniously with the natural environment but – even more remarkable – it was possible to act in such a manner as to 'aid the fertility of the earth through means that experience and industry revealed as the most convenient'. For this it was imperative to reconcile economic action with environmental reality, seeking to learn the 'most adequate and natural [use] of each plot'. An actively malign stance had to be replaced by an actively benign one. In this manner it was possible to foresee the possibility of a beneficial and progressive renewal of Brazilian social life. More specifically, Navarro proposes three basic procedures: a) the introduction of the plough, to revive worn-out soils and to endow agriculture with a sense of permanence – as opposed to the nomadism of forest burning; b) the reform of industrial hearths, in order to reduce their consumption of firewood and increase the productivity of sugar-cane mills; and c) the conservation of forests, by means of reserves and incentives to plant trees (Navarro, 1799: 15–19).

The plough was a symbol of a rational and rooted mode of agriculture, free from the evils of forest burning and nomadism. Old plots, abandoned to noxious weeds after successive predatory efforts, could be reclaimed with the plough: 'if [the farmers] again return to their huts they will find many treasures hidden below the roots of grasses and ferns. Only the iron plough can find these treasures and choke those poisonous and useless roots that have sucked away all the substance of the land'. The introduction of the plough would revive 'a great portion of the lands lying around the large population centres, which have been resting indolent and abandoned'. It would thus be possible to reduce the high prices for food, which had increased immensely in the Minas Gerais of the late 18th century, and to acclimatise in Brazil trees and animals brought from Europe, especially sheep (Navarro, 1799: 14 and 18).

The conservation of forests, another basic aspect of his proposal, depended first of all on the reform of industrial hearths used in sugar-cane processing. Their rudimentary technology caused excessive consumption of firewood. It would also be necessary to plant fast-growing trees and to use sugar-cane bagasse as fuel for the hearths. Farmers should be stimulated to plant fruit trees, palm trees and medicinal plants. Wood lots located near cities would be declared public trusts and exploited in a rational manner by municipal councils. Finally, the 'most serious concern' should be dedicated to the conservation of forests adjacent to the sea and to rivers, in order to 'provide the wood needed for ships and public uses'. These forests should be marked out and cared for as state patrimony (Navarro, 1799: 19).

Anticipating the discussion made in the next section, it is easy to notice the main theoretical matrix of such a project: the French physiocratic school of political economy, with its defence of agrarian production as the only true basis for social progress.[6] It is significant that Navarro's economic programme does not include mining, the major source of wealth in 18th century Minas Gerais. This was not accidental. Rural improvement was at the core of his Arcadian and physiocratic sensibility. Actually, he had no sympathy for the economy of mining. He criticises the men who 'started to destroy the land in order to retrieve from its bowels those treasures that were more agreeable to their ambition'. This behaviour had caused damage to city dwellers, who had to pay higher prices for subsistence goods (Navarro, 1799: 12). This was typical of the physiocratic critique of mining, branded as wavering, provisional, prone to disorganise price and monetary systems. Brazil's future, in Navarro's optimistic perspective, could do without this type of risk. The adoption of the above mentioned measures would be enough to turn Brazil into 'the richest and most fortunate [country] in the entire world', making it capable of 'harvesting, without difficulty, yellow wheat, sweet honey and aromatic balm' (Navarro, 1799: 19).

II.

Navarro's concepts were not brand new in the European and colonial contexts, but neither were they trivial. We are faced with a highly stimulating intellectual phenomenon when we consider that in 18th century Brazil someone was discussing ideas so germane to current ecological reflections – such as the image of the earth as an integrated and live reality, the global destructive impact of human action, the risk of social collapse on account of environmental degradation, and the need to promote a sustainable form of development. We can, surely, imagine Navarro as an isolated and individual phenomenon, a rare example of eco-visionary foresight blossoming in the remote backlands of Minas Gerais. The truth, however, is very different. The documentary evidence to be shown demonstrates that he is not an isolated phenomenon, but part of a consistent intellectual tradition of 'political-environmentalism'[7] in Brazil through the 18th and 19th centuries. This tradition has been ignored by international histories of ecological thought and, more surprisingly, by Brazil's own cultural memory. We can realise how little we know about the origins of the ecological sensitivity of the modern world when we ponder the discovery of such an ancient lineage of Brazilian thinkers, stretching all the way back to the 18th century, concerned with the destruction of forests, the depletion of soils, climatic changes and other environmental damage. From 1786 until 1888, according to my researches, at least 38 Brazilian authors wrote regularly about these problems, always pointing to the socially negative consequences of the destruction of the natural environment (Pádua, 1997). The theoretical framework present in almost all these writers, including the ones discussed in the present article, deserves some initial comments. First of all, they adopted a strong political bias. The natural environment was defended not because of general ethical or aesthetic reasons, but because of its importance for nation-building, for the survival and growth of Brazilian society. Natural resources were the greatest tool for Brazil's future development and should be treated carefully. To waste such a treasure would be a historical crime which should be combated by the public authorities. The main tone was always anthropocentric, scientificist and economically progressive. Destruction of nature was not understood as a 'price of progress' but as a 'price of backwardness'. It was considered the legacy of centuries of colonial exploitation. The main panacea for achieving environmental sanity, in this sense, would be the coming of modern technologies and productive practices. In the particular case of Brazil, contrary to the views that try to link the origins of environmentalism with the Romantic culture, the natural environment was first defended, sometimes heroically, by pragmatic and utilitarian intellectuals.

In order to understand the cultural context from which this whole tradition emerged, including Navarro's text, we need to reconstruct the historical lines which aided the genesis of a political discussion about the environmentally predatory nature of the Brazilian social establishment. Until the end of the 18th century, and during the entire colonial period, very few voices were raised in perception, far less in condemnation, of this fact. Since 1780, however, a theoretical movement in this direction began to take shape. It had a clearly defined epicentre: the Universidade de Coimbra after the occurrence of the curriculum reform of 1772, ordered by the progressive prime minister Marquis of Pombal. This reform pulled Portuguese academe away from traditional medieval scholastics and directed it to the new concepts of natural philosophy and political economy which were spreading in Europe. The Portuguese state itself promoted the introduction of this 'Enlightened' set of ideas in Portugal, more specifically a certain reading of such ideas. This was part of a semi-official project of cultural and economic modernisation. Despite its being launched during the long tenure of the Marquis of Pombal (1750–77), I consider this project 'semi-official' because it did not have the complete and permanent support of Portugal's ruling elite. Its trajectory was filled with turns, advances and retreats. The promoters of the reforms were always at odds with the representatives and the beneficiaries of traditionalist ideas and practices. The kings swayed in their support of the two groups, both of which were usually represented in cabinets. Several times a progressive minister was succeeded by a traditionalist one, and vice-versa. Rodrigo de Sousa Coutinho, paradigm of an enlightened and progressive minister – compared by Brazilian writer Hipólito José da Costa to 'a clock that is always ahead of time' – was succeeded as Minister of the Navy and of Ultramarine Possessions, a post he occupied between 1796 and 1801, by the Viscount of Anadia, whom the same Hipólito José da Costa considered to be 'a clock that is always late' (Cited by Maxwell, 1995 [1973]: 257).

This semi-official condition, together with the unstable basis of support, helped shape an enlightened culture that was flexible and politically moderate. 'Illumination' was interpreted more as a practical instrument of scientific progress and economic development than an utopia of revolutionary emancipation of the human race. In this context, the force of an Enlightenment committed to confrontation, radicalism and republicanism was quite limited. Even this prudent and instrumental version of the Enlightenment was harshly resisted in Portugal, as evidenced by the '*viradeira*', the conservative reaction that followed Pombal's fall from power.

At the close of the 18th century, however, a certain degree of development of natural sciences in Portugal was already irreversible – if nothing else, because of its important economic dimension. For example, in Brazil the production of precious metals, the main source of metropolitan income, was waning, and it was becoming clear that it would not recover if rudimentary methods continued to be employed. The study of geology and the development of new mining technologies became high priorities, as they brought the hope of finding new deposits and revitalising old mining sites. Brazilian agriculture also displayed a great potential for improvement, despite its low productivity. Revolutionary crises were destabilising old centres of colonial agricultural production, such as Haiti, and new opportunities were opening up in the international scene. Traditional Brazilian crops, such as cotton and sugar cane, were temporarily strengthened, despite their limited capacity for growth.

The best minds noticed that true progress in Brazilian agriculture required two movements which depended on scientific research. First, exogenous species had to be acclimatised in the colony. Incidentally, this was a central topic on the late 18th century economic agenda. Translocation of species from one region of the globe to another, with the support of botanical gardens to guarantee their survival, was in high order in colonialist countries such as France, England and the Netherlands. Portugal was clearly behind in this matter: only at the beginning of the 19th century did it begin to create botanical gardens in Brazil,[8] while French Guyana, certainly not the most important French colony, had had a well developed botanical garden, called 'La Gabrielle', since the previous century.[9] Second, better knowledge of Brazilian nature was urgently needed, in order to assess the economic usefulness of still unknown native species. The Portuguese empire was equally behind schedule in this matter. Ever since the 16th century systematic inventories of useful minerals, plants and animals of the entire world were being published in Europe, specially those found in the far eastern colonies. However, practically nothing was known about the very rich Brazilian territory, because the scattered and vague accounts of chroniclers were not an appropriate record. Brazil's colonial economy had been built, in reality, with little regard to local species. The option had been to use the territory – and the temporary fertility supplied by the burning of its enormous forest biomass – as a mere support for monocultures of exotic species brought in from the oriental tropics.[10]

At this historical juncture, however, Portuguese intellectuals and politicians started to perceive the need to promote the systematic study of Brazilian nature. This new mentality could be found in the Universidade de Coimbra and in the Academia Real das Ciências de Lisboa [Lisbon Royal Academy of Sciences], created in 1779, centres of knowledge that started to receive a growing number of youths from the Brazilian social elite. The great majority of these students – about 1,242 Brazilians attended the Universidade de Coimbra between 1772 and 1882 (Moraes, 1940) – did not become active intellectuals. But a minority of them formed the so-called Luso-Brazilian 'enlightened generation', the first group of Brazilian intellectuals trained in scientific knowledge and in the pragmatic and progressive spirit of European Enlightenment (Dias, 1969; Maxwell, 1973).

From this small elite emerged the first intellectuals systematically concerned with environmental destruction in Brazil. The major mentor of this group was the Italian naturalist Domenico Vandelli (1735–1816), a friend and correspondent of Linnaeus, who was invited by the Portuguese government to participate in the reform of the Universidade de Coimbra. This invitation was not by chance, because Vandelli, being a member of the more moderate Italian Enlightenment, was used to the presence of Catholicism and aristocracies. Even so, given the prevalence of traditionalism in Portuguese culture, his intellectual impact was deeply invigorating. He became a scientific and cultural energiser, participating in the creation of the Jardim Botânico d'Ajuda [Ajuda Botanical Garden] and the Academy of Sciences (Munteal Filho, 1993). Furthermore, he became famous as the grand master of Portuguese naturalism, training an entire generation of researchers (including many Brazilian ones). Under his personal direction, several of these students combed the interior of Portugal and of its colonies, collecting specimens and doing scientific research.[11]

Vandelli spread an intellectual synthesis that combined the physiocratic doctrine with the economy of nature. According to one author, he taught 'following the book of Buffon and the *Systema Naturae* of Linnaeus' (Ferreira, 1988: 27. Cited by Figueirôa, 1997: 45). The 'economy of nature', as systematised by Linnaeus is a basic part of the chain of scientific work that led, in the 19th century, to what came to be known as 'ecology' (Worster, 1994: chapter 2). It argued the existence of a system of interdependent balances between the several components of the natural world, in a manner that gave each component a function relevant to collective dynamics. This outlook was at the bottom of several critical analyses made in the 18th and 19th centuries of the impact of human action on the environment. It was in this cultural environment that the influential 'desiccation theory', for example, became widely known. It was developed by the cumulative efforts of naturalists such as Halles, Buffon and Duhamel du Monceau. It was the first modern scientific concept about climatic changes induced by humans, because it related the loss of vegetation to the reduction of humidity, of rainfall and of springs in certain territories (Grove, 1995: 164). The critique of deforestation, based on this thesis, gained a new conceptual and political status, because the climatic damages caused by deforestation could generate serious economic consequences.

It was precisely from all these theoretical frameworks that Vandelli started to criticise explicitly and recurrently the environmental destruction under way in the Portuguese world. Examining the situation of Portuguese wood-lots in his *Memória sobre a Agricultura de Portugal e de suas Conquistas* [*Memorial about the Agriculture of Portugal and its Conquered Lands*], published in 1789, he states that 'rarely are they planted and the older ones lack adequate care for their conservation and growth' (Vandelli, 1990 [1789a]: 128).[12] The loss of floral cover on hilly terrain, on the other hand, made them 'ever more sterile' on account of erosion. Deforestation thwarted their being 'supported in several planes in order to avoid the waters from rolling down with much speed', with the result that the waters 'not only take with them salts and oils, but precisely the most fertile land' (Vandelli, 1990 [1789a]: 129). This critique becomes much more severe, however, when Vandelli starts to reflect about environmental damage in Brazil, because the colonisation of the land was combining two negative and apparently opposite elements: under-settlement and over-exploitation. Vandelli's progressive stance in economic matters made him disgusted with the fact that 'the immense country of Brazil [was] almost deserted of people and uncultivated' (Vandelli, 1990 [1789c]: 144).[13] He was even more disgusted because, even with such slight occupation, the environmental integrity of the territory was continuously being destroyed:

> agriculture is expanding along the borders of rivers in the interior of the country, but it does so in a manner that in the future will reveal itself harmful. It consists in burning ancient forests whose wood, because of the ease of transportation by means of the river themselves, would be very useful for naval construction, or for extracting dyes, or for cabinet making. Once these forests are burned, they are cultivated for two or three years, while the fertility produced by the ashes lasts, until the diminished fertility makes

them abandon the plots in order to burn new sections of forests. Thus they continue destroying the forests along the rivers.

(Vandelli, 1990 [1789a]: 131)

In a different text, also published in 1789, entitled *Memória sobre Algumas Produções Naturais das Conquistas* [*Memorial about Some Natural Productions from the Conquered Lands*], Vandelli criticises this manner of deforestation from another standpoint. It is not only an agronomically incorrect method but also a process that destroys still unknown components of tropical flora, aborting the possibilities of their future use through the application of scientific research:

Among the plants from conquered lands, there are many unknown to botanists, basically very useful trees, or trees useful for building ships, houses and useful objects, or for extracting dyes. However, they will become rare and their transportation will become difficult in Brazil. This is explained by the habit introduced of burning large plots of forests on the borders of the rivers for the cultivation most of the corn or cassava, extinguishing the fertility of these plots in a few years and requiring new burns, leaving behind land that was earlier cultivated. Thus are destroyed immense trees that are useful and can be easily transported.

(Vandelli, 1990 [1789b]: 147)

Notice that Vandelli's perspective does not contain any kind of nature cult or romantic overflow in the face of its manifestations. The destruction of the natural environment is criticised for utilitarian and political reasons, based on a clearly pragmatic and anthropocentric perspective. Slash-and-burn agriculture is bad because it is unsustainable, because it does not preserve the fertility of the soil, because in the future it will reveal itself to be damaging. The extinction of arboreal species is undesirable because it is bad for industry – ship-building, etc. The important thing here was the correct construction of an economy and a society, neither of which could be built upon such a precarious and devastated basis.

Such precariousness, on the other hand, was present not only in environmental practices, but also in social structures. Vandelli initiates a lineage of criticism of slavery as the basis of Brazilian colonial economy, although in an implicit and cautious tone. When he comments upon Brazilian agriculture, for example, he notes that 'all agricultural tasks are performed by Black slaves, and no White will condescend to being a farmer – the major reason why agriculture in Brazil will never grow very much' (Vandelli, 1990 [1789a]: 131).

In another text, when he suggests an effort to 'pacify and civilise the Indians and make them used to agriculture', he explains this policy by the need to make Brazilian economy 'less dependent on so many Blacks, who in time will become so expensive that it will be hardly worth transporting them to Brazil' (Vandelli, 1990 [1789c]: 145). All these topics would later be taken up by several of his Brazilian students, initiating an intellectual tradition that tried to associate environmental criticism with socioeconomic criticism in the Brazilian colonial context.

It is important to note that Vandelli was never in Brazil, and that his remarks were derived from information received through his correspondents. His concerns were therefore built upon his close association with a group of his Brazilian students. This mechanism was reinforced when each of his students returned to Brazil, having first-hand contact with the destruction in progress. This was the context in which the first treatises on political environmentalism were written in Brazil.

It is significant that these writers were not concentrated in one area of Brazil, but were spread over many regions. This helped increase the richness and diversity of their observations. The major names of this initial period were Manuel Arruda da Câmara (1752–1811), in Pernambuco; Baltasar da Silva Lisboa (1761–1840) and Manuel Ferreira da Câmara Bittencourt e Sá (1762–1835), in Bahia; José Gregório de Moraes Navarro (?) and José Vieira Couto (1752–1827), in Minas Gerais; Antônio Rodrigues Veloso de Oliveira (1750–1824), in Maranhão and later in São Paulo; João Severiano Maciel da Costa (1769–1833), in Rio de Janeiro. José Bonifácio de Andrada e Silva (1763–1838), certainly the most important member of the group, distinguishes himself from the others because of his late return to Brazil. While they returned from their European studies before the end of the 18th century, or right at the beginning of the 19th century, Bonifácio stayed in Europe and involved himself in several academic and administrative tasks. After his return to Brazil, in 1819, Bonifácio eventually became Minister of the Kingdom and Foreign Affairs and the head of the cabinet that led the country to political emancipation in September of 1822. In this position he made a systematic effort to pull together a project of reform and development for Brazil, and conservation of natural resources was one of its major components (for a deeper analysis of Bonifácio's ideas and political work, and his close connections with the intellectual group discussed in this article, see Pádua, 1987 and Pádua, 1999).

Going back to the environmental discussions in Portugal, however, it is important to notice that concern over the destruction of natural resources was not limited to academic circles. It spilled over into the concerns of political leaders. In this matter, as in others, Rodrigo de Sousa Coutinho was a key actor. Coutinho envisaged a federalisation of the Portuguese empire, with Brazil as the seat of the crown, and this increased his concern with the fate of Portugal's largest colony.[14] Its potential should be carefully studied by the natural sciences, both by *in situ* expeditions and by the remittance of Brazilian specimens to Portugal, for adequate examination. Its agriculture should be stimulated by means of the diversification of cultures, the acclimatisation of exotic plants, technological development and the instruction of farmers.[15] Mining should be revitalised by the introduction of improved techniques and geological knowledge.[16] Finally, it was necessary to form an intellectual and administrative elite, born in Brazil, capable of directing the country's progress, without losing its fidelity to the Portuguese sovereign.[17] Coutinho was personally involved in the recruiting of a select set of young Brazilians. He became their mentor, supported their studies, heard their counsel and opinions, and handed them scientific and political tasks. Many of the authors who founded Brazilian political environmentalism shared this double condition: disciples of Vandelli and *protégés* of Sousa Coutinho.

In line with this idea of preparing Brazil to become the future seat of the empire, it was necessary to leave behind the brutal and coarse exploration of resources practised since the early days of the colony. Coutinho's understanding of this is clear in the letter of instructions that he sent to Manoel Ferreira da Câmara Bittencourt e Sá, in 1800, when he went to Bahia to tend matters pertaining to his family's business. Sá, about whom we shall say more later on, was one of Coutinho's favourite *protégés*. He had joined Bonifácio in a long programme of geological studies in several European nations, starting in 1790. In 1800 he was appointed to be the General officer for Mines and Diamonds in Minas Gerais and Serro do Frio, the first Brazilian to occupy the position.

In the above mentioned letter, written before Sá's appointment, he was given a set of tasks very illustrative of the cultural environment under discussion. Among other things, he should stimulate prospecting in search of new mines; work along with the local botanical garden in the acclimatisation of the Pará breadfruit in Bahia; and encourage, by means of the introduction of new technologies, the cultivation of peppers, cinnamon, hemp, cassava and sugar. A specially relevant task, in face of the subject of this article, was to confront forest destruction:

> His Royal Majesty also orders you, despite your personal interest as a land owner, to examine the plans and proposals established for the conservation of wood lots and forests of Cairu, and to observe if the owners really have the right to practice such large clear-cutting and terrible burns ... About such clearcuts and burns, in the benefit of the cultivation of cassava, His Royal Majesty orders you to alert land owners and make them see the great advantages that they would enjoy by substituting so absurd a method for the better system of a regular culture, such as the ones in the Antilles, from which abundant productions of cassava are obtained.

The letter closes with an observation that sums up Coutinho's general political understanding of the environmental issue:

> Bear always in mind that principle of eternal truth: Mines and Forests must be regulated by scientific principles, in which their general utility is computed, and not abandoned to the interests of private owners who, in these cases, and in them only, can act against public utility, in a remarkable exception to the principles of political economy.
>
> (Coutinho, 1800)

There are several interesting elements in this letter. Cassava farmers from the region of Cairu, near Ilhéus, in Bahia, were ravaging the Atlantic Forest. It was necessary to find fair criteria to evaluate their rights in face of the rights of the state. Aside from establishing these criteria, the matter could be solved by educating the farmers, who were probably ignorant of the existence of more modern and less destructive techniques (the reference to the Antilles shows that Coutinho was aware of environmental conservation practices in other tropical regions, and hoped for their application in Brazil). The most significant aspect from the theoretical point of view, however, was the discussion about the limits of the market economy. Coutinho admits that, according to the 'principles of political economy', private interests in general do not conflict with the public interest. There is, however, a 'remarkable exception', related precisely to the environmental issue. In this matter the potential for conflict between private action and 'public utility' is strong. It is therefore necessary that public authority should regulate access to natural resources according to 'scientific principles' that take into account their collective utility, instead of 'abandoning' them to private interests. Indeed, this was one of the central veins of the nascent Brazilian political-environmental critique.

III.

Since 1786, in the context of the intellectual and political environment discussed above, several intellectuals born in Brazil started to produce texts about the same environmental topics focused on by Vandelli and Coutinho, but presenting their own interpretations. In order to understand the common position of this group and to avoid mistaken interpretations, some general comments are required. First of all, we must understand their basic position about the 'Brazilian question'. In the transition between the 18th and the 19th centuries Brazil was experiencing a 'colonial crisis'. The impossibility of keeping the social and political stability of such a big country through the old methods of colonial domination was becoming clearer all the time. Furthermore, the rudimentary technologies and social practices established by the old colonial economy were unable to promote economic growth and to organise a proper use of the vast natural resources of the Brazilian territory.

In face of this reality a strong political debate began. The alternatives discussed covered a spectrum that went from the conservative permanence of pure colonialism (based on metropolitan monopoly) to a position in favour of a universal Luso-federalism, in which each territory would be considered a 'province of the monarchy', to use Sousa Coutinho's expression (cited by Mendonça, 1958: 277). The concept of the political independence of Brazil was almost absent from this debate (at least in an explicit manner). A local attempt at political emancipation in Minas Gerais, in 1786, was firmly suppressed. The dominant project among the Brazilian intellectual and political elite at that moment, including the authors discussed in this article, was to stress the urgent need to break away from the old colonial pattern and promote the endogenous progress of Brazilian society and economy without severing ties with the Portuguese state. This project was partially achieved in 1815, when Brazil ceased to be a colony and received the status of a 'united kingdom' linked to Portugal. In 1822, however, when it became clear that the new Constitutional Assembly in Portugal was planning to reduce the autonomy attained by Brazil – and even downgrade it again to the status of colony – the country's ruling elite adopted the proposal of a complete breakaway and independence from Portugal. The authors analysed in this article, however, were living in a political environment prior to this turning point. It was a moment of historical transition – with all the usual associated ambiguities – in which a certain Brazilian identity was starting to take intellectual shape. Place of birth was not an irrelevant matter in this complex interplay of identities. These authors many times identified themselves as Brazilians, despite their training and public activities in the Portuguese *polis*. It is significant that when breaking away from Portugal became imminent, in the early 1820s, all survivors of the group participated in the movement that led to the construction of an independent state.

But the peculiar identity of the writers mentioned above was not in their position about Brazilian independence. Their main particularity was emphasising the environmental aspects of Brazilian colonial condition and its prospects for autonomous development. The majority of intellectuals identified with the Luso-Brazilian enlightenment did not have a concern – or did not express such a concern – about environmental destruction. It was perfectly possible to incorporate parts of the enlightenment ideal, for example economic progressivism and scientific-technological efficacy, disconnected from any concern with environmental destruction. Attention to the environment was clearly a minority affair, despite the fact that those who did pay attention to it were far from occupying marginal political positions, specially José Bonifácio. At that moment there was not any definite *corpus* of environmental critique, but only a few theoretical sources – such as physiocracy and nature's economy – that, if properly combined, could aid reflection about the environment as a political problem. There was also a highly challenging objective context, because predatory and short-sighted routines prevailed in Brazil. Such a context was not, however, a sufficient condition for the emergence of an environmental critique, and accordingly such an outlook did not grow in the majority of the authors who observed it. To understand the emergence of this critique it is necessary to look closely at the specific profile of a group of intellectuals who for cultural and sociological reasons that need to be better investigated in the future, developed a special sensitivity regarding the topic of environmental destruction, opening a tradition that managed to persist in Brazil during the 19th century.

A crucial text for the establishment of this tradition was the *Discurso histórico, político e econômico dos progressos e estado atual da filosofia natural portuguesa, acompanhado de algumas reflexões sobre o estado do Brasil* [*Historical, political and economic discourse about the progress and current state of Portuguese natural philosophy, together with some reflections about the state of Brazil*], published in 1786 by Baltasar da Silva Lisboa. This text can be taken as a first synthesis, or a first programmatic manifesto of what I am calling the Brazilian environmental-political tradition. The approach, the topics and the proposals presented by him were recurrently recovered by many later writers. Lisboa, a doctor in Law graduated from Coimbra, was born in Bahia.[18] He played to perfection the role that Sousa Coutinho had envisioned for the new Brazilian elite. He was openly loyal to the Portuguese state, considering himself, as a Brazilian, a legitimate heir of its political and cultural hertiage. However, it was not difficult to notice, specially in the second part of his text, his special interest in the Brazilian question, and his search for a path which would lead to the development of Brazil. This was the type of patriotism that Coutinho considered acceptable, and even necessary, to the political project of the Portuguese empire.

Lisboa, as was typical of his intellectual group, had an almost messianic confidence in the transforming power of scientific rationality and natural philosophy. Accordingly, he begins with a critical analysis of the highs and lows of natural philosophy in Portuguese history, since Roman times until the reform of the Coimbra University and the creation of the Academy of Sciences.[19] The renovation under way was considered highly benign, mainly in political terms. Natural philosophy is 'the science that contributes the most to the common good' and its development has immediate social effects, causing 'agriculture to be more florescent, the arts to be more polished and perfect, the population to grow, the factories to be more stable'. The Portuguese nation, with its economy in decay, could 'invert its bad image among peoples', once it adopted 'natural history as the moral and the politics of all its districts, cities and villages' (Lisboa, 1786: 30–36).

The second part of the book is much more concrete and full of proposals, discussing the manner by which the progress of natural philosophy could help the 'vast continent of America discovered three centuries ago'. Brazil indeed needed urgent change. Agriculture was practised in the country 'in the most despicable manner that one can imagine'. It ignored the use of the plough. Work was still performed by 'the poor slaves who, badly instructed, naked, tyrannised, many times starved to death – how should they be concerned with the fortune of their owners?' (Lisboa, 1786: 39 and 48). In the production of sugar, productivity was meagre and hearths were poorly built. All this led to a great waste of resources:

> The immense quantity of wood wastefully employed in the manu-
> facturing of sugar is impossible to understand. The problem
> is in the construction of the hearths, which demand one load of
> wood for each load of sugar-cane. The adequate construction
> of reverberatory hearths would solve this problem, which causes
> great losses to farmers and masters of mills, because those who do
> not possess large forests do not manufacture sugar and those
> who do have such forests in the future will let their mills go idle
> on account of lack of firewood, because this is confirmed by
> experience.
>
> (Lisboa, 1786: 47–50)

The solution to this state of affairs required a general policy of reform. Some reforms would have a wide social impact, as in the case of the incorporation of Africans and Indians into the productive process in a rational manner. The author is in this respect essentially pragmatic and displays no sentimentalism nor cultural respect for these social groups (except for a certain admiration for the Indians' practical wisdom about tropical nature). Lisboa speaks from a cultural position assumed to be superior – Western rationalism. He had no doubt about who was civilised and who needed to be civilised. The key word in his model was incorporate into civilisation, as far as possible, those who were excluded (such as Africans, Indians and the ignorant land owners and free farmers).

This point deserves to be stressed, because it appears again and again in the other authors. Not even his strictly humanitarian suggestions display any cultural relativism or unselfish ethic. The reduction of violence against Africans and Indians was a political and economic necessity. Africans, for example, should be treated with moderation – without 'the criminal abuses exceedingly employed' by the majority of slave owners – receiving instruction about religion and marriage (so that they 'would not continue with crimes and excesses of sensual passions'). They should also be allowed one day per week to work for their own subsistence (instead of spending Sundays 'drunken and indulging in the vices typical of their natural weakness'). This policy of 'good morals and provident economy' would make the slaves 'more loyal to and more friendly with their masters' (Lisboa, 1786: 53–55).

As to the Indians, it was necessary 'to civilise them and save their souls'. The best way to do this was the North American manner: 'multiply their needs ever more, so that they will be forced to associate with more industrious neighbours'. Their incorporation in economic production was a vested interest of the state, who should not allow them to live 'in large villages filled with a clergy who are indifferent to these issues'. The cultivation of cochineal, for example, could be entrusted to the Indians 'in exchange of liquor and several trinkets that they like so much'. However, their highest importance would be as a source of knowledge about Brazilian nature. Lisboa knew that European knowledge was limited, because 'we ignore completely many other [plants], but we are aware that the Indians know many that can be used as antidotes to many diseases'. Scientific expeditions should, therefore, seek knowledge from Indians 'pacified with kindness and goods'. This task could not be postponed any longer, because the key to the country's progress was information about its natural productions. It was urgent to 'disclose all the bounteousness that nature chose to hide in those paradises, in which it seems that she decided to show all her power, as she did in no other place in the world' (Lisboa, 1786: 67–68).

In the best style of the times, Lisboa classified the potential utility of nature according to its three kingdoms. First of all, it was necessary to increase productive knowledge about native plant species, also acclimatising other useful species brought in from other parts of the world. Established cultures should be consolidated by means of more intelligent and rational methods. Cotton, in particular, was a 'new and powerful branch of industry and commerce', because England was establishing 'thousands of factories, modelled on those of Asia' and 'Europe as a whole has approved the use of such manufactured products'. The plough, pulled by cattle or horses, would be well suited to Brazilian *massapê* soils, increasing productivity. New cultures, such as rice, indigo, coffee and grapes, should be enthusiastically stimulated.

In the animal kingdom, a more productive animal husbandry industry was needed, yielding also butter and cheese. Lisboa complains about the predatory treatment of domesticated animals, such as 'the habit of killing bulls, cows and calves indiscriminately, only to fulfil a certain number of hides, resulting in reduction of the herd and in bad quality of the hides'. He was also concerned with the treatment of wild animals. Deer were abundant in the hinterlands, but 'as they are killed indiscriminately at all times, their numbers will dwindle in the future'. The great potential of fisheries was frustrated by rudimentary practices in the conservation and preparation of the catch. In consonance with his physiocratic background, Lisboa examines very briefly the mineral kingdom, mentioning only that mines should be run by 'philosopher magistrates' and that there was an important potential to be explored in the Serra dos Órgãos (Lisboa, 1786: 55–66).

By comparing Lisboa and Navarro, we can see that a well-defined project for Brazil was emerging. Some proposals appear in both authors, such as conserving wood, reforming hearths and introducing the plough. This last point will be present in the debate all the way up to the end of the 19th century, the plough having become a symbol of a rational and non-predatory agriculture, a counter-example to the hegemony of the slash-and-burn practices.[20] The two authors differ, however, when Lisboa expresses social concerns that Navarro avoided (except in passing). In this respect, future texts followed more the lines of Lisboa. The issues of incorporating the Indians and of the better treatment of Africans, for example, were reworked by several authors, gaining their most elaborate treatment in the works of José Bonifácio written after 1819, when environmental criticism took an explicitly anti-slavery attitude and established a causal connection between slave work and the destruction of nature (Pádua, 1999).

Lisboa's book should therefore not be considered a summary of the original tradition of Brazilian political environmentalism, because many new ideas and proposals were later added – Lisboa himself making some of the new contributions. The book should be taken as a first large step in this line of thought, that only now is starting to be historiographically reconstituted.

IV.

There is no space for a detailed discussion of the other texts. I will mention only a few illustrations of their literary and theoretical richness. First of all, it is important to notice that they become more and more radical. No longer produced in Portugal – as were Vandelli's treatises and Lisboa's first text – where impressions of Brazilian environmental problems could somewhat fade, the new texts were written in the field, so to say, in direct contact with exploitative practices found in several regions of Brazil.

This point gains a specially interesting analytical dimension if examined in the light of Richard Grove's findings (Grove, 1990; 1995) that establish a strong link between the colonial condition and the origins of environmentalism. Grove argues, based on a wealth of primary documents, that the most intense and comprehensive perceptions of environmental degradation, specially since the 18th century, occurred in the European colonies located in the tropics. He demonstrated that in certain regions, such as Mauritius, the Caribbean, India and South Africa – he did not study Latin America – ecological perceptions became important to administrators and naturalists of the 18th and 19th centuries, prompting the emergence of public policies aimed at neutralising environmental problems. The theoretical sources that informed such policies were similar to those of the Luso-Brazilian authors: for example, physiocracy, the economy of nature and the desiccation theory.

The large scale of the productive systems established in tropical regions translated into swift and deep demographic, biological and geological upheaval.[21] The intensity of this process generated critical environmental degradation, in which the contrast between destructive dynamics and the natural environment of the tropics – fragile, complex and unfamiliar to European eyes – was starkly clear. The first political analyses about the unsustainability of colonial productive systems appeared in the context of this collision between certain emerging elements of European culture and colonial realities.

The Brazilian case presents an interesting aspect to be considered within such a comparative framework. Contrary to the cases studied by Grove, in which environmental issues were considered and confronted by scientists and administrators born in the European colonialist countries, generally employed by colonial companies and governments, in Brazil this reflection was developed by locally born intellectuals, members of the local elite who later participated actively in Brazil's political independence. Political motivations were diverse, despite similar theoretical influences.

The Brazilian writers, when returning from their sojourn in Europe, felt deeply moved and challenged when they rediscovered the rustic reality of their country of origin. For example, the physician and botanist Manoel Arruda da Câmara, writing from Pernambuco in 1797, explained to minister Sousa Coutinho the reasons that were delaying the dispatch of scientific information that he had asked for: 'there is the vastness of the backlands which I must cross, and the deserted places and absence of a mail service, and the strong rains and swollen rivers that I will have to overcome with all my strength' (Câmara, 1982 [1797]: 239). There was in these words a sense of sacrifice and mission.

The landscape of the rediscovered country almost induced gloom. The same Câmara, in his *Memória sobre a Cultura dos Algodoeiros* [*Memorial about the Cultivation of Cotton Trees*], published in 1799, was shocked by the fact that the cultivation of sugar-cane, which required 'the deepest knowledge of physics and chemistry', was left to 'inept and stupid men in whose hands the landowner trusts his fortune'. Firewood was cut and taken as if to a 'place of sacrifice'. Every time the author had the 'unhappy experience of being present at such a catastrophe', he felt as if he 'was witnessing a dissipate and prodigal son consuming in a few hours the abundance that a laborious father had taken from the earth with the strength of his arm' (Câmara, 1982 [1799]: 113).

Câmara's reaction, typical of his intellectual group, was to develop studies and experiments seeking more efficiency in the production of sugar and cotton. He also tried to discover native plants that could open up new perspectives for agriculture and the economy in general. One of these plants was the '*almécega*', which he found in the Pernambuco backlands. Its pitch had several useful applications. The scientific validity of this discovery was not enough, however, to guarantee its economic use. His text *Ofício sobre a Almécega e a Carnaúba* [*Letter about Almécega and Carnaúba*], published in 1809, shows that the author, also in those backlands, had to deal with what he called, in general terms, 'ignorance', something that discouraged him deeply. Despite the fact that the wood of the almécega was not very useful, the species was threatened by 'the ignorance of the people' who 'relentlessly cut it down in the many agricultural plots opened in the native forests'. The tree was threatened also by the fires that '"bums" and ill-famed hunters set to the woods, with the aim of thinning out the brush so that they can ride their horses without difficulty'. This problem could only be solved by the 'forbidding such destruction of virgin forests, in which *almécegas* are abundant, and also by forbidding the setting of such fires, something that can only be accomplished if some legal punishment is given to violators' (Câmara, 1982 [1809]: 230).[22]

Writing from Ilhéus, in Bahia, in 1789, the already mentioned Manoel Ferreira da Câmara Bittencourt e Sá, spoke of a country 'covered mostly by thick forests that its inhabitants were daily striving to destroy, in exchange for the short utility of one to four crops … and without using their precious woods for construction, dyes and craftwork' (Sá, 1990 [1789]: 3). Farmers were satisfied with the 'mediocre contentment' of producing cassava and rice for the market of Salvador, Bahia's capital, instead of profiting from the introduction of new cultures such as sugar-cane, cacao and the liqueurs of tropical fruits. Or, maybe, more fisheries, specially whales and turtles, or even the wood industry. The author was well conscious of the environmental risks of these improvements. In the case of whaling, for example, Sá criticises the mistakes of the whalers, specially the 'ignorant belief that without the killing of the young whales the mothers cannot be caught'. He also notes that the scarcity of whales in other areas was causing English and North American boats to hunt in Brazilian waters. The problem could only be solved by adopting whaling methods that did not kill the younger whales (Sá, 1990 [1789]: 42).

A similar alert was given about the wood industry. The author condemns the daily waste of valuable wood burned in needless fires. Such wood should be used in a rational manner, conserving forests and replanting trees. Precisely the opposite was happening in the region, in which 'there is no record of the planting of a single tree used daily in construction or as fuel' (Sá, 1990 [1789]: 45). The matter was political enough, and even had an international dimension, for a serious intervention by the state, so that the industry could proceed in an adequate manner:

Therefore, I believe that it will be in the interest of the state not only to publish mere orders, because some have already been published, although with little effect, but to also appoint officers to take care of and regulate the indiscriminate cutting of woods, forcing owners of seaboard properties to conserve those woods fit for construction, given that they occupy such small sections of their holdings and will not bring losses to their plantations. He also must force the owners to plant and reproduce these trees, so that each one has a certain number of the mentioned species. If these measures had been taken earlier ... we would not be forced to beg and buy for steep prices the oaks of Pennsylvania, for the construction of our military vessels.

(Sá, 1990 [1789]: 45)[23]

A few years later, this advice by Sá, particularly in reference to vessels of war, was partially taken by the Portuguese government. In March, 1797, under Sousa Coutinho's authority, the crown sent royal decrees to the governors of some of Brazil's provinces, dealing with the issue of the conservation of forests and of hardwoods. The decrees were sent at least to the provinces of Paraíba, Rio Grande de São Pedro and Bahia, this last one being the most detailed and complete.[24] The content of these documents is about the same. They all open with the same rationale, that 'the woods and the trees for construction are of the highest interest to the royal navy', and can also be a good source of revenue to the royal treasury in case the navy organised 'regular cuts of those woods for the purpose of commerce with foreign nations'. Thus, it was necessary to 'take all precautions for the conservation of the forests of the state of Brazil, and avoid their ruin and destruction'. The decrees determined that all forests and wood lots along the seaboard and navigable rivers that ran into the sea were owned exclusively by the crown. These areas could not be given away as grants and the ones that had been granted should be taken back by the crown, compensating owners with new grants of land in the interior. The decrees also made owners responsible for the conservation of the royal trees, and ordered that 'those who set fires and destroy the woods' should suffer severe punishments (Sousa, 1934: 20–24).

There is not enough space to discuss the dynamics and eventual results of this essay in environmental policy in colonial Brazil.[25] There is a consensus that it failed in its basic goals. Nonetheless, it is probable that it helped to reduce, for some time, the rate and the scale of devastation, at least in some regions. One aspect deserves attention here. The policies adopted by Sousa Coutinho, in 1797, were strongly influenced by the network of Brazilians with whom he was in touch. These decrees were, to be true, a specific and narrow response, if compared to the broader discussion under way. What was being debated was nothing less than the need for a general reform in the predatory nature of the Brazilian economy, while these decrees dealt only with the supply of wood to royal shipyards. Nonetheless, this was not a minor matter, as Europe was going through deep turbulence generated by great military conflicts. Other countries were doing the same, seeking to guarantee supplies for their vessels of war (Albion, 1926). But Sousa Coutinho clearly acted because he became convinced that forest practices in the colony were not sustainable and because he feared the extinction of Brazil's forests. His decision was therefore shaped by the intellectual debate under examination.

A key character in this entire episode was, once again, Baltasar da Silva Lisboa, who then lived in Portugal, after spending a few years in Brazil. He combined a solid training as law scholar with good knowledge of forest botany, and was trusted by Coutinho. In May of 1797 he was appointed to the post of auditor of the jurisdiction of Ilhéus and magistrate in charge of forest conservation – a sort of high-ranking forest ranger. While in this position, which he occupied until 1818, he made detailed studies in mapping and compiled a flora inventory of the local Atlantic Forest, besides adopting procedures for its conservation and rational use. He had many conflicts with the local elite, especially loggers and cassava farmers. His policies suffered several changes throughout the period and generated much controversy, specially regarding the right of the state to preserve forests located on private holdings.

This conflict between state and private interests gave a special theoretical dimension to the debate between Lisboa and the intellectual spokesman for forest owners in Cairu, José de Sá Bittencourt e Aciolli. This character was a brother of Manoel Ferreira da Câmara Bittencourt e Sá and a member of Brazil's enlightened generation. After being jailed for his involvement in the 1789 anti-Portuguese conspiracy in Minas Gerais, he was released and eventually established himself as a logger and farmer in the region of Ilhéus. Despite his political past, he managed to establish direct connections with Sousa Coutinho, who appointed him to be the inspector of the saltpetre mines of Monte Alto and ordered him to build a road connecting the Bahian coast to that section of the hinterland. Aciolli was, therefore, an intellectually and politically influential adversary for Lisboa.

In June of 1799, Aciolli published an anonymous document entitled *Observações sobre o Plano Feito para a Conservação das Matas da Capitania da Bahia* [*Observations about the Plan Written for the Conservation of Forests of the Province of Bahia*], containing many criticisms of Lisboa's policies.[26] The author defended the interests of the landowners with eclectic arguments. He pulls together liberal principles and a list of concrete threats that curiously resemble those voiced today whenever the state tries to regulate deforestation activities in Amazonia. The important point is that Aciolli at no point denies the validity of the conservation of forests, demonstrating that this concept had already reached a degree of consensus among the contenders. His argument is the defence of the property rights of 'those people who live there'. Besides, he maintains that these landowners could do a better job than the state in terms of conserving forests. According to this view, farmers and loggers had a rational interest in preserving the resources located on their properties, as long as they had the guarantee of retaining the land and the liberty to manage their business.[27]

The text later contradicts this argument, because it contends that without deforestation it would be impossible to develop conventional economic production of the region. This prepares the context for the threats. Restricting the destruction of forests would cause wood to become scarce because loggers would be ruined, and cassava flour to become expensive, as farmers would also be ruined. The restrictions would bring other evils, such as unemployment and the reduction of royal revenues. Aciolli recognises that cassava production requires the use of dense forests, and not second-growth plots, in order that soils could be fertilised and ants be excluded (he was pinpointing the type of forests that needed to be burned). The permanence of this production system was a considerable political issue, because cassava was the basic staple of the local population. According to Aciolli, it was therefore necessary to 'strike a balance' between intended conservation and the forest destruction required for economic progress. The elimination of forests would not be, he argued, entirely negative because they could aid in the improvement of the region's 'very rainy climate' which had caused 'many difficulties to the first settlers'. This was a curious inversion of the desiccation theory (Aciolli, 1799).

To avoid the economic collapse of Ilhéus, without putting in risk the supply of wood to the shipyards, Aciolli suggests that the state set up forest preserves further South in the province, in the region of Porto Seguro, in lands that were almost void of population. In short, the state preserves would be beneficial, but only if they were located far away from the forests that Aciolli and his friends were using. Doctrinal coherence was not the strong point of the text. What is historically significant is its having been, in the words of Morton, 'one of the first occasions in which Brazilian elites used the classic doctrines of economic liberalism to defend their interests' (Morton, 1978: 56).

Lisboa, ironically brother of the Viscount of Cairu, the father of Brazilian liberalism, followed a completely different theoretical direction in his response. He eloquently defended the precedence of the public interest over private ones. His enlightened politics were closer to the tradition of the authoritarian modernisation of the Marquis of Pombal than to any 18th century school of liberalism. Although he does not use the term, Lisboa bases his argument on the concept of *raison d'Etat*. The supply of wood to royal shipyards is within the scope of elementary concerns such as the security and the survival of the political community. War vessels 'sustain the independence and the power of the throne'. All sectors of society depend on these two traits, including the land owners who complained about conservation measures. Without these war vessels, the 'many private parties' would not be able to 'trade the outputs of their industry in the metropolis', neither to 'acquire through their agricultural output the goods that they are capable of buying'. The monarchy, in the name of the general good, had the right to 'create an impenetrable barrier to the defective ambition of the colonists, who did not wish to cultivate without destruction and who ... destroyed such important lands with iron and fire'. To make this right even more legitimate, the conservation magistrate cited old laws from the times of Portuguese absolutism, such as the so-called 'Regimento do Monteiro-Mor', dated from 1605. It established the control of the crown over forests in order to preserve game, and it could be extended by inference to the preservation of trees.[28] Lisboa also resorts to the experience of other European nations, where 'the most intelligent men and the most illuminated governments' were decreeing the conservation of forests as a guarantee for their navies (Lisboa, no date, 12–13).

Lisboa sees the state as the grand agent of public rationality. He thus criticises the minority of land owners who always profited from 'the wood they took from private forests and those owned by the Indians' and who did not wish to be deprived of 'the advantages that their ambition and interests promise'. This group desired that 'Your Highness does not own any forests in the vicinity of the cities, that Your vessels of war depend on the whim and the ambition of middlemen, who will become the controllers of the public power of the monarchy' (Lisboa, no date, 14). Lisboa argued that the monarchy represented an autonomous and superior entity that could never be controlled by private interests. The monarchy should also have a privileged role in the occupation of geographic space so as to exercise its beneficial control over society as a whole. Based on this logic, Lisboa expresses irony about Aciolli's proposal of preserving forests in the South of the province, far away from urban centres:

> They wish that the Royal Navy have access only to the forests located in the remote parts of the coast, inhabited by savage Indians and by escaped slaves. Even then this property would not be safe because these inhabitants ... might well claim their rights over them and request compensation for the losses suffered in their agriculture. As in this century of so many novelties there have been publicists and doctors who wrote expressly about the rights of animals, who knows if they would not also recognise the legitimate rights of the orangutans, tigers and *surucucus*[29] of the dense jungles to complain about violence and request compensation for their losses in these remote lands in which they were living?
>
> (Lisboa, no date, 15)

This quotation is important to understand the intellectual tradition under examination. Lisboa's immediate arguments refer to the pretence that there could be private interests more important than those of public authority. If farmers refused to accept this authority, why would other sectors not behave in the same manner (including Indians and escaped slaves)? Moreover, if this possibility exists, why not extend it to animals? This last ironical punch reveals the anthropocentric character of Brazil's original political environmentalism. Lisboa scorns the debates about the rights of animals, which some philosophers were starting to engage in. For him the natural environment does not have any intrinsic value, but only a grand instrumental value. Its conservation is essential for the satisfaction of social needs. This is the motive of Lisboa's fight against the destruction of the forests. For him, forests are a political object, a resource required for the expression of a political project. The debate centred, therefore, not on the ethical opposition of the rights of humans *versus* the rights of non-humans, but on the political opposition of an instrumental, predatory and short-sighted view of nature and an equally instrumental, but prudent and sustainable, view of nature.

Critiques about the inconsequential actions of private interests were made at the same time by authors living in Minas Gerais, another fundamental section of the Brazilian colonial economy. In the year 1799, when Navarro published his *Discourse*, José Vieira Couto wrote his *Memória sobre a Capitania de Minas Gerais* [*Memorial about the Province of Minas Gerais*], in which he presented a deeply critical analysis of the regional situation, underlined by environmental concerns. The main objective of the text was to discuss the decline of mining and ways to reinvigorate it. The author thought that the decline was due above all to technical incompetence. The development of a 'national metallurgical craft', with modern machinery and technology, could revive mining, because enough ore remained to be exploited. Diversification of production was the key to the matter, with more attention to the exploration of iron ores.

Improvement of the transportation system was another important aspect, and this could be achieved by using the natural trails of the rivers and by constructing channels between them and the coast. New roads should be opened to substitute current ones, which were in very bad shape. Besides, new means of transportation should be adopted, with the introduction of new animals capable of hauling cargoes, like the camel and the buffalo.[30] A native solution could be the tapir, which could be domesticated and trained to haul cargoes. These measures should be complemented by a general economic development programme, stimulated by the state on the basis of tax breaks that would later be compensated by the increase in revenues caused by improved collective welfare (Couto, 1848 [1799]: 320–25).

Another aspect of this reform programme should be taken into account: the treatment of the natural environment. Couto did not point out the environmental problems created by mining, or perhaps he deliberately decided to avoid the issue.[31] In reference to agriculture and forests, though, his evaluation was probably the most eloquent among contemporary texts:

> It seems that it is time to pay attention to these precious forests, these amenable woods that the Brazilian farmer is threatening with total burning and destruction, with an axe in one hand and a firebrand in the other. A barbarian agriculture, that is also much more expensive, has been the cause of this general conflagration. The farmer gazes around and sees two or more leagues of forests, as if he were looking at nothing, and even before he finishes reducing them to ashes he is again gazing far away to take destruction elsewhere. He has no affection nor love for the land that he cultivates, because he knows well that it will not last long enough for his children. The land, on its side, does not smile at him, nor offers him the gracious sight of waving yellow ears to soothe his eyes. A harsh field, covered with stumps and thorns, is what remain in his property.
>
> (Couto, 1848 [1799]: 319)

Despite the Arcadian and poetic tone of this striking excerpt, as we follow Vieira Couto's reasoning we see that his environmental concern was much more political than aesthetic. The problems caused by deforestation and farmers' rootlessness affected the future of the province. Firewood and lumber were already scarce and this scarcity could nullify the growth potential of mining. Metallurgical industries required much wood for construction and fuel, besides charcoal, and would not be feasible if forest reserves were located too far away. The author himself had inspected 'layers of excellent iron ore' that 'will never be useful to anybody because the woods are so far away' (Couto, 1848 [1799]: 319).

The solution, according to Couto, was a total ban on the deforestation of wood lots around villages and the conservation of at least half of the wood lots on more remote properties. This policy would bring obvious benefits to agriculture and society. Farmers 'would be forced to plough and to apply manure to the land', abandoning slash-and-burn practices. In this manner, their 'remaining wood lots would be conserved for their own utility and for the utility of their sons and the state'. This forest conservation policy could furthermore lead to an authentic transformation of social dynamics, because 'properties would then become much more permanent, the population would settle down and stop wandering, agriculture would improve and we would see that this scarcity of firewood and lumber would not be so deadly to the future construction of our foundries' (Couto, 1848 [1799]: 320).

Couto's text becomes even more interesting from the point of view of the *ethos* of modern ecological thinking. Immediately after his strong protest against predatory agriculture and forest destruction, the author discloses his utopia for the future of the region:

> I think I can already see a new horizon, a new sky: Thousands of hearths cover the plains and release thick billows of smoke to the clouds. The hills are being mined and their rich entrails are vomited through their small mouths. The cacophony of a thousand machines strike my ears, a laborious, content and joyful people walks the surface of the earth in large groups.
>
> (Couto, 1848 [1799]: 320)

There is reason for surprise at this excerpt. What seems to be the nightmare of today's environmentalist – 'thick billows of smoke' and the 'cacophony of a thousand machines' – seems to be the dream of this old writer from Minas Gerais, the same man who was able to write the strong protest against deforestation quoted above. Few passages reveal so clearly that, for the intellectual tradition under examination, environmental destruction was not seen as the price of progress, but as the price of backwardness. Economic progress was not seen as a threat to the natural environment. What really degraded and destroyed the land were archaic and ignorant practices, inherited from colonial times, and they could be corrected only by modern technologies and projects. It is true that such projects are rarely so explicitly industrial as in this particular text; following the physiocratic ideal, they usually seek a modern agricultural society.

Besides, one can argue that the environmental innocence of Vieira Couto's industrialism is not an evaluation, nor the result of an actual experience. It is a fictional and vague picture of the industrial world that actually existed. His view would probably have changed if he had had the opportunity – as others did – to observe directly the impacts of the industrial city on the natural environment (Clayre, 1977). Even if we accept this counterfactual point, the text remains significant, if for nothing else because it is informed by a perception of the existence of the new social landscape produced by the Industrial Revolution. More than a defence of an industrial landscape, what the text reveals is a strong desire for progress, a devotion to modernity.

The same confidence in progress appears, in a much more ambiguous form, in the writings of Moraes Navarro. We saw that this writer from Minas Gerais was, at the time, the most keen Brazilian observer of the universal dimension of environmental problems. The problem of an essential contradiction between humanity and the planet, with the possibility of collapse of those societies that destroyed their own material conditions of existence, contrasted with the optimistic and progressive philosophy of history typical of the Enlightenment, including its Luso-Brazilian version.

390

This contradiction was a basic dilemma in Navarro's writings. He affirmed, for example, a strong faith in the regenerative powers of the earth. Despite cumulative bad management throughout history, especially Brazilian colonial history, the fertility of the earth would always be able to renew itself when human beings started to treat it properly. On the other side, human societies went through similar phases of historical evolution. In relation to Portugal, Brazil was in its infancy. The Portuguese, after having damaged the fertility of their land over a long historical span, had learned new ways, becoming better cultivators of their plots and carefully conserving 'the remains of those wood lots that they had unthinkingly destroyed' (Navarro, 1799: 8–10).[32] Brazilians would tend to do the same when they matured.

The basic ambiguity of this line of thought is in the premise, essentially metaphysical, that 'the land, despite its antiquity, never loses its vitality'. The fact is that several passages seem to contradict this possibility. If colonists insisted in their predatory ways, for example, the future of the country would be dreadful, because it 'would lose its natural resources, or see them decrease sharply, and the men would finally be forced to cultivate the land that they so mistakenly abandoned and to conserve the remaining trees, but they would not have even the seed of many of them'. Actually, this was the reality in some parts of the colony: 'look around the edges of the larger cities in the province of Minas Gerais and try to find in any of them some of those precious trees that in earlier times were the most beautiful ornament, and you will not find even signs of their ancient existence' (Navarro, 1799: 10–13). Actually, the author is saying that destruction can be irreversible, because many components of the Brazilian flora were being extinguished forever. Therefore, the ability of the earth to bounce back was not so complete. In an important part of the text, Navarro tries to confront this ambiguity, but does not solve it. In a comment about the actions of colonisers, he states that

Some will say that this behaviour of the men in Brazil is very useful and profitable because without it no advantage could be derived from those immense forests, the secret home of animals and plants; the great variety of trees and herbs would not be known, neither would their utility and virtues; the rich treasures hidden in the earth would not be discovered; barbarian peoples would not be civilised; the inner and outer commerce of those vast domains would not have increased. In the end, they will say, according to our own principle, that as the land is always capable of the same production, it does not matter that men sterilise it for some time. Because when they no longer have new plots that voluntarily surrender their natural productions, after settling all the land, after extinguishing the race of wild animals and poisonous beasts, after civilising the peoples raised among feral creatures, they will then employ those methods that necessity and industry define as the most convenient to bring back to life the ancient fertility in the earth. But we answer that, following a middle ground, they could not attain all these advantages without being deprived of others that by their own fault they go on losing, and that their descendants will not be able to repair, even if they desire to do so?

(Navarro, 1799: 13)

This line of thought is conceptually confused, as one can easily see. Navarro opens a distinct possibility of following a path by which the benefits of progress could be attained without extinguishing the possibility that future generations will have a healthy environment and repair the evils of environmental degradation, if they so wish. As he is not ready to formulate a theory of the irreversibility of environmental damage, however, he is unable to produce a decisive argument in favour of changing from a predatory pattern of development to a sustainable one. The logic of this necessity would have to be based on the impossibility of the first pattern to survive for long periods, on its ability to cancel, after a certain degree of destruction, any possibility of building a sustainable alternative. This point does not become evident. It is merely indicated in the text under the guise of lost advantages that the 'descendants will not be able to repair'.

In the end, we do not learn what would be really lost if men postponed indefinitely changing the pattern of development (trusting the eternal generosity of the earth). This contradiction between enlightened optimism and the potential pessimism of Navarro's environmental criticism weakens the conceptual validity of his argument. On the other hand, however, it reveals the richness of the theoretical tradition that this article has tried to summarise. Some of its dilemmas, as we have just seen, remain as highly controversial topics in the political and philosophical agenda of the contemporary world.

Notes

My gratitude to José Drummond for his support for translation from Portuguese. I would also like to thank John Wirth, Lise Sedrez, Ricardo Benzaquen de Arajo and the two reviewers for *Environment and History* for their comments.

1 For a summary of the environmental consequences of this mining cycle, see Dean, 1995: Chapter 5.

2 The *Dicionário Bibliográfico Brasileiro* [*Brazilian Bibliographic Dictionary*], by Augusto Sacramento Blake, published in 1898, the major source of information about Brazilian writers of the past, does not even mention Navarro's dates of birth or death.

3 The booklet was published in Portugal by the Brazilian botanist friar José Mariano da Conceição Velloso, as part of a series about agriculture, aimed at land owners in Brazil. See note 15 about the nature of this editorial venture.

4 Aster, the Greek goddess who departed from the earth in protest against human wickedness, was recurrently used as an image in post-Renaissance European thought, sometimes with political purposes. Yates (1975) presented an important study on this subject.

5 This fact has not been totally ignored by Brazilian historiography, but in general it has been underestimated. Some authors looked into the topics of 'dead cities' and nomadic agriculture that abandoned destroyed soils in search of new forest to be burned. For a synthesis, see Pádua, 1997: chapter 2. Current research in environmental history will bring new light to these issues.

6 For a good analysis of the physiocratic ideas see Grandamy, 1973.

7 I am aware of the possible anachronism implied in the use of this expression. Anyway, I take it to identify an analysis of the relationship between society and the natural environment that gives a special concern to its importance for the construction, survival and fate of a political community.

8 See Segawa, 1996 about the first botanical gardens in Brazil. Rio de Janeiro's fashionable 'Passeio Público' was built between 1779 and 1783, but its functions were more urbanistic than botanical. Royal decrees, signed by the minister Sousa Coutinho, determining the creation of true botanical gardens were sent to Belém in 1796, and to Olinda, Salvador, Vila Rica e São Paulo, two years later. None of them were actually established, though. Rio de Janeiro's important botanical garden was created only in 1808.

9 Dean, 1995: 126. This garden was later put under Portuguese control, between 1809 and 1817, when Cayenne was occupied, in reprisal to the invasion of Portugal by Napoleonic troops. A considerable quantity of botanical materials were transferred from this facility to Brazil, including a variety of sugar-cane that became known as 'caiana' (from Cayenne).

10 The exploitation of brazil-wood, in the first decades of colonisation, was an exception to this rule, despite its quite limited economic impact.

11 The best known of these expeditions, at least in the Brazilian case, was directed by a student of Vandelli, Alexandre Rodrigues Ferreira, who explored Amazonia between 1783 and 1791. It should be noted, however, that this quest for new knowledge about the natural world was relatively timid in Portugal, if compared to the efforts of other colonialist countries of the time. Suffice it to recall that Ferreira's expedition went through countless difficulties in terms of operational and political support. On this subject, see Moreira Neto, 1983.

12 In a significant footnote, Vandelli states that 'it would be necessary to apply to this kingdom the laws that France enforces in relation to its wood lots'. This example reveals the impact of the forest ordinances edited by Colbert in 1669, on the formation of 18th century political environmentalism. About this matter, see Glacken, 1967: 491. It is interesting to record, however, that a great amount of forest destruction occurred in France after the 1789 revolution, which came to be cited as a counter-example. About this point see Corvol, 1989 and Grove, 1995: 259.

13 Vandelli manifested a typical physiocratic dislike of mining, declaring that mines 'should not be the major concern and occupation in Brazil' and that 'the greater part of the richness to be gained from colonial conquests should come from other natural productions originated by agriculture or other things as offered by nature'. This did not preclude the compromising suggestion about the need to create a 'wise regulation' for mining activities or even the employment of machines to drain mined perimeters. Vandelli 1990 [1789c]: 154.

14 Coutinho forwarded his proposal to make Brazil the seat of the crown in 1803 (Maxwell, 1995 [1973]: 257).

15 The task of publishing books useful to Brazil's agrarian development was given to the naturalist and friar José Mariano da Conceição Velloso, who published several booklets, including Navarro's 'Discurso'. Velloso also published a type of practical encyclopedia entitled *O Fazendeiro do Brasil* [*The Farmer of Brazil*]. Coutinho sent several lots of these agronomic books to the governors of Brazil's provinces, so that they could be sold to farmers. It seems that the experience was not successful. A correspondence signed in 1800 by the governor of São Paulo, Antônio Mello Castro e Mendonça, informed the minister that 'nobody is willing to buy a single book, so that many of the books that have circulated were donated by me.' ... Cited by Lyra, 1994: 88.

16 Coutinho's 'Discurso sobre a Verdadeira Influência das Minas dos Metais Preciosos na Industria das Nações' ['Discourse about the True Influence of Precious Metals Mines in the Industry of Nations'] is commonly cited. He states that mining should not be neglected, going against the physiocratic position that it caused the ruin of the national economy. See Coutinho, 1990 [1789].

17 Maxwell (1995 [1973]: 254) argues that such an effort to co-opt the young learned men also had in mind to avoid them becoming involved in anti-Portuguese rebellions.

18 A relevant piece of information is that Baltasar was the younger brother of José da Silva Lisboa, the Viscount of Cairu, famous introducer of liberal economic doctrines in 19th century Brazil.

19 In this respect, Lisboa renders a special tribute to Vandelli. See Lisboa, 1786: 16.

20 For a historical discussion about the introduction of the plough in Brazilian agriculture, see Holanda, 1994 [1956]: ch. II-5. For an analysis of the continuing debate about the topic of the plough in the second half of the 19th century, see Pádua, 1998. It is curious that the potential environmental damage caused by the plough, as noticed in other countries, was not perceived by the Brazilian authors, even because it was not a concrete reality in that country. It remained a kind of distant technological utopia.

21 The case of Latin America is treated in Tudela, 1990 and Castro, 1994.

22 The author also defended the prohibition of cutting *carnaúba* trees, commonly used in the construction of corrals and fences. He argued that the use of the tree's wax would be much more beneficial to the economy (Câmara, 1982 [1809]: 231).

23 In 1807, almost 20 years after the publication of this text, a group of farmers wrote letters to the Senate of Bahia in answer to queries it had posed about the major problems affecting the agriculture of that area. Sá's letter revealed his continuing concern with forests. Most of the letter had a liberal perspective, but Sá mentions the conservation of forests as a just and necessary exception to 'the right of each to behave as he will'. He defends the need of a strong conservationist legislation, although he states his scepticism about its results. See Sá 1821 [1807]: 96–97.

24 The three decrees are reproduced in the historical collection of forest legislation compiled by Souza, 1934. Apparently, other governors received similar decrees. The governor of São Paulo, Antônio de Mello Castro e Mendonça, certainly received a similar document at that time. It was based on this document that he wrote the 'Providências Interinas para a Conservação das Matas e Paus Reais da Costa desta Capitania' ['Provision Measures for the Conservation of the Forests and Royal Trees of this Province']. See Mendonça, 1915 [1799].

25 An informative synthesis, centred on the case of Bahia, is given by Morton, 1978.

26 The section of the letter of Sousa Coutinho to Manoel Ferreira da Câmara Bittencourt e Sá, cited on section II, above, refers precisely to this conflictive situation. The minister asked Sá to make a fair evaluation of the problem, despite knowing that his brother was a participant in the conflict. He requests also that Sá convince landowners of the benefits related to the voluntary adoption of conservation practices. See Coutinho, 1800.

27 This argument has been universally contradicted by historical evidence in forested areas subject to the conditions of open frontier.

28 The character of the 'Monteiro Mor' comes from the medieval origins of the Portuguese state. He was the man responsible for the general welfare of the forests (still today called 'montes' in the Iberian Peninsula). Royal decrees defining the tasks and rights of the Monteiro Mor had been published since the mid-15th century, but only in 1605 did the post gain an official regulation.

29 Also known as surucutinga (*Lachesis muta*), the surucucu is the largest of the poisonous snakes native to Brazil. It is curious that a man with deep knowledge of the Atlantic Forest, such as Baltasar, would mention animals that did not exist in Brazil, such as tigers and orangutans. It seems to me to be a question of terminology. By tiger he probably means the jaguar (this use was recorded in the interior of Brazil by Von Ihering, 1968: 692). His orangutan were probably the large guariba or bugio monkeys. The author was still using European zoological classifications, a proof of how little was known about the specific biodiversity of Brazilian forests.

30 The proposal to introduce camels in Brazil, specially in the semi-arid regions of the Northeast, was renewed throughout the 19th century. A concrete attempt was made in 1859, at the province of Ceará, without success (Braga, 1962: 54).

31 These effects were mentioned by several authors, even by some who were less sensitive to environmental matter. The Bishop Azeredo Coutinho, in his *Discurso sobre o Estado Atual das Minas do Brasil* [*Discourse about the Present State of Mines in Brazil*], written in 1804, states that 'the gold mines operated with water ... sterilise the lands that incidentally would be very useful to agriculture; it is therefore necessary to turn them over and make very deep furrows'. Azeredo Coutinho, 1966 [1804]: 202.

32 In this respect, Navarro disagrees with other observers, such as Vandelli, who criticised the environmental conditions of Portuguese agriculture in the 18th century.

References

1. Primary sources

Accioli, José de Sá Bittencourt e (attributed to), 1799. 'Observações sobre o Plano Feito para a Conservação das Matas da Capitania da Bahia'. Rio de Janeiro, manuscript, Biblioteca Nacional (n. I-31,31,36).

Azeredo Coutinho, José Joaquim da Cunha de, 1966 [1804]. 'Discurso sobre o Estado Atual das Minas do Brasil', in *Obras Econômicas de J. J. da Cunha de Azeredo Coutinho*. São Paulo, Editora Nacional.

Câmara, Manoel Arruda da, 1982 [1797]. 'Carta a Rodrigo de Sousa Coutinho', in José Antônio Gonsalves de Mello, org., *Obras Reunidas de Manuel Arruda da Câmara*. Recife, Fundação de Cultura.

——, 1982 [1799]. 'Memória sobre a Cultura dos Algodoeiros', in J. A. G. de Mello, op. cit.

——, 1982 [1809]. 'Ofício sobre a Almécega e a Carnaúba', in J. A. G. de Mello, op. cit.

Coutinho, Rodrigo de Sousa, 1990 [1789]. 'Discurso sobre a Verdadeira Importância das Minas dos Metais Preciosos na Industria das Nações', in Academia das Ciências de Lisboa, *Memórias Econômicas* – Volume I. Lisboa, Banco de Portugal.

——, 1800. 'Ofício de 24 de Novembro a Manoel Ferreira da Câmara, que vai para a Bahia, dando-lhe S. Majestade diversas missões a cumprir'. Rio de Janeiro, manuscript, Arquivo Nacional (n. Códice 807, Vol 1)

Couto, José Vieira, 1848 [1799]. 'Memória sobre a Capitania de Minas Gerais'. *Revista do Instituto Histórico e Geográfico Brasileiro*, Vol. 11.

Lisboa, Baltasar da Silva, 1786. *Discurso Histórico, Político e Econômico dos Progressos e Estado Atual da Filosofia Natural Portuguesa acompanhado de Algumas Reflexões sobre o Estado do Brasil*. Lisboa.

——, no date. 'Crítica à Refutação do Plano dos Cortes de Madeira'. Rio de Janeiro, manuscript, Biblioteca Nacional (n. II-34,3,36).

Mendonça, Antônio Manuel de Mello Castro e, 1915 [1799]. 'Providencias Interinas para a Conservação das Matas e Paus Reais da Costa desta Capitania'. *Documentos Interessantes para a História e Costumes de São Paulo*, Vol. 43, n. 44.

Navarro, José Gregório de Moraes, 1799. *Discurso sobre o Melhoramento da Economia Rústica no Brasil*. Lisboa.

Sá, Manoel Ferreira da Câmara Bittencourt e, 1990 [1789]. 'Ensaio de Descrição Física e Econômica da Comarca dos Ilhéus na América', in Academia das Ciências de Lisboa, *Memórias Econômicas* – Volume I. Lisboa, Banco de Portugal.

——, 1821 [1807]. 'Carta sobre a Agricultura da Bahia', in João Rodrigues de Brito, *Cartas Econômico-Políticas sobre a Agricultura e Comércio da Bahia*. Lisboa, 1821.

Vandelli, Domingos, 1990 [1789a]. 'Memória sobre a Agricultura deste Reino e de suas Conquistas', in Academia das Ciências de Lisboa, *Memórias Econômicas* – Volume I. Lisboa, Banco de Portugal.

——, 1990 [1789b]. 'Memória sobre Algumas Produções Naturais deste Reino', in Academia das Ciências de Lisboa, *Memórias Econômicas* – Volume I. Lisboa, Banco de Portugal.

——, 1990 [1789c]. 'Memória sobre Algumas Produções Naturais das Conquistas', in Academia das Ciências de Lisboa, *Memórias Econômicas* – Volume I. Lisboa, Banco de Portugal.

2. Secondary sources

Albion, R.G., 1926. *Forests and Sea Power: The Timber Problem of the Royal Navy, 1652–1862*. Cambridge, Cambridge University Press.

Barbosa, W., 1971. *Dicionário Histórico-geográfico de Minas Gerais*. Belo Horizonte, Saterb.

Braga, R., 1962. *História da Comissão Científica de Exploração*. Fortaleza, Universidade do Ceará.

Castro, G., 1994. *Naturaleza y Sociedad en la Historia de América Latina*. Panama, Cela.

Clayre, A. (ed.), 1977. *Nature and Industrialization*. Oxford, Oxford University Press.

Corvol, A. (ed.), 1989. *La Nature en Revolution – 1750/1800*. Paris

Dean, W., 1995. *With Broadax and Firebrand: The Destruction of the Brazilian Atlantic Forest*. Berkeley, Berkeley University Press.

Dias, M. O. da Silva, 1969. 'Aspectos da Ilustração no Brasil'. *Revista do Instituto Histórico e Geográfico Brasileiro*, n. 278.

Ferreira, M., 1988. 'José Bonifácio d'Andrada e Silva'. *Memórias e Notícias da Universidade de Coimbra*, n. 106.

Figueirôa, S., 1997. *As Ciências Geológicas no Brasil*. São Paulo, Hucitec.

Glacken, C., 1967. *Traces on the Rhodian Shore*. Berkeley, Berkeley University Press.

Grandamy, R., 1973. *La Physiocratie*. Paris, Mouton.

Grove, R., 1990. 'Colonial Conservation, Ecological Hegemony and Popular Resistance: Towards a Global Synthesis', in J. MacKenzie (ed.), *Imperialism and the Natural World*. Manchester.

——, 1995. *Green Imperialism: Colonial Expansion, Tropical Island Edens and the Origins of Environmentalism, 1600–1860*. Cambridge, Cambridge University Press.

Holanda, S. B. de, 1994 [1956]. *Caminhos e Fronteiras*. São Paulo, Cia. das Letras.

Lyra, M., 1994. *A Utopia do Poderoso Império*. Rio de Janeiro, Sete Letras

Maxwell, K., 1973. 'The Generation of the 1790's and the Idea of a Luso-Brazilian Empire', in D. Alden (ed.), *The Colonial Roots of Modern Brasil*. Berkeley.

——, 1995 [1973]. *A Devassa da Devassa*. Rio de Janeiro, Paz e Terra.

Mendonça, M. C., 1958 [2nd edn]. *O Intendente Câmara (1764–1835)*. São Paulo, Editora Nacional.

Moraes, F. de, 1940. 'Relação dos 1.242 alunos que frequentaram a Universidade de Coimbra de 1772 (reforma pombalina) a 1872'. *Anais da Biblioteca Nacional*, no. 62, pp. 137–305.

Moraes, R., 1969. *Bibliografia Brasileira do Período Colonial*. São Paulo, Editora da Universidade de São Paulo.

Moreira Neto, C.A., 1983. 'Introdução', in Alexandre Rodrigues Ferreira, *Viagem Filosófica ao Rio Negro*. Belém, Museu Emílio Goeldi.

Morton, F.W., 1978. 'The Royal Timber Trade in Colonial Brasil'. *Hispanic American Historical Review*, no. 58.

Munteal Filho, O., 1993. *Domenico Vandelli no Anfiteatro da Natureza*. Rio de Janeiro, Pontifícia Universidade Católica.

Pádua, J. A., 1987. 'Natureza e Projeto Nacional: As Origens da Ecologia Política no Brasil', in J. A. Pádua, org., *Ecologia e Política no Brasil*. Rio de Janeiro, Espaço & Tempo/Iuperj.

——, 1997. *A Degradação do Berço Esplêndido: Um Estudo sobre a Tradição Original da Ecologia Política Brasileira – 1786/1888*. Rio de Janeiro, Instituto Universitário de Pesquisas.

——, 1998. 'Cultura Esgotadora: Agricultura e Destruição Ambiental nas Últimas Décadas do Brasil Monárquico'. *Estudos – Agricultura e Sociedade*, n. 11.

——, 1999. 'Nature Conservation and Nation Building in the Thought of a Brazilian Founding Father: José Bonifácio (1763–1838)'. Paper presented at the 1999 Conference of the American Society of Environmental History, Tucson, Arizona.

Segawa, Hugo, 1996. *Ao Amor do Público: Jardins no Brasil*. São Paulo, Studio Nobel.

Serres, Michel, 1991. *O Contrato Natural*, 1991. Rio de Janeiro, Nova Fronteira

Souza, Paulo F. de, 1934. *Legislação Florestal, 1a Parte: Legislação Histórica 1789–1889*. Rio de Janeiro, Ministério de Agricultura.

Tudela, Fernando (org.), 1990. *Desarrollo y Medio Ambiente en America Latina y el Caribe*. Madrid, Pnuma/Mopu.

Von Ihering, Rodolfo, 1968. *Dicionário dos Animais do Brasil*. São Paulo, Editora da Universidade de São Paulo.

Worster, Donald, 1994 [2nd edn]. *Nature's Economy: A History of Ecological Ideas*. Cambridge, Cambridge University Press.

Yates, Frances, 1975. *Astraea: The Imperial Theme in the Sixteenth Century*. London, Routledge & Kegan Paul.

17

CONSERVATION MOVEMENT IN POST-WAR JAPAN

Catherine Knight

Introduction

Japan has been the target of much international criticism for its environmental practices – in particular, for its contribution to tropical forest destruction, and its driftnet fishing and whaling practices.[1] However, its domestic nature conservation practices rarely come under scrutiny in the international arena. Like most societies, Japan faces the challenge of finding the balance between the preservation of the natural environment and the social and economic needs of a nation that has undergone immense economic growth and social change, but which is at the same time constrained by the limitations of being a small, largely mountainous archipelago supporting a dense population. In this struggle to find a balance, the domestic nature conservation movement has played a pivotal role, but has remained relatively weak in terms of its influence in the social and political landscape in Japan. This paper explores the factors that have contributed to the relative weakness of the nature conservation movement in Japan. These factors fall into two distinctive, but mutually influential, categories: social (and socio-historical) factors and political factors. The paper represents an historical survey, focusing largely on the post-war decades to the end of the twentieth century.[2]

Socio-historical and social factors

This article will first explore the socio-historical and social factors contributing to the relative weakness of the nature conservation movement in Japan and the nature conservation ethic underpinning this movement. These factors are the comparatively recent emergence of discourse concerning nature conservation in Japanese society; the relatively low awareness of the ecological thinking which forms the basis of effective nature conservation practice; the historical tendency of environmental citizen movements to see

399

people, rather than the environment, as victim; and the social constraints which hamper wider participation in nature conservation organisations.

The recent emergence of the nature conservation philosophy and movement in Japan

The nature conservation movement and philosophy which underpins it has developed relatively recently in Japan, in comparison to Europe and the United States, or even Australasia. This may strike some as surprising, given the much-purported Japanese veneration of nature.[3] The Japanese have historically demonstrated this admiration of nature through poetry, paintings and numerous other artistic mediums. However, these artists and poets rarely based their work on contact with 'real' or 'wild' nature, rather their natural world was more generally comprised of the beautiful cultivated gardens in the urban environments in which they lived. Thus, this veneration was based on an aesthetic appreciation of an idealised nature – a concept quite distinct from a desire to conserve and protect the 'real' nature of Japan's forests, wetlands and waterways.[4]

In Europe and the United States, with the advent of industrialisation and the concomitant awareness of the increased human capacity for the destruction of nature, there also developed a philosophical and scientific discourse examining the relationship of human beings with nature and the ethical issues and implications connected with this relationship. In Europe, a number of scientists and philosophers emerged during the nineteenth century whose work formed the basis for the development of nature conservation and ecological philosophies. Most notably, in 1866, the word 'ecology' was coined by the German biologist Ernst Haeckel (1834–1919), who was key in helping to shift biology away from classical science and towards a more holistic (ecological) view.[5]

The United States, which like Japan, still had a large proportion of its primeval nature remaining at this time of emerging discourse in Europe, provides an insightful comparison to Japan in terms of the development of a nature conservation ethic. Well before the establishment of the first National Park in 1872, there was already an established body of academic and popular literature exploring the human relationship with nature and, more particularly, the value of the American wilderness and its wildlife. For example, as early as 1847, congressman George Perkins Marsh was calling attention to the destructive impact of human activity on the land and was advocating a conservationist approach to the management of forested lands. In 1862, he published *Man and Nature,* which became a significant influence in the conservation movement in the United States. In 1860, Henry David Thoreau was introducing aspects of what later became known as 'forest ecology'. Throughout the last half of the nineteenth century and into the early twentieth century, a popular interest in ornithology was growing through books, articles and local clubs, which provided a grass-roots base for the support of many aspects of nature conservation. Already the tradition of the hunter-conservationist was established, which was a force behind the preservation of wilderness areas as spaces for recreation and relaxation. In 1876, four years after the establishment of the US's first national park, the Appalachian Mountain Club – one of the US's first conservation-related organisations – was formed.[6]

In comparison, in Japan, there was no parallel emergence of literature and discourse on the human relationship with nature at this time, and the first national nature conservation organisation, the Nature Conservation Society of Japan, was only established well into the twentieth century, in 1951.[7] The first national parks were established in 1934, but their primary purpose was economic rejuvenation through tourism rather than the preservation of wilderness for its ecological value, and, paradoxically, their establishment often led to the degradation of these areas of wilderness through development and over-use.[8] Even today, there is little Japanese literature on nature conservation or the philosophical framework and ethical issues which underpin it. The most significant works in this field are translations of Western works, such as those of pioneers John Muir and Ernest T. Seton or contemporary writers in the field. Japanese works generally deal with specific subjects or events, rather than the wider issues of ecology or sustainable human–nature relationships.[9]

The shallow-rootedness of nature conservation philosophy and nature conservation literature and discourse in the post-war years is significant for two key reasons. As will be discussed below, when the pollution crises of the 1950s and 1960s afflicted many Japanese, the focus of the citizens' movement was firmly placed on the effects on the human victims. When the urgency of the pollution crises abated, rather than turning their interests to the damage caused by industry and development to the environment itself, these citizens' movements largely disintegrated. Secondly, without a firmly entrenched philosophy and body of thought relating to nature conservation, as the majority of the Japanese population come to live in fast-paced urban environments, often hours away from any real 'wilderness', there is little awareness of the nature that people have little contact with. Whereas in the West, the stronger entrenchment of ideas regarding the moral obligation of people to protect nature, even if it is not in their immediate neighbourhood (an idea pivotal to the Western nature conservation movement) acts to counter-balance the alienating effects of urbanisation and a modern lifestyle on city-dwellers, there is little such counter-balancing effect in Japan.

Ecological awareness among the public

It can be expected that the level of ecological awareness in any society is related to the level of academic and popular discourse on nature conservation and ecology in that society, so given the limited and recent nature of this discourse in Japan, it is reasonable to assume that awareness of ecological frameworks for understanding environmental issues may also be low. Recent surveys show a relatively high awareness and concern among Japanese regarding *environmental* issues,[10] but relatively low *ecological* awareness and concern for nature conservation. In a government survey which sought people's opinions on the reasons for protecting nature, an overwhelming majority of the respondents chose as one of their responses (multiple responses were possible): 'Because nature provides man with peacefulness and charm' (75 per cent); 42 per cent chose 'Because nature is important for children's sound growth and is a place to learn about nature'; 20 per cent chose 'Because protecting nature is important to conserve resources'; while a negligible percentage chose 'Because it is important to protect the ecosystems of fauna and flora' (three per cent). In summary, the majority of responses were based on anthropocentric rather than ecological premises for preserving nature.[11]

This apparent lack of ecological awareness can also be seen among groups that are actively interested in environmental issues. Even when there is a high level of concern about a development project with significant environmental impacts such as the building of a dam or highway, environmental opposition tends to be based not on wider ecological premises, but specific impacts, such as the extinction of one species within a habitat, often focusing on its implications for humans also. For example, a group which opposed the building of the Nagara dam in Japan's last major free-flowing river focused on the possibility that the *satsukimasu* fish might be made extinct. Further, the group concentrated on the implications its extinction would have on the livelihoods of local fishermen. Similarly, in media coverage of the Isahaya Tideland reclamation project, the *mutsugoro,* or mudskipper (*Periophthalmus pectinirostori*), became the focus of the campaign, while in fact over 300 species and an entire ecological system were at risk. This was also the case in the campaign against the construction of a golf course on the southern Amami Islands of Japan. The environmental organisation opposing the project deliberately focused its campaign on the threat to the endangered Amami black rabbit, though again, several other species and an ecosystem were at risk.[12] In employing this strategy, the organisation was able to garner strong public support for conservation efforts and was ultimately successful: the Ministry of Culture subsequently put a halt to development plans. Thus, it can be argued that by focusing on a species as an emblem of such campaigns, these organisations are simply working within the contraints of public awareness, though at the same time, opportunities to better inform the public about wider ecological implications are lost.[13]

It has been suggested that one of the reasons why Japan has been relatively unsuccessful in its nature conservation policy is its tendency to favour a technocratic and post-facto approach to environmental problems.[14] This can also be interpreted as a product of a low level of ecological awareness: environmentalists have suggested that the 'technofix' approach to solving environmental problems is not only inappropriate but also dangerous, since it fails to consider ecological limits to economic growth. While Japan's pollution abatement policy, which focuses on the development of technologies to minimise the effects of pollution, has been relatively successful, nature conservation policy, which relies on significant attitudinal and behavioural changes in society, and a greater awareness of ecological frameworks for understanding, has been less successful. The technological approach has proved advantageous to Japan not only because it does not require social change, but also because of its economic benefits: Japan has been able to sell its pollution technology on both domestic and international markets. However, there do seem to be some signs that faith in this approach to solving environmental problems is on the wane: in a 2000 ISSP survey, only 1.5 per cent of respondents believed that science would solve environmental problems without any need for people to change their lifestyles. In contrast, 43.3 per cent disagreed with this statement.[15]

The tendency to see humans, rather than the environment, as victim

Some of the most alarming cases of industrial pollution in modern times occurred in Japan during the 1950s, 1960s and 1970s during Japan's transition from post-war reconstruction to a period of rapid economic growth. The cases of severe industrial pollution in the 1950s and 1960s (which became known as the 'big four') were the two incidents of Minamata 'disease' of the late 1950s and 1960s, when chemical waste containing mercury was discharged into Minamata Bay from a fertiliser factory; Yokkaichi asthma, caused by sulphur dioxide and nitrogen dioxide emissions from the petrochemical industry; and *Itai-itai* 'disease' of the 1960s, when chemical waste containing cadmium and other heavy metals was discharged into a river. These cases of pollution caused tremendous human suffering, and not surprisingly, citizen protest tended to focus on the human victims rather than the impacts of the pollution on the natural environment.

While citizens' groups are increasingly focusing on the health and protection of the environment itself, there is still a tendency to be motivated by personal interests. This may be related to the fact that the government is more responsive to opposition based on practical (particularly economic) bases rather than more 'abstract' ecological bases. This is seen in the case of the Isahaya Bay reclamation in Kyushu, which involved the building of a seven kilometre-long dyke intended to convert the tideland flats in Isahaya Bay into farmland and freshwater reservoirs for flood control. The tideland was the biggest in Japan, home to diverse plant and animal life and an important stop-over point for a large number of migratory birds. For many years, the government had remained unmoved by sustained and vigorous opposition to the project on environmental grounds. However, in 2001, a poor *nori* (an edible seaweed) harvest from the Ariake sea, which normally constitutes 40 per cent of all the *nori* consumed in Japan, caused significant alarm throughout Japan. It was widely believed that the poor harvest was due to the sluice gates across Isahaya Bay disrupting the flow of seawater from the East China Sea, allowing plankton to flourish at the expense of the *nori*. The lack of supply and possible price increases of *nori* caused concern among government officials who had remained unmoved by the previous environmental opposition to the project: questions were tabled in parliament, newspapers gave the issue extensive coverage, and opposition party politicians joined in the protests of the *nori* harvesters. Finally, in 2002, in response to the widespread concern, the sluice gates were opened for the first time since their closure in 1997 to conduct an investigation into the cause of the poor seaweed harvests, something that widespread and sustained protest on environmental grounds had been unable to achieve.[16]

The emphasis on environmental issues affecting human wellbeing is also reflected in the focus of the Ministry of the Environment since its inception (as the Environment Agency). It was public pressure resulting from the pollution incidents of the 1950s and 1960s which led to the establishment of the Environment Agency, and pollution abatement has continued to be a key policy area for this agency. This emphasis is reflected in a survey of the annual White Papers published by the Environment Agency: the primary focus of these publications has historically been on pollution issues, and increasingly, issues such as waste management.[17]

Social constraints

There are a number of social constraints which have hampered the development of a robust non-governmental organisation (NGO) sector in Japan. In addition to there not being a strong tradition of volunteering for public causes, the pace of working life in Japan is not conducive to volunteerism; after commuting up to two or three hours or more a day and spending long hours at the office or factory, few people have the time or the energy to participate in volunteer activities. In addition, there are no formalised systems in Japan for encouraging citizens to work in NGOs, such as the case in Germany, where NGOs provide alternative work opportunities for the unemployed or those who choose not to do military service. In this environment, it has predominantly been retired people or women who are not in paid employment who have the free time to be involved in environmental organisations. Nonetheless, working hours have been on a steady decline since the early 1990s, and in 2002, the average hours worked were more than 10 per cent less than the average in 1990 (calculated using data from Statistics Bureau of Japan) – noting that these statistics do not reflect unpaid 'voluntary overtime'.[18]

It has been suggested that a misunderstanding of the role, activities, and functions of NGOs, and antagonistic attitudes toward environmental organisations have also hampered the growth of this NGO sector. However, there are signs that these attitudes are changing. A strong catalyst for change was the Great Hanshin earthquake of 1995, where people saw first-hand how effective and responsive volunteer groups were in comparison to government sectors. Since the earthquake, there has been a marked increase in volunteer activity in Japan. The rapid ageing of Japanese society has also led to the increasing realisation of the importance of the NGO sector in the face of the government's inability to cope with the increasing demands of an ageing population. According to a 2001 survey, over 32 million people reported doing some form of volunteer work over the course of a normal year – nearly 30 per cent of the adult population capable of participating in such work. This represented a 3.6 per cent increase on the figures for 1996. In addition, according to a 2003 survey, just over 60 per cent of Japanese corporations responded that they support the volunteer activities of their employees (in contrast to 35 per cent in 1993).[19]

Perhaps indicating these changing attitudes in recent years, the level of public trust in environmental NGOs is now relatively high. In a 2002 survey, about 30 per cent of respondents said that in regard to environmental pollution issues, they either strongly trusted or moderately trusted information from environmental protection groups (a level of trust higher than that indicated towards industry and government, and equal to that towards university research institutions).[20]

Clearly, the media also has a role both in alerting the public to environmental issues and giving a voice to organisations other than corporate or government organisations, and it appears that NGO activities are receiving increasing media attention. However, it has also been reported that the Japanese news media frequently use only information provided by government agencies and officials, without much effort to investigate or consult a variety of sources.[21]

Political factors

A major factor in the destruction of what remains of Japan's natural environments has been the seemingly relentless drive for economic development, particularly during the post-war rapid economic growth period. The drive for economic growth exists in many countries, but what has made it particularly damaging in terms of its impacts on the environment in Japan has been the powerful nature of the 'triumvirate' – the government, bureaucracy and industry – which has come to have a vested interest in seemingly unbridled development. Development has largely been untempered by any effective balancing forces: neither the Ministry of the Environment, the agency established to formulate and oversee environmental protection policy, nor civil society have been able to form an effective counter-balance against these powerful forces for development.

The following section will illustrate that a primary factor contributing to development at the expense of the natural environment is a lack of a pluralistic and fully participant democratic framework allowing the proponents for environmental protection to be politically effective. The political factors which contribute to this situation are: powerful development interests; political weakness of the Environment Agency; lack of effective environmental impact assessment policy; and the failure of the environmental NGO community to become institutionalised.

Powerful development interests

A key driver in the degradation of Japan's natural environment has been the pursuit of large-scale development projects, such as land-reclamation, dam building, and road and airport construction. In 1993 for example, 31.8 trillion yen of public funds (43 per cent of the national budget for that year) went to the construction industry as payment for public works. This is the product of government policy aimed at increasing public works spending and the result of a collusive system for planning and executing public works projects.[22]

This collusive system has its origins in post-war politics. Until the election to government of the Democratic Party of Japan in 2009, the governing party, the Liberal Democratic Party (LDP), had been in power almost continuously since its inception in 1955. After five decades in office, the LDP had developed an extensive network of support and patronage, linking bureaucracy, big business and the powerful construction industry. This in turn made it very difficult for opposition parties to challenge its power. In this system, there is little transparency and accountability, and corruption is common. Public funds are spent on large-scale projects using a cartel-like system, in which the purpose of development projects has less importance than the reproduction of power and the distribution of profit.[23]

The Isahaya Bay reclamation project, outlined above, vividly shows the pernicious potential of the collusive system which operates behind many of Japan's public works projects. The project was first conceived in 1952 as a means of increasing food production but it was shelved in the face of increasing rice surpluses. It was revived in 1970, primarily for the purpose of securing an adequate freshwater supply for the area, but abandoned again after strong opposition from local fishermen. It was resurrected yet again in 1983 with the objective of reclaiming 1,500 hectares of tidal land for agricultural land and the added justification of flood control.

406

Construction began in 1989, amidst intense local protest. In 1997, the dyke was completed, closing off Japan's largest remaining tidal land from the sea.

Behind the project's resurrection was the powerful construction lobby, which encouraged bureaucrats and politicians in the LDP government to push ahead with the plan. The 'encouragement' was often in the form of financial contributions: research cited by Fukatsu (1997) reveals that 15 of the 38 contractors in the Isahaya Bay project contributed a total of 27.6 million yen to the LDP chapter in Nagasaki Prefecture in 1995, while nine firms donated 1.98 million yen to the Nagasaki Governor's supporters' association.[24]

The objections raised against the project were numerous. While one of the main purposes of the project was the reclamation of farmland, by this time there was a national policy to reduce rice production and already a large area of farmland was lying fallow.[25] Local farmers also viewed the plan with scepticism, maintaining that reclaimed farmland has poor drainage and infertile soil which requires the application of large amounts of fertiliser, and that produce from such soil tends to be of inferior quality, resulting in low profit margins. An additional justification for the project was flood control: silt sedimentation raises the level of the wetlands higher than the surrounding farmland, causing flooding when there is heavy rain. Flood prevention pools, created as part of the project, were intended to prevent this. However, about a month after the tidelands were sealed off, heavy rain again caused flooding of the low-lying farmland.[26] Furthermore, conservationists claimed that the reclamation would destroy the biggest remaining tideland in Japan, habitat to a diverse range of species, including locally endemic species such as the mudskipper, and destroy the tideland's function as an important stop-over point for a large number of migratory birds, including a large population of Chinese black-headed gulls, a species facing extinction.[27]

Efforts to halt the reclamation work were initiated by a few small conservation groups, but public sentiment against the project mounted as awareness was raised through media coverage. A 1997 survey conducted by *Asahi Shinbun* (one of Japan's major national newspapers) found that 58 per cent of the 1,548 respondents believed that seawater should be allowed to flow back in to save the marine life that inhabited the tidal flats. The opposition to the project was extensive: over 250 organisations, both domestic and international, submitted formal protests to the government, asking it to halt the project. However, despite the widespread opposition and the obvious flaws in the project, the government refused to review or cancel it.[28]

The historical weakness of the Environment Agency

The imbalance caused by the power of the 'triumvirate' has been exacerbated by the historical weakness of the Environment Agency (restructured to become the Ministry of the Environment in 2000). One key factor contributing to this weakness is institutional: from its inception, its structure and staffing has not been conducive to its establishing itself as an influential agency in the political landscape in Japan.

The Environment Agency was formed in 1971. Its staff were appointed from 12 different ministries, and the upper management positions in the various divisions in the EA were held, in rotation, by managers from other ministries. Once their term was complete, they would return to their permanent position. This caused a clear conflict of interest, as officials were reluctant to support decisions which ran counter to the interests of their home ministry. In addition, the post of director general of the EA was rarely accepted by politicians who were influential in the Diet (parliament).[29]

Another factor contributing to its weakness has been a lack of public interest in environmental issues beyond industrial pollution issues. Few new major environmental laws were passed in Japan after the mid-1970s until the beginning of the 1990s, and Schreurs (2002) suggests that the primary reason for this was the decrease in public and media attention regarding the environment once newly introduced pollution controls curbed citizen protest concerning industrial pollution – the decrease in activities by the citizens' movements meant that the Environmental Agency was left with little public support. In addition, after the first oil crisis in 1973, industry resistance to further environmental regulation increased and the government was pressured to ease its environmental regulations.[30]

Historically, the Environment Agency had little regulatory and enforcement power: laws relating to the protection of endangered species, national parks and environmental impact assessments have been enacted over the years but have largely been toothless without the authority and resources to enforce them. Instead, laws relating to the environment are often enforced by the very government agency which promotes the activity being regulated, leading to obvious conflicts of interest. For example, the Ministry of International Trade and Industry promotes trade, but at the same time regulates the importation of wildlife products. Similarly, the Ministry of Construction is responsible for public works programmes, but has also been responsible for conducting environmental impact assessments for those projects. Many national parks are under the jurisdiction of the Forestry Agency, which has a clear economic interest in harvesting, rather than conserving, forests within national parks.

Nonetheless, there are signs that the preservation of the natural environment is becoming a more important policy area in Japan. The Ministry of the Environment was the only Ministry to be created in the government restructuring in 2000, and within the Ministry a Nature Conservation Bureau, which in turn includes a Wildlife Division and a Biodiversity Policy Division, has been established.[31]

Lack of rigorous environmental impact assessment

The lack, until recently, of legislation requiring environmental impacts to be assessed before commencing development projects is itself a consequence of the historical weakness of the Environment Agency. After many unsuccessful attempts by the Environment Agency to introduce such legislation, the Environmental Impact Assessment Law was enacted in 1997. Until this time there was no requirement for developers to complete independent environmental impact assessments (EIAs) – a factor that has allowed development projects to proceed with little or no consideration of the impact on the environment. Even in cases where EIAs were carried out, not only were the assessments non-binding, but they were generally carried out or contracted out by the same ministry whose role it was to execute the public works programmes. Under this system, very rarely was a major project stopped as a result of an environmental impact assessment.[32]

The new system makes EIA compulsory for all large-scale projects carried out by central government, and provides increased opportunities for public participation in the assessment process. This means that before the commencement of large-scale publicly-funded development projects such as the construction of roads, airports and power stations, project planners must conduct preliminary surveys and assessments of the potential environmental impact of the projects, and consult with local governments, citizens and other interested parties to seek their input.[33]

However, the new law has also attracted criticism: it only applies to public works carried out by the central government (not prefectural governments, other local bodies, or the private sector) and does not apply to projects already approved before the law came into force in 1999. Additionally, the law has been criticised because it views the impact assessment too narrowly: the law requires that a variety of options be provided for the *execution* of the proposed project, but does not require options at a higher, strategic level. Thus, options such as finding an alternative solution to the proposed project, or not proceeding with a project at all, are not required as part of the range of options explored.[34]

The institutionalisation of environmental NGOs

An active and participant environmental NGO community plays a vital role in the advancement of environmental policy, and in helping to balance political power – and they have a particularly important role in Japan where the pro-development triumvirate is economically and politically powerful. This is illustrated by Japan's own social history – in the 1960s and 1970s its citizens' movement made a significant contribution to the formulation of some of the strictest anti-pollution laws in the world at that time.[35]

Environmental NGOs, particularly those focusing on nature conservation, are comparatively weak in terms of membership, staff, resources and political influence, compared to other OECD countries. The vast majority are relatively small localised groups focusing on specific local issues and with limited representation on advisory councils and committees at national or prefectural levels. The largest nature conservation oriented organisations are the Japanese branch of the World Wide Fund for Nature and the Wild Bird Society of Japan, with about 50,000 members (approximately 0.04 per cent of the population) each. The Nature Conservation Society of Japan has about 22,000 individual members. There are also more than 5,000 small groups engaged in environmental protection and nature conservation, predominantly active grass-roots efforts focused on a single issue.[36]

One major difference in the environmental policy formulation process in Japan, compared with Europe and North America, is that in Japan, environmental NGOs have failed to become a central part of that process. While citizens' groups played a major role in pushing for the introduction of environmental laws in Japan in the 1960s and 1970s, they have played little part in the environmental policy changes in the last few decades. This has to a large extent been the result of barriers that have prevented the institutionalisation of the environmental NGO community. These barriers include the extreme difficulty in gaining non-profit (and therefore tax-exempt) status; legal constraints which limit funding; lack of access to public information; and lack of a framework for consultation or participation in government policy formulation.[37]

Until recently, in order to gain non-profit status, an organisation had to first obtain approval from the local or national government department which had jurisdiction over the policy area. This system clearly put the organisation at a disadvantage, because the approval was at the authority's discretion, and the authority was likely to be antagonistic towards NGO activities in its policy area. The outcome was, therefore, arbitrary, and even if approval was granted, there was potential for a loss of autonomy if the relevant authority sought to control or limit the organisation's activities. The lack of predictability in the process meant that few organisations attempted to gain non-profit status. In 1998, the Nonprofit Organisation (NPO) Law was introduced. This law substantially reduced the time and paperwork required for incorporation and makes the process more predictable: incorporation is based solely on a set of objective criteria, rather than an approval process determined at the discretion of government agencies.[38]

In 2001, new tax legislation was introduced to allow NPOs incorporated under the NPO Law to receive tax-deductible donations in some limited cases. Unfortunately, the conditions which organisations must satisfy are very strict, and few incorporated NPOs are actually approved. More than a year after the introduction of this legislation, only ten NPOs had been authorised to receive this tax privilege. Some amendments have since been made with the aim of allowing more to become authorised.[39]

The Japanese NGO community is clearly hampered by financial constraints: it is reported that the average budget for environmental lobby groups in the United States is on average twenty times that of their Japanese counterparts. Without non-profit status, the majority of NGOs support their activities primarily through membership donations (as opposed to donations from the general public or corporate donations), which, given the small size of the average NGO membership, put considerable financial constraints on their activities. This is borne out by a 1999 study, which found that 80 per cent of the organisations surveyed reported that their main difficulty was limited or unstable income.[40]

Another major barrier has been the lack of legislation allowing NGOs or individuals access to official information. Until recently, access to environmental information held by public administrations was limited. Some improvement may now be expected with the 1999 Information Disclosure Law that came into force in 2001, which requires the disclosure of government and policy information when requested. However, there is a concern that most information related to ongoing policy development will not be disclosed on the basis of a provision which allows for certain kinds of information to be excluded if it is perceived that its release might result in 'a harmful exchange of opinions, or that the neutrality of decision making might suffer'.[41]

One potentially beneficial side-effect of the Japanese government's desire to be an international leader in the areas of overseas development aid and the environment, which is closely connected with its economic and foreign policy interests, is that it has drawn increased international scrutiny of its environmental policy formulation process. Japan has attracted criticism from the international community, which has been sceptical of environmental policies formulated by the Japanese government with minimal NGO or citizen input. In particular, strong doubts have been raised regarding the authenticity of Japan's desire to be an international environmental leader when it has no major environmental NGO monitoring or providing input into its policy formulation and actions.[42]

There are also signs that the attitudes of both the government and the public towards NGOs are changing. For example, increasingly, government officials appear to be soliciting feedback from NGOs. The government, and society generally, is realising the importance of the NGO sector as a core participant in society, and, increasingly, the economy. As mentioned, a key event contributing to this realisation was the Great Hanshin earthquake of 1995, where, in comparison to the slow and ineffective bureaucratic response to the disaster, the efficiency and dedication of the more than one million volunteers was striking. In addition, in the face of a long-term economic downturn and an ageing population, the government has realised that fostering the NGO community to do the work of some government sectors makes economic sense.[43]

Conclusions

As this paper has outlined, the factors contributing to the relative weakness and ineffectiveness of the nature conservation movement in Japan in the post-war decades can be divided into two distinct, but mutually influential, categories: social/socio-historical factors and political factors.

Underpinning the socio-historical factors is the failure of a strong ideological or ethical framework for the pro-active protection of nature to develop in Japan, and connected to this, the historical tendency to see humans rather than the environment as the primary victim of environmental degradation. This has meant that when concerns over the industrial pollution incidents of 1950s, 1960s and 1970s were largely resolved through legislative measures, the environmental movement lost much of its momentum, rather than turning its attention to the protection of the natural environment itself.

In terms of political factors, the powerful nature of the pro-development triumvirate, the historical weakness of the Environment Agency, the lack of effective policy for environmental impact assessment, and, perhaps most critically, the failure of NGOs to become institutionalised, have been key contributors to a political landscape in which the forces for development prevail over the forces for the protection of the natural environment. Owing to this unbalanced nature of political power in Japan, opposition to environmental degradation has largely been ineffective in bringing about policy change or the prevention of environmentally damaging projects.

There are signs that the balance of power between pro-development and pro-conservationist forces may be beginning to change – albeit only gradually – in favour of environmental protection. First, there is now a greater political emphasis on the protection of natural environments and wildlife, as reflected in the establishment of agencies within the Ministry of the Environment concerned specifically with the protection of Japan's natural environment and biodiversity. Secondly, improvements are already being seen in the participation in, and attitudes towards, NGOs and recent legislative developments, though limited in many respects, should nevertheless facilitate greater NGO participation in policy formulation and consultation on nature conservation issues. A further development is the election to government of the Democratic Party of Japan in 2009, after five virtually continuous decades of rule by the consistently pro-development Liberal Democratic Party.[44] However, only time will tell whether these developments will translate into tangible improvements in the protection of natural environments and wildlife in practice.

Notes

1 See, for example, Kellert 1991, 299; Holliman 1990; McGill 1992; Knight 1997, 711; Linden 1989; Morioka 1997.

2 This paper explores not only the formalised nature conservation organisations which form the core of any nature conservation movement, but also the impetus to preserve and protect the natural environment on the part of the government and the public generally. It should also be noted that this paper focuses specifically on the nature conservation movement, rather than environmental movement as a whole (see Mason 1999 for an examination of the post-war development of the latter).

3 See, for example, Murota 1985; Watanabe 1974; Ishi 1992; Yasuda 1992; Anesaki 1933 and Nakamura 1964.

4 Integral to this discussion is the definition of 'nature', a word which has many definitions, including 'all natural phenomena and plant and animal life, as distinct from humans and their creations' and 'a primitive state untouched by human or civilisation'. However, in the context of this discussion of nature conservation, the former is too wide a definition, as it encompasses gardens, parks and other environments which are entirely or largely human-made, as well as exotic species of flora and fauna which pose a potential threat to indigenous species and ecosystems. At the same time, the latter is too narrow – in fact, it is unlikely that any such natural environments exist anywhere on earth. Therefore for the purpose of this discussion, 'nature' and 'natural environments' will refer to environments such as wetlands, rivers or forests which support ecological systems of flora and fauna indigenous to Japan. Some areas may be partially or substantially modified (such as a river which has been straightened or modified with concrete embankments) but still support significant biological diversity.

See Knight 2004 for an in-depth discussion of the paradox apparent in the much-propounded Japanese veneration of nature versus the ongoing degradation of nature in Japan.

5 Pepper 1996, 184.

6 Library of Congress 2002.

7 This is not to say that there were not individuals in Japan's history who were keenly concerned about human impacts on the environment. For example, Tanaka Shōzo (1841–1913), often hailed as Japan's first conservationist, campaigned tirelessly until his death for a resolution to the pollution caused by the Ashio Copper Mine. However, it is not entirely accurate to describe him as a 'nature conservationist', as his primary concern was for the farmers and villages affected by the pollution, rather than the effect on the environment itself. In any case, he was a man of action rather than of the pen, so though a significant figure in Japanese social history (especially in terms of citizen protest) he did not leave a significant legacy in respect to literature on the subject.

Similarly, eighteenth century medical doctor and philosopher Andō Shōeki (1703–62), who is most widely known for his radical rejection of the feudal order, also wrote extensively about the human relationship with nature, especially of destructive human impacts on nature. However, his writings remained virtually unknown outside a small circle of contemporary followers until they were rediscovered at the turn of the twentieth century. Even then his works did not begin to be the object of widespread study until after World War Two, and it was more recently that his ecological ideas have received attention (Akiyama and Allen 1998, 282). Furthermore, as Morris-Suzuki notes, in Andō's writings 'nature' (*shizen* in Japanese) refers to 'far more than "the physical environment": Rather, it is the metaphysical concept implying the self-existent, the ground of all being' (Morris-Suzuki 1998, 40).

8 The objective of the original law relating to national parks in Japan, the National Parks Law (1931), was to 'preserve areas of outstanding beauty, while contributing towards the health, recreation and cultural education of Japanese citizens' (Article 1, National Parks Law). National parks were for the most part selected for their general appeal as places of scenic beauty and their potential to contribute to national prestige and tourism, as opposed to their ecological value. The two exceptions were the Akan and Daisetsuzan Parks of Hokkaidō, which were selected because they were places characterised by primeval nature worthy of preservation (Hatakeyama 2005, 205). After World War Two, a number of 'quasi-national parks' were established under the Natural Parks Law (1957), particularly near the main cities, mainly for recreation purposes (Sutherland & Britton 1980, 6; Hatakeyama 2005, 207–8). See Ishikawa (2001), Hatakeyama (2005) and Knight (2004) for a discussion of the function of national parks in Japan. This law was enacted against a background of government initiatives and policies to encourage the development of the tourism and leisure industry. Natural parks were seen as an important aid in the development of tourism, particularly during this post-war period when rebuilding the economy was a priority.

9 The lack of emphasis on nature conservation is also reflected in government literature on the environment. A survey of the State of the Environment White Papers published by the Environment Agency between the years 1977 to 2000, reveals little discussion of nature conservation issues. Where wildlife and wildlife habitats are discussed, it has predominantly been in terms of 'the sustainable management of resources'.

10 For example, in the 2000 International Social Survey Programme (ISSP) survey, 50 per cent of respondents had either a strong or moderate interest in environmental issues. A further 43.5 per cent said that they had some interest in environmental issues (Aramaki 2001, 57).

11 Environment Agency 1993, 101.

12 McGill 1992; Ohkura 2003; Fukatsu 1997; Domoto 1997.

13 While this might be said of many nature conservation campaigns internationally, it is an especially prominent feature of campaigns in Japan.

14 While it is difficult to objectively assess the success or otherwise of a nation's performance in respect to its nature conservation policies and initiatives, endangered species data acts as one indicator. For example, of the approximately 200 mammal species found in Japan, over a quarter are extinct, critically endangered, endangered or vulnerable. Of about 700 bird species, more than 100 are extinct, critically endangered, endangered or vulnerable. Of about 300 fresh or brackish water fish species, 79 are extinct, critically endangered, endangered or vulnerable (Ministry of the Environment 2006). Even when a species faces extinction, the official response in the past has been less than effective. For example, in the case of the Japanese crested ibis (*Nipponia nippon*), it was only in 1981, when the bird had dwindled to a few individuals, that any decisive efforts to conserve the species were made. However, while large sums of money were spent on a captive breeding programme on Sado Island, the programme failed, with all the ibises taken into captivity dying by 2003. Even had international best practice been followed (according to Brazil, the advice and assistance of specialists in successful breeding programmes elsewhere in the world was ignored) the ibises may have been too old, too few in number,

and too contaminated with pesticides to breed successfully by the time any decisive action was taken (Brazil 1992, 332–33).

15 Danaher 1996; McGill 1992; Aramaki 2001, 13.
16 Watts 2001; *The Japan Times* 25 April 2002.
17 Schreurs 1996. The survey I undertook was of a selection of White Papers published between 1977 to 2000.
18 Holliman 1990, 286–87; McCormack 1996, 80; Foljanty-Jost 2005, 112; Statistics Bureau of Japan 2003a.
19 Holliman 1990, 286; Schreurs 1996; Menju 2002; Ogura 2004, 24.
20 Hirao 2003; Aramaki 2001.
21 Menju 2002; Feldman 1993, cited in Ohkura 2003.
22 McCormack 1996; Fukatsu 1997; Mason 1999.
23 McCormack 1996, 33–34; Fukatsu 1997, 21.
24 Fukatsu 1997; Crowell and Murakami 2001.
25 In 1998, for example, over 45,000 hectares of farmland was abandoned or converted to another land-use, and this trend has continued at a similar, if slightly lower rate in subsequent years (Statistics Bureau of Japan 2003b).
26 The Ministry of Agriculture, Forestry and Fisheries (the ministry overseeing the project) subsequently claimed that the project was only supposed to provide 'partial' protection from flooding (Fukatsu 1997, 32).
27 Fukatsu 1997, 30–31; Stanley 2002.
28 Fukatsu 1997, 30. The sheer extent of this protest illustrates the fact that failure to protect important natural environments in Japan cannot be explained simply by a lack of concern for the environment. The protest was sustained, extensive – emanating from many sectors of society, not just environmental groups – and the arguments against the project were numerous, sound and persuasive. It illustrates the extent of the barrier represented by the current political system based on vested interests. The same pattern can be seen in the case of other development projects, such as the Nagara River dam project.
29 Oyadomari 1989, 29.
30 Mason 1999, 189; Schreurs 2002, 75; Oyadomari 1989, 29.
31 Schreurs 2002, 5.
32 OECD 2002, 58, 180, 280; Tanaka 2001; McGill 1992.
33 OECD 2002, 58; MOE n.d.
34 Yoshida Masahito 2004, pers. comm.; Tanaka 2001; OECD 2002: 40, 52, 180.
35 Schreurs 2002; OECD 2002, 145–46; Mason 1999; Schreurs 1996.
36 OECD 2002, 31, 174, 182; Brazil 1992.
37 Mason 1999; Schreurs 2002: 22–23.
38 Schreurs 1996; Craft 2000; *The Japan Times* 14 June 2001; Itoh and Shimada 2003; Japan NPO Center n.d.
39 Japan NPO Center n.d.; *The Japan Times* 14 June 2001; Itoh and Shimada 2003.
40 *The Japan Times* 14 June 2001; Schreurs 1996; Craft 2000.
41 OECD 2002, 179; Nakamura 2000, 45.
42 Schreurs 1996.
43 Schreurs 1996; Craft 2000; Brehm 2002; Menju 2002.
44 Though it is too early to tell what implications this will have for nature conservation policy in Japan, the early signals in terms of the new government's position on environmentally destructive construction projects have been positive. In September 2009, on its first day in office, the DPJ announced its decision to

halt the Yamba Dam, a highly controversial project that has been promoted by the LDP government since 1952.

References

Akiyama, Ken and Allen, Bruce 1998. 'Pre-modern Japanese nature writing: the example of Andō Shōeki'. In Patrick D. Murphy (ed.), *Literature of Nature: An International Sourcebook* (Chicago: Fitzroy Dearborn Publishers), 281–83.

Anesaki, Masaharu 1933. *Art, Life, and Nature in Japan*. Westport, Conn.: Greenwood Press.

Aramaki, Hisashi 2001. Yoronchōsa ripōto: Tsuyomaru kankyō haki e no kikikan. (Mounting concern for the environment: From the results of the ISSP's international comparative study: Japan). *Hōsō kenkyū to chōsa* (*The NHK Monthly Report on Broadcast Research*) 5: 56–69.

Brazil, Mark 1992. 'The wildlife of Japan: A 20th-century naturalist's view'. *Japan Quarterly,* July–September 1992.

Brehm, Vicky 2002. 'Development NGOs in Japan: Facing rapid change'. *Informed: NGO funding and policy bulletin* 6 (May), 12–14. Retrieved 14 April 2004 from http://www.intrac.org/Intrac/docs/6Informed.pdf.

Craft, Lucille 2000. 'Japan's nonprofits carve out a space of their own'. *The Japan Times,* 28 September. Retrieved 26 April 2004 from http://www.japantimes.co.jp/cgi-bin/getarticle.pl5?eo20000928a2.htm.

Crowell, Todd and Murakami Mutsuko 2001. 'Public works time bombs'. *AsiaWeek. com* 27(6). Retrieved 1 August 2003 from http://www.asiaweek.com/asiaweek/magazine/nations/0,8782,98449,00.html.

Danaher, Michael 1996. 'What price the environment? An analysis of Japanese public awareness of environmental issues'. Paper presented at the 1996 Asian Studies on the Pacific Coast (ASPAC) Conference, University of Alberta, Edmonton, Canada, 21–23 June 1996.

Domoto, Akiko 1997. *Report on biodiversity submitted to Rio+5 Summit*. Retrieved 18 March 2004 from http://www.globeinternational.org/archives/earthsummit/earth5rio-biodiversity.html.

Environment Agency (Japan) 1977. *The State of the Environment in Japan 1977*. Tokyo: Environment Agency.

—— 1984. *Kankyō hakushō 1984 (Environmental White Paper 1984)*. Tokyo: Environment Agency.

—— 1988. *Kankyō hakushō 1988 (Environmental White Paper 1998)*. Tokyo: Environment Agency.

—— 1993. *The State of the Environment in Japan 1992*. Tokyo: Environment Agency.

—— 2000. *Kankyō hakushō 1999 (Environmental White Paper 1999)* (vols 1–2). Tokyo: Environment Agency.

Foljanty-Jost, Cesine 2005. 'NGOs in environmental networks in Germany and Japan: the question of power and influence'. *Social Science Japan Journal,* **8**(1): 103–17.

Fukatsu, Hiroshi 1997. 'Tideland project brings waves of controversy'. *Japan Quarterly,* October–December.

Hatakeyama, Takemichi 2005. *Shizen hogohō kōgi (Nature Conservation Law)* (2nd edn). Sapporo: Hokkaidō University Books Publication Society.

Hirao, Sachiko 2003. 'Alternative career rewarding but low-paid: Fledgling social-service NPOs gain foothold'. *The Japan Times.* Retrieved 23 April 2004 from http://www.japantimes.co.jp/cgi-bin/getarticle.pl5?nn20030503b4.htm.

Holliman, Jonathan 1990. 'Environmentalism with a global scope'. *Japan Quarterly,* July–September.

Ishi, Hiroyuki 1992. 'Attitudes toward the natural world and the whaling issue'. *Japan Foundation Newsletter,* **XIX**(4): 1–11.

Ishikawa, Tetsuya 2001. *Nihon no shizen-hogo (Nature Conservation in Japan).* Tokyo: Heibonsha.

Itoh, Satoko and Shimada, Ema, eds. 2003. 'New legal reform efforts receive mixed welcome'. *Civil Society Monitor,* **8**: 1–4. Retrieved 30 April 2004 from http://www.jcie.or.jp/civilnet/monitor/8.html.

Japan NPO Center n.d. *The law to promote specified non-profit activities* (*NPO law*). Retrieved 30 April 2003 from http://www.jnpoc.ne.jp/English/answers/answers.html.

Japan Times, The 14 June 2001. *NPOs rising but still short on cash: Expert.* Retrieved 16 June 2003 from http://www.japantimes.co.jp/cgi-bin/getarticle.pl5?nn20010614b1.htm.

Japan Times, The 25 April 2002. *Isahaya gates open for seaweed probe.* Retrieved 23 January 2004 from http://www.japantimes.co.jp/cgi-bin/getarticle.pl5?nn20020425a2.htm.

Kellert, Stephen. 1991. 'Japanese perceptions of wildlife'. *Conservation Biology,* **5**(3): 297–308.

Knight, John 1997. 'A tale of two forests: reforestation discourse in Japan and beyond'. *The Journal of the Royal Anthropological Institute,* **3**(4): 711–30.

Knight, Cath 2004. *Veneration or destruction? Japanese ambivalence to nature, with special reference to nature conservation.* Unpublished Masters Thesis, University of Canterbury.

Library of Congress, The 2002. *The Evolution of the Conservation Movement.* Retrieved 15 June 2004 from http://memory.loc.gov/ammem/amrvhtml/.

Linden, Eugene 1989. 'Putting the heat on Japan – Accused of ravaging the world's forests and seas, Tokyo starts to clean up its act'. *Time,* 19 July.

Mason, Robert 1999. 'Whither Japan's environmental movement? An assessment of problems and prospects at the national level'. *Pacific Affairs,* **72**(2): 187–207.

McCormack, Gavan 1996. *The Emptiness of Japanese Affluence.* St Leonards, N. S. W.: Allen & Unwin.

McGill, Douglas 1992. 'Nature in the mind of Japan'. *The Sunday New York Times Magazine,* 4 October.

McKean, Margaret 1981. *Environmental Protest and Citizen Politics in Japan.* Berkeley: University of California Press.

Menju, Toshihiro 2002. *Historical background and current issues for NGOs in Japan.* Paper presented at UK-Japan NGO dialogue conference. 26–28 November 2002. Retrieved 29 April from http://www.japan-uk-ngolink.org/PDFs/conference/NGO_conferenceDay1_pm.pdf.

Ministry of the Environment (Japan) n.d. *Encouraging Independent Environmental Conservation Activities by a Variety of Organizations.* Retrieved 24 March 2004 from http://www.env.go.jp/en/org/pamph/07.pdf.

Ministry of the Environment (Japan) 2006. *Annual Report on the Environment in Japan*. Retrieved 20 June 2008 from http://www.env.go.jp/en/wpaper/2006/index. html.

Morioka, Takashi 1997. 'Japan Driftnet Fishing'. *TED Case Studies*, **4**(1). Retrieved 12 March 2004 from http://www.american.edu/projects/mandala/TED/driftjap.htm.

Morris-Suzuki, Tessa 1998. *Re-Inventing Japan: Time, Space, Nation*. Armonk, N.Y.: M.E. Sharp.

Murota, Yasuhiro 1985. 'Culture and the environment in Japan'. *Environmental Management*, **9**(2): 105–12.

Nakamura, Hajime 1964. *Ways of Thinking of Eastern Peoples: India, China, Tibet, Japan*. Honolulu: East-West Centre Press.

Nakamura, Madoka 2000. 'Toward the public interest? Transformation of the policy community in Japan'. *NIRA (National Institute for Research Advancement) Review*, **7**(4). Retrieved 30 April 2004 from http://www.nira.go.jp/publ/review/ 2000autumn/nakamura.pdf.

Nature Conservation Society of Japan (Nihon Shizen Hogo Kyōkai) 2006. *NACS-J no tokuchō* (The characteristics of NACS-J). Retrieved 1 April 2007 from http:// www.nacsj.or.jp/nacsj/index.html.

Ogura, Yuka 2004. "Volunteer Work'. *Asia Pacific Perspectives*, **2**(2): 24.

Ohkura, Yoshiko 2003. 'The roles and limitations of newspapers in environmental reporting. Case study: Isahaya Bay land reclamation project issue'. *Marine Pollution Bulletin*, **47**: 237–45.

Organisation for Economic Co-operation and Development (OECD), ed. 2002. *Environmental Performance Reviews: Japan*. Paris: OECD

Oyadomari, Motoko 1989. 'The rise and fall of the nature conservation movement in Japan in relation to some cultural values'. *Environmental Management*, **13**(1): 23–33.

Pepper, David 1996. *Modern Environmentalism: An Introduction*. Routledge: London.

Schreurs, Miranda 1996. *International environmental negotiations, the state, and environmental NGOs in Japan*. Paper for Harrison Program on the Future Global Agenda, August 1996. Retrieved 16 May 2003 from http://www.gdrc.org/ngo/jp-envi-ngo.html.

Schreurs, Miranda 2002. *Environmental Politics in Japan, Germany, and the United States*. Cambridge: Cambridge University Press.

Stanley, Michael 2002. 'The death of wetland'. *Japan Inc*, November. Retrieved 1 August 2003 from http://www.japaninc.net/article.php?articleID=933.

Statistics Bureau of Japan 2003a. Chapter 12: Labour. *Statistical Handbook of Japan*. Retrieved 12 August 2004 from http://www.stat.go.jp/english/data/ handbook/c12cont.htm#chal2_4.

Statistics Bureau of Japan 2003b. *Statistical Handbook of Japan*. Retrieved 19 May 2004 from http://www.stat.go.jp/data/kokusei/2000/kihonl/00/zuhyou/a001.xls.

Strong, Kenneth 1977. *Ox Against the Storm: A Biography of Tanaka Shozo, Japan's Conservationist Pioneer*. Vancouver: University of British Columbia Press.

Sutherland, Mary and Britton, D. Guyver 1980. *National Parks of Japan*. Tokyo: Kodansha International.

Tanaka, Akira 2001. 'Changing ecological assessment and mitigation in Japan'. *Built Environment*, **27**(1): 35–41.

Watanabe, Masao 1974. 'The conception of nature in Japanese culture'. *Science,* **183**: 279–82.

Watts, Jonathan 2001. 'Seaweed dries up in Japan'. *Guardian Unlimited,* 8 February. Retrieved 12 December 2001 from http://www.guardian.co.uk/elsewhere/journalist/story/0,7792,435489,00.html.

Yasuda, Yoshinori 1992. *Nihon bunka no fūdo (The climate and geography of Japanese culture).* Tokyo: Asakura Shoten.

18

THE AUTHORITARIAN BIOLOGIST AND THE ARROGANCE OF ANTI-HUMANISM

Wildlife conservation in the third world

Ramachandra Guha

Where will be taxonomists and evolutionists when cows and corns dominate the earth?

—Hugh Iltis, writing in 1967

If biologists want a tropics in which to biologize, they are going to have to buy it with care, energy, effort, strategy, tactics, time and cash.

—Daniel Janzen, writing in 1986

Conservation and biology are interdependent and inseparable because biology is at the heart of all phases of conservation and is the ultimate arbiter of its success and failure.

—David Ehrenfelds, in his editorial in *Conservation Biology*, 1987

Any grandiose plan for the conservation of wildlife without adequate provision for human interests is doomed to fail. Conservation in developing countries often has to be a compromise between scientific idealism and practical reality.

—Raman Sukumar, in his doctoral dissertation of 1985

I

When India became independent, in 1947, it had less than half-a-dozen wildlife reserves; it now has in excess of four hundred parks and sanctuaries, covering over 4 per cent of the country and there are proposals to double this area. Wildlife conservation controls big territory and is now big business too. Nor is this country exceptional in this regard. In response to a growing global market for nature tourism, and egged on by strong domestic pressures, other Asian and African nations have undertaken ambitious programmes to conserve and demarcate habitat and species that need to be 'protected for posterity'.

One might, at a pinch, identify five major groups that together fuel the movement for wildlife conservation in the Third World. The first are the city-dwellers and foreign tourists who merely season their lives, a week at a time, with the wild. Their motive is straightforward: pleasure and fun. The second group consists of ruling elites who view the protection of particular species (e.g. the tiger in India) as central to the retention or enhancement of national prestige. Willing on this process are international conservation organisations, such as the IUCN and the WWF, which work with a sense of mission at 'educating' people and politicians to the virtues of biological conservation.

A fourth group consists of functionaries of the state forest or wildlife service mandated by law to be in physical control of the parks. While some officials are genuinely inspired by a love of nature, the majority—at least in India—are motivated merely by the power and spin-off benefits (overseas trips, for example) that come with the job. The final group are biologists, who believe in wilderness and species preservation for the sake of 'science'.

These five groups are united in their hostility to the farmers, herders, swiddeners and hunters who have lived in the 'wild' well before it became a 'park' or 'sanctuary'. They see these human communities as having a destructive effect on the environment, their forms of livelihood aiding the disappearance of species and contributing to soil erosion, habitat simplification, and worse. Their feelings are often expressed in strongly pejorative language.

Touring Africa in 1957, one prominent member of the Sierra Club sharply attacked the Maasai for grazing cattle in African sanctuaries. He held the Maasai to be illustrative of a larger trend, wherein 'increasing population and increasing land use,' rather than industrial exploitation, constituted the main threat to the world's wilderness areas. The Maasai and 'their herds of economically worthless cattle,' he said, 'have already overgrazed and laid waste too much of the 23,000 square miles of Tanganyika they control, and as they move into the Serengeti, they bring the desert with them, and the wilderness and wildlife must bow before their herds.'[1]

Thirty years later, the WWF initiated a campaign to save the Madagascar rainforest, the home of the Ring Tailed Lemur, the Madagascar Serpent Eagle, and other endangered species. Their fund-raising posters had spectacular sketches of the lemur, and the eagle, and of the half-ton Elephant Bird which once lived on the island but is now extinct. Man 'is a relative newcomer to Madasgascar,' noted the accompanying text, 'but even with the most basic of tools—axes and fire—he has brought devastation to the habitats and resources he depends on.' The posters also had a picture of a muddy river with the caption: 'Slash-and-burn agriculture has brought devastation to the forest, and in its wake, erosion of the topsoil.'[2]

The poster succinctly summed up the conservationist position with regard to the tropical rainforest. According to this position, the enemy of the environment is the hunter and farmer living in the forest, who is too short-sighted for his, and our, good. This belief (or prejudice) has informed the numerous projects, spread across the globe, to constitute nature parks by throwing out the original *human* inhabitants of these areas, with scant regard for their past or future. All this is done in the name of the global heritage of biological diversity. Cynics might conclude, however, that tribals in the Madagascar or Amazon forest are expected to move out only so that men in London or New York can have the comfort of knowing that the lemur or toucan has been saved for posterity—evidence of which is then provided for them by way of the wildlife documentary they can watch on their television screen.

II

Let me now focus on the motives and motivations of one of the aforementioned groups: the conservation biologists. Biologists have, of course, been in the vanguard of the environmental movement in our time. The author of the work that by common consent sparked modern environmentalism was Rachel Carson, a biologist. So were numerous other scholars and writers who contributed to shaping the environmental debate of the sixties and seventies. I have in mind, for example, Garrett Hardin, Paul Ehrlich and Ray Dasmann in the United States; C.J. Brejér in the Netherlands; F. Fraser Darling and Julian Huxley in the United Kingdom; and Bjorn Gillberg and Hans Palmstierma in Sweden (these examples could be multiplied).

Biology is a science that in three major respects differs from the disciplines of physics and chemistry. First, biologists are taught to look for interdependence in nature, viewing individual life forms not in isolation, but in relation to one another. Ever since Darwin, biologists have also been oriented towards a longer time frame, thinking in aeons and generations rather than months and years. Finally, biologists have a direct professional interest in species other than humans; as ornithologists, botanists and zoologists, they are, willy-nilly, more alert to the interests of bird, plant or animal life. It must be said at once that this interest in other species sometimes blinds them to the legitimate interests of the less fortunate members of their own.

The impatience with other humans is especially marked among conservation biologists, for whom farmers and forest-dwellers have come to represent a messy obstacle to the unimpeded progress of scientific research. A 'seeming goal of humanity,' writes Daniel Janzen in the *Annual Review of*

Ecology and Systematics, 'is to convert the world to a pasture designed to produce and sustain humans as draught animals. The challenge, in which the tropical ecologist is a general, knight, foot soldier, and technical specialist, is to prevent humanity from reaching this goal. *The true battle, is, however, to re-programme humanity to a different goal.* The battle is being fought by many more kinds of professionals than just ecologists; however, it is a battle over the control of interactions, and by definition, the person competent at recognising, understanding, and manipulating interactions is an ecologist.'[3]

While the article's military metaphors and its appearance in a prestigious scientific journal are noteworthy, Janzen was only reiterating a well-worn theme. Over twenty years ago, a similar claim had been made by a botanist from the University of Wisconsin:

> If there is anybody who should provide leadership in the preservation movement it is the systematic or environmental biologist. ... We are not only citizens and humans, each with individual desires. We are not only trained taxonomists and ecologists, each perhaps wishing to preserve the particular organisms with which we work. But we, the taxonomists and ecologists, are the *only ones in any position to know* the kinds, the abundance and the geography of life. This is a knowledge with vast implications for mankind, and therefore vast responsibilities. When nobody else knows, we do know where the wild and significant areas are, we know what needs to be saved and why, and only we know what is threatened with extinction.[4]

Consider, finally, a recent assessment of global conservation by Michael Soulé, which complains that the language of policy documents has 'become more humanistic in values and more economic in substance, and correspondingly less naturalistic and ecocentric.' Soulé seems worried that in theory (though certainly not in practice!) some national governments and international conservation organisations (or ICOs) now pay more attention to the rights of human communities. Proof of this shift is the fact that 'the top and middle management of most ICOs are economists, lawyers, and development specialists, not biologists.' We have here a sectarian plaint, a trade union approach to the problem spurred by an alleged 'takeover of the international conservation movement by social scientists, particularly economists.'[5]

Soulé's essay, with its talk of conspiracies and takeover bids, manifests the paranoia of a community of scientists which has a *huge* influence on conservation policy but wants more: it wants no less than to be the sole dictator. A scholar acclaimed by his peers as the 'dean of tropical ecologists' has expressed this ambition more nakedly than most. I have already quoted from a paper published by Daniel Janzen in the *Annual Review of Ecology and Systematics*; let me now quote from a report he wrote on a new National Park in Costa Rica, whose tone and thrust perfectly complements the other, ostensibly 'scientific' essay. 'We have the seed and the biological expertise: we lack control of the terrain,' wrote Janzen in 1986. He was able to remedy this situation for himself by raising enough money to purchase the forest area needed to create the Guanacaste National Park.

One can only marvel at Janzen's conviction that he and his fellow biologists know all, and that the inhabitants of the forest know nothing. He justifies the taking over of the forest and the dispossession of the forest farmer by claiming that: 'Today virtually all of the present-day occupants of the western Mesoamerican pastures, fields and degraded forests are deaf, blind and mute to the fragments of the rich biological and cultural heritage that still occupies the shelves of the unused and unappreciated library in which they reside.'[6]

This is an ecologically updated version of the White Man's Burden, where the biologist (rather than the civil servant or military official) knows that it is in the native's true interest to abandon his home and hearth and leave the field and forest clear for the new rulers of his domain—not the animals he once co-existed with, but the biologists, park managers and wildlifers who shall now collectively determine how the territory is to be managed. In Costa Rica we only have Janzen's word for it, but elsewhere we are better placed to challenge the conservationist's point of view. A remarkable recent book on African conservation by Raymond Bonner, *At the Hand of Man*, has laid bare the imperialism, unconscious and explicit, of western wilderness lovers and biologists working on that luckless continent. Some of his conclusions are:

> Above all, Africans [have been] ignored, overwhelmed, manipulated and outmanoeuvred—by a conservation crusade led, orchestrated and dominated by white Westerners.

Livingstone, Stanley and other explorers and missionaries had come to Africa in the nineteenth century to promote the three C's—Christianity, commerce and civilisation. Now a fourth was added: conservation. These modern secular missionaries were convinced that without the white man's guidance, the Africans would go astray.

> [The criticisms] of egocentricity and neo-colonialism ... could be leveled fairly at most conservation organisations working in the Third World.
>
> As many Africans see it, white people are making rules to protect animals that white people want to see in parks that white people visit. Why should Africans support these programs? ... The World

Wildlife Fund professed to care about what the Africans wanted, but then tried to manipulate them into doing what the Westerners wanted: and those Africans who couldn't be brought into line were ignored.

Africans do not use the parks and they do not receive any significant benefits from them. Yet they are paying the costs. There are indirect economic costs—government revenues that go to parks instead of schools. And there are direct personal costs [i.e., of the ban on hunting and fuel-collecting, or of displacement].[7]

The remarks of a Zambian biologist, E.N. Chidumayo, reinforce Bonner's conclusions:

Many conservation policies in Africa tended to serve foreign interests, such as tourism and safari hunting, and largely ignored African environmental values and cultures. In fact, the only thing that is African about most conventional conservation policies is that they are practiced on African land.[8]

Bonner's book focuses on the elephant, one of the half-a-dozen or so animals that have come to acquire 'totemic' status among western wilderness lovers. Animal totems existed in most pre-modern societies, but as the Norwegian scholar Arne Kalland points out, in the past the injunction not to kill the totemic species applied only to members of the group that worshipped it. Hindus do not ask others to worship the cow, but those who love and cherish the elephant, seal, whale or tiger try and impose a world-wide prohibition on its killing. No one, they say, anywhere, anytime, shall be allowed to touch the animal they hold sacred even if (as with the elephant and several species of whale) scientific evidence has established that small-scale hunting will not endanger its viable populations and will, in fact, save human lives put at risk by the expansion, after total protection, of the *lebensraum* of the totemic animal. The new totemists also insist that their species is the 'true, rightful inhabitant' of the ocean or forest, and ask that human beings who have lived in the same terrain (and with the animals) for millennia be taken out and sent elsewhere.[9]

III

To turn now to an ongoing controversy in my own bailiwick. The Nagara-hole National Park in southern Karnataka has an estimated 40 tigers, towards the protection of which species has been directed enormous amounts of Indian and foreign money and attention.

Nagarahole is also home to about 6,000 tribal people, who have been in the area longer than anyone can remember, perhaps as long as the tigers themselves. The Karnataka state Forest Department wants the tribals out, claiming they destroy the forest and kill wild game. In response, the tribals answer that their demands are modest, consisting in the main of fuelwood, fruit, honey and the odd quail or partridge. They do not own guns, although coffee planters living on the edge of the forest do. Maybe it is the planters who poach the big game, they ask. In any case, if the forest is for tigers only, they query, why have forest officials invited India's biggest hotel chain, the Taj, to build a resort inside the park?

Into this controversy jumped a green missionary passing through Karnataka. John G. Robinson works for the Wildlife Conservation Society in New York, for whom he oversees 160 projects in 44 countries. He conducted a whistle-stop tour of Nagarahole and called a press conference in the state capital, Bangalore. Throwing the tribals out of the park, he said, was the only means to saving the wilderness. In Robinson's opinion, 'Relocating tribal or traditional people who live in these protected areas is the single most important step towards conservation.' Tribals, he explained, 'compulsively hunt for food,' and compete with tigers for prey. Deprived of food, tigers cannot survive, and 'their extinction means that the balance of the ecosystem is upset and this has a snowballing effect.'[10]

All over India, the management of parks has sharply posited the interests of poor tribals who have traditionally lived in them, against those of wilderness lovers and urban pleasure seekers who wish to keep parks 'free of human interference'—that is, free of other humans. These conflicts are being played out in the Rajaji sanctuary in Uttar Pradesh, Simlipal in Orissa, Karma in Madhya Pradesh, Melghat in Maharashtra and in numerous other locations.[11] In all these instances, Indian wildlifers have ganged up with the Forest Department to evict the tribals and rehabilitate them far outside the forests. In this endeavour they have drawn sustenance from western biologists and conservation organisations, who have thrown the prestige of science and the power of the dollar behind the crusade.

A partisan of the tribal might answer Robinson and his ilk in various ways. He might note that tribals and tigers have co-existed for centuries; it is the demands of cities and factories that have of late put unbearable pressures on the forest, with species after species being put on the endangered list. Tribals are being made the scapegoats, while the real agents of forest destruction—poachers, planters, politicians, profiteers—escape notice. As Robinson flies off to the next project on his list of 160, he might reflect on his own high-intensity lifestyle, which doubtless puts a greater stress on the world's resources than dozens, perhaps hundreds of forest tribals.

The tribal partisan might further point out that even as plans are afoot to evict the tribals from Nagarahole, the Taj group is being welcomed in to build its hotel. Meanwhile, the Forest Department has applied for American money to build seven patrol stations and a network of roads connecting them. This, it is claimed, is necessary for greater vigilance against poachers;

what it will in fact do is open out the forest still further to outside penetration. Our tribal partisan might argue, finally, that a policy which treats forest dwellers as enemies rather than partners can only be counter-productive. What this policy will encourage, in time, is poachers and smugglers of ivory and sandalwood who can count on tribal acquiescence in the battle against the common enemy, the Forest Department.[12]

All this has been more eloquently stated by the anthropologist Verrier Elwin. In 1963, having made his home among the tribals and forests of India for some thirty years, Elwin wrote deploring the 'constant propaganda that the tribal people are destroying the forest.' He asked pointedly how the tribals:

> could destroy the forest. They owned no trucks; they hardly had even a bullock-cart; the utmost that they could carry away was some wood to keep them warm in the winter months, to reconstruct or repair their huts and carry on their little cottage industries.

Who then was (and is) the real culprit? Elwin tells us of the 'feeling amongst the tribals that all the arguments in favour of preservation of forests are intended to refuse them their [rights]. They argue that when it is a question of industry, township, development work or projects of rehabilitation, all these plausible arguments are forgotten and vast tracts are placed at the disposal of outsiders who mercilessly destroy the forest wealth with or without necessity.'[13]

IV

The main difference between Verrier Elwin's time and ours is the growing influence of wildlife fanatics. In the past, the tribal was expected to give way to the juggernaut of Development, so that his forest abode could be claimed by iron mines, steel plants, and large dams. That gospel has now been given an added spin by the gospel of Total Conservation, in which the interest of the tiger is always elevated above the interest of the tribal.

That Elwin reversed this order of priority is not unrelated to the fact that his discipline of social anthropology tends to place the concerns of humans, especially vulnerable humans, above all else (and all others). But these conflicts must not be reduced to a matter of which discipline privileges which species. More sociologically sensitive biologists, for instance, have warned of the dangers of neglecting, in programmes of wilderness and wildlife conservation, the rightful concerns of the communities that live in and around protected areas.

Let me quote from three such scientists, writing in 1949, 1977 and 1994 respectively. First, a statement from the botanist M.S. Randhawa, notable for its alertness to farmers' interests and also for its then conventional categorisation of 'useful' and 'harmful' species:

With the liquidation of the feudal order ... the problem of wildlife preservation has acquired a new significance. Whatever may be the faults of princes and rajahs, it must be said to their credit that they preserved the wild animals and forests of their states rather well. With the growing demands of cultivators who want to save their crops from harmful animals, there is need of clear formulation of policy. There is immediate need of initial survey of all proposed National Parks areas. While there is necessity of maintenance of good vegetational balance and preservation of rich flora and fauna in the National Park areas, the general wildlife policy must be such as will not prejudice the use of developed agricultural land. The interests of the cultivator and the lover of nature must be harmonised.

The apprehensions of farmers that the National Parks and Nature Reserves will develop into uncontrolled sanctuaries where pests and weeds will be allowed to flourish, and which will spread into surrounding agricultural lands must be allayed. The biologist must give lists of harmful and useful birds and animals. While the friends of the cultivator should be encouraged in the National Parks, the enemies must be exterminated. The biologist should also give a finding whether campaigns should be started for the destruction of wild boars, porcupines, monkeys, bats and parrots who cause enormous damage to crops and gardens. Before any such campaigns are started, it should be ascertained whether wholesale destruction of certain birds or animals may not have harmful repercussions, on account of the upsetting of [the] balance of power between various organisms.[14]

The great ornithologist, Salim Ali, came straight to the point, without any recourse to a dubious division between good and bad species:

No conservation laws or measures can succeed fully unless they have the backing of informed public opinion, which in our case means the usually illiterate village cultivator. In other words, unless we can make the villager understand, and convince him of the logic in expecting him to preserve the tiger or leopard that has deprived him of maybe his sole wordly possession—the cow, which moreover provided the meagre sustenance for himself and his family— how can we induct his willing cooperation? Similarly, how can we expect him to see any sense in being asked not to destroy the deer or pig that have ravaged the crops which he has toiled for months to raise, and on which all his hopes are banked? Admittedly this is going to be a very difficult task, but I believe it is not impossible if we could but find the right approach. We have never really tried enough. Devising a realistic strategy is now a challenge to all conservationists.[15]

Finally, some remarks of the ecologist Raman Sukumar, whose work on the Indian elephant has highlighted the conflicts—as manifest in incidents of man-slaughter and the destruction of crops—between large animals protected in parks and farmers who live on the periphery:

> It is both unrealistic and unjust to expect only a certain section of society, the marginal farmers and tribals, to bear the entire cost of depredatory animals. We have to work towards ameliorating the impact of wildlife on people if conservation of wildlife and their habitats is to gain acceptance among such people who interact with these in their daily lives. ... Today the local people see sanctuaries or national parks as simply the pleasure resorts of the affluent. There is urgent need to reorient management of our wildlife reserves so as to pass on economic benefits to local communities. ... If an adequate proportion of the income derived from tourism is retained by the local economy there would be increased motivation for people to value wildlife and their habitats. ... It is time we take bold new approaches towards reconciling economic development with conservation.

With regard to the elephant–human conflict in southern India, Sukumar has been more than forthcoming with 'bold new approaches'. He urges proper and just compensation for the loss of life (which varies, depending on the province, from a niggardly Rs 2000 to Rs 15,000) and for damage to crops. He also thinks that in some cases, trenches and electric fences might dissuade elephants and other large mammals from trespassing into habitations and fields. Most radically, he states that 'wildlife populations that come into severe conflict with human interests may have to be directly managed to keep their levels below tolerable limits.'

He goes on to explain what the euphemism 'directly managed' actually means:

> It is clear that the adult male elephants are inherently more predisposed to raiding crops as a consequence of social organisation. The removal of an adult male elephant from the population would have a far greater effect in reducing crop-damage (by a factor of 20 in economic terms) and saving human lives than the removal of an elephant from a family herd. Our understanding of demographic processes in such polygynous species also show that the loss of a certain proportion of males is not likely to affect the intrinsic rate of growth of the population. The removal of females from

the population would certainly reduce its growth rate. Hence, the selective culling of male elephants identified as inveterate crop raiders or rogues would be the best form of population management.[16]

These recommendations are the outcome of years of careful and patient scientific work, yet they have been unable to find acceptance. For Salim Ali's hopes notwithstanding, most conservationists remain uninterested in working towards a 'realistic' strategy. Forest Departments will not pay proper compensation, claiming that it would open the floodgates to all kinds of rustics with all manner of forged claims. Other biologists, and wildlife lovers in general, will not countenance any talk of 'culling', on moral grounds—all life is sacred—or on instrumental ones: which species will we have to manage next?[17]

Meanwhile, the tension around national parks continues. Angered by conservationists, public and private, villagers in Karnataka have aided the notorious sandalwood and elephant smuggler Veerappan, who at least takes better care of their stomachs than the state. So elephants raid crops and take the occasional life, while Veerappan cheerfully eludes the thousands of security personnel who have tried to catch or kill him for a decade.

Conflicts such as these have led the more thoughtful Indian biologists to reject the notion that species and habitat protection can succeed only through the punitive guns-and-guards approach favoured by a majority of wildlife conservationists, both Indian and foreign. Some ecologists, like Raman Sukumar, have sought to resolve conflicts between large mammals and humans; others, like Madhav Gadgil, have tried to move biodiversity conservation away from a privileging of large mammals towards a more inclusive and decentralised approach that would also honour and revive traditional systems of nature conservation such as sacred groves. Sociologists with rich field experience, such as Ashish Kothari, have pleaded for a more democratic system of park management in which the voices of local communities would ring out loud and clear.

These conservationists by no means wish to see a world completely dominated by cows, corn and those who raise them. They have time for the tiger and the rainforest, and also want to protect those islands of nature not yet fully conquered by humans. Their plea, however, is to recognise wilderness protection as a distinctively North Atlantic brand of environmentalism, whose export and expansion must be done with caution, care, and above all, with humility. In the poor and heavily populated countries of the South, protected areas cannot be managed with guns and guards but must, instead, take full cognisance of the rights of the people who have lived in (and oftentimes cared for) the forest long before it became a national park or a World Heritage Site.[18] As Raman Sukumar might put it, we need to save agriculture from elephants as much as protect elephants from men.

In addition, the present philosophy and practice of conservation is flawed in a scientific as much as a social sense.[19] National park management in much of the Third World is heavily imprinted by the American experience. In particular, it takes over two axioms of wilderness thinking: the monumentalist belief that wilderness has to be 'big, continuous wilderness' and the claim that *all* human intervention is bad for the retention of diversity. These axioms have led to the constitution of huge sanctuaries, each covering thousands of square miles, and a total ban on human ingress into the 'core' areas of national parks. At the same time, little or no thought has been given to the conservation of diversity outside these strictly protected areas.

These axioms of 'giganticism' and 'hands off nature', though sometimes cloaked in the jargon of science, are simply prejudices. When it is realised that the preservation of *plant* diversity is possibly more important than the preservation of large mammals, a decentralised network with many small parks will begin to make far greater sense. The network of sacred groves in India traditionally fulfilled some of these functions. Yet modern wilderness lovers are in general averse to reviving that system: apart from rationalist objections, they are in principle opposed to local control, preferring instead centralised land management. The belief in a total ban on human intervention is equally misguided. Studies show that the highest levels of biological diversity are often found in areas with some (though not excessive) intervention. In opening up new niches to be occupied by insects, plants and birds, partially disturbed ecosystems can have a greater diversity than untouched areas.

The dogma of total protection can have tragic consequences. In 1982, scientists forbade villagers from exercising traditional grazing rights in the Keoladeo National Park in Bharatpur—when villagers protested, police opened fire, killing several of them. When the ban was enforced in following years, the population of key bird species (e.g. waterfowl and the Siberian crane) actually declined. Grazing, by keeping down the tall grass, had helped these species forage for insects. Grazing was thus beneficial to the park, but the pill was too bitter to swallow and even in subsequent years scientists have refused to lift the ban.[20]

V

The present essay is a companion piece to a polemic I published some years ago in the US journal *Environmental Ethics*. In that essay, I was scathing about 'deep ecology', an ideology then hegemonic among American environmentalists. I argued that deep ecology's master distinction, anthropocentric/biocentric, was of little use in understanding the dynamics of environmental degradation in the real world. I had also shown that deep ecology's claims to be a philosophy of universal significance were spurious, made possible only by twisting the thought of non-western thinkers (Lao Tsu and Gandhi, for example) completely out of context. I had suggested, finally, that the noble, apparently disinterested, motives of deep ecologists fuelled a territorial ambition—the physical control of wilderness in parts of the world other than their own—which led inevitably to the displacement and harsh treatment of the human communities who dwelt in these forests.[21]

Surprisingly, the article evoked a variety of responses, both for and against it. The veteran Vermont radical, Murray Bookchin, who was engaged in a polemic with American deep ecologists, offered a short (three-line) letter of congratulation. A longer (30 page) response came from the Norwegian philosopher Arne Naess, the originator of the term 'deep ecology'. Naess felt bound to assume responsibility for the ideas I had challenged, even though I had distinguished between his emphases (more sympathetic to the poor) and those of his American interpreters and followers. Other correspondents, less known but no less engaged, wrote in to praise and to condemn.[22] Over the years, the essay has appeared in some half-a-dozen anthologies, as a voice of the 'Third World', the token and disloyal opposition to the reigning orthodoxies of environmental ethics.

In the North American context mine was a rare dissenting voice, yet the arguments of my 1989 essay made perfect sense to many of my Indian colleagues—indeed, it could not have been written in the absence of conversations over the years with scientists such as Sukumar and Gadgil. Perhaps it attracted attention because it constituted one of the first attacks on a form of 'trans-nationalism' generally considered benign. After all, we are not talking here of the Marines, with their awesome firepower, or even of the World Bank, with its power of wealth and its ability to manipulate the governments of developing countries. These are men (and more rarely, women) who come preaching the equality of all species, who worship all that is good and beautiful in nature. What could be wrong with them?

Seven years later, I see no reason to revise my characterisation of deep ecology as 'conservation imperialism'. The specious nonsense about equal rights of all species cannot hide the plain fact that green missionaries are possibly more dangerous, and certainly more hypocritical, than their economic or religious counterparts. The globalising advertiser and banker works for a world in which everyone, including himself, regardless of class or colour, is in an economic sense an American—driving a car, drinking Pepsi, owning a fridge and a washing machine. The missionary, himself having discovered Christ, wants all pagans to share in the discovery. The conservationist wants to 'protect the tiger (or whale) for posterity, yet expects *other* people to make the sacrifice.

Moreover, the processes unleashed by green imperialism are well nigh irreversible. For the consumer titillated into eating Kentucky Fried Chicken can always say, 'once is enough'. The Hindu converted into Baptism can decide later on to revert to his original faith. But the tribal people, thrown out of their homes by the propaganda of the conservationist, are condemned to the life of an ecological refugee, which for many forest people is a fate next only to death. For the Chenchu hunter-gatherers who have been 'asked' to make way for a tiger reserve in the Indian state of Andhra Pradesh, the problem is that 'they have to pay for the protection of tigers while no one pays for the conservation of their communities.' As one Chenchu told a visitor from the state capital, 'If you love tigers so much, why don't you shift all of them to Hyderabad and declare that city a tiger reserve?'[23]

Notes and references

1 Lee Merriam Talbot, 'Wilderness Overseas', *Sierra Club Bulletin,* vol. 42, no. 6, 1957.

2 These quotes are from a WWF poster on display at the School of Forestry and Environmental Studies, Yale University in the summer of 1989.

3 Daniel H. Janzen, 'The Future of Tropical Ecology', *Annual Review of Ecology and Systematics,* vol. 17, 1986, p. 307, emphasis added.

4 Hugh Ilitis, 'Whose Fight is the Fight for Nature', *Sierra Club Bulletin,* vol. 9, no. 9, 1967, pp. 36–37, emphasis added.

5 Michael Soulé, *The Tigress and the Little Girl* (manuscript of forthcoming book), chapter vi, 'International Conservation Politics and Programs'.

6 Daniel H. Janzen, *Guanacaste National Park: Tropical Ecological and Cultural Restoration,* Editorial Universidad Estatal a Distancia (San Jose: 1986). See also David Rains Wallace, 'Communing in Costa Rica', *Wilderness,* no. 181, Summer 1988, which quotes Janzen as wishing to plan 'protected areas in a way that will permanently accommodate solitude seeking humans as well as jaguars, tapirs, and sea turtles'. These solitude seeking humans might include biologists, backpackers, deep ecologists, but not, one supposes, indigenous farmers, hunters or fishermen.

7 Raymond Bonner, *At the Hand of Man: Peril and Hope far Africa's Wildlife,* Alfred A. Knopf, (New York: 1993), pp. 35, 65, 70, 85, 221.

8 E.N. Chidumayo, 'Realities for Aspiring Young African Conservationists', in Dale Lewis and Nick Carter (eds.), *Voices from Africa: Local Perspectives on Conservation,* World Wildlife Fund, (Washington: 1993), p. 49.

9 Arne Kalland, 'Seals, Whales and Elephants: Totem Animals and the Anti-Use Campaigns', in *Proceeedings of the Conference on Responsible Wildlife Management,* European Bureau for Conservation and Development, (Brussels: 1994). Also the same author's 'Management by Totemisation: Whale Symbolism and the Anti-Whaling Campaign', *Arctic,* vol. 46, no. 2, 1993.

10 *The Deccan Herald,* Bangalore, 5 November 1995.

11 A useful countrywide overview is provided in Ashish Kothari, Saloni Suri, and Neena Singh, 'Conservation in India: A New Direction', *Economic and Political Weekly,* 28 October 1995.

12 'Tribals Ready for Confrontation over Nagarahole Resort', *The Times of India* (Bangalore edition), 30 August 1996.

13 Verrier Elwin, *A New Deal far Tribal India,* Ministry of Home Affairs, New, Delhi, 1963.

14 M.S. Randhawa, 'Nature Conservation, National Parks and Bio-Aesthetic Planning in India', Presidential Address, Section on Botany, in *Proceedings of the Thirty-sixth Indian Science Congress* (Allahabad: 1949), pp. 87–103.

15 Salim Ali, 'Presidential Letter: Wildlife Conservation and the Cultivator', *Hornbill,* April–June 1977.

16 R. Sukumar, 'Wildlife-Human Conflict in India: An Ecological and Social Perspective', in R. Guha (ed.) *Social Ecology,* Oxford University Press, (New Delhi: 1994), The empirical research from which these recommendations flow is reported in Sukumar's *The Asian Elephant: Ecology and Management,* Cambridge University Press, (Cambridge: 1989); also the thesis on which the book is based, *Ecology of the Asian Elephant and its Interaction with Man in South India,* Centre for Ecological Sciences, Indian Institute of Science, (Bangalore: 1985).

17 'Culling' is contrary to the ideology of 'deep ecology' that provides philosophical cover to authoritarian biologists and conservationists. Another unfortunate case concerns the crocodiles raised on the Madras Croc Bank by Romulus Whitaker and his colleagues. They have successfully raised thousands of crocodiles in captivity—and now await permission from the Government of India to harvest a species that they have convincingly demonstrated is no longer 'endangered'. Permission has not been forthcoming, despite the fact that it will generate substantial amounts of foreign exchange to the state (from the sale of leather bags and the like) and provide employment and income to the Irula tribals with whom the Croc Bank works.

18 For thoughtful suggestions as to how the interests of wild species and the interests of poor humans might be made more compatible, see M. Gadgil and P.R.S. Rao, 'A System of Positive Incentives to Conserve Biodiversity', *Economic and Political Weekly,* 6 August 1994.

19 See Ramachandra Guha, 'The Two Phases of American Environmentalism: A Critical History', in Frederique Apffel-Marglin and Stephen Marglin (eds.) *Decolonising Knowledge: From Development to Discourse,* Clarendon Press (Oxford: 1996).

20 In the famous Valley of Flowers, high up in the Himalaya, a ban on grazing has reportedly led to the local extinction of several species, for much the same reason.

21 Ramachandra Guha, 'Radical American Environmentalism and Wilderness Preservation: A Third World Critique', *Environmental Ethics,* vol. 11, no. 1, Spring 1989.

22 I speak here of private communications: published responses to my essay include David M. Johns, 'The Relevance of Deep Ecology to the Third World: Some Preliminary Comments', *Environmental Ethics,* vol. 12, no. 2, 1990; J. Baird Callicott, 'The Wilderness Idea Revisited: the Sustainable Development Alternative', *The Environmental Professional,* vol. 13, no. 2, 1991.

23 K. Balagopal, 'A Little More of the Same', *Seminar* (New Delhi), issue 412, December 1993. Making the same point, albeit in more gentle language, are villagers in the Indonesian island of Timpaus. As reported by Harald Beyer Broch, 'Some islanders have heard that foreign organisations work for protection of crocodiles, and that they succeed to the point that it is difficult to sell crocodiles in Indonesia today. Many of the present villagers said they would like these protectionists to live in villages where crocodiles are a threat, as they were in Timpaus some twenty years ago. That experience would probably have

made them change their opinion. It might be easier to want to protect animals that you never encounter, than those that may eat you next day'. Harald Beyer Broch, 'Local Resource Dependency and Utilisation: Environmental Issues as seen from Timpaus, Indonesia', paper presented at the Workshop on Environmental Movements in Asia, Leiden, 27–29 October 1994.

INDEX

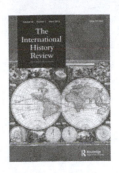